CHANGE NOTICE

THESE ARE SUPERSEDING OR SUPPLEMENTARY PAGES TO SAME PUBLICATION OF PREVIOUS DATE

Insert these pages into basic publication
Destroy superseded pages

NAVAIR 01-85ADA-1

A-6 INTRUDER PILOT'S
FLIGHT OPERATING INSTRUCTIONS
NATOPS FLIGHT MANUAL
NAVY MODEL
A-6A, B, C/KA-6D/A-6E
AIRCRAFT

Grumman Aerospace Corporation
NOas59-0259C
N00019-74C-0006

This document is subject to special export controls and each transmittal to foreign governments, foreign nationals or agents thereof may be made only with the prior approval of NAVAIRSYSCOMHQ, Washington, D.C.

This manual is sold for historic research purposes only, as an entertainment. It is not intended to be used as part of an actual flight training program. No book can substitute for flight training by an authorized instructor. The licensing of pilots is overseen by organizations and authorities such as the FAA and CAA. Operating an aircraft without the proper license is a federal crime.

ISSUED BY AUTHORITY OF THE CHIEF OF NAVAL OPERATIONS AND UNDER THE DIRECTION OF THE COMMANDER, NAVAL AIR SYSTEMS COMMAND

Copyright ©2009 Periscope Film LLC
All Rights Reserved
ISBN #978-1-935327-76-9   1-935327-76-3

Section index:
1. THE AIRCRAFT
2. INDOCTRINATION
3. NORMAL PROCEDURES
4. FLIGHT CHARAC
5. EMER PROCEDURES
6. ALL-WEA OPERATION
7. COMM PROCEDURES
8. WEAPONS SYSTEMS
9. FLT CREW COORD
10. NATOPS EVAL
11. PERFORM DATA
12. INDEX & FOLDOUTS

1 August 1974
Change 2   1 October 1975

NAVAIR 01-85ADA-1

Reproduction for non-military use of the information or illustrations contained in this publication is not permitted. The policy for military use reproduction is established for the Army in AR 380-5, for the Navy and Marine Corps in OPNAVINST 5510.1B, and for the Air Force in Air Force Regulation 205-1.

LIST OF EFFECTIVE PAGES

Insert latest changed pages; dispose of superseded pages in accordance with applicable regulations.

NOTE: On a changed page, the portion of the text affected by the latest change is indicated by a vertical line, or other change symbol, in the outer margin of the page.

Total number of pages in this manual is 980 consisting of the following:

Page No.	# Change No.	Page No.	# Change No.	Page No.	# Change No.
Title	2	1-68B Blank	2	3-58 – 3-59	2
A	2	1-69	0	3-60	0
B	2	1-70 – 1-70A	2	3-61	2
Letter	0	1-70B Blank	2	3-62	0
Fly 1	2	1-71 – 1-72	2	3-62A – 3-62B	2
Fly 2 Blank	2	1-73 – 1-88	0	3-63	2
i – iv	0	1-89 – 1-90A	2	3-64	0
v – viii	2	1-90B Blank	2	3-65	2
ix – x deleted	2	1-91 – 1-92	2	3-66 – 3-72	0
xi – xiii	2	1-93	0	3-73 – 3-74	2
xiv – xv	0	1-94 – 1-96B	2	3-75 – 3-79	0
xvi Blank	0	1-97	2	3-80 – 3-84B	2
1-1 – 1-6	2	1-98 – 1-101	0	3-85	2
1-7 – 1-8	0	1-102 – 1-103	2	3-86 – 3-107	0
1-9	2	1-104 – 1-105	0	3-108	2
1-10	0	1-106	2	3-109	0
1-11 – 1-12A	2	1-107 – 1-112	0	3-110 – 3-110B	2
1-12B Blank	2	1-113	2	3-111 – 3-114	0
1-13	2	1-114 – 1-118	0	3-115	2
1-14 – 1-23	0	1-119	2	3-116	0
1-24	2	1-120 – 1-123	0	3-116A	2
1-25	0	1-124	2	3-116B Blank	2
1-26 – 1-26A	2	1-125 – 1-126	0	3-117 – 3-118A	2
1-26B Blank	2	1-127	2	3-118B Blank	2
1-27	2	1-128	0	3-119 – 3-137	0
1-28 – 1-32	0	1-129	2	3-138	2
1-33 – 1-34A	2	1-130 Blank	2	3-139	0
1-34B Blank	2	2-1 – 2-2	0	3-140	2
1-35	2	3-1 – 3-2	2	3-141 – 3-142	0
1-36 – 1-37	0	3-3 – 3-7	0	3-143	2
1-38	2	3-8 – 3-9	2	3-144	0
1-39	0	3-10 – 3-21	0	3-145 – 3-150	2
1-40	2	3-22 – 3-26	2	3-151 – 3-152	0
1-41 – 1-48	0	3-27 – 3-30	0	3-153	2
1-49 – 1-50A	2	3-31	2	3-154	0
1-50B Blank	2	3-32 – 3-48	0	4-1 – 4-25	0
1-51	0	3-49	2	4-26 Blank	0
1-52 – 1-52D	2	3-50	0	5-1	2
1-53	2	3-50A – 3-50B	2	5-2 – 5-10	0
1-54 – 1-62	0	3-51 – 3-52	0	5-11 – 5-12A	2
1-63 – 1-64	2	3-53	2	5-12B Blank	2
1-65 – 1-66	0	3-54 – 3-57	0	5-13 – 5-15	0
1-67 – 1-68A	2			5-16 – 5-17	2
				5-18 – 5-22	0

Zero in this column indicates an original page.

A   Change 2

NAVAIR 01-85ADA-1

LIST OF EFFECTIVE PAGES

Page No.	# Change No.	Page No.	# Change No.	Page No.	# Change No.
5-23	2	8-153 – 8-154A	2	FO-23	0
5-24 – 5-52	0	8-154B Blank	2	FO-24 Blank	0
6-1 – 6-8	0	8-155 – 8-156	2	FO-25	2
7-1 – 7-2A	2	8-157 – 8-165	0	FO-26 Blank	2
7-2B Blank	2	8-166 – 8-166A	2	FO-27	2
7-3	2	8-167 – 8-174	0	FO-28 Blank	2
7-4 – 7-7	0	8-174A – 8-174B	2	FO-29	0
7-8 – 7-10A	2	8-175 – 8-180	0	FO-30 Blank	0
7-10B Blank	2	8-181	2	FO-31	0
7-11 – 7-12A	2	8-182 – 8-189	0	FO-32 Blank	0
7-12B Blank	2	8-190 – 8-191	2	FO-33	2
7-13	0	8-192 – 8-198	0	FO-34 Blank	2
7-14 – 7-14A	2	9-1 – 9-7	0	FO-34A	2
7-14B Blank	2	9-8 Blank	0	FO-34B Blank	2
7-15 – 7-18A	2	10-1 – 10-13	0	FO-35	2
7-18B Blank	2	10-14 Blank	0	FO-36 Blank	2
7-19 – 7-20	2	11-1 – 11-115	0	FO-37	2
7-21 – 7-23	0	11-116 Blank	0	FO-38 Blank	2
7-24 Blank	0	11-117 – 11-135	0	FO-39	0
8-1 – 8-2	2	11-136 – 11-137	2	FO-40 Blank	0
8-3 – 8-62	0	11-138 – 11-182	0	FO-41	0
8-63	2	Index-1 – Index-4A	2	FO-42 Blank	0
8-64 – 8-103	0	Index-4B Blank	2	FO-43	2
8-104	2	Index-5 – Index-9	2	FO-44 Blank	2
8-105	0	Index-10	0	FO-45	2
8-106 – 8-108B	2	Index-11	2	FO-46 Blank	2
8-109	0	Index-12	0	FO-47	2
8-110	2	Index-13 – Index-23	2	FO-48 Blank	2
8-111 – 8-112	0	Index-24 – Index-26	0		
8-113 – 8-116A	2	FO-1	2		
8-116B Blank	2	FO-2 Blank	2		
8-117 – 8-118B	2	FO-3	0		
8-119 – 8-122	0	FO-4 Blank	0		
8-123	2	FO-5	2		
8-124	0	FO-6 Blank	2		
8-125 – 8-126H	2	FO-7	2		
8-127 – 8-128	2	FO-8 Blank	2		
8-128A	2	FO-9	2		
8-128B Blank	2	FO-10 Blank	2		
8-129	2	FO-11	2		
8-130 – 8-131	0	FO-12 Blank	2		
8-132 – 8-132A	2	FO-12A	2		
8-132B Blank	2	FO-12B Blank	2		
8-133	2	FO-13	2		
8-134	0	FO-14 Blank	2		
8-134A – 8-134B	2	FO-14A	2		
8-135	0	FO-14B Blank	2		
8-136 – 8-138A	2	FO-15	0		
8-138B Blank	2	FO-16 Blank	0		
8-139 – 8-140D	2	FO-17	2		
8-141 – 8-142A	2	FO-18 Blank	2		
8-142B Blank	2	FO-19	2		
8-143	0	FO-20 Blank	2		
8-144 – 8-148G	2	FO-20A	2		
8-148H Blank	2	FO-20B Blank	2		
8-149 – 8-152A	2	FO-21	0		
8-152B Blank	2	FO-22 Blank	0		

Zero in this column indicates an original page

Change 2   B

INTERIM CHANGE SUMMARY

The following Interim Changes have been canceled or previously incorporated in this manual:

INTERIM CHANGE NUMBER(S)	REMARKS/PURPOSE
A-6A, B, C 1 thru 62	Previously incorporated or canceled.
KA-6D 1 thru 19	Previously incorporated or canceled.
A-6E 1 thru 15	Previously incorporated or canceled.

The following Interim Changes have been incorporated in this Change/Revision:

INTERIM CHANGE NUMBER	REMARKS/PURPOSE
63	Modify limitations, Section I, Part 4

Interim Changes Outstanding - To be maintained by the custodian of this manual:

INTERIM CHANGE NUMBER	ORIGINATOR/DATE (or DATE/TIME GROUP)	PAGES AFFECTED	REMARKS/PURPOSE

DEPARTMENT OF THE NAVY
OFFICE OF THE CHIEF OF NAVAL OPERATIONS
WASHINGTON, D.C. 20350

1 August 1974

LETTER OF PROMULGATION

1. The Naval Air Training and Operating Procedures Standardization Program (NATOPS) is a positive approach toward improving combat readiness and achieving a substantial reduction in the aircraft accident rate. Standardization, based on professional knowledge and experience, provides the basis for development of an efficient and sound operational procedure. The standardization program is not planned to stifle individual initiative, but rather to aid the Commanding Officer in increasing his unit's combat potential without reducing his command prestige or responsibility.

2. This manual standardizes ground and flight procedures but does not include tactical doctrine. Compliance with the stipulated manual procedure is mandatory except as authorized herein. In order to remain effective, NATOPS must be dynamic and stimulate rather than suppress individual thinking. Since aviation is a continuing, progressive profession, it is both desirable and necessary that new ideas and new techniques be expeditiously evaluated and incorporated if proven to be sound. To this end, Commanding Officers of aviation units are authorized to modify procedures contained herein, in accordance with the waiver provisions established by OPNAVINST 3510.9 series, for the purpose of assessing new ideas prior to initiating recommendations for permanent changes. This manual is prepared and kept current by the users in order to achieve maximum readiness and safety in the most efficient and economical manner. Should conflict exist between the training and operating procedures found in this manual and those found in other publications, this manual will govern.

3. Checklists and other pertinent extracts from this publication necessary to normal operations and training should be made and may be carried in Naval Aircraft for use therein. It is forbidden to make copies of this entire publication or major portions thereof without specific authority of the Chief of Naval Operations.

W.D. Houser

W.D. HOUSER
Vice Admiral, USN
Deputy Chief of Naval Operations
(Air Warfare)

TABLE OF CONTENTS

Section I	AIRCRAFT	1-1*
Section II	INDOCTRINATION	2-1
Section III	NORMAL PROCEDURES	3-1*
Section IV	FLIGHT PROCEDURES	4-1
Section V	EMERGENCY PROCEDURES	5-1
Section VI	ALL WEATHER OPERATION	6-1
Section VII	COMMUNICATION EQUIPMENT AND PROCEDURES	7-1
Section VIII	WEAPONS SYSTEM	8-1*
Section IX	FLIGHT CREW COORDINATION	9-1
Section X	NATOPS EVALUATION	10-1
Section XI	PERFORMANCE DATA	11-1
	ALPHABETICAL INDEX	X-1
	FOLDOUT ILLUSTRATIONS	FO-1

* SEE SUPPLEMENTAL NATOPS FLIGHT MANUAL NAVAIR 01-85ADA-1A FOR ADDITIONAL DATA

FOREWORD

SCOPE

The NATOPS Flight Manual is issued by the authority of the Chief of Naval Operations and under the direction of Commander, Naval Air Systems Command in conjunction with the Naval Air Training and Operating Procedures Standardization (NATOPS) Program. This manual contains information on all aircraft systems, performance data, and operating procedures required for safe and effective operations. However, it is not a substitute for sound judgment. Compound emergencies, available facilities, adverse weather or terrain, or considerations affecting the lives and property of others may require modification of the procedures contained herein. Read this manual from cover to cover. It is your responsibility to have a complete knowledge of its contents.

APPLICABLE PUBLICATIONS

The following applicable publications complement this manual:

NAVAIR 01-85ADA-1A (Supplemental Natops Flight Manual)
NAVAIR 01-85ADA-1B (Checklist)
NAVAIR 01-85ADA-1F (Functional Check Flight Checklist)
NAVAIR 01-85ADA-1T (Tactical Manual)
NAVAIR 01-85ADA-1T(A) (Supplemental Tactical Manual)
NAVAIR 01-85ADA-1T(B) (Tactical Pocket Guide)

HOW TO GET COPIES

AUTOMATIC DISTRIBUTION

To receive future changes and revisions to this manual or any other NAVAIR aeronautical publication automatically, a unit must be established on an automatic distribution list maintained by the Naval Air Technical Services Facility (NATSF). To become established on the list or to change existing NAVAIR publication requirements, a unit must submit a Mailing List Request for Aeronautic Technical Publications (NAVAIR Form 5605/3, Part II) to NATSF, 700 Robbins Ave., Philadelphia, Pa. 19111, listing requirements or changes thereto in accordance with the instructions contained on the request form. For additional information, refer to NAVAIRINST 5605.4 series and NAVSUP Publication 2002, Section VIII, Part C.

ADDITIONAL COPIES

Additional copies of this manual and changes thereto may be procured by submitting Form DD 1348 to Naval Publications and Forms Center, Philadelphia in accordance with NAVSUP Publication 2002, Section VIII, Part C.

UPDATING THE MANUAL

To ensure that the manual contains the latest procedures and information, NATOPS review conferences are held in accordance with OPNAVINST 3510.11 series.

CHANGE RECOMMENDATIONS

Recommended changes to this manual or other NATOPS publications may be submitted by anyone in accordance with OPNAVINST 3510.9 series.

Routine change recommendations are submitted directly to the Model Manager on OPNAV Form 3500-22 shown on the next page. The address of the Model Manager of this aircraft is:

> Commander
> Medium Attack Wing One
> Naval Air Station Oceana
> Virginia Beach, Virginia 23460

Change recommendations of an URGENT nature (safety of flight, etc.) should be submitted directly to the NATOPS Advisory Group Member in the chain of command by priority message.

YOUR RESPONSIBILITY

NATOPS Flight Manuals are kept current through an active manual change program. Any corrections, additions, or constructive suggestions for improvement of its content should be submitted by routine or urgent change recommendation, as appropriate, at once.

NATOPS FLIGHT MANUAL INTERIM CHANGES

Flight Manual Interim Changes are changes or corrections to the NATOPS Flight Manuals promulgated by CNO or NAVAIRSYSCOM. Interim Changes are issued either as printed pages, or as a naval message. The Interim Change Summary page is provided as a record of all interim changes. Upon receipt of a change or revision, the custodian of the manual should check the updated Interim Change Summary to ascertain that all outstanding interim changes have been either incorporated or canceled; those not incorporated shall be recorded as outstanding in the section provided.

CHANGE SYMBOLS

Revised text is indicated by a black vertical line in either margin of the page, adjacent to the affected text, like the one printed next to this paragraph. The change symbol identifies the addition of either new information, a changed procedure, the correction of an error, or a rephrasing of the previous material.

NATOPS TACTICAL CHANGE RECOMMENDATION						
OPNAV FORM 3500/22 (5-69) 0107-722-2002					DATE	
TO BE FILLED IN BY ORIGINATOR AND FORWARDED TO MODEL MANAGER						
FROM (originator)					Unit	
TO (Model Manager)					Unit	
Complete Name of Manual/Checklist	Revision Date	Change Date	Section/Chapter	Page	Paragraph

Recommendation (be specific)

☐ CHECK IF CONTINUED ON BACK

Justification

Signature	Rank	Title

Address of Unit or Command

TO BE FILLED IN BY MODEL MANAGER (Return to Originator)	
FROM	DATE
TO	

REFERENCE
a. Your Change Recommendation Dated

☐ Your change recommendation dated _____ is acknowledged. It will be held for action of the review conference planned for _____ to be held at _____

☐ Your change recommendation is reclassified URGENT and forwarded for approval to _____ by my DTG _____

/S	MODEL MANAGER	AIRCRAFT

A-ODG-4

Foreword   NAVAIR 01-85ADA-1

WARNINGS, CAUTIONS, AND NOTES

The following definitions apply to "WARNINGS", "CAUTIONS", and "NOTES" found through the manual.

WARNING

An operating procedure, practice, or condition, etc., which may result in injury or death, if not carefully observed or followed.

CAUTION

An operating procedure, practice, or condition, etc., which may result in damage to equipment if not carefully observed or followed.

Note

An operating procedure, practice, or condition, etc., which is essential to emphasize.

WORDING

The concept of word usage and intended meaning which has been adhered to in preparing this Manual is as follows:

"Shall" has been used only when application of a procedure is mandatory.

"Should" has been used only when application of a procedure is recommended.

"May" and "need not" have been used only when application of a procedure is optional.

"Will" has been used only to indicate futurity, never to indicate any degree of requirement for application of a procedure.

NAVAIR 01-85ADA-1

AIRCRAFT CONFIGURATION A-6A/B/C

CONFIG-URATION	EFFECTIVITY NUMBER	SERIAL NUMBER	CONFIG-URATION	EFFECTIVITY NUMBER	SERIAL NUMBER
200	27	149941	373	373	155642
A-6B MOD 1	30	149944	↓	374	155643
A-6B	35	149949		375	155644
A-6B MOD 1	41	149955		376	155645
A-6B	43	149957		377	155646
A-6B	45	151558	A-6C	379	155648
A-6B	49	151562	373	380	155649
A-6B	51	151564	↓	382	155651
A-6B	52	151565	A-6C*	384	155653
200	55	151568	373	385	155654
A-6B MOD 1	78	151591		386	155655
A-6B MOD 1	128	151820		387	155666
200	153	152600		389	155658
200	159	152606		390	155659
A-6B MOD 1	170	152617	A-6C*	391	155660
200	172	152619	373	392	155661
310	248	152939	A-6C*	393	155662
	263	152954	373	395	155664
	266	154126	↓	396	155665
	270	154130	A-6C	398	155667
	273	154133	373	399	155668
	277	154137	↓	400	155669
	287	154147	A-6C*	401	155670
	299	154159	373	402	155671
	303	154163	↓	403	155672
	309	154169	373	406	155675
	310	154170	A-6C*	407	155676
	311	154171	373	409	155678
	315	155584	↓	410	155679
	316	155585		411	155680
	323	155592	A-6C	412	155681
	326	155595	373	413	155682
	327	155596	↓	414	155683
	330	155559	A-6C*	415	155684
	331	155600	373	416	155685
310	333	155602	↓	417	155686
	339	155608		418	155687
	341	155610	A-6C	419	155688
	343	155612	373	420	155689
	346	155615		422	155691
	351	155620		423	155692
	352	155621	373	425	155694
	354	155623		426	155695
	355	155624		428	155697
	356	155625		429	155698
	358	155627	↓	430	155699
310	*359	155628	451	433	155702
A-6B PAT	360	155629		434	155703
A-6B PAT	361	155630		435	155704
A-6B PAT	362	155631		437	155706
310	363	155632		438	155707
	367	155636		439	155708
↓	368	155637		441	155710
			451	442	155711

*A-6C EQUIPMENT REMOVED

Change 2   v

AIRCRAFT CONFIGURATION CONT'D

CONFIG-URATION	EFFECTIVITY NUMBER	SERIAL NUMBER	CONFIG-URATION	EFFECTIVITY NUMBER	SERIAL NUMBER
451	443	155712	451	468	157009
↓	444	155713	↓	469	157010
	445	155714		470	157011
	446	155715		471	157012
	447	155716		472	157013
	448	155717		473	157014
	449	155718		475	157016
	450	155719		476	157017
	454	156995		478	157019
	455	156996		480	157021
	456	156997		482	157023
	459	157000		483	157024
	460	157001		484	157025
	461	157002		485	157026
	462	157003		486	157027
	464	157005		488	157029
	465	157006			

KA-6D

EFFECTIVITY NUMBER	SERIAL NUMBER	EFFECTIVITY NUMBER	SERIAL NUMBER
CONTRACTOR MODIFIED			
K-1	151582	K-30	152913
K-2	151579	K-31	151821
K-3	151589	K-32	151792
K-4	151570	K-33	151801
K-5	151566	K-34	151809
K-6	152592	K-35	151789
K-7	151791	K-36	151810
K-8	152934	K-37	152911
K-10	151583	K-38	152921
K-11	152618	K-39	152611
K-12	149945	K-40	151823
K-13	151793	K-41	152919
K-14	149942	K-42	149952
K-15	151783	K-43	152632
K-16	149964	K-44	151813
K-18	151826	K-45	152906
K-20	151827	K-46	152628
K-21	152894	K-47	151808
K-22	151824	K-48	151787
K-23	151576	K-49	152914
K-24	151575	K-50	152920
K-26	152910	K-52	152896
K-27	151818	K-54	151819
K-28	151795		
NAVY MODIFIED			
NK-1	149951	NK-5	152624
NK-2	151581	NK-6	152927
NK-3	151572	NK-7	152625
		NK-8	152893

AIRCRAFT CONFIGURATION CONT'D

A-6E MOD

EFFECTIVITY NUMBER	SERIAL NUMBER	EFFECTIVITY NUMBER	SERIAL NUMBER	EFFECTIVITY NUMBER	SERIAL NUMBER
M1	152907	M43	152915	M85	155598
M2	149956	M44	154162	M86	155597
M3	151592	M45	152596	M87	154158
M4	151804	M46	152620	M88	152947
M5	152607	M47	152642	M89	152942
M6	149948	M48	152930	M90	154151
M7	152905	M49	149943	M91	154167
M8	151807	M50	155635	M92	152953
M9	152923	M51	152646	M93	154146
M10	152587	M52	152908	M94	154136
M11	152584	M53	155581	M95	154161
M12	152621	M54	155590	M96	154134
M13	152928	M55	152936	M97	154148
M14	152635	M56	151782	M98	155591
M15	152640	M57	155616	M99	155606
M16	152895	M58	152912	M100	154124
M17	152904	M59	155604	M101	154144
M18	152916	M60	152925	M102	154168
M19	152933	M61	152902	M103	154131
M20	151573	M62	155633	M104	154128
M21	152935	M63	155657	M105	155582
M22	151802	M64	155619	M106	154135
M23	151811	M65	155589	M107	155674
M24	152623	M66	152931	M108	157004
M25	151812	M67	151784	*M121	149953
M26	152585	M68	152610		
M27	152918	M69	152924		
M28	151814	M70	152614		
M29	152929	M71	154140		
M30	152591	M72	154156		
M31	151593	M73	152641		
M32	149946	M74	152583		
M33	154142	M75	152950		
M34	149950	M76	155638		
M35	152603	M77	154132		
M36	152630	M78	152599		
M37	152948	M79	154154		
M38	151790	M80	152945		
M39	155586	M81	154129		
M40	155583	M82	152634		
M41	152593	M83	152941		
M42	155588	M84	155617		

*TRAM AIRCRAFT

AIRCRAFT CONFIGURATION CONT'D

A-6E PROD

EFFECTIVITY CODE	SERIAL NUMBER	EFFECTIVITY CODE	SERIAL NUMBER
1	158041	43	159180
2	158042	44	159181
3	158043	45	159182
4	158044	46	159183
5	158045	47	159184
6	158046	48	159185
7	158047	49	159309
9	158049	50	159310
10	158050	51	159311
11	158051	52	159312
12	158052	54	159313
13	158528	56	159314
14	158529	58	159315
15	158530	59	159316
16	158531	60	159317
17	158532	53	159567
18	158533	55	159568
19	158534	57	159569
20	158535	61	159570
21	158536	62	159571
22	158537	63	159572
23	158538	64	159573
24	158539	65	159574
25	158787	66	159575
26	158788	67	159576
28	158790	68	159577
29	158791	69	159578
30	158792	70	159579
31	158793	*71	159895
32	158794	72	159896
33	158795	73	159897
34	158796	74	159898
35	158797	75	159899
36	158798	76	159900
37	159174	77	159901
38	159175	78	159902
39	159176	79	159903
40	159177	80	159904
41	159178	81	159905
42	159179	82	159906

*TRAM AIRCRAFT

AIRCRAFT CONFIGURATION - CONTINUED

A-6E MOD

EFFECTIVITY NUMBER	SERIAL NUMBER	EFFECTIVITY NUMBER	SERIAL NUMBER
M49	149943	M61	152902
M32	149946	M17	152904
M6	149948	M7	152905
M34	149950	M1	152907
M2	149956	M52	152908
M20	151573	M58	152912
M3	151592	M43	152915
M31	151593	M18	152916
M56	151782	M27	152918
M67	151784	M9	152923
M38	151790	M69	152924
M22	151802	M60	152925
M4	151804	M13	152928
M8	151807	M29	152929
M23	151811	M48	152930
M25	151812	M66	152931
M28	151814	M19	152933
M74	152583	M21	152935
M11	152584	M55	152936
M26	152585	M37	152948
M10	152587	M75	152950
M30	152591	M71	154140
M41	152593	M33	154142
M45	152596	M72	154156
M35	152603	M44	154162
M5	152607	M53	155581
M68	152610	M40	155583
M70	152614	M39	155586
M46	152620	M42	155588
M12	152621	M65	155589
M24	152623	M54	155590
M36	152630	M59	155604
M14	152635	M57	155616
M15	152640	M64	155619
M73	152641	M62	155633
M47	152642	M50	155635
M51	152645	M63	155657
M16	152895		

AIRCRAFT CONFIGURATION - CONTINUED

A-6E PROD

EFFECTIVITY CODE	SERIAL NUMBER	EFFECTIVITY CODE	SERIAL NUMBER
1	158041	36	158798
2	158042	37	159174
3	158043	38	159175
4	158044	39	159176
5	158045	40	159177
6	158046	41	159178
7	158047	42	159179
8	158048	43	159180
9	158049	44	159181
10	158050	45	159182
11	158051	46	159183
12	158052	47	159184
13	158528	48	159185
14	158529	49	159309
15	158530	50	159310
16	158531	51	159311
17	158532	52	159312
18	158533	54	159313
19	158534	56	159314
20	158535	58	159315
21	158536	59	159316
22	158537	60	159317
23	158538	61	159570
24	158539	62	159571
25	158787	63	159572
26	158788	64	159573
27	158789	65	159574
28	158790	66	159575
29	158791	67	159576
30	158792	68	159577
31	158793	69	159578
32	158794	70	159579
33	158795	71	159580
34	158796	72	159581
35	158797		

GLOSSARY

A

ac	Alternating Current
ACLS	Automatic Carrier Landing System
ACU	Armament Control Unit
ADC	Air Data Computer
ADF	Automatic Direction Finder
ADL	Armament Datum Line
AFC	Airframe Change
	Automatic Frequency Control
AFCS	Automatic Flight Control System
AMCS	Airborne Missile Control System
AMTI	Airborne Moving Target Identification
AOA	Angle of Attack
APC	Approach Power Compensator
AVC	Automatic Velocity Correct
	Avionics Change

B

BIT	Built-In Test
BNCB	Bombardier Navigator's Control Box

C

C	Centigrade
CA	Contact Analog
CAINS	Carrier Aircraft Inertial/Navigation System
CAS	Calibrated Airspeed
C/B	Circuit Breaker
CCA	Carrier-Controlled Approach
CCU	Computer Control Unit
cg	Center of Gravity
COP	Computer Optical Positioning
CSD/S	Constant-Speed Drive/Starter
CVA	Aircraft Carrier (Attack)

D

DA	Drift Angle
dc	Direct Current
DC	Drift Corrected
DDU	Digital Display Unit
DG	Directional Gyro
DMI	Discrete Message Indicator
DR	Dead Reckoning
DRO	Discrete Readout
DRS	Detection and Ranging Set
DVRI	Direct View Radar Indicator

E

ECM	Electronic Countermeasures
EGT	Exhaust Gas Temperature

F

F	Fahrenheit
FAC	Forward Air Controller
FCLP	Field Carrier Landing Practice
FF	Fuel Flow
FLIR	Forward-Looking Infrared

G

g	Acceleration Due to Gravity
GCA	Ground-Controlled Approach
GCBS	Ground-Controlled Bombing System
GLO	Ground Lock-On
GS	Groundspeed

H

HSI	Horizontal Situation Indicator

I

ICS	Intercommunications
IFF	Identification Friend or Foe
IFR	Instrument Flight Rules
INS	Inertial Navigation System
IMN	Indicated Mach Number
IMU	Inertial Measurement Unit
ISA	International Standard Atmosphere
ITA	Initial Turn Angle

K

KCAS	Knots Calibrated Airspeed
KIAS	Knots Indicated Airspeed
KTAS	Knots True Airspeed

L

LASER	Light Amplification by Simulated Emission of Radiation
LAWS	Low-Altitude-Warning System
LGB	Laser Guided Bomb
LO	Lock-On
LOX	Liquid Oxygen
LRD	Laser Rangefinder Detector
LSD	Least Significant Digit
LSO	Landing Signal Officer

M

MAC	Mean Aerodynamic Chord
max	Maximum
MSD	Most Significant Digit
MSL	Mean Sea Level
MTV	Moving Target Velocity
MVC	Manual Velocity Correct

N

NATOPS	Naval Air Training and Operating Procedures
NFO	Naval Flight Officer
nmi	Nautical miles
NTDS	Naval Tactical Data System

GLOSSARY

O

OAP	Offset Aimpoint
OAT	Outside Air Temperature
ORT	Operational Readiness Test

P

PA	Power Approach
PCB	Pilot's Control Box (Pilot's Control Panel)
PCU	Pedestal Control Unit
PHD	Pilot's Horizontal Display
PPI	Plan Position Indicator
prf	Pulse Repetition Frequency
psi	Pounds per Square Inch
PSU	Power Supply Unit

R

RA	Radar Altimeter
RAT	Ram-Air Turbine
RHU	Right-Hand Unit
rpm	Revolutions per Minute
RS	Roll Summed

S

SAC	System Analysis Code
SIF	Selective Identification Feature
SINS	Ship's Inertial Navigation System
SL	Sea Level
SRTC	Search Radar Terrain Clearance
SRTT	Search Radar Target Tracking

T

TACAN	Tactical Air Navigation
TAS	True Airspeed
TC	Terrain Clearance
TDTA	Target Data Terrain Avoidance
TH	True Heading
TILT	Missed Message
T/R	Transformer Rectifier
TRAM	Target Recognition Attack Multisensor
TSP	Turret Stabilized Platform
TV	Television

U

uhf	Ultrahigh Frequency
UTM	Universal Test Message

V

VFR	Visual Flight Rules
VGI	Vertical Gyro Indicator
VDI	Vertical Display Indicator
VSI	Vertical Speed Indicator
VTR	Video Tape Recorder

W

WRA	Weapon Replaceable Assembly
WST	Weapons System Trainer

NAVAIR 01-85ADA-1

A-6A / A-6B / A-6E Intruder

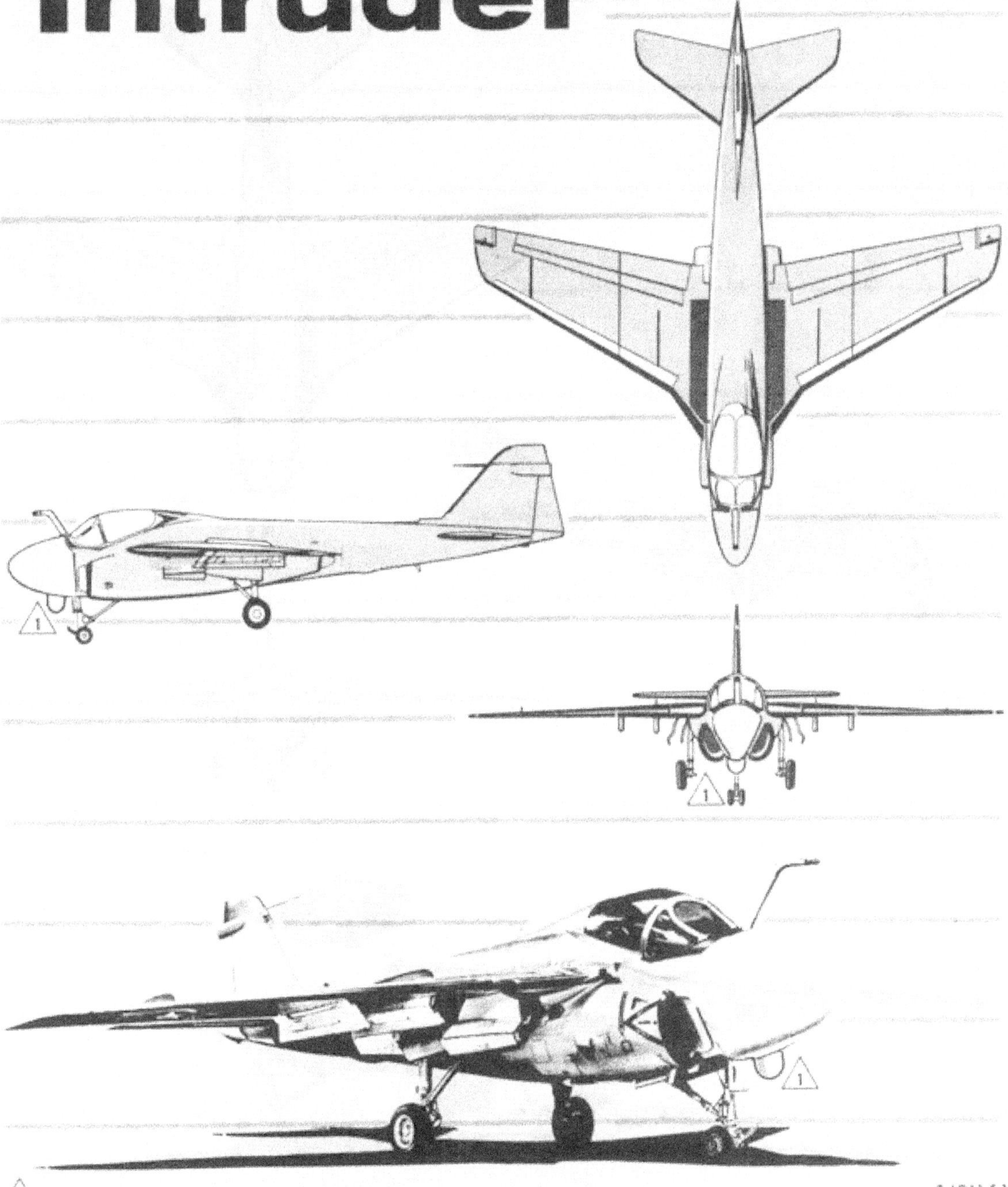

⚠ 1 A-6E 159895 AND ON AND A-6E MOD 121 AND ON

Frontispiece NAVAIR 01-85ADA-1

A-6C Intruder

Figure 1-0 (Sheet 2)

NAVAIR 01-85ADA-1

KA-6D TANKER

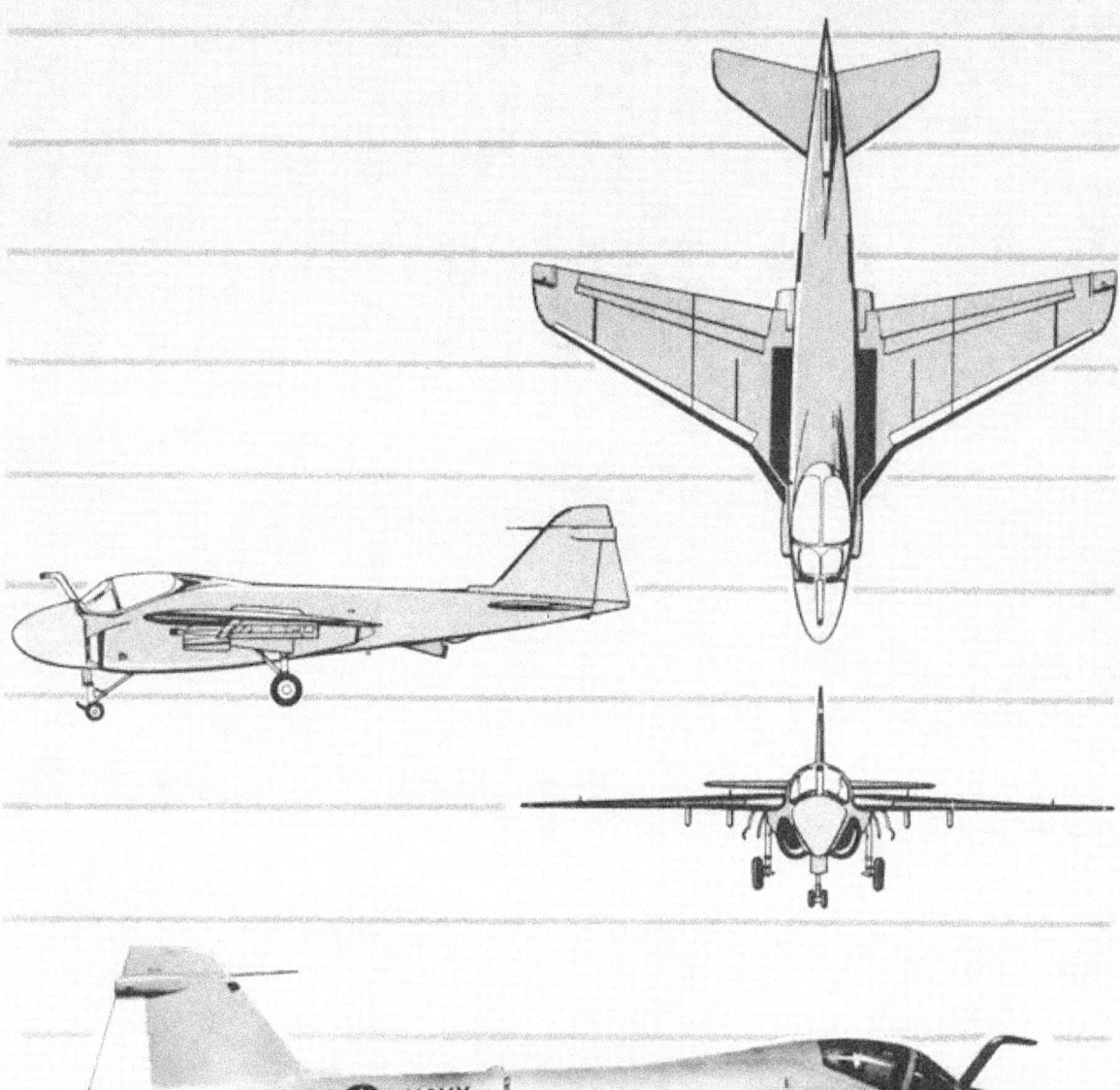

Figure 1-0 (Sheet 3)

NAVAIR 01-85ADA-1 AIRCRAFT

section I
AIRCRAFT

TABLE OF CONTENTS

PART 1 GENERAL DESCRIPTION	1-2
Aircraft	1-2
General Arrangement	1-2
Aircraft Weight	1-2
Cockpit Layout	1-2
Weapon/Store Stations	1-2
Technical Directives	1-3
Main Differences	1-3
Aircraft Dimensions	1-3
Engine	1-6
PART 2 SYSTEMS	1-8
Powerplant Systems	1-8
Throttles	1-8
Ignition System	1-8
Constant Speed Drive/Starter System	1-10
Engine Oil System	1-11
Engine Bleed-Air System	1-11
Engine Instruments	1-13
Engine Fuel Control System	1-14
Primary Aircraft Systems	1-17
Aircraft Fuel Supply System	1-17
Air Refueling System	1-23
Electrical Power Supply System	1-24
Hydraulic Power Supply System	1-39
Flight Controls	1-42
Auxiliary Aircraft Systems	1-49
Automatic Flight Control System	1-49
Approach Power Compensator System	1-51
Automatic Carrier Landing System	1-52
Speed Brakes	1-53
Landing Gear System	1-54
Nose-Gear Launch System	1-57
Wing-Fold System	1-58
Wheel Brake System	1-59
Arresting-Hook System	1-61
Flight Instruments and Indicator Lights	1-62
Angle-of-Attack System	1-62
Pitot-Static System	1-63
Attitude Instruments	1-66
Compass System	1-69
Miscellaneous Instruments	1-70
Caution, Warning and Advisory Lights	1-71
Canopy	1-72
Escape System	1-76
Ejection Seat MK GRU-5	1-76
Ejection Seat MK GRU-7	1-82
Environmental Control System	1-89
Cockpit Air-Conditioning and Pressurization System	1-89
Auxiliary Environmental Systems	1-93
Defogging	1-94
Windshield Wash	1-94
Rain-Removal (Anti-Ice) System	1-95
Equipment Cooling	1-95
Ground Cooling System (A-6E)	1-97
Engine Anti-Icing	1-97
Oxygen System	1-100
Lighting Systems	1-100
Interior Lighting	1-102
Exterior Lighting	1-102
Miscellaneous Equipment	1-103
PART 3 AIRCRAFT SERVICING	1-107
Aircraft Servicing	1-107
Danger Areas	1-107
Turning Radius and Ground Clearance	1-107
Power Requirements	1-107
Gear Stowage	1-110
PART 4 AIRCRAFT OPERATING LIMITATIONS	1-115
Engine Limitations	1-115
Airspeed Limitations	1-115
Instrument Markings	1-116
Equipment Cooling	1-119
Acceleration Limitations	1-119
Center-of-Gravity Limitations	1-124
Gross Weight Limitations	1-124
External Store Limitations	1-127
Maneuvers	1-127

Change 2   1-1

AIRCRAFT
General Description

NAVAIR 01-85ADA-1

part 1 General Description

AIRCRAFT

INTRODUCTION

The A-6A, A-6B, A-6C and A-6E Intruders are two-place, twin-engine, subsonic midwing monoplanes manufactured by the Grumman Aerospace Corporation, Bethpage, Long Island, New York. The aircraft are designed for true all-weather attack and can carry a payload of 8 1/2 tons. A wide variety of weapons can be delivered without the crew ever having seen the ground or the target. The aircraft can be air-refueled and the A-6A, A-6B, and A-6E can be used as a tanker. The KA-6D aircraft is a modified A-6A that retains the basic A-6 structure, powerplant, and associated airframe systems, without the all-weather weapons delivery systems. The KA-6D has a primary mission of refueling, while retaining a secondary capability of visual attack bombing. The aircraft is capable of transferring large quantities of fuel at a rapid rate.

The principal differences between the A-6A and the A-6B are in the equipment installed for navigation and weapon delivery and in the primary weapons delivered. The A-6C differs from the A-6A in that it has additional sensors and a centerline pod. Refer to Section VIII, NAVAIR 01-85ADA-1A, Supplemental NATOPS Flight Manual for a detailed listing of differences. The principal differences between the A-6E and A-6A are the installation in the A-6E of an improved computer that is faster and has a greater memory capacity; a search radar with track capabilities; and an improved weapon release system. The equipment-cooling system has been revised to accommodate the improved avionics, and a closed-circuit equipment-pressurization system installed. Two 30 kVA generators supply electrical power. The A-6E TRAM configured aircraft (A-6E 159895 and ON and A-6E Mod M121 and ON) represents further improvements over the A-6E, including added memory capability in the computer, the addition of provisions for a forward-looking infrared sensor and a laser detection and ranging set, and an additional air-conditioning turbine for equipment cooling. In addition, these aircraft have been equipped with a new inertial navigation system, complete mode 1 automatic carrier landing capability, an improved communications, navigation, identification system, and provisions for the Condor missile system. See figure 1-2.

The A-6 Series aircraft is powered by two Pratt Whitney, axial-flow, turbojet engines, and is characterized by a large nose radome and sweptback wings. The aircraft has arrested-landing capabilities, and, for a jet aircraft, has a relatively slow approach and landing speed. A single-point ground refueling capability shortens turnaround time and eases the normal fueling process.

The aircraft, from a flight standpoint, is essentially a hydraulic aircraft. Generally, the hydraulic systems are controlled electrically; the major departures from this being the actuation of the flight control servo-actuators, manual canopy operation, emergency landing-gear actuation, and wheel-brake operations. In these operations, the hydraulic selector valves and servo-actuators are directly positioned by the pilot.

The change of complete loss of essential functions due to battle damage or system malfunction is minimized in the electrical and hydraulic systems by the use of automatic isolation of less important electrical loads, redundant hydraulic power systems, and tandem actuators.

GENERAL ARRANGEMENT

Figure FO-1 represents the general placement of the components within the aircraft.

AIRCRAFT WEIGHT

The zero fuel/zero store weight of the A-6A and A-6B is approximately 28,300 pounds. A-6E 158041 thru 159574 weigh approximately 27,800 pounds, 159575 thru 159579 approximately 27,400 pounds and the TRAM provisioned A-6E weighs approximately 28,300 pounds. The A-6C weights approximately 30,000 pounds and the KA-6D approximately 27,300 pounds. Consult the applicable Handbook of Weight and Balance for exact weight of any series aircraft.

COCKPIT LAYOUT

The aircraft accommodates a two-man crew consisting of the pilot and bombardier/navigator in a staggered side-by-side seating arrangement. Aircraft without AFC 119 are equipped with two MK GRU-5 ejection seats. Aircraft incorporating AFC 119 are equipped with two MK GRU-7 rocket-assisted ejection seats. Figures FO-2 and FO-3 provide typical cockpit layout.

WEAPON/STORE STATIONS

The A-6A, A-6B, KA-6D, and A-6E are configured with four wing pylons and a centerline store station for a total of five external store stations. The A-6C is limited to the use of the four wing pylons due to the pod on the centerline. The necessary electrical connections, fuel lines, and valves are housed in the pylons and the centerline store station. The wing pylons are fitted with AERO 7A ejector racks and the centerline store is fitted with either an AERO 7A or an AERO 7B ejector rack. These racks are capable of being loaded with a variety of weapons, adapters, launchers, bomb racks, and ejector racks.

NAVAIR 01-85ADA-1

AIRCRAFT
General Description

The AERO 7A is capable of carrying weights up to 3500 pounds; the AERO 7B is capable of carrying weights up to 3600 pounds. Refer to Section VIII for a description of the weapon release system and to NAVAIR 01-85ADA-1T and -1TA A-6A Tactical Manual and Supplemental Tactical Manual for details of the various weapons that can be carried.

The A-6B also can carry the Standard ARM on a LAU-77A/A ejector launcher, which is loaded on the AERO-7A racks on the wing stations. Refer to Section VIII, NAVAIR 01-85ADA-1A, Supplemental NATOPS Flight Manual for details.

TECHNICAL DIRECTIVES

Figure 1-1 is a form to be used to show those technical directives (AFC, AVC, etc.) that apply to the aircraft and that have been incorporated in this manual. As changes are made to the aircraft, those that affect aircraft operation or pilot-bombardier/navigator need-to-know information will be entered on this form.

MAIN DIFFERENCES

For main differences between A-6A, A-6B, A-6C, KA-6D, A-6E and A-6E TRAM, see figure 1-2.

AIRCRAFT DIMENSIONS

See figure 1-3 for aircraft dimensions.

SUMMARY OF APPLICABLE TECHNICAL DIRECTIVES

AFC NUMBER	CLASS	TITLE	INCORPORATED	VISUAL MEANS OF IDENTIFICATION
102	R	External Power Monitor	15 Apr 1968	Reset switch on external power panel
119	U	Rocket-Assisted Ejection Seat	1 July 1971	MK GRU-7 seat
126A	U	KD-2 Camera	1 Apr 1970	Modified DVI hood
137	U	Ram-Air Turbine Frequency Monitor	15 Apr 1968	-
148	U	Key Light Control Modification	15 Apr 1968	Three-position pylon light switch
161	R	Automatic Carrier Landing System	1 Oct 1975	ACLS controls
171	R	APR-25 Installation	15 Sept 1968	APR-25 panel
175	U	Search Radar-Target Tracking	15 Mar 1969	SR track switch
183	R	Backup Flight Controls Hydraulic System	15 Mar 1969	Backup hydraulic test switch
185	U	Canopy Actuation System Improvement	15 Mar 1969	Three-position canopy switch
195	U	A-6B Mod 1	15 Sept 1971	TIAS controls
197	U	ALE-29A Chaff Dispenser Set	15 Mar 1969	ALE-29 panel
199	R	Approach Power Compensator System	15 Mar 1969	APCS switch and light
206	R	Flush-Mounted Refueling Receptacle	1 Sept 1969	Flush receptacle
209	U	AN/ALQ-100 Destruct System Modifications	1 Sept 1969	-
230	U	Automatic Carrier Landing System	1 Dec 1972	ACLS panel and indicator

Figure 1-1 (Sheet 1)

Change 2   1-3

AIRCRAFT
General Description

NAVAIR 01-85ADA-1

SUMMARY OF APPLICABLE TECHNICAL DIRECTIVES Contd.

AFC NUMBER	CLASS	TITLE	INCORPORATED	VISUAL MEANS OF IDENTIFICATION
244	U	Increased Carrier Landing Gross Weight	1 July 1971	
256	U	LB-31A Strike Camera Circuitry	1 Dec 1972	Camera control
263	U	ECM Update	1 Mar 1972	ALR-45/50 panel and lights
264	U	WSHLD AIR (Rain Removal) Caution Light	1 Mar 1972	Added caution light
268	U	Bleed-air isolation Valves and CNI Auxiliary Blower	1 Mar 1972	Bleed-air switches
269	U	Relocation of MA-1 Compass Gyroscope and Modification of Cabin Dump Panel	1 Aug 1974	Cabin dump panel
279	R	Video Tape Recorder Installation	1 Dec 1972	Recorder panel
281	U	ALE-29 Safing Pin and Flag	1 Mar 1972	Flagged pin aft of pilot's boarding ladder
287	U	ECM Update	1 Dec 1972	New ECM panel
296	U	D-704 Overpressurization Protection	1 Aug 1974	-
298	U	Response Valve Circuit Logic	1 Aug 1974	-
299	R	Relocation of D-704 Control Panel	1 Aug 1974	Observer's instrument panel
332	R	Side-Pylon Mounted Sidewinder	1 Aug 1974	COOL/FIRE switch
352	R	Modification of Fuel Dump Circuit	1 Aug 1974	DUMP/WG VENT circuit breaker
368	U	ALE-39 Countermeasures Dispenser	1 Mar 1975	ALE-39 panel
391	R	ADC Power Interrupt	1 Oct 75	CNI MASTER switch
AVC NUMBER				
658	U	Search Radar AMTI Improvement	15 Apr 1968	Operation of AMTI control
758	U	ASQ-61 Power Supply Overheat Cutout	15 Apr 1968	Operation of computer
1105	U	AN/APS-107B Modification	15 Sept 1970	-
1342	R	Reduction of Carrier Alignment Time	1 Dec 1972	-
AAC NUMBER				
592	R	AWW-1 Fuze Function Control Change	1 Aug 1974	-

Figure 1-1 (Sheet 2)

MAIN DIFFERENCES TABLE

	A-6A	A-6B	A-6C	KA-6D	A-6E	A-6E TRAM
ECM EQUIPMENT	FOR ECM DIFFERENCES REFER TO NAVAIR (01-85ADA-1A)					
20 KVA GENERATORS	X	X	X	—	—	—
30 KVA GENERATORS	—	MOD 1	—	X	X	X
MK-GRU-5 EJECTION SEATS	X	X	X	X	—	—
MK-GRU-7 EJECTION	AFC 119	AFC 119	AFC 119	AFC 119	X	X
BACK-UP HYDRAULIC SYSTEM	AFC 183	AFC 183	X	AFC 183	X	X
THREE POSITION CANOPY SWITCH	AFC 185	AFC 185	AFC 185	AFC 185	X	X
APCS AN/ASN-54 (V)	AFC 199	—	X	AFC 199	X	X
ACLS AN/ASW-25 (MODE II)	AFC 230	—	AFC 230	AFC 230	—	—
BALLISTICS COMPUTER AN/ASQ-61A	X	MOD 1	X	—	—	—
GENERAL PURPOSE COMPUTER AN/ASQ-133	—	—	—	—	X	—
SEARCH RADAR AN/APQ-92	X	X	X	—	—	—
SEARCH RADAR AN/APQ-148	—	—	—	—	X	—
TRACK RADAR AN/APQ-112	X	X	X	—	—	—
INERTIAL NAVIGATION SYSTEM AN/ASN-31	X	X	X	—	X	—
NAVIGATION COMPUTER AN/ASN-41	—	—	—	X	—	—
VIDEO TAPE RECORDER AN/USH-17 (V)	—	—	AFC 279	—	X	X
PROVISIONS FOR LB-31A STRIKE CAMERA	AFC 256	—	AFC 256	—	—	—
TIAS	—	MOD 1	—	—	—	—
DIRECTION FINDER AN/ASD-4	—	—	X	—	—	—
INFRARED DETECTING AN/AAS-28	—	—	X	—	—	—
TELEVISION CAMERA AN/AXD-4	—	—	X	—	—	—
OPTICAL SENSOR PLATFORM	—	—	X	—	—	—
ADDITIONAL AIR CONDITIONING	—	—	—	—	—	X
ACLS (MODE I)	—	—	—	AFC 161	—	X
RECONFIGURED CNI	—	—	—	—	—	X
CAINS AN/ASN-92	—	—	—	—	—	X
GENERAL PURPOSE COMPUTER AN/ASQ-155	—	—	—	—	—	X
SEARCH RADAR AN/APQ-156	—	—	—	—	—	X
DRS AN/AAS-33 PROVISIONS	—	—	—	—	—	X
CONDOR AGM-53	—	—	—	—	AFC 344	X

[1] A-6E 159895 AND ON AND A-6E MOD M121 AND ON

Figure 1-2

AIRCRAFT DIMENSIONS

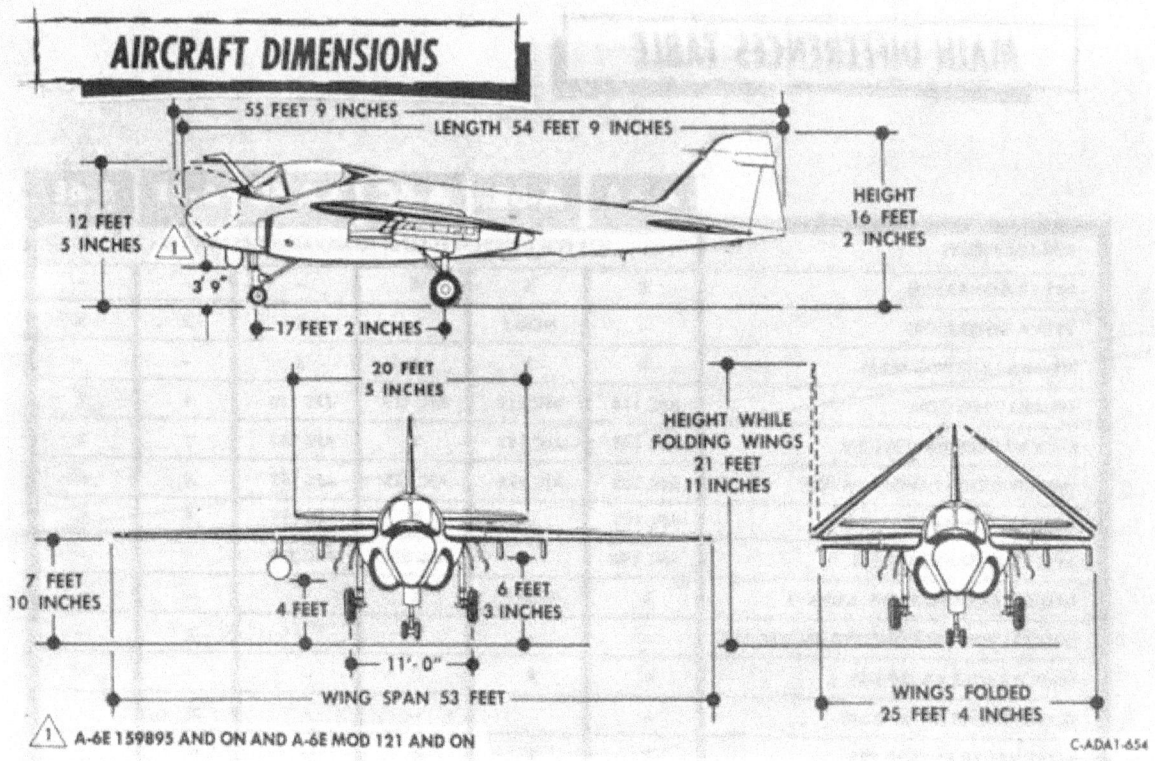

Figure 1-3

ENGINE

The aircraft is powered by two J52 P-8A/B, non-afterburning, axial-flow, turbojet engines (figure 1-4). At sea level (installed), the J52 P-8 engine develops approximately 7,700 pounds normal static thrust and 8,700 pounds military rated static thrust. The engines have a split, twelve-stage, axial-flow compressor, and a unit can-annular combustion chamber, and a split two-stage turbine. An engine bleed control system minimizes the possibility of compressor stall by automatically unloading any unusable air conditions encountered in the compressor. The compressed air supply for the aircraft is bled from the twelfth stage of the compressor. After initial start, part of this compressor air is used to drive the constant-speed drive starter (CSD/S) for starting the second engine. Twelfth-stage compressor bleed air is also used for CSD/S oil cooling on the ground, CSD/S generator function, air conditioning, engine vortex-removal jets, rain removal, and hydraulic tank pressurization. The rpm of the high-pressure turbine is governed by the engine fuel control. For a description of engine operation, refer to Section IV of this manual.

Figure 1-4

AIRCRAFT Systems NAVAIR 01-85ADA-1

 Systems

POWER PLANT SYSTEMS

THROTTLES

The throttles on the left console in the cockpit (figure 1-5), are mechanically linked to the engine fuel control units. Throttle movement does not directly affect fuel flow, but acts as one of four inputs to the fuel control units. The throttles have three placarded positions: OFF, IDLE, and MAX POWER. The idle range is reached by moving the throttle to the first stop, then around and forward of the stop (around the horn). The MAX POWER position corresponds to military thrust, and is the forward stop position of the throttles. The OFF position cuts off fuel to the engines.

The right throttle head houses four or five switches. The ICS switch is the upper switch on the throttle head and is used for various interphone functions. The speed-brakes switch is in the semicircular protrusion on the inboard face of the throttle head. Underneath the speed-brakes switch is the mike button, which is used for radio communications. In aircraft with the ALE-29A chaff dispenser, a chaff-dispense button is on the forward face of the right throttle. An air-start switch is on the aft face of both throttle heads, and is used for engine starts when airborne.

CAUTION

No provision is made in the fuel control for stabilized engine rpm in the event the throttle linkage becomes disconnected from the fuel control. If a disconnection occurs, vibration may cause the fuel control for the respective engine to assume any power setting between cutoff and military power.

Note

The APCS electromechanical actuators are located on the engines, and the throttle linkage failure may have occurred between an electromechanical actuator and the throttle. If so, the APCS switch may be held in the ENGAGE position and the desired throttle position obtained by varying AOA and releasing the APCS switch when set. Desired throttle positions may be set in this manner throughout the flight for all portions of the profile. The APCS should also be available for a normal landing approach.

THROTTLE FRICTION LOCK LEVER

A friction lock lever on the inboard side of the throttle quadrant is used to prevent the throttle from creeping. Moving the lever forward increases friction and moving it aft reduces friction. The full aft position is the off position.

Note

- The approach power compensator system will not operate unless the throttle friction lock lever is in the off position.

- Activation of the throttle friction lock lever with the approach power compensator system engaged will automatically disengage the APCS.

IGNITION SYSTEM

Each engine is provided with a dual ignition exciter unit for ground start, and for airborne continuous and air-start ignition. The ground start continuous ignition exciter unit is powered by the primary 115 V ac bus and provides high-energy (20-joule) ignition. When cranking an engine for starting, high-energy ignition is provided through igniter plugs in number 4 and 7 cans when the throttle is moved from OFF to IDLE. When the engine starts and accelerates to approximately 48% rpm, ignition automatically cuts out.

AIR - START BUTTONS

The air start buttons on the aft face of each throttle grip (figure 1-5) provides high-energy ignition to the respective engine for air start. When either button is held depressed, essential 115 V ac power, through the L or R EMERG IGN circuit breaker on the pilot's left circuit breaker panel, is provided to the ignition exciter unit, which in turn provides high-energy ignition through the igniters in burner cans number 4 and 7.

WARNING

Essential ac power must be available for air-start ignition.

1-8

ENGINE CONTROLS AND INDICATORS

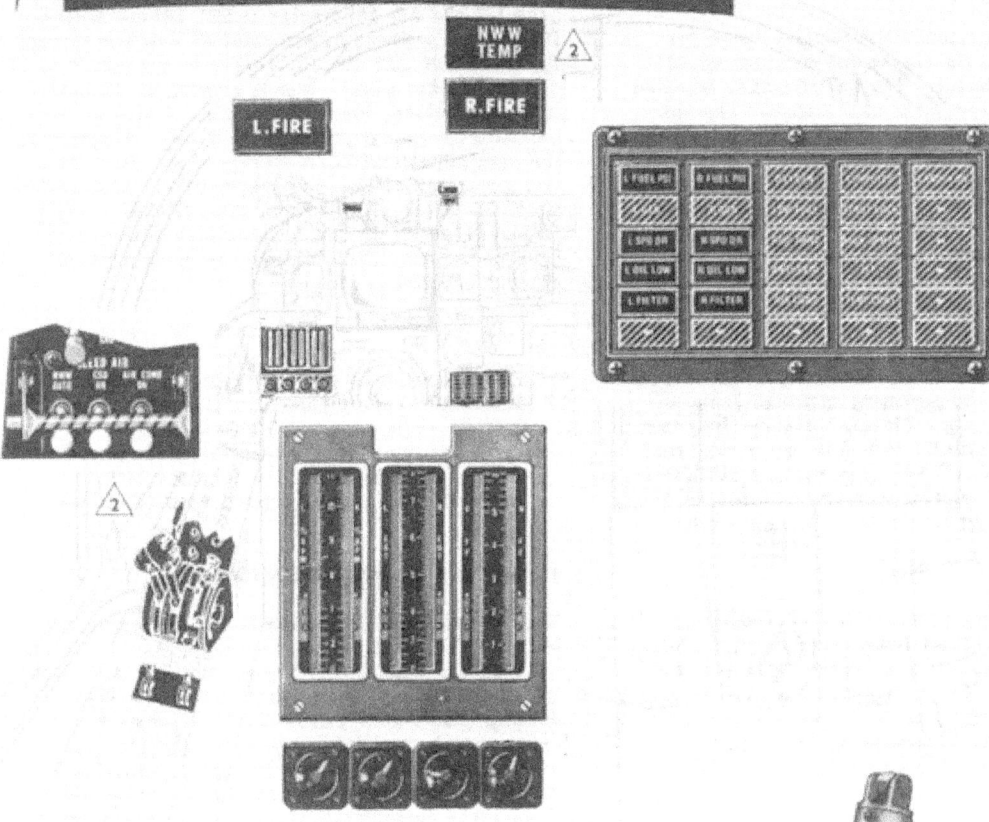

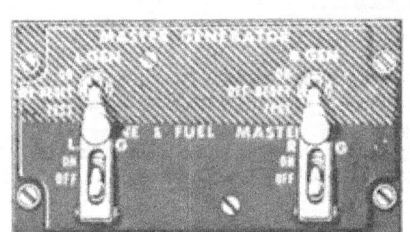

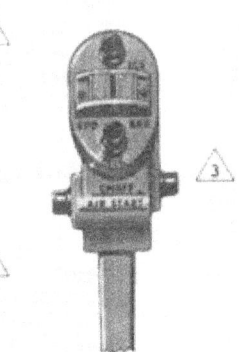

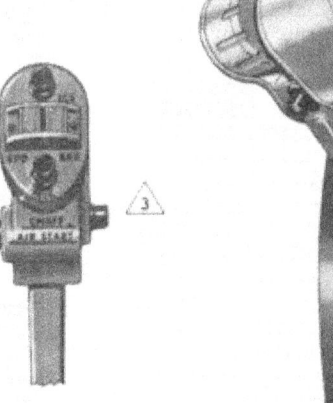

 AIRCRAFT NOT INCORPORATING AFC NO. 268

 A-6E 158533 AND ON AND AIRCRAFT INCORPORATING AFC 268

A-6A, B, C 155703 AND ON AND AIRCRAFT INCORPORATING AFC NO. 197
A-6E 158041 AND ON AND A-6E MOD M1 AND ON

Figure 1-5

AIRCRAFT
Systems

CONSTANT-SPEED DRIVE/ STARTER SYSTEM

A CSD/S (constant-speed drive/starter) provides starting torque for the engine and constant-speed drive for the generator. The CSD/S unit is mounted on the accessory section of each engine. The unit incorporates an air-driven turbine, differential transmission, and its own lubrication system. For engine start, the air turbine is driven from an external pneumatic source (or through cross-bleed from an operational engine). After the engine is started, the unit automatically goes into constant-speed drive and delivers engine torque to drive the generator. The differential transmission automatically maintains a constant generator speed with varying engine speed. To drive the generator with the engine shut down, the air turbine is driven automatically by air through cross-bleed from the operating engine or from an external power source. The air turbine drives the differential transmission, which in turn drives the generator. The CSD/S is controlled by a SPEED DRIVE switch and malfunctions are indicated by lighting of a SPD DR caution light in the cockpit.

Note

In aircraft which have engines incorporating IPPB No. 185 (smokeless burner cans), IDLE rpm may be too low at altitudes above approximately 15,000 feet to maintain constant generator speed. To ensure that generators do not drop out due to underfrequency output, maintain at least 65% engine rpm at 15,000 feet and above.

SPEED DRIVE SWITCHES

The speed drive switches are on the fuel management panel (figure 1-8) in aircraft not incorporating AFC No. 268 and on the master generator panel (figure 1-5) in aircraft incorporating AFC No. 268. The switches identified as L and R are three-position toggle switches with positions NORM, SHUTOFF, and a momentary RESET. The NORM position directs essential 28 V dc power to arm the engine crank switch and energizes a solenoid to open the pneumatic regulator shutoff valve for engine cranking. The OFF position deenergizes the solenoid, which permits the pneumatic regulator shutoff valve to close and prevents any CSD/S operation. The momentary RESET position is for ground operation of the generator without the engine operating. Positioning the switch to RESET momentarily, then to NORM, directs essential 28 V dc power to bypass the engine crank switch and energize the solenoid to open the pneumatic regulator shutoff valve, which permits air pressure to be used exclusively for driving the generator.

If both generators become inoperative in flight, the standby battery will keep the solenoid valve energized open and the generators engaged.

SPEED DRIVE LIGHTS

The speed drive lights on the annunciator panel (figures 1-5 and FO-11) display L-SPD DR and R-SPD DR and are powered by essential 28 V dc bus through the CAUTION LTS circuit breaker on the pilot's main circuit breaker panel. Steady glowing of the light indicates failure, low oil pressure, or high oil temperature for the respective CSD/S unit. Flashing of the light indicates CSD/S overspeed and the respective generator will become inoperative. At altitudes above 20,000 feet, a random, dim, flickering light indicates low oil pressure due to high altitude. A descent to lower altitude should be made prior to other corrective procedures.

Note

During zero-g or negative-g flight, either flashing or steady glowing of the speed drive lights may be expected. This does not necessarily indicate failure within the speed drive unless the indication persists after the aircraft has returned to positive-g conditions.

ENGINE & FUEL MASTER SWITCHES

The left and right engine and fuel master switches (figure 1-5) have two positions: ON and OFF. In the ON position, when either crank switch is depressed, the engine and fuel master switch will energize a holding relay. Power from the switch bypasses the crank switch, maintaining power to the speed drive switch after the crank switches are released. Other circuits in the start cycle are also energized, but since these circuits constitute automatic sequencing and cannot be controlled by the pilot, they are not discussed in this manual.

The engine and fuel master switches also open the fuel system gate valves and start the fuel boost pump. The OFF position of the switches deenergizes the engine circuits, closes the fuel system gate valves, and energizes circuits which shut down the fuel boost pump.

ENGINE CRANK BUTTONS

The engine crank buttons on the throttle quadrant (figure 1-5) are momentary pushbutton switches placarded PUSH TO CRANK. The left or right button is used to initiate the start cycle in the respective engine. With the appropriate engine fuel master switch ON and the speed drive switch in NORM, depressing a crank button completes a circuit through the gear/hook circuit breaker and opens the pressure regulator shutoff valve on the respective CSD/S unit. This allows air pressure to drive the CSD/S unit for engine start. After engine start, the crank circuit is deenergized. Both engines cannot be started simultaneously; however, either engine can be started first.

ENGINE OIL SYSTEM

Each engine is provided with a self-contained, hot-tank, high-pressure oil system for lubrication of the engine bearings and accessory drives. Oil from the tank, which has a usable capacity of 3.4 gallons, flows to the pressure pump in the accessory drive gearbox. The oil, at 45±5 psi pressure, is filtered and directed to the fuel-oil cooler and the oil nozzles in the bearing compartments. Oil will bypass the fuel-oil cooler, or the filter, if either becomes blocked. Five scavenger pumps pick up the used oil and return the oil to the tank. Air in the oil tank and bearing compartments is de-oiled at the centrifuge in the accessory drive gearbox, and excess internal pressure is vented overboard. Refer to Servicing Data, figure 1-39. Maximum oil consumption is .28 gallon per hour in a 10-hour period.

OIL QUANTITY INDICATING SYSTEM

The oil quantity indicating system is used to warn the aircrew of low oil, which could cause engine failure due to oil starvation. The system consists of two oil-level sensor probes installed in each engine oil tank, left and right low-oil caution lights on the annunciator panel, and press-to-test buttons on the master test panel. For oil system failure procedures, refer to Section V.

OIL LOW WARNING LIGHTS

During press-to-test, lighting of an OIL LOW warning light on the annunciator panel indicates oil quantity from 5 to 12 1/2 quarts ±1 quart. If the light comes on other than during press-to-test, the usable oil quantity is less than 5 ±1 quart.

OIL QUANTITY PRESS-TO-TEST BUTTONS

Oil quantity can be checked either airborne or during ground operations by depressing the LOX/FUEL/OIL test buttons on the master TEST panel. When the button is depressed, the OIL LOW lights on the annunciator panel come on to indicate oil quantity between 5 and 12 1/2 quarts in the respective oil tank. No light on, with the test button depressed, indicates oil quantity above 12 1/2 quarts. If the light comes on without depressing the button, there is less than 5 quarts in the indicated tank. The OIL LOW lights can be checked by depressing the FIRE/OIL test button, which applies power directly to the lights on the annunciator panel, through the amplifier, bypassing the sensors and sensor relays.

Note

- Oil quantity below 12 1/2 quarts ±1 quart requires engine servicing and should be reported as a discrepancy and corrected before the next takeoff.

- The LOW OIL warning light is valid only after engines scavenge.

OIL-PRESSURE INDICATOR

The oil pressure instrument is a synchro-repeater-type instrument that receives its signals from an engine-mounted oil pressure transmitter. The instrument is marked in units from 0 to 10 with a multiplier of 10, giving a range of 0 to 100 psi. The range between 35 and 50 is the normal oil pressure range; 35 psi is a minimum for ground idle conditions. Normal flight pressure is 40 to 50 psi, and is marked by a wider band and the letter N.

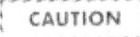

CAUTION

In addition to low oil quantity warning lights, a pressure dropdown by the indicators is also warning of an impending engine failure from oil starvation.

Aircraft maneuvers producing positive g or negative and zero g may cause engine oil pressure to deviate above or below the accepted operating range. This should be considered a normal response provided that the oil pressure returns to normal following completion of the maneuver. See prohibited maneuvers Section I Part 4 for zero/negative g time limitations.

ENGINE BLEED-AIR SYSTEM

The bleed-air system (figure 1-6) supplies high-temperature, high-pressure air from the twelfth compressor stage of the engines to the environmental control system, vortex-removal system, anti-g system, canopy seal system, hydraulic reservoir pressurization system, the fuel-cell pressurization system, and in A-6E 159895 and ON and A-6E Mod M121 and ON, the aft refrigeration unit. The functional control of the bleed air is initiated by the requirements of each individual system and the flow, temperature, and pressure are regulated by the system. Normally both engines supply air for the operation of these systems, but when necessary, single-engine operation supplies sufficient air for their operation. The system ducting is insulated to protect the airframe structure from heat radiation. Check valves in the ducting prevent back flow into the nonoperating engine during starting and single-engine operation. In A-6E 158533 and subsequent and those aircraft incorporating AFC 268, a break in the bleed-air ducting can be isolated by dividing the system into three sectors and stopping the air supply with the isolation valves, engine shutdown, or a combination of both. Temperature sensors in each sector provide warning in the event of a break.

BLEED-AIR ISOLATION VALVES

In aircraft incorporating AFC 268, three motor-driven butterfly bleed-air isolation valves divide the bleed-air system into three isolated sectors. An additional high-temperature sensor is included in the nosewheel well area. In aircraft with an aft refrigeration unit, high temperature sensors are also located in the aft equipment bay. Three switches to control these valves are on the bottom of the fuel management

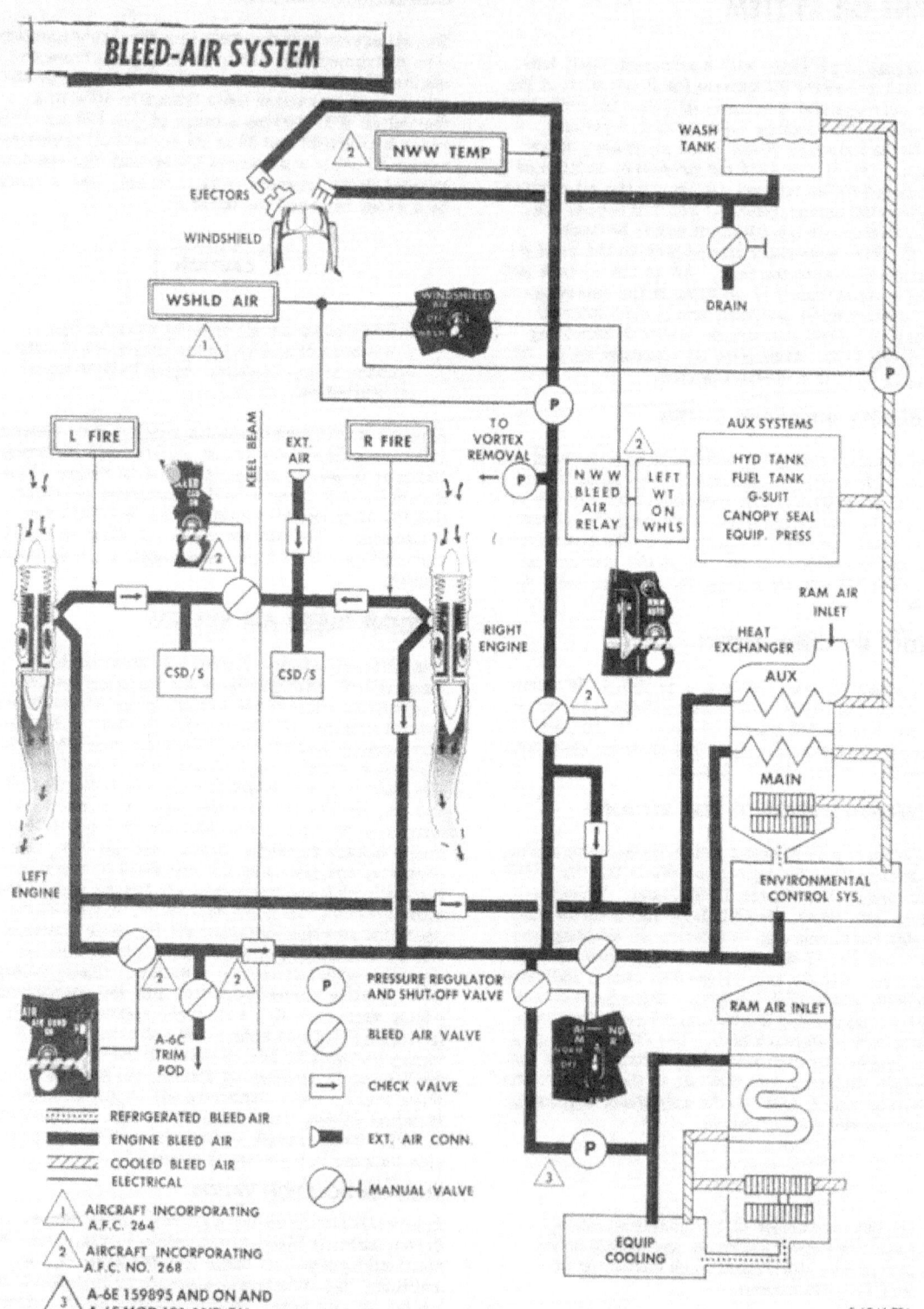

Figure 1-6

control panel (figure 1-8) and are supplied electrical power from the 115 V ac essential bus through the BLEED AIR circuit breaker on the B/N's circuit breaker panel.

Allow 5 seconds between actuations of the bleed-air isolation valves to permit the valve motors to cool.

BLEED-AIR SYSTEM CONTROLS AND INDICATORS

NWW Switch/TEMP Light

The NWW switch controls the nosewheel well bleed-air isolation valve in the forward right engine bay. The NWW valve blocks all bleed air from the nosewheel well in the event of a break in that area as indicated by lighting of the NWW TEMP light. When airborne with the NWW switch in the AUTO position, 115 V ac power from the BLEED-AIR circuit breaker through the nosewheel well bleed-air relay opens the NWW bleed-air isolation valve whenever the WINDSHIELD switch on the AIR CONDITIONING panel is in the AIR position. On the ground in the AUTO position, the valve is open through the left weight-on-wheels switch to supply the vortex-removal system and the rain-removal system when selected. The OFF position overrides any other commands and closes the valve.

CSD Switch

The CSD switch controls the CSD bleed-air isolation valve on the left side of the keel beam in the crossbleed manifold between the CSD/S's. If a break occurs in the cross-bleed manifold, it allows isolation of the two sources of bleed air so that shut-down of the affected engine will remove the supply of air to the leak.

AIR COND Switch

The AIR COND switch controls the air-conditioning bleed-air isolation valve in the left engine bay, and in A-6E 159895 and ON and A-6E Mod M121 and ON, the aft bleed-air shutoff valve in the right engine bay. If a break occurs in the ducting to the environmental control system, it allows isolation of the two sources of bleed air so that shutdown of the affected engine will remove the supply of air to the leak.

AFT TEMP Caution Light

In A-6E 159895 and ON and A-6E Mod M121 and ON, temperature-sensing elements, similar to those in the engine compartments and nosewheel well, follow the routing of hot engine bleed-air lines in the aft equipment bay. When an overtemperature condition exists, a signal is generated that lights the AFT TEMP caution light on the pilot's center instrument panel. The light, when on, indicates a possible leak in the hot engine bleed-air ducting. Airflow can be shut down by placing the AIR COND bleed-air switch on the fuel management panel to OFF. The detection system and caution light are tested by depressing the FIRE/OIL TEST switch.

ENGINE INSTRUMENTS

All the engine instruments are grouped together to the left of the horizontal display. The % RPM, EGT, and FF indicators are parallel-tape instruments. The power trim and oil-pressure instruments are circular indicators, mounted below the engine instrument group. All the instruments are marked white against black background. When cockpit lights are used, the markings appear red against a black background.

ENGINE RPM INDICATOR

A signal is developed by a tachometer generator and is compared with dc voltage from a reference potentiometer. The signal is amplified and used to drive a motor generator, which positions a white tape on the face of rpm indicators. The indicator reads percent of standard (12,052) engine rpm. The scale on the indicator is marked in 10% increments from 0% to 70%, and 1% increments, on an expanded scale, from 70% to 110%.

EXHAUST GAS TEMPERATURE INDICATOR

Exhaust gas temperature is sensed by thermocouples, which compare the generated dc signal with a reference current. The difference signal is converted to alternating current and used to drive a motor generator. As in the % RPM indicator, the motor generator drives a tape across the EGT scale. The indicator is marked in 50° C increments from 0° to 400° and 700° to 900°, and in 10° increments from 400° to 700°.

POWER TRIM INDICATOR

The power trim indicator for each engine (figure 1-5) displays temperature-corrected pressure ratio. The face of each indicator is marked PT and accommodates a single pointer. A gray arc with the extremities marked H and L is centered at the 9-o'clock position. When the pointer indicates within the arc during the MAX POWER check prior to takeoff, the engine pressure ratio is satisfactory for takeoff. Indications beyond the arc in the H or L area indicate the engine is over- or undertrimmed. Exhaust gas pressure transmitters on each engine, the total air-temperature probe, and the air data computer provide signals through the power trim computer to the indicators. The system is powered by the monitored 28 V dc bus. In flight (weight off wheels), the indicators are inoperative and the pointers out of sight behind masks.

Note

On aircraft 155599 and ON, the pointer on the power trim indicator will rotate under the following conditions:

1. When engines are off and electrical power is applied to the indicator at ambient temperatures below 75° F.

2. When engines are running and rpm is:

- Below 80% with ambient temperature between -40° and +10° F.
- Below 75% with ambient temperature between 20° and 30° F.
- Below 70% with ambient temperature between 40° and 50° F.
- Below 10% with ambient temperature above 70°.

These power trim indicators are accurate in the usable range when the pointer provides a steady indication.

ENGINE FUEL CONTROL SYSTEM

The engine fuel control system (figure 1-7) is identical for both engines and schedules fuel from the engine-driven fuel pumps to the combustion chambers. The amount of fuel metered is measured at the fuel flow transmitter, which is coupled electrically to the fuel flow indicator on the pilot's instrument panel (figure FO-2, Sheets 1, 2 and 3). Caution lights for each engine on the annunciator panel indicate when low fuel pressure or filter bypass conditions exist.

ENGINE FUEL CONTROL

The engine fuel control can be divided into a computing and metering section. The computing section monitors throttle position, burner pressure, engine speed, and compressor inlet temperature. This is translated into a fuel demand that is relayed to the metering section, which meters the correct amount of fuel from the engine fuel pump to the fuel-pressurizing and dump valve.

FUEL PRESSURIZING-AND-DUMP VALVE

The fuel pressurizing and dump valve senses fuel pressure and directs fuel to the primary and secondary fuel nozzles in the combustion chamber. Both primary and secondary fuel nozzles are used when the engine is in the operating range and fuel pressure is normal. During engine starts, low starting fuel pressure is directed to the primary fuel nozzle only. When the throttles are retarded to OFF, the pressurizing-and-dump valve stops the fuel flow from the engine fuel control and drains the primary fuel manifold overboard.

FUEL HEATER

The fuel heater is an automatically controlled unit that prevents ice from forming in the engine fuel system. This is accomplished by maintaining the minimum temperature of the fuel entering the fuel pump filter at 10°C. The fuel heater is on the bottom of the diffuser case, just forward of the pressurizing-and-dump valve and is accessible when the forward engine access door is open. The main parts of the heater are: the heat exchanger, fuel bypass valve, air-regulator valve, and the override valve. Fuel leaving the impeller stage of the engine-driven fuel pump flows around the heat exchanger core over the temperature-sensing elements of the air regulator and servo override valves, and reenters the fuel pump at the filter inlet. If the fuel passages around the heat exchanger core become restricted, a bypass valve in the heater housing opens to allow fuel flow to the engine.

FUEL FILTER LIGHT

The fuel filter lights on the annunciator panel (figure 1-8) displays L FILTER and R FILTER and are powered by the 28 V dc essential bus through the CAUTION LTS circuit breaker on the main circuit breaker panel. Lighting of either light indicates the fuel filter for the respective engine is obstructed. A pressure switch completes a circuit to the light when a minimum of 5 psi differential pressure exists between the inlet and outlet of the fuel filter.

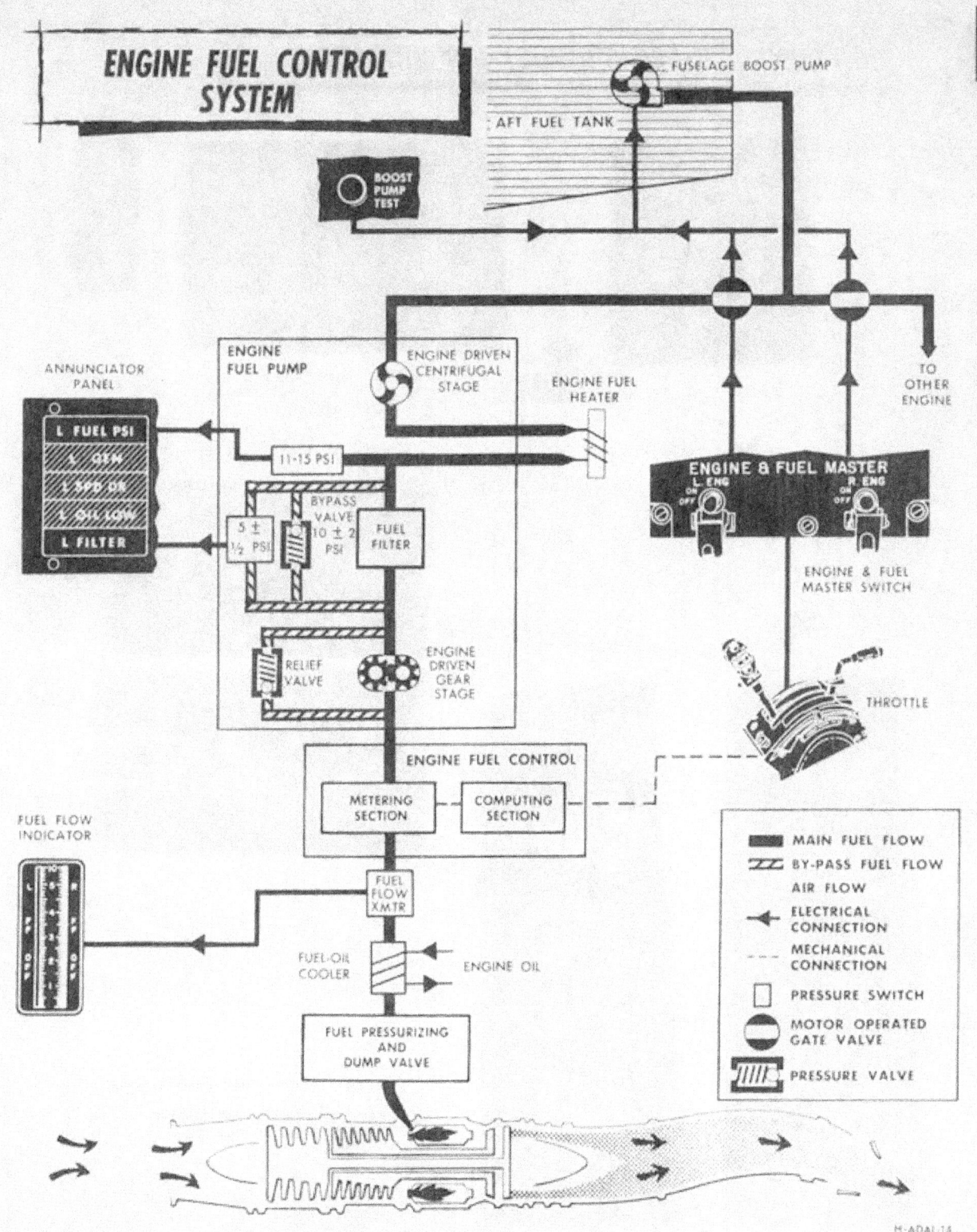

Figure 1-7

AIRCRAFT SYSTEMS
NAVAIR 01-85ADA-1

FUEL SUPPLY SYSTEM CONTROLS AND INDICATORS

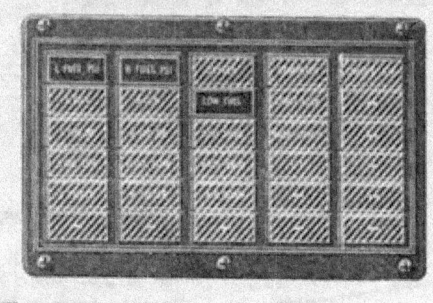

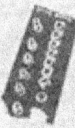

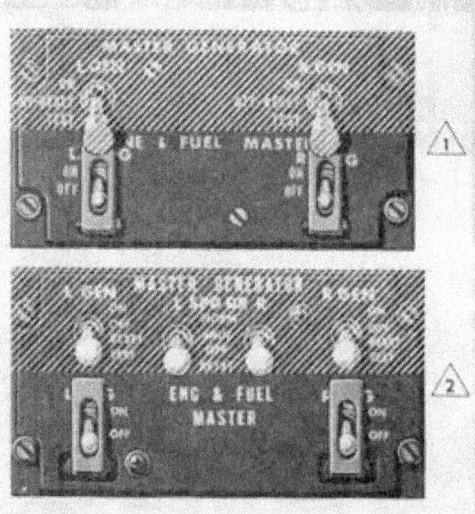

1. AIRCRAFT NOT INCORPORATING AFC NO. 268
2. A-6E 158533 AND ON AND AIRCRAFT INCORPORATING AFC NO. 268

Figure 1-8

NAVAIR 01-85ADA-1

AIRCRAFT
Systems

PRIMARY AIRCRAFT SYSTEMS

AIRCRAFT FUEL SUPPLY SYSTEM

The aircraft fuel supply system (figure FO-4) provides JP-4 or JP-5 fuel to the engine-driven fuel pumps and can be replenished in flight or used to refuel another aircraft. Refueling is accomplished through a single-point pressure refueling nozzle on the ground, or the air-refueling probe located at the aircraft centerline forward of the windshield.

The fuselage tanks include forward and aft self-sealing cells and a bladder-type mid cell. Manifolds integrate the fuselage cells and allow gravity fuel flow to the aft cell.

The wing tanks include two outboard wet tanks, one in each outer wing panel, and an inboard wet wing tank spanning from wingfold to wingfold. Transfer from all wing tanks is simultaneous and is controlled by the tank pressurization switch on the fuel management panel. See figure 1-9 for fuel tank capacities.

FUEL MGMT CONTROL PANEL

The fuel management control panel on the pilot's left console (figure 1-8) provides controls for pressurization and transfer of wing and drop-tank fuel, selectors for fuselage, wing and drop-tank fuel quantity indications, switches for fuel dumping, ground and air-refueling, and a boost pump test button.

Fuel Ready Switch

The FUEL READY switch on the fuel management panel (figure 1-8) is a three-position toggle switch with positions placarded FLT, OFF, and GRD that is used for receiving fuel in flight or for ground fueling. Placing the switch in FLT stops internal transfer of fuel by venting wing and drop tanks (or air-refueling store) to permit the aircraft to receive fuel during air-refueling operations. Fuel is taken on as it is during single-point ground fueling. In OFF, the valves return to their normal configuration. The GRD position permits the aircraft to be fueled with the single-point refueling system.

> **CAUTION**
>
> The normal flight position for this switch is OFF. Wing and drop-tank fuel will not transfer if the FUEL READY switch is in the FLT position or GRD position. Wing and drop tank fuel will not transfer if the FUEL READY switch is in the GRD position with the ground refueling power switch in FUEL or DEFUEL position.

ENGINE FUEL FEED SYSTEM

The aft cell of the fuselage tanks supplies fuel through a service tank boost pump and motor-operated gate valves to the engine fuel pumps. The aft cell is divided into two compartments by a baffle and inverted flight check valves. The check valves allow fuel to flow into the bottom part of the cell, which is essentially a service tank. The boost pump that supplies fuel to the engine pumps is in the service tank, ensuring fuel supply to the engine for a limited time for any one flight maneuver. Fuel from the forward and mid fuselage cells is gravity-fed to the lower part of the service tank through a one-way check valve. Fuel under bleed-air pressure is fed from wing and drop tanks to the forward fuselage tanks.

The service tank boost pump is controlled by the engine and fuel master switches on the master generator panel (figure 1-8). When either switch is placed ON, a relay deenergizes, closing a circuit to the boost pump. In this way, a relay failure in the aircraft will not affect boost pump operation. The engine and fuel master switches also control motor-operated gate valves. There is one gate valve for each engine in the manifold to the engine-driven fuel pump. The OFF position of the engine and fuel master switch electrically closes the valve; the ON position drives the valve open. If there is a power failure, the valve will remain in the last selected position.

Boost Pump Test Button

The boost pump test button on the fuel management control panel (figure 1-8) placarded BOOST PUMP TEST is for ground checking the operation of the main tank boost pump and the centrifugal element of the engine-driven boost pumps. When the button is depressed, primary 115 V ac power is removed from the main tank boost pump, shutting it off. Before engine start, the main tank boost pump test circuit is checked by depressing the button, shutting off the electrically driven main tank boost pump.

> **CAUTION**
>
> To preclude an engine fire, if an engine flames out during this test, the appropriate engine fuel master switch should be positioned to OFF before releasing the fuel boost pump test button.

Lighting of the L and R LOW FUEL PRESS lights indicates that the main tank boost pump test circuit did in fact shut off the boost pump. After engines are started, the centrifugal stage of the engine-driven fuel boost pump is checked by depressing the button, shutting off the electrically driven main tank boost pump. Lighting of either the L or R LOW FUEL PRESS lights indicates failure of the centrifugal stage of the respective engine-driven fuel boost pump by its failure to maintain fuel pressure.

> **CAUTION**
>
> DO NOT DEPRESS BOOST PUMP TEST BUTTON IN FLIGHT as an engine will flame out if the centrifugal stage of an engine-driven boost pump has failed.

1-17

AIRCRAFT
Systems

NAVAIR 01-85ADA-1

FUEL QUANTITY DATA TABLE

DATE: 1 MAY 1965
DATA BASIS: ESTIMATED

TANKS	TOTAL CAPACITY		APPROX. USEABLE FUEL IN LEVEL FLIGHT	
	GALLONS	POUNDS	GALLONS	POUNDS
FUSELAGE (MAIN) TANKS	1,326	9,016	1,309	8,900
INTERNAL WING TANKS	1,018	6,923	1,010	6,868
TOTAL FUSELAGE PLUS INTERNAL WING	2,344	15,939	2,319	15,768
EACH DROP TANK OR AIR REFUELING STORE	300	2,040	295.5	2,009

NOTE

TOTAL AIRCRAFT FUEL READ ON THE FUEL QUANTITY GAGE TOTALIZER EXCLUDES THE AIR REFUELING STORE.

WEIGHTS ARE BASED ON 6.8 POUNDS PER GALLON OF JP-5 FUEL, STANDARD DAY CONDITIONS.

D-ADA1-17

Figure 1-9

ENGINE FUEL PUMP

A two-stage fuel pump on the accessory drive gearbox supplies boosted fuel pressure to the engine fuel control. The pump consists of a positive-displacement gear-type pumping element and an impeller booster. If the fuel filter, between the pumping element and the impeller, becomes blocked, fuel will be directed around the filter automatically by the filter bypass. Two pressure switches, which control the low fuel-pressure and filter bypass caution lights, are also located between the pump stages.

LOW FUEL PRESSURE LIGHTS

The low fuel-pressure lights on the annunciator panel (figure 1-8) display L FUEL PSI and R FUEL PSI and are powered by the essential 28 V dc bus through the CAUTION LTS circuit breaker on the main circuit breaker panel. A pressure switch downstream of the centrifugal stage of the engine-driven pump completes a circuit to the light when the pressure is below approximately 12 to 14 PSI. At lower altitudes (below 20,000 feet), the centrifugal stage of an engine-driven pump or the main tank boost pump alone can maintain sufficient fuel pressure for engine operation and keep the light out. At higher altitudes (above 20,000 feet), failure of the centrifugal stage of an engine-driven pump will turn on the light for its respective engine, and failure of the main tank boost pump will turn on the lights for both engines. A reduction in power and descent to lower altitude should turn off the light and prevent an engine flameout.

FUEL FLOW INDICATOR

A fuel flow transmitter, powered by essential 115 V ac, 400-Hz current, translates fuel flow into an electrical signal. The signal is fed to the transformer and stepped up to drive a motor generator. The motor generator, in turn, drives a tape across the FF indicator. The fuel flow indicator reads pounds per hour (PPH) and is marked in 100-PPH increments up to 5,000 PPH. Above 5,000 PPH and up to 10,000 PPH, the scale is marked in 1,000-PPH increments and is compressed into a smaller linear distance.

FUEL PRESSURIZATION, TRANSFER, AND VENT SYSTEM

Fuselage Tanks

The fuselage fuel cells are maintained at a positive pressure of 1.25 to 2.0 psi above ambient pressure by ram air inducted through an inlet scoop on the upper aft fuselage. This pressurization ensures a head pressure to the fuselage boost pump and prevents cell collapse.

Wing and Drop Tanks

Under normal flight conditions, gear up and locked, the integrated pressurization transfer-and-vent features of the fuel supply system function automatically. Pressurization is furnished by cooled bleed air from the engines twelfth-stage compressor. In the event of double engine failure and the FUEL READY switch is in other than OFF, place the switch OFF prior to ejection. The wing tanks are pressurized to 7 psi and the drop tanks to 25 psi. Without pressurization, fuel cannot be transferred. Low wing-tank pressure is indicated by the wing-tank pressure caution lights on the fuel management panel. When going from unpressurized to pressurized tanks, there is a slight delay before the low wing-tank pressure caution lights go out because of the time needed to cycle the tank relief valves and pressurize the tanks. Limited control over the pressurization, transfer, and vent system is possible through the use of the tank pressurization switch, wing drop-tank transfer switch, and ship tank switch.

Tank Pressurization Switch

This switch is on the fuel management panel (figure 1-8) and has three positions: ORIDE, NORM, and OFF. In ORIDE, wing pressure-relief valves will close regardless of landing gear position and the pressure regulators will open to pressurize the tanks. With gear down, aircraft on the deck, and ORIDE selected, wing-tank pressurization is 7 psi. With aircraft airborne, gear up or down, and ORIDE selected, wing tanks are pressurized to 12 psi. The OFF position of the tank pressurization switch will prevent pressure buildup by holding the vent relief valve open under all flight conditions. With the switch in the NORM position and the landing gear up and locked, tank pressurization is regulated automatically. The tank pressurization switch is primarily for preflight check of fuel transfer capability.

CAUTION

During ground operation, if the tank pressure switch is actuated to ORIDE when the air-conditioning master switch is OFF, hot engine bleed air will be pumped into the wing tanks. This will damage the O-ring seals in the zero-leak check valves, permitting fuel to flow into the auxiliary heat exchanger, the hydraulic tank, vent suit, canopy seal, and electronic equipment in the nosewheel well as well as the engine bleed air lines. However, this situation will not occur while airborne due to sufficient ram air cooling.

Note

With landing gear down, wing and drop-tank fuel cannot be transferred or dumped unless the tank pressurization switch is set to ORIDE.

Outbd/Inbd WG PSI Lights

The wing-tank pressure lights on the fuel management panel (figure 1-8) display OUTBD WG PSI and INBD WG PSI and are powered by the essential 28 V dc bus. Lighting of either or both lights indicates air pressure in the respective wing tanks is below approximately 6 psi and fuel is not transferring, or is transferring at a reduced rate. The light circuit is completed by pressure switches in the respective wing tanks.

Wing Drop-Tank Transfer Switch

The wing-drop tank transfer switch (figure 1-8) on the fuel management panel has three positions: INBD, OUTBD, and NORM. The INBD position closes shut-off valves in the outboard drop tanks and the centerline tank and allows fuel to transfer from the inboard tanks. With the switch in the OUTBD position, the inboard and centerline shutoff valves are closed and fuel is transferred from the outboard tanks. Fuel transfers simultaneously from all the drop tanks with the switch in the NORM position. All drop-tank fuel transfers to the forward fuselage cell, except when dumping wing-tank fuel.

CAUTION

Tests have indicated that possible overpressurization of the fuselage fuel tanks may occur if all four drop tanks empty simultaneously. No reported instances have occurred to date; however, the following mandatory drop-tank selection procedure must be adhered to in flight for those affected aircraft:

1. Place wing-drop-tank transfer switch on INBD until inboard drop tanks empty.

2. After inboard drop tanks have emptied, place switch in NORM for remainder of flight.

3. If configured with four or more drop tanks, and only two are fueled, then NORM should be selected since only the two will empty simultaneously.

4. Three conditions exist during which drop tank transfer switch is to be placed in NORM when all drop tanks contain fuel:

   a. When fuel is being dumped.

   b. When aircraft is serving as a tanker and fuel is being transferred to receiver aircraft.

   c. Fewer than four drop tanks are installed.

Note

In aircraft not incorporating AFC No. 158, with the tank pressurization switch set to OFF, or the landing gear down, fuel will syphon from the fuselage tank to the drop tanks if inboard tanks are configured and the wing-tank transfer switch is set to OUTBD, or if outboard tanks are configured and the wing-tank transfer switch is set to INBD.

FUEL QUANTITY INDICATING SYSTEM

The fuel quantity indicating system consists of fuel capacitance sensor units mounted in the fuel tanks, a fuel quantity gage, fuel quantity selector buttons, and an indicator test button and an independent low fuel quantity caution light. The capacitance sensor units compensate for changes in fuel density and present a signal to the gage proportional to fuel quantity in pounds. The system is powered by essential 28 V dc power through the TURN/SLIP circuit breaker on the main circuit breaker panel and essential 115 V ac power through the LOX/FUEL QTY circuit breaker on the pilot's left console circuit breaker panel.

Fuel Quantity Gage

The fuel quantity gage (figure 1-8) on the pilot's instrument panel displays three simultaneous indications of fuel quantity. A digital totalizer in the lower part of the instrument face provides a continuous indication of total pounds of fuel on board. Two rotating needles indicate on a circular scale that is graduated in increments of 200 pounds up to 3,000 pounds and 500-pound increments from 3,000 to 10,000 pounds. The main needle indicates pounds of fuel in the main tank. The selectable needle indicates pounds of fuel in the main, wing, or any of the five drop tanks as selected by buttons on the fuel management panel. For fuel quantity gage tolerance scale, see figure 1-10.

Note

Unreliable totalizer and selectable needle indications should not be construed as a complete failure of the fuel quantity indicating system. The main needle can continue to be reliable and should be closely monitored to ensure proper fuel transfer.

Fuel Gage Selector Buttons

Seven FUEL GAGE selector buttons on the fuel management control panel (figure 1-8) are placarded R

FUEL QUANTITY GAGE TOLERANCE SCALE

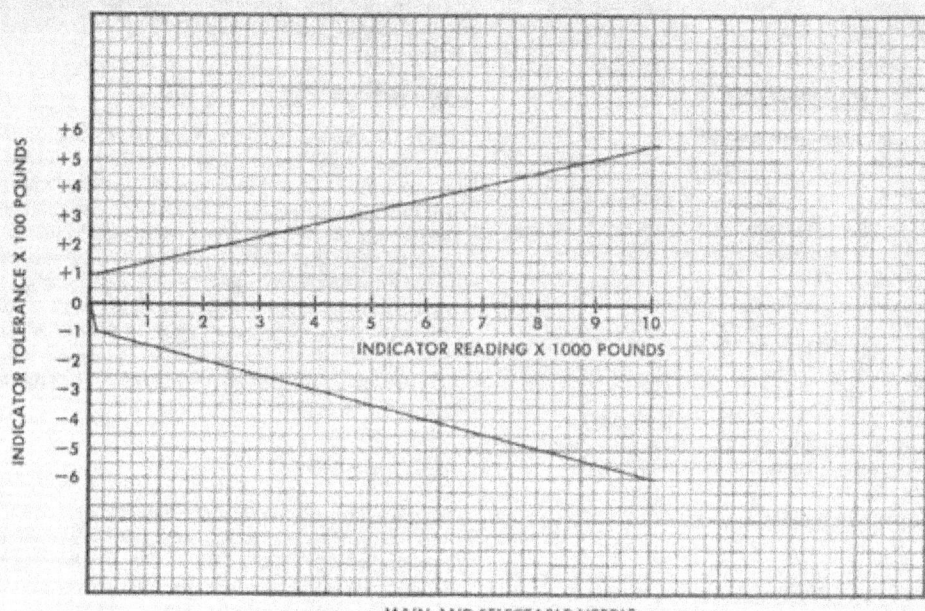

MAIN AND SELECTABLE NEEDLE

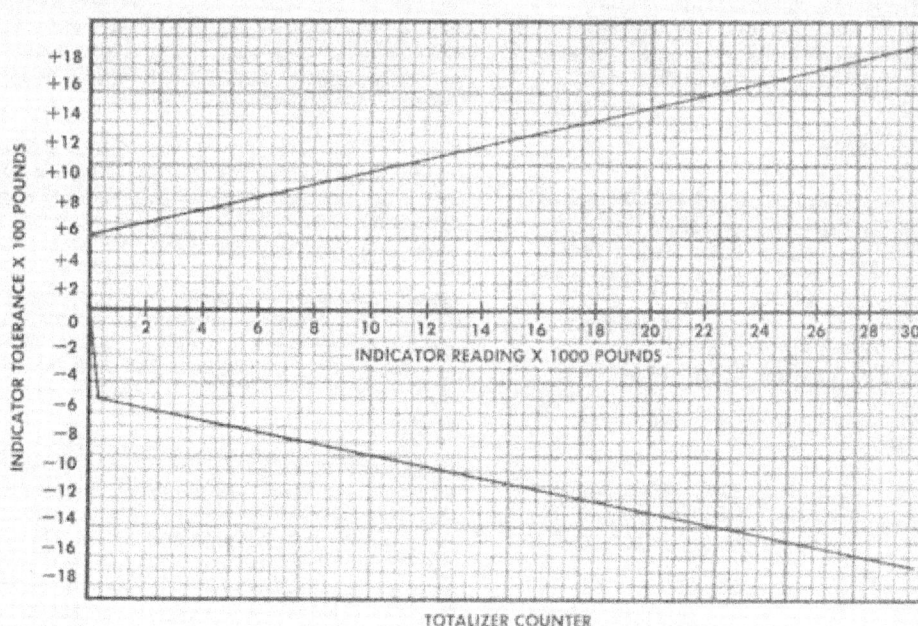

TOTALIZER COUNTER

Figure 1-10

AIRCRAFT
Systems

OUTBD, R INBD, L INBD, L OUTBD, CTR, WING, and MAIN. Depressing a particular button cancels the previous selection and selects that particular tank for presentation of fuel quantity on the fuel quantity indicator by the selectable needle. The depressed button rotates 45° and serves as a visual indication of the selected tank.

WARNING

If the selectable needle is reflecting wing fuel, and wing fuel does not transfer, it is possible to misread the wing fuel needle as fuselage fuel quantity, and not recognize fuselage fuel decreasing to zero.

CAUTION

To prevent damage to the fuel quantity gage, a selector button should be selected at all times. If a selector button is not selected, the gage will continue to motorize against the zero stop and burn out.

Note

Unless Accessory Change 86 is incorporated depressing the center store selector button with an in-flight refueling store on the centerline station will cause the selectable needle to go to zero regardless of fuel quantity in the store.

Low Fuel Caution Light

The low fuel caution circuit is highly reliable and is independent of the fuel quantity indicating system. A separate thermal resistance bridge circuit energizes the LOW FUEL caution light on the annunciator panel. The thermal resistors are part of a liquid-level sensor mounted in the aft fuselage fuel tank. When the thermal resistors are exposed to air, a relay is deenergized, allowing electrical power to reach the LOW FUEL caution light. When the thermal resistors are immersed in fuel, the relay is energized, turning off the caution light.

The thermistor will turn on the LOW FUEL caution light when the remaining fuel level is between 1,360 to 1,660 pounds of fuel, under the following conditions:

1. Aircraft attitude - 4° nose up

2. Fuel flow (maximum range cruise at 10,000 feet) - 1,460 lb/hour/engine

3. Aircraft weight - 30,000 pounds

Under these conditions, 80 pounds of fuel will remain in the forward fuselage tank, and 1,380 pounds of fuel will remain in the aft tank. Since the thermistor is in the aft tank, an increase in nose-up attitude that permits all the fuselage fuel to flow to the aft tank will delay a low-fuel indication until there is only 1,380 pounds of fuel remaining. This is 80 pounds below the 1,460 plus 200 minus 100 pounds desired. A decrease in the 4° nose up attitude will result in more than 1,460 plus 200 minus 100 pounds of fuel remaining at the time the LOW FUEL caution light comes on.

LOX/FUEL/OIL Press-To-Test Button

The LOX/FUEL/OIL press-to-test button on the MASTER TEST panel (figure 1-8) is provided to test the operation of oxygen quantity gage, OXYGEN light, and fuel quantity gage. Depressing the button causes the digital counter and the two needles on the fuel quantity gage and the needle on the liquid oxygen gage to move toward zero and the OXYGEN light on the annunciator panel to come on. In aircraft incorporating OIL LOW lights, depressing this button is also a check of oil quantity. Lighting of either OIL LOW light on the annunciator panel indicates engine oil servicing is required.

FUEL DUMPING SYSTEM

Aircraft fuel can be dumped overboard simultaneously from the fuselage tanks and the wing tanks. The wing drop tanks and the centerline drop tank or the air-refueling pod can be jettisoned, or if the tanks are to be retained, fuel from the wing drop tanks must be transferred to the outboard wing tanks. The centerline drop tank or the air-refueling store fuel must be transferred to the fuselage tank. Drop tank transfer occurs automatically. To transfer fuel from the refueling pod, the ship tank switch must be in the FROM STORE position.

Wing fuel dumping is controlled by the wing dump switch (figure 1-8). Placing the switch in DUMP opens the wing dump valves and allows tank pressure to build to 12 psi for quicker dumping. Optimum wing fuel dumping is achieved at cruise attitude, 4° to 4 1/2° nose up. While flying in this attitude, approximately 6,300 pounds of wing fuel can be dumped in 5 minutes. Due to drain-down time, it takes approximately 3 minutes to dump the remaining dumpable fuel, 554 pounds. The fuel leaves the aircraft through manifolds on the trailing edge of each wingtip.

When dumping wing fuel while flying at nose-down attitudes, the dump rate becomes increasingly slower. With decreasing attitude, dumping becomes sporadic because air pressure is lost when the dump valve inlet, in the trailing edge, is uncovered and the amount of trapped fuel becomes increasingly larger. The amount of trapped fuel ranges from approximately 140 gallons trapped at 0° flight attitude to the total wing fuel (1,018 gallons) at 10° nose down.

Flight test has shown that the disturbance in the airflow over the wing caused by the wing-tip speed brakes when they are extended is sufficient to significantly disrupt the pattern of fuel flowing from the wings during dump. For this reason, wing fuel should be dumped with the wing-tip speed brakes closed.

Fuselage fuel dumping is selected with the fuselage (FUS) dump switch. The transfer-and-dump pumps in the forward and aft cells operate to increase the dump rate. With fuselage cells full, dumpable fuel is pumped overboard in 3.5 to 4 minutes. Due to the location of the transfer-and-dump pump in the forward cell and the standpipe in the aft cell, a certain amount of fuel remains in the fuselage tank after dumping is completed. At cruise attitude (4 1/2° nose up or 12 1/2 units on the AOA indicator), approximately 3600 pounds remain in the A-6A, B, C, and A-6E, and approximately 2700 pounds in the KA-6D. A slight dive will increase fuel remaining. A slight climb, an airspeed change, or any other maneuver resulting in an increased angle of attack during dump will decrease the fuel remaining to a minimum of 2400 pounds. The fuselage fuel is dumped through a dump vent outlet at the lower aft end of the fuselage.

Purging of fuel vapor from the wing tanks is automatic. No purging is provided for the drop tanks.

Fuselage Dump Switch (FUS)

The DUMP position of the two-position fuselage switch on the fuel management panel (figure 1-8) starts the forward and aft fuel transfer pumps and opens the fuselage dump gate valve. Power to drive the forward pump comes from the monitored 115 V ac bus. The rear pump is powered by 115 V ac from the primary ac bus. The NORM position of the switch cuts electrical power to the transfer pumps and drives the fuselage dump gate valve closed.

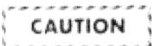

CAUTION

Place the fuselage dump switch to NORM after dumping fuselage fuel to prevent the transfer pumps from overheating.

Wing-Dump Switch

The wing dump switch has two positions: DUMP and NORM. When DUMP is selected, power is supplied to the wing dump valves, the wing tank gate valves, and the wing tank pressure regulators. The regulators boost pressure to 12 psi in the wing tanks for dumping. The wing gate valves are powered closed, preventing fuel transfer to the fuselage tanks. Leaving the switch in DUMP will hold the wing dump valves open. The NORM position of the wing dump switch powers the wing dump valves closed, and allows the wing-tank pressure regulator to pressure the tanks at 7 psi with the landing gear retracted.

Note

- When refueling in flight at a low fuel state, placing the WING DUMP switch to the DUMP position will allow all received fuel to enter the fuselage cells and centerline tank if installed where it is immediately available to the engines.

- Return wing dump switch to NORM prior to landing to prevent dumping fuel on deck.

AIR REFUELING SYSTEM

The aircraft can receive fuel in flight from a drogue-equipped tanker, or serve as a tanker and deliver fuel in flight to a probe-equipped receiver aircraft. Air-refueling flight procedures are found in Section IV, Part 4, of this manual, and the Air Refueling NATOPS manual. Air-refueling charts are available in Section XI, Part 3. A description of the air-refueling tanker system is presented in Section VIII.

AIR REFUELING (RECEIVER)

During air-refueling, fuel flows through the receiver aircraft probe nozzle under pressure and is distributed to each tank in the same manner as it is through the single-point refueling (system) receptacle. The amount of fuel flow is determined by the number of empty or partially full receiver tanks. As each tank is filled, float-operated shutoff valves stop the flow of incoming fuel.

Fuel flow rates vary in accordance with the fueling pressure at the refueling-probe nozzle and the number of tanks filling. The maximum rate is approximately 325 gpm when all tanks are filling. The refueling shutoff valves are designed to withstand surge pressures that current tankers produce.

Air Refueling Probe Light

A red air-refueling probe light is installed to illuminate the air-refueling probe for night operation. The light is forward of the cockpit canopy and left of the aircraft centerline and is aimed a the tip of the refueling probe. Placing the TAXI/PROBE light switch on the master light control panel (figure 1-36) to ON directs electrical power to the probe light when the landing gear are up and locked.

Refueling Valve Manual Control Handle

A refueling valve manual control handle is provided to open or close the refueling gate valve (figure FO-4) manually in the event of electrical failure. Located between the pilot and B/N, the handle is mounted in a slotted guide on the bulkhead adjacent to the right side of the main circuit breaker panel. The handle is placarded REFUELING VALVE MANUAL CONTROL and has two detented positions marked OPEN (up) and CLOSE (down).

Note

In-flight actuation of the REFUELING VALVE MANUAL CONTROL HANDLE in the event of complete electrical failure will permit refueling of fuselage tanks only. The wing tanks will still remain pressurized.

If operated with electrical valve failure only (not total electrical failure), all tanks will be filled.

AIRCRAFT
Systems

NAVAIR 01-85ADA-1

ELECTRICAL POWER SUPPLY SYSTEM

The normal electrical power supply in the A-6A, A-6B/Mod 0/1 and A-6C (figure FO-5) is provided by the two engine-driven 115/200 V ac generators (alternators) rated at 20 kVA. In the A-6B Mod 1, KA-6D, and A-6E, the engine-driven generators are rated at 30 kVA. Transformer/rectifiers convert 115 V ac to 28 V dc for aircraft electrical requirements. Normally each engine drives one generator by a pneumatic mechanical constant-speed drive/starter unit (CSD/S). If an engine fails, bleed air from the operating engine (rpm above 75%) will automatically be directed to the CSD/S of the inoperative engine. Each generator is controlled by a switch on the master generator panel (figure FO-2). The CSD/S is controlled by a speed drive switch on the fuel management control panel (figure FO-2) in aircraft not incorporating AFC 268 and on the master generator panel (figure FO-2) in aircraft incorporating AFC 268.

Note

In aircraft that have engines incorporating IPPB 185 (smokeless burner cans), idle rpm may be too low at altitudes above approximately 15,000 feet to maintain constant generator speed. To ensure that generators do not drop out due to underfrequency output, maintain at least 65% engine rpm at 15,000 feet and above.

The system is protected by supervisory control panels that sense abnormal voltage conditions and automatically deenergize the affected generator. A battery is provided as an auxiliary source of dc power for the CSD/S and the assist-spin recovery system. If both generators fail, an emergency electrical power system (ram-air turbine generator) is available to provide power for the operation of essential equipment. An external power receptacle is provided for starting engines or operating electrical systems by ground power.

CIRCUIT BREAKERS

Circuit breaker panels are located in the cockpit (figure 1-11 Sheets 1 thru 4) and external throughout the aircraft (figure 1-12 Sheet 1 thru 9). Panels particular to the A-6B or A-6C as well as A-6A panels modified for the A-6B or A-6C are shown in figure 1-13 Sheets 1 and 2). In the cockpit, the main and bombardier/navigator's circuit breaker panels are installed in an inverted position to facilitate reading the placards. Key cockpit circuit breakers are shown in figure 1-14.

Pushbutton-type circuit breakers protect the electrical supply system and associated components from an overloaded circuit. The appropriate circuit breaker will pop and isolate a circuit or component that draws too much current, thus preventing equipment damage and possible fire.

The numeral on the button indicates the amperage (amp) rating. The three-phase or gang-bar circuit breakers can be set so that two phases only are engaged. To prevent equipment malfunction, ensure all three phases of the gang bar are engaged.

CAUTION

Do not hold in circuit breakers that repeatedly pop out. Forceably holding the circuit breaker in may result in irreparable damage to the equipment or possible fire.

Note

In the event of equipment malfunction, it is recommended that the applicable circuit breaker be disengaged until qualified maintenance personnel have repaired the defective equipment.

EXTERNAL POWER

External three-phase power is supplied to the ac power distribution system through a standard six-pin receptacle on the right side of the fuselage. The electrical systems are protected against incorrect phase-sequenced ground power by a phase-sensing relay In A-6A, B, C 154170 and ON and aircraft incorporating AFC 102, the phase-sensing relay is replaced by an external power monitor, which protects the systems against over- and undervoltage, over- and underfrequency, and incorrect phase rotation in the ground power supply. The two-position external power monitor control switch labeled RESET, NORMAL is on the external power panel.

ELECTRICAL POWER DISTRIBUTION

Electrical power is distributed to the various electrical components through a series of buses. The buses are arranged to group equipment of equivalent significance. In this way, any failure in the system can be automatically directed toward the areas of least importance. Generally, the essential buses power all the equipment necessary to fly the aircraft, the primary buses power equipment necessary to complete the mission, and the monitored bus powers the convenience circuits.

When both generators are operating, the right generator supplies the primary ac buses and, through the emergency power transfer relay, supplies the essential ac buses. The left generator, through its line contactor, energizes the monitored transformer/rectifier (T/R) and the 115 V ac monitored bus. The T/R, in turn, powers the 28 V dc monitored buses. The right generator through its line contactor, energizes the primary T/R and the primary and essential ac buses.

The primary T/R supplies power to the dc primary and through the dc emergency transfer relay to the

NAVAIR 01-85ADA-1

AIRCRAFT
Systems

COCKPIT CIRCUIT BREAKER PANELS

A-6A/B/C TYPICAL

5 PILOTS LEFT CONSOLE CIRCUIT BREAKER PANELS

3 B/N AUXILIARY CIRCUIT BREAKER PANEL

2 B/N AUXILIARY CIRCUIT BREAKER PANEL

⚠1 155642 AND ON AND AIRCRAFT INCORPORATING A.F.C. NO. 217

⚠2 149941 THROUGH 155641 NOT INCORPORATING A.F.C. NO. 217

⚠3 AIRCRAFT INCORPORATING A.F.C. NO. 119

⚠4 AIRCRAFT INCORPORATING A.F.C. NO. 268

⚠5 AIRCRAFT INCORPORATING A.F.C. NO. 230

1 BOMBARDIER/NAVIGATOR'S CIRCUIT BREAKER PANEL

4 MAIN CIRCUIT BREAKER PANEL

O-ADA1-21

Figure 1-11 (Sheet 1)

1-25

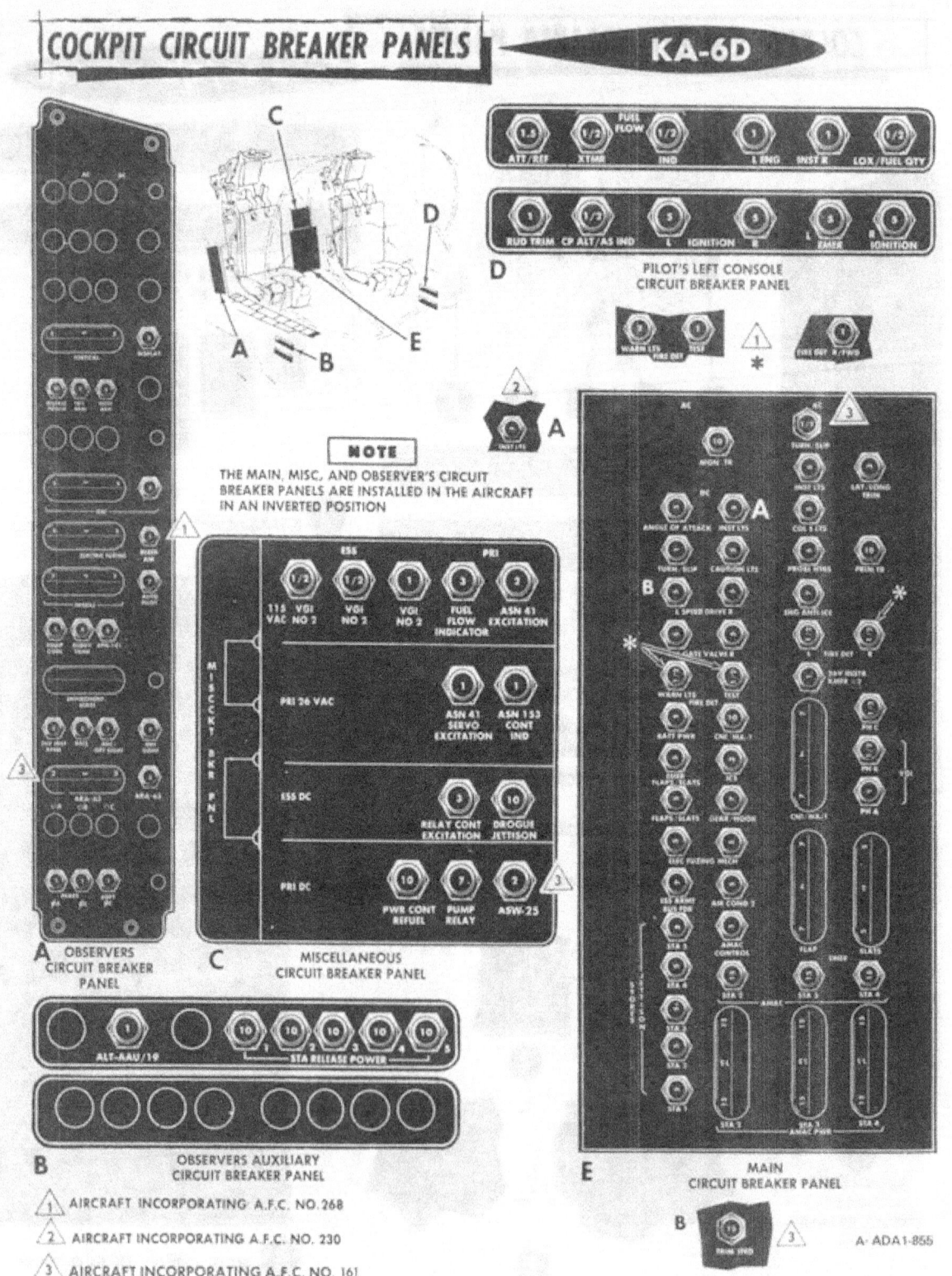

Figure 1-11 (Sheet 2)

NAVAIR 01-85ADA-1

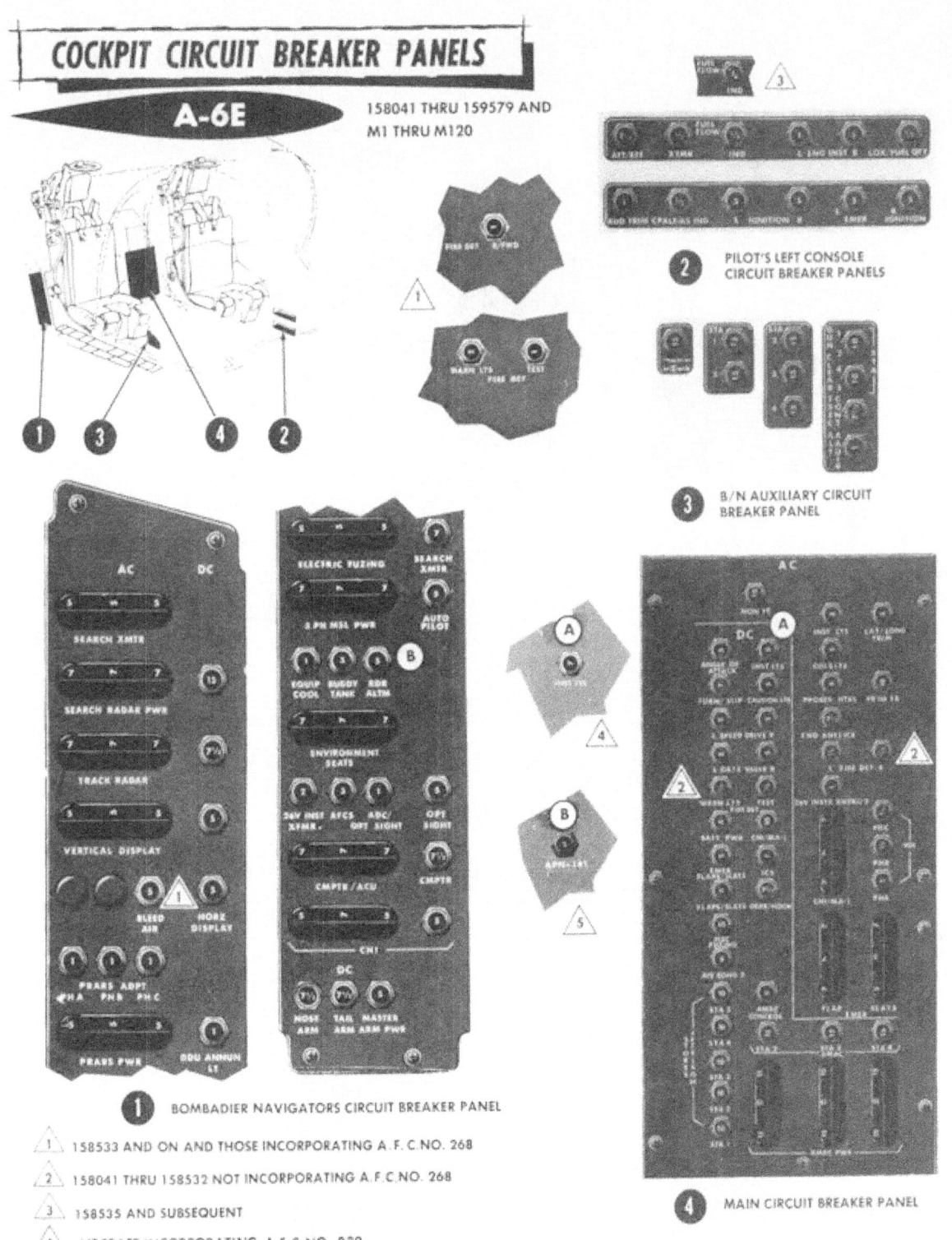

Figure 1-11 (Sheet 3)

NAVAIR 01-85ADA-1

COCKPIT CIRCUIT BREAKER PANELS CONT.

A-6E
159895 AND ON AND M121 AND ON

1. BOMBARDIER NAVIGATORS CIRCUIT BREAKER PANEL

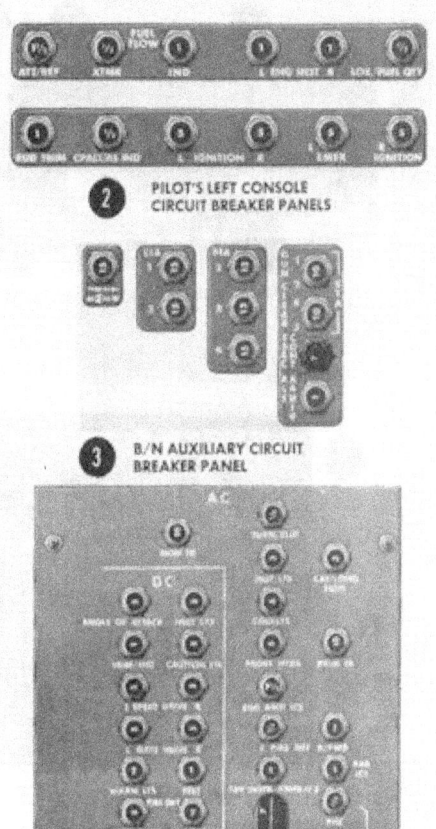

2. PILOT'S LEFT CONSOLE CIRCUIT BREAKER PANELS

3. B/N AUXILIARY CIRCUIT BREAKER PANEL

4. MAIN CIRCUIT BREAKER PANEL

Figure 1-11 (Sheet 4)

AIRCRAFT
Systems

NAVAIR 01-85ADA-1

EXTERNAL CIRCUIT BREAKER PANELS

A-6A/B/C TYPICAL

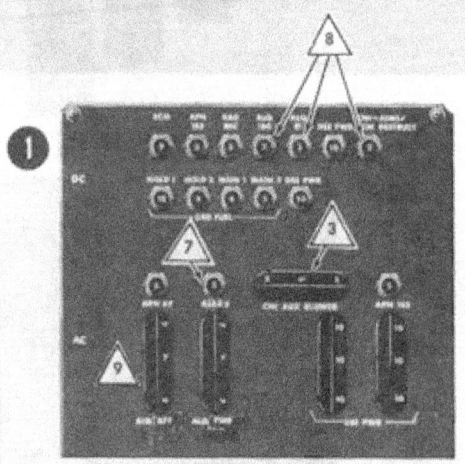

AFT BAY CIRCUIT BREAKER PANEL

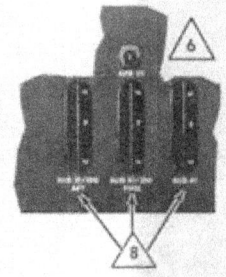

AC - DC POWER CIRCUIT BREAKER PANEL

Figure 1-12 (Sheet 1)

EXTERNAL CIRCUIT BREAKERS CONT.

A-6A/B/C TYPICAL

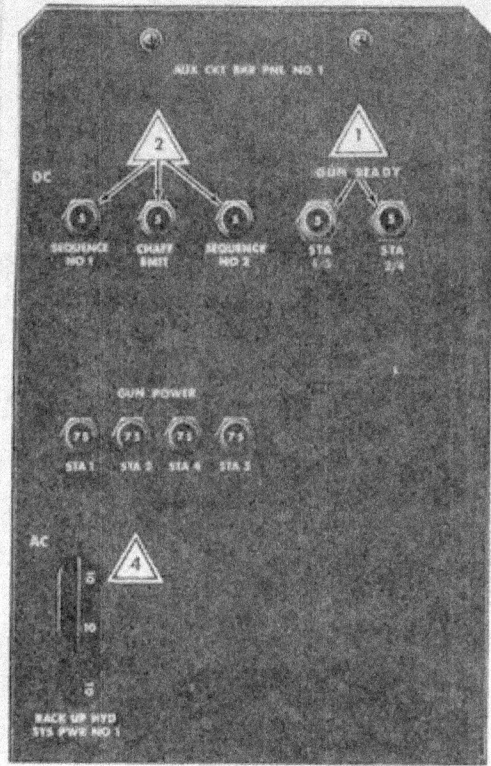

AUXILIARY AFT BAY CIRCUIT BREAKER PANEL NO. 1 (LEFT SIDE) 155640 AND ON AND AIRCRAFT INCORPORATING A.F.C. NO 183

 155642 AND ON INCORPORATING A.F.C. NO. 119

 155703 AND ON AND AIRCRAFT INCORPORATING A.F.C. NO. 197

 AIRCRAFT WITHOUT A.F.C. NO. 183 INCORPORATING A.F.C. NO. 268

 AIRCRAFT WITH A.F.C. NO. 183 AND INCORPORATING A.F.C. NO. 268

 AIRCRAFT INCORPORATING A.F.C. NO. 256

 AIRCRAFT NOT INCORPORATING A.F.C. 263

 AIRCRAFT INCORPORATING A.F.C. NO. 263

 AIRCRAFT NOT INCORPORATING AFC NO. 287

 AIRCRAFT INCORPORATING A.F.C. NO. 287

AUXILIARY AFT BAY CIRCUIT BREAKER PANEL NO. 2 (RIGHT SIDE) 155640 AND ON AND AIRCRAFT INCORPORATING A. F. C. NO. 183

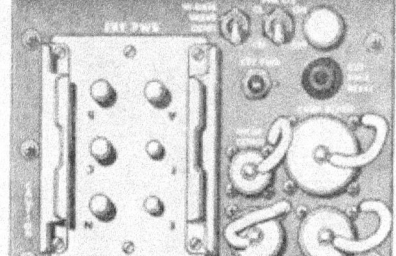

EXTERNAL POWER RECEPTACLE

Figure 1-12 (Sheet 2)

AIRCRAFT
Systems

NAVAIR 01-85ADA-1

EXTERNAL CIRCUIT BREAKERS CONT. — A-6A/B/C TYPICAL

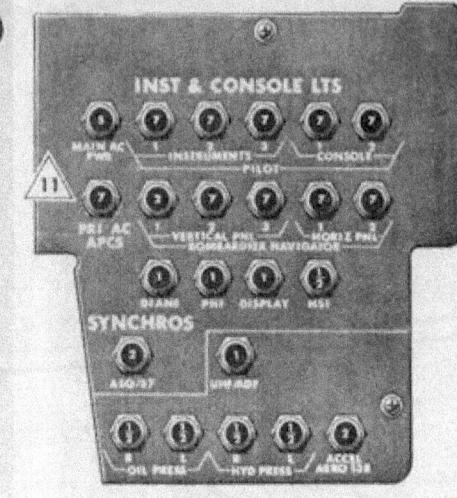

/10\	155703 AND ON AND AIRCRAFT INCORPORATING A.F.C. NO. 185
/11\	155642 AND ON AND THOSE INCORPORATING A.F.C. NO. 199
/12\	149941 THROUGH 155641 NOT INCORPORATING A.F.C. NO. 199
/13\	155721 THRU 157029 NOT INCORPORATING A.F.C. NO. 287
/14\	AIRCRAFT INCORPORATING A.F.C. NO. 352

Figure 1-12 (Sheet 3)

1-30

NAVAIR 01-85ADA-1

AIRCRAFT Systems

EXTERNAL CIRCUIT BREAKER PANELS — KA-6D

NOSE WHEEL WELL CIRCUIT BREAKERS PANELS

1. AIRCRAFT INCORPORATING A.F.C. NO. 399
2. AIRCRAFT INCORPORATING A.F.C. NO. 185
3. AIRCRAFT INCORPORATING A.F.C. NO. 352

ADA1-856-1

Figure 1-12 (Sheet 4)

AIRCRAFT
Systems

EXTERNAL CIRCUIT BREAKER PANELS (CONT.)

KA-6D

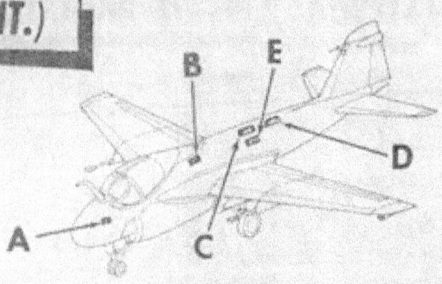

A EXTERNAL POWER PANEL

B AC/DC POWER CIRCUIT BREAKER PANEL

C AUXILIARY AFT BAY CIRCUIT BREAKER PANEL NO. 2 (RIGHT SIDE)

1. AIRCRAFT INCORPORATING A.F.C. NO. 183
2. AIRCRAFT INCORPORATING A.F.C. NO. 268
3. AIRCRAFT NOT INCORPORATING A.F.C. NO. 263
4. AIRCRAFT INCORPORATING A.F.C. NO. 263
5. AIRCRAFT NOT INCORPORATING A.F.C. NO. 287
6. AIRCRAFT INCORPORATING A.F.C. NO. 287

D AUXILIARY AFT BAY CIRCUIT BREAKER PANEL NO. 1 (LEFT SIDE)

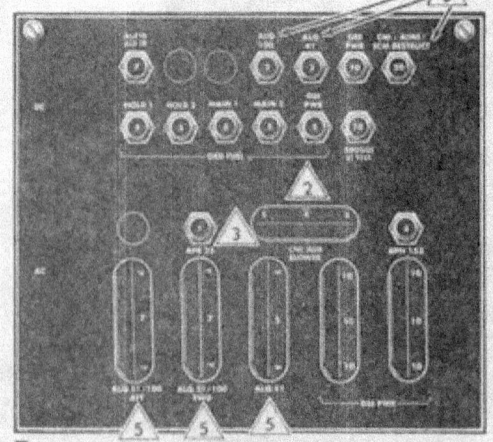

E AFT BAY CIRCUIT BREAKER PANEL

Figure 1-12 (Sheet 5)

EXTERNAL CIRCUIT BREAKER PANELS

A-6E

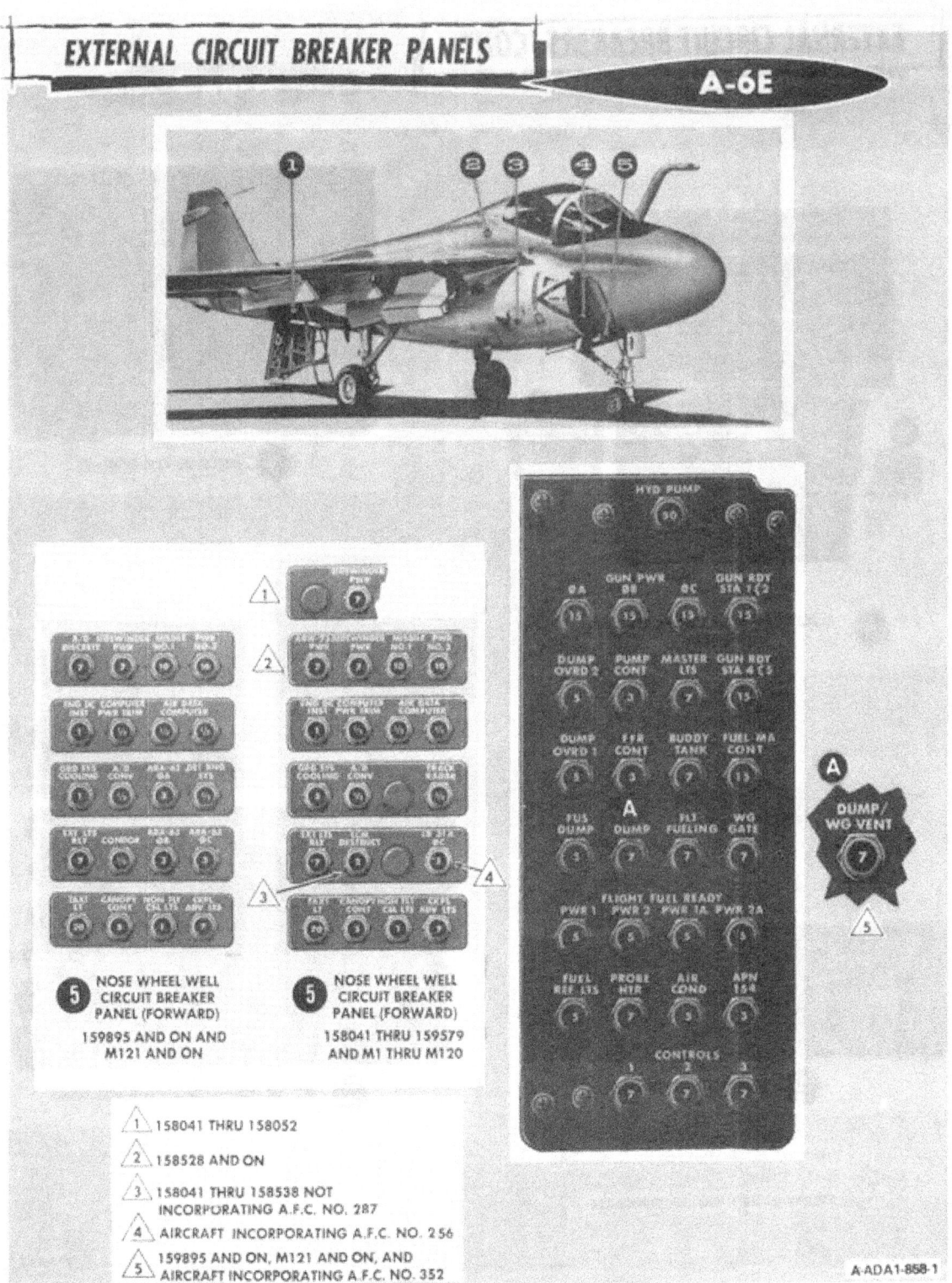

Figure 1-12 (Sheet 6)

AIRCRAFT Systems
NAVAIR 01-85ADA-1

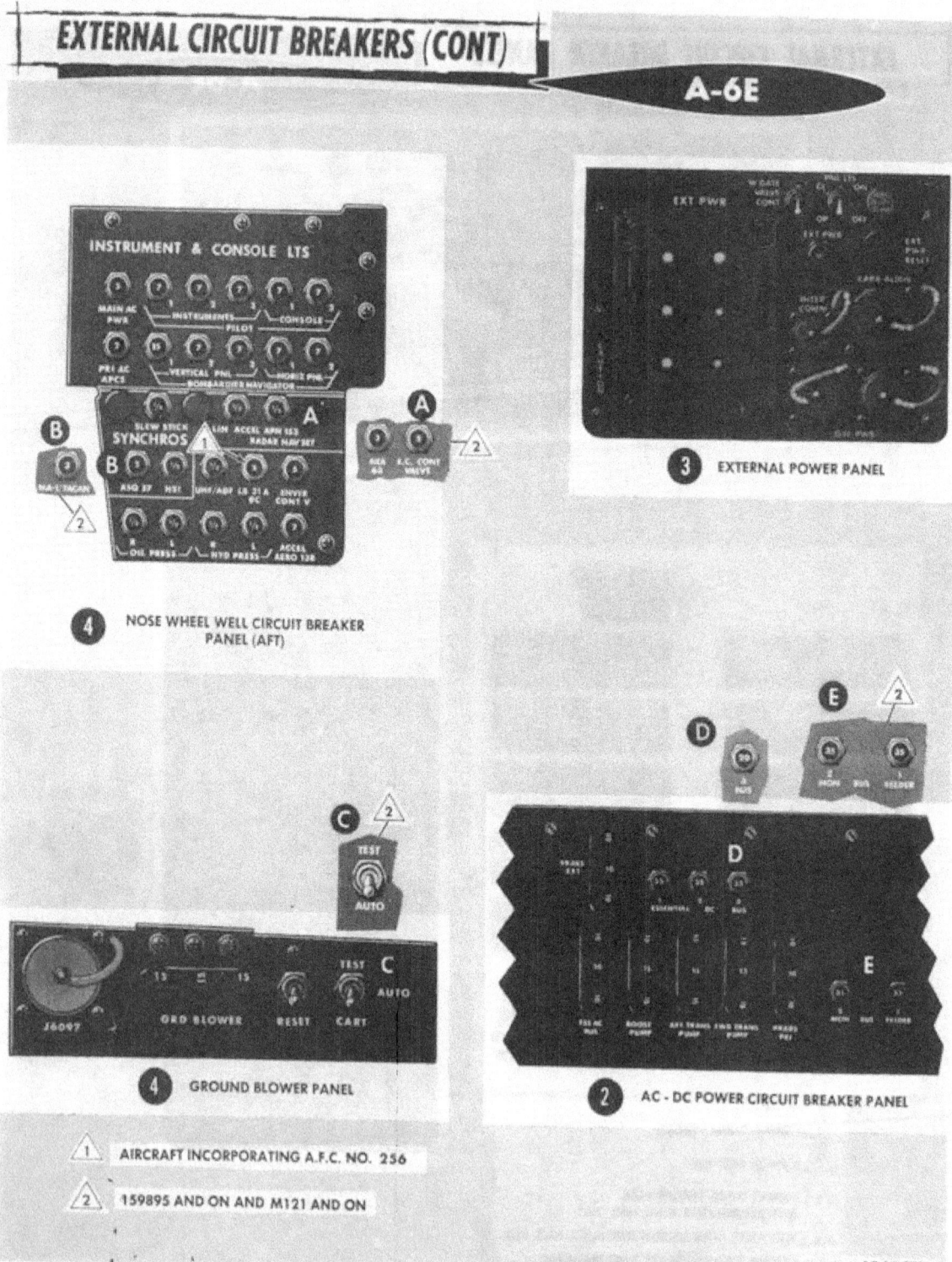

Figure 1-12 (Sheet 7)

NAVAIR 01-85ADA-1

EXTERNAL CIRCUIT BREAKERS (CONT)   A-6E

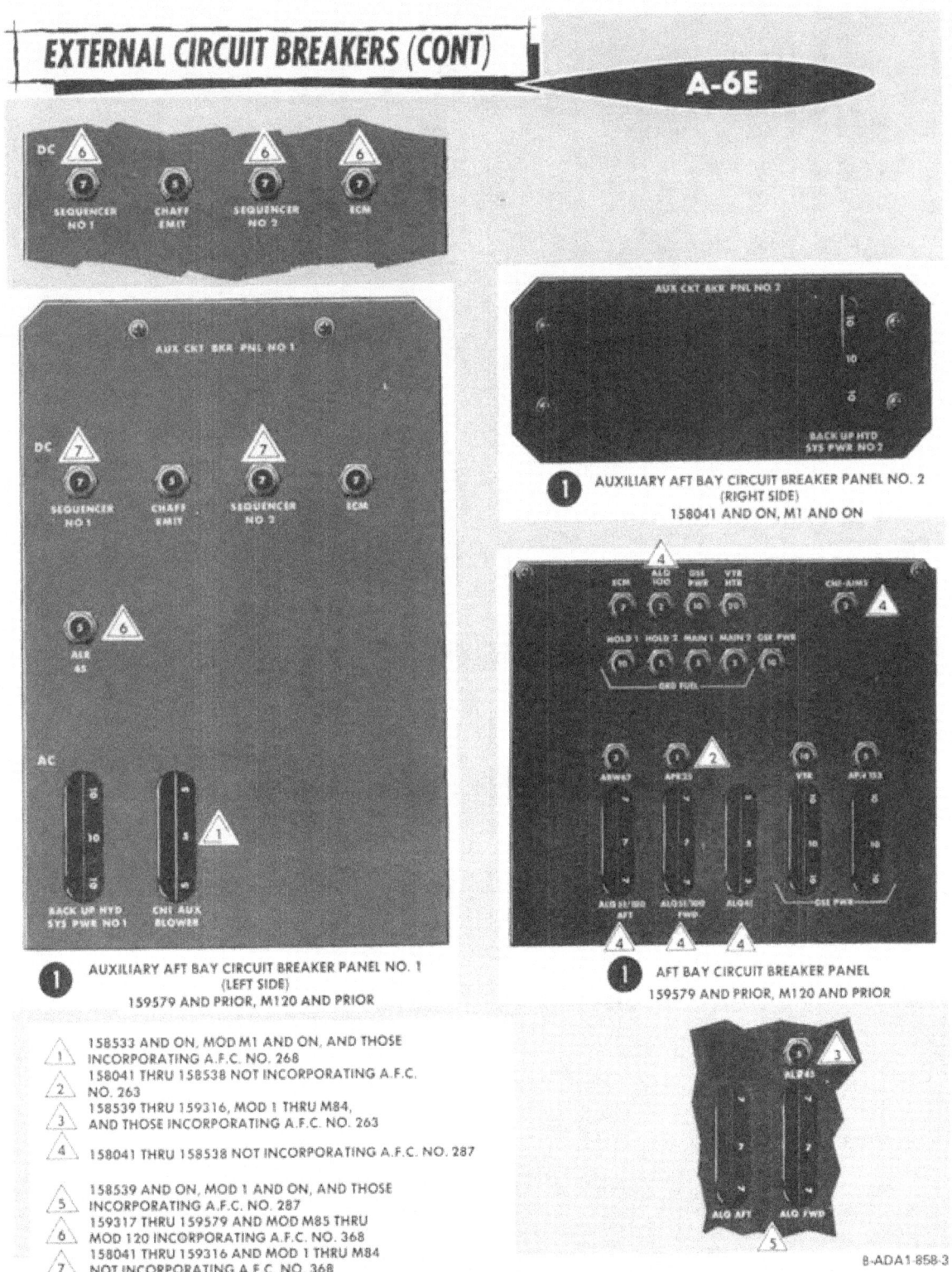

① AUXILIARY AFT BAY CIRCUIT BREAKER PANEL NO. 2
(RIGHT SIDE)
158041 AND ON, M1 AND ON

① AUXILIARY AFT BAY CIRCUIT BREAKER PANEL NO. 1
(LEFT SIDE)
159579 AND PRIOR, M120 AND PRIOR

① AFT BAY CIRCUIT BREAKER PANEL
159579 AND PRIOR, M120 AND PRIOR

△1 158533 AND ON, MOD M1 AND ON, AND THOSE INCORPORATING A.F.C. NO. 268
△2 158041 THRU 158538 NOT INCORPORATING A.F.C. NO. 263
△3 158539 THRU 159316, MOD 1 THRU M84, AND THOSE INCORPORATING A.F.C. NO. 263
△4 158041 THRU 158538 NOT INCORPORATING A.F.C. NO. 287
△5 158539 AND ON, MOD 1 AND ON, AND THOSE INCORPORATING A.F.C. NO. 287
△6 159317 THRU 159579 AND MOD M85 THRU MOD 120 INCORPORATING A.F.C. NO. 368
△7 158041 THRU 159316 AND MOD 1 THRU M84 NOT INCORPORATING A.F.C. NO. 368

8-ADA1-858-3

Figure 1-12 (Sheet 8)

EXTERNAL CIRCUIT BREAKERS (CONT)

159895 AND ON AND A-6E MOD M121 AND ON

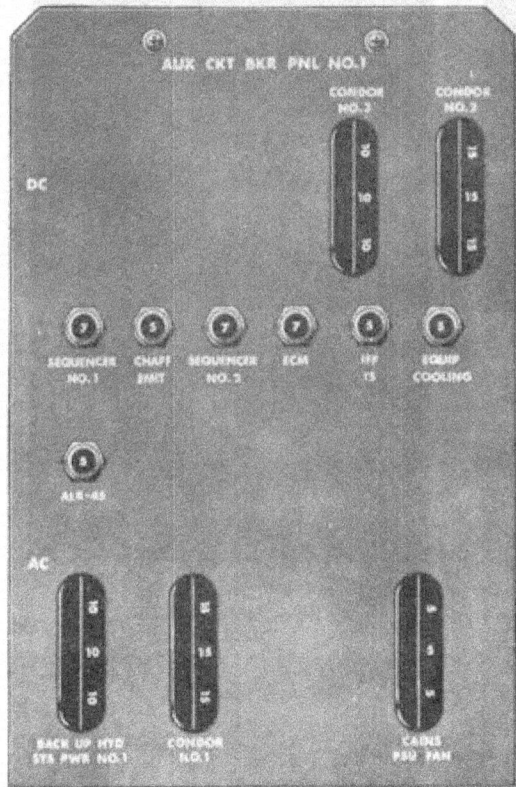

AUXILIARY AFT BAY CIRCUIT BREAKER PANEL NO. 1 (LEFT SIDE)

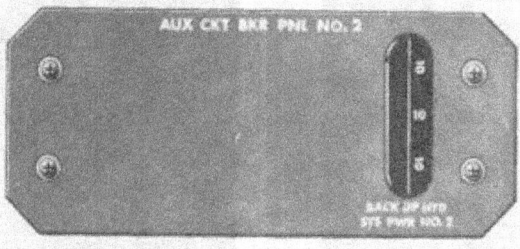

AUXILIARY AFT BAY CIRCUIT BREAKER PANEL NO. 2 (RIGHT SIDE)

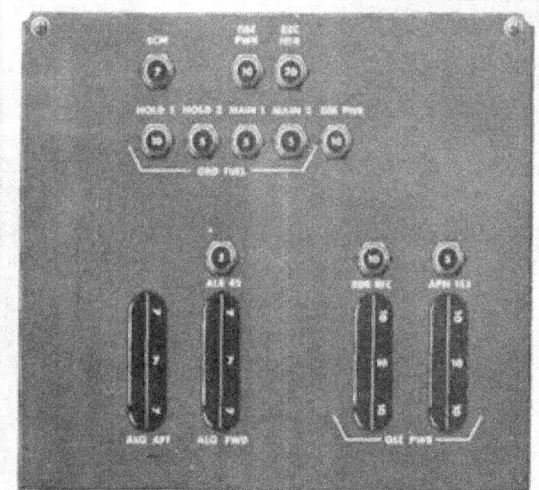

AFT BAY CIRCUIT BREAKER PANEL

Figure 1-12 (Sheet 9)

AIRCRAFT
Systems

NAVAIR 01-85ADA-1

CIRCUIT BREAKER PANELS — A-6 B/C PECULIAR

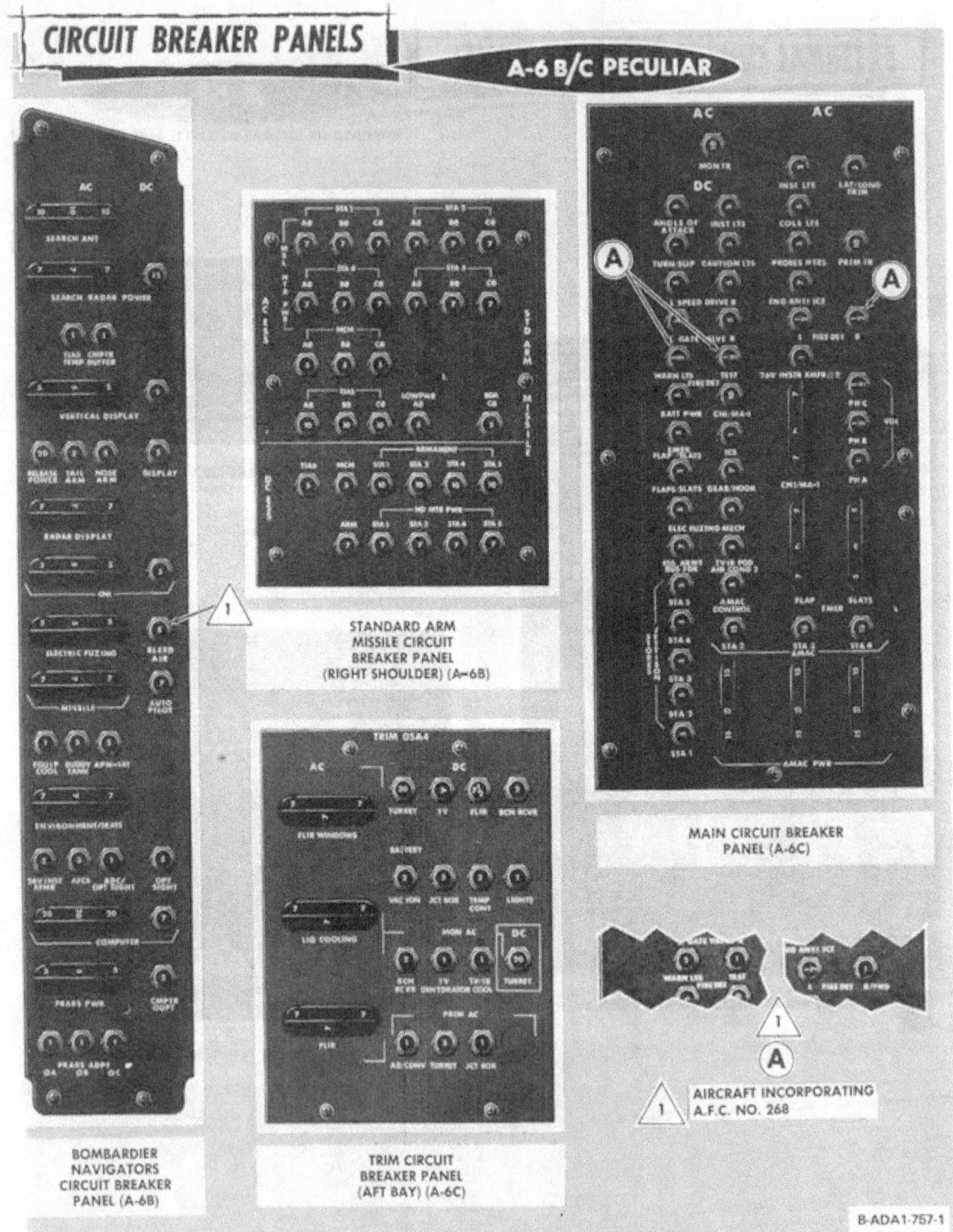

Figure 1-13 (Sheet 1)

NAVAIR 01-85ADA-1

A-6 B/C PECULIAR

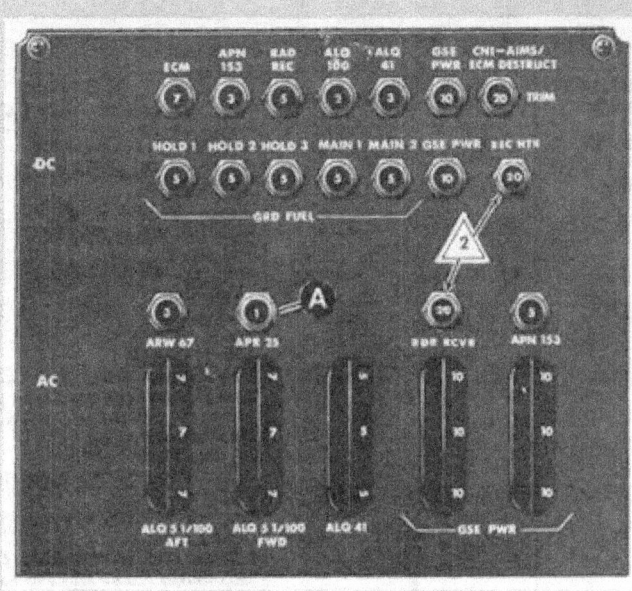
AFT BAY CIRCUIT BREAKER PANEL (A-6C)

AC - DC POWER PANEL AND TRIM
MONITOR AC CIRCUIT BREAKER PANEL (A-6C)

AUX AFT BAY CIRCUIT BREAKER
PANEL NO. 2 (A-6B)

 AIRCRAFT INCORPORATING A.F.C. NO. 268

 AIRCRAFT INCORPORATING A.F.C. NO. 279

Figure 1-13 (Sheet 2)

AIRCRAFT
Systems
NAVAIR 01-85ADA-1

KEY COCKPIT CIRCUIT BREAKERS

CIRCUIT BREAKER PLACARD	BUS	LOCATION	ITEMS ON CIRCUIT BREAKER
LAT/LONG TRIM	ESS AC	MAIN	AIR COND RAM AIR SWITCH AIR NAV COMPUTER (A-6A)
GEAR/HOOK	ESS DC #1	MAIN	SPIN ASSIST WEIGHT ON WHEELS SWITCH
L. SPD DR	ESS DC #1	MAIN	LEFT ENGINE FUEL MASTER LEFT CSD/S
R. SPD DR	ESS DC #1	MAIN	RIGHT ENGINE FUEL MASTER RIGHT CSD/S
CNI/MA-1 [1]	ESS AC	MAIN	HSI (TACAN) MA-1 ASQ-57 POWER
CAUTION LTS	ESS DC #1	MAIN	LOW ALTITUDE WARNING LIGHT (A-6E) APN-141/APN-194 INDICATOR (A-6E) WARNING LIGHTS TEST SWITCH MASTER LIGHT PANEL ANNUNCIATOR PANEL INTEGRATED POSITION INDICATOR
ANGLE OF ATTACK	ESS DC #1	MAIN	ANGLE OF ATTACK INTEGRATED POSITION INDICATOR (A-6A,B,C/KA-6D) ELECTRIC FLAP DRIVE (A-6A, B, C/KA-6D) EMERGENCY BRAKE RELAY (A-6A, B, C/KA-6D) WHEELS WARNING SWITCH (A-6E)
INST LTS	ESS AC ESS DC #1	MAIN	INSTRUMENT LIGHTS ACLS [3]
TURN/SLIP-[1] [2] TRIM/IND	ESS DC #1	MAIN	TURN AND SLIP INDICATOR RUDDER TRIM INDICATOR STABILIZER TRIM INDICATOR LOW FUEL CAUTION LIGHT IF C/B POPPED
26V INST XMFR #2	ESS AC	MAIN	MA-1 COMPASS AND CARD EGT/FF/RPM INDICATORS
26V INST XMFR	PRIM AC	B/N	L/R HYDRAULIC PRESSURE INDICATORS SEARCH RADAR RADAR RECORDER
ADC/OPT SIGHT	PRIM AC	B/N	ADC OPTICAL SIGHT CONTROL SPEED BRAKE NULL DETECTOR
TSEC CONT	ESS DC #1	B/N	KY-28
AUTO PILOT	PRIM DC	B/N OBSERVER	ADC AUTO PILOT ASQ-61 (A-6A) ASN-31 (A-6A)
MISSILE (A-6A, B, C/KA-6D)	PRIM AC	B/N OBSERVER	ICS
3 PH MSL PWR (A-6E)	PRIM AC	B/N	ICS JUNCTION BOX ARMAMENT PANEL (AWE)
PRARS ADPT PH A [1]	PRIM AC	B/N	A/D CONVERTER INS ADAPTER (A-6E)
CNI [1]	ESS AC	B/N	ASQ-57 RECEIVER AMPLIFIER POWER ARC-75 TRANSMITTER (A-6E)

[1] A-6, B, C/KA-6D AND A-6E 158041 THRU 159579 AND MOD M1 THRU M120

[2] A-6E 159895 AND ON, A-6E MOD M121 AND ON

[3] AIRCRAFT WITH AFC 230

Figure 1-14

essential dc buses and the monitored T/R supplies power to the dc monitored bus. When only one T/R is operating, the monitored bus is isolated from the system and only the essential and primary buses are energized through the transfer relay and the monitored bus is deenergized. If the right generator is inoperative, power is transferred to the essential and primary buses through the transfer relay and the monitor bus is deenergized. Ac emergency power from the ram-air turbine generator supplies the ac essential buses only and the emergency dc power through a 50-ampere emergency T/R.

AC ELECTRICAL POWER

The ac power system supplies 115/200 V, three-phase, 400-Hz, constant frequency ac power from two nonparalleled generators.

Generator Switches

The generators are controlled by two three-position toggle switches on the master generator panel (figure 1-5) and placarded ON, OFF-RESET, and TEST. The ON position supplies 28 V dc for initial generator excitation through the supervisory control panels and connects the generators to the buses after operating voltage is available. The OFF-RESET position disconnects the generator from the buses and opens the generator exciter field circuit to shut down the generator. If a generator is disconnected by overvoltage or undervoltage conditions, an attempt to reset the generator may be made by cycling the switch to OFF-RESET then ON. In the spring-loaded TEST position, the generators are energized but are not connected to the buses. The TEST position is primarily for maintenance use but can be used in flight as a troubleshooting procedure to verify generator output.

Generator Warning Lights

The generator warning lights on the annunciator panel (figure FO-11), placarded L GEN and R GEN, come on, indicating the respective generator in inoperative. Operating power is from the essential 28 V dc bus through the CAUTION LTS circuit breaker on the main circuit breaker panel.

Note

If both generators are inoperative, the generator lights will not come on unless the RAT is extended and operating.

DC ELECTRICAL POWER

Two nonparalleled, 100-ampere transformer/rectifiers (T/R) convert ac electrical power to 28 V dc electrical power for aircraft requirements. Since the dc system is dependent on the ac system, any ac system malfunction affects the dc system.

Battery

A 22.7-volt, nickel-cadmium 11-ampere-hour battery is on the right side of the fuselage in the center wing section. In addition to providing power to the spin recovery and CSD/S and ECM destruct when installed, this battery provides power for the electric-motor-driven auxiliary hydraulic pump for ground operation (weight on wheels) of the canopy, radome, extensible equipment platform, and charging the brake accumulator. Power for generator reset is provided directly to the CSD/S through the engine fuel master switches and CSD/S battery power relay. This battery is charged from the dc monitored bus and is protected by the BATT PWR circuit breaker on the main circuit breaker panel.

EMERGENCY ELECTRICAL POWER (RAT)

The emergency electrical system energizes the ac and dc essential buses. The system is powered by a ram-air-turbine-driven ac generator which, in turn, energizes a 50-ampere transformer-rectifier for the 28 V dc power. The emergency system is energized by pulling the ram-air turbine (RAT) handle (figure FO-2) on the pilot's left console. When the handle is pulled, the ram-air turbine is hydraulically positioned into the airstream above the left wing. A variable-pitch prop controls turbine speed and consequently regulates generator frequency. The emergency generator will be placed on the line automatically. If either generator becomes operative, the emergency generator will be taken off the line automatically, and the corresponding generator caution light will go out. The emergency generator is retracted by pushing down the RAT handle. The minimum operating airspeed for the RAT is 110 KIAS.

In A-6A, B, C 154170 and on and aircraft incorporating AFC No. 137, there is an underfrequency relay to delay power transfer to the aircraft electrical system until the ram-air turbine generator reaches approximately 90% of its normal speed.

Note

If the number one essential dc circuit breaker on the external port shoulder AC/DC power circuit breaker panel pops, the entire number one essential dc bus will be lost even though both main generators remain operative and power the primary and monitored buses. To restore essential dc power, the RAT must be extended. If the essential bus is not energized by RAT deployment, it will then be necessary to secure both main generators to regain essential bus power.

HYDRAULIC POWER SUPPLY SYSTEM

The aircraft hydraulic system (figure FO-6) is composed of two primary systems (the flight and combined), backup and auxiliary hydraulic systems. The four systems are independent of each other even though both the combined and flight systems power the tandem-type flight control actuators and flight control pressure determines the position of the isolation valve, which divides the combined systems into primary and secondary circuit.

AIRCRAFT
Systems

NAVAIR 01-85ADA-1

Both the combined and flight systems are powered by two 3,000 psi engine-driven hydraulic pumps (one pump on each engine).

Both the combined and flight systems are supplied with hydraulic fluid under 40-psi pressure from a piston-type reservoir, which is pressurized by engine compressor bleed air. If hydraulic power carts are attached for ground operation, the reservoirs must be pressurized from an external source.

HYDRAULIC PRESSURE GAGES

Four hydraulic pressure gages are incorporated in a single unit on the pilot's instrument panel and receive power from the 26 V ac (instrument) bus. The upper two gages, side by side, and identified as FLT, are for the two engine-driven pumps for the flight hydraulic system. The lower two gages, side by side, and identified as COMB, are for the two engine-driven pumps for the combined hydraulic system. Each indicator scale is a 120° arc with increment markers 30° apart. Each increment marker represents 1,000 psi. The 3,000 psi marker is accentuated. Pressure transmitters sense the hydraulic pressure of each pump and transmit electric signal to position the needles on the scale of the respective indicators.

FLIGHT HYDRAULIC SYSTEM

The flight hydraulic system powers one side of the tandem-type flight control actuators and the flaperon autopilot actuator. Should the combined hydraulic system fail, the flight hydraulic system is capable of delivering sufficient power to maneuver the aircraft throughout the flight envelope. At high IMN (above approximately 0.70 mach) diminished control effectiveness can be expected. Hydraulic system pressure is shown on the pressure indicators (figure FO-2 sheets 1 and 2) on the left side of the pilot's instrument panel. The top dials indicate the pressure output of the left and right engine-driven flight system pumps.

CAUTION

In aircraft not incorporating the backup flight control hydraulic system, there are no hydraulic pressure warning lights. A pressure drop in the indicator is the only warning of failure in the flight or combined systems. In aircraft incorporating the backup flight control hydraulic system, lighting of the BACK UP HYD caution lights is indication of failure of either the flight or combined system. Lighting of both the BACK UP HYD and the RUD THRO caution lights is indication of complete normal hydraulic failure.

Flight Hydraulic System Power Distribution

The flight hydraulic system powers the flight controls and AFCS.

COMBINED HYDRAULIC SYSTEM

The combined hydraulic system powers the second side of the tandem-type flight control actuators and, in addition, all other hydraulic power auxiliary devices in the aircraft (figure FO-6). In order to prevent a fluid leak in any of the auxiliary devices from draining the system and thus leaving only a single system for powering flight controls, an isolation valve is added to divide the combined system into a primary circuit supplying the flight controls and a secondary circuit supplying auxiliary equipment. The hydraulic pressure indicators indicate the pressure output of the left and right engine-driven combined system pumps.

Primary Combined Hydraulic System

The primary combined hydraulic system powers the flight controls, RAT accumulator, and retract, spin recovery, speed brakes, TRIM pod (A-6C), air-refueling system (KA-6D) and DRS turret (A-6E 159895 and ON and A-6E Mod M121 and ON i.e., TRAM configured aircraft).

Secondary Combined Hydraulic System

The secondary combined hydraulic system powers the canopy, flaps, slats, landing gear, flaperon popup, wing fold, antiskid, nosewheel steering, hook (retract), strut lock, and normal wheel brakes.

Isolation Valve and Switch

The isolation valve divides the combined system into primary and secondary circuits, and is both automatically and manually controlled. Manual pilot control is by the two-position switch on the landing-gear handle (figure 1-18). In the LDG position, the combined secondary system is pressurized in addition to the primary system and all auxiliary hydraulic devices are operated. In the FLT position, only the primary flight controls, speed brakes, spin recovery, AFCS, RAT, TRIM pod (A-6C), air-refueling system (KA-6D) and DRS turret (A-6E TRAM) are powered.

Note

- After takeoff and when landing gear, flaps, and slats have been fully retracted, the pilot should select the FLT position on the switch.

- Either the combined primary or the flight hydraulic system alone will power the flight controls throughout the flight envelope except at high IMN.

A bar on the landing-gear handle pushes the isolation valve switch to the LDG position when the landing gear handle is placed DN. If the pilot has not selected FLT after takeoff, and the flight hydraulic system fails, the isolation valve is spring-loaded to automatically cut off pressure to the combined secondary hydraulic system. If electrical power is lost to the valve with normal flight hydraulic pressure available, the valve will open, allowing the secondary circuit to be pressurized.

Note

A flight system failure will deenergize the isolation valve to close off the combined secondary system. It will then be necessary to use emergency landing gear, emergency flaps/slats, and auxiliary brakes to land the aircraft.

COMBINED SYSTEM AUXILIARY PUMP OPERATION

A handpump in the combined hydraulic system is available to operate the canopy, wheel brakes, the extensible equipment platform, and the radome when the engine-driven pumps are not operating. An electrically driven hydraulic pump is also provided which will power the same equipment as the handpump during ground operation.

The handpump can be operated from either the cockpit or the nosewheel well. The electrically driven pump may be operated from the cockpit, nosewheel well, or for canopy operation from either boarding-ladder well. Operation of the canopy from the nosewheel well is limited to handpump operation. The handpump and the electrically driven hydraulic pump will deliver 3000 psi at very low flow rates. The handpump will charge the brake accumulator at any time, but the electric pump is operative only with weight on wheels. Charging rate is reduced if any additional hydraulic operation is being performed. Pressure to operate the canopy is controlled by the manual selector handle in the cockpit and nosewheel well. The nose radome and the aft extensible equipment platform are also operated through manual selector valves in the nosewheel well. Should the wheel-brake accumulator be depleted, it must be charged before other equipment can be operated.

Note

Excessive loss of combined system hydraulic fluid will render the auxiliary hydraulic pumps inoperative. Wheel-brake applications will be limited to cycles indicated on the brake cycle gage and canopy operation will then be hydraulically inoperative.

Auxiliary Hydraulic Pumps

The auxiliary hydraulic pumps operate the canopy, brake accumulator, radome, extensible equipment platform (A-6A, B, C, and A-6E), and refueling-reel access door (KA-6D).

WARNING

Ensure hydraulic pressure is applied to the retract side of the extensible equipment platform prior to unlatching and lowering.

BACK UP FLIGHT CONTROLS HYDRAULIC SYSTEM

The backup flight controls hydraulic system is incorporated in A-6E and A-6A, B, C 155640 and on and aircraft incorporating AFC No. 183. This system provides limited hydraulic power to the rudder and stabilizer actuators should both the flight and combined hydraulic systems fail. With a complete hydraulic failure, rudder will shift to full authority (35°). The system does not provide for flaperon operation.

The backup hydraulic pump motor package is powered by 115 V ac through circuit breakers on the aft bay auxiliary circuit breaker panels.

WARNING

The backup flight control hydraulic system is provided to allow a damaged aircraft to leave the combat area. With full rudder authority (35°) available, extreme caution should be exercised in executing rudder deflections. Airspeed should be reduced to less than 0.80M, since dihedral effect begins to reverse at approximately that airspeed.

Note

Loss of the generators prevents use of the backup hydraulic system. The backup hydraulic system will not operate from the RAT.

A failure in either the flight or combined system will activate its pressure switch as the pressure drops below 800±100 psi, energizing the backup motor pump and isolating a small portion of the combined system fluid. When the motor pump pressure exceeds 1000 psi, the BACK UP HYD caution lights on the annunciator panel will come on. If, in addition to the BACK UP HYD caution light, the RUD THRO light comes on, it indicates a complete hydraulic failure of both normal systems with flight controls then limited to rudder and stabilizer.

Note

- When operating on one hydraulic system only, rapid cycling of the controls will cause the BACK UP HYD light to go out momentarily, indicating that the capacity of the backup pump has been exceeded. To avoid excessive demands on the backup pump, control inputs should be kept smooth.

- When operating on the backup system only, rapid control inputs exceeding pump capacity may cause some lag in surface response against opposing loads. When the pump output pressure drops below 800 psi, the pump pressure switch opens momentarily, turning off the BACK UP HYD caution light. Therefore, monitoring this light while operating on the backup hydraulic system will indicate when pump capacity has been exceeded.

AIRCRAFT
Systems

BACK UP HYD SYS TEST Switch

In aircraft incorporating the backup flight controls hydraulic system, a backup hydraulic test switch is provided on the pilot's left console. The switch enables the pilot to check the operation of the flight system pressure switch (FLT) and the combined system pressure switch (COMB) individually before starting engines and with external electrical power connected. The switch also provides checking the hydraulic backup motor pump operation. The switch is spring-loaded to the center (OFF) position.

Note

The secondary power monitor relay prevents the back up hydraulic system from coming on with external power plugged in.

Placing the switch in either the FLT or COMB position energizes the hydraulic backup motor pump which, in turn, turns on the BACK UP HYD caution light. While testing either system, it is possible to check rudder and stabilizer movement for several cycles.

With engine running, the switch in the OFF position and both generators on the line, the BACK UP HYD caution light remaining out indicates that both pressure switches have returned to their normally open (hydraulic pressure on) position.

CAUTION

Ground operation of the backup hydraulic system should be limited only to testing of the system.

BACK UP HYD Caution Light

The BACK UP HYD caution light on the annunciator panel comes on when one hydraulic system is depressurized and the backup pump is delivering 1000 psi. The light will go out when the backup pump output pressure goes below 800 psi.

FLIGHT CONTROLS

The flight control surfaces consist of a slab stabilizer, a rudder, and upper wing surface spoilers called flaperons. The control stick and rudder pedals are linked directly to their corresponding surface actuators by a system of pushrods, bellcranks, and cables. In each case, control surface deflection is held in a fixed relationship to pilot control deflection by a proportional followup linkage. Each surface is powered by an irreversible actuator, which is controlled by an input slide valve, and which, in turn, is positioned by the pilot's control. Each control actuator is of the tandem type, and is powered by both the flight and combined primary hydraulic systems.

To provide for additional control with flaps extended, or for spin recovery, extended rudder and stabilizer travel is provided. The integrated position indicator, (figures FO-2 sheets 1, 2 and 3) on the left side of the pilot's instrument panel, indicates the condition of the stabilizer and rudder throws in addition to the configuration of the flaps/slats and speed brakes, and the landing gear. Flight controls and indicators are shown in figure 1-15.

Note

Either the combined primary or the flight hydraulic system alone will power the flight controls throughout the flight envelope. At high IMN (above approximately 0.70 mach) diminished control effectiveness can be expected.

CAUTION

Do not actuate the assist-spin recovery switch with the flaps down or lower flaps with the spin recovery system on. The spin recovery system is to be operated only with the flaps up. Operation of the system with flaps down can result in damage that will prevent reselection of cruise control throws.

ARTIFICIAL FEEL

The irreversible control actuators require that artificial feel be provided to the pilot for all three flight control systems. This feel is obtained entirely through the use of mechanical devices, and does not require mach or g-sensing to be fed in by electronic equipment.

Longitudinal System

Artificial feel is provided by the following devices:

STATIC FORCE FEEL - Is provided by a double-acting bungee that produces a greater breakout force gradient near stick neutral, and a lower gradient to full deflection. Breakout forces exceed the 1 1/4-pound autopilot stick switches.

FLIGHT CONTROLS AND INDICATORS

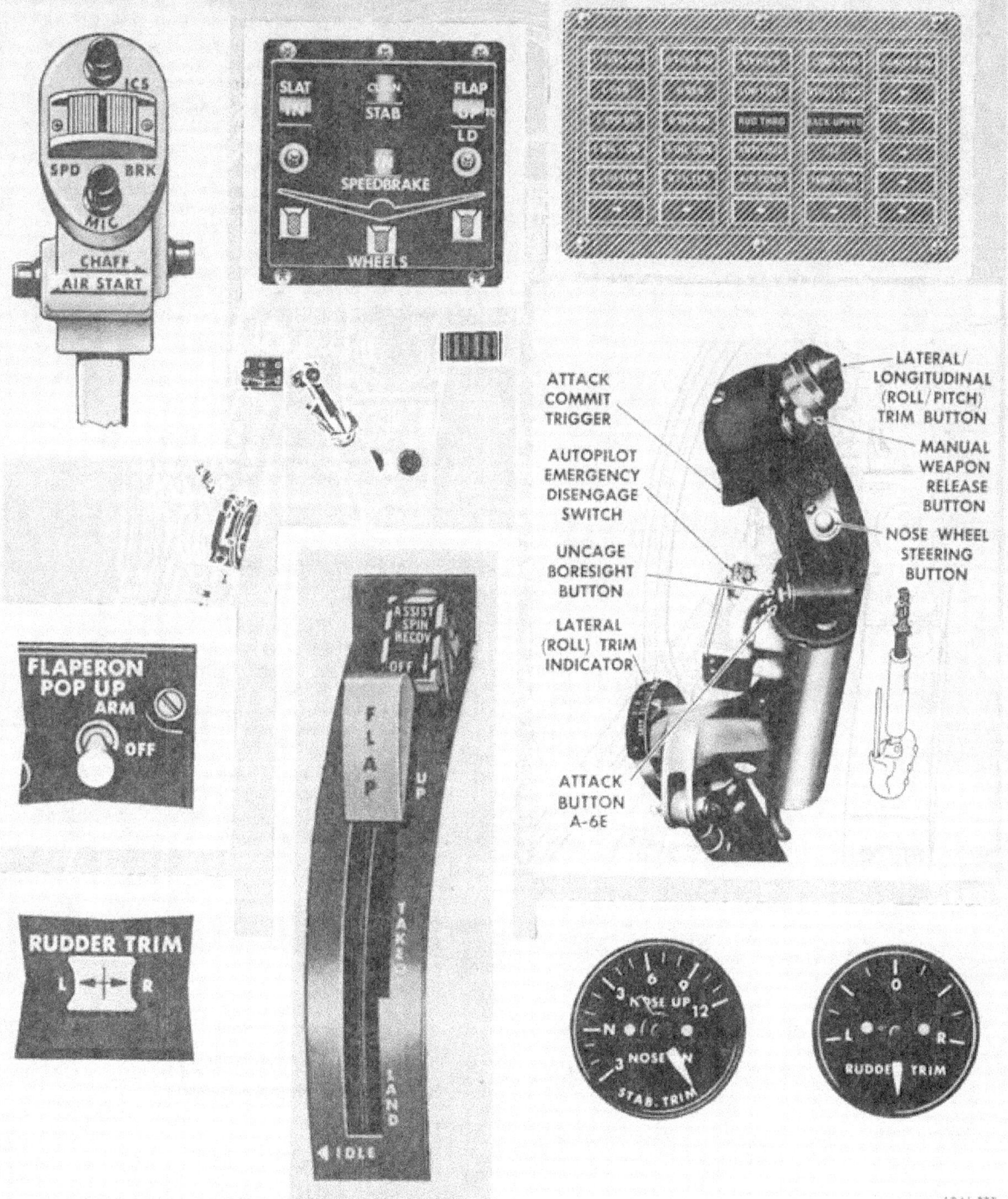

Figure 1-15

AIRCRAFT
Systems

MANEUVERING FORCE - Is provided by a g-sensing bobweight at the base of the control stick, and on the control linkage aft of the pilot's seat.

DYNAMIC PITCH DAMPING - Is provided by pitch acceleration-sensing bobweights, both fore and aft of the center of gravity.

STICK RATE DAMPING - Is provided by a leaf spring and eddy-current damper. The eddy current damper is a magnetic-mechanical device that produces a resisting torque proportional to stick velocity. If a damper fails, a clutch can be overridden for control system operation.

Lateral System

Artificial feel is provided by the following devices:

STATIC FORCE FEEL - Is provided by a double-acting bungee similar to, but with lower force level than, the longitudinal bungee. Control preload at neutral is equal to the AFCS force cutout switch settings.

LATERAL RATE DAMPING - Is provided by an eddy-current damper identical to the longitudinal damper, except for the gear train into the system linkage.

Directional System

Artificial feel is provided by the following device:

FORCE FEEL - Is provided by a double-acting bungee of much higher preload and rate than the feel bungees in the other axis.

Three-Axis Damping

Pitch, roll, and directional oscillations are minimized through the use of the AFCS. By placing the on/off switch ON with the automatic stability augmentation switch in STAB AUG, automatic stability augmentation inputs are directed to the hydraulic power actuators in series with the pilot's command. Because the inputs to the hydraulic actuators are in series, they are not felt by the pilot.

CONTROL STICK

The control stick is the primary flight control for the aircraft's longitudinal and lateral axis. Since the flight controls are hydraulically powered, an artificial feel system is used to simulate in-flight stick loads. In manual and stability augmentation flight modes, the stick applies a mechanical input to the flaperon and stabilizer hydraulic actuators for control surface movement. Refer to the discussion on flight controls, Section IV, for more detailed information relating the stick to control surface movement, and to the discussion on lateral trim. The control stick grip has several switches and buttons to provide maximum efficiency is mission performance. See figure 1-15. The lateral and longitudinal trim button, weapon release button, and nosewheel steering button are easily operated by the thumb. The attack commit trigger is actuated by the forefinger and the uncage boresight button can be actuated by the fourth finger. The 1.1±0.2-pound autopilot-disengage switches are located in the column. The grip moves to a slight degree independent of the control stick. When this occurs, the autopilot-disengage switches are actuated. Although the autopilot emergency disengage switch is on the lower portion of the control stick, it is within easy reach of the right hand.

Note

Refer to Section VII Weapons Systems for description of the weapon release button, the attack commit trigger, and the attack button.

Lateral/Longitudinal (Roll/Pitch) Trim Button

The roll/pitch trim button on the stick grip (figure 1-15) is a five-position switch spring-loaded to the off (center) position. The up and down positions control pitch trim through an electromechanical actuator that repositions the stabilizer feel device (bungee) to a new no-load position. The left and right positions control roll trim through an electromechanical actuator that repositions the flaperon feel device to a new no-load position. The lateral trim indicator is on the forward base of the control stick. Total flaperon deflection, through use of the trim button, is 9° up at a rate of approximately 0.8° per second. Total stabilizer deflection, through use of the trim button; with flaps up is 3/4° leading-edge-up to 9.5° leading-edge-down; with flaps down, 1/2° leading-edge-up to 22° leading-edge-down.

WARNING

If the trim button comes off, exercise extreme caution. The exposed probe will produce a severe shock.

Note

In the event of a trim button malfunction, occasional use of the AFCS AUTO MODE will assist the pilot in overcoming excessive trim requirements due to attitude, configuration, and/or airspeed changes.

Autopilot Emergency Disengage Switch

This normally closed pushbutton switch (figure 1-15) provides emergency release of the AFCS. It is mounted on the junction box beneath and to the right of the pilot stick grip. The pushbutton is marked AUTOPILOT OFF and is coded with yellow and black barber pole stripes. Depressing this pushbutton disengages all AFCS control functions and returns all controller switches to their disengaged position.

Nose-Wheel Steering Button

The spring-loaded nosewheel steering button on the pilot's control stick grip must be depressed to keep nosewheel steering (figure 1-15). It is used to engage normal nosewheel steering. When the nosewheel steering circuit is energized, the nosewheel steering selector valve is positioned to direct combined hydraulic system pressure to the steering control valve.

Lateral (Roll) Trim Indicator

The lateral (roll) trim indicator on the forward side of the stick grip adapter (figure 1-15) indicates the trimmed position of the flaperons. The scale is calibrated in three units left and right of zero (neutral) and is mechanically operated.

FLAPERONS

Flaperons are used for lateral control. Stick movement to the left of neutral results in the left flaperon being raised with the right flaperon remaining neutral. Conversely, stick movement to the right of neutral results in the right flaperon being raised and the left flaperon remaining neutral. Maximum flaperon deflection is 51°.

The flaperons are divided on each wing at the wing fold. A mechanical interlock prevents the wing-fold system from being unlocked unless the flaperons are near neutral. Conversely, when the wing-fold handle is actuated, a mechanical stop prevents the flaperons from being actuated.

Flaperon Pop-Up Switch

A flaperon pop-up feature is available for decreasing ground roll after landing. The flaperon will pop up to the 39±3° position. The flaperon pop-up switch on the pilot's left console (figure 1-15) is a two-position switch that provides control over flaperon pop-up. The OFF position deactivates pop-up. The ARM position electrically arms the flaperons for pop-up. In order to complete the circuit, the left weight-on-wheels switch must be actuated, the throttles retarded to idle, and the wings spread and locked.

Note

Control stick movement is limited laterally to 1 inch left and right when flaperons are popped up.

Flaperon Autopilot Actuator

The flaperon autopilot actuator is a hydraulic servo unit that receives inputs from the control stick and the autopilot. The input information is converted to a mechanical movement, which, in turn, actuates the flaperons.

Note

In the event of actuator malfunction, there is a ball lock detent that permits disengagement of the actuator.

HORIZONTAL STABILIZER

Longitudinal control is provided by the horizontal stabilizer. To provide maximum control and help prevent overstress under all flight conditions, actuation of the flaps results in an increase in stabilizer travel. The normal travel range of the stabilizer is 1.5° leading-edge-up to 9.5° leading-edge-down; with flaps down, the range is increased to 1.5° leading-edge-up to 24° leading-edge-down.

In aircraft incorporating the backup flight controls hydraulic system, stabilizer operation and control is available if both the flight and combined hydraulic systems are inoperative.

Note

Backup system control rate for stabilizer operation is approximately 10% of normal.

Stabilizer Position Indicator

The stabilizer position indicator on the integrated position indicator on the main instrument panel (figure 1-15) indicates available stabilizer travel by presenting a symbol of a stabilizer for full travel, and the word CLEAN for restricted travel. The indicator is powered by the essential 28 V dc bus through the CAUTION LIGHTS circuit breaker on the right circuit breaker panel.

> **CAUTION**
>
> Restricted stabilizer travel at low speed could result in inadequate pitch control and full stabilizer travel at high speed could cause structural failure.

Horizontal Stabilizer Trim

The stabilizer is trimmed by actuating the trim button on the control stick grip (figure 1-15). The button controls a two-speed irreversible electromechanical actuator, which varies the neutral position of the feel bungee. For manual operation, high trim speed is used, giving approximately 1° per second rate of stabilizer displacement. During autopilot operation, the slow speed is used, producing a stabilizer change at the rate of approximately 1/20° per second. With flaps up, the trim limits are 3/4° leading-edge-up to 9.5° leading-edge-down; flaps down 1/2° leading-edge-up and 22° leading-edge-down.

Horizontal Stabilizer Trim Gage

The stabilizer trim gage (figure 1-15) indicates horizontal stabilizer trim position from 3 units nose down to 12 units nose up. The letter N on the gage represents the neutral position of the stabilizer surface (3° leading-edge-down) in flaps down position. A signal is generated by a position transmitter that drives a dc motor that positions the pointer.

Horizontal Stabilizer Hydraulic Power Actuator

The hydraulic power actuator for the horizontal stabilizer is unique in reference to the primary flight control actuators. The actuator has provisions for a parallel mode of operation in conjunction with the AFCS.

RUDDER

Directional control is provided by a single rudder. Similar to the design features of the longitudinal controls, the lowering of the flaps mechanically provides additional rudder travel. With the flaps up, rudder travel is 4° either side of neutral; with the flaps down, rudder travel is 35° either side of neutral. The rudder is controlled by rudder pedal displacement or by AFCS input.

The rudder actuator linkage is protected from high winds when the aircraft is parked by an arrangement that permits full 35° rudder travel when the flight and combined hydraulic systems are depressurized. Full 35° rudder travel is available when both the flight and combined hydraulic systems are inoperative.

Note

Backup system control rate for the rudder is approximately 30% of normal.

Rudder Pedals

Conventional rudder pedals, with toe-action braking, are used in the aircraft. Moving the rudder pedals transmits a mechanical input to the rudder actuator. The actuator, in turn, utilizes hydraulic power to deflect the rudder.

In addition to providing manual directional control, the pedals are also used for steering the aircraft on the ground. The nosewheel steering feature is actuated manually by depressing the nosewheel steering button (figure 1-15) and automatically when the weight-on-wheels switches are closed and the arresting hook is down.

The rudder pedals are adjustable a total of 9 inches fore and aft, in 1-inch increments.

Rudder Trim Switch

The rudder trim switch on the pilot's left console controls an irreversible electromechanical actuator that varies the neutral position of the mechanical linkage, for directional trim. Full trim corresponds to 4° of rudder travel either side of neutral, flaps up and 7° either side of neutral, flaps down.

Rudder Trim Gage

The rudder trim gage (figure 1-15) indicates rudder position from four units left to four units right. A signal generated by a position transmitter drives the pointer on the indicator.

ASSIST-SPIN RECOVERY SWITCH

The assist-spin recovery switch (ASSIST-SPIN RECOV) enables the pilot to select extended rudder and stabilizer throw for maximum control surface deflection without lowering the flaps. The switch, which is on the forward right edge of the throttle quadrant (figure 1-15), is guarded, and has two positions. The aft (guarded) position is OFF. The forward position electrically energizes a selector valve to port hydraulic fluid to a shift cylinder. This cylinder mechanically shifts the tail control surfaces into an extended throw condition (±35° rudder, 1 1/2° to 24° stabilizer). Power for the cylinder is supplied by the combined primary hydraulic system.

CAUTION

- Do not actuate the assist-spin recovery switch with the flaps down or lower flaps with the spin recovery system on. The spin recovery system is to be operated only with the flaps up. Operation of the system with flaps down can result in damage that will prevent reselection of cruise control throws.
- Reselection of cruise control throws after spin recovery should be done below 300 KIAS while anticipating a nose-down pitch change.

Rudder Throw Caution Light

The RUD THRO caution light on the annunciator panel comes on whenever extended rudder travel is actuated in the clean configuration, or the assist-spin recovery switch is actuated.

In A-6E, A-6A, B, C, 155640 and on and aircraft incorporating AFC No. 183 (backup flight controls hydraulic system), lighting of both the RUD THRO caution light and the BACKUP HYD caution light indicates that both the flight and combined hydraulic systems are inoperative. Under these circumstances, flight control is limited to rudder and stabilizer only.

WING FLAPS AND SLATS

The wing flaps are semi-Fowler type slotted flaps and work in conjunction with the wing slats to provide additional lift during takeoff and landing. Both the flaps and the slats are divided at wing-fold and cannot be actuated unless the wing lockpin switch is energized. Power for driving the flaps and slats in normal operation is supplied by the combined secondary hydraulic system.

There are two flap actuators for each flap panel. The actuators are mechanically linked to a central gearbox in the right wing root. The hydraulic brake of the gearbox maintains the position of the flap panel regardless of air loads. A planetary gear arrangement in the gearbox, working with the hydraulic brake, permits the flap actuators to be driven from hydraulic or electrical (emergency) power sources.

The rudder and stabilizer shift mechanisms for increasing control surface movement are also actuated through the flap gearbox. The stabilizer is shifted by a cable wound on a cable drum that is mounted on a shaft extending from the gearbox. The rudder shift cable is routed through the stabilizer shaft sector, and is reloaded as the stabilizer shifts to the dirty configuration. Relaxed cable tension permits springs to withdraw the rudder cam step and allow full (±35°) rudder deflection.

Note

If the stabilizer shift cable parts, the stabilizer and rudder shift will be spring-loaded to either the clear or dirty configuration depending on location of shift sector (less or more than halfway shifted) prior to cable failure.

As in the flap system, the slat main gearbox transforms hydraulic power to mechanical power through a hydraulic motor driven by the combined hydraulic system. There is one slat actuator for the inner slat panel and two for the outer slat panel for a total of six actuators. Interconnecting pins ensure equal slat extension on both wings.

Flap Lever

A three-position flap lever to the right of the throttles (figure 1-15) controls the operation of the flaps and slats. Positioning the flaps handle to the LAND position actuates a switch, powered by the 28 V dc essential bus. This completes a circuit to the solenoid-operated hydraulic selector and flap brake valves. The brake in the gearbox releases and the selector valve directs hydraulic pressure to the down side of the flap hydraulic motor. Similarly, actuation of the flap handle closes the slat switch, completing a circuit to a solenoid-operated selector and slat brake valves. The brake in the gearbox releases and the selector valve directs hydraulic pressure to the down side of the slat hydraulic motor. The flaps will extend to 40° down, and the slats will extend to 27.5° down (full down). Limit switches open the electrical circuits to the flat and slat selector and to the brake valve solenoids. Both brakes are spring-loaded to the locked position as a fail-safe feature.

When the flap lever is moved to the TAKE-OFF position, an electric circuit is completed to the solenoid selector and to the brake valve to direct hydraulic pressure to either the extend or retract side of the flap hydraulic motor and releases the flap brake. If the flaps are down, the retract side of the hydraulic motor is energized. When the flaps reach 30°, a limit switch deenergizes the solenoid selector valve and the brake valves, stopping retraction. If the flaps are up, the extend side of the hydraulic motor is energized. The solenoid selector valve and the brake valve are deenergized by the 30° limit switch when the flaps reach 30° down. With the flaps initially full down and the flap lever moved to TAKE-OFF, the slats remain full down. If the flaps are initially UP, a circuit is completed to the slat solenoid selector valve and brake valve. The brake is released and hydraulic pressure is directed to the extend side of the flap motor.

Positioning the flap lever to UP, with flaps and slats extended, actuates flap and slat switches, which energize the respective solenoid selector valves. The selector valves then direct hydraulic pressure to the retract side of the hydraulic motors. When the flaps reach full up, limit switches deenergize the selector valve solenoids and the hydraulic motors stop.

1-47

WARNING

The pilot must ensure that the flap lever is fully seated in the desired detent and aircraft flap and/or slat configuration is confirmed with the integrated position indicator. Flaps and/or slats may be positioned to the TAKE-OFF or UP position without the flap lever being seated in the detent selected. Any movement of the flap lever to a position between the UP and TAKEOFF detents may cause the flaps and/or slats to assume a position not intended.

Note

The maximum recommended airspeeds for flap normal extension are:

TAKEOFF	250 KIAS for 30° flaps
LAND	200 KIAS for 40° flaps

Emergency Flap Switch

The emergency flap switch on the throttle quadrant (figure 1-5) is a three-position, square toggle switch with positions placarded UP, OFF, and DN. The emergency flap switch provides flap and slat operation when the flight or combined hydraulic systems fail. Making a selection with the emergency flap switch will override the flap lever selection. When the switch is placed down (DN), power is supplied by the 28 V dc essential bus to the hydraulic brake selector valves, ensuring hydraulic brake lock configuration. Simultaneously, circuits are completed to the 115 V ac primary emergency flap and slat motors. As these electric motors are energized, the electric brakes are released, permitting emergency flap and slat operation. Cam-operated limit switches deenergize the emergency motors when the flaps and slats reach the fully extended position. For retracting the flaps and slats, the emergency flap switch is placed in the UP position. Again, the hydraulic brake selector valves are energized, ensuring hydraulic brake lock configuration, and the electric brake locks are released, permitting emergency flaps and slat operation. The phasing of the emergency ac motors is changed, reversing the motors, and retracting the flaps and slats. The motors will be deenergized when the cam-operated upper limit switches are actuated. The OFF position opens the circuits to the emergency motors and stops emergency flap and slat operation.

CAUTION

- Emergency extension of the flaps to the terminal (LAND) position above 160 KIAS may result in a burned-out clutch in the gear box and complete loss of flap operation. It is permissible to commence flap extension by the emergency flap switch at any speed up to the structural limitation (200 KIAS for LAND position) of the flaps; however, airspeed deceleration to below 160 KIAS must be continued as the flap extension process continues toward LAND position.

- The emergency flap switch should not be used for normal flap operations. The flap and slat motors may be damaged by continuous use.

- Activation of the emergency flaps/slats switch is independent of the wing-fold interlock. Inadvertent operation of the switch can therefore produce damage to the slats when the wings are not fully spread and locked.

- Allow 3 minutes rest between emergency flap switch actuation. If it is necessary to cycle the emergency flap switch repeatedly, limit use to five cycles. One cycle is defined as 45 seconds extension, 3 minutes rest, 45 seconds retraction, 3 minutes rest. Abuse of motors will result in loss of the emergency actuating system.

- The emergency flap/slat switch should be returned to OFF when the flaps have reached the desired position.

Note

- Insure that the position of the flap lever corresponds with the desired flap position before engaging the emergency switch. If hydraulic power should be restored, the flaps would be driven to the position selected by the flap lever. Regardless of the position of the flaps, making a selection with the emergency flaps switch overrides the flap lever selection.

- Emergency extension of the flaps to T/O may result in extension beyond the T/O position. An attempt to return to the T/O position will result in retraction of the slats during the period that the emergency flap switch is activated, resulting in a partially retracted slat condition.

Flap and Slat Indicators

The flap and slat indicating windows are on the integrated position indicator on the pilot's instrument panel (figure 1-15). The flap window indicator shows that the flaps are 30° or 40° down by using position lines and a flap outline. When the flaps are in transition or power is OFF, a barber pole will appear in the window.

Note

Above 180 KIAS (approximately), the flaps may not fully extend to the TAKE-OFF position. Above 140 KIAS (approximately) the flaps may not fully extend to the LAND position. In either situation, the flap indicator will display a barber pole until airspeed is reduced.

The slat window displays a slat when the slats are 27.5° down. As in the flap window, a barber pole will appear when the slats are in transition or power is OFF. The indications are identical for normal or emergency operations.

NAVAIR 01-85ADA-1

AIRCRAFT Systems

AUXILIARY AIRCRAFT SYSTEMS

AUTOMATIC FLIGHT CONTROL SYSTEM

The automatic flight control system (AFCS) is an electromechanical system that provides three-axis stability augmentation, three-axis attitude control, and mach hold or altitude hold, as selected by the pilot. A-6E 159895 and ON and A-6E Mod M121 and ON and aircraft with AFC 161 have the AN/ASW-40 AFCS. All other aircraft have the AN/ASW-16.

STABILITY AUGMENTATION MODE (STAB AUG)

The stability augmentation mode (STAB AUG) provides improved control of the aircraft by automatically damping oscillations about the pitch, roll, and yaw axes. In this mode, the stabilizer flaperons, and rudder are actuated proportionately in response to pitch, roll, and yaw rates respectively. Movement of the control surfaces is not transmitted to the control stick or rudder pedals. The only evidence of STAB AUG action is improved aircraft stability.

STAB AUG is considered the manual mode of AFCS operation in that the pilot manually flies the aircraft with stick and rudder pressure.

AUTO MODE

The pilot relief mode (AUTO) is the basic hands-off operating mode of the AFCS. Mode selection is made by placing the AUTO/STAB AUG switch in the AUTO position. The AFCS will remain engaged only if the pitch and roll modules are properly aligned with the attitude reference selected by the compass switch and the ac operating voltage of the AFC is within limits.

Note

- The AFCS should either be secured or placed in the STAB AUG mode before switching into or out of MAG/VGI (A-6A, B, C, and A-6E) or REF 1/REF 2 (KA-6D) to prevent abrupt or unexpected attitude changes during a change in reference signals to the AFCS.

- In AUTO mode, the manual trim button on the control stick grip is deactivated and its functions are performed automatically. Manual rudder trim is available in all modes. If, in the AUTO mode of operation, the stick is grasped, the system reverts to STAB AUG operation, during which manual trim may be accomplished. AUTO mode is resumed when the stick is released.

In the AUTO mode, the AFCS provides pitch attitude hold and heading hold. If AUTO is selected at bank angles in excess of 5°, it will hold a constant bank angle. The system will hold any bank angle between 5° and 60°. If the 60° limits are exceeded, the AFCS will automatically return the aircraft to 60°. Automatic heading hold may be inhibited in A-6E 159895 and ON and A-6E Mod M121 and ON by selecting HDG OFF. In addition, heading command from the attack/navigation system is available in the AUTO MODE in these aircraft by selecting ROLL CMD.

Pitch limits are 25° nose up and 60° nose down. If these limits are exceeded, the AFCS will automatically return the aircraft to the nearest limit of the pitch range. When forces of 1.1±0.2 pounds are applied to the control stick, the AFCS reverts to the STAB AUG mode. When control stick pressure is released, AUTO mode is reengaged and the aircraft will again hold a constant pitch attitude and a constant heading or bank, depending on bank angle existing when control stick pressure is released. If the bank angle is less than 5°, the AFCS will level the aircraft and hold a constant heading. If the bank angle is greater than 5° when stick pressure is released, the AFCS will hold the existing bank angle.

Additional pilot relief functions incorporated in AUTO mode are described below.

ALTITUDE HOLD

When altitude hold (ALT) is selected, the pitch attitude of the aircraft is controlled by pressure altitude signals from the air data computer. The AFCS retains its fully automatic features and in addition maintains the aircraft at an altitude corresponding to the barometric pressure existing at the time ALT is selected. Control stick pressure interrupts altitude hold and the system reverts to the STAB AUG mode. When control stick pressure is released, altitude hold is reengaged and the aircraft will again maintain a constant altitude.

Note

- It is recommended that the aircraft be in approximately level flight before engaging the altitude control. Using the altitude hold feature to level off from climbs or descents in excess of 1000 feet per minute will probably result in an error in the level-off altitude. Repeated use of altitude hold at high vertical speeds will result in wearing of the clutch in the altitude hold module of the air data computer.

- Selecting ALT when the aircraft is on the deck will result in an apparent pitch trim runaway. This is characteristic of the AFCS and does not indicate a malfunction.

MACH HOLD

The mach hold function maintains the mach number existing at the time of mach hold engagement. In this mode, a signal from the air data computer commands a pitch-up or pitch-down whenever the airspeed is

Change 2   1-49

above or below the selected mach number. Mach hold and altitude hold cannot be selected simultaneously. Selection of either function automatically disengages the other.

Longitudinal pressure on the control stick interrupts mach hold. When pressure on the control stick is released, the AFCS returns to mach hold and will again hold the existing mach number.

Note

- Mach hold should not be engaged until mach number is stabilized.

- During extended periods of mach hold operation at a constant throttle setting, the aircraft will climb slowly due to weight loss through fuel consumption. This is normal and can be corrected by reducing thrust.

- Selecting MACH when the aircraft is on the deck will result in an apparent pitch trim runaway. This is characteristic of the AFCS and does not indicate a malfunction.

ROLL COMMAND

The roll command function is available in the ASW-40 AFCS. This function allows the digital computer to command the AFCS to fly the aircraft to a heading to make good a selected target or track. Fully automatic hands-off control of the aircraft in roll is achieved by the AFCS in response to computer steering error inputs in the form of bank commands. The roll command function is energized when ROLL CMD is selected, but the switch is mechanically latched into the ROLL CMD position only as long as a computer roll command discrete is present and the AFCS is in AUTO.

AUTOPILOT CONTROL PANEL - AN/ASW-16

The autopilot control panel, placarded AUTOPILOT, is on the center console (figure 1-16). The controls consist of three solenoid-held toggle switches, two solenoid-held pushbuttons, and one momentary-on pushbutton. The toggle switches are placarded ON/OFF, AUTO/STAB AUG, and CMD ON/OFF. Pushbutton switches are placarded ALT, MACH, and RETURN TO LEVEL. The RETURN TO LEVEL and CMD ON/OFF switches are currently inoperative. The other controls and their functions are discussed under the description of the various operating modes available to the pilot.

Autopilot Switch

This two-position, solenoid-held toggle switch is interlocked with the AUTO/STAB AUG switch, which is spring-loaded to the STAB AUG position. In its normal operating position (ON), the switch engages the three-axis damper function of the STAB AUG mode. This switch must be engaged to permit selection of any of the automatic functions.

(A-6E 159895 AND ON AND A-6E MOD M121 AND ON)

Figure 1-16

Note

- After positioning AUTOPILOT ON/OFF switch to ON, and thereby engaging STAB AUG mode, wait at least 30 seconds before engaging either of the AUTO mode functions, to permit the gyros to reach operating speed.

- In order to engage the AFCS with a minimum of transients, the lateral position of the pilot's control stick should be neutral when the autopilot switch is set to ON and it should be left in neutral for 3 to 6 seconds after the AFCS is engaged to permit the servo ram to engage completely.

AUTO/STAB AUG Switch

This two-position, solenoid-operated toggle switch is placarded AUTO and STAB AUG. It is interlocked with the ON/OFF switch and is spring-loaded to the STAB AUG position. It can be placed in the AUTO position only when the ON/OFF switch is engaged. With AUTO selected, the ALT or MACH functions may be engaged.

ALT Button

The solenoid-held ALT button is used when the AFCS is in the AUTO mode, to select the altitude hold function, permitting the pitch attitude of the aircraft to be controlled in response to pressure altitude signals from the air data computer to maintain the barometric pressure existing at selection. Deselection of AUTO causes the button to disengage.

MACH Button

The solenoid-held MACH button is used when the AFCS is in the AUTO mode, to select the MACH hold function, permitting the pitch attitude of the aircraft to be controlled in response to mach signals from the air data computer to maintain the mach number existing at selection. Deselection of AUTO causes the button to disengage.

AUTOPILOT CONTROL PANEL - AN/ASW-40

The autopilot control panel, placarded AUTOPILOT, is on the center console (figure 1-16). The controls consist of four three-position, solenoid-held toggle switches and two two-position solenoid-held toggle switches. The three-position toggle switches are placarded ACL/OFF/PCD, ALT/OFF/MACH, HDG OFF/NORM/ROLL CMD, and MAG VGI/COMP IN/COMP OUT. The two-position switches are placarded ON/OFF and AUTO/STAB AUG.

Autopilot Switch

This two-position, solenoid-held toggle switch placarded ON/OFF is interlocked with the AUTO/STAB AUG switch, which is spring-loaded to the STAB AUG position. In its normal operating position (ON), the switch engages the three-axis damper function of the STAB AUG mode. This switch must be ON to engage any of the automatic functions of the AFCS.

Note

- After positioning the AUTOPILOT ON/OFF switch to ON, and thereby engaging STAB AUG mode, wait at least 30 seconds before engaging any of the AUTO mode functions, to permit the gyros to reach operating speed.

- In order to engage the AFCS with a minimum of transients, the lateral position of the pilot's control switch is set to ON and it should be left in neutral for 3 to 6 seconds after the AFCS is engaged to permit the servo ram to engage completely.

AUTO/STAB AUG Switch

This two-position, solenoid-operated toggle switch is placarded AUTO and STAB AUG. It is interlocked with the ON/OFF switch and is spring-loaded to the STAB AUG position. It can be placed in the AUTO position only when the ON/OFF switch is engaged. With AUTO selected, the ALT, MACH, or ROLL CMD functions may be engaged.

ACL/OFF/PCD Switch

This three-position, solenoid-held toggle switch is used with AUTO selected to enable response to pitch and roll commands from the ACLS. In the ACL position, the AFCS is coupled to and receives pitch and roll signals through the AN/ASW-25 Data Link. With ACL selected, the AFCS is in the parallel mode of operation. In this mode, the autopilot input signal will result in a maximum stabilizer travel of ±7.8° together with corresponding control stick travel. When the pilot applies a force of 10 pounds in pitch or 7 pounds in roll to the control stick, the AFCS reverts to the STAB AUG mode. When control stick pressure is released, the AFCS remains in STAB AUG.

Note

- If either the AFCS fails to revert to STAB AUG or the control stick fails to move with pilot pitch inputs or both, ACL can be disengaged and normal control stick movement restored by application of rapid fore and aft input of approximately 50 pounds at the stick grip. Turn off the AFCS and continue the flight in manual.

- ACL may also be disengaged by use of the AFCS emergency disconnect switch.

Automatic disengagement of the ACL mode occurs when autopilot command signals exceed normal operating inputs or when the stabilizer actuator servo ram receives a hard over signal causing the main ram to actuate a rate switch. Either disengagement causes the AFCS to revert to STAB AUG. In the OFF position, the data link interface is disengaged. The PCD position is not operational.

ALT/OFF/MACH Switch

This three-position solenoid-held toggle switch is used with AUTO selected to engage either the altitude-hold or the mach-hold function of the AFCS. When the ALT position is selected, the pitch attitude of the aircraft is controlled in response to pressure altitude signals from the air data computer to maintain the barometric pressure existing at selection. Selecting MACH permits aircraft pitch attitude to be controlled in response to mach inputs from the air data computer to maintain the mach number existing at selection. Deselection of AUTO causes the switch to move to OFF.

HDG OFF/NORM/ROLL CMD Switch

This three-position solenoid-held toggle switch is used with AUTO selected, to disable heading hold or to enable response to roll command signals from the digital computer AN/ASQ-155.

When HDG OFF is selected, the AFCS provides only pitch attitude hold in the AUTO mode. Selecting

NORM enables the heading hold function of the AUTO mode.

Selecting ROLL CMD permits the AFCS roll axis to respond to heading commands from the digital computer, with bank angle authority limited to ±30°.

Attitude Reference Switch

This three-position, toggle switch is placarded MAG/VGI, COMP IN, and COMP OUT. Functions of the switch are described in Section VIII of this manual.

AFCS Out Light

The AFCS OUT caution light on the approach indexer comes on with ACL selected when the autopilot has reverted to the STAB AUG mode.

AFCS EMERGENCY DISCONNECT

The AFCS emergency disconnect switch is on a junction box immediately below and to the right of the control stick grip. The switch is marked AUTO PILOT OFF and is coded with yellow and black barber-pole stripes. When the disconnect is actuated momentarily, electric power is disconnected from all AFCS circuits. Any switches or pushbuttons on the AFCS control panel that are engaged automatically return to the OFF position.

Note

In the event of any unusual vibrations or oscillations in the flight controller or if a malfunction is suspected, actuate the emergency disconnect to eliminate the AFCS as a cause. Any AFCS switches or pushbuttons that do not return to the OFF positions after actuating the emergency disconnect should be positioned to OFF manually or the autopilot circuit breaker on the bombardier/navigator's circuit breaker panel should be pulled, or both.

APPROACH POWER COMPENSATOR SYSTEM

The approach power compensator system (APC) AN/ASN-54(V) is installed in A-6E, A-6A 155642 and on an aircraft incorporating AFC No. 199. The primary purpose of the APC is to maintain an airspeed that will result in a constant average angle of attack. The system consists of the approach power control set, angle-of-attack transmitter, stabilizer position transducers, control switches, and a warning light.

When engaged, the APC automatically sets the throttles at the calculated thrust, regardless of previous setting needed to maintain the aircraft at the proper angle of attack. The precise throttle setting will depend upon aircraft gross weight, bank angle, flight path angle, and temperature setting selected. The APC uses acceleration measured perpendicular to the glide path, angle-of-attack error, and stabilizer position inputs to control throttle movement. If the pitch angle is changed to achieve a desired glide path, the throttles will automatically move as required to correct for the change in aircraft attitude. However, engine speed will not increase above 99% rpm or decrease below 75%. Furthermore, the system is damped to prevent excessive throttle movement when flying through heavy turbulence.

Manual throttle operation is available with the system turned off, and an emergency override feature allows the pilot to manually disengage the system by applying a forward or aft force of 10 to 12 pounds to the throttles. The system may also be disengaged by moving the throttle friction lock lever forward out of the off position, by selecting OFF or STBY with the APC power switch, or actuating the weight-on-wheels switch. Therefore, the pilot is assured final override authority if the system malfunctions or when a missed wire (bolter) occurs during carrier landing.

Note

- After disengaging the APC, the pilot will have to manually reselect ENGAGE with the APC power switch.

- If the throttles do not come free after attempting to disengage the APC by the normal methods, a force of 35 to 55 pounds applied to the throttles manually disengages the system. This emergency procedure damages the APC actuators, which must be repaired before the system is used again.

APC POWER SWITCH

The APC power switch on the ANTI-SKID/FLAPERON POP UP panel, is a three-position toggle switch placarded OFF, STBY, and ENGAGE. In the OFF position, all power to the system is removed and the throttles must be manually positioned. In the STBY position, power is supplied to the throttle computer. However, the control amplifier is not active and the throttles must be manually positioned. In the ENGAGE position, the system will automatically control the engine thrust by varying throttle position. The power switch is held in the ENGAGE position by a holding coil. If a malfunction causes a disengagement, the power switch will automatically move to STBY position and the APCS STANDBY light will come on.

WARNING

It is possible to engage the APC in any configuration. Engaging the APC at high power settings in the clean configuration will cause a rapid retardation of power to less than 75% rpm.

Note

- The APC will not engage unless the throttle friction lock lever is in the OFF position, full aft.

- STBY should be selected 60 seconds prior to ENGAGE to allow the throttle computer to adjust its output to a predicted level and thereby reduce throttle transients when ENGAGE is selected. Selecting ENGAGE without stopping at STBY is not harmful to the system. However, the pilot should anticipate increased throttle transients and a longer time before the desired thrust setting is established.

AIR TEMPERATURE SWITCH

The air-temperature switch is a three-position toggle switch placarded COLD, STD, and HOT. It allows the pilot to change the computer gain as a function of outside temperature. Since thrust developed for any given throttle setting varies with outside air temperature, the correct gain should be selected before engaging the APCS. The COLD position will be used when temperature is below 40°F (+4°C) and the HOT position when the temperature is above 80°F (+26°C). When the temperature is between 40°F and 80°F (+4°C and +26°C), the STD position is used.

Note

Selecting the wrong gain may degrade APC performance; however, the system will compensate and maintain stable operation.

APCS STANDBY LIGHT

The APCS STANDBY light on the approach indexer illuminates when the system is disengaged and is in the STBY position. The light can be extinguished by engaging the system or by turning the system off. The primary purpose of the light is to warn the pilot that the APC has disengaged and returned to the standby position. Depressing the LTS WARN press-to-test button on the pilot's master test panel will check for operating circuitry of the light.

AIRCRAFT
Systems

NAVAIR 01-85ADA-1

AUTOMATIC CARRIER LANDING SYSTEM

The automatic carrier landing system (ACLS) is installed in A-6E 159895 and ON, A-6E Mod M121 and ON in KA-6D aircraft with AFC 161 and, with a lesser capability in aircraft incorporating AFC 230. The ACLS consists of an airborne subsystem and a shipboard subsystem with most of the required equipment being aboard ship.

AIRBORNE SUBSYSTEM

The airborne subsystem in all ACLS-equipped aircraft includes the AN/ASW-25B Data Link receiver and associated controls and indicators. In addition, the aircraft with full capability have a modified APN-154 Radar Beacon, the AN/ASW-40 AFCS, and the AN/ARA-63 ILS Receiver. See figures 1-17 and 1-17A.

SHIPBOARD SUBSYSTEM

The shipboard subsystem is composed of an AN/SPN-10/42 Computer interfaced with the naval tactical data system (NTDS), AN/SPN-10/42 Radar, and data link transmitter. A shore-based AN/SPN-42T1 is used for indoctrinating pilots in ACLS procedures and is identical to the shipboard system except for ship stabilization and deck motion compensation.

APPROACH MODES

Several ACLS approach modes are available depending on aircraft modifications. These modes are as follows:

- Mode I Approach - Automatic coupled AFCS approach from acquisition to touchdown on the carrier flight deck.

Hands-off capability is accomplished by interfacing the data link with the automatic flight control system and the approach power compensator (figure 1-17B).

The carrier's landing radar system (AN/SPN-42) tracks the aircraft and the radar computer compares aircraft position with desired aircraft position. The aircraft's position is then corrected to fly the desired glide path by commands from the naval tactical data system (NTDS). These commands are transmitted over the UHF data'link to the aircraft's AN/ASW-25 Data Link receiver, which then directs pitch and roll commands to the automatic flight control system.

In addition to carrier control of the aircraft, discrete messages are transmitted and displayed on the pilot's discrete message indicator. These messages provide the pilot information relative to the progress of the landing approach and direct actions required of the flight crew. The carrier's AN/SPN-42 also transmits azimuth and elevation glide slope error

ACLS CONTROL PANEL AND INDICATORS

AIRCRAFT INCORPORATING AFC 230

TYPICAL

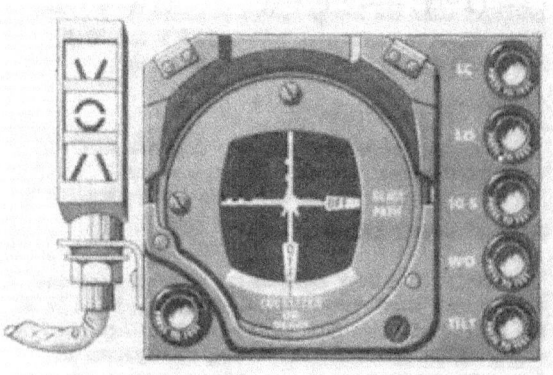

AFT BULKHEAD CONSOLE

Figure 1-17

NAVAIR 01-85ADA-1

AUTOMATIC CARRIER LANDING SYSTEM CONTROLS AND INDICATORS

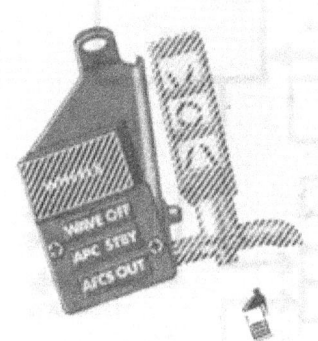

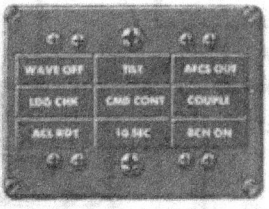

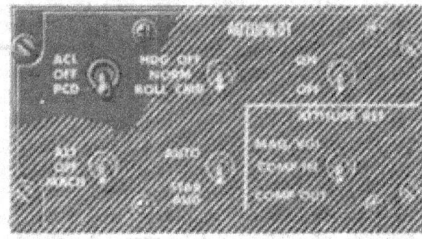
LOCATED ON AFT CENTER CONSOLE-TOP

Figure 1-17A

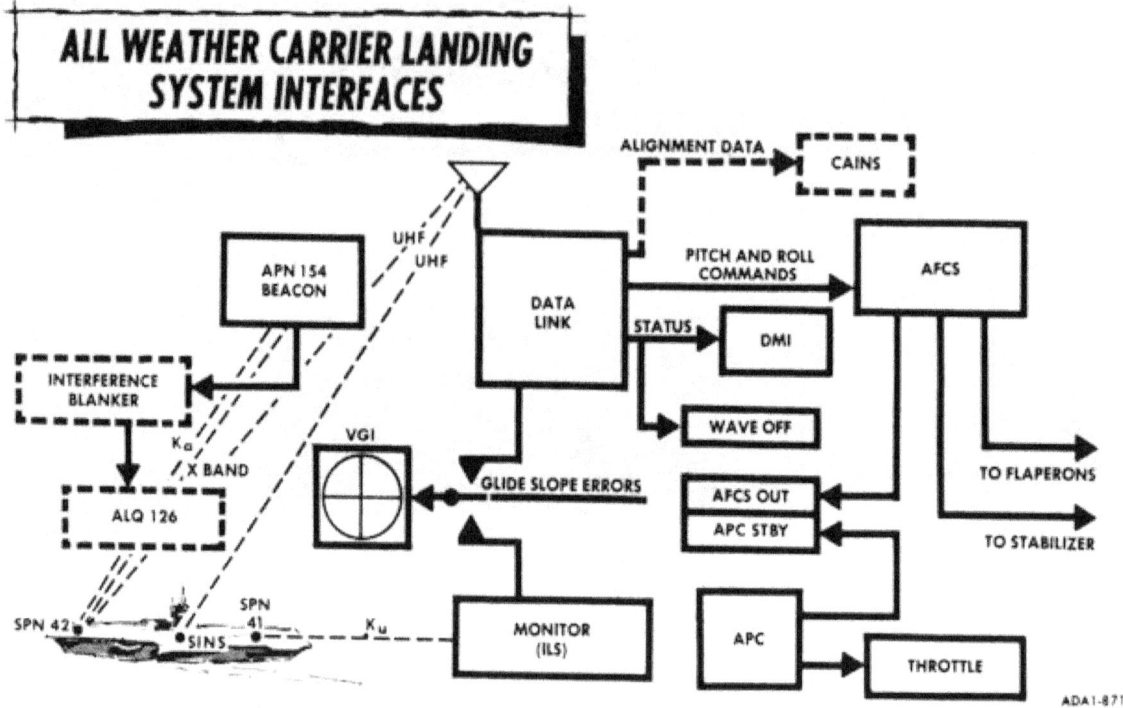

Figure 1-17B

signals to the aircraft's data link receiver, which are displayed by the cross pointers on the vertical gyro indicator. When an operational AN/SPN-41 is available aboard the carrier, the pilot may elect to monitor the approach through the AN/ARA-63 ILS Receiver by selecting MON on the VGI DIS switch on the pilot's miscellaneous panel. In this case, aircraft bank and pitch commands continue to be received from the AN/SPN-42, while independant lateral and vertical glide slope deviations are displayed on the vertical gyro indicator as received from the AN/SPN-41 through the AN/ARA-63 Receiver and may be used as a crosscheck. The pilot may take control at any time and continue the approach in Mode II.

- Mode IA Approach - Automatic coupled AFCS approach from acquisition to 200 feet and 1/2 mile minimums; manual approach to touchdown.

- Mode II Approach - Uncoupled approach in which the pilot flies the aircraft in response to the ACLS course indicator pointers as in an ILS. Use of APCS is optional for a Mode II Approach.

- Mode III Approach - Manual controller talkdown approach requiring no special aircraft equipment onboard.

Aircraft with AFC 230 have Mode II and capability. A-6E 159895 and ON and A-6E Mod M121 and ON and KA-6D aircraft with AFC 161 are equipped for all modes.

ACLS CONTROLS AND INDICATORS

DATA LINK Panel

The DATA LINK panel provides the controls for operation of the data link receiver. In aircraft with AFC 230, it is on the aft bulkhead (observer's instrument panel KA-6D) and on the pilot's left console in the fully capable A-6E. The ON/OFF/AUX ON toggle switch when in the ON position provides power from the essential 28 V dc bus for system operation. The AUX ON position is inoperative. The TEST/NORM/A-J mode switch provides normal system operation when in the NORM position. The TEST position provides a self-test feature, which will function only in the presence of a universal test message (UTM) from a ground- or carrier-based transmitter. With the proper data link frequency selected on the FREQ SELECT switches, the ACLS course pointers will cycle every 6 seconds from fly-up-and-right to a fly-down-and-left, indicating proper data link operation. As the pointers cycle down and left, the WO (wave-off) light on the discrete message indicator panel will come on. The A-J position is inoperative.

ACLS Course Indicator

The ACLS course indicator (ID-351) horizontal and vertical pointers present glide path and azimuth errors (actual displacement from approach path) in relation to aircraft position represented by a miniature aircraft in the center of the instrument. The vertical and horizontal pointer OFF flags will be displayed and the needles will show a zero glide slope and centerline error whenever AN/SPN-10/42 Radar is not locked on the aircraft.

The vertical gyro indicator ID-1791 (figure 1-17A), on the pilot's center instrument panel, in A-6E 159895 and ON and A-6E Mod M121 and ON, and KA-6D with AFC 161, provides the pilot pitch and roll indications with respect to an artifical horizon. In addition, vertical (azimuth) and horizontal (glide slope) pointers are super-imposed across the face of the instrument to indicate lateral (heading) and vertical (glide slope) errors during carrier approach. The instrument is self-contained with respect to pitch and roll indications. Glide slope and heading error indications are transmitted from the shipboard AN/SPN-42 or AN/SPN-41 to deflect the pointers toward the desired track. Either the data link or AN/ARA-63 Receiver may be used to control the cross pointers, by means of the VGI DIS switch on the pilot's miscellaneous panel. When the switch is placed in D/L, the cross pointers are driven through the data link receiver. When the switch is placed in MON, the pointers are driven through the AN/ARA-63 Receiver.

The cross pointers are activated through the data link when the ON-OFF-AUX ON switch on the data link control panel is set to ON, the proper frequency is set, the TEST-NORM-AJ switch is in the NORM or AJ position, and the data link receives a valid label 6 message from the AN/SPN-42 with no TILT and no WAVEOFF discretes. The cross pointers are activated through the ARA-63 Receiver when the power switch on the ARA-63 control is set to ON and the shipboard AN/SPN-41 is locked on. When not activated, the cross pointers are driven out of view behind masks at the bottom and right side of the instrument.

A system test is provided by means of the TEST-NORM-AJ switch on the data link control panel. To conduct the test, a universal test message (UTM) must be transmitted from land- or carrier-based equipment. When the switch is held in the TEST position, cycling of the cross pointers from fly-up-and-right to fly-down-and-left every 6 seconds indicates the system is operational.

A conventional turn-and-slip indicator is provided at the base of the instrument. The turn needle is powered by a remote rate gyro.

A test pushbutton is at the base of the instrument. Depressing the pushbutton causes the turn needle to indicate a double-needle-width turn and drives the cross pointers into view to show zero azimuth and glide slope error.

Discrete Message Indicator Panel

The discrete message indicator panel in aircraft with AFC 230 (figure 1-17) contains five lights, which provide the pilot with additional information during an ACLS approach. The LC (landing check) light comes on when the proper aircraft address has been inserted in the SPN-10/42 by the controller and indicates the pilot should perform the landing check. The LO light indicates the radar is locked on. At this time, the horizontal and vertical OFF flags disappear and the horizontal and vertical pointers on the ACLS course indicator present aircraft relative position from glide slope and centerline. The flashing WO (wave-off) light indicates an unsatisfactory approach path or carrier equipment failure. WO signals may also be initiated by the final controller (between lock-on and touchdown), PRI-FLY (between 9 seconds and 1.5 seconds from touchdown), and the LSO (between 1 mile and touchdown). The 10-S (10-second) light comes on approximately 10 seconds from touchdown and indicates deck motion compensation is being added to glide path commands. The TILT (missed message) light comes on within 2 seconds after the last valid flight path command message is received. The TILT light will also be on prior to aircraft address insertion by the controller and will go out when the LC light comes on.

In A-6E 159895 and ON and A-6E Mod M121 and ON and KA-6D with AFC 161, the discrete message indicator contains nine indicator lights, which provide the pilot with information necessary to complete or abort a carrier approach. The function of each light is as follows:

WAVE OFF (flashing red) - Indicates the aircraft has deviated beyond limits from the azimuth or glide slope path or that there has been a failure of the carrier approach equipment. It also may be triggered by the LSO for conditions he considers unsafe.

LDG CHECK (yellow) - Lights when the proper aircraft address has been inserted in the carrier's AN/SPN-42 by the controller and indicates that the pilot should complete the landing checklist.

ACL READY (yellow) - Indicates that the aircraft has arrived at the radar acquisition window and the radar is locked on. The signal, which is transmitted automatically by the shipboard AN/SPN-42, indicates that azimuth and glide slope errors are being transmitted.

Change 2   1-52C

AIRCRAFT Systems

TILT (red)	-	Alerts the pilot to any loss of current command inputs to the data link. If steering commands received by the data link are not updated for any 2-second period during the approach, the TILT light comes on. This discrete automatically disengages the AFCS if it is coupled. The TILT light will also be on prior to the time the shipboard controller inserts the proper aircraft address in the AN/SPN-42 and will go out when the LDG CHECK light comes on.
CMD CONT (yellow)	-	Indicates the AN/SPN-42 is transmitting pitch and bank commands.
10 SEC (yellow)	-	Lights approximately 12.5 seconds prior to touchdown to indicate that ship's motion has been added to glide slope information and D/L commands.
AFCS OUT (red)	-	Indicates the autopilot has uncoupled from the data link mode. Light will go out when AFCS is recoupled or after 20 seconds have elapsed.
COUPLE (yellow)	-	Indicates the pilot can couple the autopilot to data link commands.
BCN ON (yellow)	-	Indicates cockpit beacon switch is on and Ka/X band loop is closed.

VGI DIS Switch

The two-position VGI DIS toggle switch on the pilot's miscellaneous panel is provided on A-6E 159895 and ON and A-6E Mod 121 and ON to permit the pilot to select the source of course and glideslope signals driving the VGI pointers. With the switch at the D/L position, the pointers will be positioned by error signals from the ship's SPN-42 radar. With MON selected, independent course and glideslope signals received by the ARA-63 will be displayed, permitting a cross check of a Mode I approach or as an alternate source for a Mode II approach.

RADAR BEACON AUGMENTOR RECEIVER

In A-6E 159895 and ON and A-6E Mod M121 and ON and KA-6D with AFC 161, the APN-154 Radar Beacon is provided with a Ka-Band augmentor receiver to enable the APN-154 to reply to and extend the tracking capability of the ship's SPN-42 radar. The augmentor is turned on by setting the mode selector switch to ACLS. The augmentor receiver may be tested by depressing and holding the ACLS TEST button/light on the radar beacon panel (figure 1-17A). If the augmentor tests good, the light in the button comes on.

AN/ARA-63 ILS RECEIVER

The ILS receiver is used with the carrier-based AN/SPN-41 (C-scan) transmitters for manual instrument and landing approaches or an independent monitor (figure 1-17B) during ACLS approaches. The system operates in the K_u band, between 15.4 and 15.7 GHz, on any of 20 channels selected by the pilot. Channel selection is made on the ARA-63 control panel (figure 1-17A) on the left console.

The aircraft system receives and decodes glide slope, azimuth and elevation signals, which are displayed on the VGI if the VGI DIS switch is set to MON. Operating range is approximately 20 miles and warmup time is a minimum of 1 minute. Electrical power requirements are 28 V dc and three-phase 115 V ac from the primary bus through ARA-63 circuit breakers on the forward and aft nosewheel well circuit breaker panels (A-6E) and the observer's circuit breaker panel (KA-6D).

ARA-63 Control Panel

The ARA-63 control panel provides all the controls for operating the ILS receiver.

CHANNEL Selector - A rotary selector switch permitting any of 20 channels to be tuned.

BIT Button - A momentary-action pushbutton permitting self-test of the ARA-63 when the button is pressed and held. A valid test is indicated on the VGI (when the VGI DIS switch is at MON) by the vertical pointer slowly oscillating on the right side of the display, then on the left side. The horizontal pointer remains stationary in the center of the VGI.

POWER switch - A two-position lever-lock switch marked ON and OFF. With OFF selected, the ARA-63 is turned off.

Indicator Light - Comes on when ARA-63 is on and receiving.

SPEED BRAKES

The wing-tip speed brakes consist of a set of split trailing-edge surfaces at the tip of each wing, outboard of the flaps. When fully deflected, the brakes open to an included angle of 120° (60° per each half). The individual brake surfaces are approximately 2 ft. x 4 ft. panels making a total of 32 sq. ft. total braking area for the airplane. The lower speed brake is attached to the wing by two external fixed hinges. The upper surface is attached to the wing by two adjustable tension links at the same wing station as the lower hinges. The surfaces are interconnected at three points. This configuration has been optimized to yield symmetric deflection of the upper and lower brake surfaces. The primary consideration affecting the overall design of the speed brakes controls has been to obtain close synchronization between left- and right-hand wing brakes. This consideration led to the incorporation of flow regulators and electrical transmitters. Essentially the actuation is as follows:

The pilot operates a momentary switch in the cockpit, which selects a position of the solenoid-controlled hydraulic slide valve. Power is then transmitted to the speed-brake surfaces by single tandem-type hydraulic cylinders in each wing tip via the flow regulators. (This power is from the combined hydraulic system.) Consequently, primary synchronization is initially provided by the flow regulators, which control rate and position of the surfaces within 10%.

Fail-safe features have been added at several levels. If for any reason the surfaces become asymmetric by more than 8°, an electrical synchronization system will actuate to retract the surfaces. This would close the surfaces in 2 1/2 seconds from full open. Pilot operation of wing-tip speed brakes can be regained by cycling the wing-tip speed-brake control switch to retract. In the event of loss of electrical or hydraulic power or both, the system will go to a closed selection. The pilot has the option of selecting closed at all times. Whenever the surfaces are in the closed position, ball locks in the speed-brake actuation cylinder hold the surfaces even with loss of hydraulic pressure.

The flow regulators in the hydraulic system have been selectively fitted to provide good control of synchronization and minimize the transients during all failure conditions. The normal speeds of operation are 5.0 seconds out and 2.5 seconds in.

SPEED-BRAKE POSITION INDICATOR

The speed-brake position indicator, part of the integrated position indicator on the pilot's instrument panel, indicates position of the speed brakes. The word IN appears when the speed brakes are stowed. Barber poles appear whenever the brakes are in transition, partially extended, or the indicator loses electrical power. Fully extended wing-tip speed brakes are indicated by black dots on a white background. The indicator is supplied by the essential 28 V dc bus and protected by the CAUTION LTS circuit breaker on the main circuit breaker panel.

FAIL-SAFE PROVISIONS

Fail-safe provisions exist at several levels. If electrical power is lost, the system will go to a closed selection. Whenever the speed brakes are closed, ball locks in the speed-brake actuation cylinder hold the brakes closed, even if hydraulic pressure is lost.

Note

The speed brakes must be fully closed to permit engagement of the ball locks. A hydraulic failure with brakes extended will result in the brakes closing to a trial position which is not sufficiently closed for the locks to engage. It is recommended that the speed-brake selector switch be left in the retract position when not in use.

For most types of system failure, the electrical asymmetry sensors will react and retract the brakes. It is noted that there is no practical protection for either a mechanically jammed speed-brake surface or jammed hydraulic selector valve. The sizable airloads on the speed brakes will tend to close them against any but the most severe interference. Extensive experience has not produced any failure of this type.

Note

Normal operation of the stability-augmentation yaw damper will provide an increased margin of safety for yaw transients induced by asymmetric wing-brake deflections.

SPEED-BRAKE SWITCH

A three-position thumb switch with retract, neutral, and momentary extend positions is in the right throttle head, and controls actuation of the speed brakes. Positioning the switch forward retracts the speed brakes; holding it aft extends them. Momentary operation of the switch produces partial extension and will show a barber pole on the integrated position indicator. In the center (temporary hold) position, return flow of hydraulic fluid is blocked from both the extend and retract sides of the speed-brake cylinders, hydraulically locking the speed brakes.

Note

The normal position of the three-position switch is retract.

SPEED-BRAKE TEST SWITCH

The speed-brake test switch is a toggle switch on the left console placarded NORM and TEST. The switch is spring-loaded in the NORM position. The TEST position provides a check of the speed-brake null-detector system and is selected prior to takeoff.

To make the speed-brake test, proceed as follows:

1. Speed-brake switch aft to extend speed brakes.
2. Select TEST position - brakes should retract immediately.

LANDING GEAR SYSTEM

LANDING GEAR CONTROLS AND INDICATORS

The aircraft has a fully retractable tricycle landing gear. When the gear is up and locked, the wheel wells are covered flush to the aircraft with the landing gear doors. The system is electrically controlled by the 28 V dc essential bus and is powered to the extend and retract position by the secondary circuit of the combined hydraulic system. A pneumatic system powered by four air bottles charged to 2,450 psi provide a one-shot extend cycle in the event of a hydraulic failure. A number of indicators are provided to warn of unsafe landing gear operation.

Note

The landing gear is structurally capable of withstanding being extended into the slipstream up to 250 KIAS. However it will not necessarily lock down at this speed. The design of power requirements to drive the gear and doors to the down and locked position against airloads is based on the selection to down being made at 200 KIAS or less.

Wheels Warning Light

The WHEELS warning light on the windshield bow (figure 1-18) will flash any time all three landing gear are not down and locked with both throttles retarded to less than 24 1/2° above idle (approximately 82.5%), and the flaps are not retracted.

Note

Whe WHEELS warning light will flash on the approach to landing with the landing gear down and locked if only RAT power is available. This is normal operation since the landing gear downlock relay is powered from the primary dc bus.

Wheels Transition Light

The wheels transition light to the right of the landing gear handle (figure 1-18) will glow any time the landing gear handle is first selected UP or DOWN, and will continue to glow until the position of all three gears agree with the position of the handle, and all three gears are either up or down and locked.

Landing Gear Position Indicator

The integrated position indicator on the left side of the pilot's instrument panel (figure 1-18) displays the position of each landing gear as follows:

GEAR UP - The word up appears in the appropriate window when the main gear uplock switches and the forward door switches are closed; nose gear uplock switch closed.

GEAR DOWN - A picture of a wheel appears in the appropriate window when the main gear and the nose gear are down and locked.

GEAR TRANSITION - A barber-pole indication will appear in the appropriate window when the uplock or downlock switches, or the main gear forward door switch is not closed.

LANDING GEAR CONTROLS AND INDICATORS

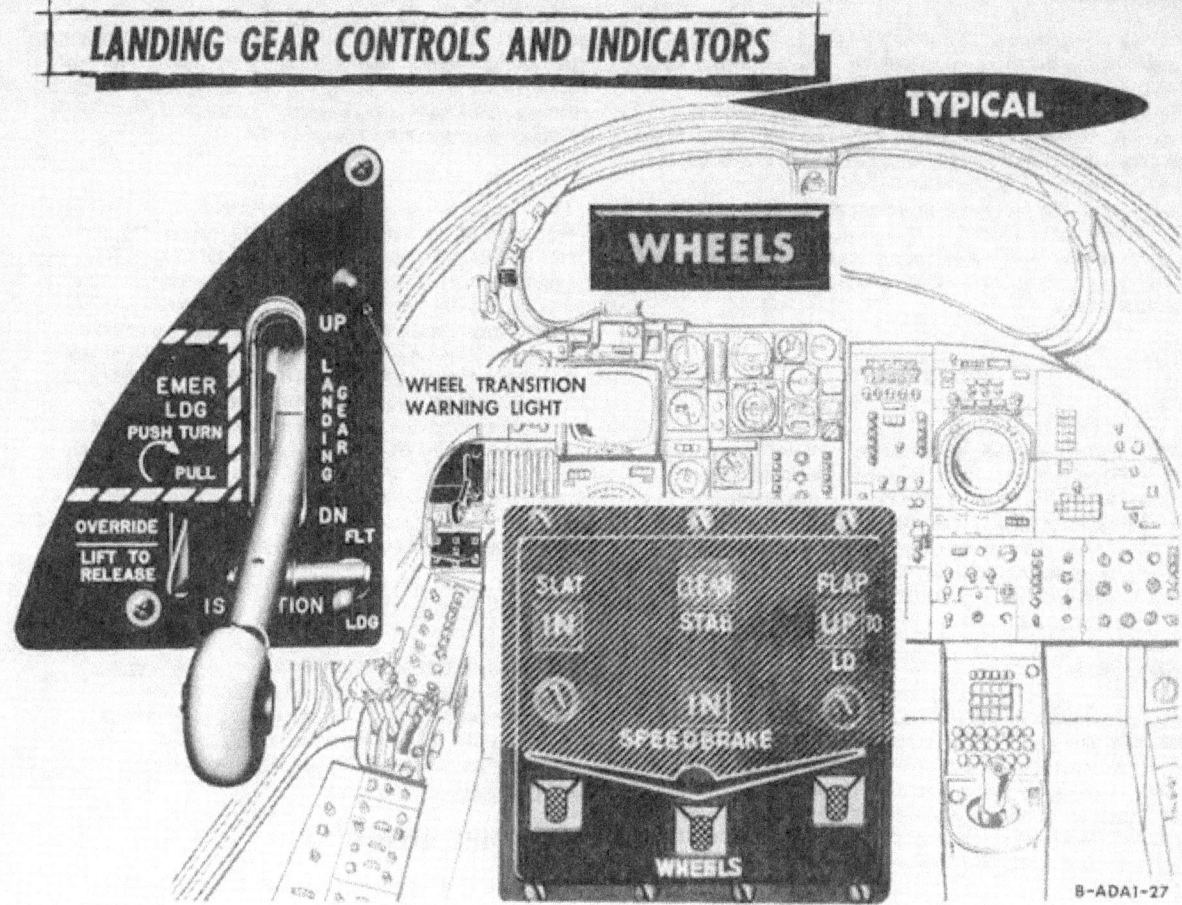

Figure 1-18

Note

The approach light indexer will not light until all gear are down and locked.

Landing Gear Handle

The landing gear handle (figure 1-18) is on the left side of the pilot's instrument panel. The wheel-shaped handle actuates a switch that electrically positions the landing-gear selector valve to the selected position.

CAUTION

Dump cabin pressure before lowering the landing gear above 8,000 feet. Automatic pressurization begins at this altitude, and the possibility of jamming the nose-gear door exists when the gear is actuated with the aircraft pressurized. The cabin may be repressurized after the nose gear has been extended.

Inadvertent gear-up selection, when the aircraft is on the deck, is prevented by the left nutcracker weight-on-wheels switch, which energizes a landing-gear handle lock solenoid. This solenoid throws a latch, which mechanically locks the landing-gear handle in the DN position. If the lock remains in place after takeoff, it can be mechanically repositioned by lifting the override lever to the left of the landing-gear handle.

Note

If the gear is raised by overriding the gear-handle downlock latch, the flaperon pop-up should be disarmed to prevent its inadvertent actuation while airborne if the throttles are fully retarded. The left weight-on-wheels switch, which controls the gear-handle down latch, is a series link in the flaperon pop-up arming circuit.

AIRCRAFT
Systems

MAIN GEAR

Cycling of each gear from both up- and downlocked positions is accomplished through hydraulic and mechanical actuation of the main gear mechanism. When the landing gear handle is placed in the DN position, hydraulic pressure is directed in a sequence controlled by hydraulic valves and mechanical linkage, to open the forward main gear dooes, rear doors, release uplocks and position the downlocks. The wheel is rotated by a drag brace that mechanically rotates the strut cylinder and wheel as the gear is actuated. The main gear extends and retracts hydraulically.

CAUTION

When cycling the gear, allow sufficient time (approximately 7 seconds) for the landing gear to complete a half cycle (i.e. from full up to full down) before attempting a reversal. If the direction is reversed before the door is fully opened, the gear linkage will not have completed its travel and the forward gear door may fail.

NOSE GEAR

The nose gear is hydraulically interconnected with the main gear and is actuated hydraulically to the position selected on the landing gear handle. Motion of the nose gear during retraction is aft and up into the nosewheel well. As the nose gear extends or retracts, mechanical linkages actuate the nosewheel uplock, downlock, and the nosewheel well doors.

CAUTION

Upon lowering the gear handle, if an immediate nose gear indication is received, a failed gear down Micro Switch is indicated and the reading is unreliable. A visual nose-gear-down confirmation prior to landing is recommended.

EMERGENCY LANDING GEAR EXTENSION

Emergency air bottles furnish the power necessary to lower the landing gear in the event of a hydraulic or electrical failure. This one-shot system is powered by nitrogen pressure (2,450 psi) stored in four compressed nitrogen bottles. Pushing in, rotating 90° clockwise, and pulling out the landing gear control handle at least 2 to more than 3 inches to the overcenter position actuates the emergency gear-down valve (release valve) on the bottle in the nosewheel well. Pressure from the nosewheel well bottle, in turn, discharges the three other bottles. All bottles are manifolded on the fill side for single-point pressurizing. However, each bottle has a separate function during the extension cycle.

The nose gear actuator is pressurized to extend, thus opening the uplock and opening the doors by a mechanical linkage. Pressure will power the nose strut to full extension, where the downlock is spring-loaded to the locked position. This same air bottle powers the aft main gear door actuators by a separate line, and opens the main landing gear dump valve. This dump valve vents all system actuators to prevent a hydraulic lock from opposing the gear extend sequence.

Main gear extension is accomplished by pressure from two other bottles separately opening the right and left forward doors by opening the door latch cylinders and pressurizing the door extend cylinders. Opening of the forward doors mechanically releases the aft main gear doors to be opened by pressure from the nose gear bottle. Opening of both aft main doors then permits pressure from the fourth bottle to release both main gear uplocks. The aft door emergency uplock timer check valves are in series so that unless both doors are opened, neither uplock is pressurized. When unlocked, the main gear free-falls to the down position, where the downlock cylinders are spring-loaded to the lock position. Cockpit indications are the same as during normal gear extension.

Note

The landing gear handle must be pulled out with sufficient force and extension to ensure actuation of the emergency air bottles. Extension of the gear handle may be in excess of 3 inches depending on control rigging.

NOSE-WHEEL STEERING

Directional control of the aircraft on the ground is possible through nosewheel steering or conventional differential braking action. Shimmy damping is available in either mode of operation through the use of restrictors in the steering mechanisms. The nosewheel steering will power the lower strut barrel up to approximately 56° and return to center. To permit tighter turns with differential braking, the lower strut will disengage a spring-loaded lock-pin (tog-lock) at approximately 63° of lower strut rotation. The lower strut is now free to swivel and will remain so until the tog-lock is realigned and reengages the upper strut detent.

Nosweheel steering is engaged when the steering button on the control stick grip is depressed and the weight-on-wheels switch on the main landing gear is closed. Steering is also engaged automatically when the arresting hook is extended and the weight-on-wheels switch is closed. When selected, steer unit rotation is proportional to rudder pedal deflection, full pedal begin required to obtain full 56° steering. Since full rudder travel is obtained only with flaps extended, there will be rudder pedal force buildup with flaps up (steering limits are unaffected).

When the nosewheel steering button is depressed, the nosewheel steering selector valve is energized, allowing hydraulic fluid from the secondary circuit of the combined hydraulic system to pressurize the steering control valve and position an internal shuttle valve. The steering control valve is mechanically linked to the rudder pedals. When the rudder pedals are actuated, hydraulic fluid is directed through the control valve, around the shuttle valve, and into the appropriate side of the power chamber. The power chamber is mechanically linked to the nosewheel; therefore, rotation of the output shaft in the power chamber turns the nosewheel. When hydraulic pressure is cut off, a centering spring on the nosewheel strut centers the nosewheel and repositions the internal shuttle valve. Check valves provide a closed circuit between the power chamber and a restrictor in the shuttle valve. This closed hydraulic circuit effectively dampens any shimmy. It should be noted that steering unit deflection will follow pedal deflection only so long as the steering switch is depressed. When the steering button is released, or when aircraft power is lost, the lower strut will remain at approximately the same angle since there is little centering with the weight on the wheels. When reengaging, the transient will be mild if the pedals and the steering unit are at the same rotation angle as the lower strut. If however, the pedals have been centered, the lower strut will produce a moderate jolt when the steering switch is selected on.

When the tog-lock has been disengaged by turning past 63°, the steering switch will have no effect as long as the lower strut is free swiveling. The reengaging jolt will again be mild or severe when the tog lock reengages the detent, depending on the relative position of the lower strut and the upper steering unit. Braking will sometimes be necessary to center the lower strut sufficiently to reengage the tog-lock. If the nosewheel steering is deflected when the main wheels leave the ground, a centering spring will center the nosewheel, providing the tog-lock is engaged.

CAUTION

Failure of the tog-lock to reengage will result in a free swiveling nosewheel, which can produce a nose-gear jam when the gear is retracted.

Nose-Wheel Steering Button

The spring-loaded nosewheel steering button on the pilot's control stick grip (figure 1-15) must be depressed to keep nosewheel steering (figure 1-44). It is used to engage normal nosewheel steering. When the nosewheel steering circuit is energized, the nosewheel steering selector valve is positioned to direct combined hydraulic system pressure to the steering control valve.

NOSE-GEAR LAUNCH SYSTEM

The components necessary for a catapult launch are on the nose gear. A launch bar (figure 1-19) mounted forward of the nose gear serves the dual purpose of

guilding the aircraft to the shuttle from the lead-in track and attaching the aircraft to the shuttle. A bellcrank, aft of the nose-gear strut, attaches the aircraft to the catapult through an attachable holdback bar and release element. The release element will fail at 53,000 pounds of tension. A lifter spring is compressed by the bellcrank as a thrust moment is exerted by the aircraft to engage the launch bar and shuttle. After the release element is broken, the spring applies a force to a lifter pushrod through the holdback bellcrank, repositioning the launch bar when the aircraft clears the shuttle.

To stow the launch bar within the nosewheel well after landing gear retraction, a second launch bar retraction stage is needed to raise the launch bar to the full up position. This is done by mechanical linkage from the nose-gear drag brace to the launch bar. When the gear is extended, the linkage is moved out of the way and the launch bar drops to its intermediate position.

If the launch bar fails to reach its intermediate position after launch, retraction of the landing gear will move the launch bar through the secondary retraction stage in a position to engage the launch bar uplatch.

CATAPULT GRIP

The nose strut oleo is locked during a launch to provide clearance between large centerline stores and the deck hardware, and to minimize strut loads. This

NOSE GEAR LAUNCH BAR

A-ADA1-159

Figure 1-19

AIRCRAFT
Systems

is accomplished by actuating the catapult grip (figures FO-2 sheets 1, 2 and 3) forward of the throttles. With the shuttle engaged and the throttles advanced to takeoff, the catapult grip is rotated 90° to the right and pulled up. A strut-lock switch is actuated by the catapult grip. This switch electrically positions the strut-lock valve. Hydraulic pressure is directed to the strut, positioning the collar over the bleed holes of the shock strut. This locks the strut for launch. After launch, the catapult grip, which is spring-loaded, is released, opening the strut-lock switch. The strut-lock selector valve is actuated, venting the strut-lock line to return. This allows the collar to uncover the bleed holes for normal strut operation.

CAUTION

The catapult grip must be used (pulled out and up) for all catapult launches, since proper grip position is required for nose-strut stiffening. Failure to use the catapult grip will result in catapulting with a soft nose strut and may cause structural damage to the aircraft or the centerline stores.

NOSE STRUT INDICATOR

When the aircraft launch bar is lowered to engage the catapult, the launch bar switch will arm the strut annunciator light. When the throttle is advanced past normal cruise position to full power, and the catapult grip is not positioned, the strut-lock light (figure FO-11) will come on. Positioning the catapult grip will lock the strut (hard position) and turn off the strut-lock warning light. When the gear is extended, the lock light will come on, through the weight-on-wheels relay, with the flaps DOWN, the throttles below approximately 82.5%, and the nose strut HARD.

LAUNCH BAR INDICATOR

When the aircraft is in flight (no weight on wheels) and the launch bar is not up and latched, or the nose gear is cocked more than 8°, the nosewheel window on the integrated indicator will read TOW LINK, and the indexer and exterior approach lights will flash.

CAUTION

With a cocked nose gear, the normal launch bar procedure of recycling the landing gear may result in structural damage by jamming the nose-gear wheel in the nosewheel well.

WING-FOLD SYSTEM

The combined secondary hydraulic system supplies the power for wing folding. The flight hydraulic system must also be pressurized to hold the combined system isolation valve open.

A double locking device at the wing-fold selection control is integrated with the wing fold handle and flight controls to prevent inadvertent damage to control surfaces spanning the wing fold line. If the control stick is not in a neutral position, a mechanical flaperon interlock will prevent the wing-fold handle from being actuated. The wing-fold handle in turn, must be actuated to position the mechanism on the lock cylinder to allow retraction of the hydraulically operated wing lockpins. A wing lockpin switch controls the operation of a selector valve, which directs hydraulic pressure to the lockpins. However, if the flaps and slats are extended, the electric circuit to the wing lockpin selector valve is opened, overriding the UNLOCK position of the wing lockpin switch. Conversely, the flap, slat, and flaperon pop-up circuits are opened when the wings are unlocked. When the wing-fold handle is not stowed, the control stick is restricted laterally by the wing-fold interlock.

WING-FOLD HANDLE

The wing-fold handle (figures FO-2 sheets 1, 2 and 3) is mounted flush in the center console. The arm of the handle extends forward and down the right side of the console, where it is attached to a pivot point. Actuation of the wing-fold handle occurs in steps and is tied in with the wing lockpin switch.

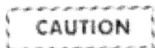

CAUTION

If the wing lockpin switch is in the lock position, actuation of the wing-fold handle to the down position is not possible.

WING LOCKPIN SWITCH

The wing lockpin switch is under the wing-fold handle in the center console. The switch has two positions: UNLOCK and LOCK.

WING-FOLD OPERATION

The wing-fold handle rotates the mechanical lock to a position that enables the hydraulic lockpins to be actuated, and positions the wing-lock warning flaps on each wing. The wing lockpin switch actuates a solenoid-operated hydraulic selector valve, which directs combined system pressure to the four lockpin cylinders at the wing-fold joint, and opens the flap, slats, and flaperon pop-up electrical circuits. The hydraulic pressure at the lock cylinder retracts the wing lockpins. As the lockpins retract, they remove the mechanical stops of the wing-fold handle. The wing-fold handle can now be moved to the full forward position. By moving the wing-fold handle full forward the wing-fold selector valves are positioned by mechanical linkage, directing combined hydraulic system pressure to the wing-fold actuating cylinders. The wings are folded by the two opposed actuating cylinders in each wing acting on a bellcrank at the wing-fold joint.

CAUTION

Wing-tip speed brakes, slats, and flaperons should be checked visually for retraction before folding the wings.

WING-SPREAD OPERATION

The reverse sequence of events occurs in spreading the wings. Squeeze the wing-fold handle and move it aft to the first stop, and wait for all spread motion to cease. The wing-fold selector valve directs hydraulic pressure to retract the wing-fold actuating cylinders. When the wings are fully spread and all spread motion has ceased, the wing lockpins switch should be actuated to LOCK. In the LOCK position, the wing lockpin selector valves direct flow to the wing-spread timer check valves (one in each wing). When the wings reach the fully spread position, the wing-fold timers open, pressurizing the wing lockpin cylinders. Simultaneously, the structural wing fittings release the mechanical detents that prevent lockpin extension until the lockpins and holes are aligned. When the lockpin holes are aligned, the pins extend. This locks the wings and removes the mechanical stops of the wing-fold handle. Moving the handle flush to the console mechanically locks the hydraulic lockpin and stows the wing-fold warning flags. If any of the lockpins fail to go home, the flags will remain up and the wing-fold handle cannot be stowed.

WHEEL BRAKE SYSTEM

The main wheel brakes are hydraulically powered, multiple disk brakes. An artificial feel system is provided to simulate pedal forces. A brake selector handle is provided for pilot selection of normal, auxiliary, or emergency/park brake operation. The normal brakes are powered by the combined secondary hydraulic system. The auxiliary and emergency/park brakes are powered by a hydraulic brake accumulator. The accumulator is pressurized by the handpump and, in aircraft incorporating it, the electrically operated auxiliary hydraulic pump will also pressurize the accumulator. Accumulator pressure is displayed on a brake cycle gage in number of brake cycles remaining. An antiskid system is available only with normal brakes.

BRAKE SELECTOR HANDLE

The brake selector handle (figure 1-20) is a T-shaped handle displaying BRAKE that is used to select the mode of brake operation. The handle mechanically positions a three-way valve for the brake modes.

Normal Braking

With the brake selector handle in (full forward) and vertical, the brake selector valve ports combined secondary hydraulic system pressure to the brake control valves. The brake control valves actuated by the pilot's feet on the toe brakes meter hydraulic pressure to the wheel brakes. The antiskid system may be employed with normal braking.

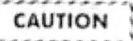

CAUTION

After heavy or repeated brake applications, such as encountered in practice landings, a 5- to 10-minute cooling period should be permitted in the air, with the gear extended between landings.

Auxiliary Braking

With the brake selector handle in (full forward) and horizontal (rotated 90° clockwise), the brake selector valve ports brake accumulator hydraulic pressure to the brake control valves. The brake control valves actuated by the pilot's feet on the toe brakes meter hydraulic pressure to the wheel brakes. Brake pedal feel will be the same as normal breaking without antiskid. The antiskid system will be inoperative even if it is switched on. Auxiliary brake applications are limited by the capacity of the accumulator and a priority valve. A fully charged accumulator will provide approximately fifteen auxiliary brake applications. The priority valve reserves the last four to seven applications exclusively for emergency/park brake applications.

Emergency/Park Brakes

When the brake selector handle is out (pulled aft) in either the vertical or horizontal position, the brake selector valve ports brake accumulator hydraulic pressure directly to the wheel brakes, locking the wheels. With the selector valve in this position, if the hydraulic handpump is actuated, pressure will be applied directly to the wheel brakes.

Note

Pull the brake selector handle AFT with a clockwise motion. Pulling the handle AFT with a slight counterclockwise movement may cause the handle to bind and prevent brake actuation.

CAUTION

- If the brakes are overheated by prolonged or repeated braking, application of the emergency/park brakes may fuse the brakes and lock the wheels.

- When releasing the emergency/parking brake, ensure that the brake selector handle does not bind and remains vertical after positioning the handle in by applying counterclockwise motion. Failure to do so may prevent complete relief of parking brake pressure, resulting in dragging brakes. Taxi shall not be attempted if the handle binds or rotates clockwise from the vertical position.

AIRCRAFT
Systems

NAVAIR 01-85ADA-1

WHEEL BRAKE CONTROLS AND INDICATOR

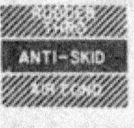
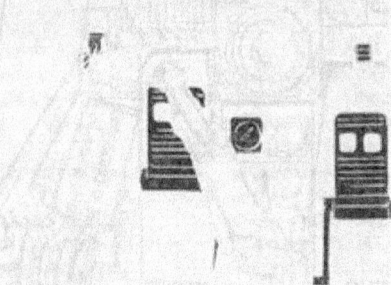

AIRCRAFT NOT INCORPORATING AFC NO. 199

A-6A, B, C 158642 AND ON AND AIRCRAFT
INCORPORATING AFC NO. 199

Figure 1-20

Brake Cycles Gage

The brake cycles gage on the main instrument panel (figure 1-20) is a direct-reading pressure gage connected to the brake accumulator. The scale is calibrated in number of brake cycles (applications) remaining. The red area below 4, marked EMER, is reserved exclusively by a priority valve for emergency/park brake operation and is not available for auxiliary brake operation.

Note

The number of brake cycles indicated on the gage is an approximation. When auxiliary brakes are selected, avoid pumping brakes, as each reduction in brake pressure depletes the accumulator. A smooth application of the brakes with constantly increasing pedal pressure will result in optimum braking.

ANTI SKID SYSTEM

The antiskid system used in conjunction with the normal brake system increases high-speed braking efficiency. The system, through the right weight-on-wheels switch, prevents landing with brakes locked and permits application of full brake pedal force before touchdown for obtaining minimum stopping distances. The possibility of tire blowout is minimized and tire life and wheel balance is prolonged.

Note

Normal braking is not available with antiskid selected until the right weight-on-wheels switch is actuated.

The system is selected by a pilot-operated toggle switch and powered by the primary 28 V dc bus.

The major components are skid detectors in each wheel axle, an antiskid control box, and an antiskid control valve between each brake control valve and its respective wheel brake. The skid detectors sense wheel rotation speed and send proportional signals to the antiskid control box. An incipient skid is detected as a difference in wheel rpm. Under this condition, the antiskid valve for the slow-turning wheel relieves hydraulic pressure permitting the wheel to rotate freely; then the pressure is reapplied over a short time interval (approximately 2 seconds). A locked wheel is detected when one wheel is not turning, and the other is turning above 150 rpm (approximately 11 knots). Under this condition, the brake pressure to the locked wheel is released, then reapplied at a slightly power pressure. If a brake release signal exceeds 3.5 seconds, the antiskid system will become inoperative and the antiskid light in the cockpit will come on.

ANTI-SKID Switch

The ANTISKID switch (figure 1-20) is a two-position toggle switch with positions placarded ON and OFF. The ON position provides primary 28 V dc power to energize the system provided the brake selector handle is in the NORMAL position. The OFF position deenergizes the system. If the ANTISKID light comes on, the system may be energized again by cycling the switch to OFF, then ON.

Note

- Antiskid is available only when normal brakes are selected.
- Antiskid does not operate below 11 knots.
- Antiskid is inoperative when the ANTISKID light is lit.
- Erratic antiskid brake operation may indicate overheated brakes and impending brake lock.
- Use antiskid for normal takeoff and landings only. For taxiing, the antiskid switch should be OFF.

ANTI-SKID Light

The ANTI-SKID light on the annunciator panel (figure 1-20) displays ANTI-SKID and is powered by the essential 28 V dc bus through the CAUTION LTS circuit breaker on the main circuit breaker panel. Lighting of the light indicates that the antiskid system is inoperative as a result of a brake release signal exceeding 3.5 seconds, the brake selector handle being out or rotated, the antiskid toggle switch being off, or a failure of the antiskid system.

ARRESTING-HOOK SYSTEM

The arresting-hook system provides carrier landing capability and arrested landing capability on runways equipped with arresting gear. It may also be used for aborted takeoff on suitably equipped runways. The hook is released from the up position by a cable operated up-hook release. A fail-safe feature automatically releases the hook if the release cable parts. When released, the hook is extended to the trail position by dashpot pressure assisted by gravity. The dashpot also dampens hook bounce and acts as a shock absorber during cable engagement. The system incorporates hook retraction ability and a hook transition indicator light.

Note

When the arresting hook is extended, the nosewheel steering system is armed and will engage on landing when the main gear weight-on-wheels switches are actuated.

HOOK-RELEASE HANDLE

The hook-release handle on the pilot's instrument panel (figure FO-2 Sheet 1, 2 and 3) is marked ARG HOOK PULL and is shaped to be grasped by the fingers from the bottom. Pulling the handle aft pulls a cable that releases the hook uplock. (The aft position of the handle also disarms the hook lift switch circuit.) The hook is extended by dashpot pressure assisted by gravity. When the handle is released, it is reset by spring action and the hook-lift switch is rearmed.

There is no emergency operation of the arresting-hook system as such, but a fail-safe feature automatically releases the hook if the hook-release cable snaps. To stow the hook when the automatic release feature is actuated, pressurize the combined secondary hydraulic system and momentarily depress the hook-lift button. By cycling the hook to the stowed position, hydraulic pressure will be maintained to the lift cylinder until the hook-release handle is pulled or power is taken off the aircraft. The hook-release handle must be in its normal flight position before the hook can be retracted. A switch in the release handle closes a circuit to the hook-lift button when the release handle is stowed. Normal operation of the indicating circuits is not affected by a failure of the release cable.

HOOK-LIFT BUTTON

The hook-lift button on the pilot's instrument panel (figure FO-2 Sheets 1, 2 and 3) is placarded HOOK LIFT and incorporates an integral hook transition light. Depressing the button momentarily when the hook is extended energizes a solenoid valve that ports combined secondary hydraulic pressure to the arresting-hook lift cylinder, which retracts the hook. Electric power is provided by the essential 28 V dc bus through the GEAR/HOOK circuit breaker on the main circuit breaker panel. A holding relay keeps the valve energized until the hook-down switch, located behind the hook-release handle, is deenergized during the first 1/8-inch of handle travel.

CAUTION

Do not depress the HOOK LIFT button while the hook is engaged in the arresting gear. Doing so may break the hook bumper cable.

Note

A short-circuit condition in the hook-lift circuitry can result in a continuous hook-lift signal to the solenoid controlling the hook-lift cylinder. As long as the hydraulic system isolation valve switch is in the flight position, hydraulic pressure is not available to the hook-lift cylinder, and the hook will lower normally. However, when the isolation valve switch is moved to the landing position by lowering the landing gear or placing the switch to the landing position, the arresting hook will raise since hydraulic pressure is now available to the hook-lift cylinder. The arresting hook can be lowered by pulling the gear/hook circuit breaker on the center console circuit breaker panel and then pulling the hook-release handle. This procedure does not affect hydraulic pressure to the landing gear after the gear is ascertained to be down and locked. Under these conditions, the approach lights and angle-of-attack indexer will flash. Positioning the hook bypass switch to the touch-and-go position will prevent a flashing approach light and indexer.

Hook Transition Light

The hook transition light is incorporated in the hook-lift button (figure FO-2 Sheets 1, 2 and 3) and powered by the primary 28 V dc bus through the CKPT ADV LTS circuit breaker on the nosewheel circuit breaker panel. The light comes on during hook transition on both extension and retraction.

HOOK BYPASS SWITCH

The HOOK BYPASS switch on the pilot's left console (figure FO-2 Sheets 1, 2 and 3) is a three-position toggle switch with position placarded TOUCH-GO, ARREST, and TEST. The TOUCH-GO position, used for non-arrested landings, bypasses the flashing feature of the approach lights and indexer when the aircraft is in a landing configuration with the hook retracted. The ARREST position, used for arrested landings, arms the flashing feature of the approach lights and indexer for appropriate operation when a landing configuration is established. The flashing will continue until the hook is released. The TEST position tests the flashing circuit of the approach lights and indexer.

Dashpot Pressure Gage

The dashpot pressure on the left side of the aft fuselage is a direct-reading gage that presents the pneumatic pressure in the hook dashpot. The gage is divided into three increments: low, normal, and high. Normal preflight indication, with hook up, should be in the normal range.

FLIGHT INSTRUMENTS AND INDICATOR LIGHTS

ANGLE-OF-ATTACK SYSTEM

The angle-of-attack system (figure 1-21) measures the angle between the longitudinal axis of the aircraft and the relative wind. A sensor on the right side of the fuselage forward of the wings consist of a probe that lines up with the airstream, and a potentiometer pickoff that converts the position of the probe to electrical signals. The signals are compared to a rebalance potentiometer and the error signal is used to drive a servomotor in the angle-of-attack instrument. The servomotor drives the instrument pointer and rotates a series of cam-actuated switches that control the visual presentations of angle-of-attack and approach indexer to the pilot and the approach light to the LSO. Sensor heat for icing conditions is controlled by the pitot heat switch in the cockpit.

ANGLE-OF-ATTACK INDICATOR

The angle-of-attack indicator is on the upper left side of the pilot's instrument panel (figure 1-21). The pointer is driven by a servomotor and rotates over a card graduated from 0 to 30 units. Optimum angle-of-attack for landing approach is marked by a light area of the 3-o'clock position on the instrument. The units do not reflect angle-of-attack in degrees. A readout window on the instrument face will indicate OFF if there is no power to the servomotors.

APPROACH LIGHTS

The approach lights are controlled by switches actuated by the angle-of-attack indicator cam, and give qualitative information on angle-of-attack to the LSO. The lights are on the forward nose wheel door, and are green (high angle-of-attack), amber (optimum angle-of-attack), and red (low angle-of-attack).

During an arrested landing, with the hook bypass switch in ARREST, the approach light will flash when the arresting hook is not in trail and the landing gear is down and locked.

APPROACH INDEXER

The cam-operated switches in the angle-of-attack indicator also control the approach indexer left of the pilot's windscreen (figure 1-21). In aircraft incorporating AFC No. 230, a second indexer is attached to the ACLS course indicator (ID-351). Three lamps glow red through apertures on the face of the indexer, giving approach information. The upper arrow is for high angle-of-attack, the lower arrow for low angle-of-attack, and the circle is for optimum angle-of-attack. When both an arrow and circle appear, an intermediate position is indicated. During an arrested landing, with the hook bypass switch in ARREST, the approach indexer will flash

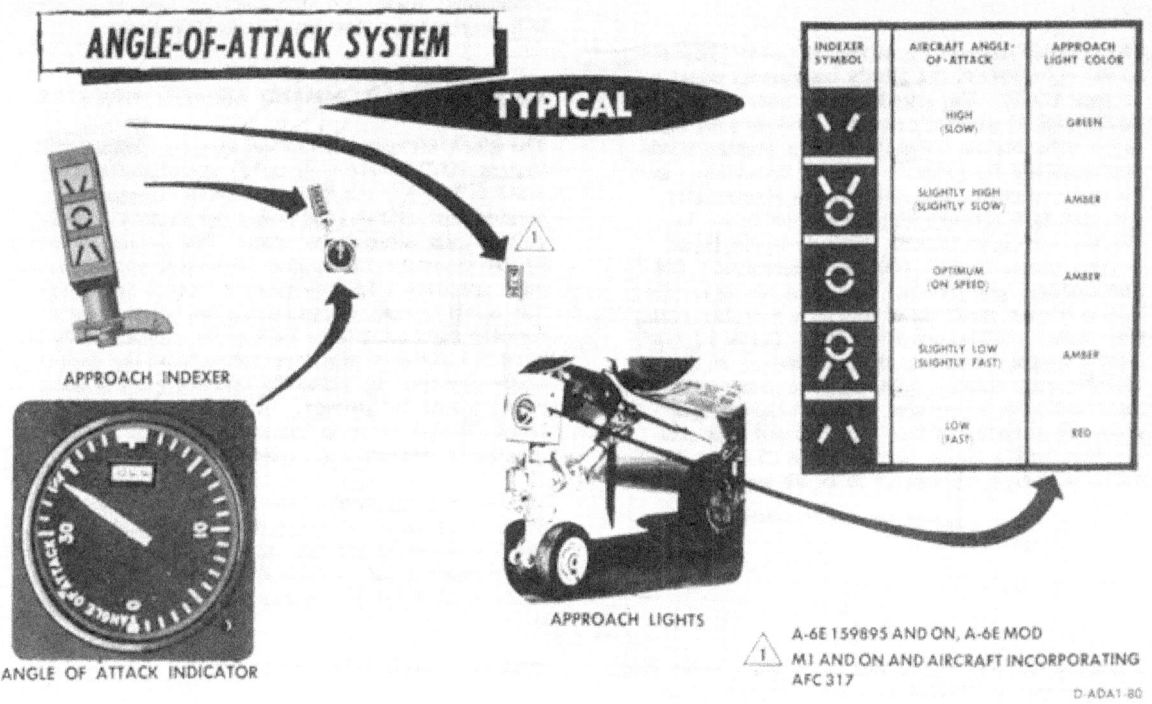

Figure 1-21

when the arresting hook is not in trail and the gear is extended. To ensure that the approach index lights are operating, depress the lights warning button on the master test panel. Intensity of the approach indexer lights is adjustable using the thumbwheel on the master lights panel.

Note

The approach lights and approach indexer are disabled until all gear are down and locked.

PITOT-STATIC SYSTEM

The pitot-static boom is on the vertical stabilizer. Pitot pressure is impact air pressure developed as the result of the relative wind velocity and is measured at the opening in the forward end of the sensor. Static pressure, which is a function of altitude and temperature, is measured through a series of small openings on the side of the sensor. Pitot pressure is used in the air data computer and the mach airspeed/command/airspeed indicator. Static pressure is used in the air data computer, servoed barometric altimeter, mach/airspeed/command airspeed indicator, and vertical velocity indicator. To prevent or eliminate icing, the pitot-static sensor is electricall heated.

Note

- In A-6E 159895 and ON and A-6E Mod M121 and ON, the air data computer receivers power only if the MA-1/ADC switch on the cabin dump panel is at ON.
- In A-6E incorporating AFC 391, the CNI MASTER switch must be in other than the OFF position for the ADC to operate.

PITOT HEAT SWITCH

The pitot heat switch, on the air-conditioning control panel (figure 1-33), is a two-position switch marked ON and OFF. Placing the switch ON allows the electrical power to be supplied from the 28 V dc primary bus to a conventional heater in the pitot tube. It also allows, through the left weight-on-wheels switch, heat to be provided to the angle-of-attack probe, and the total-temperature probe.

AIRCRAFT
Systems

NAVAIR 01-85ADA-1

SERVOED BAROMETRIC ALTIMETER

The servoed barometric altimeter (AAU-19A) is on the right side of the pilot's instrument panel (Figure FO-2). The standby mode uses an aneroid mechanism to present pressure altitude with normal barometric setting correction. The standby mode is considered the primary mode of operation. In the servoed mode, the altimeter is electrically operated by a synchro signal received from the air data computer (ADC). Altitude is displayed in digital form by a 10,000-foot counter, a 1,000-foot counter, and 100-foot drum. A single needle also indicates hundreds of feet on a circular scale, with center graduations of 50 feet. Below 10,000 feet, a diagonal warning symbol appears on the 10,000-foot counter. A barometric pressure setting (baroset) knob is provided to insert barometric pressure in inches of Hg. The baroset knob has no effect on the digital output (Mode C) of the ADC, which is always referenced to 29.92 inches Hg.

The altimeter has a pressure mode and a servo mode of operation, controlled by a self-centering mode switch placarded STBY and RESET respectively. In the pressure mode of operation, the altimeter displays altitude directly from the static system (uncorrected for position error) and operates as a standard pressure altimeter. In the servo mode, the altimeter displays altitude, corrected for position error, from the synchro output of the ADC altitude module. A dc-powered internal vibrator is automatically energized while in the STBY mode to minimize errors due to friction in the display mechanism.

The servo mode of AAU-19A operation is selected by placing the mode switch to RESET for 1 to 3 seconds, with ac power on. During STBY operation, a red STBY flag appears on the dial face. The altimeter will automatically switch to STBY operation when there is an electrical interruption longer than 3 seconds, an electrical failure in the altimeter or ADC, or significant differences exist between indicated and actual altitude. The altimeter automatically switches to STBY to protect system components and this should not be construed or relied upon as a fail-safe feature. The STBY mode of operation may be selected manually by placing the mode switch in STBY. During STBY operation, it is possible for the transponder to continue to transmit altitude information (corrected for position error) on Mode C, while the altimeter is displaying altitude uncorrected for position error.

The altimeter should agree within ±75 feet of field elevation in both modes, and the servoed and standby reading shall agree within ±75 feet. In addition, the allowable difference between servoed mode reading of two AAU-19 altimeters is 75 feet at all altitudes.

The standby modes should be used for critical flight evolutions: night/IFR ship and field takeoff/landings; IFR penetrations; low level night/IFR flight.

MACH/AIRSPEED/COMMAND AIRSPEED INDICATOR

The mach/airspeed/command airspeed indicator (figure FO-2 Sheets 1, 2, and 3) is calibrated from mach 0.5 to 2.0 and 80 to 650 knots airspeed. Indicated airspeed is read under the pointer, which rotates over a nonlinear scale. The pointer is driven by the pressure differential derived from comparing pitot pressure with atmospheric (static) pressure. The mach number is read using the pointer and a rotating card calibrated with mach number. The card is rotated by static pressure from the pitot-static system. By using the rotating card in conjunction with the pointer, the necessary relationship is established between indicated airspeed and atmospheric pressure to produce a mach number.

Maximum mach number and minimum airspeed indices are controlled by the mach limit knob on the lower left side of the instrument. The minimum airspeed index is set by rotating the knob and the maximum mach is set by pushing the knob in and rotating it.

VERTICAL SPEED INDICATOR

A standard vertical velocity indicator (figure FO-2 Sheets 1, 2, and 3) is mounted on the right side of the pilot's instrument panel. The instrument operates on a pressure differential. Static pressure from the pitot system enters the diaphragm inside the instrument case. The instrument case itself contains static air, which passes through a restriction. Because of the restrictor, change in altitude causes the air pressure in the diaphragm to increase or decrease more rapidly than air pressure in the instrument case. The resulting difference in pressure is converted to a vertical velocity and is displayed as feet per minute up or down on the instrument face. The needle is damped to minimize oscillation and is mechanically stopped at the extreme travel limits. The range of the instrument is from 0 to 6,000 feet per minute up or down, with the first 1,000 feet graduated in 100-foot increments and the remainder in 500-foot increments.

RADAR ALTIMETER SYSTEM

Note

In A-6E 158041 thru 158792, and MOD M 1 thru M 12, the AN/APN-141 radar altimeter is installed. A-6E 158792 and ON, and MOD M 13 and subsequent have provisions for incorporation of either the AN/APN-141 or the AN/APN-194 radar altimeter.

The radar altimeter is a low-altitude, pulsed, range-tracking radar that measures the surface or terrain

1-64   Change 2

clearance below the aircraft. Altitude information is developed by radiating a short-duration rf pulse from the transmit antenna to the earth's surface, and measuring the time interval until rf energy returns through the receiver antenna and is detected in the receiver. The altitude information is continuously presented to the pilot, in feet of altitude, on the dial of an indicator (figure 1-22).

The radar altimeter has two modes of operation. In the search mode, the system successively examines increments of range until the complete altitude range is searched for a return signal. When a return signal is detected, the system switches to the track mode and tracks the return signal, giving continuous altitude information. When the radar altimeter drops out of the track mode of operation, the OFF flag appears and the indicator will drop behind a mask at the base of the instrument. The altimeter remains inoperative until a reliable signal is received from the receiver-transmitter, at which time the altimeter will again indicate the actual altitude above the terrain.

Reliable system operation in the altitude range of 10 to 5,000 feet for the APN-141 and 0 to 5,000 feet for the APN-194 permits close altitude control at minimum altitudes. The system is inoperative in banks of more than 30°, in climbs or dives of more than 50° and when the reflected signal is otherwise too weak.

The system includes the height indicator and warning light (figure 1-22) mounted on the pilot's instrument panel, a low-altitude aural warning tone (LAWS), the radar receiver-transmitter installed on the rudder actuator access door, and two antennas (transmit and receive) mounted in the rudder actuator access door and in the aircraft skin just forward of the same access door.

RADAR ALTIMETER HEIGHT INDICATOR

This indicator is on the pilot's instrument panel (figure 1-22) and contains the only operating control in the system. The indicator displays radar altitude above the earth's surface on a single-turn dial that is calibrated from 0 to 5,000 feet in increasing increments. This permits greater definition at lower altitudes.

POWER/SELF-TEST/POSITIONING CONTROL

This control is located in the lower left corner of the indicator. This control is a combination power switch, self-test switch, and positioning control for the low-altitude limit index (limit bug). The adjustable limit index outside the calibrated scale can be preset to a desired altitude and used as reference for flying at fixed altitudes. By depressing and holding the indicator control knob in flight, the self-test circuit is energized and the indicator will read 5±5 feet on the APN-141 and 100±10 feet on the APN-194 radar altimeter. During self-test, the green light on the face of the APN-194 will also light. Normal operation is resumed by releasing the control knob.

OFF Flag

The OFF flag in the middle of the indicator is actuated either electronically or mechanically. It is energized electronically when the altitude signal becomes unreliable and exceeds a threshold voltage. Mechanical actuation of the OFF flag is accomplished when the altitude pointer rotates beyond 5,000 feet and actuates the OFF flag switch (figure 1-22).

LOW-ALTITUDE WARNING SYSTEM (LAWS)

The low-altitude warning system provides a low-altitude warning light and low-altitude aural alarm tone available to the pilot. The system is activated when the aircraft descends below the height set on the limit index of the height indicator, and should be used as an aid to search radar terrain clearance.

In addition, an aural tone and a radar altimeter failure light provide warning of radar altimeter unreliability.

Note

In order for the B/N to hear the aural tone, the pilot must select ALT 1 on his ICS control panel.

Low-Altitude Aural Warning

The low-altitude aural warning alarm provides a 2-second tone through the pilot's headset and the B/N's headset if the pilot has ALT 1 selected on his ICS control panel. The tone is audible if the aircraft descends below the height set on the limit index of the height indicator.

The low-altitude signal alternates between 700 and 1700 Hz at a 2-Hz rate while the unreliable signal alternates between 700 and 1700 Hz at an 8 Hz rate. The volume of the tone must be set prior to flight, since there is no external control that can be adjusted during flight.

Low-Altitude Warning Lamp

The red low-altitude warning lamp is below the radar altimeter. The low-altitude warning lamp will light whenever the aircraft altitude falls below the pilot's preset limit indexer.

Radar Altimeter Failure Light

A radar altimeter failure light glows RA in black letters on a red background in the lower half of the vertical bar on the right side of VDI. When the output of the radar altimeter is less than 1 volt (20 feet) or greater than 26.5 volts (5000 feet) the light will be lit. Circuitry may be tested by depressing the LTS WARN button on the master test panel.

LAWS PREFLIGHT CHECK

1. The intercommunications set must be on and operating for the signals to be heard through the pilot's headset.

RADAR ALTIMETER

Figure 1-22

2. Turn the radar altimeter on and set the altitude limit index at 25 feet. On initial turn-on, the OFF flag appears and the pointer moves behind the mask. Check that the radar altimeter failure light (RA) is on and the radar altitude curtain on the VDI is not in view.

3. After warmup (1 to 5 minutes) the OFF flag disappears and the pointer moves from behind the mask to an altitude between 0 and 10 feet. As the pointer passes the preset limit index altitude, the low-altitude signal is heard in the pilot's headset and the low-altitude warning light comes on. At this time, the radar altimeter failure light comes on and the altitude curtain disappears.

ATTITUDE INSTRUMENTS

VERTICAL DISPLAY INDICATOR (VDI)

The vertical display indicator (VDI), referred to as the ADI in the A-6C (analog display indicator or attitude directional indicator) is the primary attitude reference indicator. The display (contact analog) is a television-like picture of artificially generated ground and sky texture which meet to form the reference horizon. A video bank angle marker with a fixed index mark, fixed pitch attitude markers, and movable video pitch trim markers are provided. The viewing area is approximately 30° in elevation and 50° in azimuth and simulates the view through the front cockpit window, enabling the pilot to fly the aircraft during all visibility conditions. Additional symbology provided on the contact analog display and the terrain avoidance display (A-6A, B, C, and A-6E) are described in Section VIII.

VERTICAL DISPLAY CONTROL

The vertical display control panel (figure 1-23) on the pilot's left console (KA-6D) contains all the controls for operation of the vertical display indicator. In the A-6A, B, C, and A-6E the controls are located on the pilot's control panel on the pilot's instrument panel. Additional controls on the pilot's control panel are described in Section VIII.

Brightness/Contrast Controls

The BRIGHTNESS/CONTRAST controls are used to vary the brightness and contrast of the display. The BRIGHTNESS knob controls the overall brightness of the display. The CONTRAST knob controls the relative video contrast of the greys and blacks on the display scope.

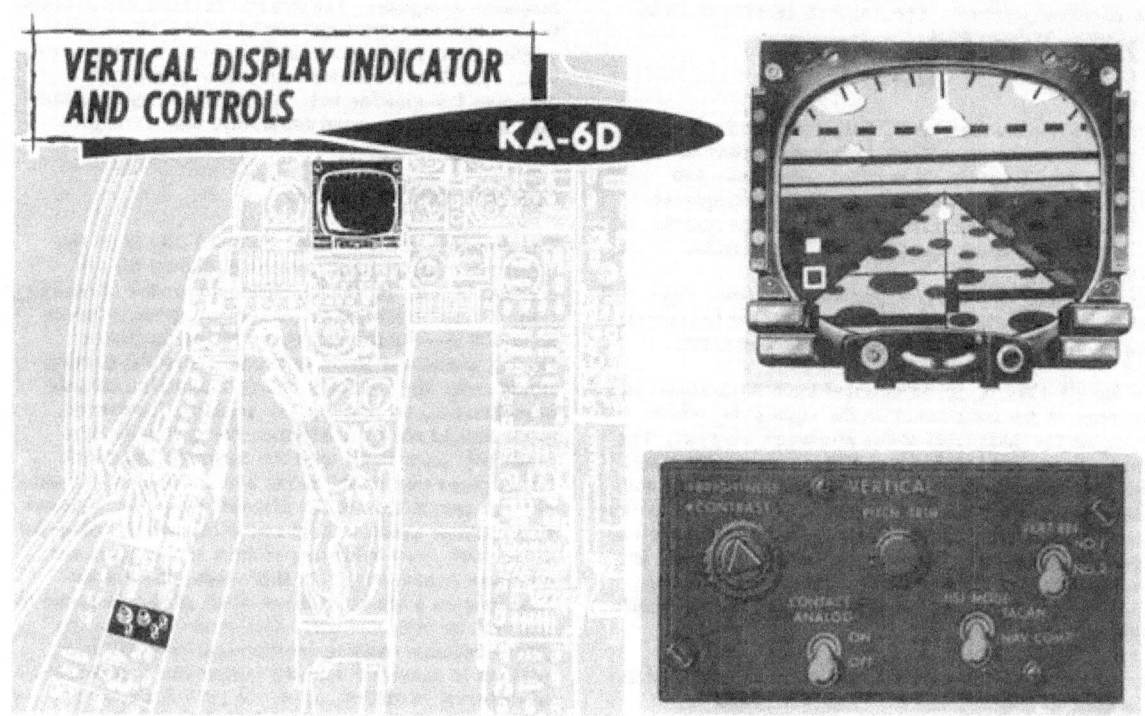

Figure 1-23

Pitch Trim Knob

The PITCH TRIM knob controls the vertical position of the elevation cursors.

Display Selector Buttons (A-6A,B,C,E)

The DISPLAY selector buttons allow a choice of contact analog (CONT ANALOG) and search radar terrain clearance (TC) displays. The standby button (STBY) keeps the vertical display in readiness for a mode selection. The TC CAL button selects the terrain clearance calibration display. With the OFF position selected, no power is supplied to a vertical display system.

Contact Analog Switch (KA-6D)

The contact analog switch is a two-position toggle switch marked ON and OFF. Placing the switch to ON presents the contact analog display on the VDI.

VERT REF Selector (KA-6D)

The VERT REF selector is a two-position toggle switch marked No. 1 and No. 2. The No. 1 position selects No. 1 vertical reference for the VGI and No. 2 vertical reference for the ADI. The No. 2 position selects No. 2 vertical reference for the VGI and No. 1 vertical reference for the ADI.

HSI Mode Switch (KA-6D)

The HSI mode switch is a two-position toggle switch marked TACAN and NAV COMP. The TACAN position displays range and bearing information to the selected TACAN station on the HSI. The NAV COMP position displays range and bearing information to the selected station (D_1 or D_2) on the HSI.

VERTICAL GYRO INDICATOR (VGI)

The VGI MM-3 (figure FO-2 sheets 1, 2, and 3) or ID-1791/A (figure FO-3 sheet 4) indicates to the pilot the flight attitude of the aircraft. Pitch and roll indications are displayed by a sphere in relation to a fixed minature aircraft symbol. The sphere is light-colored above the artificial horizon bar, black below the bar, and is marked in 5° pitch increments in both directions, beginning at the horizon bar. Roll indications are given by a marker that moves around the periphery of the sphere. The marker moves across a linear scale that is graduated in 10° increments to 30° and then in 30° increments to 90°.

The sphere is positioned by servomechanisms that receive signals from a remote, independent gyro reference. Rolls through 360° are possible without tumbling the gyro. The gyro will flip 180° at 90° of pitch from straight and level flight, but will return to normal after passing through the extreme pitch angles. A warning flag will appear whenever there is no power to the indicator, and will remain displayed for approximately 1 minute (MM-3) or 30 seconds (ID-1791/A) after initial power is applied. The flag does not indicate the condition of the instrument. On the MM-3, a gyro fast-erect button (figure FO-2) to the lower left of the instrument speeds up the erection process. The flag will be visible while the button is depressed.

Note

On KA-6D without AFC 161, the gyro fast-erect button speeds the erection process of the No. 1 and No. 2 vertical references and must be held down until erection is completed. The fast erection rate is 5° per minute and the normal erection rate is 1 1/2° per minute.

On the MM-3, a pitch trim knob on the lower right face of the instrument is used to adjust the horizontal bar of the sphere to the fixed miniature aircraft.

On the ID-1791/A, an adjustment knob is provided at the base of the instrument on the right side, which controls the pitch trim of the miniature aircraft. The knob, placarded PULL TO CAGE, is also used to cage the gyroscope so that the horizon line is parallel with the wings of the miniature aircraft. Caging the instrument momentarily during warmup speeds the erection process somewhat. Turning the knob to the right to its limit raises the miniature aircraft 5°. Rotating it to the left to its limit of travel moves the miniature aircraft down 10°.

A conventional turn-and-slip indicator is provided at the base of the instrument. The turn needle is powered by a remote rate gyro.

The glide slope and azimuth pointers of the ID-1791/A are activated when the ON/OFF/AUX ON switch and the TEST/NORM/AJ switch on the data link control panel are turned respectively to ON and NORM and the shipboard AN/SPN-42 Radar is locked on. At all other times, the pointers are driven out of view behind masks at the bottom and right side of the instrument.

A test pushbutton is at the base of the instrument. Depressing the pushbutton causes the turn needle to indicate a double-needle-width turn and drives the cross pointers into view to show zero azimuth and glide slope error.

TURN-AND-SLIP INDICATOR MD-1

The turn and slip indicator (figure FO-2 Sheets 1, 2, and 3) gives the pilot information on the rate of turn of the aircraft around its vertical axis and the turn coordination. The driving mechanism for the pointer is a permanent-magnet type, dc, governor-controlled gyro motor. A needle-width deflection of the pointer will produce a 360° turn in 4 minutes. Pointer motion is damped by an air dashpot and is deflected in the direction of the turn. The inclinometer portion of the instrument contains damping fluid and a ball that moves from center in an uncoordinated turn.

COMPASS SYSTEM MA-1

The MA-1 compass system may be used as a directional gyro corrected for apparent drift due to the earth's rotation, or as a directional, gyro-stabilized, magnetic compass. The system is generally operated in the slaved or gyro-stabilized mode, which automatically corrects inherent gyro errors of the system. The MA-1 compass system consists of a compass transmitter unit, a directional gyro assembly, an amplifier servo assembly, and a compass control panel.

COMPASS CONTROL PANEL

The compass control panel (figure 1-24) is on the observer's instrument panel (KA-6D) or the aft console (A-6A, B, C, E). The two modes of operation, magnetic slaved or directional gyro, provide accurate directional reference for all latitudes. During periods of flight in areas where the earth's fields make the readings on any magnetic compass questionable, as in the polar regions, the slaved mode should not be used since the gyro will automatically align itself with the incorrect magnetic fields generated by the earth and subsequently transmit erroneous data to the aircraft systems. Operation in these areas is best accomplished by using the directional gyro operating without inputs from the compass transmitter. In this mode, the system functions as a standard directional gyro. Because of inherent system stability, this mode of operation offers reliable heading information over extended periods of operation without subsystem references. At different latitudes, apparent gyro drift varies, with the smallest amount of drift being at the equator and the greatest amount in the polar regions. In the directional gyro mode, with the proper latitude selection made on the control panel, the gyro is made to precess at a rate required to overcome gyro drift at the selected latitude.

The compass system is actuated by power being applied to the essential bus. A power failure indication or a hold indication in the form of a red flag labeled OFF is displayed in the control panel synchronizer window above the selected switch. During normal operation, this flag will disappear 10 seconds after application of power. After 3 minutes warmup, the selector switch should be positioned to the mode of operation required to accomplish the mission.

Note

- In A-6A, B, C, and KA-6D aircraft incorporating AFC 253, when ground power is applied, the MA-1 compass is disabled until one of the following occurs:

  1. At least one aircraft generator is on the line
  2. The MA-1 switch on the AC/DC relay panel is activated.

- On A-6E 158795 thru 159579; MOD M21 thru M120 and aircraft incorporating AFC 269 or AFC 391, the CNI MASTER switch must be in other than the OFF position for MA-1 compass system operation.

- On A-6E 159895 and ON and MOD M121 and ON, the MA-1/ADC switch must be at ON to operate the MA-1 compass system.

Compass Selector Switch

This three-position rotary switch on the compass panel has positions for FREE S LAT, SLAVED, and FREE N LAT. In the SLAVED positions, the compass is supplied with inputs from the compass transmitter, relative to the earth's magnetic field. In the FREE S LAT and FREE N LAT positions, the information supplied by the compass transmitter is considered unreliable and the system operates as a directional gyro precessing at a rate required to compensate earth's normal rotation.

Pull-To-Set Control

This control permits realignment of the radio-magnetic indicator unit. The spring-loaded control is pulled out and rotated until the desired heading appears under the indicator cursor.

Note

During reset operation, the autopilot will be automatically disconnected while this knob is pulled out, permitting normal aircraft operation when introducing heading change information.

Figure 1-24

Latitude Select Control

The latitude selector knob marked SET TO LAT on the compass control panel is used to rotate a circular dial at the base of the knob. The dial is numbered from 0° to 90° of latitude. The latitude selector control is operative in the FREE N LAT and FREE S LAT selector switch positions only, and is used to select the latitude in which the aircraft is operating.

Synchronizer Window

This indicator is on the compass control panel and affords readout indications as to system operation. During periods of system power malfunction, warm-up, and shutdown, a red flag appears in the window to denote that the system is inoperative. During normal operation, the red flag is retracted and a white bar aligns itself with the fixed arrow marker above the indicator window. Positioning of the bar under the arrow indicates satisfactory system alignment only during the SLAVED mode operation.

COMPASS SYSTEM OPERATION

Gyro Operation (SLAVED)

1. Selector switch - SLAVED (requires 3 munutes warmup).

2. Pull-to-set knob - OUT
Rotate control until approximate magnetic heading of aircraft is under radiomagnetic indicator cursor.

3. Pull-to-set knob - RELEASE
When pull-to-set knob is released, indicator should align itself with exact magnetic heading of aircraft. A visual indication of system alignment is given when white bar is below arrow on indicator window. Oscillation of white bar during slaved mode is a normal condition and indicates satisfactory operation of system.

Note

There are two null positions of the knob 180° apart. An indication of the correct null position is movement of the white bar in the same direction that the knob is turned.

Gyro Operation (UNSLAVED)

1. Selector switch - FREE N LAT or FREE S LAT as required.

2. Pull-to-set knob - OUT
Rotate control until desired heading of aircraft is set under cursor of radio-magnetic indicator.

AIRCRAFT
Systems

3. Latitude selector control - ADJUST
Set this control to reflect degrees latitude at which aircraft will be flying. This affords automatic compensation for apparent drift of gyro due to earth's rotation.

Note

During free gyro operation, the synchronizer indicator window has no significance. If free gyro operation must be used for extended periods, reset the gyro whenever an accurate heading reference can be determined.

HORIZONTAL SITUATION INDICATOR

The horizontal situation indicator (HSI) (figure 1-25), on the pilot's instrument panel, provides range and bearing information, and course deviation. TACAN bearing (azimuth) information is provided by the small needle head (bug) that moves around the perimeter of the compass card. The HSI needles are identified by the difference in shape: the TACAN needle is a solid triangular indicator; the UHF needle is a broken triangular indicator. When the command radio is in the ADF mode the UHF indicator reflects the magnetic bearing to the selected UHF transmitter. The TACAN indicator reflects the magnetic bearing to the selected TACAN station. The displacement of the UHF or TACAN needle indicates the heading of the aircraft with respect to the individual ground installation. The course bar on the HSI shows the direction of the ground site with respect to the aircraft.

With a power loss, a red OFF flag appears in the window on the face of the instrument and a mask covers the distance counter. The distance counter is also covered when the TACAN is in REC or with a loss of DME when T/R is selected. A range display in the upper left corner shows the number of nautical miles away from the station. When the radio signal is not readable, a mask covers the numerals. An arrow will simultaneously indicate a TO or FROM direction, depending on whether the aircraft is flying toward or away from the ground station. If the power to the azimuth ceases, the TO/FROM arrow will disappear from view. The heading set knob manually adjusts the heading marker. With the course set (CRS SET) knob, the pilot can set in the desired course. Loss of 115 V ac essential power to the TACAN will cause the red OFF flag to show in the indicator face. With air-to-air TACAN ranging selected, the TACAN bearing pointer provides no valid indications.

| **WARNING** |

The UHF/ADF (APR-48) antenna is on the under side of the starboard engine intake beneath the B/N boarding ladder. With landing gear extended, the UHF/ADF magnetic bearing indication displayed on the HSI may be up to 40° in error.

1-70 Change 2

NAVAIR 01-85ADA-1

STANDBY COMPASS

A conventional standby compass is above the center of the aircraft instrument panel. It is a semifloat-type compass suspended in compass fluid. A pair of magnets attached to the compass card align with the earth's magnetic field to present magnetic heading indications. Extraneous magnetic fields are minimized by built-in permanent magnets. A compass correction card containing corrections for instrument error for various headings is found above the standby compass.

MISCELLANEOUS INSTRUMENTS

ACCELEROMETER B-6

The B-6 accelerometer (figure FO-2 Sheets 1, 2, 3, and 4) is a direct-reading instrument used to measure the accelerations of the aircraft along its vertical axis. The dial is graduated in g units from -5g to +10g. The normal reading of the instrument at rest is +1g. The instrument has three pointers. The main pointer gives a continuous indication of the vertical acceleration of the aircraft. The other two pointers stop at the maximum positive acceleration and maximum negative acceleration reached during any specific maneuver. These pointers will remain fixed until reset to +1g by depressing the knob on the lower left corner of the instrument.

G METER

The g meter (figure FO-2 Sheets 1, 2 and 3) displays the magnitude of normal accelerations in g units. A sensor unit in the left wheel well transmits potentiometer pickoff information from the position of a spring-loaded mass to a servomotor. The servomotor positions the instrument marker, which moves vertically across the instrument face. The range of the instrument is -5g to +10g.

Note

This instrument is not included in A-6E 159895 and ON and MOD M121 and ON or KA-6D with AFC 161.

CLOCKS

Two mechanical, integrally lighted 8-day clocks with 12-hour elapsed-time capability are provided. The winding and setting knob is in the lower left corner of the instrument; the elapsed-time setting knob is in the upper right. Successive depressions of the elapsed-time setting knob will start, stop, and reset the sweep second hand and elapsed-time hand to the 12-o'clock position.

OUTSIDE AIR TEMPERATURE INDICATOR

The outside air-temperature indicator (OAT) on the lower right corner of the bombardier/navigator's instrument panel has a single pointer dial calibrated in 5° increments from -50°C to +75°C. The temperature bulb aft of the right intake duct is a resistance-type sensor. The bulb and indicator are powered by the 28 V dc monitor bus through the ENG DC INST circuit breaker in the nosewheel well.

CAUTION, WARNING, AND ADVISORY LIGHTS

The caution, warning, and advisory lights (figure FO-11) include the pilot's indicator lights and the bombardier/navigator's indicator lights. Lighting of a particular light is applicable to the system and a condition associated with it. The description and function of each light is incorporated under the applicable system.

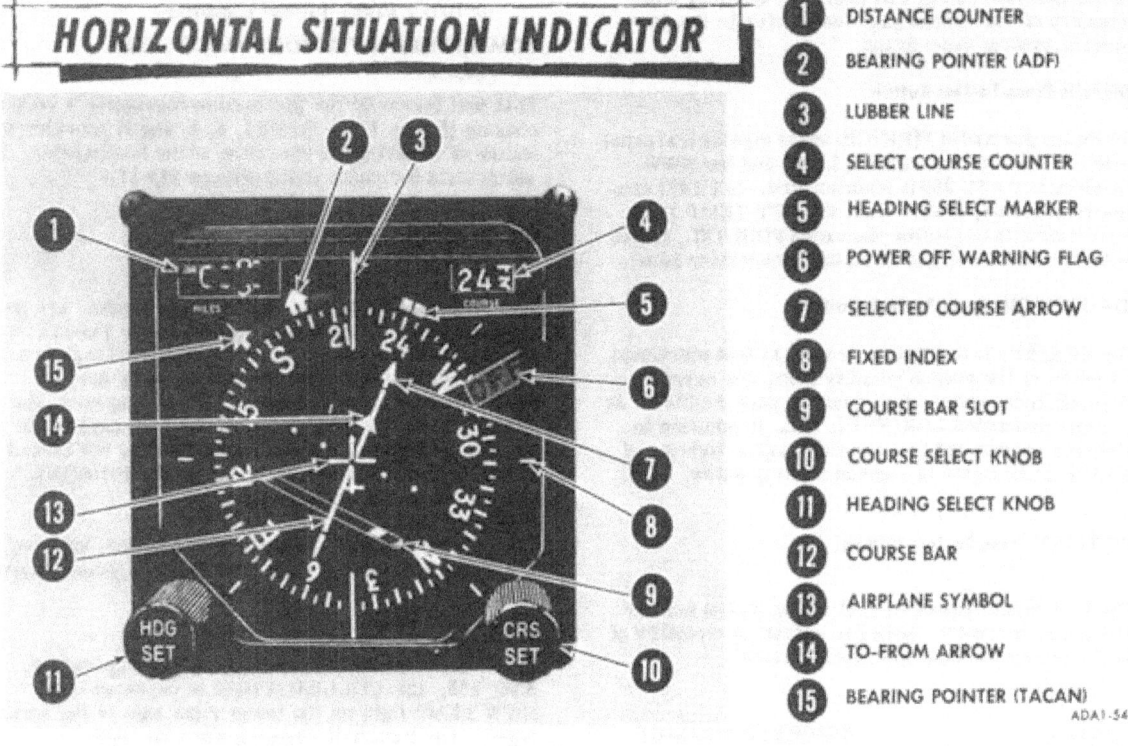

Figure 1-25

ANNUNCIATOR PANEL

The annunciator panel (figure FO-11) on the lower center portion of the pilot's instrument panel provides caution lights for the various aircraft systems. Lighting of a particular light advises of a malfunction or emphasizes a particular condition of the applicable system, and will cause the master caution lights to flash. When the master caution lights are reset, the annunciator light will remain on until the discrepancy is corrected.

The lights are powered by the essential 28 V dc bus through the CAUTION LTS circuit breaker on the main circuit breaker panel.

MASTER CAUTION LIGHT AND RESET BUTTON

The master caution light on the left of the optical sight (figure FO-2 Sheets 1, 2 and 3), and the other at the top center of the bombardier/navigator's instrument panel (figure FO-3 Sheets 1, 2, 3, and 4).

will give a flashing indication whenever a caution light on the annunciator panel comes on. The master caution reset button will turn the master caution light off, and rearm the circuit for any subsequent caution lights.

CAUTION

Due to the proximity of the emergency stores jettison button, care should be exercised to prevent inadvertent stores jettisoning (figure FO-2 Sheets 1, 2, 3, and 4).

Note

In A-6E 159895 and ON and A-6E Mod M121 and ON, the master caution circuitry is reset by pressing the light.

MASTER TEST PANEL

The master test panel (figure FO-2 Sheets 1, 2, and 3) is in the center of the pilot's instrument panel adjacent to the annunciator panel, and contains three press-to-test buttons. The primary purpose of the master test panel is to check the circuitry of the warning and caution lights by means of the LTS WARN and the FIRE/OIL test buttons. The LOX/FUEL/OIL test button will check the quantity gage circuitry of the oxygen gage test; refer to the applicable system description.

FIRE/OIL Press-To-Test Button

The button placarded FIRE/OIL on the master test panel turns on the two fire warning lights and the NWW TEMP light if AFC 268 is incorporated. In TRAM configured aircraft, it also tests the AFT TEMP light. In aircraft with this button placarded FIRE/OIL, it also turns on the low-oil lights on the annunciator panel.

LOX/FUEL/OIL Press-To-Test Button

The LOX/FUEL test button is used to test electrical circuitry of the oxygen quantity gage, the oxygen warning light, and the fuel quantity gage needles. In aircraft placarded LOX/FUEL/OIL, in addition to checking oxygen and fuel quantity gages, lighting of the OIL LOW lights is a check of oil quantity.

LTS WARN Press-To-Test Button

The LTS WARN press-to-test button on the master test panel is used to check for operating circuitry of the following warning and caution lights:

ATTACK
MASTER CAUTION
COLLISION
APPROACH INDEXER
ANNUNCIATOR PANEL
ARM WEAPON
APCS STBY
AFCS OFF
WAVE OFF
WHEELS WARNING
WHEELS TRANSITION

DISCRETE MESSAGE
  INDICATOR
HOOK LIFT
OUTBD WG PSI
INBD WG PSI
RADAR ALTIMETER
  FAILURE
TERRAIN CLEARANCE
RESELECT (A-6E)
COMPLETE (A-6E)

Note
The platform light is not wired to the pilot's or B/N's press-to-test circuitry.

BOMBARDIER/NAVIGATOR'S MASTER TEST (A-6A,B,C,E)

This test button on the bombardier/navigator's right console (figure FO-3 Sheets 1, 2, 3, and 4) provides a means of checking the circuitry of the bombardier/navigator's indicator lights (figure FO-11).

FIRE WARNING LIGHTS

Two fire warning lights, one for each engine, are on opposite sides of the optical sight (figure FO-11). The lights will come on when the heat-sensing elements, which are placed where excessive heat is likely to occur, are grounded. If a fire occurs, the semiconductor section of the sensing element heats up, decreasing resistance, and grounding the circuit. The circuit can also be grounded by the FIRE/OIL test button on the master test panel.

The system includes a short discriminator; however, if a short occurs, the light may flash on momentarily.

NWW TEMP LIGHT

In A-6E 158533 and ON and aircraft incorporating AFC 268, the COLLISION light is replaced by a NWW TEMP light on the lower right side of the optical sight. The light will come on when the heat-sensing element array placed near the bleed-air ducting in the nosewheel well and radome areas senses excessive heat. The light is tested by the FIRE/OIL press-to-test button.

COLLISION LIGHT

The collision light, located on the lower right side of the optical sight, has no operational function. AFC 268 replaces the collision light with the NWW TEMP light.

CANOPY

The aircraft canopy is operated by hydraulic pressure and can be controlled externally or from the cockpit. It can also be jettisoned or manually released from the cockpit or through external controls for crash rescue.

CANOPY OPERATION

CANOPY SELECTOR VALVE

In A-6A, B, C 149941 thru 155702 and KA-6D aircraft not incorporating AFC 185, the canopy selector valve is a two-position, detented, solenoid-operated selector valve positioned by the cockpit canopy switch, the boarding ladder switches, or the manual selector handles in the cockpit and nosewheel well. In A-6A 155703 and ON, and aircraft incorporating AFC 185, the canopy selector valve is a three-position, spring-loaded return-to-neutral, open-center, solenoid-operated selector valve positioned by the cockpit canopy switch, the boarding ladder switches, or the manual selector handles in the cockpit and nosewheel well.

When the canopy selector valve is positioned to open, hydraulic pressure from the combined system is initially directed to the canopy seal selector valve, dumping air pressure from the canopy seal so that the canopy can be opened. Pressure is then directed to the open side of the canopy actuating cylinder, opening the canopy. When the valve is positioned to close, the sequence is reversed and the canopy is closed and the seal is inflated.

When the engines are running, combined system pressure is provided by the engine-driven pumps. Otherwise, an external source of hydraulic pressure may be used, or combined system fluid can be pressurized by means of the handpump or the electrically driven auxiliary hydraulic pump.

In aircraft with the three-position selector valve, the valve must be held in the selected position manually or electromechanically until the desired action has been completed or it will return to the neutral position, releasing the pressure to the canopy actuating cylinder and stopping the action of the canopy.

CANOPY SWITCH

The CANOPY switch (figure 1-26) on the right side of the pilot's instrument panel is used for normal operation of the canopy.

AFC No. 185 Not Incorporated

In aircraft with the two-position canopy selector valve, the CANOPY switch is a two-position toggle switch marked OPEN and CLOSE. When aircraft primary dc electrical power on line, moving the switch energizes a solenoid on the canopy selector valve, positioning the valve and permitting hydraulic pressure to move the canopy to the selected position. CANOPY switch position does not affect selector valve position with external electrical power connected.

WARNING

Ensure that personnel are clear of the canopy while disconnecting external power.

Note

Before applying aircraft electrical power, the CANOPY switch should be positioned to agree with the position the canopy to prevent inadvertent canopy actuation.

AFC No. 185 Parts 1 and 3 Incorporated

In aircraft with the three-position canopy selector valve, the CANOPY switch (figure 1-26) is a three-position, spring-loaded, return-to-neutral toggle switch marked OPEN and CLOSE. With aircraft electrical power on the line, moving the switch to the desired position actuates a solenoid on the canopy selector valve, permitting hydraulic pressure to move the canopy to the selected position as long as the switch is held in the desired position. A magnetic holding feature holds the canopy switch in the close position and is activated approximately 1/2 inch prior to the canopy reaching its fully closed position. The canopy switch will remain the closed position until aircraft electrical power drops off the line or the switch is repositioned manually. With the aircraft on external power, the canopy switch must be held in either the open or close position to expect canopy action.

AFC No. 185 Part 1 Incorporated

In aircraft with AFC 185 Part 1 only incorporated, the canopy switch is a three-position, spring-loaded, return-to-neutral toggle switch marked OPEN and CLOSE. With external electrical power on the line, moving the switch to either the OPEN or CLOSE position actuates a solenoid on the canopy selector valve, permitting hydraulic pressure to move the canopy to either the OPEN or CLOSED position as long as the switch is held in that position. Release of the switch will return it to neutral and stop canopy action. On aircraft power, the switch must be held open to activate the canopy open.

WARNING

On aircraft power, the CANOPY switch is held in the CLOSE position, when selected, and the canopy will complete its travel to the CLOSE position unless the CANOPY switch is manually repositioned OFF.

Canopy Switch Caution Light

In aircraft with the three-position canopy selector valve, a light on the annunciator panel shows CANOPY SW any time aircraft primary dc electrical power is on the line and the CANOPY switch is not at CLOSE.

MANUAL CANOPY HANDLE

Two manual selector handles, one on the pilot's pedestal (figure 1-26) and one in the nosewheel well, are used to position the canopy selector valve when aircraft electrical power is not on the line. From the cockpit, pushing the handle full in moves the valve to close and pulling the handle to full out moves the valve to open.

In aircraft with the two-position canopy selector valve, the electrically selected position of the valve can be overridden by the manual handle, but when aircraft electrical power is put on the line, the valve will assume the position electrically selected by the CANOPY switch.

WARNING

Actuating the manual canopy selector handle to the closed position after engine shutdown will close the canopy if engines are still windmilling. Serious injury can result from premature closing of the canopy before aircrewmen are clear of the cockpit area.

1-73

AIRCRAFT
Systems

NAVAIR 01-85ADA-1

CANOPY CONTROLS AND INDICATORS

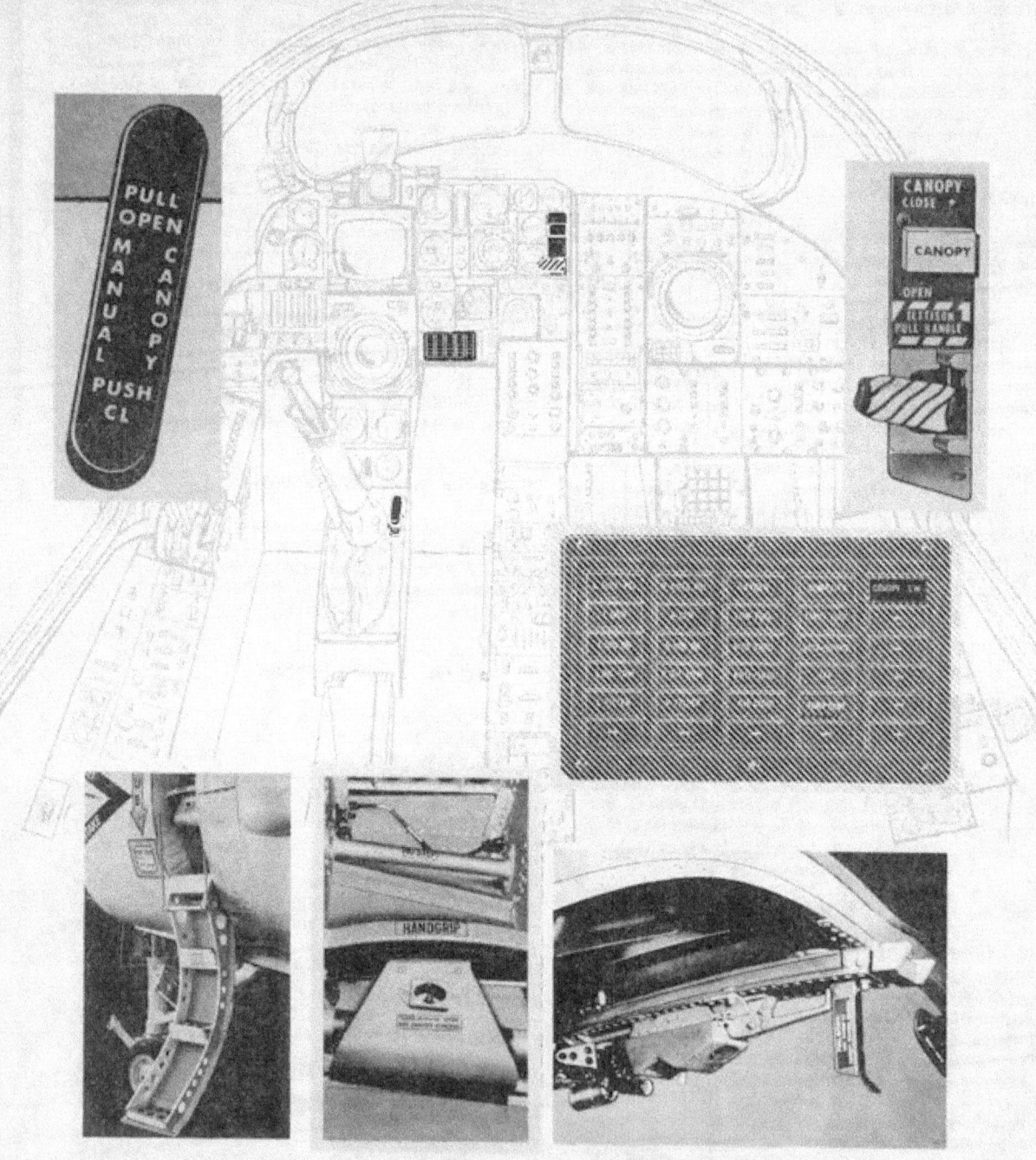

Figure 1-26

Note

If the manual canopy selector handle is actuated while operating on aircraft electrical power, the position of the cockpit electrical switch will determine the canopy position when the handle is released.

In aircraft with the three-position canopy selector valve, the manual handle must be held in position until the canopy reaches the desired position.

BOARDING-LADDER SWITCHES

Two three-position, spring-loaded, return-to-neutral switches, one in each boarding-ladder well, are provided for external operation of the canopy. These switches are placarded AUX CANOPY CONTROL. Holding either switch in the OPEN or CLOSE position actuates the canopy selector valve and operates the electric-motor-driven pump to move the canopy to the selected position.

Ensure canopy area is clear before actuating boarding-ladder switches.

AUXILIARY HYDRAULIC PUMPS

When the engines are secured, combined system fluid can be pressurized to operate the canopy by means of the handpump or the battery-powered electric-motor-driven pump. The canopy selector valve is positioned by the manual canopy handle or the boarding-ladder switches.

Hand Pump

Two handles, one in the nosewheel well and one in the cockpit on the left side of the center console, are used to operate the handpump, which provides combined system pressure to operate the canopy.

Electric-Motor-Driven Pump

The electric-motor-driven pump provides combined system pressure for canopy operation on the ground and is operated by a pushbutton switch in the cockpit placarded AUX HYD PUMP MOTOR, or by the boarding-ladder switches. In aircraft with the two-position canopy selector valve, the pushbutton switch is on the pilot's pedestal in the upper left corner. In aircraft with the three-position canopy selector valve, the push-button switch is on the handpump handle stop on the left side of the center console.

Note

Ensure that personnel are clear of the canopy while connecting or disconnecting external power.

CANOPY REMOVAL (MANUAL)

If the canopy seal has first been deflated, the canopy can be removed manually by pulling the manual release handle on the canopy beam (figure 1-26) (or the external T-handles on the aft end of the canopy) disconnecting the canopy from the hydraulic actuating piston. The canopy can then be slid off the tracks and removed.

The canopy seal is best deflated by cracking the canopy slightly with the hydraulic handpump or the electric-motor-driven pump. This opens the canopy seal selector valve, dumping air pressure from the seal and frees the canopy for opening.

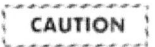

Do not attempt to operate the canopy hydraulically after the manual release handle has been pulled until the actuating piston has been reconnected.

In an emergency, if the seal cannot be deflated by the normal means and it is inpractical or impossible to jettison the canopy, the seal may be deflated by puncturing it with a knife. Cutouts for this purpose are provided in the seal retainer on both sides of the cockpit at a location approximately even with the B/N's backrest.

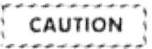

Manual canopy removal is not intended as a normal method of egress and if used, should be entered in the yellow sheet (OPNAV FORM 3760-2) to ensure corrective action or appropriate inspection is completed.

EMERGENCY CANOPY JETTISON

The emergency canopy jettison system uses pressure from a precharged air bottle to fire an explosive charge placed in the canopy actuating cylinder. When the charge is fired, a rod within the piston rod will drive the canopy and its retaining mechanism off the canopy track.

Note

Although canopies have safely separated from the aircraft above 220 KIAS, no flight test data are available on jettisoning the canopy above this airspeed.

Canopy Jettison Handle

The canopy jettison handle (figure 1-26), on the right side of the pilot's instrument panel is used to jettison the canopy. Pulling the handle releases air from a precharged bottle to pneumatically activate an explosive charge in the canopy actuating cylinder. The canopy jettison handle is guarded with a safety pin, which is removed prior to flight. For detailed procedures on escape, see Section V of this manual.

ESCAPE SYSTEM

Safe escape from the aircraft is by individually controlled MK GRU-5 ejection seats or by MK GRU-7 rocket-assisted ejection seats for each crewmember. The seats are not interlocked with the canopy and may be ejected through the canopy. The seat catapult guns are equipped with rain seals, which will permit underwater ejection in extreme emergency.

The MK GRU-7 seats are capable of safe ejection on the deck at zero airspeed; the MK GRU-5 can provide safe ground-level ejection at speeds in excess of 100 knots. Either type provides safe escape in straight-and-level flight throughout the operational envelope of the aircraft.

WARNING

At speeds in excess of 500 KIAS, straight-and-level flight, a minimum altitude of 100 feet is necessary for safe ejection with the MK GRU-5 seat.

Capabilities of the seat are shown in Section V. Preflight procedures and location of safety pins are shown in Section III. Ejection procedures are discussed in Section V.

EJECTION SEAT MK-GRU 5

The seat (figure 1-27) consists of a main beam assembly composed of two vertical and three horizontal members, plus the following components and assemblies: a drogue parachute container assembly with headrest, primary firing mechanism, and attached face curtain, drogue gun, time-release mechanism, shoulder-harness reel mechanism and dual attached leg-restraint cord assemblies, emergency oxygen bottle, ventilated parachute back pad, ventilated seat pan, PK-2 pararaft kit and lap belt assembly, and the seat bucket vertical and tilt adjustment actuators. Ejection of either seat sets the IFF/SIF modes 1 and 3 to emergency and actuates the equipment destruct system when installed.

EJECTION SEAT OPERATION

The ejection sequence (figure 1-28) is started by pulling the face-curtain firing handle or the lower ejection handle. When either firing handle is pulled, the catapult sear is withdrawn and shoulder-harness reel locks in its present position. When the catapult gun fires, the expanding gases drive the catapult tubes upward and eject the seat and occupant from the aircraft. As the seat rises, the occupant's legs are pulled back into the leg pads and the restraint cords are pulled tight. As the seat continues to rise, tension shears rivets (securing the cords to the deck), freeing the cords from the aircraft. The occupant's legs remain secured to the seat by snubbers wedging against the restraint cord, preventing any flailing of the occupant's legs. The occupant's legs remain secured to the seat until the time-release mechanism actuates a plunger, freeing the occupant's legs before separation from the seat. While the seat is going up the rail, the following events occur:

- The drogue-gun trip rod is pulled.
- The time-release mechanism trip rod is pulled.
- The emergency oxygen bottle is activated.
- The IFF/SIF emergency code is activated.

One second after the drogue-gun trip rod is pulled a small controller drogue chute is drawn from the pack by a metal piston fired from the drogue gun. The controller drogue chute then pulls the stabilizer chute out of its container. The stabilizer chute is secured to the seat by a scissor shackle until released by the time-release mechanism. During ejection, the occupant is held in the seat by upper restraint straps, lap belt, and leg-restraint cords.

Deployment of the personnel parachute and separation of the occupant from the seat are delayed by the time-release mechanism until the occupant has descended from the upper atmosphere or until expiration of a 2.0-second time delay. When the seat is below an altitude of 10,000 to 14,500 feet (barostat setting of particular model seat), the time-release mechanism starts a 2.0-second time delay, after which the time-release mechanism releases the drogue parachute from the scissors shackle, allowing the drogue chute to pull out the personnel parachute withdrawal line and deploy the personnel parachute. At the same time, the harness restraints, lap belt, leg restraints, survival kit, upper block of the personnel services disconnect, and face curtain are unlocked. The occupant is then free to be pulled from the seat sticker clips by the line stretch of the main parachute as the seat rotates away. When the occupant is free from the seat, he makes a normal parachute descent with his survival kit connected to him by the lap belt/harley buckle.

MANUAL SEAT SEPARATION

If the time-release mechanism fails, the crewmember can manually separate from the seat by pulling up and aft on the emergency restraint release (front right side of seat bucket). Rotating the emergency restraint release releases the lap belt, the leg-line straps, parachute container, survival kit, and personnel services disconnect. The occupant must push free of the seat and manually deploy the personnel parachute by locating and pulling the parachute ripcord.

WARNING

The personnel parachute must be deployed manually if the harness emergency restraint release has been pulled.

EJECTION CONTROLS

Face-Curtain Handle

The automatic ejection sequence is initiated by pulling the face-curtain handle located immediately aft and above the occupant's head (figure 1-27). When the face-curtain handle is pulled, the firing mechanism is actuated and the primary cartridge is detonated.

Note

The seat is fired after approximately 13 inches of face-curtain travel.

Lower Ejection Handle

The lower ejection handle is on the front of the seat bucket, between the occupant's legs (figure 1-26).

The sequence of personnel parachute deployment remains the same, since both the face-curtain handle and the lower ejection handle initiate seat firing by extracting the sear from the ejection-gun firing mechanism.

WARNING

If the face-curtain firing handle does not actuate the ejection seat, the face-curtain handle should be held while the lower ejection handle is actuated, to prevent the possibility of entanglement with the drogue gun when it fires.

Note

The seat is fired after approximately 2 1/2 inches of lower ejection handle travel.

PARACHUTE

The parachute is in a rectangular back pack aft of the occupant. The parachute pack is attached to the seat by two retention straps that run from the seat bucket locks, through the parachute pack, and to the shoulder-harness reel mechanism, where they attach. On ejection, the straps are automatically released at both points by the time-release mechanism. The parachute pack is attached to the occupant by two straps connected to the Koch fittings of the integrated torso harness.

Time-Release Mechanism

The time-release mechanism is on the right side of the ejection-seat headrest and is armed upon ejection by a time-release mechanism trip rod which is secured to the trip rod bracket.

The time-release mechanism comprises a g-controller to prevent both the deployment of the personnel parachute and occupant separation from the seat at high g forces, and an altitude-sensing barostat, to prevent premature deployment of the parachute at high altitudes. Between 10,000 and 14,500 feet depending on model of seat and at deceleration of 4.5 g's or less, the time-release mechanism releases the drogue parachute from the shackle scissor, and through the personnel parachute withdrawal line deploys the pilot's personnel parachute. At the same time, the harness restraints, leg restraints, upper blocks of the personnel services disconnects, and face curtain are released. The occupant is then free to be pulled from the seat sticker clips by the opening shock of the main parachute.

PARACHUTE WITHDRAWAL LINE

The parachute withdrawal line is connected from the personnel parachute to the seat drogue parachute. In normal ejection, this line is pulled out by the drogue parachute after the time-release mechanism activates to deploy the personnel parachute.

EMERGENCY RESTRAINT RELEASE

This control is the black-and-yellow striped handle forward on the right side of the seat bucket (figure 1-27). In the forward and down (locked) position, the occupant and his personal equipment are secured to the seat. When the emergency restraint release is lifted and rotated to the aft and up (unlocked) position, the occupant and his personal equipment are disconnected from the seat except for the sticker clips and the personnel parachute withdrawal line. The emergency restraint release simultaneously releases the lap-belt harness locks, shoulder harness reel straps, dual leg-restraint cords, the right and left personnel services disconnects. The face-curtain handle and lower ejection handle are automatically locked and ejection cannot be accomplished.

WARNING

The emergency restraint release may be manually repositioned to the unactuated position, which will:

1. Enable the occupant to unlock the face curtain handle.

2. Automatically unlock the lower ejection handle.

In this situation the lap belt harness locks and shoulder harness reel straps, dual leg-restraint cords, and right and left personnel services disconnects will remain released. Ejection in this condition would be extremely hazardous and is not recommended.

This control will normally be in the forward position. Emergencies such as ditching, over-the-side bailout, or failure of the time-release mechanism will require operation of this control. For detailed information regarding specific use of the emergency restraint release, refer to Section V of this manual.

Shoulder Harness Lock Lever

This control is on the left side of the seat. In the forward position, forward movement of the occupant is restricted and any slack created by rearward

AIRCRAFT
Systems

NAVAIR 01-85ADA-1

EJECTION SEAT

MK GRU-5 SEAT

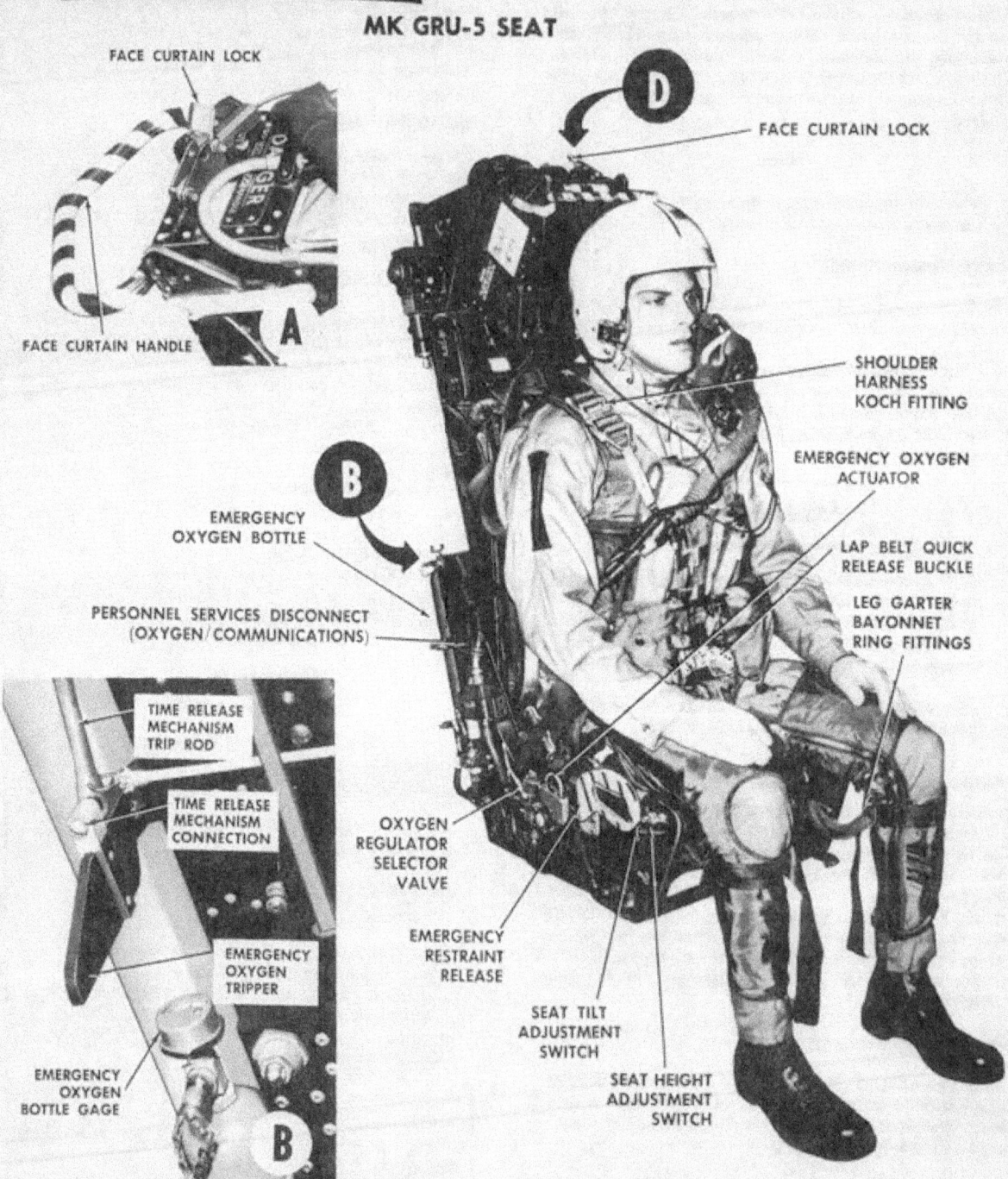

Figure 1-27 (Sheet 1)

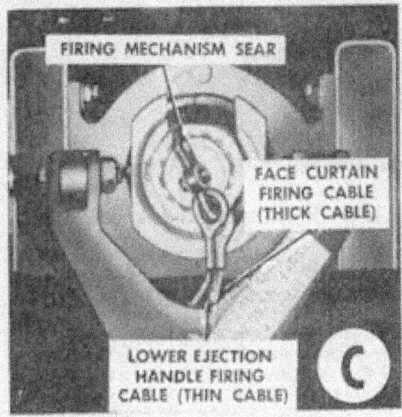

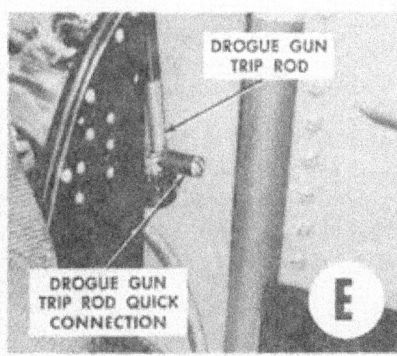

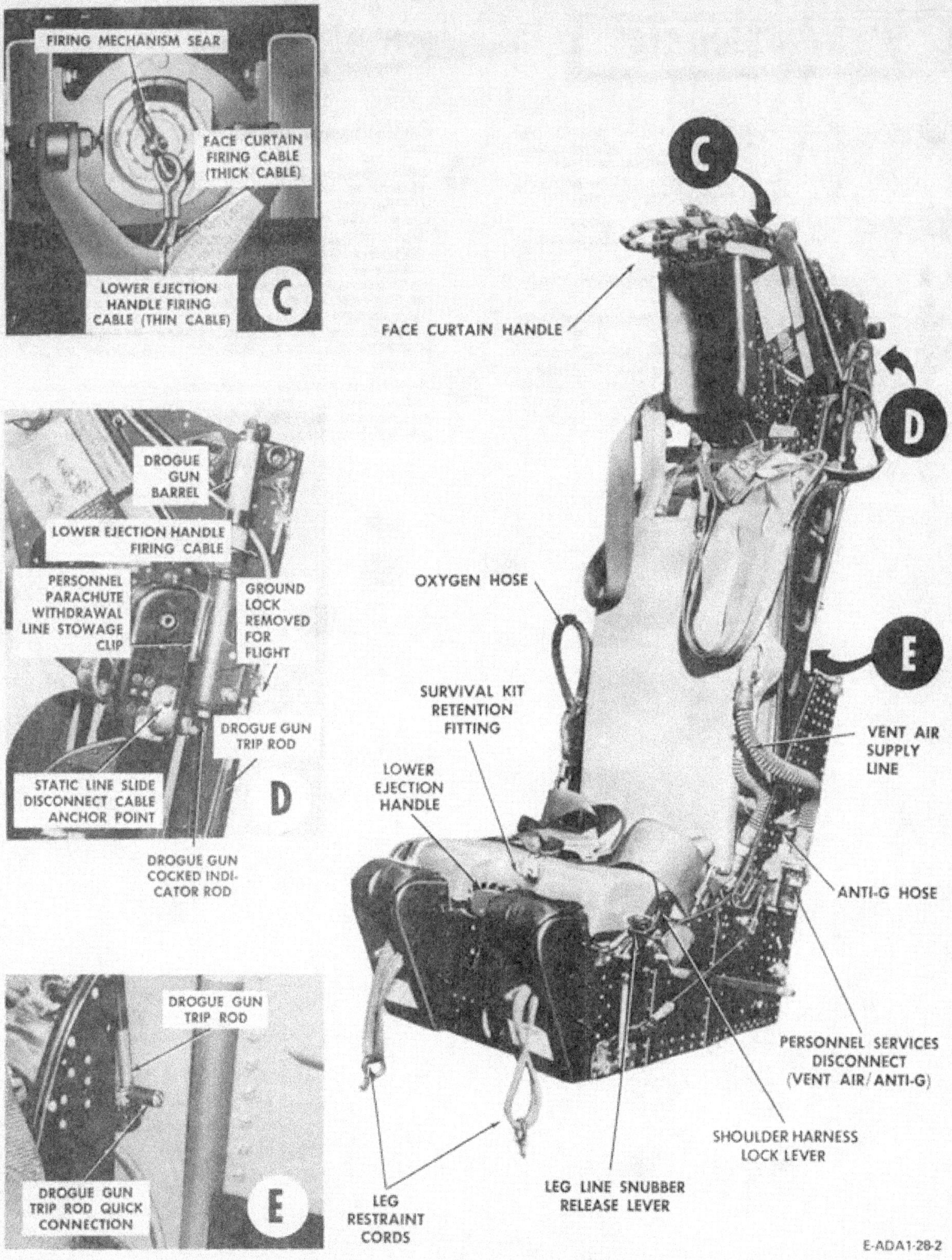

Figure 1-27 (Sheet 2)

AIRCRAFT
Systems

NAVAIR 01-85ADA-1

EJECTION SEQUENCE — MK GRU-5

1. INITIAL EJECTION: EMERGENCY OXYGEN RELEASED, IFF EQUIPMENT DESTRUCT SWITCH ACTUATED, SHOULDER HARNESS LOCKED, LEG RESTRAINTS WITHDRAWN AND LOCKED AND TIME RELEASE AND DROGUE GUN MECHANISMS ARE TRIPPED AS SEAT LIFTS OUT OF COCKPIT.

2. DROGUE GUN FIRES ONE SECOND AFTER EJECTION; DROGUE PISTON WITHDRAWS CONTROLLER DROGUE PARACHUTE.

3. CONTROLLER DROGUE DEPLOYS AND WITHDRAWS STABILIZER DROGUE.

4. STABILIZER DROGUE DEPLOYS, STABILIZING AND DECELERATING SEAT AND OCCUPANT.

5. ABOVE 13,000 FEET OR 14,500 FEET (DEPENDING ON SEAT MODEL): BAROSTAT SECURES TIME RELEASE ESCAPEMENT MECHANISM UNTIL COMPLETION OF DESCENT TO LOWER ALTITUDE, DROGUE PARACHUTE RETENTION SHACKLE REMAINS LOCKED TO SEAT BY RESTRAINT SCISSOR AND SEAT AND OCCUPANT DESCEND THROUGH HIGHER ALTITUDES ON DROGUE PARACHUTES ONLY.

6. BELOW APPROXIMATELY 10,000 FEET OR 11,500 FEET (DEPENDING ON SEAT MODEL) AND DECELERATION OF 4.5g OR LESS: BAROSTAT FREES TIME RELEASE ESCAPEMENT MECHANISM. TIME RELEASE MECHANISM SUBSEQUENTLY RELEASES DROGUE SHACKLE RESTRAINT SCISSOR, OCCUPANT'S UPPER AND LOWER HARNESS RESTRAINT, LEG RESTRAINTS AND UPPER BLOCKS OF PERSONNEL SERVICES DISCONNECTS. RELEASE OF SHACKLE PERMITS CONTINUED PULL OF DROGUE PARACHUTES ON LINK LINES TO RELEASE FACE CURTAIN RESTRAINT, AND MAIN PERSONNEL PARACHUTE. OCCUPANT REMAINS ATTACHED TO SEAT BY STICKER CLIP RETENTION OF LOWER RESTRAINT HARNESS ON SEAT BUCKET.

7. LINE STRETCH OF MAIN PARACHUTE PULLS OCCUPANT, SURVIVAL KIT AND LOWER RESTRAINT HARNESS FREE OF STICKER CLIPS. SEAT FALLS FREE. OCCUPANT DISCARDS FACE CURTAIN AND CONTINUES NORMAL PARACHUTE DESCENT.

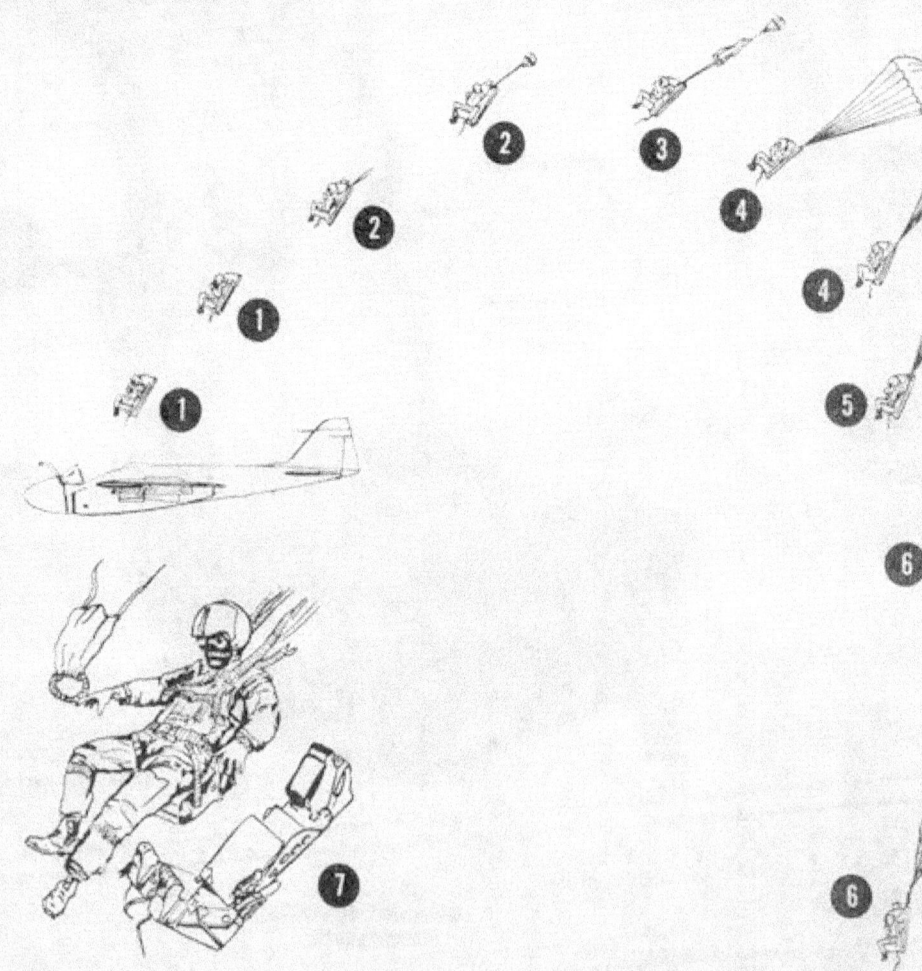

Figure 1-28

movement is taken up by the shoulder-harness reel. The control is locked in this position by using the detent. Once unlocked with manual control, the spring-loaded center position, the occupant can move forward freely, unless the reel locks owing to excessive forward velocity. When the forward velocity decreases, the shoulder straps must be released by repositioning the control. Both straps feed from the same shaft and it is impossible for one to lock without the other. If the reel is locked manually, the control must be positioned full aft to the unlock position to allow forward movement.

LEG GARTER

The leg garter and leg-restraint cords keep the occupant's legs firmly against the leg rests during ejection. The garter is placed around the leg above the calf and below the knee. It should be tight enough so it does not slip down over the calf.

The leg-restraint cords are attached to the aircraft deck and routed through the snubber box seat structure. They are then passed through garter rings and snapped into the leg-line locks. The garter rings are snapped into the bayonet fitting when strapping in.

Leg-Line Snubber Release Lever

The leg-line snubber-release lever is forward on the left side of the seat bucket. When moved forward, this control provides slack in the dual leg-restraint cords.

WARNING

If this lever is jammed in the forward position, manual or automatic separation from the seat is unlikely.

EMERGENCY OXYGEN

An emergency oxygen bottle (1,800 psi) attached to the right side of the ejection seat is automatically actuated on ejection. When the seat rises during ejection a lever on the bottle is tripped by a striker arm, which opens the oxygen valve. The oxygen flows through the seat-mounted regulator, where it is metered through the normal oxygen inlet line.

Note

The emergency oxygen supply will last approximately 10 minutes. The duration will depend upon altitude and breathing rate.

Emergency Oxygen Actuator

The emergency oxygen actuator is the green handle on the right side of the seat, immediately aft of the emergency restraint-release (figure 1-27). This control is used to actuate the emergency oxygen system if the normal system fails.

LR-1 PARARAFT

The LR-1 pararaft kit (figure 1-29) is attached to the lap belt and stowed in the seat bucket. The LR-1 pararaft survival kit contains a one-man life raft, and additional survival equipment as listed and/or required in the latest directives or regulations, or both.

Note

The LR-1 pararaft kit has a quick-disconnect fitting that must be released to open the raft.

PERSONNEL SERVICES DISCONNECT

Oxygen/Communications Disconnect

The oxygen/communications disconnect is mounted on the right side of the seat and serves both the oxygen and communications lines. The seat occupant's personnel oxygen and communication equipment terminates in a block that is plugged and locked into the seat. The aircraft oxygen and communications lines also terminate in this block. This block is unlocked by the time-release mechanism and pulled free when the occupant separates from the seat upon deployment of the personnel parachute, or actuation of emergency restraint release.

Vent/Air/Anti-G

A vent line (exposure suit/back pack pad) and anti-g line personnel services disconnect is mounted on the left side of the seat. The disconnect is unlocked by the time-release mechanism and pulled free when the occupant separates from the seat upon deployment of the personnel parachute, or actuation of emergency restraint release.

SEAT ADJUSTMENT

Seat adjustment is controlled by two three-position, momentary-contact switches (figure 1-27) on the right side of the right thigh support. The direction of switch movement corresponds to the direction of seat movement. Seat adjustment is limited to 5 inches of vertical movement and 10° of tilt.

WARNING

Head and neck injury may occur during ejection or canopy jettison if the seat is not adjusted properly. Do not allow the top of the helmet to project above the level of the face curtain.

CAUTION

The seat height-adjustment actuator motors are intermittent-duty motors. The height actuator motor has a duty cycle of 30 seconds on and 10 minutes off. The tilt actuator motor has a duty cycle of 1 minute on and 15 minutes off.

LR-1 LIFE RAFT

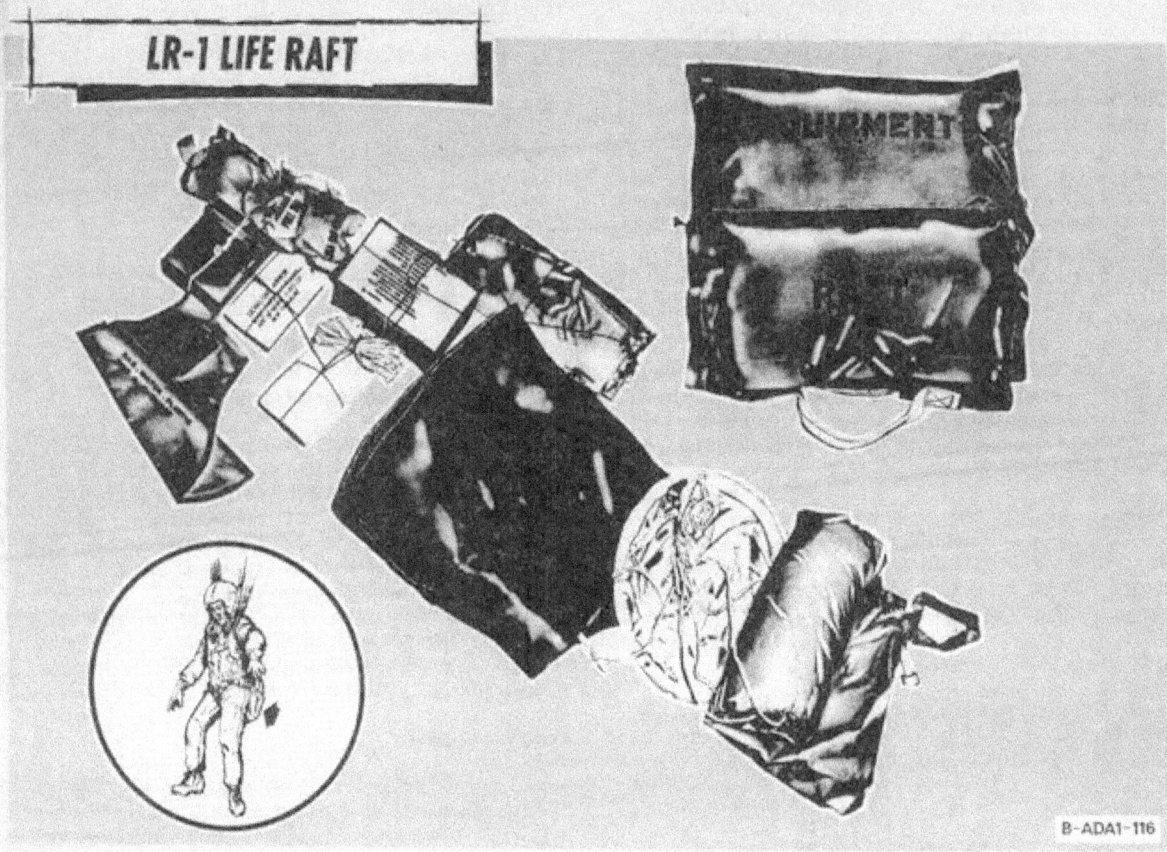

Figure 1-29

LAP BELTS

The lap belt is attached to the seat bucket by two lap belt locks and two sticker clips. The LR-1 pararaft kit is attached to the lap belt and stowed in the seat bucket.

SEAT HARNESS

The seat harness is compatible with a modified integrated torso harness and consists of an adjustable back pad, seat pan, LR-1 pararaft kit, lap belt, two shoulder-harness-reel straps, and two parachute retention straps. The reel straps attach to the occupant's parachute risers. On ejection, they are automatically released by the time-release mechanism. Dual leg-restraint cords hold the occupant's legs securely against the thigh rest extensions on the front face of the bucket assembly. The leg garters are attached to the restraint cords by bayonet ring fittings.

EJECTION SEAT MK-GRU 7

The seat (figure 1-30) consists of a main beam assembly composed of two vertical beams and three horizontal members plus the following components and assemblies: a seat-stabilizer drogue-parachute container assembly with headrest; firing mechanism and attached face curtain and lower ejection handle; parachute withdrawal line guillotine; drogue gun; time-release mechanism; powered shoulder harness-reel mechanism; and attached leg-restraint cord assemblies; ventilated parachute back pad; ventilated seat cushion; RSSK-7 survival kit with emergency oxygen bottle; and the seat bucket actuators. Each seat contains an emergency restraint release, a 28-foot personnel parachute and container, and a rocket motor that is triggered by a gas-generating initiator.

A powered retraction shoulder-harness reel that is actuated by the face-curtain handle or the lower ejection handle ensures that the occupant is pulled back into the seat during ejection. Ejection of either seat sets the IFF/SIF modes 1 and 3 to emergency and actuates the equipment destruct system when installed.

EJECTION SEAT OPERATION

The ejection-seat operation sequence (figure 1-31) is initiated by pulling the face-curtain handle or the lower ejection handle. When either firing handle is pulled, the catapult sear and shoulder-harness reel sear are withdrawn. The powered shoulder-harness reel pulls the occupant back into the seat to an upright position. When the catapult gun fires, the expanding gases drive the catapult tubes upward and eject the seat and occupant from the aircraft. As the seat rises, the leg-restraint cords are pulled tight, pulling the occupant's legs back into the leg pads. As the seat continues to rise, tension built up shears rivets (securing the cords to the deck), freeing the cords from the aircraft. The occupant's legs remain secured to the seat by snubbers wedging against the restraint cord, preventing any flailing of the occupant's legs. The occupant's legs remain secured to the seat until the time-release mechanism actuates, freeing the occupant's legs prior to separation from the seat. While the seat is going up the rails, the following events occur:

- The drogue-gun trip rod is pulled.
- The time-release mechanism trip rod is pulled.
- Personnel services disconnect lanyard is pulled.
- The emergency oxygen bottle is activated.
- The IFF/SIF emergency code is activated.
- The rocket-motor initiator lanyard is pulled.

When fully extended, the rocket-motor initiator lanyard fires the rocket motor under the seat.

One-half second after the drogue-gun trip rod is extracted, a small controller drogue chute is drawn from the pack by a metal piston fired from the drogue gun. The controller drogue chute then pulls the stabilizer chute out of its container. The stabilizer chute is secured to the seat by a scissor shackle until released by the time-release mechanism.

During ejection, the occupant is held in the seat by upper restraint straps, lap restraints, and leg-restraint cords. Deployment of the personnel parachute and separation of the occupant from the seat are delayed by the time-release mechanism until the occupant has descended from the upper atmosphere or until expiration of a 2.0-second time delay.

When the seat is below an altitude of 11,500 to 14,500 feet (barostat setting), the time-release mechanism starts a 2.0-second time delay, after which the time-release mechanism releases the drogue parachute from the scissors shackle, allowing the drogue chute to pull the personnel parachute withdrawal line out of the guillotine and deploy the personnel parachute. At the same time, the shoulder harness restraints, leg restraints, survival kit, and face curtain are unlocked. The occupant is then free to be pulled from the seat sticker clips by the line stretch of the main parachute as the seat rotates away. When the occupant is free from the seat, he makes a normal parachute is free from the seat, he makes a normal parachute descent with his (RSSK-7) survival kit connected to him by the integrated torso harness.

MANUAL SEAT SEPARATION

If the time-release mechanism fails, the crewmember can manually separate from the seat by pulling up and aft on the emergency restraint-release (front right side of seat bucket). Rotating the emergency restraint-release up and aft fires the guillotine severing the personnel parachute withdrawal line and releasing the shoulder-harness restraint straps, the lower restraint, the leg-line straps, parachute container, and survival kit. The occupant must push free of the seat and manually deploy the personnel parachute by locating and pulling the parachute ripcord.

WARNING

The personnel parachute must be deployed manually if the emergency restraint-release has been pulled.

EJECTION CONTROLS

Face-Curtain Handle

The automatic ejection sequence is initiated by pulling the face-curtain handle immediately aft and above the occupant's head. When the face-curtain handle is pulled, the firing mechanism sear and the powered shoulder harness reel sear are mechanically withdrawn and the primary and shoulder harness reel cartridges are fired. As the seat rises, the drogue-gun and time-release mechanism sears are extracted by trip rods and the emergency IFF and equipment destruct (when installed) are activated.

Note

The seat is fired after approximately 7 inches of face-curtain travel.

Lower Ejection Handle

The lower ejection handle is on the front of the seat bucket, between the occupant's legs. The sequence of operation remains the same.

WARNING

If the face-curtain handle does not actuate the ejection seat, the face-curtain handle should be held while the lower ejection handle is actuated, to prevent the possibility of entanglement with the drogue gun when it fires.

AIRCRAFT
Systems

NAVAIR 01-85ADA-1

EJECTION SEAT

MK GRU 7

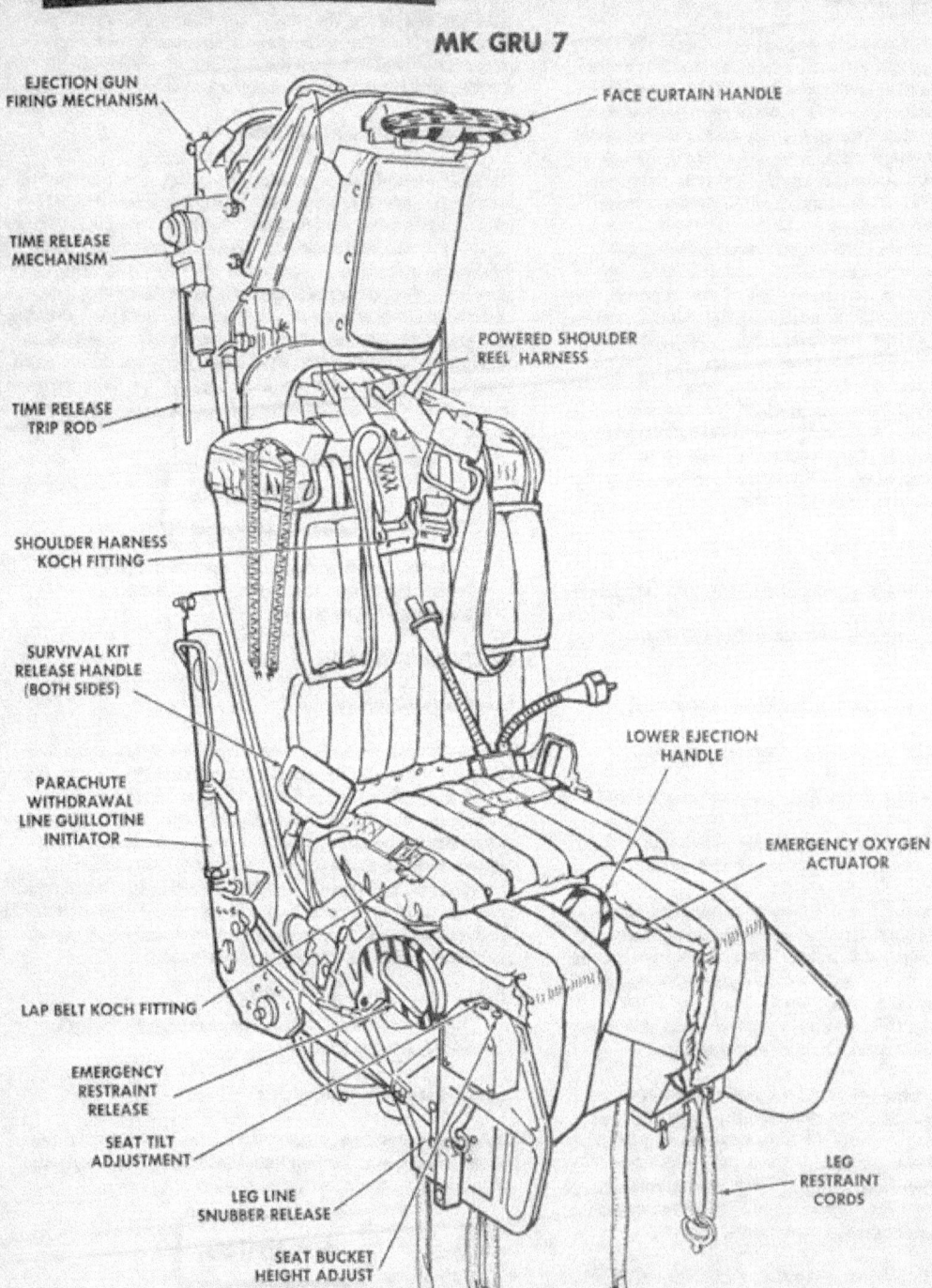

Figure 1-30 (Sheet 1)

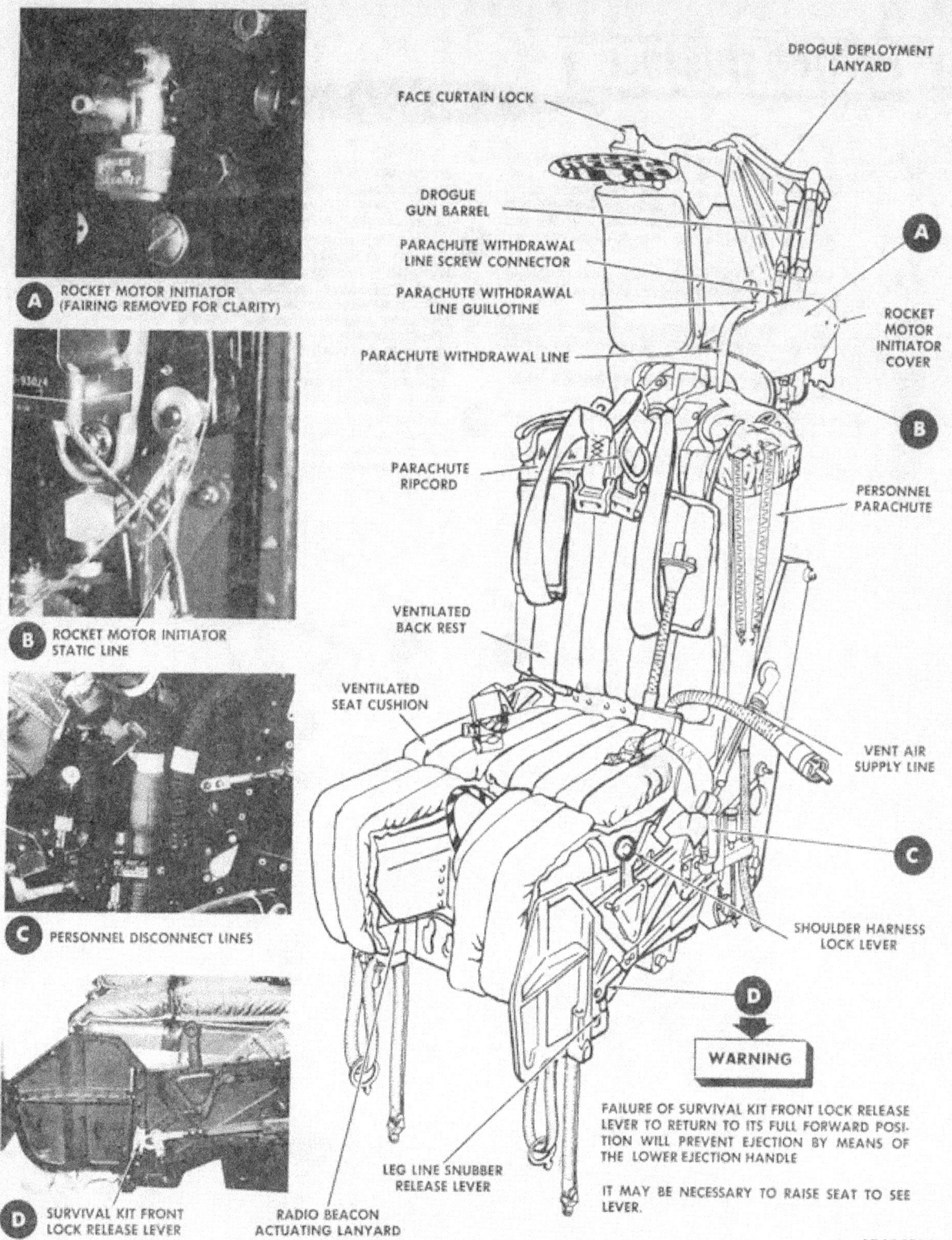

Figure 1-30 (Sheet 2)

AIRCRAFT
Systems

NAVAIR 01-85ADA-1

EJECTION SEQUENCE

MK GRU-7

1. INITIAL EJECTION: EMERGENCY OXYGEN RELEASED, IFF, EQUIPMENT DESTRUCT SWITCH ACTUATED, SHOULDER HARNESS RETRACTED AND LOCKED, LEG RESTRAINTS WITHDRAWN AND LOCKED AND TIME RELEASE AND DROGUE GUN MECHANISMS ARE TRIPPED AND PERSONNEL SERVICES AND ROCKET MOTOR LANYARDS ARE PULLED AS SEAT LIFTS OUT OF COCKPIT.

2. ROCKET MOTOR INITIATOR SEAR WITHDRAWN BY EXTENDED LANYARD, GAS DRIVES ROCKET MOTOR FIRING MECHANISM, IGNITING MOTOR.

3. DROGUE GUN FIRES ONE HALF SECOND AFTER EJECTION; DROGUE PISTON WITHDRAWS CONTROLLER DROGUE PARACHUTE.

4. CONTROLLER DROGUE DEPLOYS AND WITHDRAWS STABILIZER DROGUE.

5. STABILIZER DROGUE DEPLOYS, STABILIZING AND DECELERATING SEAT AND OCCUPANT.

6. ABOVE 14,500 FEET: BAROSTAT SECURES TIME RELEASE ESCAPEMENT MECHANISM UNTIL COMPLETION OF DESCENT TO LOWER ALTITUDE. DROGUE PARACHUTE RETENTION SHACKLE REMAINS LOCKED TO SEAT BY RESTRAINT SCISSOR AND SEAT AND OCCUPANT DESCEND THROUGH HIGHER ALTITUDES ON DROGUE PARACHUTES ONLY.

7. BELOW APPROXIMATELY 11,500 FEET: BAROSTAT FREES TIME RELEASE ESCAPEMENT MECHANISM. TIME RELEASE MECHANISM SUBSEQUENTLY RELEASES DROGUE GUN SHACKLE RESTRAINT SCISSOR, OCCUPANT'S SHOULDER HARNESS RESTRAINTS, LAP BELT, LEG RESTRAINTS, PARACHUTE CONTAINER AND SURVIVAL KIT. RELEASE OF SHACKLE PERMITS CONTINUED PULL OF DROGUE PARACHUTES ON LINK LINES TO RELEASE FACE CURTAIN RESTRAINT AND MAIN PERSONNEL PARACHUTE. OCCUPANT REMAINS ATTACHED TO SEAT BY STICKER CLIP RETENTION OF LOWER RESTRAINT HARNESS ON SEAT BUCKET.

8. LINE STRETCH OF MAIN PARACHUTE PULLS OCCUPANT, SURVIVAL KIT AND LOWER RESTRAINT HARNESS FREE OF STICKER CLIPS. SEAT FALLS FREE. OCCUPANT DISCARDS FACE CURTAIN AND CONTINUES NORMAL PARACHUTE DESCENT.

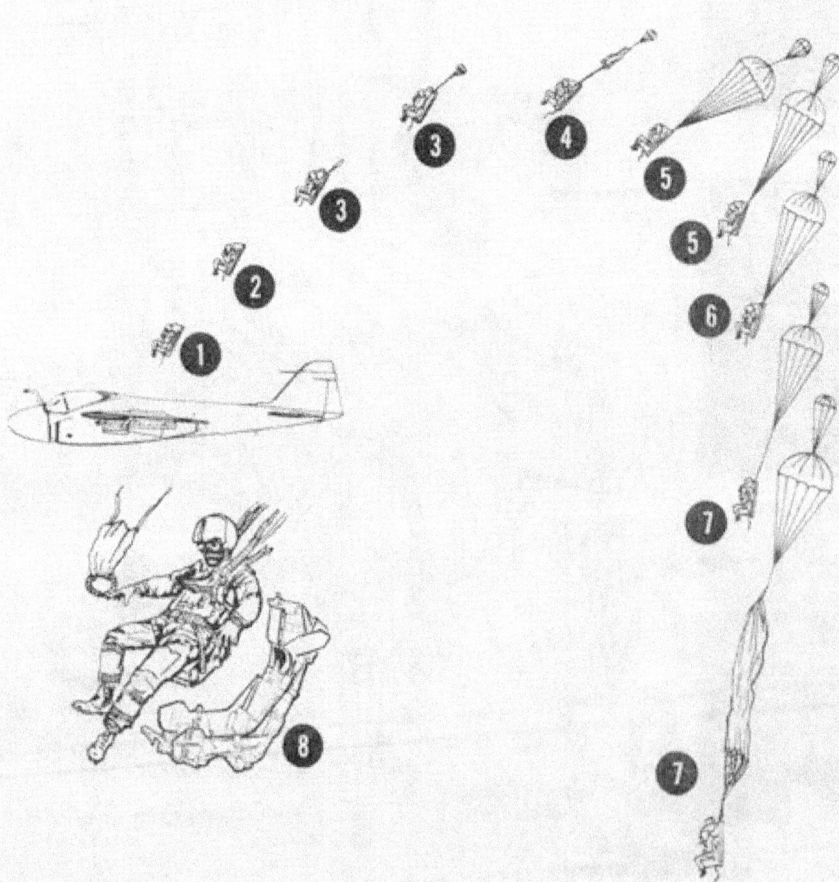

Figure 1-31

Note

The seat is fired after approximately 2 inches of lower ejection handle travel.

PARACHUTE

The personnel parachute is contained in a rectangular back pack aft of the occupant. The parachute pack is attached to the seat by two lock-in fittings. On ejection, the locks are automatically released by the time-release mechanism at both points. The parachute pack is attached to the occupant by two risers connected to the top Koch-fittings of the integrated torso harness.

Time-Release Mechanism

The time-release mechanism is on the right side of the ejection-seat headrest and is armed upon ejection by a time-release mechanism trip rod, which is secured to the trip-rod bracket.

The time-release mechanism contains an altitude-sensing barostat to prevent premature deployment of the parachute at high altitudes. At approximately 13,000 (±1,500) feet or less, the time-release mechanism releases the drogue parachute from the scissors shackle, pulling the personnel parachute withdrawal line from the guillotine and deploying the occupant's personnel parachute. At the same time, the shoulder-harness restraints, lower restraints, leg restraints, parachute container, survival kit, and face-curtain are released.

The occupant is then free to be pulled from the seat sticker clips by the line stretch of the main parachute.

Parachute Withdrawal Line

The parachute withdrawal line is connected from the personnel parachute to the seat drogue parachute. In normal ejection, this line is pulled out by the drogue parachute after the time-release mechanism actuates to deploy the personnel parachute. The line is routed through a gas-operated guillotine that severs the line for manual seat separation.

Guillotine

The guillotine on the left side of the seat is fired by the initial travel of the emergency restraint-release. The guillotine initiator is mounted on the right aft side of the seat bucket. The guillotine severs the personnel parachute from the seat and drogue parachute; the personnel parachute must then be manually deployed by pulling the parachute ripcord.

EMERGENCY RESTRAINT RELEASE

This control is the black-and-yellow-striped handle forward on the right side of the seat bucket. In the forward and down (locked) position, the occupant and his personal equipment are secured to the seat. When the emergency restraint release is lifted and rotated to the aft and up (unlocked) position, the occupant and his personal equipment are disconnected from the seat. The initial travel of this handle fires the parachute withdrawal-line guillotine, severing the personnel parachute from the seat and drogue parachute. The personnel parachute must be manually deployed by pulling the parachute ripcord.

The emergency restraint-release simultaneously releases the lower restraint locks, personal parachute-container retention fittings, survival-kit attachment lugs and sticker clips, shoulder-harness reel straps, and leg-restraint cords.

WARNING

When the emergency release is actuated, the face-curtain handle and lower ejection handle are automatically locked and ejection cannot be accomplished. There is no provision for resetting this control in flight.

This control will normally be in the forward and down position. Emergencies such as ditching, bailout, or failure of the time-release mechanism will require operation of this control. For detailed information regarding specific use of the emergency restraint release, refer to Section V.

POWERED SHOULDER HARNESS REEL

Each seat has a powered shoulder harness reel that is fired when ejection is initiated. The initiator is fired by mechanically extracting the sear that positions the occupant to an upright position during ejection with minimum shock. The shoulder-harness reel straps are connected to the parachute risers and the upper torso harness.

Shoulder Harness Lock Lever

This control is on the left side of the seat. In the forward position, forward movement of the occupant is restricted and any slack created by rearward movement is taken up by the reel. The control is locked in this position by using the detent. In the spring-loaded center position, the occupant can move forward freely, unless the reel locks owing to excessive forward velocity. Upon releasing tension on the straps following automatic lock-up, the straps are released without the necessity of repositioning the manual control. Both straps feed from the same shaft and it is impossible for one to lock without the other. If the reel is locked manually, the control must be positioned full aft to the unlock position to release the straps.

LEG GARTER

The leg garter and leg-restraint cords are used to keep the occupant's legs firmly against the leg rests during ejection. The leg garter is placed around the leg above the calf and above the ankle. It should be tight enough so it does not slip down over the calf.

AIRCRAFT
Systems

> **CAUTION**
>
> The lower strap should contain the release fitting.

The leg-restraint cords are attached to the aircraft deck and routed through the snubber box seat structure. They are then passed through garter rings and snapped into the leg-line locks. The garter rings are snapped into the bayonet fitting when strapping in. Leg-line snubbers are released by pulling the release lever on the forward side of each snubber box.

EMERGENCY OXYGEN

An emergency oxygen system in the survival kit is actuated during ejection by a cable connected from the personnel services disconnect to the automatic emergency oxygen actuator. The cable is disconnected from the survival kit after oxygen release and the oxygen flows through the occupant's personnel oxygen regulator to mask.

> **Note**
>
> The emergency oxygen supply will last approximately 15 minutes. The duration will depend upon altitude and breathing rate.

Emergency Oxygen Actuator

The emergency oxygen system actuator is a green ring on the top left thigh support of the survival kit. This control is provided to actuate the emergency oxygen system if the normal system fails.

SURVIVAL KIT

The survival kit is packed in a rigid two-piece container (RSSK-7) (figure 1-32) stowed in the seat bucket. The RSSK-7 survival kit contains a one-man life raft, and additional survival equipment as listed and/or required in the latest directives and/or regulations.

PERSONNEL SERVICES DISCONNECTS

Supply lines from the aircraft for the oxygen, communications, anti-g, and ventilation systems terminate at the personnel services disconnect, which is attached to the left side of the seat bucket by a quick-release pin. Quick-disconnect fittings connect the supply lines to the lines in the seat, which serve the occupant. The oxygen and communications lines connect to a distribution point in the left rear corner of the survival kit. The emergency oxygen lanyard is also attached to the personnel services disconnect. When the seat is ejected, a lanyard pulls the pin securing the personnel services disconnect to the seat. This releases the disconnect and further upward travel of the seat causes the supply lines to be disconnected at their quick-release fittings and the emergency oxygen lanyard to be pulled, actuating the emergency oxygen supply.

SEAT ADJUSTMENT

Seat adjustment is controlled by two three-position, momentary-contact switches on the right side of seat bucket. The direction of switch movement to adjust the seat is marked near the switches. Seat adjustment is limited to 5 inches of seat bucket vertical movement and 10° of tilt.

> **WARNING**
>
> Head and neck injury may occur during ejection or canopy jettison if seat is not adjusted properly. Do not allow the top of the helmet to project above the level of the face curtain.

> **CAUTION**
>
> The seat-tilt and height-adjustment actuator motors are intermittent-duty motors. The tilt actuating motor has a duty cycle of 1 minute on and 15 minutes off. The height actuating motor has a duty cycle of 1 minute on and 10 minutes off.

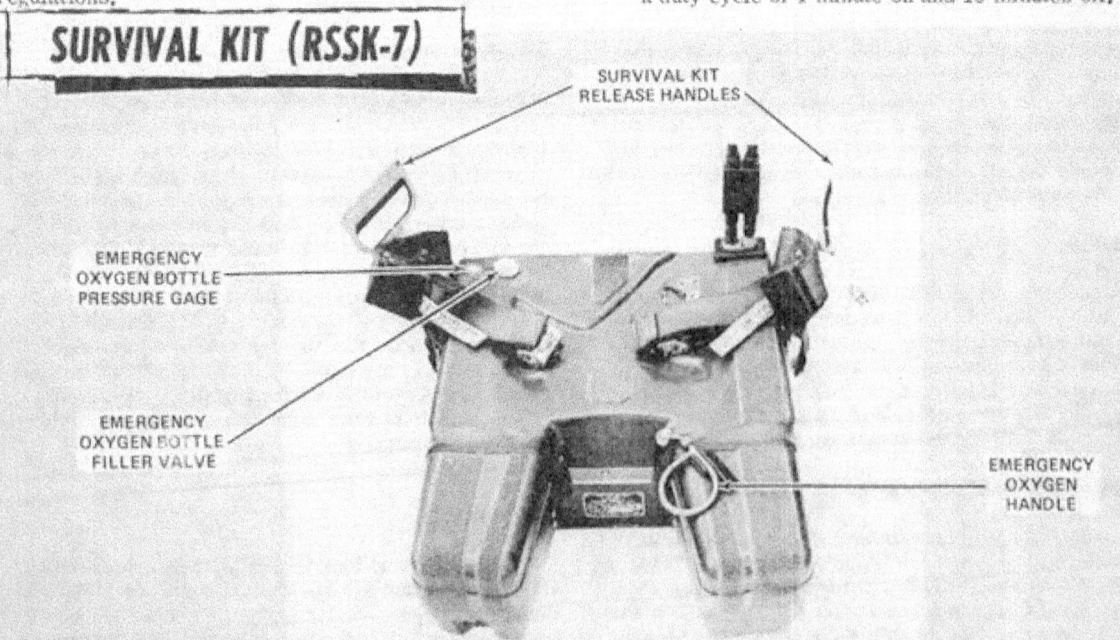

Figure 1-32

ENVIRONMENTAL CONTROL SYSTEM

The environmental control system (figure FO-7) regulates the environment of the crew and the electronic equipment. The system provides cockpit air-conditioning and pressurization, windshield and canopy defogging, electronic equipment cooling and pressurization, and windshield-washing, de-icing, seat cushion ventilation, and rain-removal. In addition, pressurized air is furnished for auxiliary systems such as canopy seal inflation, operation of the anti-g suit bladders, and suit or seat-cushion ventilation as well as hydraulic reservoir and fuel-tank pressurization. In TRAM provisioned aircraft (A-6E 159895 and ON and A-6E Mod 121 and ON), the existing air-cycle refrigeration unit has been augmented by the addition of a second unit in the aft equipment bay. The additional unit is required for the cooling of electronic equipment that has been incorporated in these aircraft.

High-pressure hot bleed air is taken from the twelfth stage of each engine compressor and is passed through the main bleed-air shutoff valve to the air-cycle refrigeration unit, which cools it. On A-6E 158533 and ON and aircraft incorporating AFC 268, the hot bleed air is passed through the air-conditioning bleed-air isolation valve and the main bleed-air shutoff valve to the air-cycle refrigeration unit which cools it. In TRAM aircraft, bleed air from the air-conditioning bleed-air isolation valve also is passed through the aft bleed-air shutoff valve to the aft air-cycle refrigeration unit, where it is cooled. Bleed-air check valves permit system operation with only one engine running.

Bleed air entering the forward air-cycle refrigeration unit passes through the main and auxiliary heat exchangers, where ram air, entering through the right wing intake scoop, is circulated around the fins of the heat exchangers to cool the bleed air and then is dumped overboard. The cooled bleed air passes through the mass flow-control valve to drive the cooling turbine. Since energy is extracted to drive the turbine, this further cools the air. The cooling turbine drives the ram-air exhaust fan.

In TRAM aircraft, high-pressure hot bleed air is taken from the twelfth stage of each engine compressor and is ducted to the main and auxiliary sections of the forward air-cycle refrigeration unit heat exchanger, the aft bay air-cycle refrigeration unit heat exchanger, and directly to the rain-removal system. Bleed air entering the forward and aft refrigeration units passes through the heat exchangers, where ram air circulates around the fins of the heat exchangers to cool the bleed air and is then dumped overboard. In both the forward and aft systems, the cooled bleed air passes through a mass flow-control valve to drive the cooling turbine. Since energy is extracted to drive the turbines, the air is cooled further. The cooling turbine drives the ram-air exhaust fans. The forward unit provides air for cockpit air-conditioning and pressurization; DRS turret pressurization; canopy defogging; anti-g; vent-suit cooling; and hydraulic reservoir, fuel tank, canopy seal, and windshield-wash pressurization. Exhaust air from the cabin provides cooling for equipment in the nose radome. The aft unit provides cooling air for electronic equipment in the aft equipment compartment, right and left shoulder compartments, nosewheel well, cockpit, and nose radome.

COCKPIT AIR-CONDITIONING AND PRESSURIZATION SYSTEM

The cockpit air-conditioning and pressurization system either automatically or manually maintains cockpit temperature and pressure within the limits of crew safety and comfort. To accomplish this, the system forces a mixture of dehumidified refrigerated bleed air and hot engine bleed air into the cockpit. In the automatic mode, a temperature-control system, consisting of temperature switches, selectors, sensors and associated valves, and an electronic controller automatically maintain the mixture temperature after temperature selection is made. Correct cockpit pressure is controlled by a pressure regulator and a safety valve. All controls for operating the system are on the AIR CONDITIONING control panel (figure 1-33), except for the cabin dump switch on the CABIN DUMP panel (figure 1-33).

AUTOMATIC COCKPIT AIR-CONDITIONING

In the automatic mode, the cockpit is furnished temperature-controlled air by the environmental control system. For proper temperature control, both hot engine bleed air and refrigerated, dehumidified bleed air are provided. Thus the temperature of the cockpit air is regulated by a mixture of hot and refrigerated air. These are mixed by means of a dual temperature-control valve in the hot line and in the cold line. The action of the mass flow-control valve assists in stabilizing cabin air at the temperature selected on the AIR CONDITIONING control panel. For example, if the cabin temperature decreases with the dual temperature-control valve at full cold, the portion of the valve in the cold line begins to close. As this occurs, the mass flow controller, downstream of the cooling turbine, senses a pressure increase and begins to close the mass flow-control valve. This results in a decreased flow through the cooling turbine, increasing the temperature of air delivered to the dual temperature-control valve.

MANUAL COCKPIT AIR-CONDITIONING

The dual temperature-control valve can be operated manually by a toggle switch on the AIR CONDITIONING control panel. If the air-conditioning system fails or shuts down, ram air, ducted from the heat exchanger inlet scoop, can be selected for ventilation and limited pressurization of the cockpit.

AIRCRAFT
Systems

NAVAIR 01-85ADA-1

ENVIRONMENTAL CONTROL SYSTEM CONTROLS AND INDICATORS — TYPICAL

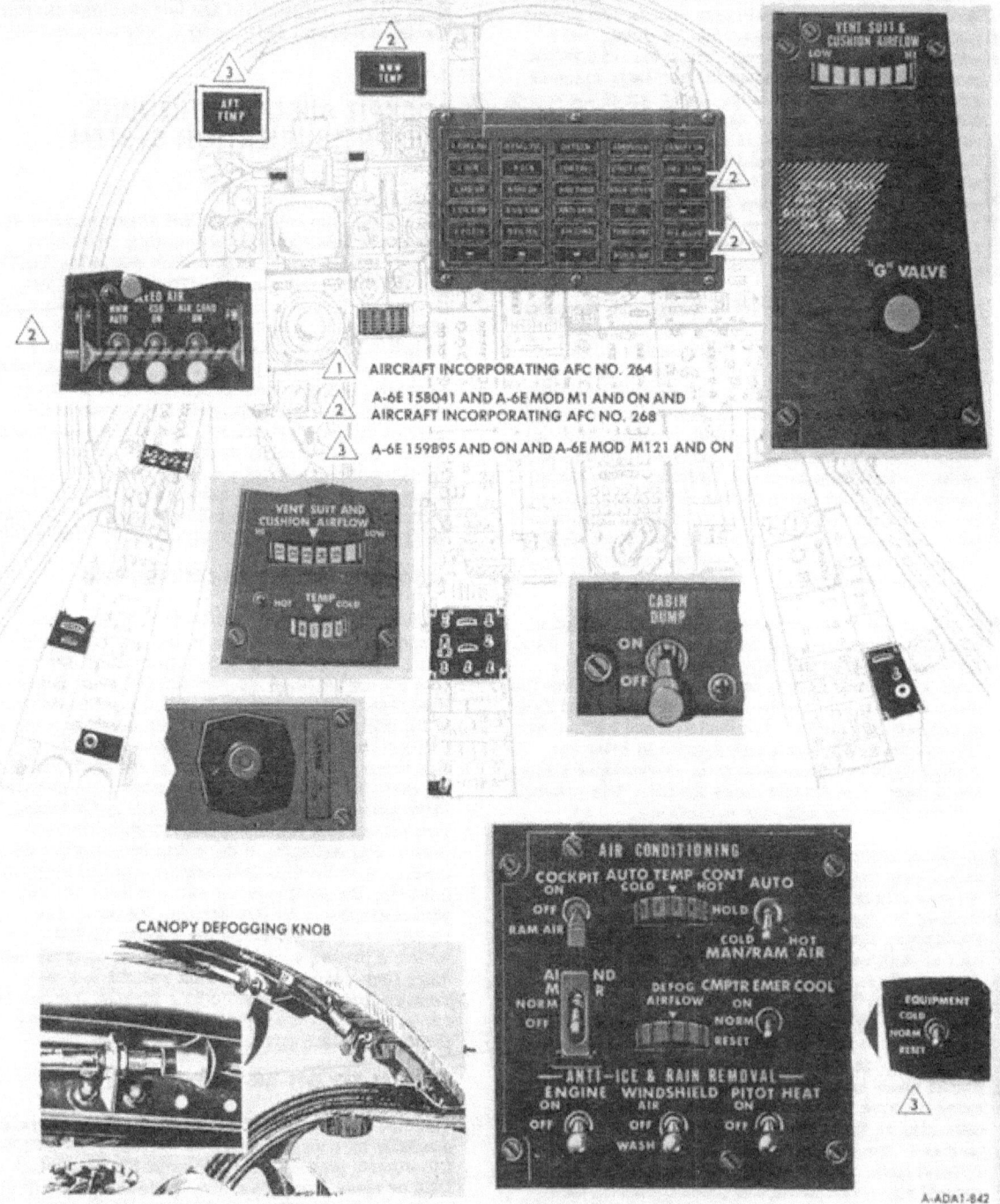

1. AIRCRAFT INCORPORATING AFC NO. 264
2. A-6E 158041 AND A-6E MOD M1 AND ON AND AIRCRAFT INCORPORATING AFC NO. 268
3. A-6E 159895 AND ON AND A-6E MOD M121 AND ON

Figure 1-33

1-90 Change 2

COCKPIT PRESSURIZATION

Air from the refrigeration unit enters the cockpit under sufficient pressure to provide adequate cockpit pressurization. Cockpit pressurization, automatically initiated at 8,000 feet, is controlled by the cabin air-pressure regulator. The regulator controls the discharge rate of the air from the cockpit. After the aircraft reaches 8,000 feet, the regulator valve partially closes and maintains a cockpit altitude pressure of 8,000 feet until an aircraft altitude of 23,000 feet has been reached. Above an altitude of 23,000 feet, the regulator maintains 5 psi pressure differential. (See figure 1-34.) The regulator discharge air assists in cooling various electronic equipment in the nose compartment and nosewheel well. If the regulator should fail, the cockpit air-pressure safety valve automatically dumps when the cockpit pressure differential exceeds 5.5 psi. The safety valve is also capable of negative pressure relief to prevent excessive negative pressure during dives, when the ambient pressure is increasing faster than cockpit pressure is increasing. The safety valve, which dumps into the atmosphere, may also be operated manually by the crew, if desired.

AIR-CONDITIONING CONTROL PANEL

Air-Conditioning Master Switch

The air-conditioning master switch is a two-position (NORM and OFF) toggle switch on the AIR CONDITIONING control panel (figure 1-33). The switch is guarded to the NORM position. With the canopy switch closed (or open with AFC 185 installed), placing the switch to NORM deenergizes the electrical circuit to the main bleed-air shutoff valve, permitting the valve to open if the engine is providing air at 8 psi or more, and the air-conditioning caution light (AIR COND) to go off. Hot engine bleed air is now available for operation of the various environmental systems. Placing the switch to the OFF position allows electrical power to close the shutoff valve, thus shutting off the supply of hot engine bleed air to the environmental system.

CABIN PRESSURE SCHEDULE

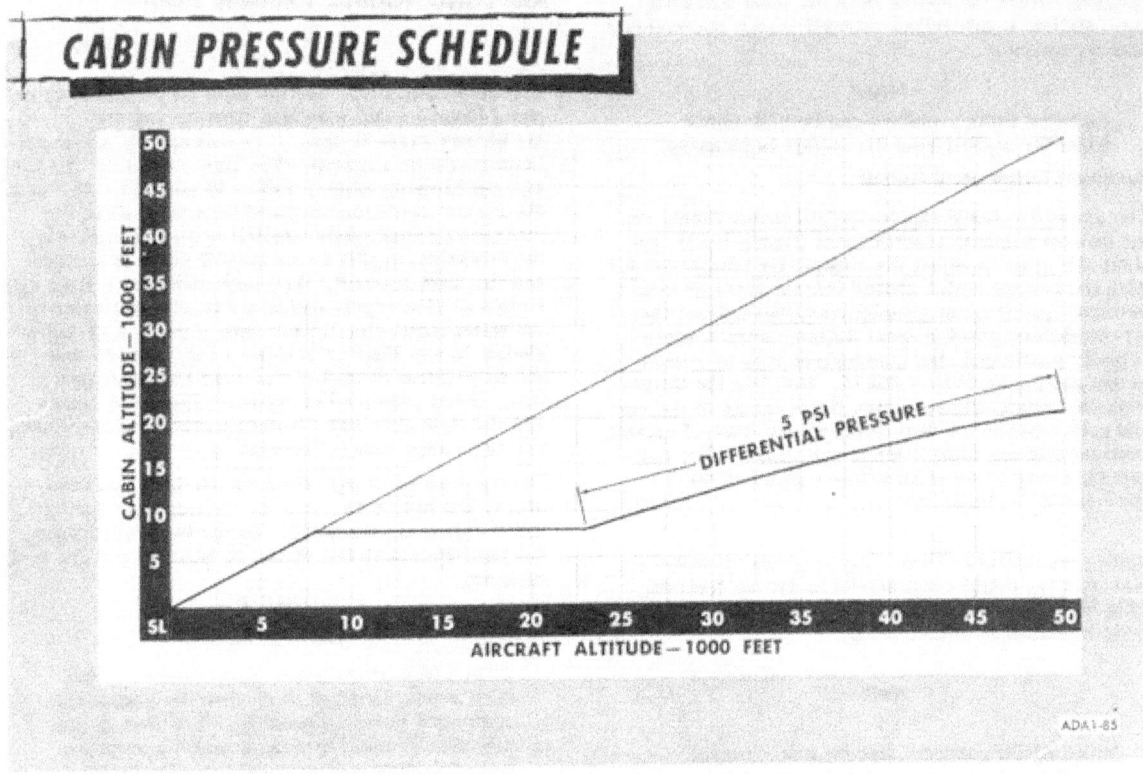

Figure 1-34

> **CAUTION**
>
> Fuel tank and anti-g suit pressurization lines bypass the main bleed-air shutoff valve. During ground operations, do not actuate either the g-valve test button or the ORIDE position of the tank pressure switch unless the air-conditioning master switch is in the NORM position and, in TRAM aircraft, the air-conditioning cockpit switch is in the ON position. Heat damage to O-ring seals in the fuel check valves may occur. Damage to these seals will permit fuel to flow into the auxiliary heat exchanger, the hydraulic tank, vent suit, canopy seal, and electronic equipment in the nose and nosewheel well as well as the engine bleed-air lines.

Note

The hot engine bleed-air line to the rain-removal system bypasses the main bleed-air shutoff valve. The system may still be operated with the air-conditioning master switch at OFF.

A spring-loaded guard over the air-conditioning master switch prevents inadvertent operation of the switch to OFF. Before placing the switch to OFF, the guard must be lifted.

Air-Conditioning Cockpit Switch

The cockpit switch, on the AIR CONDITIONING control panel (figure 1-33) is a three-position toggle switch marked ON, OFF, and RAM AIR. With an engine running, the canopy switch closed, (except in aircraft with the three-position canopy selector valve) and the air-conditioning master switch at NORM, placing the cockpit switch ON engages the air-conditioning and pressurization system by energizing the dual temperature-control valve and deenergizing (opening) the cabin shutoff valve. Depending upon the setting on the automatic temperature-control thumbwheel, conditioned air flows into the cockpit.

> **CAUTION**
>
> In TRAM aircraft, during ground operation of the air-conditioning system with an engine running, the air-conditioning cockpit switch must be kept at ON to ensure sufficient airflow to prevent hot engine bleed air from entering the environmental systems serviced by the forward unit.

Placing the cockpit switch OFF energizes (closes) the cabin shutoff valve, and drives the dual temperature-control valve to the full hot position. This prevents any airflow to the cockpit. The RAM AIR position closes the cabin shutoff valve and drives the dual temperature-control valve to the full hot

AIRCRAFT
Systems

NAVAIR 01-85ADA-1

position. When the switch is in the RAM AIR position, airflow is controlled manually using the manual/ram air switch.

Note

Reduced cabin pressure can be maintained when the manual/ram air switch is actuated.

Automatic Temperature Control

The automatic temperature-control thumbwheel, on the air-conditioning control panel (figure 1-33), enables the crew to adjust the cockpit air temperature. With the canopy switch closed (except aircraft with the three-position canopy selector valve) and the other air-conditioning and pressurization controls appropriately positioned, the thumbwheel may be moved to any setting between 0 and 14. Rotating the thumbwheel automatically regulates the openings of the hot and cold sides of the dual temperature-control valves, thus varying the cockpit air temperature. The temperature may be selected within a range of 60° to 80°F (15.6° to 26.1°C).

Before leaving the chocks, the automatic temperature-control thumbwheel should be set as desired. This will allow the automatic air-conditioning controls to stabilize while taxiing.

Note

In the AUTO position, temperature control should be set at the maximum cold position while the engines are at idle power.

Manual Ram Air Switch (Man/Ram Air)

The manual ram-air switch on the air-conditioning control control panel (figure 1-33) is a four-position toggle switch marked AUTO, HOLD, COLD, and HOT. The AUTO position is selected to place the dual temperature-control system in the automatic mode and thus allow control of the cockpit air temperature as selected by the automatic temperature-control thumbwheel. Placing the switch to HOLD removes the dual temperature-control valve from automatic control. The switch is spring-loaded to HOLD when AUTO is not selected. Momentarily holding the switch in COLD or HOT alters the positions of the hot and cold sides of the dual temperature-control valves accordingly, to change the cockpit air temperature. When released, the switch springs back to HOLD and the dual temperature-control valve remains fixed. The COLD and HOT positions should be toggled intermittently to avoid overshooting the desired position.

With RAM AIR selected on the air-conditioning cockpit switch, airflow is controlled manually through the MAN/RAM switch, which opens and closes the ram-air valve. The temperature of the air from an external refrigerated source can be controlled manually through this switch.

AIR-CONDITIONING CAUTION LIGHT

The air-conditioning caution light on the annunciator panel (figure 1-33) indicates whether the main bleed-air shutoff valve is open or closed and the air-conditioning system engaged. The light comes on when the air-conditioning master switch is placed to OFF and the shutoff valve is energized (closed). When the air-conditioning master switch is placed to NORM, the electrical supply to the shutoff valve is opened and the light goes off. The air-conditioning light also comes on if overpressurization occurs upstream of the water separator. When this occurs, a pressure switch in the ducting activates the forward and aft compartment shutoff valve to the open position. After pressure is reduced, the valve closes and the light goes out. If overpressurization recurs, the same sequence is repeated.

During periods of high ambient humidity and temperature, the light may come on momentarily during rapid engine acceleration. Under these conditions, the light should go out within 10 seconds and not come on again.

CAUTION

If the AIR COND caution light comes on, the crew should be alert to protect the electronic equipment from overheating. The flow of conditioned air into the cockpit and the overflow from the computer pedestal, if apparently normal both quantitatively and qualitatively and whether or not the COMPUTER overheat light is lit, may serve as a indication of an otherwise adequately functioning system. An arbitrary reflex decision to shut down essential gear predicated solely upon lighting of the subject light may be neither desirable nor necessary.

Note

The AIR COND caution light may come on momentarily when the throttles are advanced. This is a normal indication unless the light remains on.

CABIN DUMP SWITCH

The cabin dump switch (figure 1-33) is on the CABIN DUMP panel on the center console and allows the crew to manually dump cabin pressure. Placing the switch ON allows electrical power to energize the cabin dump solenoid. This, in turn, causes the safety valve to open and the cockpit pressure to be dumped. With the switch OFF, the cabin dump solenoid is deenergized, the valve is closed, and normal cockpit pressurization is obtained.

NORMAL OPERATION

Note

Except in aircraft with the three-position canopy selector valve, the canopy must be closed to energize the air-conditioning and pressurization system. It is recommended that this be done before leaving the chocks while engines are at idle setting.

1. Air-conditioning master switch - NORM
2. Cockpit air-conditioning switch - ON
3. MAN/RAM AIR switch - AUTO
4. Automatic temperature-control thumbwheel - SET at 0

Initially set temperature controls as desired. After the system stabilizes, select desired setting.

MANUAL OPERATION

Note

Except in aircraft with the three-position canopy selector valve, the canopy must be closed to energize the air-conditioning and pressurization system.

1. Air-conditioning master switch - NORM
2. Cockpit air-conditioning switch - ON
3. MAN/RAM AIR switch - TOGGLE AS DESIRED, then HOLD

AUXILIARY ENVIRONMENTAL SYSTEMS

The environmental control system provides hot bleed air and refrigerated, dehumidified bleed air for anti-exposure suit or seat-cushion ventilation and for anti-g suit operation. Personnel services disconnects are provided in both seats for these purposes.

ANTI-EXPOSURE SUIT AND SEAT CUSHION VENTILATION

The pilot and the bombardier/navigator receive a mixture of dehumidified refrigerated air and engine bleed air to ventilate their anti-exposure suits or seat cushions. The controls for the suit and seat cushions are on the vent suit and cushion control panel (figure 1-33). The bombardier/navigator has no temperature control; however, he will receive air at the temperature selected by the pilot. The pilot's airflow thumbwheel must be moved toward HI to receive temperature-controlled air.

Vent Suit and Cushion Airflow Control

The pilot's airflow thumbwheel on the vent suit seat cushion control panel (figure 1-33) controls the amount of airflow to the pilot's ventilated anti-exposure suit or seat cushion. With the air-conditioning master switch at NORM, rotating the thumbwheel toward HI energizes (opens) the flow-control valve and activates the temperature-control system. This allows a mixture of hot engine bleed air from the refrigeration unit to pass to the pilot's and bombardier/navigator's cushion. The bombardier/navigator has a similar control on the right console but it has provisions only for regulating airflow and cannot start the system operating.

Vent Suit and Cushion Temperature Control

The temperature (TEMP) thumbwheel on the vent suit and cushion panel (figure 1-32) controls the temperature of the airflow to the pilot's and bombardier/navigator's ventilated anti-exposure suits or seat cushions. With the air-conditioning master switch at NORM, rotating the temperature thumbwheel to HOT or COLD sets the temperature, which the vent suit temperature-control system maintains.

Normal Operation of Vent Suit and Cushion

1. Air-conditioning master switch - NORM
2. Airflow thumbwheel - TOWARD HI
3. Temperature thumbwheel - AS DESIRED

ANTI-G SUITS

Cooled engine bleed air from the auxiliary heat exchanger is piped to the anti-g valves in the left and right consoles. The anti-g valves regulate pressure to the anti-g suits to a maximum of 10 psi and allow the suits to be inflated under varying pressures in proportion to the amount of g force exerted on the aircraft and occupants. As the g force decreases, the anti-g valves register a corresponding decrease in the pressure admitted to the suits. Excess pressure is exhausted into the cockpit. Air from each anti-g valve reaches its suit through personnel services disconnects in the respective seat. The suit bladders may be inflated at any time by depressing the button on top of the valve. Releasing the button allows the valve to close and the pressure in the suit to be exhausted.

G Valve Test

The g valve test buttons on the pilot's left console (figure 1-33, immediately aft of the vent suit and cushion airflow control and the bombardier/navigator's right console, aft on the outboard side (figure 1-33) provide means of testing the proper operation of anti-g suits.

Depressing the g-valve test button provides the necessary air pressure to inflate the anti-g suit bladder. Releasing the button will automatically stop further airflow to the suit and permit the anti-g suit bladder to deflate.

WARNING

Ensure that the air-conditioning master switch is in the NORM position and in TRAM aircraft, the air-conditioning cockpit switch is at ON, prior to depressing the g-valve test button. Hot engine bleed air will be pumped through the anti-g suit if the test button is depressed when the air-conditioning master switch (or, in TRAM aircraft, the air-conditioning cockpit switch) is OFF and the aircraft is on the deck.

DEFOGGING

A mixture of engine compressor bleed air, and air cooled by the main section of the refrigeration unit heat exchanger can be directed to the inside surfaces of all transparent cockpit areas to prevent fog formation. The amount of defog air is monitored by the defog pressure regulator, which is controlled by the defog airflow thumbwheel. The temperature-control valve automatically maintains the defogging air at a temperature of 115°C (240°F) within a tolerance of ±2.8°C (±5°F) for any stabilized flight conditions, and at a tolerance of ±5.6°C (±10°F) while the aircraft is experiencing varying flight conditions.

CANOPY DEFOGGING

The defog airflow is directed to the windshield and side panels any time the system is operating. To direct defog airflow to the canopy, the canopy defog knob must be moved forward (ON). Before descending after prolonged cold-soaking, the defog airflow thumbwheel should be actuated toward HI and the defog knob should be moved to full ON (figure 1-33).

Defog Airflow Thumbwheel

The defog airflow thumbwheel on the air-conditioning control panel (figure 1-33) allows the crew to engage the defogging system and regulate the pressure of the defog air to the transparent cockpit areas. With the canopy closed and the air-conditioning master switch at NORM, turning the thumbwheel to the right engages the defogging system. The defog pressure-regulator shutoff valve becomes energized, opens the valve, and allows temperature-controlled air to flow through the system to the cockpit diffusers. As the thumbwheel rotation is continued, the flow of air to the transparent areas is increased. Conversely rotating the thumbwheel to the left decreases the flow of air to these areas. The air supply to the canopy is automatically shut off when the canopy is opened.

Canopy Defog Knob

A manual canopy defog knob (figure 1-33), on the upper center structure of the canopy, permits the crew to modulate, or shut off completely, portions of total defogging flow delivered to the canopy diffusers. This is accomplished by means of a pushpull cable connected to a butterfly valve. Moving the knob aft (OFF) decreases airflow to the canopy and increases windshield airflow.

OPERATION OF DEFOGGING

1. Air-conditioning master switch - NORM
2. Defog airflow thumbwheel - AS DESIRED
3. Canopy defog knob - AS DESIRED.

WINDSHIELD SWITCH

The windshield switch on the air-conditioning control panel (figure 1-33) has positions marked AIR, OFF, and WASH, and is spring-loaded from WASH to OFF (spring-loaded to OFF from either position with AFC 264). See figure 1-6 for a functional diagram. Electrical power for the windshield switch comes from the 28 V dc primary bus through the AIR COND circuit breaker on the nosewheel well circuit breaker panel.

CAUTION

- Placing the WINDSHIELD switch to AIR on the ground at high power settings may cause the windshield to crack.
- Allow 5 seconds between actuations of the WINDSHIELD switch to permit cooling of the nosewheel well bleed-air isolation valve motor.

Note

- In aircraft incorporating AFC 264, the WSHLD AIR light will come on when the WSHLD AIR switch is placed in the AIR position.
- In A-6E 158533 and ON and aircraft incorporating AFC 268, the nosewheel well bleed-air isolation valve will open if the NWW bleed-air switch on the fuel management panel is in AUTO.

WINDSHIELD WASH

Placing the WINDSHIELD switch to the WASH position electrically energizes the windshield-washing regulator and dump valve. The valve allows bleed-air, cooled by the auxiliary heat exchanger, to pressurize the 1 1/2-gallon fluid tank. The 50-50 water-methanol mixture from the tank is forced through five nozzles onto the pilot's windshield as long as the switch is held to WASH. When released to OFF, the valve shuts off the bleed-air and dumps the pressure in the tank.

Operation of Windshield Wash

1. Windshield switch . . . . WASH
2. Windshield switch . . . . AIR

RAIN REMOVAL (ANTI-ICE)

Placing the windshield switch to the AIR position electrically energizes the rain-removal pressure-regulator shutoff valve; the WSHLD AIR light (AFC 264) on the annunciator panel; and if AUTO is selected on the NWW switch (AFC 268), the nose-wheel well bleed-air isolation valve. Bleed-air passes from the isolation valve through the regulator in the rain-removal valve, is mixed with ambient air by two ejectors, and then directed in a broad stream across the pilot's windshield.

Operation of Rain Removal (Anti-Ice)

1. Windshield switch .... WASH
2. Windshield switch .... AIR

CAUTION

Operation of the rain-removal system is not recommended on a dry windshield or above 200 KIAS. Operation on the ground at high power settings may cause the windshield to crack.

EQUIPMENT COOLING

The equipment-cooling system employs ram air, refrigerated air, and a controlled mixture of refrigerated air and hot engine bleed air to cool electronic equipment in various sections of the aircraft. With an engine running, operation of the equipment-cooling system is automatic. In A-6A, B, C, KA-6D, A-6E through 159579, and A-6E Mod through M120, the air-conditioning master switch must be on for the equipment-cooling system to operate. In A-6E 159895 and ON and A-6E Mod M121 and ON, operation of the system is independent of the air-conditioning master switch requiring only that the air-conditioning bleed air switch be at ON.

Airflow is controlled by a combination of temperature sensors and flow-control valves, by sonic venturis, and by the equipment-cooling pressure regulator. (See figure FO-7.)

COMPUTER EMERGENCY COOLING (A-6A, B, C, E) THRU 159579 AND A-6E MOD THRU M120)

If the computer inlet air temperature exceeds 150°F, the computer thermal switch will deenergize, automatically completing a circuit to the COMPUTER overheat caution light and computer cooling shutoff valve. The computer shutoff valve will then close, preventing hot bleed air from flowing and allowing cooled bleed air to be ducted to the ballistics computer.

When duct temperature drops below 150°F, the computer overheat caution light will go out; however, the computer shutoff valve will remain closed. To restore automatic computer cooling, the computer emergency cooling (CMPTR EMER COOL) switch on the AIR CONDITIONING control panel (figure 1-33) must be actuated to RESET.

Computer Emergency Cooling Switch

The computer emergency cooling switch on the AIR CONDITIONING control panel (figure 1-33) is a three-position toggle switch placarded ON, NORM, and RESET. In the NORM position, automatic temperature control of computer air is provided, or in the event of temperature-control malfunction, unregulated cooled air is directed to the computer.

The RESET position is used to restore automatic computer cooling in the event of automatic temperature-control malfunction (COMPUTER overheat light coming on momentarily, then going off).

The ON position is used if continuous unregulated cooling airflow is desired.

The computer emergency cooling switch is inoperative in the KA-6D.

COMPUTER Overheat Light (A-6A, B, C)

The COMPUTER overheat caution light is on the annunciator panel (figure 1-33). In A-6A, B, C, a momentary light (on and then off), indicates a shift of computer cooling from regulated to unregulated temperature control. A steady light indicates failure of temperature-control regulation and a failure of the emergency cooling system. Setting the computer emergency cooling switch to ON should select unregulated cooling airflow and turn off the light.

CAUTION

- If the COMPUTER caution light on the annunciator panel remains on, secure the computer.

- If the COMPUTER caution light remains on after the computer is secured, a computer temperature control valve failure is indicated. To prevent damage to the computer and possible smoke and fumes in the cockpit, the AIR COND MASTER switch should be set to OFF. Unnecessary electronic equipment should be secured to prevent damage.

The A-6E COMPUTER light on the annunciator panel comes on when the temperature of the computer has exceeded a safe level.

CAUTION

If the COMPUTER light comes on, the computer should be secured immediately to prevent damage.

The COMPUTER overheat caution light is inoperative in the KA-6D.

AIRCRAFT
Systems

Temperature Control Light (A-6E)

The TEMP CONT caution light is on the annunciator panel (figure 1-33). A momentary light (on and then off), indicates a shift of computer cooling from regulated to unregulated temperature control. A steady light indicates failure to temperature-control regulation and a failure of the emergency cooling system. Setting the computer emergency cooling switch to ON should select unregulated cooling airflow and turn off the light.

> **CAUTION**
>
> If the TEMP CONT caution light remains on, a computer temperature control valve failure is indicated. To prevent damage to the computer and possible smoke and fumes in the cockpit, the AIR COND MASTER switch should be set to OFF. The COMPUTER light may be expected to come on. The computer and any unnecessary electronic equipment should be secured to prevent damage.

COMPUTER PURGE (A-6A,B,C)

In aircraft incorporating AFC 135, a high-temperature air purge system is provided to aid in eliminating moisture from the computer units and raise their temperature to prevent condensation in and on them. This purge operates automatically when the computer, search radar, and track radar are turned off with air-conditioning on.

EQUIPMENT COOLING (A-6E TRAM CONFIGURED)

In A-6E 159895 and ON and A-6E Mod M121 and ON (TRAM configured aircraft) the equipment-cooling system provides properly conditioned air to specially cooled electronic equipment in the aft equipment compartment, left and right shoulder compartments, cockpit, nose radome, and nosewheel well. The system uses hot bleed air from the engines and refrigerated bleed air from the aft air-cycle refrigeration unit in the aft equipment compartment. Engine bleed air flow to the equipment-cooling system is controlled by the aft bleed-air shutoff valve. This valve is controlled by the AIR COND BLEED AIR switch on the fuel management panel and thermal switches in the equipment-cooling system. The AFT BLEED caution light on the annunciator panel comes on when this valve is closed. Hot engine bleed air flows to the air-cycle refrigeration unit to be cooled and through the aft equipment cooling temperature-control valve to a mixing chamber, where it is mixed with refrigerated air to provide air of the proper temperature.

Refrigerated air from the aft air-cycle refrigeration unit is also used to cool the aft equipment compartment if ram-air temperature is excessive. When the ram-air thermal switch is activated by a temperature of $125° \pm 5°F$, the normally closed aft equipment compartment shutoff valve is opened, permitting refrigerated air to flow to the compartment.

Should the temperature in the equipment-cooling duct exceed 150°F, a thermal switch opens, causing the TEMP CONT caution light to come on and the equipment-cooling temperature-control valve to close, blocking the flow of hot bleed air to the mixing chamber, thus providing only refrigerated air to the system. When the temperature is reduced to below 150°, the TEMP CONT light goes out; however, the equipment-cooling temperature-control valve remains closed until the EQUIPMENT switch on the AIR CONDITIONING control panel is momentarily actuated to reset.

AFT BLEED Caution Light

The AFT BLEED caution light on the annunciator panel comes on when the aft bleed-air shutoff valve in the main bleed-air duct in the right engine compartment is closed. If this light is lit, electronic equipment must be shut down to prevent overheat damage.

EQUIPMENT Switch

The EQUIPMENT switch is a three-position toggle switch on the AIR CONDITIONING control panel marked COLD, NORM, and RESET. In the NORM position, automatic temperature control of equipment cooling air is provided, or in the event of temperature-control malfuction, unregulated cooled air is provided. The RESET position is used to restore automatic operation of the system after the TEMP CONT light has gone off. The COLD position closes the equipment-cooling temperature-control valve, directing unregulated refrigerated air to the system.

COMPUTER Overheat Light

The COMPUTER light on the annunciator panel comes on when the temperature of the computer has exceeded a safe level.

> **CAUTION**
>
> If the COMPUTER light comes on, the computer should be secured immediately to prevent damage.

TEMP CONT Caution Light

The TEMP CONT caution light on the annunciator panel comes on when an overtemperature in the equipment-cooling system has caused the equipment-cooling temperature-control valve to close, directing only refrigerated air to the system. The light remains on until the temperature in the equipment cooling duct is reduced to less than 150°F. The light should go out in approximately 30 seconds, the time required for the valve to close. If the light remains on for more than 30 seconds, a failure of the thermal switch or the equipment-cooling temperature-control valve is indicated. If the thermal switch has failed, setting the EQUIPMENT switch to COLD should close the valve and turn off the light.

> **CAUTION**
>
> If the TEMP CONT light remains on more than 30 seconds after selecting COLD, a failure of the equipment-cooling temperature-control valve is indicated. To prevent overheat damage, set the AIR COND BLEED shutoff valve to OFF and secure electronic equipment.

TRIM POD ENVIRONMENTAL CONTROL SYSTEM (A-6C)

A separate environmental control system is provided in the TRIM pod, which uses engine bleed air to produce conditioned air for pod heating, cooling, pressurization, and window defogging. The turret air temperature is maintained by an additional liquid cooling unit (powered through the TV/IR POD AIR COND 2 circuit breaker on the main circuit breaker) and air circulating fans.

> **CAUTION**
>
> In aircraft incorporating AFC 268, the TRIM pod environmental control system is inoperative with the left engine shut down or with the AIR COND bleed-air isolation valve closed.

TV/IR Cooling Switch

The TV/IR COOLING switch is a three-position toggle switch on the center console marked OFF, NORM, and RESET, which controls the engine bleed-air valve and turns on the POD CLG light. Selecting

OFF closes the engine bleed-air valve. The NORM position permits automatic operation of the engine bleed-air valve. The RESET position is used to reset the valve for automatic operation in the event of malfunction. There is no provision for manual operation of the engine bleed-air valve.

Pod Cooling Light

The POD CLG light on the annunciator panel comes on steady to indicate that the engine bleed-air valve is closed, the liquid coolant temperature exceeds 150°F, or coolant pressure is below 2 psi. When the POD CLG light comes on, the pod environmental control system is shut down, but the sensors remain on. The light flashes if the system is dead-ended.

> **CAUTION**
>
> If the POD CLG light comes on and cannot be reset, the TV and IR sensors should be shut down to prevent equipment damage.

The operation of the light may be tested by depressing the pilot's LTS WARN button.

Turret Hot Light

The TUR HOT light on the annunciator panel comes on to indicate that the air temperature in the turret that houses the optical sensor platform and FLIR and LLLTV receivers is above 135°. When the light comes on, the TV and IR sensors are secured automatically. The ECS remains on. The operation of the light may be checked by depressing the pilot's master test button. If the TV/IR POD AIR COND 2 circuit breaker becomes disengaged, power will be lost to the liquid cooling pump. The air-cycle machine will continue to run, but the TUR HOT light as well as the COMPUTER light will come on. If the POD CLG light was on, it will go out.

GROUND COOLING SYSTEM (A-6E)

The ground cooling system provides cooling air for specially cooled electronic equipment when operating on external power.

GROUND COOLING (A-6E 158041 THRU 159579 AND MOD M1 THRU M120)

The ground cooling system automatically provides cooling air to components of the computer, radar, INS, and CNI. The ground blower operates to draw in outside air when the right generator is OFF, external power is applied, and either the search radar POWER switch, the COMPUTER power switch on the DDU, or the CNI MASTER switch is set ON.

> **CAUTION**
>
> When the right generator is on the line, the ground blower is automatically turned OFF and equipment-cooling air is supplied by the engines. During ground operation with engines running and the ground blower OFF, the radar units in the nose radome are cooled by cabin discharge air. Operation of the radar with the canopy OPEN and the ground blower OFF must be limited to no more than 5 minutes.

Provisions are made to connect external cooling air when ambient temperature exceeds 103°F or when the aircraft is in an enclosed, poorly ventilated area.

Equipment protection circuits are provided to warn of overheating in the computer and to shut down both the sensitive electronic equipment and the ground blower. When temperatures in the pedestal control unit exceed 176°F, or temperatures exceed 230°F in the computer or analog-to-digital converter, the COMPUTER light comes on and power to the computer, the analog-to-digital converter, the radar, and the CNI package is interrupted. The light will remain on until the equipment cools to below the overheat temperature. After sufficient cooling, power may be restored by depressing the RESET button on the ground cooling panel in the nosewheel well.

Ground Cooling Switch

The ground cooling toggle switch on the ground cooling panel in the nosewheel well has three positions marked TEST, AUTO, CART. The TEST position is used to test the operation of the ground blower. The CART position permits use of the ground cooling system with external cooling air. The ground blower does not operate when CART is selected. The normal AUTO position permits the system to operate in the automatic mode.

Note

The ground cooling switch automatically returns to the AUTO position when external electric power is turned off.

GROUND COOLING (A-6E 159895 AND ON AND MOD M121 AND ON)

The ground cooling system automatically provides cooling air to components of the radar; inertial navigation system (CAINS); communications, navigation, and identification (CNI); detection and ranging set (DRS); and computer. Automatic operation of the system occurs when external electrical power is applied, any of the above systems are operating, and the AUTO/TEST switch on the ground blower panel in the nosewheel well is set to AUTO.

The system contains two cooling fans: a ground blower in the nosewheel well, and the CAINS PSU fan in the left shoulder compartment. External cooling air may be applied when ambient temperature is excessive or the aircraft is in an enclosed, poorly ventilated area. In this case, a low-pressure switch downstream of the ground cooling inlet turns the cooling fans off when pressure of the external cooling air is applied. The pressure switch turns the fans on when external air is shut off.

If an overtemperature condition occurs in any of the specially cooled electronic equipment during ground operation, power to all of the specially cooled electronic systems will be cut off. After the affected equipment has cooled below operating limits, the specially cooled electronic equipment can be enabled by momentarily placing the RESET switch on the ground blower panel in the RESET position.

The TACAN has a separate fan, which operates whenever the TACAN is on.

Ground Cooling Panel

The ground cooling panel in the nosewheel well contains the circuit protection and controls for the ground cooling system.

TEST/AUTO switch - Selecting TEST operates the ground cooling fans with no equipment operating. Selecting AUTO enables automatic operation of the system.

RESET switch - Momentarily selecting RESET restores electrical power to specially cooled equipment if the equipment has cooled sufficiently after an overtemperature has caused a power interruption.

ENGINE ANTI-ICING

An independent system for preventing or removing ice at the engine inlet guide vanes is provided on each engine. Hot air, taken directly from the compressor, is ducted to the vane area when the pilot anticipates icing conditions. The engine anti-ice switch controls the engine anti-ice system. (See figure 1-33.)

ENGINE ANTI-ICE SWITCH

The engine anti-ice switch is a two-position toggle switch (ON and OFF) on the AIR CONDITIONING control panel (figure 1-33). Placing the switch ON allows electrical power to energize the anti-icing air shutoff valve, which opens to allow hot engine bleed air to be distributed to the guide vanes.

CIRCUIT PROTECTION

Several circuit breakers protect the components of the environmental control system. The AIR COND circuit breaker in the nosewheel well provides 28 V dc from the primary bus while 28 V dc from the essential bus goes through the AIR COND 2 circuit breaker on the main circuit breaker panel. Power from the 115 V ac essential bus is provided through the LAT LONG TRIM circuit breaker on the main circuit breaker panel. The ENVIRONMENT SEATS and EQUIP COOL circuit breakers on the bombardier/navigator's circuit breaker panel provide 115 V ac from the primary bus. The BLEED AIR circuit breaker on the B/N's circuit breaker panel supplied 115 V ac from the essential bus to the bleed-air isolation valves. On non-TRAM A-6E aircraft, the CNI AUX BLOWER circuit breaker on the auxiliary aft bay circuit breaker panel supplies 115 V ac from the primary bus to the CNI auxiliary cooling blower. On TRAM configured A-6E, the EQUIP COOLING circuit breaker and the CAINS PSU FAN circuit breaker on the auxiliary aft bay circuit breaker panel provide 28 V dc and 115 V three-phase ac from the primary bus.

PITOT HEAT

The pitot heat switch, on the AIR CONDITIONING control panel (figure 1-33), is a two-position switch marked ON and OFF. Placing the switch ON allows electrical power to be supplied from the 28 V dc primary bus to a conventional heater in the pitot tube. It also allows, through the left weight-on-wheels switch, heat to be provided to the angle-of-attack and total-temperature probes when airborne.

OXYGEN SYSTEM

The liquid oxygen system delivers gaseous oxygen to the crew to enable them to operate above 10,000 feet altitude and to maintain peak body efficiency at altitudes above 5,000 feet. In the MK GRU-5 ejection seat, the system delivers oxygen mixed with cockpit ambient air up to an altitude of approximately 30,000 feet; however, 100% oxygen is available at any time. Above 30,000 feet, an aneroid device in the system automatically closes off the entrance of ambient air. In the MK GRU-7 ejection seat, 100% oxygen is provided at all times. The oxygen source of the system is a supply of liquid oxygen stored in a 10-liter oxygen converter in the aft equipment compartment. In addition, the converter installation has provision for the installation of a second similar converter for use during long-range missions. System pressure is maintained at 70 to 100 psi by pressure-opening and pressure-closing valves on the converter and by a system relief valve. See figure 1-35 for oxygen duration.

AIRCRAFT
Systems

Liquid oxygen is converted into gaseous oxygen and is delivered through a single line to the heat exchanger and plenum assemblies on the aft sloping bulkhead of the cockpit. In the plenum, temperature-conditioned oxygen is stored before being delivered through the shutoff valves to the seat-mounted personnel services disconnects. On the MK GRU-7 seat, a line from the personnel services disconnect goes to a distribution point in the left rear corner of the survival kit. The emergency oxygen supply also connects to this point. The oxygen regulators, one for each crewmember, govern the pressure and flow of gaseous oxygen to the face mask of the seat occupant.

OXYGEN QUANTITY GAGE

The oxygen quantity gage (figure FO-2 sheets 1, 2 and 3) at the top right side of the pilot's instrument panel indicates the quantity of liquid oxygen in the converter. The gage reads 20 liters maximum, so as to be usable when two converters are used.

OXYGEN CAUTION LIGHT

The oxygen caution light on the annunciator panel (figure FO-11) indicates that sufficient pressure is not being maintained, or that the liquid oxygen indicator is 2 liters or less. When the oxygen pressure drops below 50 psi, a pressure switch, attached to one of the oxygen pressure lines, is closed. This allows electrical power to turn on the oxygen warning light.

LOX/FUEL/OIL Press-To-Test Button

Pressing the LOX/FUEL/OIL press-to-test button on the master test panel causes the oxygen quantity gage to drop to zero and the oxygen warning light to come on.

SEAT MOUNTED OXYGEN REGULATOR

In aircraft incorporating the MK GRU-5 ejection seat, a diluter-demand oxygen regulator (Bendix 29255 series) in the right side of each ejection seat (figure 1-27) allows the pilot and the bombardier/navigator to direct oxygen flow to their face masks as desired.

The regulator automatically provides positive-pressure breathing above a cabin pressure altitude of approximately 35,000 feet and during ejection above that ambient altitude.

Oxygen Regulator Selector Knob

This control is on the top of the regulator assembly (figure 1-27) and is used to position the internal valve assembly and the aneroid. The knob is rotated counterclockwise to the full UP position to get diluter-demand operation of the regulator. Rotating the knob clockwise repositions the valve, permitting 100% oxygen flow to the mask.

WARNING

During in-flight emergencies such as cockpit or electrical fires, the oxygen regulator selector valve should be positioned for 100% oxygen flow to prevent smoke and fumes from being inhaled.

PERSONAL OXYGEN REGULATOR

In aircraft incorporating the MK GRU-7 ejection seat, each crewmember is provided with a personal-issue oxygen regulator that is compatible with his mask and the aircraft oxygen system.

OXYGEN SUPPLY LEVERS

The oxygen levers on the pilot's left console and bombardier/navigator's right console are two-position lever switches marked ON and OFF and are used to engage the crew's oxygen system. Lifting the lever handle out against the pressure of the lever handle spring disengages the lever from its notch and allows it to be placed ON. This opens the pilot's oxygen shutoff valve, permitting oxygen under pressure to flow through the valve. Placing the lever OFF closes the valve and stops all oxygen flow through the valve.

EMERGENCY OXYGEN SUPPLY

In aircraft incorporating the MK GRU-5 seat, each ejection seat is equipped with a cylinder of compressed oxygen capable of supplying emergency oxygen for approximately 10 minutes (figure 1-27). Each seat is equipped with a pull-type lanyard for switching to emergency oxygen operation.

Since the emergency oxygen supply is attached to the MK GRU-5 seat, oxygen will not be available subsequent to seat separation during an ejection sequence. Therefore, the oxygen mask must be disconnected from the helmet at that time to permit normal effortless breathing. This is particularly important before water entry to avoid inhalation of water.

In aircraft incorporating the MK GRU-7 ejection seat, each survival kit is provided with a cylinder of compressed oxygen capable of supplying emergency oxygen for approximately 15 minutes. A manual control is provided to actuate the emergency supply in the event the aircraft system fails or is depleted.

NAVAIR 01-85ADA-1

AIRCRAFT Systems

OXYGEN DURATION CHART

MAN HOURS OF OXYGEN REMAINING - 100%

CABIN ALTITUDE	LITERS LIQUID O₂										LESS THAN 1
	10	9	8	7	6	5	4	3	2	1	
35,000 FEET and above	32.2	29.0	25.7	22.6	19.3	16.1	12.9	9.6	6.4	3.2	EMERGENCY DESCEND TO ALTITUDE NOT REQUIRING OXYGEN
30,000 FEET	25.5	23.0	20.4	17.9	15.3	12.8	10.2	7.6	5.1	2.5	
25,000 FEET	20.5	18.4	16.4	14.3	12.3	10.2	8.2	6.1	4.1	2.0	
20,000 FEET	16.5	14.8	13.2	11.5	9.9	8.2	6.7	4.9	3.3	1.6	
15,000 FEET	13.4	12.1	10.7	9.4	8.0	6.7	5.3	4.0	2.6	1.3	
10,000 FEET	11.0	9.9	8.8	7.7	6.6	5.5	4.4	3.3	2.2	1.1	
8,000 FEET	10.3	9.3	8.2	7.2	6.2	5.1	4.1	3.1	2.1	1.0	
5,000 FEET	9.2	8.3	7.4	6.5	5.5	4.6	3.7	2.8	1.8	.9	
SEA LEVEL	7.6	6.8	6.0	5.3	4.5	3.8	3.0	1.9	1.5	.7	

NOTE

- WHEN TWO PERSONS ARE USING OXYGEN, DIVIDE THE NUMBER OF HOURS REMAINING BY TWO.
- DURATION DATA SHOULD BE USED AS A GUIDE ONLY SINCE OXYGEN CONSUMPTION VARIES WITH THE INDIVIDUAL.
- CONVERSION OF LIQUID O_2 TO GASEOUS O_2 IS 860 LITERS OF GASEOUS TO 1 LITER OF LIQUID O_2
- CONSUMPTION RATES ARE BASED ON MIL 1-19326B
- CONSUMPTION RATES SHOWN ARE FOR 1 MAN.

Figure 1-35

AIRCRAFT
Systems

NAVAIR 01-85ADA-1

Since the emergency oxygen supply is in the survival kit, oxygen is available during the parachute descent; however, the mask should be removed after the parachute opens to prevent suffocation after the oxygen supply is depleted.

Emergency Oxygen Manual Control

In aircraft incorporating the MK GRU-5 ejection seat, a ring attached to the individual emergency oxygen bottle through a cable and linkage assembly on the right side of each ejection seat (figure 1-27) allows the pilot and bombardier/navigator to actuate an emergency oxygen supply. Pulling the ring opens a valve, allowing oxygen to pass through the regulator and on to the mask.

In aircraft incorporating the MK GRU-7 ejection seat, the emergency oxygen supply is actuated manually by pulling a green ring on the inside left thigh of the survival kit. When the ring is pulled, a cable opens the valve on the emergency oxygen cylinder allowing oxygen to flow to the regulator. The ring and cable come free when the valve opens.

Note

The emergency oxygen supply is automatically actuated when the Martin-Baker seat is ejected.

LIGHTING SYSTEMS

INTERIOR LIGHTING

The interior lighting system provides maximum controlled lighting for the instrument panels and consoles, and consists of the pilot's lighting system, bombardier/navigator's lighting system, and the aft equipment bay dome light and switch.

The pilot's lighting system consists of the flight instrument lights, console lights, indexer light, floodlights, kneeboard light, utility light, and daylight floodlights. The system provides the pilot with complete control over the lighting of his instrument panel and consoles as well as the intensity of all caution and advisory lights.

The bombardier/navigator's lighting system consists of the bombardier/navigator's instrument panel lights, bombardier/navigator's console lights, and the utility light. The system provides the bombardier/navigator with complete control over the lighting of his instrument panel and console.

The aft equipment bay dome light and switch system is on the top of the aft equipment bay and provides lighting of the bay for maintenance personnel. This light can be turned on only when external electrical power is supplied to the aircraft.

Electrical power for lighting of all flight instruments is supplied by the 28 V dc and 115 V ac essential buses, and power for lighting of all other instruments comes from the 28 V dc and 115 V ac monitored buses. Power for the utility light is supplied by the essential bus. All controls for operation of the pilot's internal lighting system except the kneeboard, utility, and daylight floodlights are on the master light panel, and those used for the bombardier/navigator's lighting system are on the internal lights panel.

Daylight Floodlights

Four daylight floodlights are mounted on the canopy bow to minimize the possibility of flash blinding due to lighting or to nuclear blast (with or without the radiation shield). Two 40-watt lamps are oriented to illuminate the pilot's and the bombardier/navigator's instrument panels. Two 20-watt lamps illuminate the left and right consoles. The lights are controlled by a three-position switch on the aft side of the canopy bow. The positions of the switch are BRIGHT (forward), OFF (center), and DIM (aft).

Utility Lights

There are three utility lights in the cockpit. Two of the lights are on either side of the cockpit on the cockpit longerons. The third light is overhead on the canopy bow. Each light has an individual ON/OFF switch, a rheostat control, and the option of red or white filter and flood or spot illumination. Alligator clips and swivel mountings allow the lights to be placed in any convenient location for maximum use.

Pilot's Kneeboard Light

The pilot's kneeboard light (figure 1-36) is on the canopy bow and directs a beam of light to the pilot's right knee. The light is controlled by an individual ON/OFF switch mounted on the light.

Bombardier/Navigator's Map Light

The bombardier/navigator's map light is on the lower right side of the canopy. An ON/OFF rheostat switch is used to place the light on or off.

PILOT'S INTERIOR LIGHT CONTROLS

Flight Instrument Lights Control

The pilot's flight instrument lights thumbwheel is on the master light panel (figure 1-36) and controls the lighting of the flight instruments on the pilot's instrument panel and the caution and advisory lights. Rotating the flight instrument thumbwheel to dim lights the instruments at a low intensity, whereas with the thumbwheel at bright, they will light with maximum intensity. Provisions are incorporated into the pilot's flight instrument lighting circuitry so that the flight instrument lights must be lit before nonflight instruments may be lighted. This control also actuates the warning light dimming circuits. The warning lights are dim when the instrument thumbwheel is in the full bright position and bright when the thumbwheel is in the dim position.

1-100

LIGHTING CONTROLS

OVERHEAD UTILITY AND FLOODLIGHTS

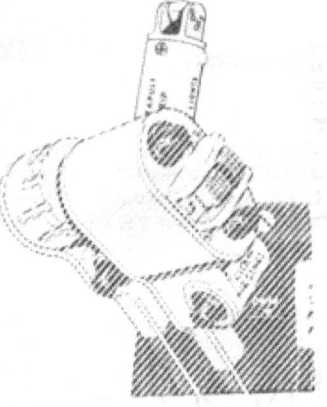

A-6A,B,C 149941 THRU 154169 NOT INCORPORATING AFC NO. 148

Figure 1-36

AIRCRAFT
Systems

Console Lights Control

The pilot's console lights control on the master light panel (figure 1-36), controls the illumination of the pilot's left and center consoles and the optical sight-head elevation thumbwheel. With the flight instrument thumbwheel set at either dim or bright, rotating the console thumbwheel to dim lights the instruments on the pilot's left and center consoles at a low intensity. Conversely, rotating the thumbwheel to bright lights the instruments at maximum intensity.

Approach Indexer Light Control

The indexer light thumbwheel on the master light panel (figure 1-36) controls the lighting of the approach light indexer. With the flight instrument thumbwheel set at either dim or bright, rotating the indexer thumbwheel to dim lights the indexer at a low intensity. Conversely, rotating the thumbwheel to bright lights the indexer at maximum intensity.

BOMBARDIER/NAVIGATOR'S INTERIOR LIGHT CONTROLS

The lighting control panel (figure 1-36) is on the bombardier/navigator's right console, immediately aft of the oxygen control panel. The function of each of the control switches is provided in the following paragraphs.

INTERIOR LIGHTING CONTROL PANEL

Panel Light Control

The panel light control (figure 1-36), permits the bombardier/navigator to adjust the intensity of the control panel lighting. The control has OFF and bright (BRT) positions, with intermediate positions offering varying degrees of panel light intensity.

Console Light Control

The console light control (figure 1-36) permits the bombardier/navigator to adjust the right console lighting. The control has DIM and bright (BRT) positions, with intermediate positions offering varying degrees of console light intensity.

Note

The console cannot be lighted until the panel light control has first been rotated ON.

Floodlight Control Switch

The floodlight control switch (FLOOD) (figure 1-36) is a three-position toggle switch that controls the floodlights below the canopy sill and below the glare shield. The switch provides for three operating conditions: bright (BRT), DIM, AND OFF.

Daylight Floodlight Switch

The daylight floodlight switch (DAY FLOOD LTS) (figure 1-36) is a three-position (BRT, OFF, and DIM), switch on the aft side of the canopy bow, that may be actuated by the pilot or bombardier/navigator. When the switch is placed to BRT or DIM, two 40-watt lamps are oriented to illuminate the pilot's and bombardier/navigator's instrument panels and two 20-watt lamps illuminate the left and right consoles. Under normal conditions, the daylight floodlights switch will be in the OFF position and should be used only when there is need for a high-intensity source of light.

EXTERIOR LIGHTING

Position, formation, anticollision, refueling probe, and taxi lights make up the aircraft exterior lighting. The position lights are in the leading edge of the right and left wings, in the trailing edge of the pylons at stations 1 and 5, and in the tail of the aircraft. The right-wing position light is green, the left-wing position light is red, the pylon position lights are amber, and the tail position light is white. Provisions have been made to permit the pilot to send visual code with the pylon lights. The formation lights are: a yellow light on either side of the fuselage (aft of the wing trailing edge), a red light on the left wing tip, and a green light on the right wing tip. Each of the wing tip formation lights contains two lenses: one in the upper portion of the wing tip and the other in the lower portion. Two anticollision lights, one on the vertical stabilizer and one on the nose-gear door fairing, are used on the aircraft. The nose-gear light automatically goes off when the nose gear is extended. Each of the anticollision lights contains two rotating lamps and a red lens. (For tanker missions a green lens is substituted.) The taxi is on the nose-gear door fairing. All controls for the exterior lights are on the master light panel (figure 1-36), except the exterior lights master switch pushbutton, which is on the catapult grip.

Anticollision Light Switch

The anticollision light switch controls the anticollision lights on the vertical stabilizer and on the nosegear door fairing. On A-6E 159895 and ON, and A-6E Mod M121 and ON, the anticollision lights are on the vertical stabilizer and on bottom of each engine cowling. The switch is a two-position toggle switch on the master light panel (figure 1-36) and has positions marked ON and OFF. Placing the collision light switch ON directs 115 Vac power from the primary bus to the anticollision lights.

When the landing gear is extended, the anticollision light relay becomes energized and the anticollision light on the nose-gear door fairing goes off. In the KA-6D, the anticollision lights are generally green for identification purposes.

Exterior Lights Master Switch

The exterior lights master switch is a two-position toggle switch on the end of the catapult grip marked ON/OFF. With the exception of the anticollision lights, no external lights can be turned on until the exterior lights master switch has been set to ON.

Pylon Light Controls

The pylon position lights may be operated from the master light control panel by a momentary KEY pushbutton switch or pylon toggle switch marked ON, OFF, and KEY, when the external lights master switch on the catapult grip is ON.

In aircraft with the momentary pushbutton switch, power is applied to the pylon position lights whenever the button is depressed, permitting them to be keyed to send visual code. As an aid to signalling, the KEY LT indicator light glows whenever the pylon lights are on.

In aircraft with the toggle switch, holding the switch to the momentary KEY position causes the pylon lights and the KEY LT indicator light to come on, permitting the pylon lights to be keyed to send visual code. Selecting the OFF position removes power from the pylon lights. The lights may still be operated by means of the air-refueling control panel master switch when the pylon switch is off. Selecting the ON position applies power to the pylon lights, permitting their use as position lights.

Wing Light Switch

The wing light switch, on the master light panel (figure 1-36), controls the position lights on the right and left wings. The switch is a three-position toggle switch marked BRT, OFF, and DIM. With the exterior lights master switch pushbutton actuated to ON, placing the wing position light switch to BRT turns the wing position lights on bright, using 28 V dc power from the monitored bus. Placing the switch to DIM puts a resistor in series with the lights and dims them.

Tail Light Switch

The tail light switch controls the position light on the tail. The switch is a three-position toggle switch on the master light panel (figure 1-36) and is placarded BRT, OFF, and DIM. With the exterior lights master switch actuated to ON, placing the tail position light switch to BRT turns the tail position light on bright, using 28 V dc power from the monitored bus. Placing the switch to DIM turns on the light at a dimmed intensity.

Key Light and Key Pushbutton

The KEY light and KEY pushbutton on the master light panel (figure 1-36) allows the crew to signal with the pylon position lights. Depressing the key pushbutton causes the pylon position lights to come on. The key light reproduces the signal being displayed by the pylon position light. The master lights switch on the catapult grip must be on for the above operation.

Formation Light Switch

The formation light switch on the master light panel (figure 1-36) is a three-position toggle switch marked BRT, OFF, and DIM. The switch controls the formation lights on either side of the fuselage and at the left and right wing tips. With the external lights master switch pushbutton actuated to ON, placing the formation light switch to BRT connects 28 V dc power from the monitored bus to all formation lights. Selecting the DIM position of the switch dims the lights by putting a resistor in series with them.

Taxi Light Switch

The taxi light switch on the master light control panel (figure 1-36) is a two-position, bar-type switch placarded ON and OFF. The switch controls the taxi light on the nose-door fairing. Placing the switch ON directs electrical power to turn on the taxi light when operating with landing gear down and locked.

In aircraft with the switch placarded TAXI/PROBE, it also controls the air-refueling probe light on the forward fuselage. Placing the switch ON directs electrical power to turn on the air-refueling probe light when landing gear is up and locked. With the landing gear down and locked, the taxi light is lit.

MISCELLANEOUS EQUIPMENT

ARMOR PLATE

Armorplate is located on the engine access door below the engine accessory sections, below the fuel shutoff valves, below the elevator and rudder hydraulic actuators, on the wings below the flaperon actuators, and below the ECM equipment in the tail section (figure 1-37).

FLAK CURTAINS

The aircraft has provisions for installation of flak curtains or small arms shields. Canopy curtains are installed in the lower left and right sides of the sliding canopy. A slide fastener along the top forward edge may be zippered open and the curtain folded down to improve visibility (figure 1-38). Additional protection is installed against the fuselage

ARMOR PLATE

INSTALLATION OF ARMOR PLATE FOR VULNERABLE FLIGHT CONTROL AREAS

1. FUEL CONTROLS
   (External plates over engine access doors)

2. FLAPERON ACTUATORS
   (External plates below each wing)

3. FUEL VALVES
   (Internal plates wishbone area)

4. ECM EQUIPMENT
   (Internal plates)

5. ELEVATOR and RUDDER ACTUATORS
   (External plates)

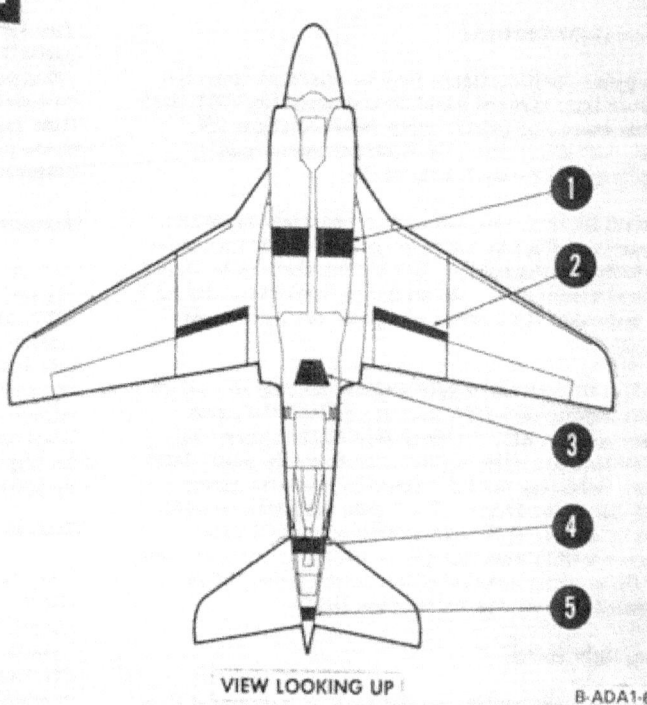

VIEW LOOKING UP

Figure 1-37

FLAK CURTAINS AND RADIATION SHIELD

FLAK CURTAINS

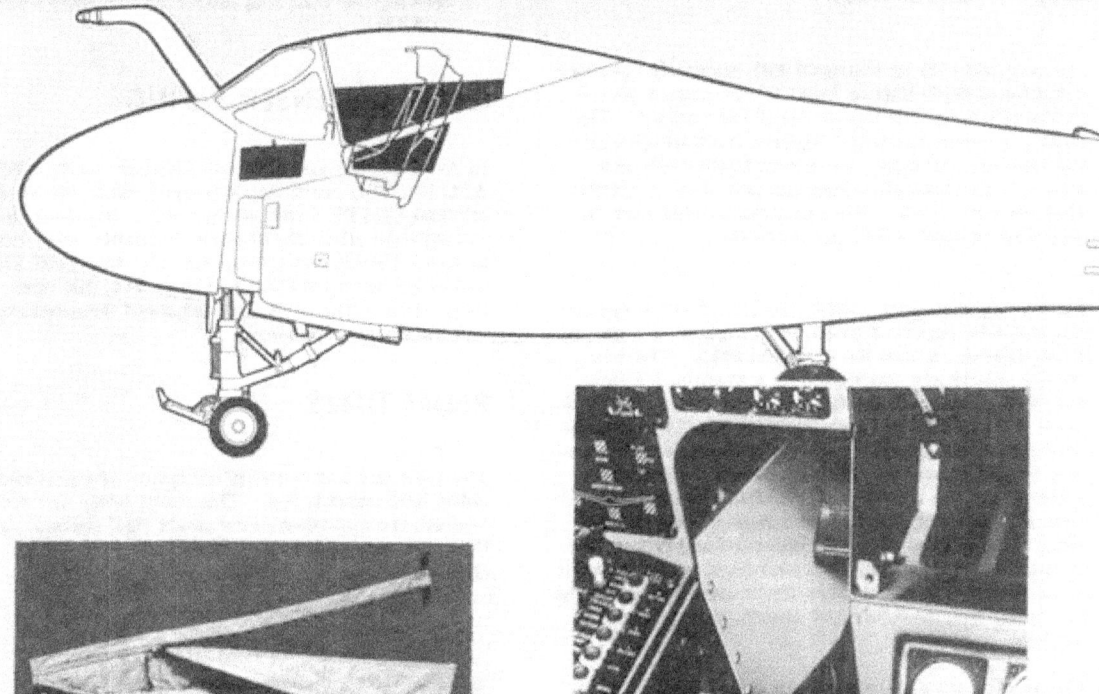

CANOPY FLAK CURTAIN (TYPICAL)

LEFT RUDDER SCUFF PLATE SHIELD

RADIATION SHIELDS

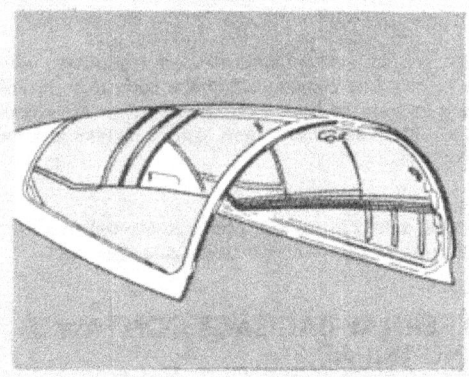

EXTEND TELESCOPING SECTIONS

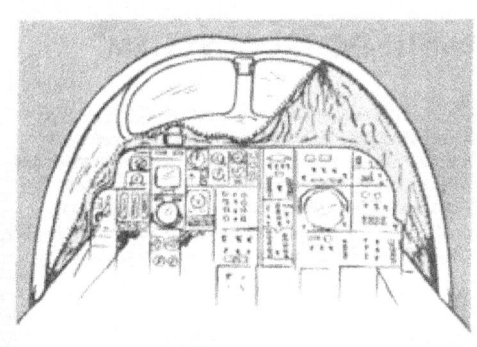

ZIP-UP FORWARD LINING

Figure 1-38

above the pilot's and bombardier/navigator's consoles. A flak shield is also available for installation on the pilot's left rudder scuff plate (figure 1-38).

RADIATION SHIELDS

The aircraft may be equipped with manually operated radiation shields (figure 1-38) to completely shield off the glass-enclosed portions of the cockpit. The shields present an opaque surface from which light and heat are reflected, providing flight crew protection from flash blindness and heat during special weapons deliveries. The radiation shields may be closed or opened at will during flight.

The canopy radiation shield consists of two fixed and two movable panels of molded fiber glass at each side of the canopy, inside the enclosed area. The two sliding panels are suspended on a system of tracks and rollers between the canopy spine and a fixed side panel. When stowed, both movable panels telescope inside a fixed aft panel. When the shields are in use, they extend forward to the canopy bow, completely blanking out the canopy. The shield assemblies in each side of the canopy move independently of each other and must be manually unlocked and positioned by the pilot and bombardier/navigator. The forward movable panel automatically locks when moved to the full open, half open, or full closed (canopy arch) position.

The windshield radiation shield is an aluminized fiber glass cloth that is attached to the glare shield mounted on top of the instrument panel underneath the windshield. A zipper assembly attached along the entire inner surface of the windshield bow permits the curtain to be drawn up to this position when zippered up by the bombardier/navigator and by the pilot. When closed, it completely shields off the windshields.

EQUIPMENT DESTRUCT SYSTEM

The aircraft is equipped with a system for automatically destroying certain communications and electronic countermeasures equipment. The destruction system when installed operates automatically off the aircraft battery when the ejection seats are fired, when the aircraft is subjected to 60 to 80 g's laterally, or when the aircraft is immersed in salt water.

Ground safing provisions are as follows:

- In aircraft not incorporating AFC No. 281, inserting a flagged pin in the receptacle marked ECM SAFE aft of the left boarding ladder renders the destruct system inoperative.

- In A-6A 155702 and ON, and A-6E 158528 and ON incorporating AFC No. 281, a guarded two-position ECM maintenance safe toggle switch marked ARM and SAFE is in the left boarding-ladder well. When the boarding ladder is down, the switch may be set to SAFE for maintenance. Stowing the boarding ladder moves the switch to ARM.

CHAFF DISPENSER SAFING

In A-6E 158528 and ON, and aircraft incorporating AFC No. 281, inserting a flagged pin in the receptacle marked CHAFF SAFE aft of the left boarding ladder renders the ALE-29/39 chaff dispenser inoperative. In A-6A 155701 and prior, KA-6D, and A-6E 158052 and prior incorporating AFC No. 281, the same flagged pin safes both the equipment destruct system and the chaff dispenser.

RELIEF TUBES

The pilot and bombardier/navigator are provided with individual relief tubes. The relief tubes are stowed beneath the crewmembers' seats (MK GRU-5) or on the right side of the crewmember's seats (MK GRU 7).

Failure to properly stow the relief tube (MK GRU-5 only) on the clamp provided could result in inadvertent firing of the ejection seat or jamming of the emergency harness-release mechanism.

STOWAGE CONTAINERS

Covered rations and data storage containers are on the pilot's left console aft of the optical sight control panel and on the bombardier/navigator's right console. The containers have hinged covers and locking wing nuts.

Ground safety locks and pins are stowed in a compartment in the pilot's boarding-ladder well.

EXTERNAL BAGGAGE CONTAINER (CNU-188/A)

The external baggage container is a modified Aero-1C fuel tank, containing two shelves, mounted center and aft. For external baggage container limitations, see A-6 Tactical Manual NAVAIR 01-85ADA-1T. For detailed loading instructions, see NAVAIR 11-1-CNU-188A-1.

part 3 Aircraft Servicing

AIRCRAFT SERVICING

The following servicing data is provided to lend assistance if the aircraft lands at a strange field or the maintenance crews are unfamiliar with the aircraft. See figure 1-39 for servicing diagram.

Note

When operating in and out of military airfields, consult the current DOD IFR Supplement for compatible servicing units, fuel, etc.

AIRCRAFT FUELING

The aircraft can be fueled and defueled on the ground through a single-point pressure adapter (figure 1-39). The ground fueling and defueling operation is controlled at the fueling station control panel (figure 1-39). The switches on the fueling station control panel operate shutoff valves in the aircraft fuel system, thereby controlling fuel flow into or out of the internal fuel cells of the fuselage, integral wing tanks, and air-refueling store. The aircraft can be fueled with wings folded or spread; however, in order to empty the outboard wing tanks, the wings must be spread during defueling operations.

PNEUMATIC PRESSURES

1. Ram-air turbine accumulator . . . . . 500 psi
2. Combined hydraulic accumulator . . 2,000 psi
3. Flight hydraulic accumulator . . . . 2,000 psi
4. Wheel-brake accumulator . . . . . 800±50 psi
5. Canopy jettison pressure . . . . 2450±100 psi bottle
6. Arresting-hook dashpot pressure . . 1,000 psi (dry nitrogen)
7. Emergency landing gear bottles (dry nitrogen) 2,450 ± 100 psi

8. Landing-gear strut pressures

    a. Nose gear . . . . . 350 psi (dry nitrogen)

    b. Main gear . . . . . See strut nameplates

9. Pneumatic starting compressor. . . 100 lb at 50 psi
10. Equipment pressure . . . . . . 600-2800 psi
11. Surge suppressor . . . 70 psi (dry nitrogen) (KA-6D)

DANGER AREAS

See figures 1-40 and 1-41.

TURNING RADIUS AND GROUND CLEARANCE

See figure 1-42.

POWER REQUIREMENTS

Power requirements for shipboard and shore-based operations are as follows (figure 1-43):

1. Pneumatic starting and electrical power - 23 kVA
2. BACE (all black boxes) - 21 kVA
3. Air Force power units providing 28 V dc require the use of an adapter.

RESERVOIR CAPACITIES

Reservoir capacities are as follows:

1. Flight hydraulic system reservoir - 0.74 gallon.

AIRCRAFT
Aircraft Servicing

NAVAIR 01-85ADA-1

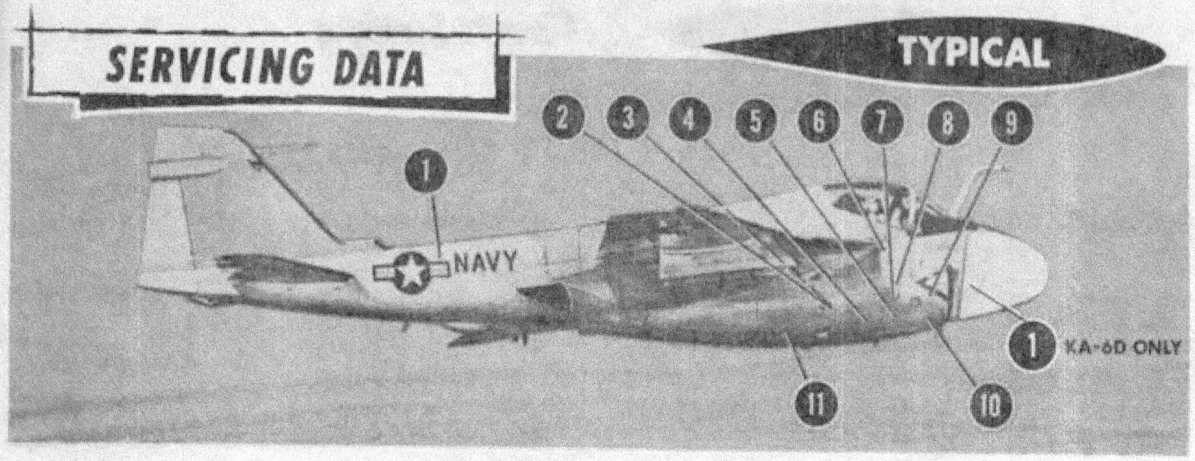

* FUEL GRADE SELECTOR ON ENGINE FUEL CONTROL MUST BE SET FOR GRADE OF FUEL USED

** OIL MIL-L-7808 SHOULD BE USED WHEN GROUND TEMPERATURES ARE -40°C (-40°F) AND BELOW IN WHICH COLD STARTING CAN BECOME A PROBLEM

* FUEL	MIL-J-5624 (JP-5 OR JP-4)
HYDRAULIC FLUID	MIL-H-5606
LIQUID OXYGEN	MIL-O-27210 (TYPE II)
OIL	MIL-L-23699 ** MIL-L-7808
WINDSHIELD WASH METHANOL	MIL-O-M-232D

① LIQUID OXYGEN FILLER VALVE

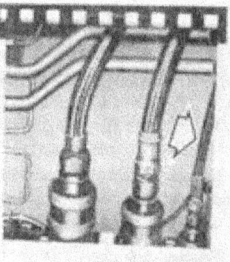
② FLIGHT HYDRAULIC SYSTEM FILLER LINE (RIGHT SIDE)

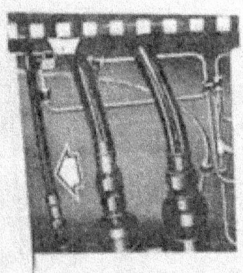
③ COMBINED HYDRAULIC SYSTEM FILLER LINE (LEFT SIDE)

④ ENGINE STARTING RECEPTACLE

⑤ CSD/S FILLER

H-ADA1-30-1

Figure 1-39 (Sheet 1)

1-108

NAVAIR 01-85ADA-1

AIRCRAFT
Aircraft Servicing

⑥ EXTERNAL COOLING AIR CONNECTION

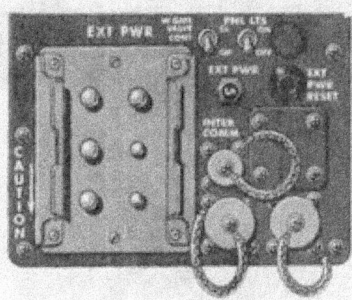
⑦ KA-6D EXTERNAL ELECTRICAL RECEPTACLE

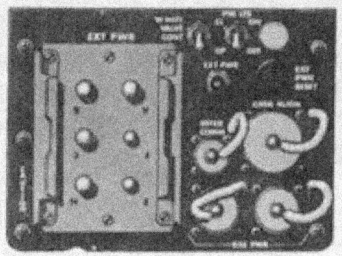
⑦ A-6A,B,C/A-6E EXTERNAL ELECTRICAL RECEPTACLE

⑧ REFUELING STATION CONTROL PANEL

⑨ WINDSHIELD WASH TANK FILLER

⑩ AIRCRAFT FUELING RECEPTACLE

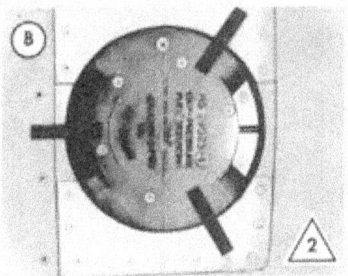
⑩ AIRCRAFT FUELING RECEPTACLE

⑪ OIL SYSTEM FILLER

△1 A6A,B,C 155719 AND PRIOR AND KA6D
△2 A6A,B,C 155720 AND SUBSEQUENT

NOTE

FOR SERVICING THE A-6C TRIM POD REFER TO NAVAIR 01-85ADA-2-1 GENERAL INFORMATION AND SERVICING

Figure 1-39 (Sheet 2)

1-109

RADAR TRANSMISSION DANGER AREAS

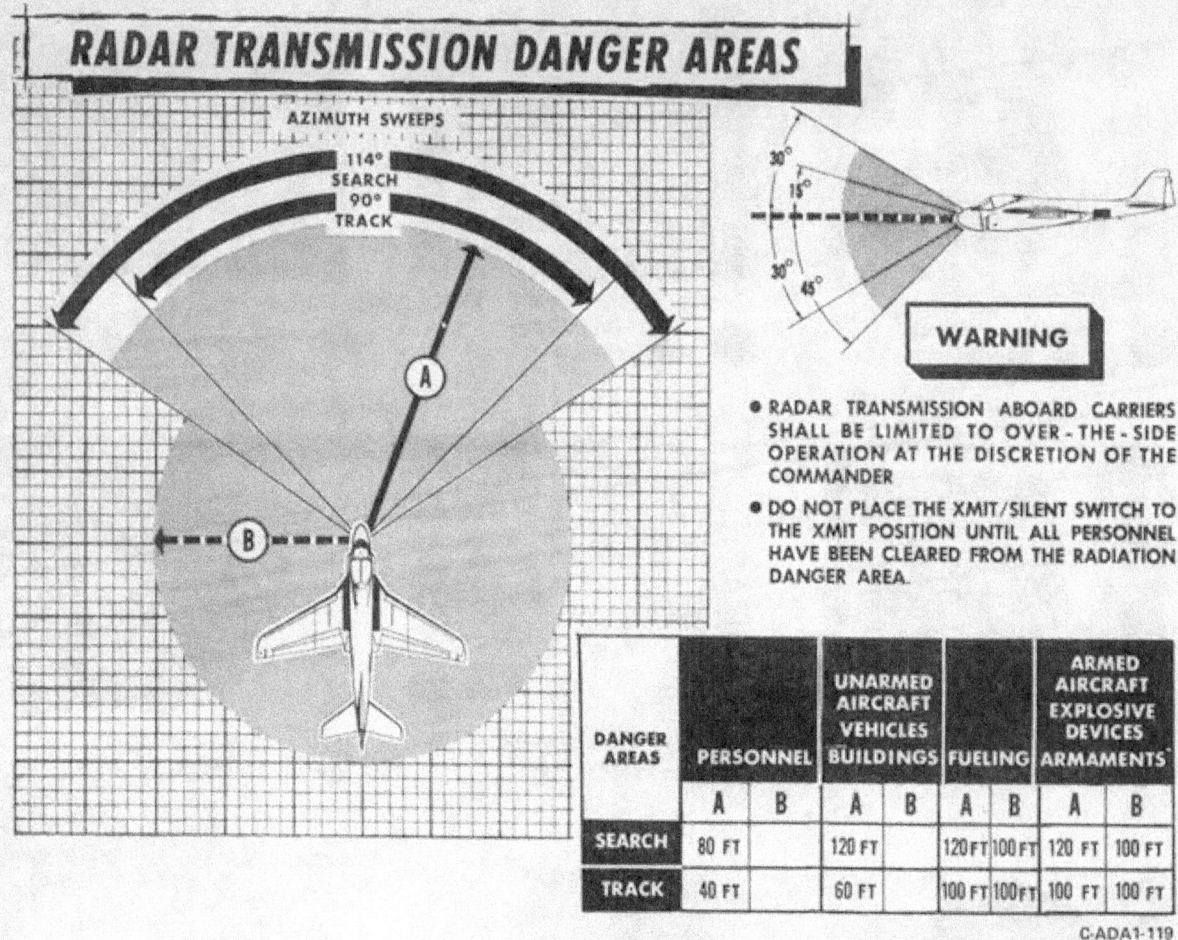

Figure 1-40

2. Combined hydraulic system reservoir - 3.34 gallons.
3. Oxygen converter - 10 liters
4. Auxiliary oxygen converter - 10 liters
5. Smoke abatement tank - 0.9 gallon

TIRES

Tires sizes for the aircraft are:

Main - 36x11-24 P.R. Type VII

Nose - 20x5.5-12 P.R. Type VII or 20x5.5-14 P.R.

Note

Do not mix 12 P.R. and 14 P.R. 20x5.5 tires on nosewheel.

Minimum Tire Inflation Pressure

Main - 230 psi (carrier) - As shown in figure 1-41 (land)
Nose - 290 psi (carrier) - 175 psi (land)

GEAR STOWAGE IN A-6 SERIES AIRCRAFT

The following procedure will apply to stowage of gear in A-6 aircraft.

1. No gear shall be stowed aft of extensible equipment platform in A-6 series aircraft.
2. Gear stowed in aft equipment bay of A-6 aircraft shall be secured within extensible equipment platform or, for KA-6D, forward of extensible platform in area around LOX converters. Any gear stowed within extensible platform shall be stowed in such a manner that no portion of gear protrudes above ladder rails on platform, when platform is in stowed position.
3. Gear may be stowed in forward deck section of observer's side of cockpit in KA-6D.

All gear stowed in the aforementioned areas of the aircraft shall be securely tied.

CAUTION

Care will be taken to insure gear does not restrict movement, damage, or impede the normal operation of any of the aircraft's equipment, nor is tied to an aircraft system actuator (i.e. flight control actuator, etc.).

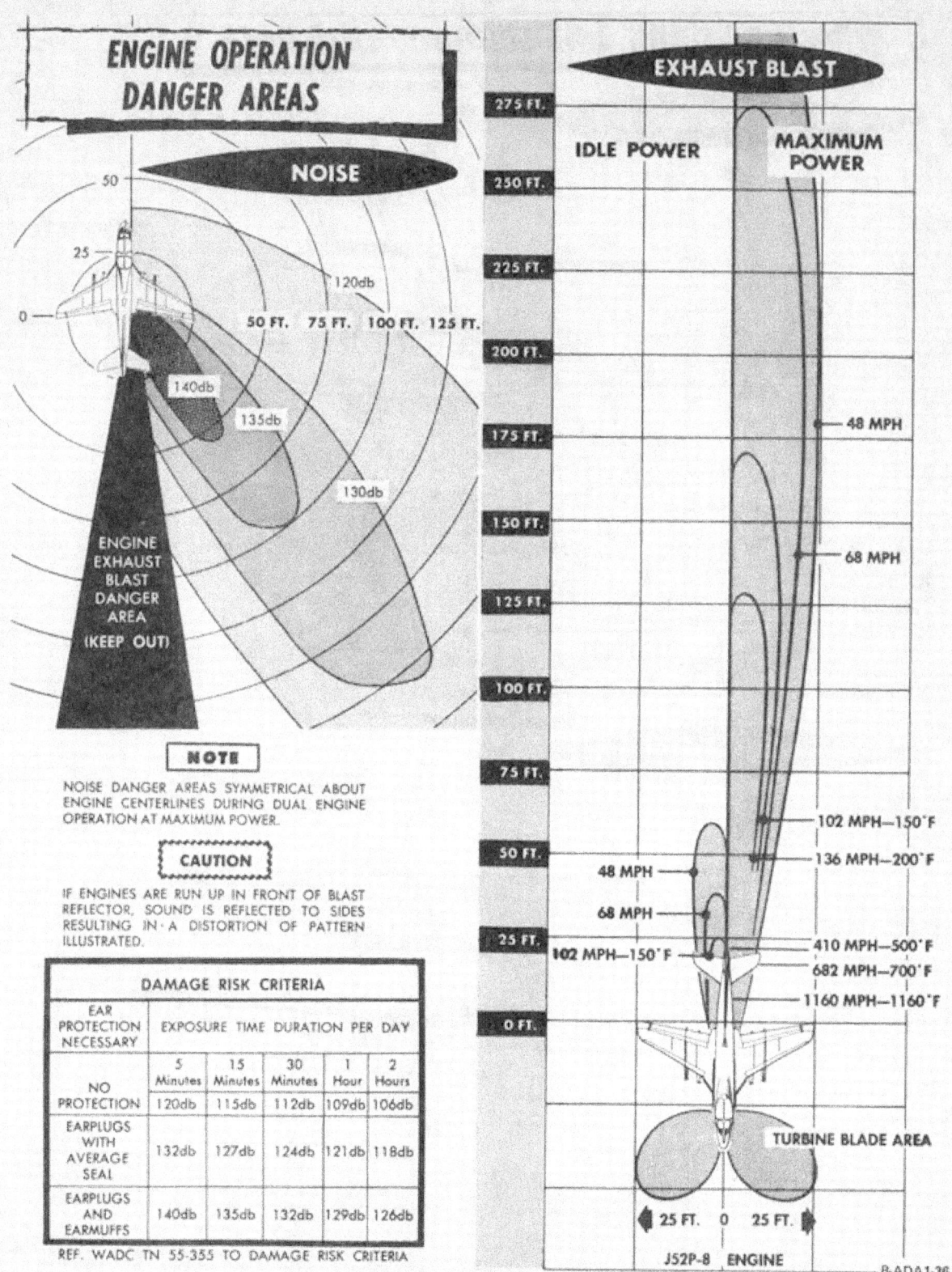

Figure 1-41

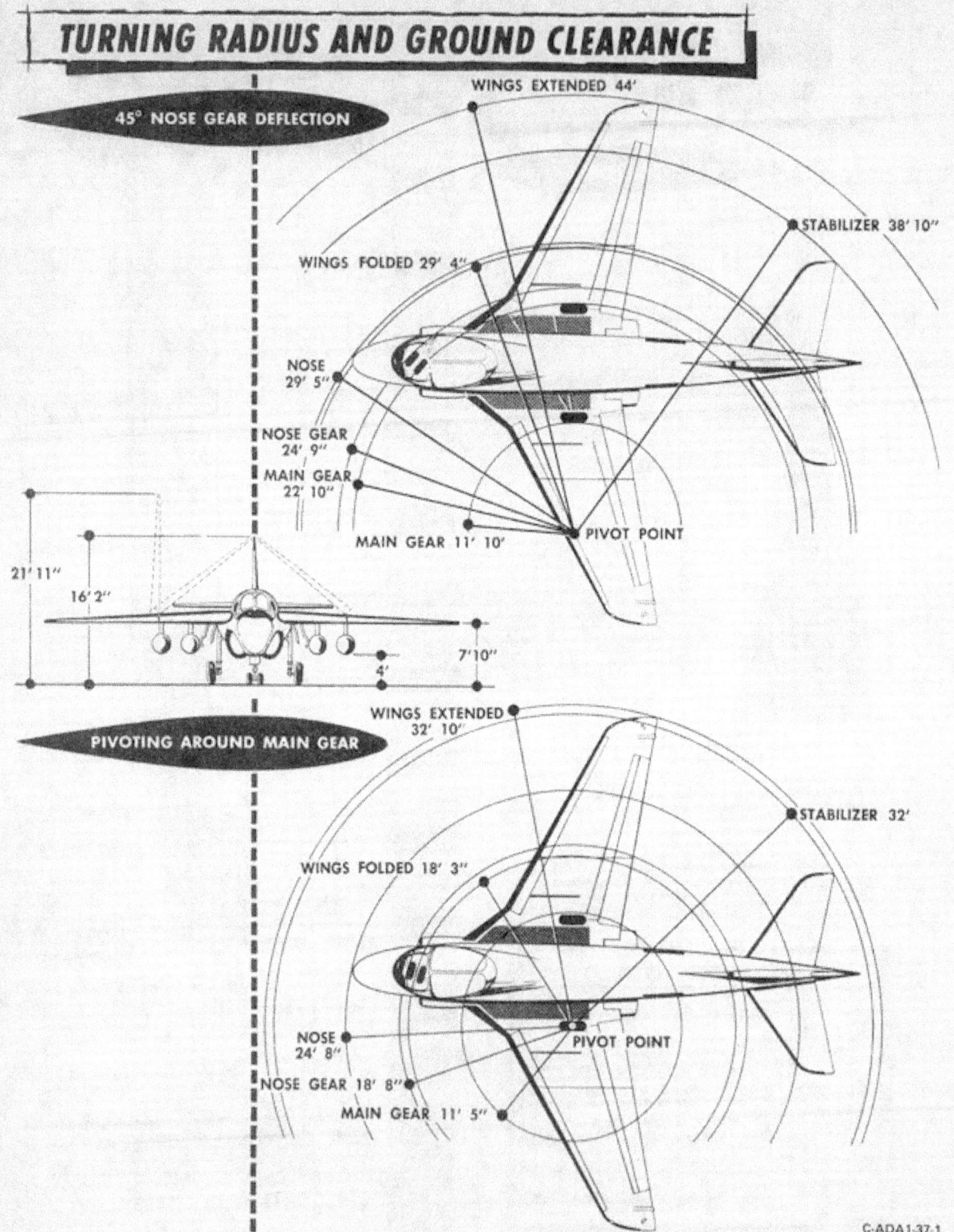

Figure 1-42 (Sheet 1)

NAVAIR 01-85ADA-1

AIRCRAFT
Aircraft Servicing

TURNING RADIUS AND GROUND CLEARANCE

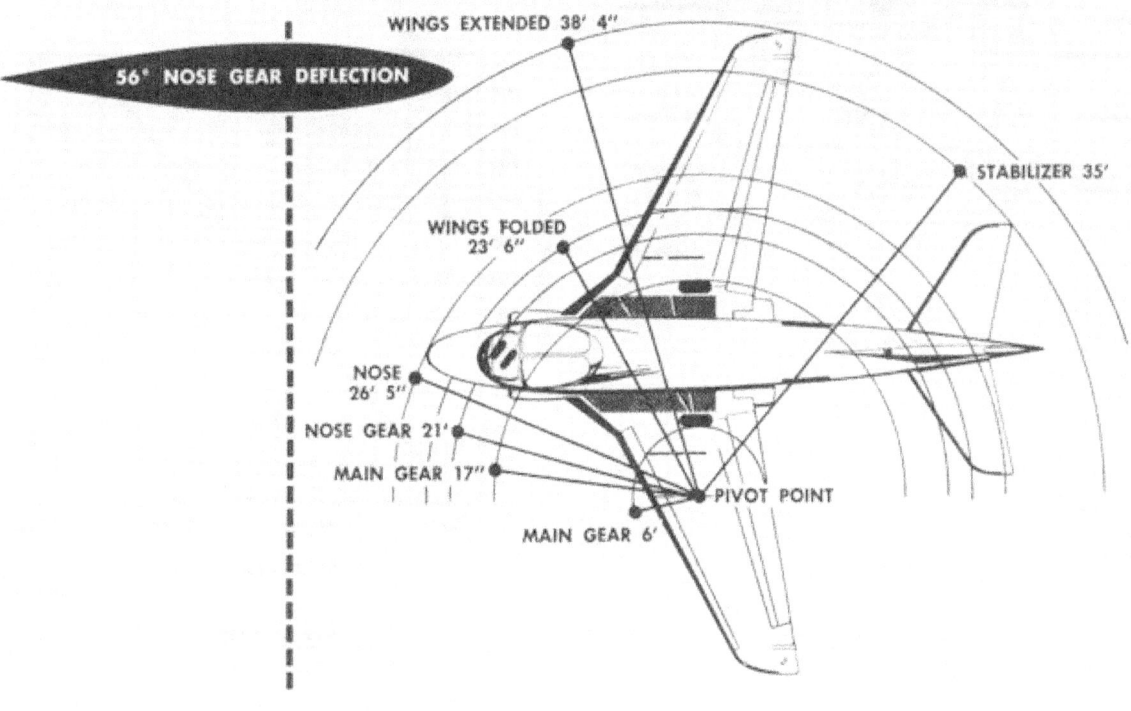

56° NOSE GEAR DEFLECTION

- WINGS EXTENDED 38' 4"
- STABILIZER 35'
- WINGS FOLDED 23' 6"
- NOSE 26' 5"
- NOSE GEAR 21'
- MAIN GEAR 17"
- PIVOT POINT
- MAIN GEAR 6'

CENTERLINE CLEARANCES

A-6A, A-6B / KA-6D / A-6E / [1] A-6E TRAM
D-704 REFUELING STORE
  CATAPULTING (59,000)
    AERO — 7A : 9", AERO — 7B : 11"
  LANDING
    AERO — 7A : 9¼", AERO — 7B : 11½"
  STATIC (53,000)
    AERO — 7A : 13¼", AERO — 7B : 15½"

[1] A-6E 159895 AND ON AND A-6E MOD 121 AND ON

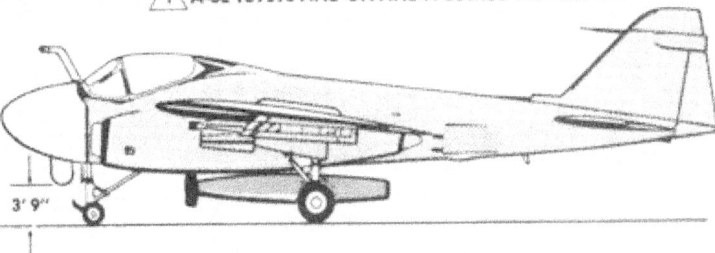

3' 9"

A-6C

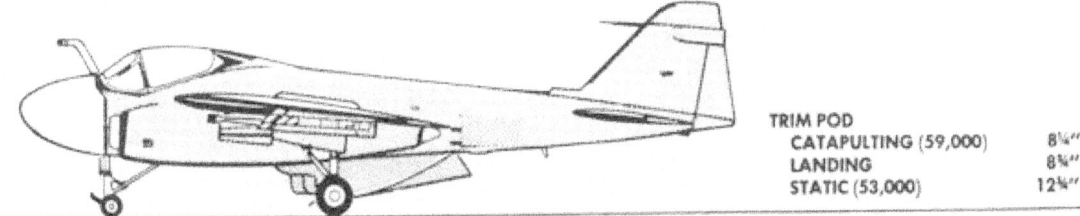

TRIM POD
  CATAPULTING (59,000)   8¼"
  LANDING   8¾"
  STATIC (53,000)   12¾"

D-ADA1-37-2

Figure 1-42 (Sheet 2)

Change 2   1-113

AIRCRAFT
Aircraft Servicing

NAVAIR 01-85ADA-1

POWER UNITS				
	PNEUMATIC STARTING	ELECTRICAL POWER	COMBINATION UNITS	AIR CONDITIONING
SHORE BASED	GTC-85-28 GTC-85-72 MA-1, MA-1A MA-2	NC-12, NC-10 MD-3 MD-3A	MA-1MP MA-2MP MA-3MP	NR-3, NR-4 NR-10
SHIPBOARD	GTC-85-28 GTC-85-72	DECK EDGE POWER NC-10		NR-3, NR-5
AGE REQUIREMENTS	40-50 PSI AT 90 TO 95 LBS PER MIN. 100° TO 425°F	115/200V 400 CPS. AC 22 KVA		3 PSI, 45 LBS PER MIN. 35 TO 50 F.

C-ADA1-714

Figure 1-43

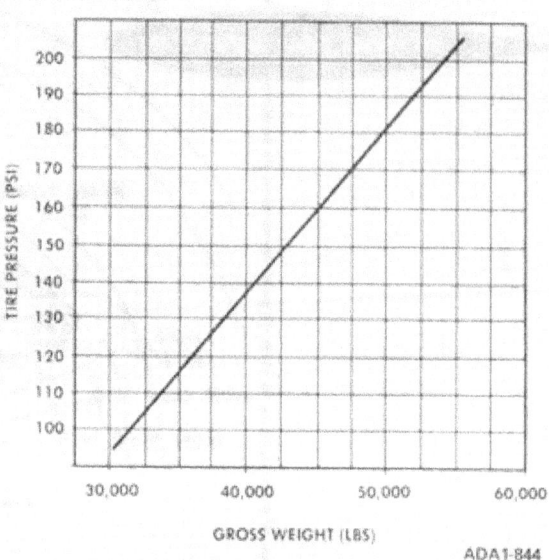

Figure 1-44

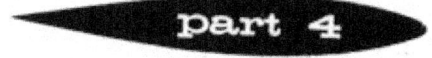

part 4 — Aircraft Operating Limitations

INTRODUCTION

This section includes the aircraft and engine limitations that must be observed during normal operation. Instrument markings giving various operation limitations are shown in figure 1-45. Some markings that are self-evident are not discussed in the text.

Note

The limitations in this section apply to A-6 series aircraft unless otherwise noted.

ENGINE LIMITATIONS

Engine limitations are shown in figure 1-46. Additional information is given in the following paragraphs.

ENGINE OVERSPEED

Should the engine overspeed limit of 102.5% on the J52-P-8 engine be exceeded the engine must be inspected for damage. Log the condition on the yellow sheet (OP-NAV Form 3760-2) to insure inspection. Should the maximum permissible engine overspeed limit of 102.9% rated rpm be exceeded on the J52-P-8 engine, the engine must be changed.

ENGINE IDLE

CAUTION

- A minimum speed of 65% should be maintained during idle letdown to insure that the generators will continue to produce required output while under high electrical loads. This may require advancement of the throttle(s) off the IDLE stop.

- A minimum engine speed of 75% should be maintained during glide/reduced power bombing runs and during high-g or high-speed maneuvers to minimize the possibility of hung accelerations/burner can blowout.

ENGINE OIL PRESSURE

Normal oil pressure is 40 to 50 psi with a minimum of 35 psi at idle. Oil pressures between 35 and 40 psi are undersirable and should be tolerated only for the completion of the flight, preferable at a reduced throttle setting. Oil pressures below normal should be reported as an engine discrepancy and should be corrected before the next flight. Oil pressures below 35 psi are unsafe and require that either the engine be shut down or a landing be made as soon as possible, using the minimum thrust required for safe flight.

ENGINE EXHAUST GAS TEMPERATURE

The engine exhaust gas temperatures (EGT) are given in figure 1-46 for starting and acceleration conditions. They are time-limited to momentary for starting and 8 minutes for acceleration. Momentary is considered a period not to exceed 15 seconds.

AIR STARTS

Refer to Air Start Envelope, Section V.

AIRSPEED LIMITATIONS

MAXIMUM AIRSPEEDS

The maximum indicated airspeed in smooth or moderately turbulent air for the aircraft in the basic configuration is the maximum attainable; i.e., the aircraft is drag-limited.

The maximum permissible airspeeds for the A-6C are as follows:

Optical sensor platform stowed . . . . .70 IMN
Optical sensor platform deployed. . . . . . .88 IMN
Optical sensor platform rotation . . . . . . 250 KIAS

Note

Basic configuration is landing gear and flaps retracted, and canopy closed.

For A-6B/Standard ARM airspeed and maneuvering restrictions, refer to Supplemental NATOPS Flight Manual NAVAIR 01-85ADA-1A.

Landing Gear

Extended . . . . 250 KIAS
Entending . . . . 250 KIAS
Retracting . . . . 200 KIAS
Emergency extension . . . . 150 KIAS

AIRCRAFT
Aircraft Operating Limitations

NAVAIR 01-85ADA-1

INSTRUMENT MARKINGS

ENGINE J52—P-8

BASED ON JP-5 FUEL

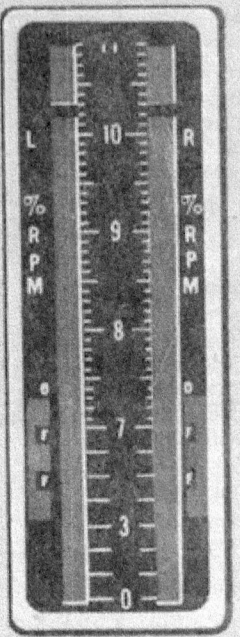

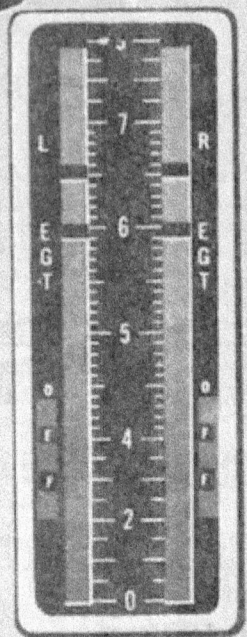

TACHOMETER

102.9% ▬▬▬ MAXIMUM OVERSPEED

EXHAUST TEMPERATURE

650°C ▬▬▬ MILITARY POWER
594°C ▬▬▬ NORMAL RATED

POWER TRIM

☐ NORMAL RANGE

OIL PRESSURE

35 PSI ▬▬▬ MINIMUM (GROUND IDLE)
35-40 PSI ☐ CAUTION
40-50 PSI ☐ CONTINUOUS
50 PSI   MAXIMUM

D-ADA1-84

Figure 1-45

ENGINE OPERATING LIMITS

J-52 P-8 ENGINES

OIL: MIL-L-23699

FUEL: MIL-J5624D
GRADE: JP-5 or JP-4

EGT LIMITS	ANY EGT LIMITS EXCEEDED SHOULD BE REPORTED AS A DISCREPANCY AND MAXIMUM TEMPERATURES REACHED AND LENGTH OF TIME NOTED.	
THRUST SETTING	MAXIMUM OBSERVED EGT (°C)	TIME LIMIT (MINUTES)
ACCELERATION	677°	8 MINUTES
MILITARY	650°	30 MINUTES (ACCELERATION TIME INCLUDED)
NORMAL RATED	594°	
90% NORMAL RATED (CRUISE)		CONTINUOUS
75% NORMAL RATED		
IDLE		
STARTING	455°	MOMENTARY

RPM LIMITS
ANY OVERSPEED LIMIT EXCEEDED SHOULD BE REPORTED AS A DISCREPANCY AND MAXIMUM RPM NOTED.

52 to 60% RPM - IDLE
102.5% RPM - OVERSPEED, Engine inspection required.
102.9% RPM - OVERSPEED, Engine change required.

OIL PRESSURE LIMITS
MIL-L-23699

35 PSI - MINIMUM AT GROUND IDLE RPM

40 PSI - MINIMUM

50 PSI - MAXIMUM

NOTES
(1) NORMAL OIL PRESSURE IS 40 TO 50 PSI, EXCEPT AT IDLE. OIL PRESSURES BETWEEN 35 AND 40 PSI ARE UNDESIRABLE AND SHOULD BE TOLERATED ONLY FOR THE COMPLETION OF THE FLIGHT, PREFERABLY AT A REDUCED THROTTLE SETTING. OIL PRESSURES BELOW NORMAL SHOULD BE REPORTED AS AN ENGINE DISCREPANCY AND SHOULD BE CORRECTED BEFORE THE NEXT TAKE-OFF. OIL PRESSURES BELOW 35 PSI ARE UNSAFE AND REQUIRE THAT EITHER THE ENGINE BE SHUT DOWN OR A LANDING BE MADE AS SOON AS POSSIBLE, USING THE MINIMUM THRUST REQUIRED FOR SAFE FLIGHT.
(2) (OIL MIL-L-7808 SHALL BE USED WHEN CONTINUOUS GROUND COLD SOAK TEMPERATURES BELOW −40°F. ARE ANTICIPATED).

Figure 1-46

AIRCRAFT
Aircraft Operating Limitations

Flaps/Slats

Takeoff position or less . . . . 250 KIAS
Land position . . . . 200 KIAS

> **WARNING**
>
> - Extreme caution should be exercised during flap retraction under heavy gross weight conditions. To avoid aircraft stall or settling due to flap retraction, do not retract the flaps below 170 KIAS for weights up to 50,000 pounds and not below 185 KIAS for weights above 50,000 pounds. At the heavier weights and under high ambient temperature conditions, acceleration and climb performance are marginal and it may be impossible to reach 185 KIAS. If 185 KIAS cannot be reached, it is recommended that external store weight be reduced in order to permit acceleration to 185 KIAS prior to flap retraction.
>
> - If a barber-pole indication on slat/flap retraction should occur after takeoff, power must be maintained at military and airspeed controlled within limits (170 KIAS or 185 KIAS as applicable) by adjusting aircraft attitude. Power reduction or diversion of attention must not be attempted until reaching safe operating altitudes.

> **CAUTION**
>
> If a wave-off is initiated with flaps in the LAND position (40°), ensure that they are retracted to the TAKE-OFF position (30°) before reaching 200 KIAS in order to prevent structural failure to the flap actuating mechanism. The flap drive system does not provide a blowback feature.

Flaps/Slats Emergency (40° LAND)

> **CAUTION**
>
> Emergency extension of the flaps to the terminal (LAND) position above 160 KIAS may result in a burned-out clutch in the gear box and complete loss of flap operation. It is permissible to commence flap extension by the emergency flap switch at any speed up to the structural limitation (200 KIAS for LAND position) of the flaps; however, airspeed deceleration to below 160 KIAS must be continued as the flap extension process continues toward LAND position.

Canopy

Opened . . . . 250 KIAS
Opening . . . . 200 KIAS
Closing . . . . 150 KIAS
Jettisoning (maximum recommended) . . . 220 KIAS

> **Note**
>
> Although canopies have safely separated from the aircraft above 220 KIAS, no flight test data are available on jettisoning the canopy above this airspeed.

Ram-Air Turbine

Extension . . . . Maximum Airspeeds
  A-6C . . . . .88 IMN
Retraction . . . . 475 KIAS
  A-6C . . . . 475 KIAS/.88 IMN

> **Note**
>
> The minimum recommended airspeed to ensure full electrical output is 110 KIAS.

Speed Brakes

Partial or Full Extension . . . Maximum Airspeeds
  A-6C . . . . .88 IMN

Rain-Removal System

Operating . . . . 200 KIAS

Internal Air Refueling Store (KA-6D)

Refueling/Drogue
Extension . . . . 220-320 KIAS/.80 IMN

Drogue Retraction . . . . . . 220-280 KIAS/.72 IMN

Altitude . . . . SL - 35,000 ft.

Hose Jettison . . . . 220-320 KIAS

Response Test . . . . . . 220-275 KIAS/.68 IMN

Air Refueling Store

Drogue Extension . . . . 300 KIAS

Drogue Retraction . . . . 250 KIAS

Drogue Unfeathering . . . . 300 KIAS

Refueling Store Jettison . . . . 300 KIAS

NAVAIR 01-85ADA-1

AIRCRAFT
Aircraft Operating Limitations

> **CAUTION**
>
> Use of an external air-refueling store on the KA-6D is prohibited unless IAFC No. 296 or AFC No. 296 is incorporated in the aircraft. If IAFC No. 296 or AFC No. 296 is installed and it is decided to transfer fuel utilizing the D-704, the TO STORE switch on the centerline refueling store panel shall remain in the OFF position until the fuel quantity in the centerline refueling store is less than 500 pounds. When the fuel in the centerline refueling store reaches 500 pounds or less, move the centerline refueling store switch to the TO STORE position to replenish the store. Monitor fuel quantity indicator closely so that switch may be returned to the OFF position as soon as the fuel quantity indicates 1500 pounds. If the tanker fuel transfer/dump pump starting relay is malfunctioning, the fuel transfer rate to the refueling centerline store could be fast enough to cause store failure if the indicated fuel in the store is permitted to go above 1,500 pounds.

EQUIPMENT COOLING

> **CAUTION**
>
> - Without the engines running or ground cooling applied, cooling air is not available. In addition, with the engines running with the canopy open, adequate cooling air for equipment in the radome area is not available. Operation without cooling of any electronic equipment requiring forced cooling should be limited to 5 minutes to prevent failure from overheating.
>
> - In the A-6E, without engines running or ground cooling applied, ground blower operation is automatic when external electrical power is applied and the search radar, computer, or CNI systems are turned on. When the right generator is on the line, the ground blower is automatically turned OFF and equipment-cooling air is supplied by the engines. During ground operation with engines running and the ground blower OFF, the radar units in the nose radome are cooled by cabin discharge air. Operation of the radar with the canopy OPEN and the ground blower OFF must be limited to no more than 5 minutes.
>
> - In the A-6E, electronic equipment should not be operated without aircraft air conditioning or external cooling air applied when ambient air temperature exceeds 103° F or when the aircraft is located in an enclosed, poorly ventilated area.

- The CNI equipment, which is normally force-cooled, is provided with an auxiliary cooling blower in aircraft incorporating AFC No. 268. The blower operates any time the AIR COND MASTER switch is OFF or the AIR COND bleed-air isolation switch is OFF.

- Do not operate the A-6C TV or IR sensors or the TRIM pod environmental control system on the ground unless engines are running and aircraft air conditioning is on or ground air conditioning is applied to the pod. In aircraft incorporating AFC No. 268, the left engine must be running and the AIR COND bleed-air switch must be ON to operate the TRIM pod environmental control system.

ACCELERATION LIMITATIONS

A-6A,B,C,E

> **CAUTION**
>
> Aircraft in which AFC No. 254 is not incorporated are restricted to a maximum normal acceleration of 5.0 g for symmetrical maneuvers and 4.0 g for asymmetric (unsymmetric or rolling) maneuvers for clean wing and all authorized wing store loads. Do not exceed g times gross weight product of 185,000 pounds for symmetric cases or 148,000 pounds for asymmetric cases above 37,000 pounds aircraft gross weight.

Except that moderate and heavy buffeting shall be avoided, the maximum permissible accelerations for flight with wing-tip speed brakes retracted are (figure 1-47 and 1-48):

Symmetrical flight . . . . -2.4 to +6.5g
Asymmetrical flight . . . . -1.0 to +5.2g

With wing-tip speed brakes extended, the maximum permissible accelerations are (figure 1-49 and 1-50):

Symmetrical flight . . . . -2.4 to +6.0g
Asymmetrical flight . . . . -1.0 to +4.8g

Whenever a MER installed on any aircraft wing station has stores loaded asymmetrically fore and aft, observe the following carriage limits:

Rack Asymmetry (LB)	Acceleration (G)
600 to 1,200	-1.0 to +4.5
1,200 to 1,800	-1.0 to +3.5
1,800 or greater	-1.0 to +2.5

Change 2   1-119

AIRCRAFT
Aircraft Operating Limitations

NAVAIR 01-85ADA-1

ACCELERATION LIMITATIONS

WING TIP SPEED BRAKES RETRACTED

AIRCRAFT CONFIGURATION:
WING TIP SPEED BRAKES
RETRACTED

DATE: 1 FEB 1972
DATA BASIS: FLIGHT TEST

REMARKS
ENGINE(S): (2) J52-P-8

FUEL GRADE: JP-5
FUEL DENSITY: 6.8 LB/GA

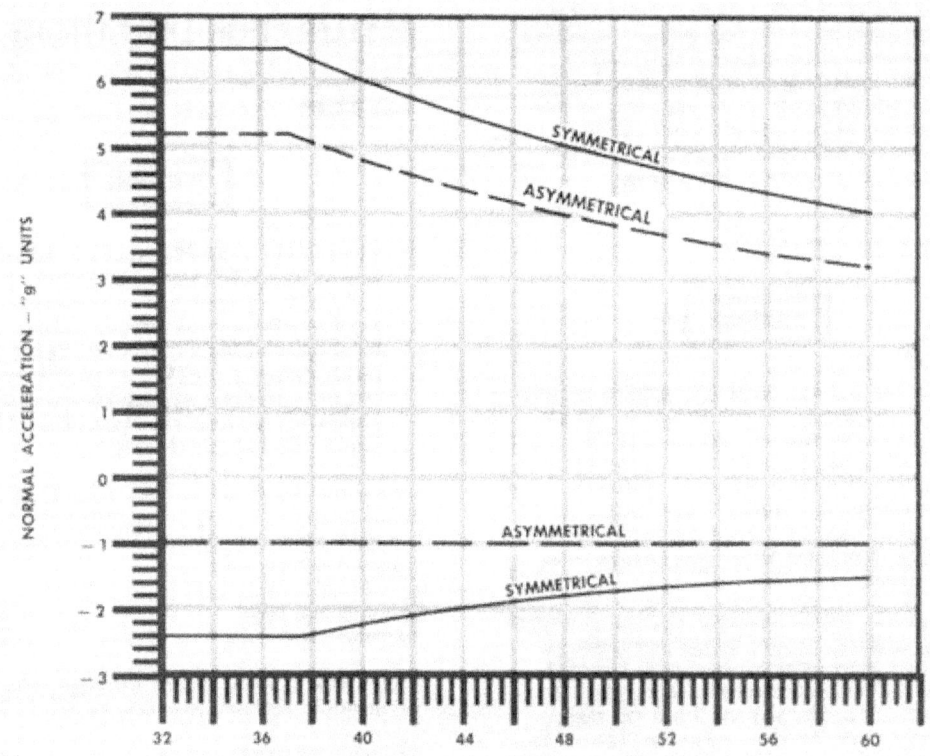

GROSS WEIGHT — 1000 POUNDS

CAUTION

- A-6A, B, C/KA-6D aircraft in which AFC No. 254 is not incorporated are restricted to a maximum normal acceleration of 5.0 g for symmetrical maneuvers and 4.0 g for asymmetric (unsymmetric or rolling) maneuvers for clean wing and all authorized wing store loads. Do not exceed g times gross weight product of 185,000 pounds for symmetric cases or 148,000 pounds for asymmetric cases above 37,000 pounds aircraft gross weight.

- Full acceleration limits do not routinely apply to the KA-6D. See KA-6D Acceleration Limitations paragraph this section.

E-ADA1-122

Figure 1-47

NAVAIR 01-85ADA-1

AIRCRAFT
Aircraft Operating Limitations

OPERATING FLIGHT STRENGTH DIAGRAM

WING TIP SPEED BRAKES RETRACTED

AIRCRAFT CONFIGURATION:
FOR GROSS WEIGHTS
OF 37,000 LB. OR LESS

DATE: 1 FEB 1972
DATA BASIS: FLIGHT TEST

REMARKS
ENGINE(S): (2) J52-P-8

FUEL GRADE: JP-5
FUEL DENSITY: 6.8 LB/GAL

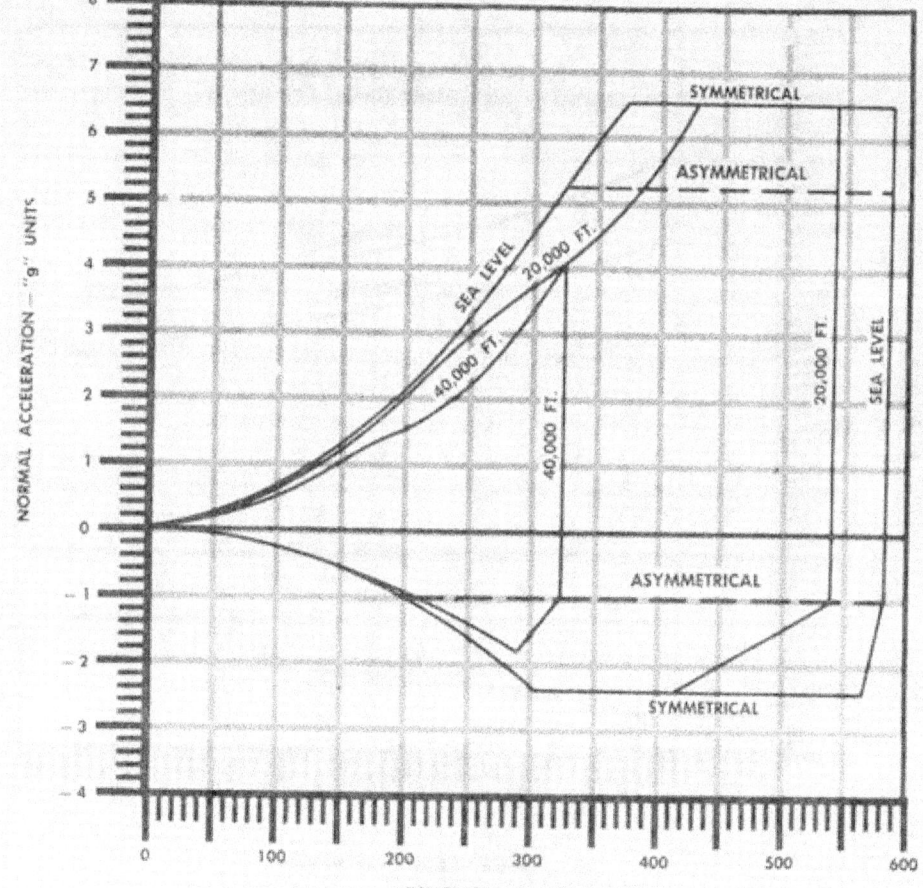

CAUTION

* A-6A, B, C/KA-6D aircraft in which AFC No. 254 is not incorporated are restricted to a maximum normal acceleration of 6.0 g for symmetrical maneuvers and 4.0 g for asymmetric (unsymmetric or rolling) maneuvers for clean wing and all authorized wing store loads. Do not exceed g times gross weight product of 185,000 pounds for symmetric cases or 148,000 pounds for asymmetric cases above 37,000 pounds aircraft gross weight.

* Full acceleration limits do not routinely apply to the KA-6D. See KA-6D Acceleration Limitations paragraph this section.

Figure 1-48

AIRCRAFT
Aircraft Operating Limitations

NAVAIR 01-85ADA-1

ACCELERATION LIMITATIONS

WING TIP SPEED BRAKES EXTENDED

AIRCRAFT CONFIGURATION:
WING TIP SPEED BRAKES
EXTENDED

DATE: 1 FEB 1972
DATA BASIS: FLIGHT TEST/ANALYSIS

REMARKS
ENGINE(S): (2) J52-P-8

FUEL GRADE: JP-5
FUEL DENSITY: 6.8 LB/GAL

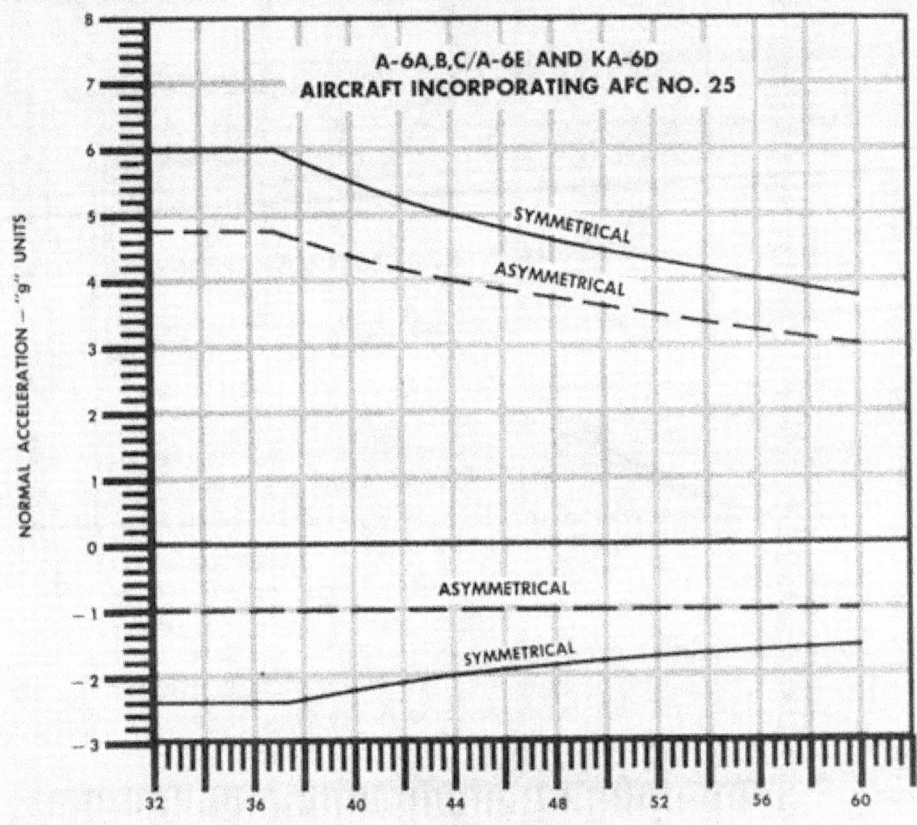

CAUTION

- A-6A, B, C/KA-6D aircraft in which AFC No. 254 is not incorporated are restricted to a maximum normal acceleration of 5.0 g for symmetrical maneuvers and 4.0 g for asymmetric (unsymmetric or rolling) maneuvers for clean wing and all authorized wing store loads. Do not exceed g times gross weight product of 185,000 pounds for symmetric cases or 148,000 pounds for asymmetric cases above 37,000 pounds aircraft gross weight.

- Full acceleration limits do not routinely apply to the KA-6D. See KA-6D Acceleration Limitations paragraph this section.

B-ADA1-126

Figure 1-49

NAVAIR 01-85ADA-1

AIRCRAFT
Aircraft Operating Limitations

OPERATING FLIGHT STRENGTH DIAGRAM

WING TIP SPEED BRAKES EXTENDED

AIRCRAFT CONFIGURATION:
FOR GROSS WEIGHTS
OR 37,000 LB. OR LESS

DATE: 1 FEB 1972
DATA BASIS: FLIGHT TEST

REMARKS
ENGINE(S): (2) J52-P-8

FUEL GRADE: JP-5
FUEL DENSITY: 6.8 LB/GAL

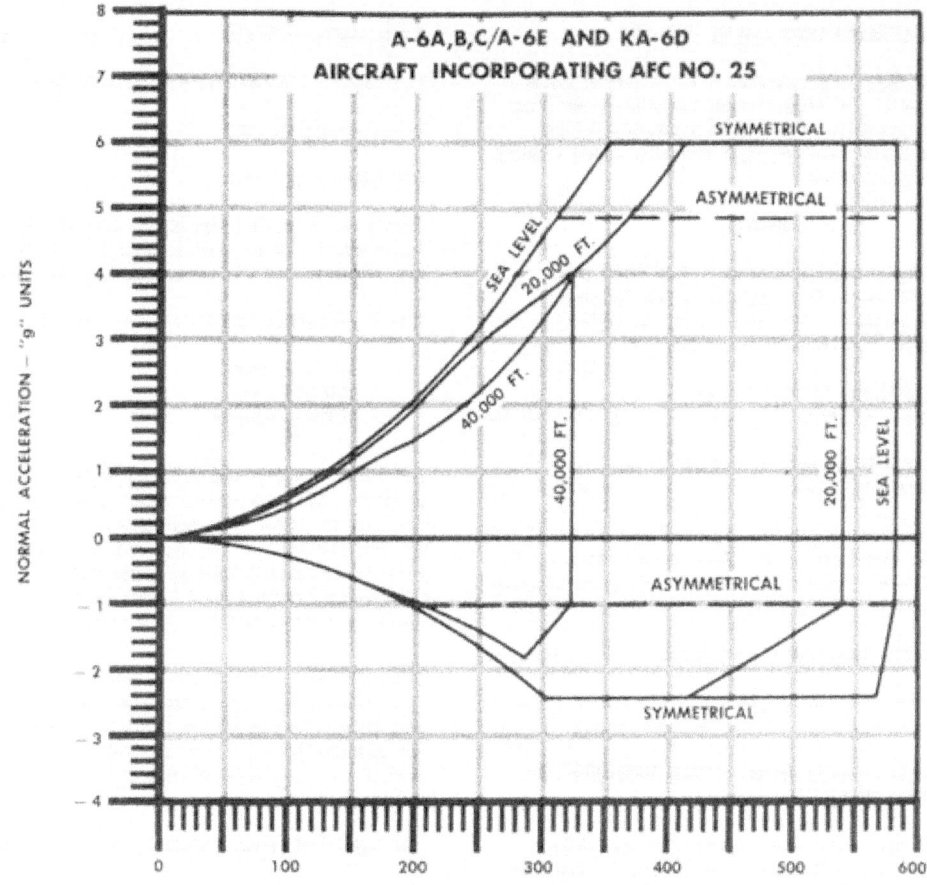

CAUTION

- A-6A, B, C/KA-6D aircraft in which AFC No. 254 is not incorporated are restricted to a maximum normal acceleration of 5.0 g for symmetrical maneuvers and 4.0 g for asymmetric (unsymmetric or rolling) maneuvers for clean wing and all authorized wing store loads. Do not exceed g times gross weight product of 185,000 pounds for symmetric cases or 148,000 pounds for asymmetric cases above 37,000 pounds aircraft gross weight.

- Full acceleration limits do not routinely apply to the KA-6D See KA-6D Acceleration Limitations paragraph this section.

C-ADA1-125

Figure 1-50

AIRCRAFT
Aircraft Operating Limitations

NAVAIR 01-85ADA-1

As gross weights are increased above 37,000 pounds (figure 1-50), the permissible accelerations are decreased in order to maintain a constant g x gross weight product. To approximate the maximum permissible accelerations at these higher gross weight conditions, reduce load factor by 0.15 g for every 1,000 pounds above 37,000 pounds.

When flying in conditions of moderate turbulence, it is essential that accelerations due to deliberate maneuvers be limited to 5.0 g in order to minimize the possibility of overstressing the aircraft as a result of the combined effects of gusts and maneuvering loads.

NORMAL ACCELERATION LIMITS (KA-6D)

The KA-6D normal acceleration limits were established based on the requirement for a 10-year wing fatigue service life. The following acceleration limitations apply to flight with wing-tip speed brakes extended or retracted:

Note

To permit adequate monitoring of wing life, acceleration loads in excess of the following shall be reported by message to NAVAIR-DEVCEN, WARMINSTER (CODE-2).

Symmetrical flight (gross weight
37,000 pounds or less) . . . . -1.0 to +3.0g

Asymmetrical flight (gross weight
37,000 pounds or less) . . . . 0 to +2.0g

For symmetrical or asymmetrical flight above 37,000 pounds, the permissible positive acceleration is decreased so that g times gross weight does not exceed 111,000 pounds.

Asymmetrical external store loading . . . . 0 to 2.0g

For asymmetrical store loading, the g times gross weight factor shall not exceed 74,000 pounds.

ACCELERATION LIMITATIONS WHEN REQUIRED BY OPERATIONAL NECESSITY (KA-6D)

In cases of operational necessity, the operational commander may authorize acceleration limitations in excess of the normal acceleration limitations.

Note

To permit adequate monitoring of wing life, acceleration loads in excess of the normal acceleration limitations shall be reported by message to NAVAIR-DEVCEN, WARMINSTER (CODE-2).

Except that moderate and heavy buffeting shall be avoided, the maximum permissible accelerations for flight with wing-tip speed brakes retracted are (figure 1-47 and 1-48):

Symmetrical flight . . . . -2.4 to +6.5g

Asymmetrical flight . . . . -1.0 to +5.2g

With wing-tip speed brakes extended, the maximum permissible accelerations are (figure 1-49 thru 1-52):

AIRCRAFT NOT INCORPORATING AFC NO. 25

Symmetrical flight . . . . -2.4 to +5.2g

Asymmetrical flight . . . . -1.0 to +4.2g

AIRCRAFT INCORPORATING AFC NO. 25

Symmetrical flight . . . . -2.4 to +6.0g

Asymmetrical flight . . . . -1.0 to +4.8g

Whenever a MER installed on any aircraft wing station has stores loaded asymmetrically fore and aft, observe the following carriage limits:

RACK ASYMMETRY (LB)	ACCELERATION (G)
600 to 1,200	-1.0 to -4.5
1,200 to 1,800	-1.0 to +3.5
1,800 or greater	-1.0 to +2.5

As gross weights are increased above 37,000 pounds (figure 1-40), the permissible accelerations are decreased in order to maintain a constant g x gross weight product. To approximate the maximum permissible accelerations at these higher gross weight conditions, reduce load factor by 0.15 g for every 1,000 pounds above 37,000 pounds.

When flying in conditions of moderate turbulence, it is essential that accelerations due to deliberate maneuvers be limited to 5.0 g in order to minimize the possibility of overstressing the aircraft as a result of the combined effects of gusts and maneuvering loads.

LANDING CONFIGURATION (ALL A-6 SERIES)

Zero g to +2.0 g is permitted in the landing configuration.

CENTER-OF-GRAVITY LIMITATIONS

MAXIMUM FORWARD C.G.

Gear Up . . . . 20.5% MAC
Gear Down (Landing) . . . . 20.5% MAC
Gear Down (Takeoff) . . . . 23.0% MAC

MAXIMUM AFT C.G.

Gear Up . . . . 28.7% MAC
Gear Down (Landing and Takeoff) . . . 29.0% MAC

NAVAIR 01-85ADA-1

AIRCRAFT
Aircraft Operating Limitations

ACCELERATION LIMITATIONS

AIRCRAFT CONFIGURATION:
WING TIP SPEED BRAKES
EXTENDED

WING TIP SPEED BRAKES EXTENDED

DATE: 18 OCT 1965
DATA BASIS: FLIGHT TEST

REMARKS
ENGINE(S): (2) J52-P-8

FUEL GRADE: JP-5
FUEL DENSITY: 6.8 LB/GAL

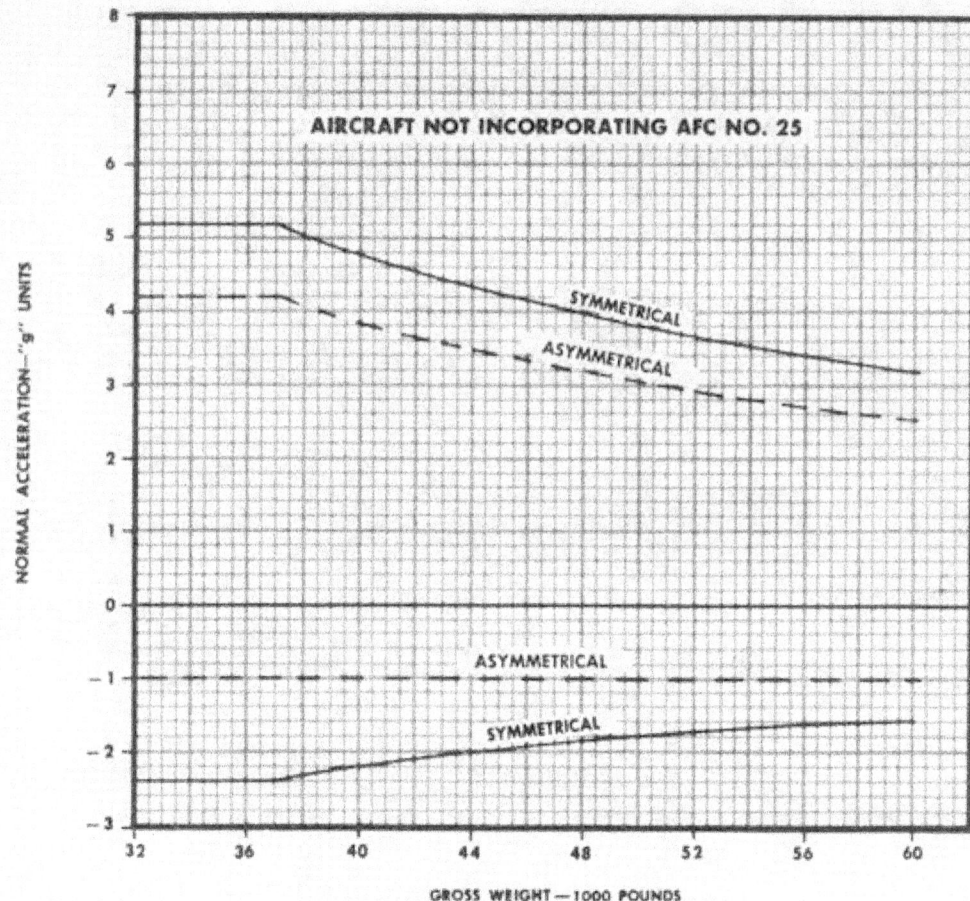

CAUTION

- Aircraft in which AFC No. 254 is not incorporated are restricted to a maximum normal acceleration of 5.0 g for symmetrical maneuvers and 4.0 g for asymmetric (unsymmetric or rolling) maneuvers for clean wing and all authorized wing store loads. Do not exceed g times gross weight product of 185,000 pounds for symmetric cases or 148,000 pounds for asymmetric cases above 37,000 pounds aircraft gross weight.

- Full acceleration limits do not routinely apply to the KA-6D. See KA-6D Acceleration Limitations paragraph this section.

ADA1-845

Figure 1-51

AIRCRAFT
Aircraft Operating Limitations

NAVAIR 01-85ADA-1

OPERATING FLIGHT STRENGTH DIAGRAM

KA-6D

WING TIP SPEED BRAKES EXTENDED

AIRCRAFT CONFIGURATION
FOR GROSS WEIGHTS
OF 37,000 LB. OR LESS

DATE: 18 OCT 1965
DATA BASIS: FLIGHT TEST

REMARKS
ENGINE(S): (2) J52-P-8

FUEL GRADE: JP-5
FUEL DENSITY: 6.8 LB/GAL

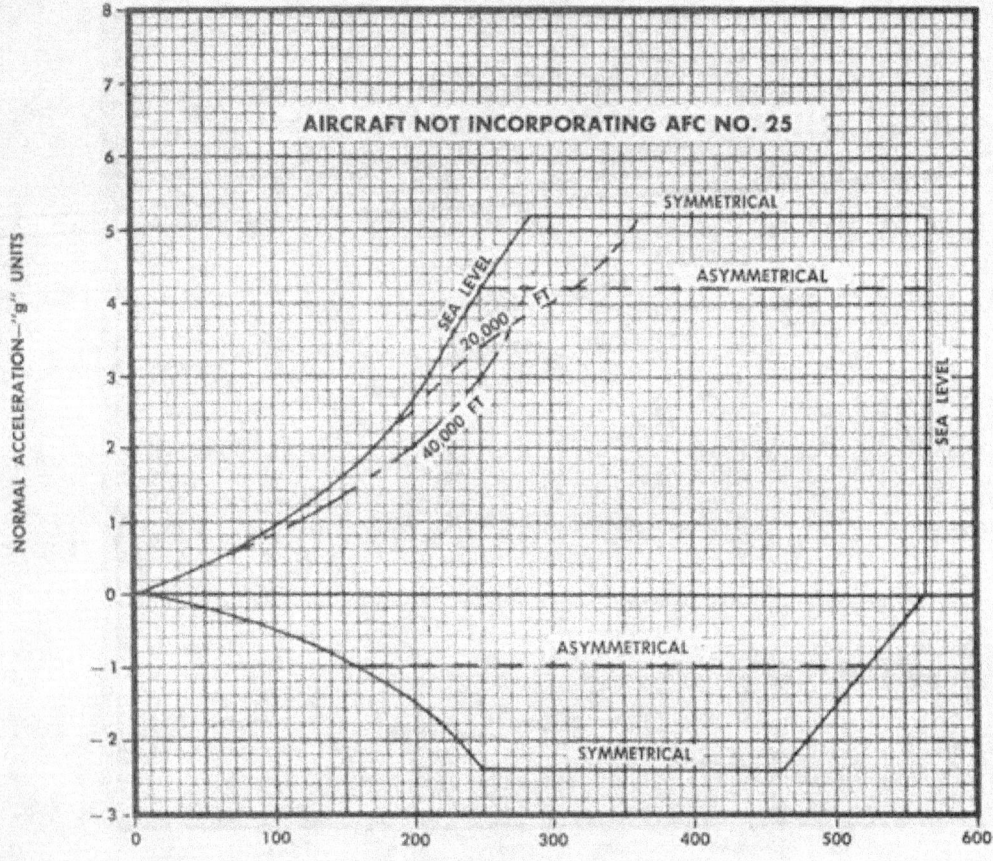

CAUTION

- A-6A, B, C/KA-6D aircraft in which AFC No. 254 is not incorporated are restricted to a maximum normal acceleration of 5.0 g for symmetrical maneuvers and 4.0 g for asymmetric (unsymmetric or rolling) maneuvers for clean wing and all authorized wing store loads. Do not exceed g times gross weight product of 185,000 pounds for symmetric cases or 148,000 pounds for asymmetric cases above 37,000 pounds aircraft gross weight.

- Full acceleration limits do not routinely apply to the KA-6D. See KA-6D Acceleration Limitations paragraph this section.

ADA1-846

Figure 1-52

GROSS WEIGHT LIMITATIONS

A-6A, A-6B, A-6C, KA-6D, A-6E

Field takeoff	60,400 pounds
Field landing (minimum rate of descent)	45,000 pounds
Field landing (other than minimum rate of descent)	36,000 pounds
Catapulting	58,600 pounds
Barricade engagement	
Shipboard	36,000 pounds
SATS (M-21)	45,000 pounds
Field arrestment	See Section V
Carrier landing and carrier arrestments (using MK 7 Mod 2 or Mod 3 arresting gear)	36,000 pounds
Carrier landing and carrier arrestments (using MK 7 Mod 1 arresting gear)	
A-6C and A-6A, A-6B with AFC No. 244	36,000 pounds
A-6A, A-6B without AFC No. 244	33,500 pounds

CAUTION

- Landings other than field landings (minimum rate of descent) are not permitted if the total weight of external stores (excluding pylons with Aero-7 but including racks), on stations 1, 2, 4, and 5 exceeds 4,000 pounds or if the sum of the weight of stores on aircraft stations 1 and 2 or on stations 4 and 5 exceeds 2,000 pounds. For asymmetric external store loadings, the static moment shall not exceed 21,150 foot-pounds.

- If the total weight of external stores (excluding pylons with Aero-7, but including racks), loaded symmetrically or asymmetrically, exceeds 800 pounds on either aircraft station 1 or 5, landings other than field landings (minimum rate of descent) should be made at a gross landing weight of 33,500 pounds or less if operating requirements permit. This will decrease the moment of inertia in roll and thereby increase the safety margin in case of high rate-of-sink, one wing low, or hard carrier landings.

- The maximum recommended gross weight for carrier landings is 33,500 pounds. A-6B Standard Arm and A-6C TRIM configurations will require increased weight to insure adequate fuel reserves. Carrier landings should be made at the minimum gross weight consistent with operational requirements. Arrested landings with fuel in internal wing tanks is not permitted except in an emergency.

CARRIER LIMITATIONS

1. CATAPULTING WITH PARTIALLY FULL INTERNAL INBOARD WING TANKS, OUTBOARD WING PANEL TANKS, OR EXTERNAL TANKS IS NOT PERMITTED.

2. CATAPULT LAUNCH AND ARRESTED LANDINGS ARE NOT PERMITTED WITH ASYMMETRIC EXTERNAL STORE LOADING IN EXCESS OF 21,150 FOOT-POUNDS OF STATIC MOMENT. THE ASYMMETRIC LOAD AT THE OUTBOARD WING STATIONS (1 OR 5) X 11.75 PLUS THE ASYMMETRIC LOAD AT THE INBOARD WING STATIONS (2 OR 4) X 7.9 SHALL NOT EXCEED 21,150 FOOT-POUNDS.

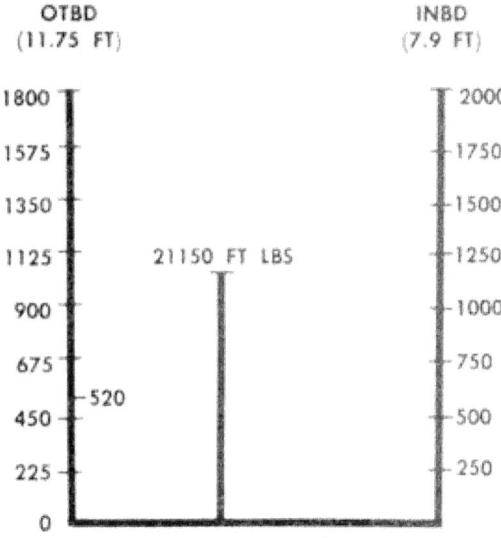

3. AERO-1D FUEL TANKS MUST BE EMPTY FOR OTHER THAN FLARED, NON-ARRESTED, FIELD LANDINGS EXCEPT IN AN EMERGENCY.

NOTE

FOR ADDITIONAL LIMITATIONS, REFER TO THE CURRENT A-6 LAUNCH AND RECOVERY BULLETINS

Figure 1-53

EXTERNAL STORE LIMITATIONS

Only the external stores listed in the A-6A Tactical Manual NAVAIR 01-85ADA-1T may be carried and released, singly or in combination to the limits shown. Operating limitations for flight, catapulting, and arrested landings with external stores are the same as the basic aircraft unless otherwise noted.

MANEUVERS

Note

For A6B/Standard ARM airspeed and maneuvering restrictions, refer to Supplemental NATOPS Flight Manual NAVAIR 01-85ADA-1A.

AIRCRAFT
Aircraft Operating Limitations

NAVAIR 01-85ADA-1

RUDDER MANEUVERS

Clean Configuration (Gear and Flaps Retracted/4° Rudder)

Full pedal sideslips are permitted to the limits of the flight envelope.

Extended Rudder Throw (35° Rudder)

Extended rudder throw can be obtained in the following modes of operation:

- Flaps extended
- Assist-spin recovery switch ON
- Flight and combined hydraulic systems depressurized (backup flight controls hydraulic system activated)

Restrictions applicable to these configurations are outlined in the following paragraphs.

Gear and Flaps Extended

Full pedal sideslips are permitted to 190 KIAS with flaps at TAKEOFF (30°) or LAND (40°).

BACKUP FLIGHT CONTROLS HYDRAULIC SYSTEM ACTIVATED

Rudder maneuvers are permitted to the limits presented in figure 1-54.

ASSIST-SPIN RECOVERY SWITCH ON

CAUTION

- The assist-spin recovery switch should be actuated only to effect recovery from a spin. Operation of the switch may impose an additional acceleration, which during an accelerated maneuver may overstress the aircraft or when operating at minimum airspeeds may pitch the aircraft up into a stall or heavy buffet.
- After spin recovery is accomplished, the limitations presented in figure 1-54 must be observed until the assist-spin recovery switch is moved to OFF.
- Positioning the switch to OFF after spin recovery should be done below 300 KIAS while anticipating a sharp nose-down trim change.

ROLLING MANEUVERS

Gear and Flaps Extended

Full stick 60° banks are permitted up to 250 KIAS with flaps at TAKEOFF (30°) and to 200 KIAS with flaps at LAND (40°).

Gear and Flaps Retracted

Full abrupt flaperon rolls and rolling pullouts are permitted up to the acceleration limits shown in figure 1-47 and 1-48 and to the maximum speed attainable and within the following additional restrictions:

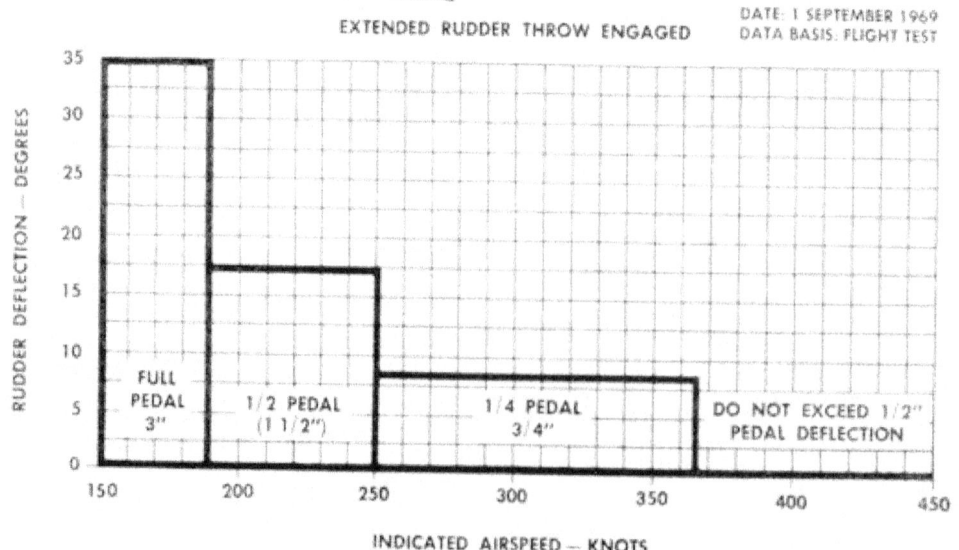

Figure 1-54

a. Not to exceed 360°.

b. With more than 1,500 pounds of fuel in an external fuel tank at stations 1 and/or 5, and/or with a full or partially full D-704 air-refueling store at station 3, lateral control motion is limited to 1/2 deflection at airspeeds in excess of 450 KIAS.

c. With the A/A37B-5 TER or A/A37B-6 MER loaded with more than 1,500 pounds of bombs at station 1 and/or 5, lateral control motion is limited to 1/2 full deflection at airspeeds in excess of 350 KIAS or 0.65 IMN, whichever is less.

d. When a MER installed on an aircraft wing station is asymmetrically loaded with stores, additional rolling limitations are imposed. A rack asymmetrical loading condition exists:

- When the total weight of stores loaded forward does not equal the total weight of stores loaded aft, or

- When the total weight loaded on rack stations 3 and 4 does not equal the total weight loaded on stations 5 and 6.

When either of the above asymmetrical loading conditions occurs, observe the lateral control motion limits shown in figure 1-55.

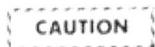 CAUTION

Exercise caution when deflecting the flaperons, as an increase in normal acceleration will result.

PROHIBITED MANEUVERS

1. Large abrupt control reversals
2. Intentional spins
3. Negative g flight in excess of 30 seconds
4. Zero g flight in excess of 10 seconds
5. Nonejected releases from MER/TER racks using curvilinear tracking runs (commonly called pipper on target tracking).

ASYMMETRICAL LOADING, ROLL LIMITS

RACK ASYMMETRY (LB)		MAX STICK DEFLECTION
A/C STATION 2 OR 4	A/C STATION 1 OR 5	
600 TO 1,200	400 TO 600	¼ THROW ABOVE 350 KIAS / .65 IMN
1,200 OR GREATER	600 TO 1,200	½ THROW ABOVE 350 KIAS / .50 IMN
	1,200 OR GREATER	COORDINATED TURNS ONLY.

Figure 1-55

Section II: INDOCTRINATION

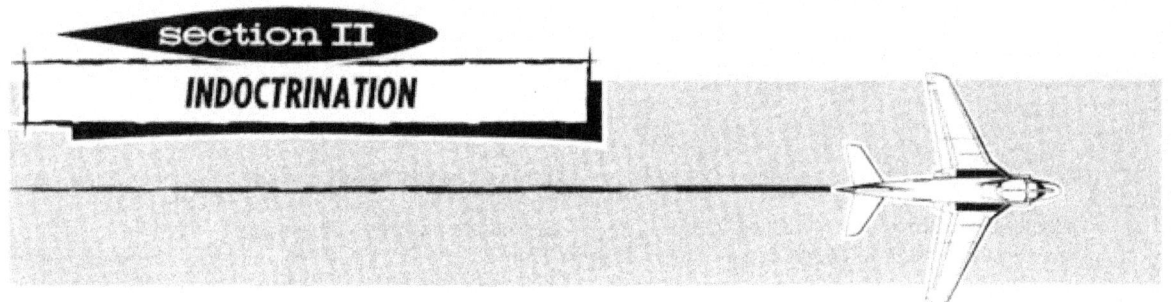

TABLE OF CONTENTS

Ground Training Syllabus	2-1
Flight Training Syllabus	2-1
Ceiling/Visibility Requirements	2-1
Initial Qualification and Currency Requirements	2-2
Requirements for Various Flight Phases	2-2
Requirements for Night/Instrument Flight	2-2
Carrier-Landing Qualifications	2-2
Minimum Crew Requirements	2-2
VIP/Orientation Flights	2-2
Personal Flying Equipment	2-2

GROUND TRAINING SYLLABUS

MINIMUM GROUND TRAINING

The ground training syllabus sets forth the minimum ground training that must be satisfactorily completed prior to operating the A-6. The ground training syllabus for each activity will vary according to local conditions, field facilities, requirements from higher authority, and the immediate unit commander's estimate of the squadron's readiness. The minimum ground training syllabus for the pilot and bombardier/navigator is set forth below.

Minimum Ground Training Requirements

The minimum ground training requirements for the A-6 pilot and bombardier/navigator, which shall be successfully completed prior to flight, are as follows:

1. NAMTD A-6 flight crew familiarization course or equivalent
2. Preflight check of the aircraft
3. Cockpit check and familiarization
4. Bailout, ditching procedure, safety, and survival equipment checkout
5. Weapons System Trainer Flight Syllabus (if available)
6. Locally prepared written examination covering appropriate emergency procedures.

The minimum ground training requirements for the A-6 observer, which shall be successfully completed prior to flight, are as follows:

1. Flight physiology training required by OPNAVINST 3710.7 series.
2. Bailout, ditching procedures, safety, and survival equipment checkout.
3. Lookout responsibilities and procedures.
4. Emergencies evaluation and use of emergency procedures checklist.
5. Hand signals (ground and flight).

FLIGHT TRAINING SYLLABUS

The flight training syllabus is designated to effect the orderly and expeditious qualification of pilots and bombardier/navigators in flying the A-6 as an aircraft, as a weapons system, and as a tanker from both carrier- and shore-based installations.

CEILING/VISIBILITY REQUIREMENTS

In general, the following pilot ceiling/visibility minimums for time-in-model apply.

Time-in-Model (hr)	Ceiling/Visibility (ft) (mi)
0 to 10	VFR (remain clear of clouds)
10 to 20	800/2; 900/1-1/2; 1,000/1
20 to 45	700/1; 600/2; 500/3
45 and above	OPNAV minimums

INDOCTRINATION

Where adherence to these minimums unduly hampers pilot training, Commanding officers may waive time-in-model requirements for actual instrument flight, provided pilots meet the following criteria:

1. Have a minimum of 10 hours in model.
2. Completed two simulated instrument sorties.
3. Completed two actual or simulated TACAN penetrations to field minimums.

INITIAL QUALIFICATION AND CURRENCY REQUIREMENTS

Initial flight qualification shall be obtained by satisfactory completion of the required course of instruction at a formal USN/USMC A-6 replacement training squadron training syllabus. Minimum requirements to maintain currency after initial qualification shall be established by the unit commanding officer but will involve as a minimum 10 hours of first pilot time and 2 takeoffs and landings in A-6 aircraft in the previous 90 days for pilots and annual NATOPS evaluation with the grade of at least conditionally qualified for pilots and B/N's. Requalification of those crewmembers whose currency has lapsed shall include appropriate ground training followed by a familiarization flight phase to include NATOPS requalification.

REQUIREMENTS FOR VARIOUS FLIGHT PHASES

Solo Flight

Solo flight is prohibited.

Night

Not less than 10 hours in model.

Cross-Country

1. Have a minimum of 25 hours in model.
2. Have a valid instrument card.
3. Have completed at least one night familiarization flight.
4. Have completed a locally prescribed aircraft servicing checkout.
5. Must be current in model.

Ferry

Ferry requirements are contained in OPNAVINST 3710.6 series.

For members of ferry squadrons, training requirements, checkout procedures, evaluation procedures, and weather minima shall be governed by the provisions contained in OPNAVINST 3710.6 (series).

REQUIREMENTS FOR NIGHT/INSTRUMENT FLIGHT

Aircraft instrumentation requirements for night and instrument flight are specified in OPNAV 3710.7 series instructions. In addition, a vertical display indicator, radar altimeter, and aligned inertial platform are required for night and instrument flight. The VDI and the inertial platform are the primary attitude reference.

CARRIER LANDING QUALIFICATIONS

Carrier landing qualifications will be in accordance with LSO NATOPS manual

MINIMUM CREW REQUIREMENTS

In the A-6A/B/C/E, the minimum crew requirements for flight shall consist of a qualified pilot and NFO. A qualified observer, when authorized by competent authority, may occupy the B/N seat during nonsystem flights.

The minimum crew in the KA-6D is a qualified pilot. However, solo flight is prohibited. The KA-6D is designed to be crewed by a pilot and an additional crewman, in order to fullfill the entire mission spectrum of the aircraft. The existing cockpit layout allows the pilot to perform all of the in-flight refueling functions and continue to maneuver the aircraft. The in-flight refueling mission therefore can be completed with a NON-NFO in the right seat. VIP/ORIENTATION flights can be performed while executing the in-flight refueling mission. Due to the myriad of possible problems and emergencies that can arise in any high-performance aircraft, right seat flights by untrained personnel should be minimized.

VIP/ORIENTATION FLIGHTS

VIP/orientation flight requirements are contained in OPNAVINST 3710.7 series.

PERSONAL FLYING EQUIPMENT

The minimum requirement for personal flying equipment is contained in OPNAVINST 3710.7 series.

In addition, the latest available flight safety and survival equipment as authorized by Aviation Crew Systems Manual, Volume 7 (Aircrew Personal Protective Equipment), NAVAIR 13-1-6.7, shall be used by crewmen for flight in A-6 aircraft.

Section III
NORMAL PROCEDURES

TABLE OF CONTENTS

PART 1 BRIEFING/DEBRIEFING	3-3
Briefing/Debriefing Responsibilities	3-3
Briefing Officer	3-3
Pilot-In-Command/Mission Commander	3-3
Operational Briefing	3-3
Preoperational Briefing	3-3
Preflight Briefing	3-3
PART 2 MISSION PLANNING	3-5
Mission Planning	3-5
Nuclear Weapons	3-5
Conventional Weapons	3-5
PART 3 SHORE-BASED PROCEDURES	3-6
Preparations for Flight	3-6
Crew Preflight Check	3-8
Ejection Seat Check	3-13
Pilot Prestart Procedures External Power On	3-21
Starting Engines	3-26
Post Start	3-28
Ordnance	3-30
Before Taxiing	3-30
Wing Spread	3-30
Control Checks	3-31
Refueling System Ground Check (KA-6D)	3-32
Attitude Gyro Check (KA-6D)	3-33
Before Takeoff	3-33
Takeoff (Ashore)	3-34
After Takeoff Climb	3-36
Cruise	3-37
Flight Characteristics	3-37
Descent	3-37
Before Landing	3-37
Landing (ASHORE)	3-38
Wave-Off	3-39
After Landing	3-40
Wing Fold	3-41
Hot Refueling	3-41
Post Hot-Seat Checklist	3-41
Engine Shutdown	3-42
PART 4 CARRIER-BASED PROCEDURES (PILOT)	3-43
Field Mirror Landing Practice	3-43
Preflight Inspection	3-43
Pattern Entry	3-43
Pattern	3-43
Night Pattern	3-43
Carrier-Based Procedures	3-44
Preflight	3-44
Post Start	3-44
Taxi	3-44
Launch Procedures	3-44
Catapult Launch	3-45
Recovery	3-46
Pattern (VFR)	3-46
Approach	3-46
Wave-Off/Bolter Pattern	3-46
Arrested Landing and Exit from Landing Area	3-48
Carrier-Controlled Approach	3-49
Automatic Carrier Landing System	3-49
PART 5 SHORE-BASED PROCEDURES (B/N)	3-53
B/N Prestart Procedures	3-53
Weapon System Preflight	3-56
Taxi	3-68
Weapon System Preflight - When in Radar Turn-Up Area A-6A, B, C	3-68
Pretakeoff	3-73
Takeoff	3-73
Airborne	3-73
Before Landing	3-74
In Chocks	3-74
A-6C Preflight	3-75
A-6C Pretakeoff	3-79
A-6C Airborne	3-79
A-6C Before Landing	3-79
A-6C In Chocks	3-79
Inertial Platform Alignment	3-80
Fixed Target Ground/Discrete Lock-On Tracking A-6A	3-85
Moving Target Detection and Acquisition A-6A	3-87
Moving Target Discrete Lock-On and Tracking A-6A	3-87
Search Radar Tracking (RTT) A-6A	3-87
Velocity Correct A-6A, B, C	3-89
Track Radar Optical Tracking (TROT) (P-7B TRIM)	3-89
Computer Optical Positioning (COP) (P-8, 6)	3-90
Boresight Mode	3-90

3-1

TABLE OF CONTENTS

Track Radar Displays A-6A, C	3-92
Attack A-6A, B, C	3-93
AN/AWW-1 Electrical Fuzing	3-101
Target Tracking A-6E	3-102
Velocity Correct A-6E	3-104
Computer Optical Positioning (COP) A-6E	3-105
Attack A-6E	3-105

PART 6 CARRIER-BASED PROCEDURES (B/N) ... 3-113
   Carrier Alignment (Automatic) A-6A, B, C . 3-113
   Carrier Alignment (Manual) A-6A, B, C . . 3-114
   Carrier Alignment (Automatic) A-6E 3-115
   Carrier Alignment (Manual) A-6E 3-117

PART 7 DEGRADED SYSTEM OPERATING PROCEDURES (A-6A, B, C) ... 3-119
   Search Radar Failure 3-119
   Automatic Frequency Control (AFC) Failure 3-119
   Magnetron Reset Button Search and Track . 3-120
   Track Radar Emergency Search Operation 3-120
   Limits to Use of Emergency Search Mode of Operation 3-120
   Emergency Search Mode Characteristics . 3-120
   Weapon Delivery in Manual Mode 3-121
   Nonsystem Laydown Bombing 3-122
   Weapon Delivery With Loss of Air Data (Emergency Straight Path) 3-123

Attack Procedures With Loss of Air Data	3-123
Weapon Delivery With Selective Data Replacement - NOMATS (P-8.6)	3-123
LAB IP and LAB Target Delivery	3-123
Valid Data Interpretation and Use	3-124
Search Radar Delivery	3-125
Coordinate System Bombing	3-125
Release Override	3-125
Alternate Modes of Navigation and Stabilization	3-126

PART 8 AIR-REFUELING PROCEDURES ... 3-128
   Air-Refueling Procedures KA-6D 3-128
   Air-Refueling (Tanker) Procedures - D-704 Store 3-132

PART 9 SATS PROCEDURES ... 3-136
   Preflight 3-136
   Taxi 3-136
   Launch Procedures 3-136
   Catapult Emergencies 3-137
   Recovery 3-137
   Wave-Off/Bolter 3-137

PART 10 FUNCTIONAL CHECKFLIGHT PROCEDURES ... 3-138
   Functional Checkflight Requirements . . . 3-138
   Pretakeoff 3-138
   In-Flight 3-146
   Landing 3-153

 Briefing/Debriefing

BRIEFING/DEBRIEFING RESPONSIBILITIES

The Commanding Officer shall ensure that every flight crew is properly and adequately briefed on all facets of the assigned mission. Through the Operations Officer, he shall assign the appropriate personnel to brief each flight, according to the mission and anticipated conditions.

BRIEFING OFFICER

The Briefing Officer assigned on the Flight Schedule shall have the overall responsibility for coordinating and conducting a proper and adequate briefing of the flight. This responsibility will be assumed by the flight leader if a Briefing Officer has not been assigned.

PILOT-IN-COMMAND/MISSION COMMANDER

Each Pilot-in-Command/Mission Commander shall ensure that an adequate briefing has been obtained, and that his crew is fully prepared for the scheduled mission.

OPERATIONAL BRIEFING

Flight crews shall be given complete, comprehensive briefings on all operations. The briefing officer shall work in conjunction with the operations officer, Air Intelligence Officer, and other officers concerned, in preparing the necessary information. He shall make optimum use of all graphic presentation devices, maps, charts, etc., which are available.

PREOPERATIONAL BRIEFING

Immediately prior to all operations of appreciable complexity and duration, a general information brief shall be given to familiarize personnel with the overall nature of the operation. The following topics shall be included:

1. The mission and objectives of the operation, and the part the squadron will play in carrying them out

2. A brief chronological breakdown of how the operation will be conducted.

3. The geographical area in which the operations will be conducted including but not limited to the following:

    (1.) BINGO FIELDS

    a. Instrument approach facilities.
    b. Runway length and arresting gear.
    c. Local terrain and obstructions.

    (2.) EMERGENCY FIELDS

    a. Fields suitable for landing but without required support equipment.
    b. Instrument approach facilities.
    c. Runway length and arresting gear.
    d. Terrain and obstructions.

    (3.) SAR FACILITIES

    a. Type.
    b. Frequencies.
    c. Locations.

4. The forces involved, both friendly and enemy, and how they will be deployed

5. The rules of engagement set down by the governing operation order

6. Search and rescue, EMCOM, and other special communications procedures which will be used, including explanation of shackles and authenticators

7. A discussion by the Briefing Officer of the principal attack tactics to be employed

PREFLIGHT BRIEFING

These briefs are presented immediately before the launching of scheduled flights, and therefore must be carried out in the most expeditious manner. It is imperative that all pilots and bombardier/navigators be in flight gear and otherwise ready for the briefing at the designated time. The brief shall include, but not be limited to the following:

Note

Information marked with an asterisk (*) shall be displayed on a status board in the briefing or ready room, and should be copied by pilots before commencement of the briefing.

NORMAL PROCEDURES
Briefing/Debriefing

1. General.
    a. Aircraft assigned, call signs, and event number.*
    b. Fuel load, stores, and aircraft gross weight.
    c. Engine start, taxi and takeoff times.
    d. Line and taxi procedures.
    e. Takeoff distance and speed, rendezvous instructions, and visual signals.

2. Mission.
    a. Primary.
    b. Secondary.
    c. Operating area.
    d. Time on station or over target.
    e. IP (Radar/Visual).
    f. Review of target and procedures.

3. Communications.
    a. Channels and frequencies.*
    b. Controlling agencies.
    c. Navigational aids.*
    d. Radio procedures and discipline.
    e. Reports required.
    f. Authenticators, IFF/SIF procedures.
    g. ADIZ procedures.
    h. EMCON conditions.

4. Participating units.
    a. Voice calls and side numbers.*
    b. Disposition.
    c. Utilization.
    d. Friendly subs and surface units.

5. Navigation and flight planning.
    a. Duty runway/predicted foxtrop corpen for launch and recovery.
    b. Takeoff.
    c. Climb-out.
    d. Mission route including planned use of all navigation systems, check point (radar/visual) restricted or danger areas.
    e. Fuel/oxygen management including bingo fuel.
    f. Marshal holding.
    g. Penetration procedures.
    h. GCA or CCA procedures.
    i. Recovery time and recovery order.*

6. Operations.
    a. Instructions for coordinating other units.

7. Weapons.
    a. Type/quantity.*
    b. Preflight.
    c. Special routes with ordnance aboard.
    d. Pattern including airspeeds and altitudes.
    e. Restrictions on use.
    f. Armament switches/arming.
    g. Minimum release/pullout altitudes.
    h. Duds, hung ordnance, dearming, and jettison procedures.
    i. Safety.

8. Weather - base, enroute, and target.
    a. Wind: direction and velocity at surface and at applicable altitudes (jet streams and contrails).*
    b. Cloud coverage: present and forecast.*
    c. Visibility.*
    d. Sea state.
    e. Water and air temperature (cold weather).*
    f. Target weather.
    g. Divert weather.

9. Emergencies.
    a. Takeoff.
    b. Radio failure.
    c. Loss of NAV aids/system.
    d. Loss of visual contact with flight.
    e. SAR procedures.
    f. System failure.

10. Air intelligence and special instructions.
    a. Friendly/enemy force disposition.
    b. Current situation.
    c. Targets.
    d. Safety precautions.
    e. Reports and authentication.
    f. Escape and evasion.

11. Miscellaneous.
    a. Other units in the area.
    b. Current NOTAMS, bulletins, and safety-of-flight information.
    c. SAR - participating units and procedures.

Part 2 — Mission Planning

MISSION PLANNING

Detailed preflight planning is essential for the success of any attack mission, consistent with the time available and the nature of the assignement.

NUCLEAR WEAPONS

Mission planning for nuclear weapons delivery shall be in accordance with NAVAIR 01-85ADA-1T, A-6A Tactical Manual.

CONVENTIONAL WEAPONS

Conventional weapons deliveries fall generally into two types:

1. Preplanned strikes on specific targets
2. Close air support, call fire, or armed reconnaissance

Preplanned Strikes

Preplanned strikes on specific targets shall be planned in the same manner as special weapons deliveries.

Close Air Support, Call Fire, and Armed Reconnaissance Strikes

Due to the tactical nature of these missions, detailed preplanning is unrealistic. Preplanning shall concentrate primarily on target area familiarization and review of weapons check list and fuel planning aids.

Shore Based Procedures

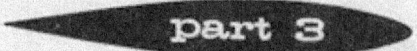

Note

- Refer to Supplemental NATOPS Flight Manual NAVAIR 01-85ADA-1A for A-6B-peculiar procedures.

- A-6C-peculiar procedures may be found in this part following the A-6 common procedures. The appropriate place in the A-6 common procedures for completing an A-6C-peculiar procedural step is indicated by A-6C in boldface type followed by the applicable step number. Eg.:

A-6C 1.

PREPARATIONS FOR FLIGHT

When both crewmembers are present, it is recommended that a thorough briefing be conducted concerning normal and emergency procedures, crew coordination, and cooperation through the planned mission. Refer to Section IX, Flight Crew Coordination.

FLIGHT RESTRICTIONS

Refer to Section I, Part 4, Aircraft Operating Limitations, and Section XI, Performance Data.

FLIGHT PLANNING

Refer to Section XI, Performance Data, to determine fuel consumption, airspeeds, power settings, and altitude required for the intended flight mission.

ACCEPTANCE OF AIRCRAFT

Review current OPNAV form 3760-2 (yellow sheet) for status and servicing of aircraft.

WEIGHT AND BALANCE

Refer to Section I, Part 4, for Aircraft Operating Limitations.

For loading information, refer to the Handbook of Weight and Balance Data, AN-01-1B-40.

CHECKLISTS

The placarded takeoff and landing checklist (figure 3-1) located in the aircraft cockpit serve as reminders for the orderly check of certain essential aircraft functions. The pilot is responsible for the completion of the checklist and acknowledgement by the bombardier/navigator is mandatory prior to take-off or landing.

ACCESS TO COCKPIT

See figure 3-2 for normal entry into the cockpit.

Figure 3-1

NAVAIR 01-85ADA-1

NORMAL PROCEDURES
Shore-Based Procedures

EXTERNAL CANOPY OPERATION

MANUAL OPERATION FROM NOSE WHEEL WELL

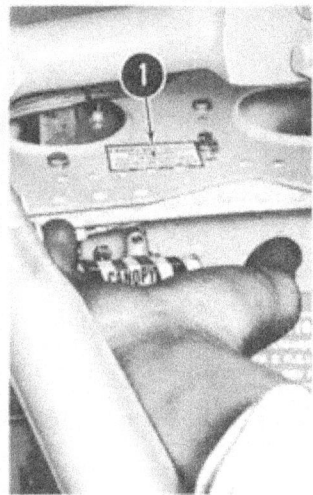
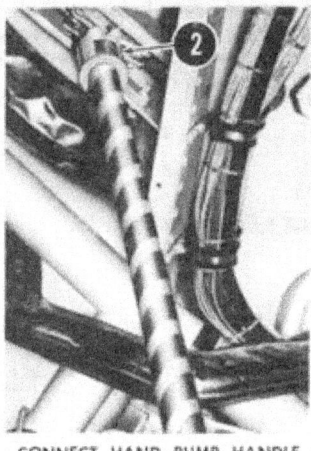

CONNECT HAND PUMP HANDLE TO HAND PUMP (45 CYCLES TO FULLY OPEN CANOPY)

1 CANOPY SELECTOR GROUND OPERATION "PUSH UP" TO OPEN—"PULL DOWN" TO CLOSE

NOTE

A-6E, A-6A 155703 AND ON AND AIRCRAFT INCORPORATING A.F.C. NO. 185. CANOPY SELECTOR HANDLE MUST BE HELD IN DESIRED POSITION TO OPERATE CANOPY.

2 HAND PUMP AND HANDLE

NOTE

BEFORE ENTERING COCKPIT OR INITIATING COCKPIT CHECKS ENSURE THAT BOTH COCKPIT CANOPY SWITCH AND MANUAL SELECTOR HANDLE ARE OPEN OR NEUTRAL

CANOPY OPERATION—BOARDING LADDER SWITCHES

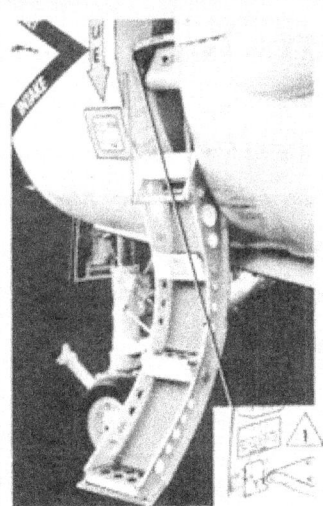
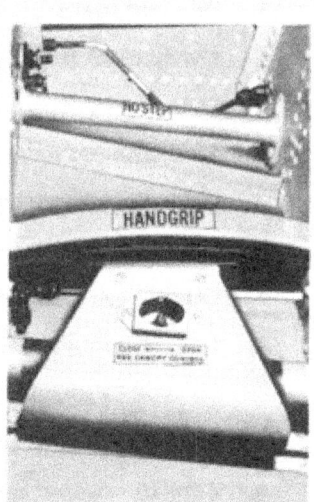

TYPICAL BOTH SIDES OF AIRCRAFT

⚠ 1 A-6E 158041 THROUGH 158538 AND A-6A 155720 THROUGH 157029 NOT INCORPORATING A.F.C. NO. 287.

E-ADA1-34

Figure 3-2

NORMAL PROCEDURES
Shore-Based Procedures

NAVAIR 01-85ADA-1

CREW PREFLIGHT CHECK

BEFORE EXTERIOR INSPECTION

> **CAUTION**
>
> Prior to ground power being applied, it is mandatory that either qualified maintenance personnel or a crewmember ensure that steps 1 through 3 have been completed.

1. Fire extinguishing .... AVAILABLE

   A-6C 1.

2. Cockpit canopy switch and manual selector handle .... OPEN OR NEUTRAL

3. Cockpit check

   a. Oxygen switches .... OFF

   b. Emergency flap switch .... OFF

   c. FUEL READY switch .... AS DESIRED

   d. Wing and fuselage dump switches .... OFF

   e. Landing-gear handle .... DOWN

   f. Trim button .... SECURE

   g. VDI and PHD .... OFF

   h. Armament switches .... OFF/SAFE

   i. Pitot heat switch .... OFF

   j. CNI MASTER switch (except A-6E TRAM) .... OFF

   k. ECM .... OFF

   l. ICIR COOLING switch .... OFF

   m. BNCB SEARCH/TRACK power switches (except KA-6D) ...... OFF

   n. Inertial platform control panel (except KA-6D) .... OFF

   o. Ground-controlled bombing system (GCBS) (except A-6E TRAM) ... OFF

   p. Internal system refueling panel (KA-6D)

      (1) POWER switch .... OFF

      (2) DROGUE jettison switch .... SAFE/GUARD CLOSED AND SAFETY-WIRED

   q. External refueling store panel (if installed)

      (1) Master/power switch .... OFF

      (2) JETTISON switch .... NORM

   r. Doppler power switch .... OFF

CONTINUED ON NEXT PAGE

NAVAIR 01-85ADA-1

NORMAL PROCEDURES
Shore-Based Procedures

CREW PREFLIGHT CHECK—CONTINUED

4. External power .... CONNECTED
5. Integrated position indicator .... MATCHES AIRCRAFT CONFIGURATION
6. Annunciator panel RUD THRO light .... ON

WARNING

If the RUD THRO light is not lit prior to start, a rudder linkage failure may have occurred.

7. Fuel, oil, and oxygen quantity .... CHECK
8. Platform (Except KA-6D) .... STBY (5 MINUTES MINIMUM)
8A. NAVIGATION panel (A-6E TRAM)
   a. MODE button .... LEVEL
   b. SINS DATA switch .... OFF

EXTERIOR INSPECTION

Perform exterior inspection as outlined below: (refer to figure 3-3)

Ⓐ NOSE AREA

1. Armament safety override switch .... OFF
2. Canopy air bottle .... 2450 PSI ±100 PSI

EXTERIOR INSPECTION

GENERAL CHECKS

THE FOLLOWING GENERAL CHECKS SHOULD BE PERFORMED THROUGHOUT THE EXTERIOR INSPECTION: CRACKS, DISTORTIONS, LOOSE FASTENERS; COVERS REMOVED; FUEL, OIL, HYDRAULIC LEAKS; ACCESS DOORS AND PANELS SECURELY FASTENED; AND EXTERNAL STORES SECURE.

NOTE

THE EXTERIOR INSPECTION NORMALLY BEGINS AT THE PILOT'S COCKPIT BOARDING LADDER AND PROGRESSES IN A CLOCKWISE DIRECTION AROUND THE AIRCRAFT. AFTER COMPLETION OF THE "AFT FUSELAGE AREA" CHECKS, REPEAT THE "CENTER FUSELAGE AND WING AREA" CHECKS FOR THE LEFT SIDE INSPECTION.

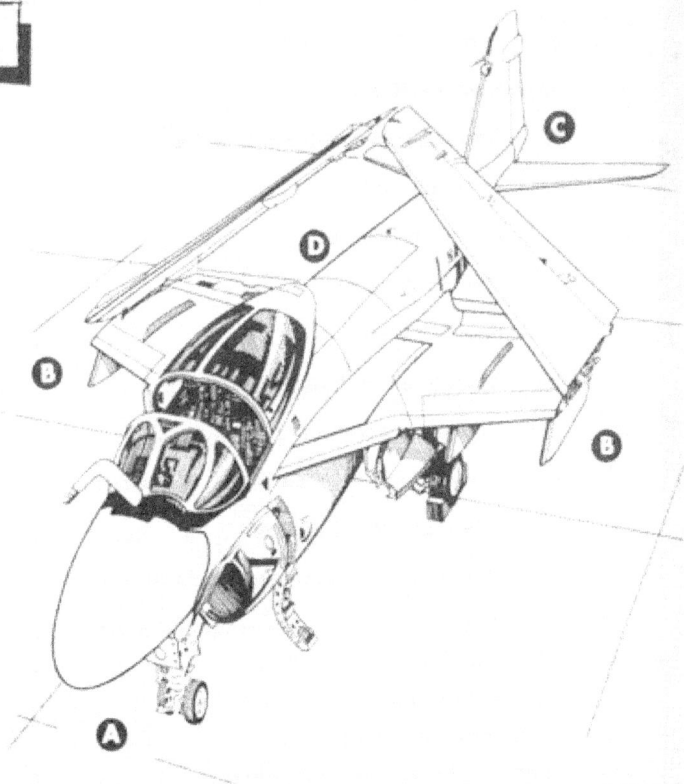

Figure 3-3

CONTINUED ON NEXT PAGE

NORMAL PROCEDURES
Shore-Based Procedures

NAVAIR 01-85ADA-1

CREW PREFLIGHT CHECK—CONTINUED

3. Canopy jettison bleeder valve plunger .... DEPRESS
    If air escapes a leak in one of the canopy jettison bottles is indicated.
    This could result in unintentional jettison of the canopy

4. Total-temperature probe... CHECK
5. Intake duct area .... CLEAR
6. Radome .... SECURE
7. Air-refueling probe... CHECK VISUALLY FOR DAMAGE
8. Nose gear... CHECK
    a. Approach, anticollision, and taxi lights .... CHECK
    b. Tires and shockstrut .... PROPERLY INFLATED
    c. Nose-gear ground safety lock .... INSTALLED
    d. Nose-gear shimmy damper .... CHECK
    e. Nose-gear steering linkage .... CHECK
    f. Nose-gear door linkage .... CHECK
    g. Nose-gear tie down.. CHECK AS REQUIRED
    h. Nosewheel cotter pins .... INSTALLED
9. Nose-gear wheel well .... CHECK
    a. Landing-gear emergency air gage................................... 2450 ±100 PSI
    b. Auxiliary brakes .... 800 PSI MINIMUM PRELOAD
    c. Circuit breakers .... IN
    d. Handpump handle .... SECURE
    e. Splash curtains .... SECURE
    f. Manual canopy handle .... UP (OPEN)
    g. Equipment pressure .... 600-2800 PSI
    h. Dehumidifier crystals (A6A, B, C only) .... CHECK (BLUE IN COLOR)
    i. Down-lock Micro Switch .... SECURE
    j. Ground blower power switch (A-6E only) .... AUTO
    k. Ground blower inlet screen (A-6E only) .... CLEAR
10. Intake duct area .... CHECK
11. Outside air-temperature probe .... CHECK
12. Angle-of-attack probe .... CHECK
13. Flight hydraulic reservoir quantity .... CHECK (THEN SECURE ACCESS PANEL)
14. Ground refueling panel .... CHECKED

CONTINUED ON NEXT PAGE

CREW PREFLIGHT CHECK—CONTINUED

    a. FWD/AFT transfer and dump pump . . . . CHECK
    b. Power switch . . . . OFF
15. Air-conditioning inlet . . . . CLEAR

Ⓑ CENTER FUSELAGE AND WING AREA

1. Forward engine access doors . . . . FLUSH WITH FUSELAGE
    a. Latch handles (6) . . . . STOWED AND LOCKED
    b. Locking pins (8) . . . . FULLY SEATED
       Check through visual inspection ports
2. Main-gear wheel well . . . . CHECK
3. Main gear . . . . CHECK
    a. Tire and shock strut . . . . PROPERLY INFLATED
    b. Main landing-gear dump valve . . . . CHECK IN
    c. Main-gear ground safety lock . . . . INSTALLED
    d. Main-gear tie down . . . . CHECK AS REQUIRED
    e. Jack pads . . . . STOWED
4. Center pylon . . . . SECURE
5. Wing pylon . . . . SECURE
6. Wing slat . . . . SECURE
7. Fuel ram-air inlet . . . . CLEAR
8. Wing-tip speed brakes . . . . CLOSED
    Ensure speed-brake ground safety lock removed.
9. Position and formation lights . . . . CHECK
10. Wing fuel dump-vent line . . . . CLEAR
11. Wing flap and flaperon . . . . SECURE
    Ensure cotter pins and safety wires installed
12. Exhaust area . . . . CLEAR
13. A-6C TRIM pod . . . CHECK FOR HYDRAULIC LEAKS AND GENERAL SECURITY, POD STOWED
14. Air-refueling store (if installed)
    a. Store propeller . . . . CHECK
    b. Hydraulic fluid level . . . . CHECK
    c. Pod fuel quantity . . . . CHECK
    d. Drogue . . . . CHECK
    e. Electrical hookup . . . . CHECK

Ⓒ AFT FUSELAGE AREA

1. Rudder and stabilizer . . . . CHECK
2. Fuselage fuel dump-vent line . . . . CLEAR
3. Arresting hook . . . . SECURE
4. Arresting-hook ground safety lock . . . . REMOVED
5. Extensible equipment platform . . . . SECURE

WARNING

Aircrews will ensure that items stowed in the aft equipment bay are properly secured to prevent damage or interference with critical components.

6. Dashpot pressure . . . . (HOOK UP) NORMAL
                                                                                                                                     (HOOK DOWN) LOW
7. Liquid oxygen vent (Except KA-6D) . . . . CLEAR
8. Doppler radome (Except KA-6D) . . . . SECURE
9. Chaff dispenser . . . . CLEAR/SECURE

CONTINUED ON NEXT PAGE

CREW PREFLIGHT CHECK—CONTINUED

Ⓓ TOP FUSELAGE, WING, TAIL AREA

1. Fuel ram air inlet .... CLEAR
2. Aft compartment air inlet .... CLEAR
3. Anti collision light .... CHECK
4. Ram-air turbine .... CHECK
   Check Cannon plug for security
5. Pitot tube .... COVER REMOVED

Note

Before entering cockpit ensure that both the cockpit canopy switch and the canopy manual selector handle are in the open position.

6. Canopy manual disconnect pin and eccentric bushing .... CHECK
   Check that eccentric bushing is in horizontal position with pins inserted and locked and T-handles stowed in clips provided. See figure 3-4.

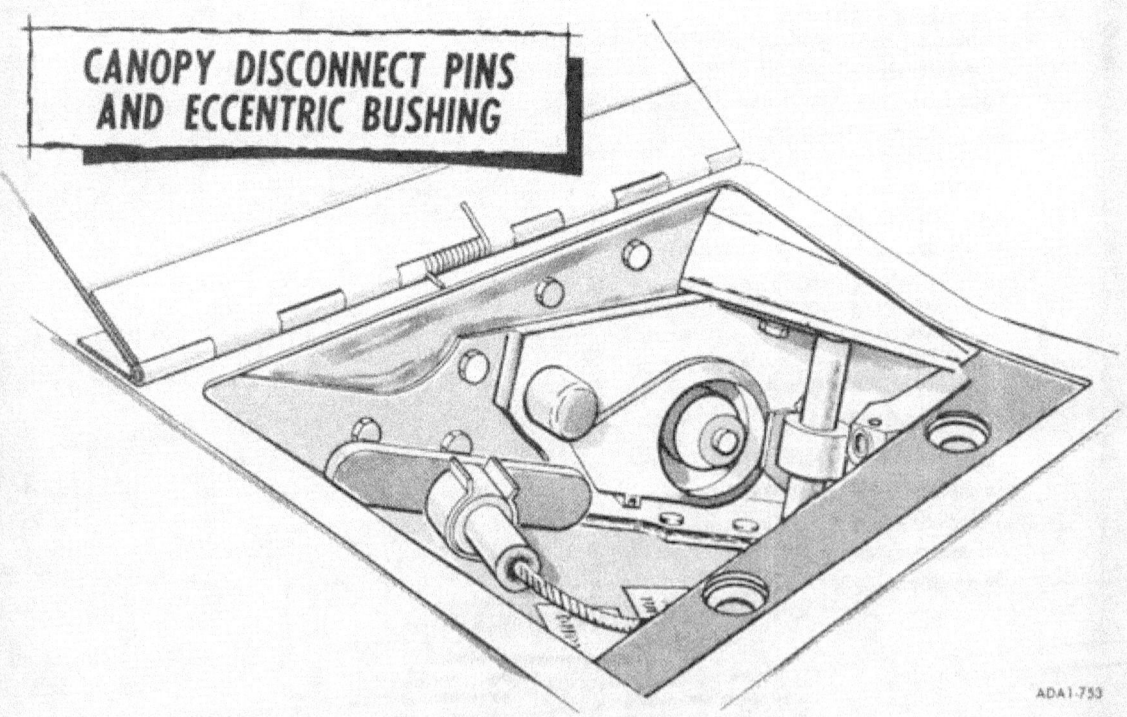

Figure 3-4

NAVAIR 01-85ADA-1

NORMAL PROCEDURES
Shore-Based Procedures

CREW PREFLIGHT CHECK—CONTINUED

7. Canopy jettison air bottle pin .... CHECK REMOVED

WARNING

If pin is difficult to remove, it may indicate the bottle
has discharged and the canopy will be jettisoned unless
the pressure is bled off.

8. Pitot/static lines (2) .... CHECK FOR PROPER CONNECTION

EJECTION SEAT CHECK

WARNING

To prevent inadvertant firing of the ejection seat or
jamming of the emergency restraint release, ensure
that the relief tube is properly stowed in the clamps
provided.

MK GRU-5 SEAT

Note

Before entering the cockpit or initiating other cockpit
checks, ensure that both the cockpit canopy switch
and the manual selector handle are in the open position.

1. Face-curtain lock and lower ejection handle guard .... UP (LOCKED POSITION)
2. Ejection-seat ground safety pins .... IN
3. Firing cables .... CONNECTED (THIN ON TOP - THICK ON BOTTOM)
4. Top latch mechanism indicator .... LOCKED
   Check that top latch mechanism plunger and indicator dowel are both flush with
   or slightly recessed from end of top latch mechanism housing.
5. Drogue-gun cocking indicator .... EXTENDED
6. Drogue-gun trip rod bolt .... INSERTED (NUT ATTACHED)

CONTINUED ON NEXT PAGE

3-13

NORMAL PROCEDURES
Shore-Based Procedures
NAVAIR 01-85ADA-1

EJECTION SEAT SAFETY PINS

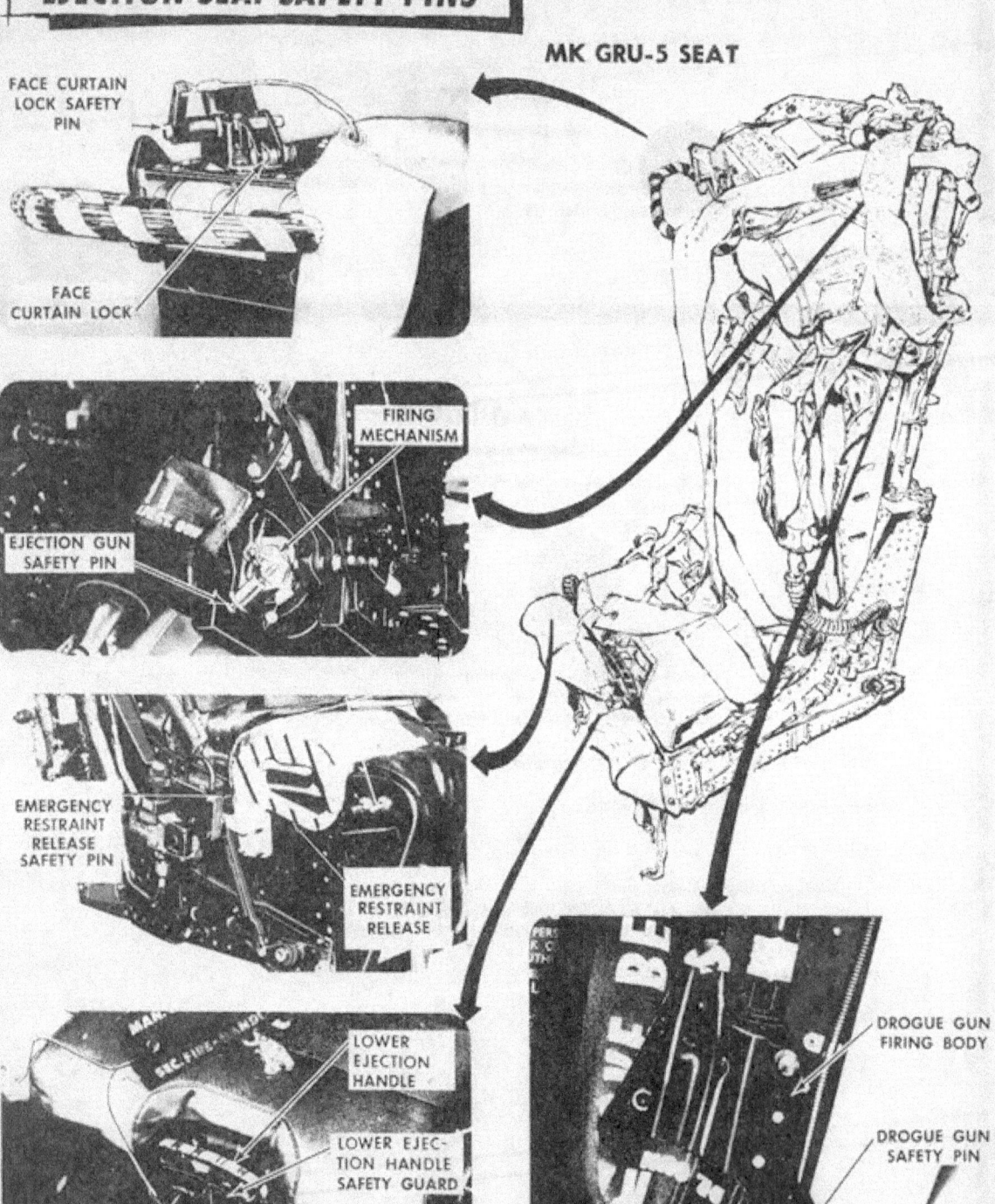

Figure 3-5

NAVAIR 01-85ADA-1 — NORMAL PROCEDURES
Shore-Based Procedures

EJECTION SEAT CHECK — CONTINUED

7. Drogue gun .... LOCKWIRED AND SEALED
8. Auxiliary ejection seat cartridges, firing mechanism .... LOCKWIRED AND SEALED
   and retaining ring
9. Slide disconnect static line cable .... CONNECTED
   Check that slide disconnect static line cable is connected to retention lug by link line pin.

WARNING

If the slide disconnect static line cable is not connected, manual separation from the seat with the personnel parachute is not possible.

10. Time-release mechanism .... LOCKWIRED AND SEALED
11. Time-release mechanism trip rod bolt .... INSERTED (NUT ATTACHED)
    Check that time-release mechanism trip rod bolt is inserted through emergency oxygen actuator with trip lever in UP position, and that nut is attached.
12. Emergency oxygen bottle .... 1,800 PSI
13. Left- and right-hand personnel services blocks .... CONNECTED
14. Personnel parachute withdrawal-line screw connector .... CHECK
    Check that personnel parachute withdrawal-line screw connector is secured and that withdrawal line is positioned over firing cables.

WARNING

If the personnel parachute withdrawal line is not securely connected, automatic deployment of the occupant's personnel parachute will not occur after ejection.

15. Parachute attachment .... HARD PULL
16. Back and seat pads .... CHECK FOR PROPER POSITIONING
17. Lap belt and shoulder harness .... SECURE (HARD PULL)
    Pull on lap belt and shoulder harness to check if firmly attached.
18. Leg-line snubber-release lever .... LOCKED (AFT)

WARNING

If the leg-line snubber-release lever is jammed in the UNLOCKED (forward) position, manual or automatic seat separation may not be possible.

19. Leg restraint .... ATTACHED TO DECK
20. Ejection-seat ground safety pins .... REMOVE (5 PINS) AND STOW

CONTINUED ON NEXT PAGE

NORMAL PROCEDURES
Shore-Based Procedures

NAVAIR 01-85ADA-1

EJECTION SEAT PREFLIGHT

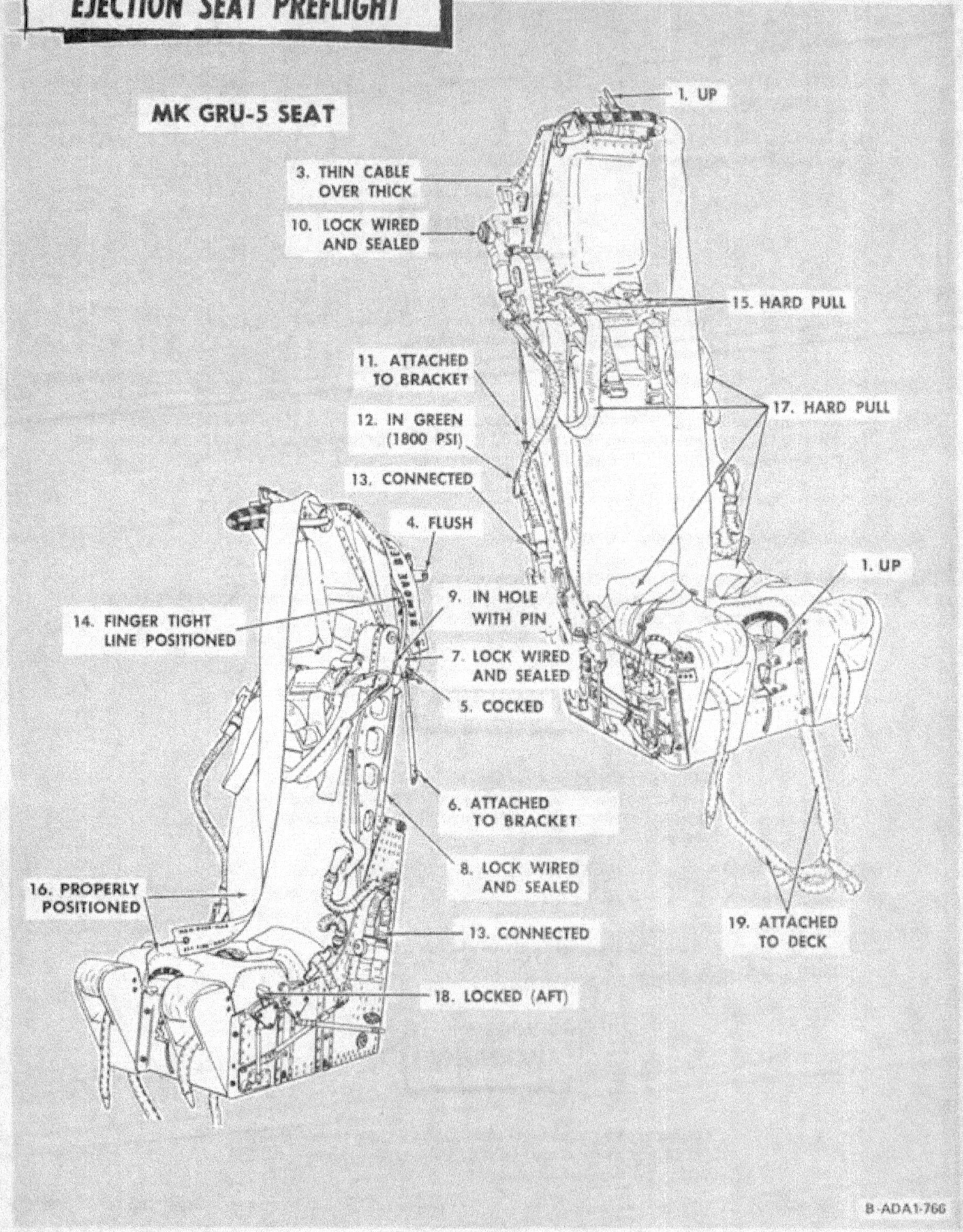

MK GRU-5 SEAT

- 1. UP
- 3. THIN CABLE OVER THICK
- 10. LOCK WIRED AND SEALED
- 15. HARD PULL
- 11. ATTACHED TO BRACKET
- 17. HARD PULL
- 12. IN GREEN (1800 PSI)
- 13. CONNECTED
- 4. FLUSH
- 1. UP
- 14. FINGER TIGHT LINE POSITIONED
- 9. IN HOLE WITH PIN
- 7. LOCK WIRED AND SEALED
- 5. COCKED
- 6. ATTACHED TO BRACKET
- 8. LOCK WIRED AND SEALED
- 16. PROPERLY POSITIONED
- 19. ATTACHED TO DECK
- 13. CONNECTED
- 18. LOCKED (AFT)

B-ADA1-766

Figure 3-6

3-16

EJECTION SEAT CHECK—CONTINUED

MK GRU-7 Seat

1. Face-curtain lock and lower ejection handle guard . . . . UP (LOCKED POSITION)
2. Ejection-seat ground safety pins (6) (7 in seats with ACC 271) . . . . INSTALLED
3. Ejection-gun firing linkage . . . . CONNECTED
   Check through the windows that the face-curtain cables are connected to the firing linkage.
4. Top latch mechanism . . . . LOCKED
   Check that top latch mechanism plunger and indicator dowel are both flush with or slightly recessed from end of top latch mechanism housing.
5. Drogue-gun trip rod . . . . SECURED
   Check that the drogue-gun trip rod is secured to the fixed ejection-gun bracket with the red painted portion covered by the trip rod outer barrel.
6. Rocket motor initiator sear extraction lanyard . . . . ATTACHED
   Check that the rocket motor initiator sear extraction lanyard is attached to the sear actuating link and the drogue gun trip rod.
7. Drogue gun . . . . LOCKWIRED AND SEALED
8. Shoulder harness reel actuating link . . . . CONNECTED
9. Parachute withdrawal line . . . . ROUTED THROUGH GUILLOTINE
10. Parachute withdrawal-line connector . . . . CONNECTED

WARNING

If the personnel parachute withdrawal line is not securely connected, automatic deployment of the parachute will not occur after ejection.

11. Rocket motor initiator . . . . LOCKWIRED AND SEALED
12. Parachute . . . . HARD PULL
13. Shoulder-harness reel straps and leg-restraint cords . . . . HARD PULL
14. Leg-restraint cords . . . . ATTACHED TO DECK
15. Emergency oxygen
    a. Emergency oxygen bottle . . . . 1,800 PSI
    b. Emergency oxygen actuator . . . . PROPERLY STOWED
16. Personnel services disconnect lanyard . . . . SECURED TO DECK
17. Survival-kit front lock release lever . . . . FULL FORWARD

CONTINUED ON NEXT PAGE

NORMAL PROCEDURES
Shore-Based Procedures

NAVAIR 01-85ADA-1

EJECTION SEAT SAFETY PINS

MK GRU 7

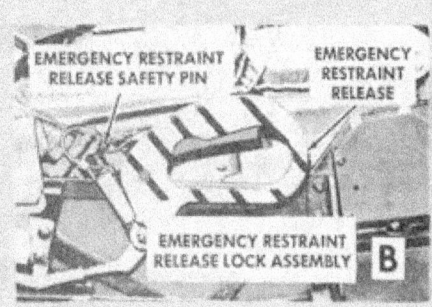

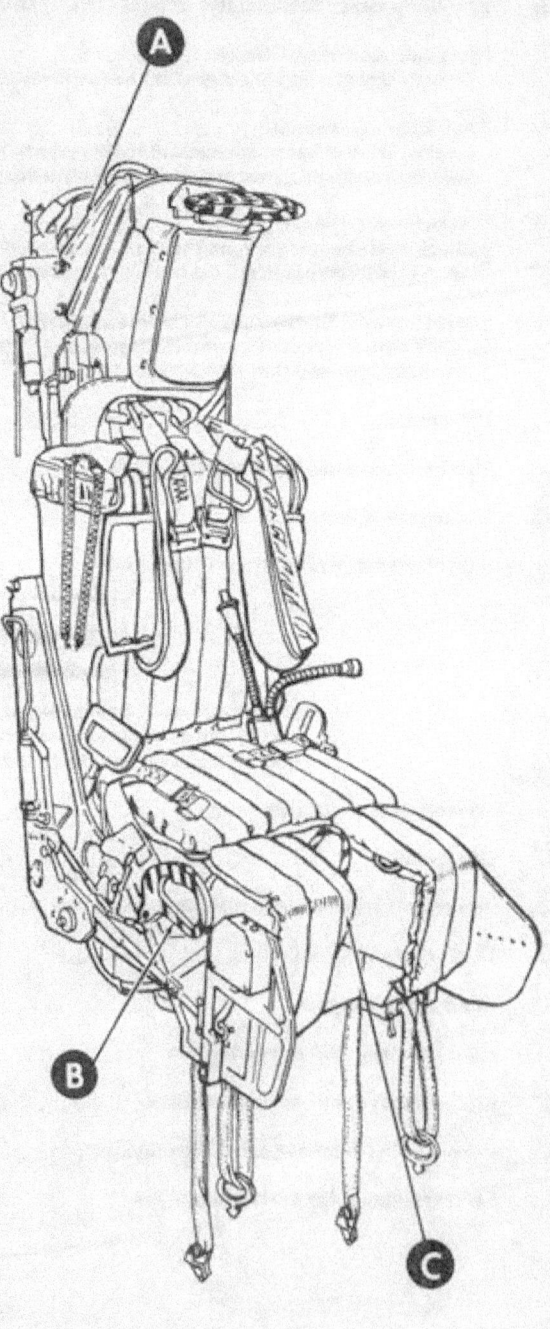

Figure 3-7 (Sheet 1)

3-18

NAVAIR 01-85ADA-1

NORMAL PROCEDURES
Shore-Based Procedures

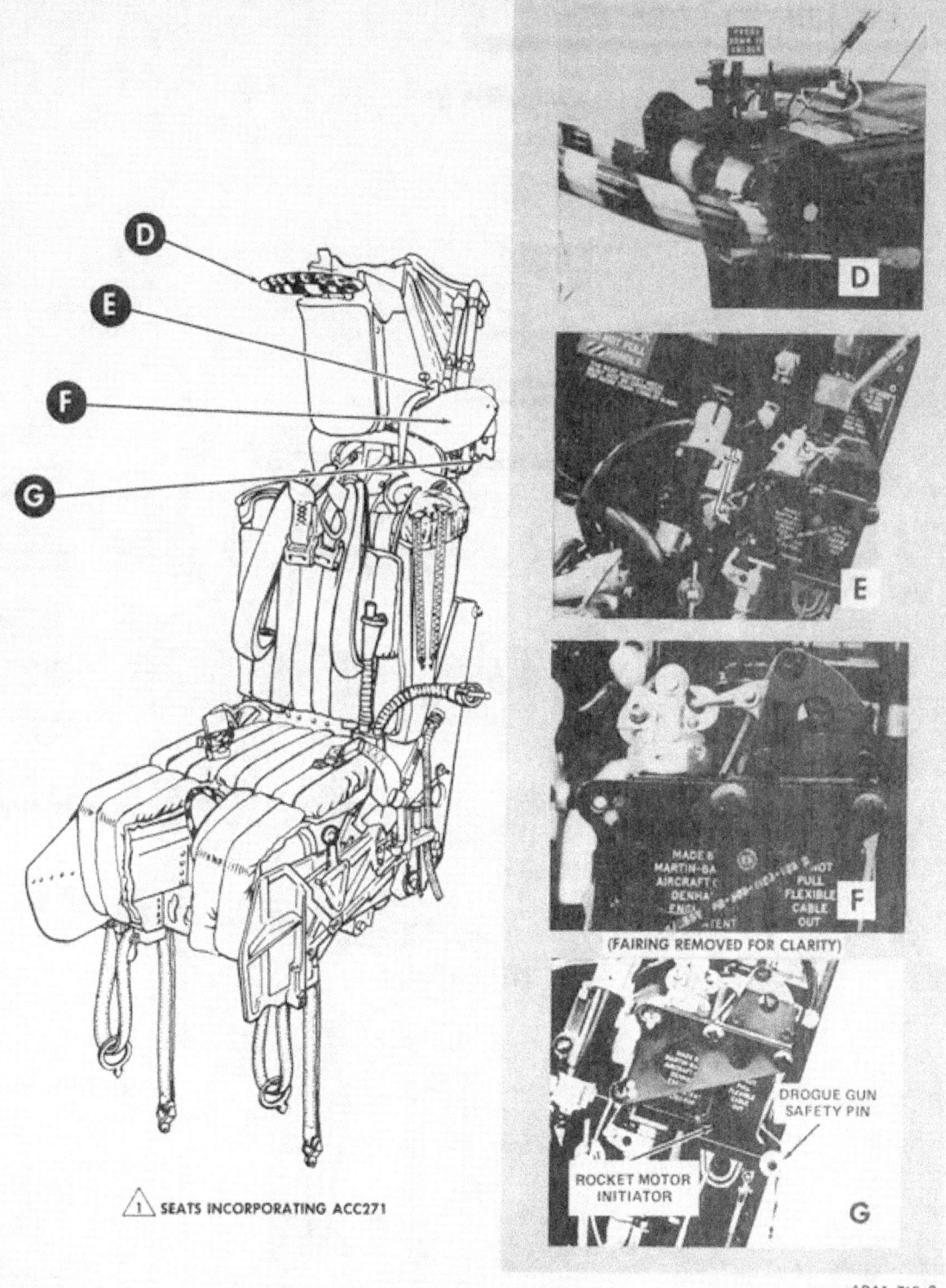

⚠1 SEATS INCORPORATING ACC271

Figure 3-7 (Sheet 2)

NORMAL PROCEDURES
Shore-Based Procedures
NAVAIR 01-85ADA-1

EJECTION SEAT PREFLIGHT

MK GRU 7

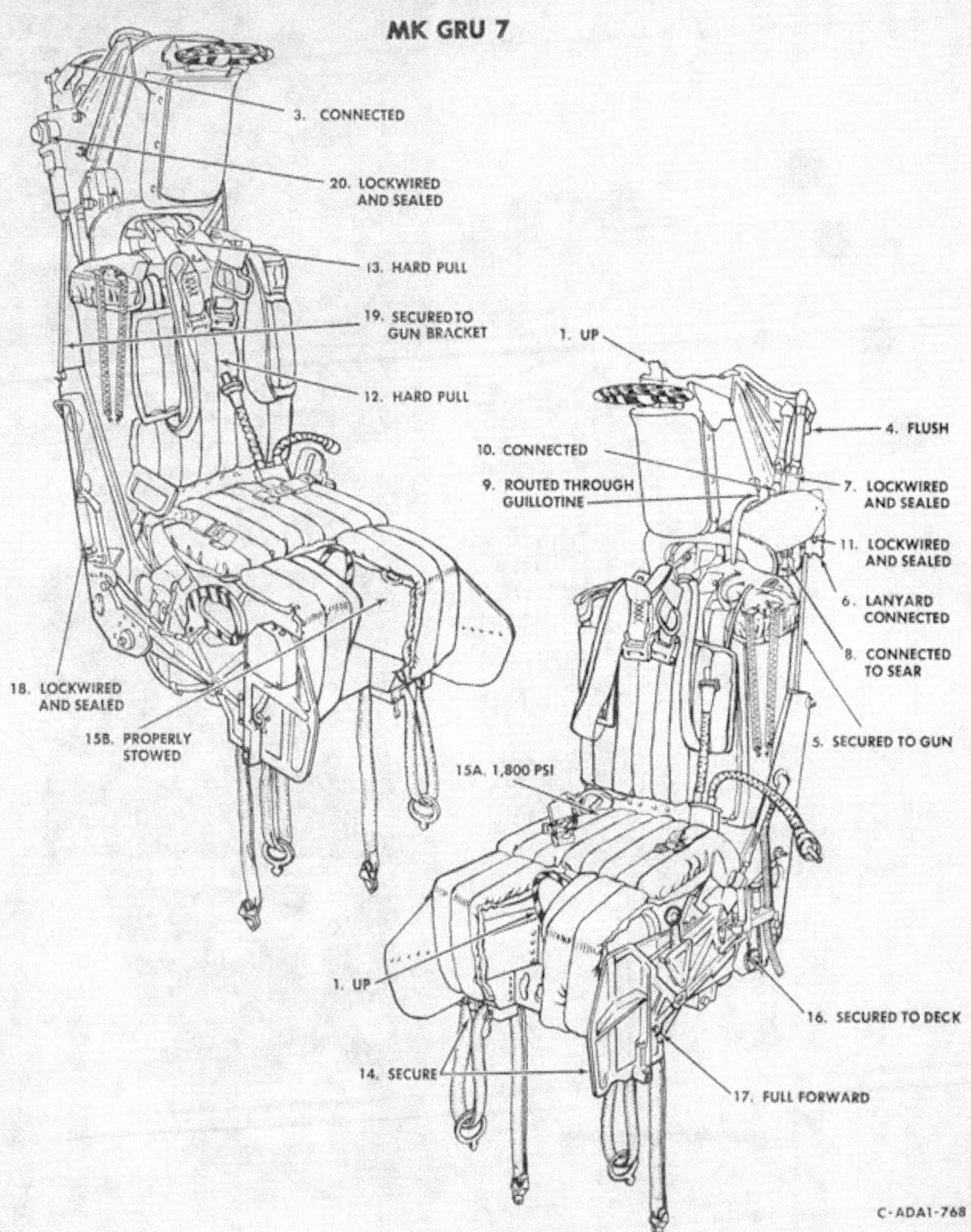

Figure 3-8

EJECTION SEAT CHECK – CONTINUED

WARNING

Failure of survival-kit front lock release lever to return to its full forward position will prevent ejection by means of the lower ejection handle.

Note

It may be necessary to raise the seat to see the lever.

18. Guillotine initiator .... LOCKWIRED AND SEALED
19. Time-release mechanism trip rod .... SECURED
    Check that the time-release mechanism trip rod is secured to the fixed ejection-gun bracket with the red painted portion covered by the trip rod outer barrel.
20. Time-release mechanism .... LOCKWIRED AND SEALED
21. Ejection-seat ground safety pins (6) (7 in seats with ACC 271) .... REMOVE AND STOW

PILOT PRESTART PROCEDURES EXTERNAL POWER ON

UPON ENTERING COCKPIT

1. Harnessing .... FASTEN

WARNING

If the survival-gear lanyard is connected (GRU-5 only), the survival equipment will hinder rapid evacuation of the cockpit during a ground emergency or ditching.

2. Helmet .... ON
3. Oxygen mask, communication connections, and anti-G suit/anti-exposure suit ..... CONNECTED
4. Seat .... ADJUST
   a. Assume ejection position, sit erect, buttocks against backrest, head firmly against headrest, spine straight, thighs against seat pan.
   b. With left hand, reach up and touch face-curtain handle.
   c. Adjust seat height so that top of helmet just clears underside of face-curtain handle.

Note

Above procedure ensures proper positioning for ejection.

5. Rudder pedals .... ADJUST

CONTINUED ON NEXT PAGE

NORMAL PROCEDURES
Shore-Based Procedures
NAVAIR 01-85ADA-1

PILOT PRESTART PROCEDURES EXTERNAL POWER ON–CONTINUED

6. Backup flight control hydraulic system .... TEST
   Place backup hydraulic test switch to FLIGHT position. BACKUP HYD light will go on. Cycle rudder and stabilizer (response indicated by plane captain's signals). Repeat for COMBINED position of switch. This test verifies operation of pressure-sensing switches in flight and combined hydraulic systems and operation of backup hydraulic motor/pump.

> **CAUTION**
>
> If the RUD THRO caution light goes out during the backup hydraulic system check, terminate the test immediately as there is no fluid in the backup hydraulic pump and pump cavitation will result.

7. Selective stores jettison switch (Except A-6E) .... SAFE
8. RAT handle .... MATCHING RAT POSITION
9. Interior and exterior lighting .... AS DESIRED
10. Anticollision light switch .... ON
11. UHF auxiliary receiver (except A-6E TRAM) .... SET AS DESIRED
12. ICS (except A-6E TRAM) .... AS DESIRED
12A. RAD/ICS panel (A-6E TRAM) .... AS DESIRED
12B. Data link (A-6E TRAM) .... OFF
12C. ACLS (A-6E TRAM) .... PROPER FREQ AND OFF
13. Vent suit and cushion airflow .... AS DESIRED
14. Optical sight unit switches (except A-6E TRAM) .... AUTO/MAN

> **CAUTION**
>
> Do not leave AUTO/OFF/MAN switch OFF during taxi or flight operation.

15. Oxygen .... CHECK
    O₂ on, with mask away from face, depress ICS then O₂ off.
16. Contact analog switch (KA-6D) .... OFF
17. HSI mode switch (KA-6D) .... TACAN
18. Vertical reference switch (KA-6D) .... NO. 1
19. Rudder trim .... SET TO ZERO
20. Hook bypass switch .... AS DESIRED
20A. VGI DIS switch (A-6E TRAM, KA-6D with APC-161) .... D/L
21. Engine and fuel master switches .... ON
    Check annunciator panel to ensure that low-fuel-pressure caution lights are out, indicating fuel boost pump operation.
22. Boost pump test button .... DEPRESS
    Check that LOW FUEL PRESSURE lights come on.
23. Right engine and fuel master switch .... OFF

CONTINUED ON NEXT PAGE

NAVAIR 01-85ADA-1

NORMAL PROCEDURES
Shore-Based Procedures

PILOT PRESTART PROCEDURES EXTERNAL POWER ON—CONTINUED

24.	Generator switches	OFF
25.	Speed drive switches	NORM
26.	Approach power compensator (when installed)	OFF
27.	Antiskid switch	OFF
28.	Flaperon pop-up switch	OFF
29.	Speed-brake test switch	NORM
30.	Emergency flap switch	OFF
31.	Throttles	OFF AND FRICTION ADJUSTED
32.	Flap lever	MATCHING FLAP POSITION
33.	Assist-spin recovery switch	OFF AND GUARDED
34.	Bleed-air isolation valves (AFC No. 268)	
	a. NWW	AUTO
	b. CSD	OFF
	c. AIR COND	ON
35.	Fuel quantity	CHECK
36.	Fuel-ready switch	OFF
37.	Fuselage dump switch	NORM
38.	Wing dump switch	NORM
39.	Wing drop-tank transfer switch	AS REQUIRED
40.	Tank pressurization	NORM
41.	Brake selector handle	OUT AND VERTICAL
42.	Landing-gear handle	DOWN (DN)
43.	Integrated position indicator	CHECK FOR PROPER INDICATIONS
44.	Radar altimeter	OFF
45.	ECM (KA-6D)	OFF
45A.	Optical sight unit switches (A-6E TRAM)	AUTO/MAN

> **CAUTION**
>
> Do not leave AUTO/OFF/MAN switch OFF during taxi.

45B.	HDG SEL switch (A-6E TRAM)	
46.	AOA indicator	OFF, FLAG NOT SHOWING
47.	Auxiliary brakes cycle gage	15 CYCLES
48.	PHD/VDI security	CHECK

CONTINUED ON NEXT PAGE

Change 2 3-23

NORMAL PROCEDURES
Shore-Based Procedures

NAVAIR 01-85ADA-1

PILOT PRESTART PROCEDURES EXTERNAL POWER ON—CONTINUED

WARNING

The VDI shall have three Phillips-head screws securing it to the mounting bracket. The PHD shall have three hex-head bolts securing it to the mounting bracket.

49. Pressure altimeter (AAU-19) .... CHECK AND SET TO STBY
50. Airspeed indicator .... CHECK AT ZERO
51. VGI .... SET TO HORIZON
52. Clock .... SET
53. VSI .... CHECK AT ZERO
54. Canopy switch .... OPEN OR NEUTRAL
55. Canopy safety pin .... REMOVE
56. All instruments .... CHECK FOR SECURITY
57. Fire/oil warning system .... TEST
    Depress FIRE/OIL test button and check lighting of left and right fire warning lights, NWW light, AFT TEMP light (A-6E TRAM) and right and left OIL LOW warning lights.
58. LOX/FUEL/OIL button .... TEST
    Depress LOX/FUEL/OIL test button. Check that oxygen quantity gage drops to zero and oxygen warning light comes on at approximately 2 liters. Pointer on fuel quantity gage moves toward zero, which is a functional test of fuel quantity indicating system. This is not a test of low-fuel warning light. Low-oil warning light check is valid only after oil scavenging.
59. Lights warning .... TEST
    Check following lights: Landing gear transition, wheels warning, hook transition annunciator panel, master caution, angle-of-attack indexers, complete and reselect (A6E), and in-flight refueling panel lights (KA-6D).
60. Manual canopy selector handle (AFC 185 not incorporated) .... CHECK UP
61. VDI (Except A-6C, KA-6D) .... STANDBY FOR 5 MINUTES

A-6C 2, 3, 4

62. ECM panel (except A-6E TRAM) .... OFF
63. Station selector switches .... OFF AND LOCKED
64. Master armament switch .... OFF AND LOCKED
65. Gun switch .... OFF/SAFE
66. Mechanical and electrical fuzing switches .... SAFE
67. Selective jettison button (A-6E) .... OUT AND GUARDED

CONTINUED ON NEXT PAGE

PILOT PRESTART PROCEDURES EXTERNAL POWER ON–CONTINUED

68.	Nuclear selector buttons (3)	OFF AND LOCKED
69.	ASN-41 Navigation computer (KA-6D)	STBY
70.	Autopilot switch	OFF
70A.	ATTITUDE REF switch (A-6E TRAM)	COMP IN
71.	UHF radios	ON (T/R G)
72.	APN-153 Doppler (KA-6D)	STBY
73.	TACAN	ON-T/R

Note

In KA-6D, for normal TACAN operation ensure that the HSI mode selector is at TACAN.

74.	IFF	STANDBY
75.	SIF	AS REQUIRED
76.	Air conditioning cockpit switch	ON
77.	Automatic temperature control thumbwheel	SET AT ZERO
78.	MAN/RAM air switch	AS DESIRED
79.	Computer emergency cooling switch (EQUIPMENT switch, A-6E TRAM) (Inoperative in KA-6D)	NORM
80.	DEFOG AIRFLOW thumbwheel	OFF
81.	Air conditioning master switch	NORM
82.	Engine anti-ice switch	OFF
83.	Windshield rain-removal switch	OFF
84.	Pitot heat switch	OFF
85.	Wing-fold handle	MATCHING WINGS

CAUTION

If wings are folded, ensure that the wing-fold handle is in the full forward position; otherwise the wings may spread as soon as hydraulic pressure is applied either during engine start or ground-rig operation.

86.	Radio mixer control box (except A-6E TRAM)	SET-UP AS DESIRED
87.	ECM tone controls (except A-6E TRAM)	AS DESIRED
88.	Cabin dump	OFF
89.	Antenna select switches (except A-6E TRAM)	AS DESIRED
90.	CNI master (except A-6E TRAM)	AS REQUIRED

CONTINUED ON NEXT PAGE

NORMAL PROCEDURES
Shore-Based Procedures

NAVAIR 01-85ADA-1

PILOT PRESTART PROCEDURES EXTERNAL POWER ON—CONTINUED

Note

On aircraft BUNO 158795 and subsequent; MOD M 21 and subsequent; and aircraft incorporating AFC No. 269, the CNI MASTER switch must be in other than the OFF position for MA-1 compass system operation.

90A.	MA-1/ADC switch (A-6E TRAM)	ON
91.	Circuit breakers (incl. C/B's under pilot's left console)	IN
92.	MA-1 compass	CHECK SYNC AND SLAVED
93.	Speech security equipment	OFF
94.	Radar beacon	STANDBY (AS REQUIRED)
95.	ACLS (when installed) (except A-6E TRAM)	PROPER FREQ AND OFF
96.	Fueling valve manual control	CHECK
97.	Hose-reel ground test switch (KA-6D)	OFF
98.	No. 2 UHF radio (KA-6D)	ON (T/R + G)

STARTING ENGINES

The engines cannot be started simultaneously; however, either engine can be started first. This procedure established starting the left engine (No. 1) first to allow checking the operation of the air-conditioning bleed-air isolation valve (AFC 268 incorporated).

CAUTION

If any of the following indications occur during an attempted engine start, a malfunction is indicated and immediate action on the part of the pilot is required:

- Abnormal engine noise or sound
- Wet start (no light-off within 10 seconds after placing throttle to idle)
- Hot start (EGT exceeds 455°C)
- Hung start (RPM will not accelerate to idle)
- Oil pressure fails to rise to 35 PSI within 30 seconds of operation
- Fire warning light comes on, or other indication of fire
- Speed-drive caution light remains ON above 40% RPM

1.	Ground turbine compressor (GTC)	ON
2.	GTC start air	AVAILABLE
	50 PSI indicated available from ground crew	

CONTINUED ON NEXT PAGE

3-26   Change 2

STARTING ENGINES—CONTINUED

> **CAUTION**
>
> If the wings are folded, grasp the wing-fold handle and ensure that the mechanical lock is unlocked and maintain positive forward pressure on the wing-fold handle until flight and combined systems indicate normal pressure.

3. Left crank switch .... DEPRESS, THEN RELEASE
   (In aircraft with AFC No. 268 only, no rotation should be obtained, indicating that the CSD bleed-air isolation valve is actually closed.

4. CSD bleed-air isolation valve (Aircraft with AFC No. 268 only.) .... ON

5. Left crank switch .... DEPRESS, THEN RELEASE
   Rotation should now begin, indicating that the CSD bleed-air isolation valve has opened. Steps 3 through 5 provide a functional check of the CSD bleed-air isolation valve.

6. At 18% RPM, left throttle .... IDLE

7. Fuel flow .... 700 TO 800 POUNDS PER HOUR

8. Exhaust temperature .... UNDER 455°

> **CAUTION**
>
> A hot start can be anticipated by observing a greater than normal fuel flow and exhaust temperature increase. Normally, the EGT tape will ride evenly or slightly below the RPM tape during a start. Whenever the EGT exceeds the RPM, a hot start can be anticipated. It is essential that the engine be shut down immediately.

9. Oil pressure .... 35 to 50 PSI

10. Idle RPM .... STABILIZED
    Check idle rpm stabilized at approximately 52% to 60% rpm depending upon ambient conditions.

11. Hydraulic pressure .... NORMAL

12. External compressed-air source .... DISCONNECT

13. Landing gear ground safety locks .... REMOVE
    Check visually with ground crewman. Ground crewman will carefully remove nose-gear ground safety lock, with entry into and exit from nosewheel well being made from starboard side of aircraft.

14. AIR COND bleed-air isolation valve (Aircraft with AFC No. 268 only) .... CHECK
    Check AIR COND bleed-air isolation valve OFF and note that cabin airflow stops, indicating that valve actually closed. Reopen valve.

15. Hook lift button .... DEPRESS

16. RAT .... RETRACT (IF EXTENDED)

CONTINUED ON NEXT PAGE

NORMAL PROCEDURES
Shore-Based Procedures
NAVAIR 01-85ADA-1

STARTING ENGINES — CONTINUED

17. Right engine and fuel master switch . . . . ON
18. Left throttle . . . . ADVANCE TO 75% RPM.
19. Start right engine as per items 5 through 11.
20. Left throttle . . . . IDLE (AFTER RIGHT ENGINE AT IDLE SPEED)
21. Right generator . . . . ON (CHECK CAUTION LIGHT OUT)
22. Left generator . . . . ON (CHECK CAUTION LIGHT OUT)
23. External electrical power . . . . DISCONNECT

POST START

1. Anti-g valve . . . . PRESS TO TEST
2. Vent suit/cushion airflow . . . . ADJUST
3. Oxygen switch . . . . ON
4. Oxygen mask . . . . ATTACHED
5. Oxygen regulator (GRU-5 only) 100%
6. Contact analog switch (KA-6D only) . . . . ON
7. Rain removal (aircraft NOT incorporating AFC No. 268) . . . . CHECK

> **CAUTION**
>
> The rain-removal system shall be checked by actuating the windshield switch to the AIR position and by holding your hand over the top of the windscreen to feel the hot air. Turn the windshield air off as soon as possible to prevent cracking the windshield. If unable to turn off the hot air, secure the engines as soon as possible.

8. NWW bleed-air isolation valve (Aircraft incorporating AFC No. 268 only.) . . . . CHECK
   Place windshield switch to AIR position, check for hot air by holding your hand over top of windscreen, and for WSHLD AIR light (AFC No. 264) on. Close NWW bleed-air isolation valve and note that hot air stops. Return NWW switch to AUTO and note that hot air is reapplied; return windshield switch to OFF and note that hot air stops.

9. Engine-driven fuel boost pump . . . . CHECK

> **CAUTION**
>
> To preclude an engine fire, if an engine flames out during this test, the appropriate engine fuel master switch should be positioned to OFF before releasing the fuel boost pump test button.

CONTINUED ON NEXT PAGE

POST START—CONTINUED

10. Radar altimeter . . . . ON AND SET
11. Canopy . . . . CLOSED

WARNING

Prior to actuating the canopy switch to the closed position, ensure that both boarding ladders are clear, that no one is on the aircraft, and that the B/N is aware that the canopy will be closed.

CAUTION

Cooling air is not available to the search/track radar while operating on internal power for more than 5 minutes with the canopy open.

12. VDI . . . . ON AND ADJUST

Note

Elevation calibration of the horizon line can be checked by going to the TEST position. When in TEST, the horizon line should match the fiducial markers.

13. Air-conditioning master switch . . . . OFF AND BACK TO NORMAL

Note

Check that ducted air to the cabin ceases and the air conditioning light comes on.

14. CNI MASTER switch . . . . ON
15. Platform (Except KA-6D) . . . . VERIFY OPERATE
16. ECM . . . . AS DESIRED

CAUTION

To preclude inadvertent chaff dispensing, before turning on ECM power, ensure that the GEAR/HOOK circuit breaker is properly seated and there are no indications of a weight-on-wheels switch failure (AOA indexer on/approach light on).

17. For carrier operations, complete the following additional steps.
    a. Tank pressure switch . . . . ORIDE
       Check wing-tank pressure lights out.
    b. Tank pressure switch . . . . NORMAL

CAUTION

To prevent damage to the aircraft during catapult launches, ensure that the wing tank pressure switch is returned to normal before taxi.

CONTINUED ON NEXT PAGE

NORMAL PROCEDURES
Shore-Based Procedures

NAVAIR 01-85ADA-1

ORDNANCE

When carrying ordnance, refer to and complete the appropriate NAVAIR checklist for type of ordnance carried. Capability and type of ordnance carried on the A-6A can be found in NAVAIR 01-85ADA-1T.

BEFORE TAXIING

1. Ordnance ground safety locks . . . . REMOVED
   Check visually with ground crewmen

2. Boarding ladders . . . . STOWED

> **CAUTION**
>
> The pilot and bombardier/navigator should visually check their respective boarding ladders up to avoid airframe damage in flight.

3. Chocks . . . . REMOVE

4. Brake selector handle . . . . CHECKED, IN AND VERTICAL
   Push brake handle in to release parking brakes. Check handle for freedom of push/pull movement and with handle in for vertical position by applying counterclockwise rotation.

> **CAUTION**
>
> If the handle binds or does not remain in the vertical position when pushed in (brake release), taxi shall not be attempted.

5. Brakes . . . . TEST
   After initial roll, apply normal brakes and test operation.

6. Nosewheel steering . . . . ENGAGE
   Engage nosewheel steering to minimize brake wear.

WING SPREAD

1. Wing-fold handle . . . . AFT, TO FIRST STOP
   (Wait for all spread motion to cease.)

2. Wing lockpin switch . . . . LOCK

3. Wing-fold handle . . . . STOW
   Move wing-fold handle aft and down flush with center console smartly with palm of hand.

4. Wing-fold warning flags . . . . CHECK RETRACTED

CONTROL CHECKS

1. Flight controls .... CYCLE SMOOTHLY AND CHECK FOR NORMAL THROW AND DIRECTION

WARNING

Takeoff shall not be attempted if stabilizer shift indicator flickers/barberpoles when the controls are rapidly cycled. The BACK-UP HYD light may flicker in aircraft incorporating AFC 183 and aircraft serial number 155640 and subsequent showing normal operation of the backup hydraulic system.

CAUTION

To prevent damage to the hydraulic pumps from cavitation, do not permit hydraulic pressure to go below 2000 psi during control checks.

2. Wing fuel pressure .... ORIDE AND CHECK LIGHTS OUT

CAUTION

Ensure that the air-conditioning master switch is in the NORM position. Hot engine bleed air will be pumped into the wing tank if the tank pressure switch is actuated to ORIDE when the air-conditioning master switch is OFF.

3. Flaps/slats .... TAKEOFF/DOWN
   While flaps/slats are in transit, observe flaperon for pop-up.

WARNING

If flaperon pop-up occurs during flap/slat operation, a pop-up valve failure is indicated and takeoff should not be attempted.

4. Speed brakes .... EXTEND
5. Autopilot .... CHECK, THEN OFF

Note

- Wait at least 30 seconds after application of power before engaging any function to permit the gyros to reach operating speed. If STAB AUG will not engage, move the control stick through full lateral throw to ensure that the AFCS is in detent.

- In aircraft with the ASW-40 if when checking ACL disengagement the AFCS fails to revert to STAB AUG or the control stick fails to move with pilot pitch inputs or both, ACL can be disengaged and normal control stick movement restored by application of rapid fore and aft inputs of approximately 50 pounds at the stick grip. Turn off the AFCS and do not use it for flight.

6. Speed brakes .... RETRACT

CONTINUED ON NEXT PAGE

NORMAL PROCEDURES
Shore-Based Procedures

NAVAIR 01-85ADA-1

CONTROL CHECKS—CONTINUED

Note

If the wing-tip speed brakes do not retract utilizing the speed-brake test switch, DO NOT extend the speed brakes in flight.

8. Wing fuel pressure .... NORMAL
9. Flight controls .... CYCLE SMOOTHLY AND CHECK FOR EXTENDED THROW AND DIRECTION
   During control stick cycling, hold stick in full aft and full forward positions. If stabilizer does not achieve full travel, secure engines and investigate.
10. Trim .... CYCLE AND SET FOR TAKEOFF
    Adjust pitch trim so that stabilizer leading edge aligns with takeoff trim reference mark painted on aft fuselage. Note pitch trim position indicator reading for future reference.
11. Flight instruments .... CHECK

REFUELING SYSTEM GROUND CHECK KA-6D

1. Refueling power switch .... ON
2. Pounds scheduled .... SET (SOME QUANTITY)
3. Drogue switch .... EXT
   Spring in drogue canister ejects drogue 1 to 2 feet.
   HYD PRESS light goes out.
   STOW/TRAIL indicator shows barberpole.
4. Hose-reel ground test switch .... FULL TRAIL
   Hold until indicator shows TRAIL and READY light comes on. HYD PRESS light remains out. With AFC 298 installed, indicator continues to show barber pole and READY light comes on.
5. Fuel transfer switch .... AUTO
6. Hose-reel ground test switch .... FUEL RANGE
   Hold until VALVE OPEN light comes on. READY light stays on: Indicator shows TRAIL on aircraft not incorporating AFC No. 298 and barber pole on aircraft incorporating AFC No. 298.
7. Reel response switch .... TEST
   Hold for about 15 seconds and release. Drogue will retract.

Note

The drogue is retracted when the reel response switch is released from the TEST position. Premature actuation of the drogue switch to RET will preclude the drogue from fully seating.

8. Drogue switch .... RET
   Indicator shows STOW, READY light goes out, HYD PRESS light comes on.
9. FUEL TRANS switch .... OFF
10. Refueling power .... OFF

NAVAIR 01-85ADA-1

NORMAL PROCEDURES
Shore-Based Procedures

ATTITUDE GYRO CHECK KA-6D

VERTICAL DISPLAY INDICATOR TEST

After warmup:

1. Contrast and brightness . . . . ADJUST
2. Symbol display . . . . CHECK
   Sky texture, ground texture, roll index, pitch index.
3. Pitch trim marker . . . . ADJUST, CHECK

VERTICAL REFERENCE CHECK

1. Vertical reference switch . . . . NO. 1
2. VGI attitude indicator approximately 3° nose up. . . . . CHECK
3. Vertical reference switch . . . . NO. 2
4. VDI horizon shift . . . . LESS THAN 0.2 INCH
5. Roll index movement . . . . LESS THAN 2

BEFORE TAKEOFF

Before takeoff, the takeoff checklist (figure 3-1) must be completed.

1. Wings . . . . SPREAD AND LOCKED
2. Trim . . . . CHECKED
   a. Rudder . . . . 0°
   b. Flaperon . . . . 0°
   c. Stabilizer . . . . 6 UNITS NOSE UP
3. Flaps . . . . TAKEOFF
   a. Slats . . . . DOWN
   b. Stabilizer . . . . SHIFTED
   c. Speed brakes . . . . IN

WARNING

The pilot must ensure that the flap lever is fully seated in the desired detent and aircraft flap slat configuration is confirmed with the integrated position indicated.

4. Fuel
   a. Quantity . . . . CHECKED
   b. Tank pressure switch . . . . NORMAL
   c. Wing pressure lights . . . . LIT
   d. Fuel ready switch . . . . OFF
5. Controls . . . . UNRESTRICTED

CONTINUED ON NEXT PAGE

NORMAL PROCEDURES
Shore-Based Procedures

NAVAIR 01-85ADA-1

BEFORE TAKEOFF—CONTINUED

6. Seats .... ADJUSTED AND ARMED
   a. Face-curtain guard .... DOWN (UNLOCKED)
   b. Lower ejection handle guard .... ROTATE CLEAR (UNLOCKED)
7. Harness .... LOCKED
8. Flaperon pop-up .... ARM

Note

Check that the flaperons go down when each throttle is moved out of the IDLE position.

9. Antiskid switch .... ON
10. Auxiliary brakes .... 15 CYCLES

TAKEOFF (ASHORE)

After taxiing to the runup area, allow the aircraft to roll straight ahead to insure nose alignment. Apply brakes and complete the following checks:

1. Pitot heat switch .... AS REQUIRED
   Set pitot heat switch as required for existing weather conditions.
2. Engine anti-ice switch .... AS REQUIRED
   Set engine anti-ice switch as required for existing weather conditions
3. RAT .... AS REQUIRED

CAUTION

Ingestion of a significant amount of water into the generator cooling scoop may result in the loss of the generator(s). Deployment of the RAT will preclude the loss of electrical power above 110 KIAS.

4. IFF/SIF .... AS REQUIRED
5. AFCS .... OFF UNTIL SAFELY AIRBORNE
6. ICS .... HOT
7. Engines .... CHECK
   Advance throttle to MAX POWER, flaperons in normal configuration, allow engine RPM to stabilize: observe that EGT, fuel flow, oil pressure, and hydraulic pressure gages are within operating limits. Check cockpit power trim indicators to insure engines are developing proper takeoff thrust.
   In the absence of reliable power trim indications, the following may be used as indication of normal engine performance.

   RPM - 97% to 100%
   EGT - 640°C to 660°C
   Fuel flow - 6500 pph to 8500 pph.

CONTINUED ON NEXT PAGE

TAKEOFF (ASHORE) – CONTINUED

Note

Engine thrust is a critical factor in heavy gross weight takeoffs under high ambient air-temperature conditions. Under these conditions, if the power trim indicators show less than the desired engine power outputs, the decision to elect takeoff must be carefully weighed against such critical factors as runway available, density altitude, critical field length and other indications of engine performance.

8. Throttle stagger 1/2 inch maximum mismatch with engines in sync at maximum power; 1/4 inch maximum mismatch at 86% rpm.

9. Controls .... CYCLED
   Controls shall be cycled rapidly while engines are operating at sufficient rpm to preclude hydraulic pump cavitation (above 75%). If any unusual airframe vibrations are experienced, takeoff shall not be attempted.

WARNING

Takeoff shall not be attempted if the stabilizer shift indicator flickers/barberpoles when the controls are rapidly cycled. The BACK-UP HYD light may flicker showing normal operation of the backup hydraulic system.

10. Nose-wheel steering .... ENGAGE

11. All caution and warning lights .... OUT

12. Bombardier/navigator .... CHECK READY FOR TAKEOFF

13. Brakes .... RELEASE

14. Nose-wheel .... CENTERED
    Use nose-wheel steering for directional control until rudder effective at approximately 80 knots.

TAKEOFF TECHNIQUE

Refer to Section XI, for rotation speeds at various gross weights. A positive climb attitude at a moderate rate of climb (1,000 to 1,500 FPM) must be established before the landing gear is retracted. Flaps/slats are raised prior to 250 KIAS. Maintain a moderate climb attitude until scheduled climb speed is attained. Refer to Section XI, for recommended maximum rate of climb. Minimum run takeoff is the same as for normal takeoff, except that the nose is raised at speeds recommended for minimum takeoff ground run; airspeed is then held constant.

CROSSWIND TAKEOFF

The use of the nose-wheel steering and normal flight control are adequate for crosswind takeoffs up to a crosswind component of 90° and 20 knots. See Section XI for chart.

NORMAL PROCEDURES
Shore-Based Procedures

AFTER TAKEOFF — CLIMB

When the aircraft is definitely airborne:

1. Landing gear . . . . UP (BELOW 200 KIAS)
   Check that wheels transition light comes on and then goes out. Check that OUT'BD WING TK PRESS and INBD WING TK PRESS caution lights are out.

   CAUTION

   The landing gear should be completely up and locked before exceeding 200 KIAS.

2. Flaps . . . . UP
   Retract flaps before reaching 250 KIAS. Check integrated position indication for flap UP and slat IN, and stabilizer shift indications.

   WARNING

   - Extreme caution should be exercised during flap retraction under heavy gross weight conditions. To avoid aircraft stall or settling due to flap retraction, do not retract the flaps below 170 KIAS for weights up to 50,000 pounds and not below 185 KIAS for weights above 50,000 pounds. At the heavier weights and under high ambient temperature conditions, acceleration and climb performance are marginal and it may be impossible to reach 185 KIAS. If 185 KIAS cannot be reached, it is recommended that external store weight be reduced in order to permit acceleration to 185 KIAS before flap retraction.

   - If a barberpole indication on slat/flap retraction should occur after takeoff, power must be maintained at military and airspeed controlled within limits (maximum of 250 KIAS and minimum of 170 KIAS or 185 KIAS as applicable) by adjusting aircraft attitude. Power reduction or diversion of attention must not be attempted until reaching safe operating altitudes.

   Note

   Remedial action for barberpoled slats may include any or all of the following at speeds above the minimum for slat retraction and up to a maximum of 250 KIAS.

   (1.) With flap lever in retracted position, apply a slight negative g.
   (2.) Momentarily acutate flap lever to takeoff position and as slats begin to extend, immediately return lever to up position.
   (3.) Momentarily actuate emergency flap switch to DOWN and as slats begin to extend, immediately set switch to UP and then OFF.
   (4.) While maintaining airspeed above minimum retraction speed, extend flaps/slats partially closed then retract. As slats approach fully closed position, momentarily apply slight negative g.

CONTINUED ON NEXT PAGE

NAVAIR 01-85ADA-1

NORMAL PROCEDURES
Shore-Based Procedures

AFTER TAKEOFF – CLIMB – CONTINUED

3. Isolation valve switch . . . . FLT
   After landing gear, flaps, and slats have been fully retracted, place isolation valve switch to FLT position.

4. Accelerate to best climb speed.

CRUISE

Cruise control data for various weights and configurations are contained in Section XI.

FLIGHT CHARACTERISTICS

See Section IV, for information on the flight characteristics of this aircraft.

DESCENT

Before descent, and after prolonged cold-soaking at high altitudes, the cockpit temperature should be increased and the defogging control turned ON. Normal penetration (letdown), as reflected in the descent charts, is in Section XI, and is normally accomplished with approximately 80% rpm at a descent speed of 250 KIAS. Speed brakes are extended and descent speed is maintained by adjusting the rate of descent.

For maximum-range glide, see Section V, Emergency Procedures. The descent speed (200 KIAS) is maintained without the use of speed brakes. Before all descents, the following checks should be performed:

1. Defog . . . . ON
2. Refile . . . . AS REQUIRED
3. Fuel . . . . CHECK

Note

Inform the bombardier/navigator when dumping fuel.

4. Weather . . . . CHECK
5. Pressure altimeter . . . . CHECK AND SET
6. Radar altimeter . . . . . ON AND CHECKED
   BELOW 5,000
   FEET AGL

CAUTION

Do not actuate the landing gear above 8,000 feet unless the cabin is depressurized.

7. Engine anti-ice . . . . AS REQUIRED
8. Pitot heat . . . . AS REQUIRED

BEFORE LANDING

The landing checklist must be completed prior to landing.

1. Harness . . . . LOCKED
2. Armament . . . . ALL SWITCHES OFF/SAFE
3. Flaperon pop-up . . . . ARM
4. Antiskid . . . . ON
5. Hook . . . . AS REQUIRED
   (Isolation switch to LAND)
6. Wheels . . . . DOWN
7. Flaps . . . . TAKEOFF
   (Check stabilizer shifted, slats down, and speed brakes extended.)

CONTINUED ON NEXT PAGE

BEFORE LANDING—CONTINUED

> **WARNING**
>
> The pilot must ensure that the flap lever is fully seated in the desired detent and aircraft flap/slat configuration is confirmed with the integrated position indicator.

> **Note**
>
> Approximately 180 KIAS and above, the flaps may not fully extend to TAKEOFF position (30°). Above 140 KIAS (approximately), the flaps may not fully extend to the LAND position. In either case, the flap indicator will display a barber pole until the airspeed is reduced.

8. Fuel .... CHECK
   Check quantity, compute correct approach airspeed, check fuel dumps NORM and wing PSI lights ON.

9. Autopilot .... OFF or STAB AUG (AS DESIRED)

10. ICS .... HOT

11. AUX BRAKES .... CHECKED 15 CYCLES

LANDING (ASHORE)

Upon touchdown

1. Throttles .... IDLE

2. Nose-wheel steering .... ENGAGE AS NECESSARY
   (below 80 KIAS)

3. Brakes .... APPLY AS REQUIRED

> **CAUTION**
>
> Overinflation of struts may prevent the steering weight-on-wheels switch on the right main strut from closing. If any difficulty is experienced with braking or steering, set the antiskid switch OFF.

TYPICAL LANDING

For a typical landing, enter the traffic pattern conforming to existing course rules. In the break, reduce power to 75% (minimum), extend the speed brakes, and transition to the landing configuration below 250 KIAS.

Complete the landing checklist (figure 3-1) by the abeam position. Reduce airspeed to appropriate speed and check for optimum AOA indications, and commence approach to landing.

Note

- Check indicated airspeed against optimum AOA. An optimum AOA indication is equal to 105 KIAS plus 2 knots for each 1000 pounds over 28,000 pounds gross weight. If external stores are carried add 2 knots.

- If a discrepancy exists between the two indications, fly the instrument showing the first optimum speed indication.

- For additional information see figure 3-9.

Use the angle-of-attack indexer and maintain the on-speed indication. Maintaining final approach power of approximately 87% at sea level rpm, and a 3° to 3 1/2° glide-slope angle will provide a normal rate of descent (approximately 700 fpm).

Upon touchdown, retard throttles to idle for flaperon pop-up operation to hold aircraft firmly on the runway. For minimum rollout distance, drop the nose and use antiskid braking. Use the rudder and nose-wheel steering for directional control of the aircraft on the landing roll. Rudder control is effective on landing roll down to speeds of 50 KIAS. Aerodynamic braking may be employed to minimize brake wear.

CAUTION

If heavy braking is used during landing or taxi, do not use the parking brakes until the brake disks have cooled. Avoid prolonged brake applications to prevent the brake disks fuzing.

REDUCING BRAKING REQUIREMENTS

If it is suspected that heavy or repeated braking will result in overheated brakes, residual thrust during taxi back to the chocks can be reduced by securing the left engine using the following procedures:

1. Left throttle . . . . OFF

2. Left engine and fuel master switch . . OFF

Note

The output from the monitored buses will be lost when either engine is shut down. This will generally make the above procedures undesirable during night operations.

WAVE-OFF

CROSSWIND LANDING

When the crosswind component is greater than 10 knots, take a longer interval and land on the upwind side of the runway. If the crab technique is used, line the aircraft up with the runway just before touchdown. The crabbing technique may produce lateral drift or skid, the amount varying with the pilot's ability to line the aircraft up at touchdown. Retard the throttles to IDLE. Rudder control is effective down to 50 knots. Do not use aerodynamic braking. Aerodynamic braking may cause the loss of directional control in a crosswind. The flaperon pop-up will hold the aircraft firmly on the runway. Nose-wheel steering can be used after the right weight-on-wheels switch has actuated.

Note

Neutralize rudder pedals before engaging nose-wheel steering.

HEAVY GROSS WEIGHT LANDINGS

As landing gross weight increases, the landing pattern should be expanded, and the approach and touchdown speeds will be increased as necessary to maintain donut on-speed indication. For gross weights above 36,000 pounds, the final approach speed should be planned for a minimum sink-rate landing.

WET RUNWAY LANDING

The procedure to be followed when landing on a wet runway is essentially the same as that for a normal landing. However, if standing water is evident or suspected, and the crosswind is not greater than 10 knots, aerodynamic braking should be employed.

The decision to wave off should be made as early as possible. If decision to wave off is made, proceed as follows:

1. Throttles . . . . MAX POWER
(Establish a positive rate of climb.

Speed brakes . . . . RETRACTED

CAUTION

If a wave-off is initiated with flaps in the LANDING position, ensure that they are retracted before reaching 200 KIAS to prevent structural failure of the flap-actuating mechanism. The flap drive system does not have a blowback feature.

AFTER LANDING

After aircraft has slowed to taxi speed:

1. IFF/SIF .... OFF

Note

Ensure that Mode 4 is in hold before securing the IFF/SIF.

2. Lower ejection - handle guard .... UP (LOCKED POSITION)
3. Face-curtain guard .... UP (LOCKED POSITION)
4. Pitot heat switch .... OFF
5. Windshield air switch .... OFF
6. Engine anti-ice switch .... OFF
7. AFCS (STAB AUG) .... OFF
8. Flaps .... UP
9. Speed brakes .... IN
10. Antiskid switch .... OFF

Note

The antiskid switch should be turned OFF for any taxiing maneuvers.

11. Flaperon pop-up switch .... OFF
12. Wing fold .... AS REQUIRED

CAUTION

Do not fold wings while taxiing. Taxiing with wings folded should be avoided when possible.

13. Radar altimeter .... OFF
14. VDI .... STDBY/OFF
15. Oxygen switch .... OFF
16. ECM .... OFF
17. ASN-41 navigation computer (KA-6D) .... OFF
18. Doppler power switch (KA-6D) .... OFF

WING FOLD

1. Wing flaps/slats/flaperon/wing-tip speed brakes . . . . RETRACTED/CHECKED VISUALLY
2. Control stick . . . . NEUTRAL
3. Wing-fold handle . . . . FORWARD TO FIRST DETENT
   Check wing-fold warning flags extended at wing fold.
4. Wing lockpin switch . . . . UNLOCK
5. Wing-fold handle . . . . FULL FORWARD

HOT REFUELING

WARNING

Do not refuel with wings folded, because of the proximity of the wing dump valves to the hot engine exhaust.

1. Wings . . . . SPREAD

WARNING

During carrier operations, it may be necessary to hot refuel with the wings folded. Do not hot refuel the outboard wing panels with the wings folded.

2. Fire extinguisher equipment . . . . AVAILABLE
3. All emitters . . . . OFF/STBY
4. Canopy . . . . CLOSED
5. Ejection seats
   a. GRU-5: shoulder harness, lap belt, leg restraints/ejection seat . . . . . UNFASTEN/SAFE
   b. GRU-7: ejection seat (remain strapped in) . . . . SAFE
6. Air-conditioning master switch . . . . CHECK ON
7. Tank pressure override switch . . . . NORM
8. Fuel-ready switch . . . . GROUND
9. Monitor appropriate frequency.
10. Boarding ladders . . . . DOWN

POST HOT-SEAT CHECKLIST

1. Harness/leg restraints . . . . FASTEN
2. Fuel-ready switch . . . . OFF
3. Engine-driven fuel pump . . . . CHECK
4. Radar altimeter . . . . ON AND SET
5. Fire/oil warning system . . . . TEST
6. LOX/FUEL/OIL button . . . . TEST
7. LIGHTS WARN button . . . . TEST
8. VDI . . . . ON AND ADJUST
9. CNI equipment . . . . CHECK AND SET
10. Ordnance ground safety locks . . . . REMOVE
11. Boarding ladders . . . . STOWED
12. Platform (except KA-6D) . . . . VERIFY IN OPERATE

NORMAL PROCEDURES
Shore-Based Procedures

NAVAIR 01-85ADA-1

ENGINE SHUTDOWN

1. Wheels .... CHOCKED
   (Get signal from ground crew that wheels are chocked.)
2. Ordnance ground safety locks .... INSTALLED
3. CNI master switch .... OFF
4. Canopy .... OPEN
5. Oil level .... CHECK
   Depress LOX/FUEL/OIL test button. Lighting of either and/or both OIL-LOW lights on the annunciator panel indicates oil quantity from 5 to 12 1/2 quarts.
6. Throttles .... IDLE, 3 to 5 MINUTES
   (Idle rpm stabilizes engine temperature)
7. Throttles .... 75% RPM for 30 SECONDS
   (75% rpm for 30 seconds scavenges oil)
8. Transfer relay and left generator phase .... CHECK
   Check proper operation of transfer relay and correct phase of left generator as follows:
   a. Right generator switch .... OFF

   Note

   Ensure that the left generator assumes the electrical load, the VGI provides proper indications, and seat adjustment operates correctly.

   b. Right generator switch .... ON
      (CHECK CAUTION LIGHT OUT)
9. Throttles .... OFF
10. Engine and fuel master switches .... OFF

> **CAUTION**
>
> Ensure the engine fuel master switches are turned off immediately after securing the throttles to ensure the fuel system gate valves close before the generators fall off the line.

11. Generator switches (after generators fall off line) .... OFF
12. Landing-gear ground safety locks .... INSTALLED

> **CAUTION**
>
> Install ground safety locks immediately after engine windmill. Do not move the aircraft until landing-gear ground safety locks are installed, as the gear may accidently collapse.

3-42

part 4 Carrier-Based Procedures-Pilot

FIELD MIRROR LANDING PRACTICE

PREFLIGHT INSPECTION

A normal preflight inspection (figure 3-3) will be conducted with specific attention being given to the struts and tire condition. Check that the hook bypass switch is in the touch-and-go position.

PATTERN ENTRY

Call "Paddles" prior to pattern entry to confirm Charlie time. Enter the break at 250 KIAS, at 800 feet above the terrain. When cleared to break and the proper interval of the aircraft ahead is assured, roll into a 60° banked turn, extend wing-tip speed brakes, reduce power to a minimum of 75%, slow to 250 KIAS, extend gear, place flaps to TAKE OFF (below 250 KIAS), and maintain 800 feet until intercepting the downwind leg. On the downwind leg, descend to 600 feet above the terrain. Slow to appropriate airspeed for gross weight and check airspeed against the angle-of-attack indicator to ensure proper calibration of the indicator and the indexer. At the 180° position, the angle-of-attack indicator should indicate "on speed." Aircraft in formation will take a 10-second break interval. Complete the landing checklist before reaching the 180° position.

PATTERN

180° Position

Begin approach by turning 15 seconds past the abeam position in order to have a 1 1/2 mile wings-level groove. Commence a slight descending turn to final, maintaining optimum angle-of-attack.

90° Position

Maintain optimum angle-of-attack at approximately 450 feet. Final adjustment to longitudinal trim should be made.

Final

At approximately 1 1/4 miles, the meatball will appear in the center of the mirror. Reduce power as necessary to establish a rate of descent that will keep the meatball centered. Glide slope corrections should be made early by smooth changes in power and stick position as required to maintain a centered meatball and optimum angle-of-attack. Control altitude with the throttle and angle-of-attack (airspeed) with the stick. Once established on the glide slope, keep the scan going, cross-checking meatball, lineup, and angle-of-attack, and make positive corrections, immediately but smoothly.

Landing

Keep the aircraft on the glide slope and centerline all the way down. Do not flare. When touchdown is made, add full power immediately and utilize the bolter technique described under Wave-off/Bolter Pattern. Climb straight ahead until reaching 300 feet. Turn downwind for the next pass when the aircraft ahead is approximately in the 10 o'clock position on the downwind leg.

Wave-Off

The pilot must initiate a wave-off whenever he believes his aircraft to be in an unsafe position. Any time a wave-off is received, either by the wave-off lights or by radio, it is mandatory and will be answered with FULL MILITARY POWER speed brakes, and a transition to climbing attitude to prevent further loss of altitude.

Bingo Fuel

Recovery at home field will be with no less than 1,450 pounds of fuel remaining.

Note

With the landing gear down, wing and drop-tank fuel cannot be transferred or dumped unless the tank pressurization switch is set to ORIDE.

NIGHT PATTERN

The night pattern and approach technique are generally the same as the day pattern with the following exceptions:

1. The pattern will be flown on instruments until visual acquisition of the meatball is made.

3-43

NORMAL PROCEDURES
Carrier-Based Procedures (Pilot)

2. A straight-in CCA-type approach at 600 feet above the terrain will be made by extending the downwind leg 30 to 45 seconds past the normal abeam position used in the day pattern.

3. For ACLS, the pattern if flown at 1200 feet or as assigned. A level turn to final is commenced 3 miles past the abeam position until a positive lock-up is achieved, then radar controlled approach to landing.

CARRIER BASED PROCEDURES

The CVA/CVS NATOPS manual and LSO NATOPS manual are the governing sources for carrier-based procedures.

PREFLIGHT

Day

A normal preflight inspection should be made with particular attention given to the landing gear, tires, hook, and underside of the fuselage for possible damage.

Occasionally, the aircraft assigned will be manned on the hangar deck. Unless the aircraft is already spotted on the elevator, it will be towed or pushed for access to the flight deck. The signal to stop a plane that is being moved by other than its own power is a whistle blast. Leave the hardhat off. Any whistle blast signifies an immediate stop. If the plane director is lost from view, stop. The aircraft will be raised to the flight deck level and either respotted or started on the elevator.

Note

Brake cycles remaining should be kept at 12 or higher by use of the auxiliary hydraulic pumps.

Night

External preflight will be made using a flashlight. In addition to normal cockpit preflight, ensure that external light switches are positioned to dim for post start light check. The master exterior lights, anticollision, and taxi light switches should always be in the OFF position before start. Set the cockpit and approach indexer lights as desired.

POST START

Day

Engines will normally be started 20 minutes before launch, and the customary functional checks will be performed. Do not let the plane directors hurry these checks. When ready, signal the plane director with a thumbs up. Chocks and tiedowns will be removed upon signal by the plane director. Hold footbrakes regardless of parking-brake position, when tiedowns and removed.

Night

After normal system checks are completed, perform exterior lights check. When ready, signal the plane director with a vertical motion of the flashlight, meaning checks are completed and the aircraft is up. If the aircraft is down, make a horizontal motion with the flashlight.

Note

Complete wing and drop-tank pressurization checks as described under POST START procedures, Section III.

TAXI

Day

Only emergency stop signals are used. Any signal from the plane director given from above the waist is intended for the pilot. Any signal given from below the waist is intended for deck-handling personnel. While taxiing, careful attention must be given to the director and his signals shall be followed explicity. Nosewheel steering permits the use of minimum power while taxiing. Taxi speed shall be slow at all times, expecially on wet decks and approaching the catapult area. Be prepared to use the emergency brake should normal braking fail.

Night

During night carrier-deck operations, the tempo of operations, both in volume and speed, is considerably reduced from day operations. Slow and careful handling of aircraft by both plane directors and pilots is mandatory. If the pilot has any doubt as to the plane director's signals, stop.

LAUNCH PROCEDURES

Day

Proper positioning on the catapult is easily accomplished if the entry is made with only enough power to maintain forward motion and the plane director's signals are followed explicity. All functional checks will be performed before taxiing into the shuttle. After the tow link is dropped to the deck and the trail bar has been attached to the aircraft and checked by squadron maintenance personnel, the aircraft shall be taxied up to the mouth of the lead-in track. The catapult director will then direct the pilot to approach the catapult track using nosegear steering and brakes. Release nosewheel steering upon signal in the track, and as the aircraft rolls forward the tow bar will drop into the shuttle and the aircraft will stop in position for shuttle tension-up.

Night

Maneuvering the aircraft for catapult hookup at night is identical to that used in day operations; however, it is difficult to determine your speed or motion over the deck. The pilot must rely upon, and follow closely, the plane director's signals.

CATAPULT LAUNCH

Day

The Pilot's ICS control will be positioned to HOT mike for all catapult launches. Ensure that the takeoff checklist is completed before entering the nose-tow approach ramp. Aircraft trim should be set to recommended setting for expected excess end airspeed. Refer to current Aircraft Launching Bulletins for A-6 aircraft. The flashing indexer warning system for tow link/cocked nosewheel indication is only valid with the hook bypass switch in the touch-and-go position after launch. Flaperon pop-up and anti skid should be OFF.

Upon receipt of the "tension up and release brakes" signal, advance the throttles to full military power, engage throttle friction, and engage the strut lock. Check all engine and flight instruments for normal indications and operation, check the STRUT LOCK light extinguished, and perform a smooth, but rapid cycle of flight controls. Ensure the B/N is ready, place the head firmly against the headrest, chin down; and render an exaggerated hand salute to the Catapult Officer. There will be a 2- to 4-second delay before catapult firing due to sequence followed by the catapult crew.

CAUTION

The catapult grip must be used (rotated inboard and pulled up) for all catapult launches, since proper positioning is necessary for nose-strut stiffening. Maximum centerline store clearance is attained when the engines are operating at maximum thrust, brakes released, and catapult grip moved to the strut-lock position. Air crews should monitor the annunciator panel for STRUT LOCK warning light out before catapult launch. Failure to use the catapult grip will result in catapulting with a soft nose strut and may cause structural damage to the aircraft or centerline stores.

Catapult launches should be planned for a 10- to 15-knot excess end airspeed. Excess end airspeed is an arbitrary safety factor added to the minimum airspeed required to effect a safe but not optimum catapult launch. The minimum airspeed was determined during shipboard carrier suitability trials and is applicable for specific gross weight and ambient temperature/wind conditions. Recommended elevator trim settings for variations in end airspeed will result in optimum climb attitude off the catapult. Launch bulletins recommend a "lightly held control stick" catapult technique be used.

After leaving the catapult, allow the aircraft to rotate to the pitch attitude (10° to 12°) resulting from the elevator trim setting. The resulting climbing attitude is the optimum for aircraft weight and, once attained, should be maintained with stick positioning and trim. The angle of attack (AOA) indicator should indicate approximately 3 o'clock. Initial climbing attitude information is also available on the VDI. After launch, maintain optimum AOA and pitch angle and monitor the airspeed and altimeter for increasing values. Retract the landing gear after becoming airborne. Retract the flaps at the recommended flaps-up airspeed for launch gross weight.

Note

The right flaperon will raise due to a reaction to the catapult's acceleration and will result in a slight right clearing turn off the catapult stroke. This should be prevented by the pilot with lateral stick input during the catapult stroke.

CAUTION

Extreme caution should be exercised during flap retraction under heavy gross weight conditions. To avoid aircraft stall or setting due to flap retraction, do not retract the flaps below 170 KIAS for weights up to 50,000 pounds and not below 185 KIAS for weights above 50,000 pounds. At the heavier weights and under high ambient temperature conditions, acceleration and climb performance are marginal and it may be impossible to reach 185 KIAS. If 185 KIAS cannot be reached, it is recommended that external store weight be reduced in order to permit acceleration to 185 KIAS before flap retraction.

Instrument scan after launch should include all flight instruments. Initial pitch attitude is immediately indicated on the VDI, VGI, and AOA. Wing position is displayed on VDI, VGI, and by the HSI if turning. Airspeed information is available and can be monitored during the catapult stroke. Vertical speed lags slightly but may be used after leaving the catapult. The altimeter, like the VSI, lags and accurate information is not immediately available. The radar altimeter is available for use immediately after launch. It must be emphasized that the most important requirement after catapult launch is the necessity to climb.

NORMAL PROCEDURES
Carrier-Based Procedures (Pilot)

> **CAUTION**
>
> Use of the vertical gyro instrument (VGI) as a primary attitude reference following catapult launches is not recommended. Due to the inherent inaccuracies and possibility of failure of the VGI, this instrument should be used for backup/emergency situations only.

Night

The procedures for catapult launch at night are basically the same as for day launches. When ready to launch, signal the Catapult Officer by placing the external light master switch to ON. The launch technique discussed under the DAY procedures is applicable. The bombardier/navigator should monitor the flight instruments until climbing through 2,500 feet.

AIRCRAFT OR CATAPULT MALFUNCTION

If it is determined that the aircraft is down after establishing military power, signal the catapult officer by shaking the head from side to side. Transmit to Pri-Fly, "Suspend (catapult number)." Never raise a hand into the catapult officer's view to give a thumbs down signal for it may be misinterpreted as a salute and the catapult fired. At night, do not turn the master light switch on. The catapult officer will relay a no-go situation to the deck edge catapult operator by crossing his forearms over his head. He will then give the release tension signal and walk in front of the wing to give the throttle back signal. Then, and only then, reduce the throttle from military power to idle and remove the head from headrest. The same signals will be used to signify a catapult malfunction.

> **CAUTION**
>
> Leave the throttle at military power until the catapult officer walks in front of the wing and signals for power to be reduced to idle.

RECOVERY

Procedures for arrival, marshal, and approach shall be in accordance with the CVA/CVS NATOPS Manual.

PATTERN (VFR)

Pattern entry shall be in accordance with the CVA/CVS NATOPS Manual. At the break, the leader shall break smartly to 60° of bank, extend wing-tip speed brakes, reduce power to a minimum of 75%, slow to 250 KIAS, extend the landing gear, flaps to TAKE OFF below 250 KIAS, and maintain 800 feet until intercepting the downward leg. Then descend to 600 feet and slow to the appropriate airspeed for gross weight and compare airspeed and angle-of-attack indicators for proper indications. At the 180° position, at 1 mile abeam the angle-of-attack should be on-speed. Subsequent aircraft on the flight shall break at 17-second intervals. Complete the landing check list before the 180° position (flaperon pop-up, and antiskid switches OFF). See figure 3-9.

APPROACH

Begin the approach by turning at the 180° position in order to have an approximate 35-second groove. Establish a 25° to 35° bank and descend to no lower than 450 feet. Meatball acquisition at 450 feet will occur near the 45° position; reduce power as necessary to maintain a rate of descent that will keep the meatball centered.

Glide slope corrections should be made early by smooth changes in power and stick position as required to maintain a centered meatball and normal angle of attack (figure 3-10). Twenty-one units may be set when operating on larger class carriers to enhance visibility during the approach. Control altitude with the throttle and angle-of-attack (airspeed), with the stick. Once established on the glide slope, keep the scan going, cross-checking meatball, line-up and angle of attack, and make positive corrections, immediately but smoothly. During the approach, cross-check meatball, angle of attack, and line-up down to touchdown. Add full power and retract speedbrakes immediately upon touchdown in anticipation of a bolter.

WAVE-OFF/BOLTER PATTERN

Day

Wave-offs will be straight up the angle deck when given close in. Pilots must bear in mind that a late wave-off is critical in that the chance of an inflight engagement is great. Therefore, the pilot will, upon receiving a wave-off signal either by radio or the wave-off lights, immediately add full military power, retract speedbrakes and transition to a climbing attitude to prevent any further loss of altitude.

A wave-off to the right will be made only when overshooting the landing line to the extreme, or for other safety considerations.

Climb straight ahead on a wave-off or a bolter, then turn to parallel the ship's recovery course on the port side. Do not cross the bow while flying upward. Be alert for other aircraft launching or entering the pattern from the break. The aircraft ahead will have priority for the turn downwind.

Night

On a wave-off or bolter, climb straight ahead on final bearing. The downwind turn will be at 1200 feet or as assigned by CCA, not exceeding 30° bank. The night pattern should be flown entirely on instruments until in a position to acquire the meatball visually. However, it is prudent to remain alert to the transmission of other aircraft and to make a brief visual check when it becomes apparent another aircraft is in close proximity.

3-46

NORMAL PROCEDURES
Carrier-Based Procedures (Pilot)

CARRIER LANDING PATTERN

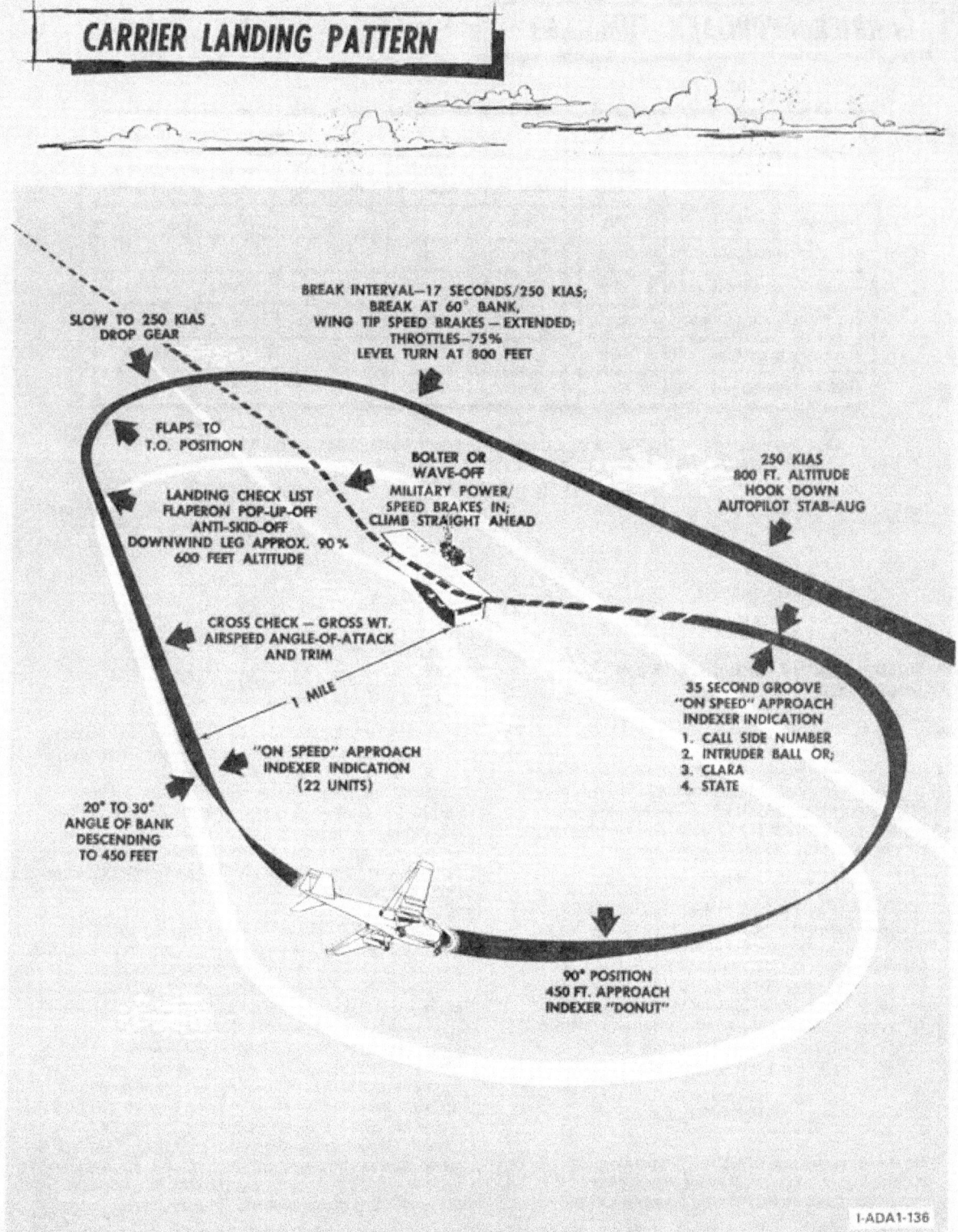

Figure 3-9

NORMAL PROCEDURES
Carrier-Based Procedures (Pilot)

CARRIER APPROACH SUMMARY

CONFIGURATION	OPTIMUM AOA	APPROACH AIRSPEED, KCAS			HOOK-TO-EYE DISTANCE, FT	
		36,000 LB GROSS WT	33,500 LB GROSS WT	28,000 LB GROSS WT	OPTIMUM AOA	OPTIMUM AOA PLUS 1 UNIT
NORMAL (T.O. FLAPS)	22	120	115	105	15.4	15.9
T.O. FLAPS/NO. SLATS	19	126	121	111	13.7	14.2
LANDING FLAPS/NO SLATS	19	122	117	107	13.7	14.2
NO FLAPS/SLATS EXTENDED	22	148	142	130	15.4	15.9
NO FLAPS/NO SLATS	20	152	147	134	14.2	14.8
SINGLE ENGINE (T.O. FLAPS)	21	123	118	108	14.8	15.3

DATA IN THIS CHART IS THE RESULT OF CARRIER SUITABILITY FLIGHT TEST EVALUATION CONDUCTED BY THE NAVAL AIR TEST CENTER, PATUXENT RIVER, MARYLAND.

Figure 3-10

ARRESTED LANDING AND EXIT FROM LANDING AREA

Day

Upon touchdown, advance the throttles to full military power and retract speed brakes. As soon as arrested, place the throttles to idle and raise the flaps. Allow the aircraft to roll back to disengage the arresting gear, then raise the hook.

Note

On CVA's with a long rollout, any holding of brakes or application of military power longer than absolutely necessary to ensure safety will result in the aircraft being hung in the gear. The hook must be in the lowered position during the subsequent pullback. Additionally, during pullback the pilot must stay off the brakes and be alert to the taxi director's signal to raise the hook.

CAUTION

Do not depress the HOOK LIFT button while the hook is engaged in the arresting gear. Doing so may break the hook bumper cable.

CAUTION

Before folding the wings, ensure that the flaps, slats, and speed brakes have been retracted.

Before shutdown, the aircraft should be cleaned up. Keep the engines running until the director signals "chocks are in place", and "cut engine". Landing-gear safety pins should be installed after shutdown. Be prepared to use the auxiliary or emergency braking if necessary.

If the aircraft is struck below to the hangar deck, keep the canopy closed and the oxygen mask on until dropped from the flight deck and signalled to shut the engines down. Open the canopy before securing the engines. After the engines are cut, normal braking will lose effectiveness and the auxiliary braking systems must be used. Remove the hardhat and follow the aircraft director's signal. Aircraft handling personnel will move the aircraft from this point. Engine rundown noise will make it very difficult to hear whistle signals; consequently, the pilot must be alert for both hand and whistle signals. Keep rolling speed slow and under control by use of brakes, keeping the cycles at 12 with auxiliary hydraulic pumps. Whenever the plane director is not in sight, stop.

Night

The same procedures for day operations should be used at night, except that immediately following arrestment, place the master exterior light switch to OFF. Taxi out to the landing area slowly. Do not stare fixedly at the plane director's wands, but use them as the center of the scan pattern.

CARRIER-CONTROLLED APPROACH

Carrier-controlled approaches shall be conducted in accordance with the CVA/CVS NATOPS Manual. A typical approach is illustrated in figure 3-11.

Holding

Aircraft will normally hold individually at 230 KIAS with the arresting hook down. Five minutes before penetration, the defog should be turned on and maximum comfortable cabin temperature should be maintained to prevent possible fogging on the windscreen and canopy.

Penetration

The aircraft will depart holding allowing approximately 700 pounds of fuel for the penetration and approach. Penetration will be accomplished as follows:

1. Throttles . . . . RETARD TO 80%
2. Nose over to establish a 4,000 foot per minute rate of descent.
3. Airspeed . . . . ACCELERATE TO 250 KIAS
4. Speed brakes . OUT, ADJUST THROTTLES
5. Call PLATFORM at 5,000 feet and reduce rate of descent to 2,000 feet per minute

At level-off altitude:

6. Speed brakes . . . . IN
7. Throttles . . . . ADJUST POWER TO MAINTAIN 250 KIAS

Final Approach

The pilot will continue to fly on instruments until the meatball is intercepted. The bombardier/navigator will normally maintain a visual lookout and will call meatball to the pilot on the ICS.

AUTOMATIC CARRIER LANDING SYSTEM

Automatic carrier landing system (ACLS) approaches apply to properly modified ASW-25 data link equipped aircraft using carrier- or shore-based SPN-10, SPN-42 or MPN-T1 ACLS facilities. Four modes of approach are available; however, use of specific modes is dependent on aircraft modifications. In mode 1 approaches, data-link-transmitted ACLS control signals are coupled to the autopilot after ACLS radar lock-on and control the aircraft until touchdown. Mode 1A approaches differ from mode 1 approaches in that data link/ACLS control signals are uncoupled 1/2 mile (approximately 200 feet altitude) from touchdown. Mode 2 approaches are pilot-controlled approaches using the data link/ACLS signals to present the pilot with the aircraft's glide slope and final bearing situation on a cockpit course indicator. Mode 3 approaches are simply a controller talk-down approach and require no special aircraft equipment onboard.

ACLS MODE 1 APPROACHES

An ACLS Mode 1 approach is illustrated in figure 3-11A. In a Mode 1 approach, the pilot flies the aircraft manually up to the point where the autopilot is coupled to the ACLS. The ACL-PCD switch on the AUTO PILOT control panel should be placed in the ACL position. To monitor the approach on the ARA-63, the ARA-63 power switch is set to PWR, the briefed channel is selected, and the DIS switch on the pilot's miscellaneous panel is set to MON.

1. Position the following controls as indicated to prepare the aircraft for data link ACL signals:

    a. Autopilot . . . . ON
    b. AUTO-STAB AUG switch . . STAB AUG
    c. Data link power switch . . . . ON
    d. TEST-NORM-AJ switch . . . . . NORM
    e. Frequency select dials . . . . As briefed
    f. ARA-63 power switch . . . . ON
    g. ARA-63 channel select control . . . . As briefed
    h. Radar beacon power switch . . . . . ON
    i. Radar beacon mode selector . . . ACLS

When the above controls are set, the discrete message indicator will indicate missed message (TILT).

2. Before or while in marshal, check the data link system for proper operation by the universal test message (UTM) check. The UTM is conducted by holding the TEST-NORM-AJ switch in the TEST position with the VGI DIS switch in the D/L position. The VGI cross pointers should drive into view and cycle between the following indications at 6-second intervals:

	Sequence 1	Sequence 2
Pitch Bar	Down	Up
Bank Bar	Left	Right
DMI	Wave Off	No lights

Change 2   3-49

NORMAL PROCEDURES
Carrier-Based Procedures (Pilot)

NAVAIR 01-85ADA-1

CARRIER CONTROLLED APPROACH (TYPICAL)

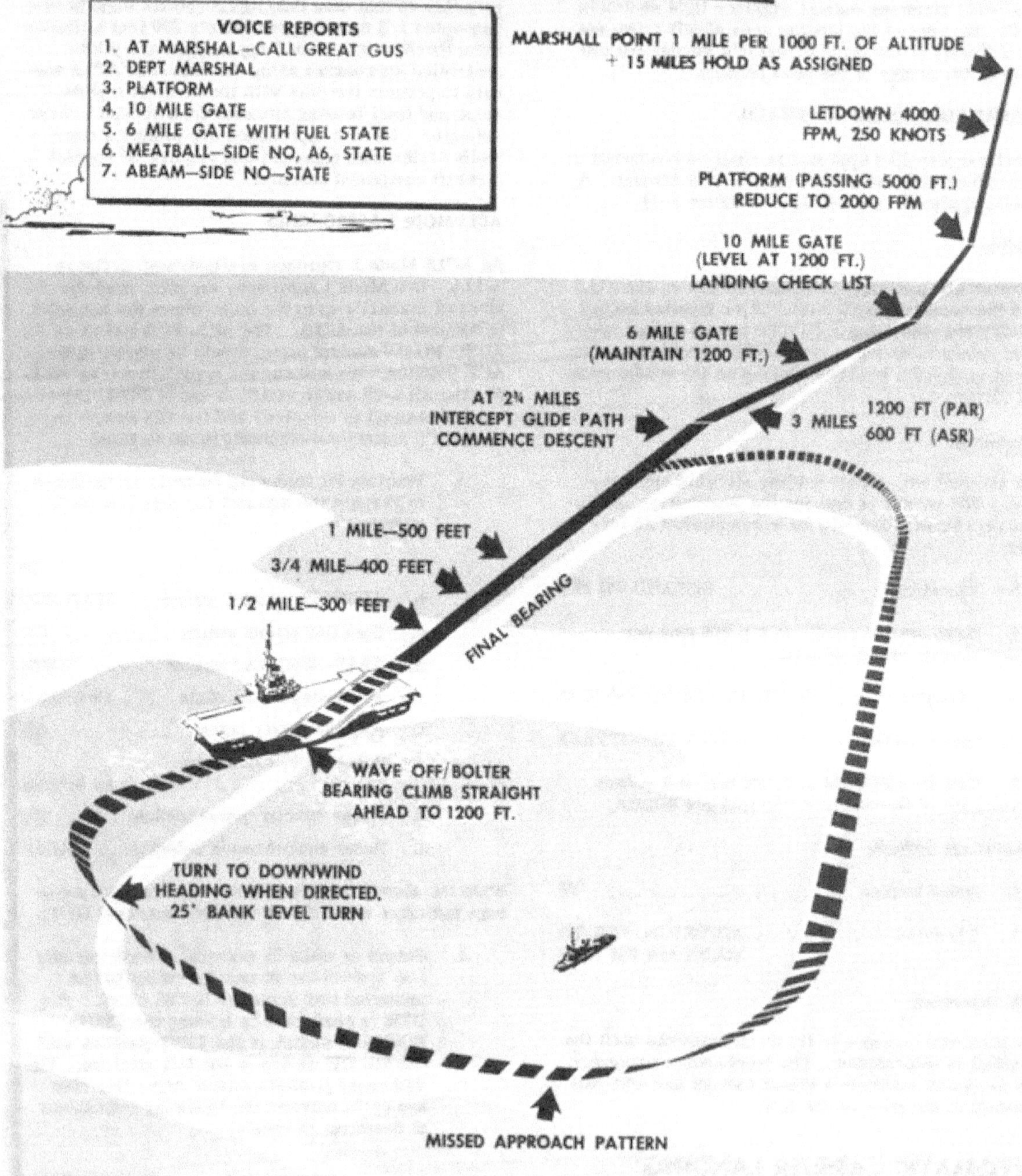

VOICE REPORTS
1. AT MARSHAL—CALL GREAT GUS
2. DEPT MARSHAL
3. PLATFORM
4. 10 MILE GATE
5. 6 MILE GATE WITH FUEL STATE
6. MEATBALL—SIDE NO, A6, STATE
7. ABEAM—SIDE NO—STATE

MARSHALL POINT 1 MILE PER 1000 FT. OF ALTITUDE
+ 15 MILES HOLD AS ASSIGNED

LETDOWN 4000 FPM, 250 KNOTS

PLATFORM (PASSING 5000 FT.) REDUCE TO 2000 FPM

10 MILE GATE (LEVEL AT 1200 FT.) LANDING CHECK LIST

6 MILE GATE (MAINTAIN 1200 FT.)

AT 2¼ MILES INTERCEPT GLIDE PATH COMMENCE DESCENT

3 MILES 1200 FT (PAR)
         600 FT (ASR)

1 MILE—500 FEET
3/4 MILE—400 FEET
1/2 MILE—300 FEET

FINAL BEARING

WAVE OFF/BOLTER BEARING CLIMB STRAIGHT AHEAD TO 1200 FT.

TURN TO DOWNWIND HEADING WHEN DIRECTED. 25° BANK LEVEL TURN

MISSED APPROACH PATTERN

Figure 3-11

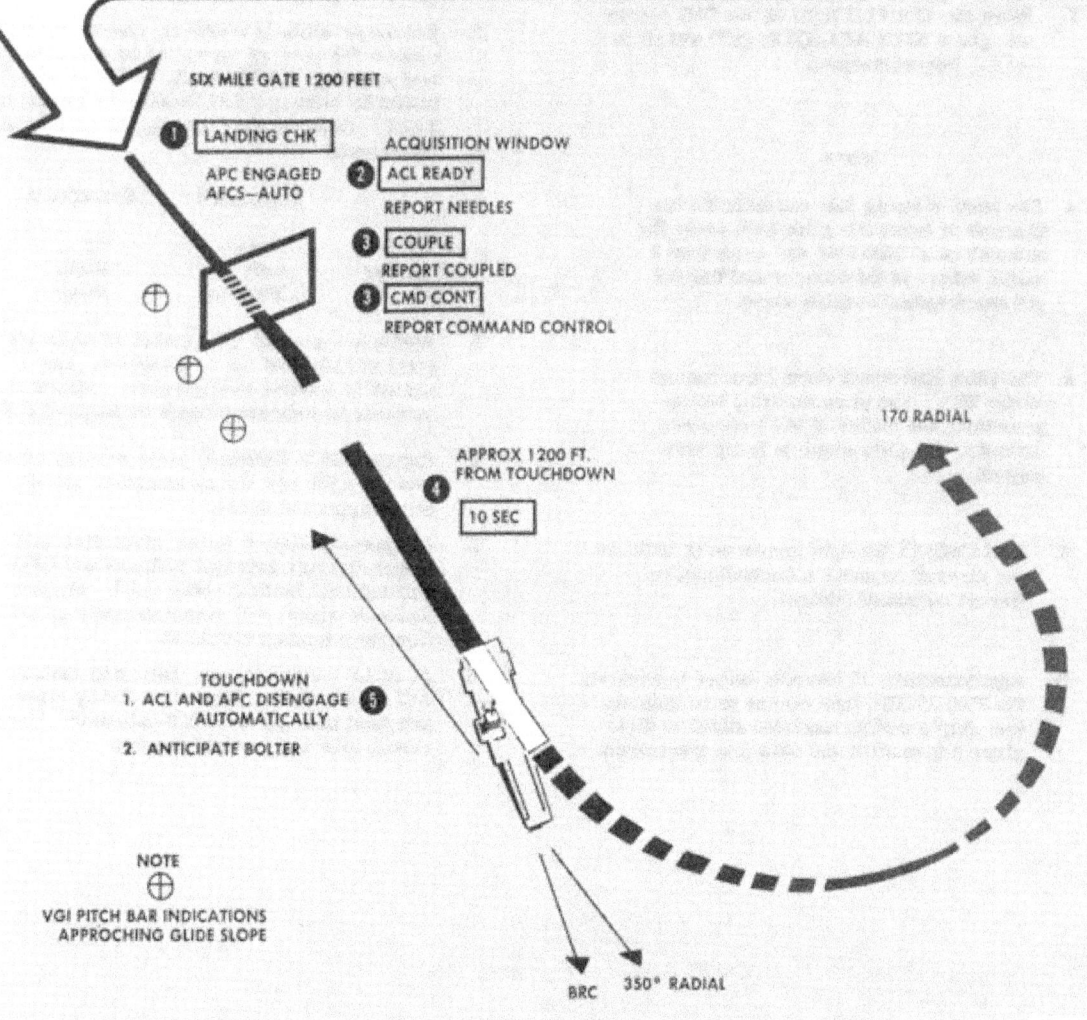

Figure 3-11A

NORMAL PROCEDURES   NAVAIR 01-85ADA-1

3. Perform a normal CCA and at the 10-mile gate, level at 1200 feet or as assigned. Change to landing configuration when the DMI LDG CHECK light comes on or earlier.

4. Engage APCS while heading inbound at 1200 feet or assigned altitude and adjust to approach airspeed.

5. At approximately 6 miles, the controller will insert the aircraft address. The LDG CHECK light comes on at this time and the TILT light goes off. The pilot should confirm landing checklist complete and report gear down.

6. At ACLS radar lock-on, the DMI will indicate ACL READY and the VGI cross pointers are driven into view. At this time, report side number and needles.

7. When the COUPLE light on the DMI comes on, place AFCS ACL/OFF/PCD switch in ACL. Report coupled.

Note

- The pitch steering bar will indicate the aircraft is below the glide path since the aircraft is at 1200 feet and more than 3 miles astern of the carrier and has not yet intercepted the glide slope.

- The pitch bar moves down from the top of the VGI. The pitch steering bar approaching the center of the instrument indicates the glide slope is being intercepted.

8. DMI CMD CONT light comes on to indicate the aircraft is under command control. Report command control.

9. Approximately 10 seconds before touchdown, the DMI 10 SEC light comes on to indicate that ship's motion has been added to glide slope information and data link commands.

ACLS MODE 2 APPROACHES

An ACLS mode 2 approach is illustrated in figure 3-12. In a mode 2 approach, the ACLS indicator (ID-351) pitch-and-bank steering bars present vertical and lateral glide-slope errors respectively in relation to the aircraft. The pilot flies the aircraft toward the steering bars as in an ILS approach. Discrete readout (DRO) panel light lighting and going out are noted in the following procedural steps.

1. Position the following controls as indicated to prepare aircraft for data link/ACLS signals:

   a. Data link power switch . . . . ON
   b. Message selector switch . . . . . NORM
   c. Frequency-select dials . . AS BRIEFED

When the controls are selected, the DRO will indicate missed message (TILT).

2. Before or while in marshal, check data link system for correct operation by universal test message (UTM) check. UTM is selected by holding TEST/NORM/AJ switch in TEST. Observe the following ACLS indicator commands:

	Sequence 1	Sequence 2
Pitch Bar	Down	Up
Bank Bar	Left	Right
DRO	Wave-off	Blank

3. Perform a normal CCA and at 10-mile gate, level at 1200 feet (or as assigned), and change to landing configuration. DRO will continue to indicate missed message (TILT).

4. Engage APCS (optional) while heading inbound level at 1200 feet (or as assigned) and stabilize approach speed.

5. At approximately 6 miles, controller will insert aircraft data link address and DRO will indicate landing check (LC). Missed-message signal will simultaneously go out. Complete landing checklist.

6. At ACLS radar lock-on, DRO will indicate ACL ready (LO). Observe a fly-up signal and final bearing on ACLS indicator. Then report side number and needles.

3-50B   Change 2

Note

- The pitch steering bar indicates erroneous information if level at 1200 feet and further than 3 miles aft of the carrier.

- Hold altitude as the pitch steering bar moves down from the top of the ACLS indicator. As the pitch steering bar approaches the center of the indicator, ease the nose over to intercept glide slope. Fly on glide slope and centerline by keeping the indicator needles centered.

7. At 1/2 mile astern or sooner (pilot's discretion), transfer to standard visual approach and make ball call.

8. If console operator does not unlock radar, 10 second will light 10 seconds prior to touchdown.

9. If aircraft exceeds ACLS limits or experiences a system malfunction, flashing wave-off (WO) light on DRO will alert pilot.

NORMAL PROCEDURES
Carrier-Based Procedures (Pilot)

NAVAIR 01-85ADA-1

ACLS MODE 2 APPROACH (TYPICAL)

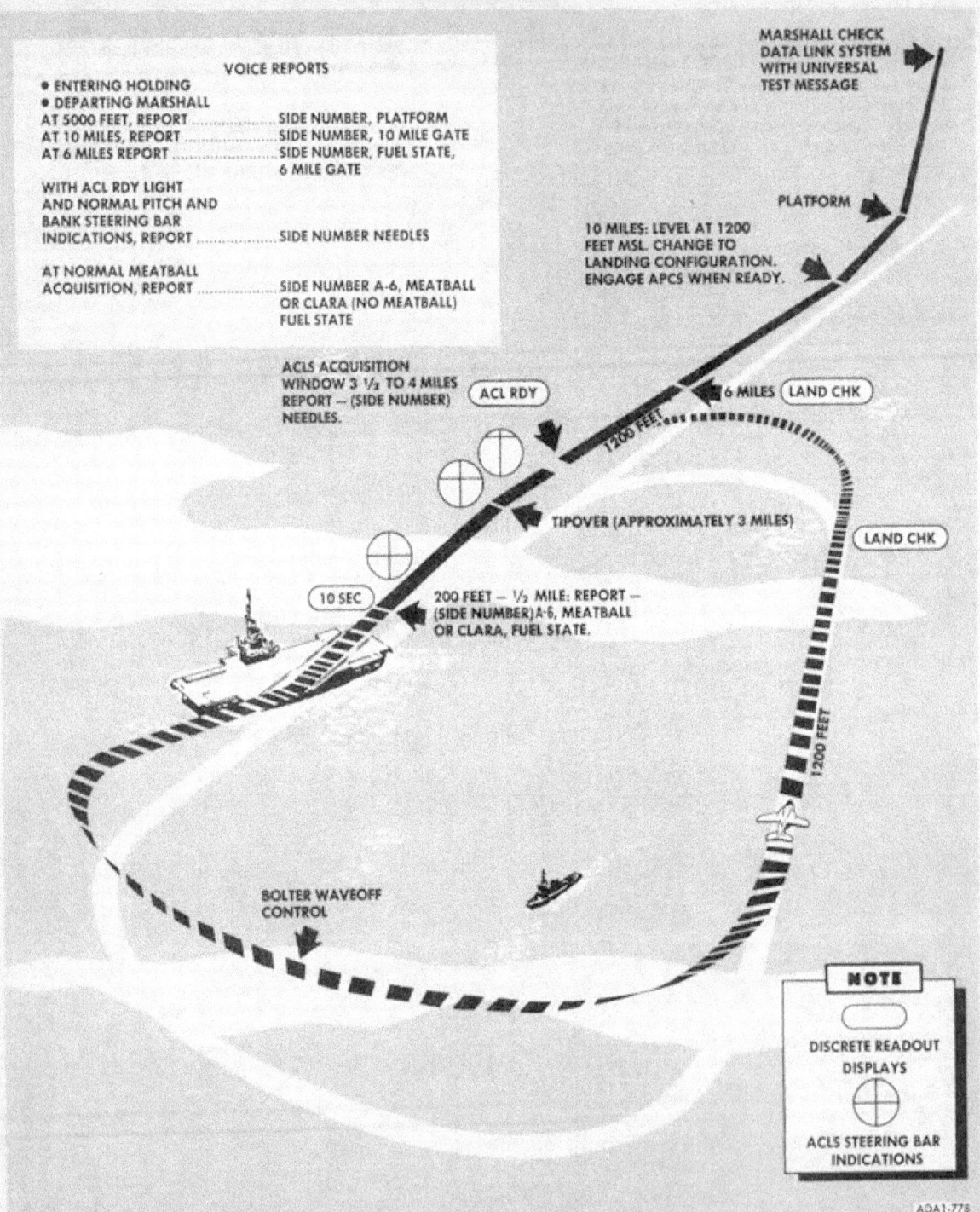

Figure 3-12

Part 5 — Shore Based Procedures (B/N)

B/N PRESTART PROCEDURES

1. Preflight checklist .... COMPLETED
2. Harnessing .... FASTEN

WARNING

If the survival-gear lanyard is connected (GRU-5 only) the survival equipment will hinder rapid evacuation of the cockpit during a ground emergency or ditching.

3. Helmet .... ON
4. Oxygen mask, communications, and anti-g suit/anti-exposure suit ..... CONNECTED
5. Seat .... ADJUST
    a. Assume ejection position, sit erect, buttocks against backrest, head firmly against headrest, spine straight, thighs against seat pan.
    b. With left hand, reach up and touch face-curtain handle.
    c. Adjust seat height so that top of helmet just clears underside of face-curtain handle.

Note

Above procedure ensures proper positioning for ejection.

6. Inertial platform alignment (as applicable) .... COMMENCED
7. Oxygen switch .... ON
    O_2 on, with mask away from face, depress ICS, then O_2 off.
8. Oxygen mask .... ATTACH TO HELMET
9. Oxygen regulator (GRU-5 only) 100%
10. Inertia reel .... CHECK
11. Vent suit-seat cushion controls .... AS DESIRED
12. Hose-reel ground test switch (KA-6D) .... OFF
13. No. 2 UHF radio (KA-6D) .... ON (T/R + G)
14. B/N circuit breaker panel .... ALL CIRCUIT BREAKERS IN
15. Chaff programmer panel .... AS DESIRED
16. RADIO control panel (RAD/ICS panel, A-6E TRAM) .... AS DESIRED
17. BOMB TONE switch .... AS DESIRED
18. Interior lights .... AS DESIRED
19. Advisory lights .... TEST
    Test all advisory lights except those on ARMAMENT panel by depressing B/N MASTER TEST BUTTON.
20. B/N's auxiliary circuit breaker panel .... ALL CIRCUIT BREAKERS IN

CONTINUED ON NEXT PAGE

NORMAL PROCEDURES
Shore-Based Procedures (B/N)

B/N PRESTART PROCEDURES—CONTINUED

A-6A, B, C

Pilot's Control Box (PCB)

21.	Mode selector switch	SRCH
22.	Brightness control	OFF (CCW)
23.	Contrast control	OFF (CCW)
24.	Persist control	OFF (CCW)
25.	PHD power switch	STBY
26.	Range marker knob	CCW
27.	Azimuth line knob	CCW
28.	Clearance switch	AS DESIRED
29.	Clearance range marker control	OFF (CCW)
30.	Flight line control	OFF (CCW)
31.	Display scale switch	AS DESIRED
32.	Display/track/boresight switch	DISPLAY
33.	MRI control	OFF (CCW)
34.	Receiver gain control	OFF (CCW)

Left Hand Panel

35.	Desired attack mode selector button	DEPRESS
36.	Intervalometer	SET
37.	Desired g-selector button	DEPRESS
38.	Release mode switch	AS DESIRED
39.	SALVO/TRN/STEP switch	AS DESIRED
40.	Rocket mode switch	AS DESIRED

Flight Mode Selector Panel

41.	Flight mode button	OFF
42.	Nav checkpoint/normal switch	NORM

CONTINUED ON NEXT PAGE

B/N PRESTART PROCEDURES—CONTINUED

43. Navigation mode button .... UNSTAB-NO STEER
44. Navigation transfer switch .... LEFT

Attack Navigation Panel (RHU)

45. Error code switch .... READ
46. Data select switch .... AS DESIRED
47. Release advance button .... OUT

Navigation Control Panel

48. Magnetic variation switch .... AS REQUIRED
49. Navigation data switch .... DATA
50. Navigation mode selector switch .... INERL
51. Manual range control .... AS DESIRED
52. Computer/manual/stop scan switch .... CMPTR
53. Fixed/moving (target) switch .... FIXED
54. Track receiver tune control .... AFC
55. Search receiver tune control .... AFC
56. Meter select button .... ANT PAT
57. Search trigger switch .... PRI
58. Search radar track switch .... OFF
59. Sync set/echo check/off switch .... OFF
60. XMIT/SIL switch .... SIL
61. Search magnetron reset button .... OUT
62. Brightness control .... CCW
63. Contrast control .... CCW
64. Video gain control .... CCW
65. Receiver gain control .... CCW
66. STC slope control .... CCW
67. STC depth control .... CCW
68. Range/azimuth marker brightness control .... CCW
69. Diff gain control .... AREA (CCW)
70. Scan rate control .... SLOW

CONTINUED ON NEXT PAGE

NORMAL PROCEDURES
Shore-Based Procedures (B/N)

NAVAIR 01-85ADA-1

B/N PRESTART PROCEDURES—CONTINUED

71.	AMTI control	OFF
72.	Azimuth stabilization control	OFF
73.	Scan angle control	FULL CW
74.	Display select button	PPI
75.	PPI RANGE switch	30-5 NM

WEAPON SYSTEM PREFLIGHT

> **CAUTION**
>
> - During preflight operations, the bombardier/navigator will ensure that the radiation danger area is clear of personnel, equipment, and other aircraft before placing the transmit/silent switch to the XMIT position.
>
> - In the A-6A, B, C, cooling air is not available to the search radar or track radar without the engines running or ground cooling applied, and radar operation may result in failure.
>
> - In the A-6A, B, C, E sufficient cooling air is not available to equipment in the radome area for more than 5 minutes operation with canopy open.

TURN-ON/PREFLIGHT A-6A,B,C

Note

- In aircraft Serial No. 154170 and subsequent and aircraft incorporating AVC No. 758, the ballistics computer is protected against overheating of the power supply. If the power supply overheats, the computer is automatically shut down. After the overtemperature condition has ceased to exist, the computer must be recycled by the bombardier/navigator to restore operation.

- In aircraft incorporating AFC No. 135, to reduce high humidity and to warm the equipment, turn-on of search and track radars and the computer should be delayed for 5 minutes with the canopy closed and the engine running

Bombardier/Navigator's Slew Control Panel

1.	Velocity-correct switch	OFF-SAVE or OFF-ERASE

Note

All radar transmissions shall conform to current Hazards of Electromagnetic Radiation to Ordnance (HERO) restrictions.

2.	FLIGHT mode selector button	FLIGHT
3.	Search radar power switch	STBY
4.	Track radar power switch	STBY

CONTINUED ON NEXT PAGE

WEAPON SYSTEM PREFLIGHT—CONTINUED

Note

The track radar/search radar and VDI require 5 minutes warmup in the STBY position.

5. CMPTR EMER COOL switch .... RESET
6. Computer error indicator .... CHECK
7. Address key release bar .... DEPRESS
   Release bar must be momentarily depressed to release any depressed address key prior to selecting another address key.
8. Address key .... DEPRESS PRES LOCA
   Depress present location address key and enter latitude, longitude, and altitude data for present position.

Note

The computer error indicator light should be on. The computer is in a digital computer off (DCO) condition and the platform is receiving correction signals from the erection controller.

9. Navigation data switch .... PRE POS
   Check readout windows for proper entries.
10. Address key release bar .... DEPRESS
11. Address key .... DEPRESS BASE
    Depress base address key and enter latitude, longitude, and altitude data for base.
12. Navigation mode selector .... BASE - NO AP
13. Navigation data switch .... ON CALL
    Check tape dials for proper entry and check range and bearing on DVI and PHD.
14. Address key release bar .... DEPRESS
15. Address key .... DEPRESS TARGET
    Depress TARGET address key and enter latitude, longitude, and altitude data for target.
16. Navigation mode selector .... PRES TGT - NO AP
    Check tape dials for proper entry and check range and bearing on DVI and PHD.
17. Address key release bar .... DEPRESS
18. Address key .... DEPRESS CHECK POINT
    Depress checkpoint address key and enter latitude, longitude, and altitude data.
19. Nav checkpoint/normal switch .... NAV CHK PT
    Check tape dials for proper entry and check range and bearing on DVI and PHD.
20. Navigation checkpoint/normal switch .... NORM
21. Address key release bar .... DEPRESS

CONTINUED ON NEXT PAGE

NORMAL PROCEDURES
Shore-Based Procedures (B/N)

NAVAIR 01-85ADA-1

WEAPON SYSTEM PREFLIGHT—CONTINUED

22. Address key .... REL ADV
    Depress release advance key and enter N-00000. Note reading of release advance in attack-navigation panel window C5. Release advance button must be engaged to read the value set.

23. Address key release bar .... DEPRESS

24. Navigation mode selector button .... UNSTAB-NO STEER
    Check range readout on DVI and PHD.

    Note

    In aircraft with the P8.6 program, the NOMATS code, UNSTAB NO STEER range, and temperature should be entered as desired, at this time.

25. Antenna pattern switch .... CHECK AND SET
    Momentarily actuate antenna pattern switch in both directions. Observe corresponding increase and decrease reading on the meter. Decrease until meter reads zero.

26. Meter selector button .... MAG FREQ-CHECK

27. Meter selector button .... XTAL CUR-CHECK

28. Meter selector button .... MAG CUR

29. Search radar brightness control .... ADJUST
    Adjust brightness control until PPI sweep is just visible on bombardier/navigator's DVI.

30. Search radar contrast control .... 3/4 to full CW

31. Search radar video gain control .... 2/3 CW

32. Search radar receiver gain control .... 3/4 CW

33. Marker brightness controls .... ADJUST (CW)
    Adjust both marker brightness controls until range markers and azimuth line are visible. Check that there are two range markers visible at 10 nmi intervals.

TURN-ON/PREFLIGHT A-6E

Bombardier/Navigator's Control Panel

Note

Before turning the search radar POWER switch to STBY, ensure that the nosewheel well area is clear.

1. TRANSMIT switch .... SIL

2. Search radar POWER switch .... STBY

Note

The search radar requires 4 to 7 minutes warmup in STBY.

CONTINUED ON NEXT PAGE

NAVAIR 01-85ADA-1

NORMAL PROCEDURES
Shore-Based Procedures (B/N)

WEAPON SYSTEM PREFLIGHT—CONTINUED

3.	BRT control	CW UNTIL SWEEP
4.	CONTRAST control	CW
5.	VIDEO/DIF gain control	CCW
6.	RCVR gain control	CW
6A.	BEACON control (A-6E TRAM)	OFF
7.	DISPLAY	PPI (APPROXIMATELY 27.5 MILES)
8.	RNG MKR/AZ MKR controls	CW TO DESIRED SETTING
	Check for two 10-mile range marks.	
9.	STC SLOPE/DEPTH controls	SET CCW
9A.	RCVR TUNE control (A-6E TRAM)	MAN
10.	SCAN RATE control	SLOW SCAN
11.	AMTI control	OFF
12.	SCAN STAB switch	ADL
13.	SCAN ANGLE control	SET AS DESIRED
14.	BEACON control (except A-6E TRAM)	OFF
14A.	AZ RANGE TRKG switch (A-6E TRAM)	OFF
15.	FREQ AGILITY switch	OFF
16.	ELEV TRKG switch	OFF
17.	RCVR TUNE control (except A-6E TRAM)	MAN
18.	Cursor control switch	MAN
19.	MAN RANGE setting	30,780
20.	METER toggle switch	RIGHT
21.	FAULT ISLN switch	OFF (CENTER)
22.	TEST MODE toggle switch	OFF (CENTER)
23.	TEST MODE button	BIT
24.	TRACK POWER switch (except A-6E TRAM)	OFF
25.	MODE switch (except A-6E TRAM)	TRACK

Note

Manual test procedures step 26 through 37 may be accomplished prior to engine start and computer ORT.

26.	TEST MODE toggle	LEFT
	Note GO light.	
27.	Test mode - SRCH	ADJUST FOR VIDEO
	Note GO light.	
28.	Display	ARE 30

CONTINUED ON NEXT PAGE

Change 2   3-59

NORMAL PROCEDURES
Shore-Based Procedures (B/N)

WEAPON SYSTEM PREFLIGHT—CONTINUED

29. MAN RNG .... ADJUST TO VIDEO
    Note range 30, 775±100

30. TEST MODE toggle .... RIGHT

31. Test mode .... ELEV TRACK
    Note GO light.

32. Test mode .... TWS
    Adjust MAN RNG for GO light 30, 780±100

33. TEST MODE toggle .... LEFT

34. Test mode .... SRCH

35. COMPT/MAN .... COMPT

36. RCVR tune .... AFC

Note

The following check may be made only if current hazards of electronic radiation to ordnance (HERO) and EMCON conditions permit.

37. Radar POWER .... ON
    a. DISPLAY .... PPI
    b. MAG CUR 8
    c. All PRF's .... CHECK
    d. XTAL CUR .... ABOUT .6
    e. All PRF's .... CHECK
    f. MAG FREQ 5
    g. ANT PATT .... NEAR
    h. Check XMTR PWR .... .4 to .8
    i. Check RCVR SENS at .5 to .8 with full RCVR gain
    j. METER toggle-right .... ANT PATT
    k. Display .... ARE 30

Digital Display Unit

1. Navigation mode select switch .... INERL
2. Navigation data switch .... DATA
3. DATA SELECT switch .... A

Armament Control Unit

1. STA readouts (STA 1-5) .... AS DESIRED
2. RELEASE mode select button .... AS DESIRED

CONTINUED ON NEXT PAGE

WEAPON SYSTEM PREFLIGHT—CONTINUED

3.	ATTACK mode select button	AS DESIRED
4.	TIME thumbwheel	AS DESIRED
5.	QUANTITY thumbwheel	AS DESIRED
6.	INTERVAL thumbwheel	AS DESIRED

Pilot's Control Panel

1.	VDI BRT/CONTRAST controls	CCW
2.	PITCH TRIM control	CCW
3.	OFFSET IMP PT/PATH BRT controls	CCW
4.	PHD BRT/CONTRAST controls (except A-6E TRAM)	CCW
5.	PHD power switch (except A-6E TRAM)	STBY
6.	RNG MKR/AZ MKR controls (except A-6E TRAM)	CCW

> **CAUTION**
>
> During preflight operations, the bombardier/navigator will ensure that the radiation danger area is clear of personnel, equipment, and other aircraft before moving the TRANSMIT switch from SIL.

> **Note**
>
> All radar transmissions shall conform to current Hazards of Electromagnetic Radiation to Ordnance (HERO) restrictions.

COMPUTER TURN-ON/TEST PROCEDURES A-6E (E 1.5 PROGRAM)

> **CAUTION**
>
> The AAU-19 altimeter should remain in STBY until the A/D converter tests have been completed.

> **Note**
>
> Turning on the right generator with the computer on may cause the computer to revert to the initial power-uptest sequence.

1. COMPUTER switch . . . . ON

   a. COMPT ERROR light: lit 4 seconds
      ATTACK light: lit 4 seconds
      DDU windows: all 0's
      TEMPORARY STORAGE window: all dashes

   b. CLEAR button . . . . DEPRESS
      All windows: 3's

   c. CLEAR button . . . . DEPRESS
      G/S/LONG window: S77777
      WIND SPEED/LAT window: S7777
      TEMPORARY STORAGE window: S777777
      All other windows: 7's

   d. CLEAR button . . . . DEPRESS
      G/S/LONG window: 11111

CONTINUED ON NEXT PAGE

NORMAL PROCEDURES
Shore-Based Procedures (B/N)   NAVAIR 01-85ADA-1

WEAPON SYSTEM PREFLIGHT—CONTINUED

Note

- All switch discretes to the computer may be checked at this time by selecting the switch and reading the corresponding code in the TEMP STORE window.
- Operational requirements may dictate that the flight program be entered at this point; however, it is recommended that the ORT be completed through the A/D converter checks on internal power. The complete computer check will be accomplished by maintenance personnel during daily checks.
- Before commencing the A/D converter checks, ensure that the VDI is in CONT ANALOG.

    e. CLEAR button .... DEPRESS
Depressing clear button starts analog-to-digital (A/D) converter test.

G/S/LONG window first reads:	012000
then	011900
then	010600

If no failures are present between 011900 and 010600:

then decreases by 100's	3400
then reads	111111

- ATTACK light lit: ADC out of tolerance/failed.
- COMPT ERROR light lit: normal accelerometer failure.

Note

- The A/D converter test is completely automatic and requires approximately 3 minutes to complete.
- Any failure during the A/D converter test stops the test and the readout in the G/S/LONG window indicates which test was failed. Depressing the CLEAR button permits the rest of the tests to be completed unless readout 120, 119, 118, 117, 064, or 063. Refer to A/D Converter Tests in Section VIII for mission impact of test failures.

2. COMPT MODE switch .... ENTER
3. ADDRESS key .... PRES LOC
   Enter present position data:
    a. Latitude and longitude of departure using POS ACTION key.
    b. Pressure altitude of departure using ALT ACTION key.
4. Navigation mode select switch .... DR
5. Velocity-correct switch .... OFF ERASE, THEN OFF SAVE
6. RELEASE bar .... DEPRESS
7. ADDRESS key .... UNSTAB
   Enter desired cursor initialization range in miles.
8. RELEASE bar .... DEPRESS
9. COMPT MODE switch .... STEER

Digital Display Unit

10. Navigation data select switch .... PRES POS
    Read correct present position entries of latitude, longitude and altitude to confirm keyboard entries.
11. Navigation data select switch .... ON CALL
    Depress UNSTAB key and read correct cursor initialization range to confirm keyboard entry.

WEAPON SYSTEM PREFLIGHT – CONTINUED

Note

The inertial platform may be placed in OPER at any time during the ORT if necessary. However, a complete evaluation of alignment accuracy requires that the computer be operating in the flight program.

COMPUTER TURN-ON/TEST (E100 PROGRAM)

Pedestal Control Unit

1. COMPT MODE switch .... STEER or TEST

   Turning the computer on in STEER enables only the automatic tests; in TEST enables the complete ORT.

2. Velocity correct switch .... OFF SAVE
3. Azimuth-Range switch .... ON

Digital Display Unit

1. DATA SELECT switch .... A
2. NAVIGATION data switch .... PRES POS
3. MAG VAR .... SET LOCAL VARIATION
4. COMPUTER switch .... ON

Note the following automatic sequence of test indications requiring approximately 40 seconds:

- COMPT error light comes on for approximately 4 seconds, then goes out.
- ATTACK light comes on for approximately 4 seconds, then COMPT ERROR light comes on. Both lights remain on for approximately 4 seconds, then go out.
- TEMP STORE windows display several test indications, then
- TEMP STORE windows read dashes (-).
- All DDU windows read 0.
- All DVRI and PAIP windows read 0.

Note

- At this time, a failed test may be repeated by pressing the SAC key on the PCU, or if TEST had been selected, the computer ORT may be continued by depressing the PCU CLEAR button.
- If STEER had been selected, at the successful completion of the automatic test, the COMPT ERROR light will come on, DDU window A5 will display the 001 SAC, and the alignment program may be entered.

Pedestal Control Unit

1. COMPT MODE switch .... ENTER
2. PRES LOC ADDRESS key .... DEPRESS
3. Present position latitude, longitude and altitude .... ENTER
4. SAC key - DEPRESS - Note that COMPT ERROR light goes out, DDU window A5 displays 0's.

CONTINUED ON NEXT PAGE

NORMAL PROCEDURES
Shore-Based Procedures (B/N)

NAVAIR 01-85ADA-1

WEAPON SYSTEM PREFLIGHT – CONTINUED

Pilot's Control Panel

1. DISPLAY button .... CONT ANALOG
2. RANGE MILES button 3
3. BRT/CONTRAST control .... ADJUST FOR NORMAL PICTURE

NAVIGATION Control Panel

1. MODE select button .... ALIGN
   Note that the ALIGN light comes on ~~after 45 seconds~~.

Note

During IMU alignment, the balance of the computer entries may be made.

Pilot's Auxiliary Indicator Panel

1. HDG SEL switch .... CMD

If the computer ORT was selected initially, proceed as follows:

1. CLEAR button .... DEPRESS
   All windows read: 3's

2. CLEAR button .... DEPRESS
   G/S LONG window reads: S 77777
   WIND SPEED/LAT window reads: S 7777
   TEMP STORE window reads: S 777777
   All other windows read: 7's

3. CLEAR button .... DEPRESS
   G/S LONG window reads: 111111

4. CLEAR button .... DEPRESS
   Depressing the CLEAR button starts the A/D converter tests requiring approximately 3 minutes. Observe the following:

   - G/S/LONG window first reads: 012100 then counts down by 100's
   - Movement of VDI symbols, actuation of lights during countdown
   - Actuation of DVRI and NAVIGATION control panel lights during countdown

If no failures:

- G/S/LONG window reads: 111111
- COMPT ERROR and ATTACK lights - OFF
- DVRI: ATTACK, RESELECT, ELEVATION, AZ-RANGE, and COMPUTER lights .... ON
- VDI: ATTACK, PLATFORM, COMPUTER, IN RANGE, and breakaway lights .... ON
  All other lights .... FLASH
- VDI: Target symbol .... ON
  steering symbol, pathway and release marker .... OFF
  Impact point .... FLASH

If G/S LONG window countdown stops before reaching 111111, see Section VIII for failure definition. Failed tests considered nonessential may be bypassed by depressing the CLEAR button.

CONTINUED ON NEXT PAGE

WEAPON SYSTEM PREFLIGHT—CONTINUED

RADAR TEST PROCEDURES A-6E

Note

The following tests are to be accomplished after computer flight program has been entered.

1. CMPT MODE .... STEER AND UNSTAB
2. AZ/RNG switch .... DISLODGE
3. Position range line on video with slew stick 30, 780±100
4. BEACON .... FULL CW

    a. RCVR gain .... CCW
       Test video disappears.

    b. BEACON .... FULL CW
       Readjust range line to video note approximately 150 feet difference.

    c. BEACON .... OFF

    d. RCVR gain .... CW
       Test video reappears.

    e. RCVR tune .... AFC

5. ELEV TRK .... ON
6. CMPT steer .... OPT TGT
   Position range line on video with slew stick 30, 780±100. ELEVATION light ON.
7. Azimuth-range switch .... ENABLE (AFT)
   Note RNG 30, 780±100. AZ-RANGE/ELEVATION lights ON, check slew inhibited.

Note

Range accuracy data obtained by ranging on the BIT video is considered accurate enough to preclude ground transmission.

8. Azimuth-range switch .... DISLODGE (FORWARD)
9. Test mode .... AMTI
   GO light, AMTI CW/then OFF. Note video dropout just out of detent, then fills in as control is rotated CW.
10. PCB .... TC
    Observe antenna pattern goes to FAR.
11. Test mode .... TC
    GO light, check TC fail light on VDI .... OFF

CONTINUED ON NEXT PAGE

NORMAL PROCEDURES
Shore-Based Procedures (B/N)

NAVAIR 01-85ADA-1

WEAPON SYSTEM PREFLIGHT—CONTINUED

12. RCVR tune .... MAN THEN AFC
    Observe TC fail light on then OFF.

13. PCB .... TEST
    Observe proper display. Select RNG 2.

14. PCB .... TC CAL
    Observe proper display with RNG 2 and 1.5 coded.

15. PCB .... CONT ANALOG

16. POWER switch .... STBY

17. Test mode .... OFF

18. CMPT steer .... UNSTAB

19. DISPLAY .... PPI

Note

All fault isolation operations must be conducted in accordance with appropriate maintenance publications and are not flight crew procedures.

Video Tape Recorder

1. Function .... STBY

2. Power .... ON

3. Test .... LAMP

4. Test .... BIT
   Wait at least 1 minute prior to checking for any failure lights.

5. Power .... OFF

OPTICAL SIGHT CHECK PROCEDURES A-6E

Sight Unit Control Panel

1. AUTO/OFF/MAN switch .... AUTO

2. Fixed and moving reticles .... ON

3. In range and breakaway displays .... TEST

Computer Control Unit Keyboard Panel

4. COMPT MODE switch .... STEER

5. UNSTAB key .... DEPRESS
   Observe that fixed and moving reticles are superimposed (within 1 1/2 to 2 mils).

COMPUTER ENTRY PROCEDURES A-6E

Computer Control Unit Keyboard Panel

1. COMPT MODE switch .... ENTER

CONTINUED ON NEXT PAGE

WEAPON SYSTEM PREFLIGHT—CONTINUED

2. ADDRESS key .... TGT 1
   Enter data for first target as follows:
   a. Latitude and longitude, using POS ACTION key.
   b. MSL altitude of target, using ALT ACTION key.

3. ADDRESS key .... OAP 1
   Enter data for target 1 offset aimpoint 1 as follows:
   a. True bearing from target to aimpoint, using BRG ACTION key.
   b. Distance from target to aimpoint in feet, using DIST ACTION key.

   Note

   - In aircraft with the E1.5 program, the OAP 1 offset distances for TGT 1 through 4 and the OAP 2 offset distances for TGT 1 through 3 are entered in feet. The OAP 2 offset distance for TGT 4 is entered in X and Y coordinates in meters.

   - In aircraft with the E100 program, OAP distances for targets 1-3 are entered in feet, and OAP bearing for targets 1-3 is entered as true bearing from target to aimpoint. OAP data for target 4 is entered as follows:

     OAP 1 - TGT 4 distance in meters, direction is entered as true bearing from OAP to target, but displayed as the reciprocal;

     OAP 2 - TGT 4 offset distance entered in meters in X and Y coordinates.

   c. Altitude difference in feet from target to aimpoint, using ALT ACTION key.

4. ADDRESS key .... OAP 2
   Enter data for target 1 offset aimpoint 2 in the same manner as OAP 1.

5. Release bar .... DEPRESS

6. Data for targets 2, 3, and 4 .... ENTER
   Enter data for additional targets and offsets as noted above.

7. Release bar .... DEPRESS

8. ADDRESS key .... NAV XPT
   Enter data for the navigation checkpoint as follows:
   a. Latitude and longitude of checkpoint using POS ACTION key.
   b. MSL altitude of checkpoint, using ALT ACTION key.

9. RELEASE bar .... DEPRESS

10. ADDRESS key .... GRD TRK
    Enter blast clearance altitude for ordnance carried using ALT ACTION key. If ground track bombing is to be used, enter ground track using BRG ACTION key.

11. RELEASE bar .... DEPRESS

12. ADDRESS key .... MAN
    Enter temperature in degrees F using TEMP ACTION key.

    Note

    Temperature displayed will be corrected so will not necessarily be the number entered.

13. RELEASE bar .... DEPRESS

14. ADDRESS key .... REL ADV
    Enter desired release advance distance or zeros using DIST ACTION key.

CONTINUED ON NEXT PAGE

NORMAL PROCEDURES
Shore-Based Procedures (B/N)
NAVAIR 01-85ADA-1

WEAPON SYSTEM PREFLIGHT—CONTINUED

15. COMPT MODE switch . . . . STEER

Digital Display Unit

16. Navigation data select switch . . . . ON CALL

Computer Control Unit Keyboard Panel

17. ADDRESS keys . . . . DEPRESS
    Depress each address key for which data was entered one at a time and read correct entries in windows in lower section of DDU.

Note

Entries for the address key depressed on the lowest row of the CCU keyboard panel will be displayed.

18. ADDRESS key . . . . UNSTAB

Digital Display Unit

19. Navigation data select switch . . . . DATA

ASN-41 NAVIGATION COMPUTER CHECK KA-6D

1. HSI mode switch . . . . NAV COMP

2. Computer function selector switch . . . . TEST
    Windspeed counter should read 231±3 knots.
    Wing direction counter should read 91±1.
    Present position latitude indicator should show South integration.
    Present position longitude indicator should show East integration.
    HSI bearing pointer No. 2 should read 30° right.

3. Computer function selector switch D2
    Set destination 2 latitude and longitude

4. Computer function selector switch D1
    Set destination 1 latitude and longitude

5. Computer function selector switch . . . . STBY

6. Magnetic variation . . . . SET
    Set magnetic variation to local value

7. Windspeed and direction . . . . SET
    Set in surface windspeed and direction

8. Present position latitude and longidude . . . . SET

APN-153 DOPPLER RADAR CHECK A-6E/KA-6D

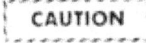

CAUTION

Ensure a minimum warmup period of 5 minutes in STBY before going to TEST.

CONTINUED ON NEXT PAGE

WEAPON SYSTEM PREFLIGHT—CONTINUED

1. Mode selector .... STBY
2. DA (drift angle) knob .... SET 20° L or R
3. GS (groundspeed) knob .... SET 350 KNOTS
4. Mode selector .... TEST
5. Within 35 seconds (maximum), GND SPEED window should read 121±5 knots and ...... DRIFT arrow should read 0°±2°.

PRE-TAXI PROCEDURES

1. Platform selector button .... OPER
2. Error code switch (A-6A, B, C)/SAC key (A-6E) .... CYCLE/DEPRESS
   Cycle error code switch/depress SAC key. Check that computer error light is out. Computer is now fully operational and is sending correction signals to platform.
3. Navigation data switch .... DATA

Note

Moving the aircraft or checking nosewheel steering before going to OPER will seriously degrade platform alignment.

4. G valve test button .... MOMENTARILY DEPRESS
5. ECM .... AS DESIRED

CAUTION

Prior to turning on the ECM power switch, ensure the gear/hook circuit breaker is properly seated and there is no indication of weight-on-wheels switch failure (angle-of-attack indexer and approach light on).

6. Doppler .... REFERENCE CHECK
7. Mission recorder
   a. Power switch .... ON
   b. Function switch .... STBY

NORMAL PROCEDURES
Shore-Based Procedures (B/N)

TAXI PROCEDURES

1. Monitor inertial heading on DVI and velocities in tape dial readouts. Wind direction should read aircraft heading ±180° on RHU, windspeed and groundspeed should approximate taxi speed.

WEAPON SYSTEM PREFLIGHT—WHEN IN RADAR TURN-UP AREA A-6A,B,C

After 5-Minute Warmup

> **CAUTION**
>
> During preflight operations, the bombardier/navigator will ensure that the radiation danger area is clear of personnel, equipment, and other aircraft before placing the XMIT/SIL switch to the XMIT position.

1. XMIT/SIL switch .... XMIT
2. Search radar power switch .... ON
3. Scan rate control .... FAST
   Position scan rate switch to fast position. Observe scan rate on DVI increase by a factor of two.
4. Scan angle control .... CCW
   Rotate scan angle control counterclockwise and observe that sweep angle on DVI decreases correspondingly.

> **Note**
>
> Check MAG CUR at PPI-30, 75 and 150 settings. Adjust meter reading to 0.8 at PPI setting that gives highest meter reading before adjustment. Insure MAG current never exceeds 0.8 at any time.

5. PPI range switch 75
   Observe change in sweep length on display, and that there are two range markers at 25 nmi intervals.
6. PPI range selector control 150
   Observe change in sweep length on display, and that there are five range markers at 25 nmi intervals. Antenna scan rate will be reduced by one half.
7. PPI range switch 5
8. Slew activate switch .... DEPRESS
   Move slew stick and note corresponding movement of indicator bug and search radar cursors.
9. DISPLAYS select button WAC/ARE-50
   Switches to SECT display when range cursor drives to less than 44 NMI; switches to ARE-50 at 27.5 nmi.

CONTINUED ON NEXT PAGE

NAVAIR 01-85ADA-1

NORMAL PROCEDURES
Shore-Based Procedures (B/N)

WEAPON SYSTEM PREFLIGHT—WHEN IN RADAR TURN-UP AREA A-6A,B,C—CONTINUED

10. DISPLAYS select button SECT/ARE-25
    Switches to ARE-25 when range cursor drives to less than 27.5 NMI.

11. DISPLAYS select button .... PPI

12. Receiver gain control .... ADJUST

13. Video gain control .... ADJUST

14. Contrast control .... ADJUST

15. Brightness control .... ADJUST

16. Meter select button .... MAG FREQ
    Use increase/decrease switch to adjust frequency as desired.

17. Meter select button .... XTAL CUR
    Note absence of needle sweep, indicating AFC lock-on.

18. PHD power switch .... ON

19. PHD BRIGHTNESS control .... ADJUST

20. PHD CONTRAST control .... ADJUST

21. PHD PERSIST control .... ADJUST

22. PHD RANGE MKRS and AZ LINE Controls .... ADJUST

23. Track radar power switch .... ON

24. Meter select button .... TRACK MAG CUR
    Check that track radar magnetron current reads 0.8. If adjustment is necessary, use track MAG CUR control on BNCB. This control may be locked in position after adjustment.

25. Meter select button .... TRACK XTAL CUR
    Note absence of needle sweep, indicating AFC lock-on.

26. Sync set/echo check switch .... SYNC SET
    Check for proper displays on DVI/PHD

27. Sync set control knob .... ROTATE/LOCK
    Rotate control knob until proper synchronization is indicated. Lock knob in proper position.

Note

A sync set performed immediately after radar turn-on may not be valid during later portions of the flight. Whenever the track radar will be used for either discrete or ground lock-on tracking, the sync set should be rechecked while airborne.

28. Sync set procedure .... COMPLETE
    Complete either procedure below

    Sync Set - Targets Not Available

    a. Track radar power switch .... STBY

    b. XMIT/SIL switch .... SIL

CONTINUED ON NEXT PAGE

NORMAL PROCEDURES
Shore-Based Procedures (B/N)

NAVAIR 01-85ADA-1

WEAPON SYSTEM PREFLIGHT—WHEN IN RADAR TURN-UP AREA A-6A,B,C— CONTINUED

    c. Range cursor .... SUPERIMPOSE OVER 10NM FIXED RANGE LINE

    d. Track radar power switch .... CYCLE
       Cycle track radar power switch between STBY and ON, observing any change in position of range cursor.

    e. Sync set control knob .... ADJUST/LOCK
       While cycling track radar power switch between STBY and ON, adjust sync set control as necessary (which moves range cursor when track radar power switch is on) until there is no visual difference in range between STBY and ON positions. Lock knob in proper position.

Sync Set-Targets Available

    a. Track radar power switch .... STBY

    b. Dislodge switch .... DISLODGE

    c. Locate close-in fixed target in search radar PPI 30.

    d. ARE-25 .... SELECT
       Adjust display for sharp target video and thin, sharp range cursor.

    e. Slew control .... ADJUST CURSORS
       Position cursors so that range cursor is under and against target.

    f. Track radar power switch .... ON
       Note any relative motion between range cursor and target video.

    g. Sync set control knob .... ADJUST/LOCK
       Adjust sync set control knob so that there is no change in position of range cursor with respect to target when track radar is on.

29. Sync set/echo check switch .... ECHO CHK
    Note number of horizontal lines on DVI.

30. Sync set/echo check switch .... OFF

31. Track radar power switch .... STBY

Aircraft 19 through 309 and Aircraft Not Incorporating AVC No. 658

32. AMTI control .... ROTATE CW AND NOTE FIXED TARGET CANCELLATION.

33. AMTI control .... OFF

Aircraft 310 and Subsequent and Aircraft Incorporating AVC 658

32. AMTI control .... ROTATE CW.
    Observe display sweep background noise disappears and no spoking or spurious signals are present. Note fixed target cancellation.

33. AMTI control .... OFF

All Aircraft

34. STC slope control .... ADJUST

35. STC depth control .... ADJUST
    Increase STC slope and depth controls (CW) observing proper reduced gain effect at near ranges.

CONTINUED ON NEXT PAGE

WEAPON SYSTEM PREFLIGHT—WHEN IN RADAR TURN-UP AREA A-6A,B,C— CONTINUED

36. Differential gain control .... ADJUST
    Adjust differential gain control, noting sharpening of target returns.
37. Search trigger switch .... SEC
    There should be little or no change in display sweep.
38. Search trigger switch .... PRI
39. PPI range knob 30
40. Computer/manual switch .... MAN
41. Azimuth cursor switch .... SLEW CW AND CCW
    Check clockwise and counterclockwise slewing of azimuth cursor
42. Manual range control knob .... CHECK AND SET
    Return computer/manual switch to CMPTR

Pilot's Control Box

43. Track mode selector switch .... DISPLAY
44. Mode selector switch .... E-SCAN
45. Clearance/range marker control .... ADJUST
46. Flight line control .... ADJUST
47. Display miles scale switch 5
    Observe display for markers and sweep.
48. Display miles scale switch 10
    Observe display for change in range and markers.
49. Mode selector switch .... SRCH

Bombardier/Navigator's Control Panel

50. Mode selector switch .... TCPPI

Pilot's Control Box

51. Clearance/range marker control .... ADJUST
    Observe display on PHD/DVI for proper presentation.
52. Display miles scale switch 5
    Observe presentation for range shift.
53. Displays selector button .... EMER SRCH

Bombardier/Navigator's Slew Grip:

54. Elevation slew switch .... ACTUATE FOR VIDEO

Pilot's Control Box

55. Receiver gain/MRI controls .... ADJUST FOR OPTIMUM DISPLAY
56. Display miles scale switch 10
    Observe display for range shift.

CONTINUED ON NEXT PAGE

NORMAL PROCEDURES
Shore-Based Procedures (B/N)

WEAPON SYSTEM PREFLIGHT—WHEN IN RADAR TURN-UP AREA A-6A,B,C—CONTINUED

57. Track radar power switch . . . . STBY

58. XMIT/SIL switch . . . . SIL

> **CAUTION**
>
> The XMIT/SIL switch should not be manipulated when the track radar power switch is in the ON position.

ADDITIONAL SYSTEM GROUND CHECKS ON SURVEYED RADAR REFLECTOR (If Available)

1. Taxi to radar turn-up spot, point aircraft ADL at surveyed reflector

2. Preparatory steps . . . . COMPLETE
   a. Track radar power switch . . . . STBY
   b. Track radar dislodge switch . . . . DISLODGE (FORWARD)
   c. Track radar DISPLAY/TRACK/BORESIGHT switch . . . . TRACK

3. Locate surveyed target on search radar

4. Record search radar range and bearing to target

5. Track radar power switch . . . . ON

6. Perform sync set. Acquire ground lock-on. Record TROT/COP check.

7. Track radar dislodge switch . . . . DISCRETE (AFT)

8. Acquire discrete lock-on. Record TROT/COP check, radar range and bearing to target, and cursor position with respect to target.

Note

The above ground checks can provide valuable preflight and post flight troubleshooting information.

NAVAIR 01-85ADA-1

NORMAL PROCEDURES
Shore-Based Procedures (B/N)

PRETAKEOFF PROCEDURES

1. Complete Takeoff Checklist with pilot using challenge and reply.

2. Check inertial heading and MA-1 heading

When aligned with runway and ready for takeoff:

3. Navigation data switch (Aircraft with ASN-31) . . . . DATA
   Check velocities 0 to 3 knots

4. Steering mode . . . . AS DESIRED

5. ICS . . . . HOT

6. Report to pilot . . . . READY FOR TAKEOFF

A-6C 1.

TAKEOFF PROCEDURES

1. Monitor pilot's instruments.
2. Monitor inertial velocities.

AIRBORNE

AFTER TAKEOFF PROCEDURES
A-6C 1, 2, 3, 4, 5

1. Flight mode selector button . . . . AS DESIRED
2. Search radar power switch . . . . ON
3. Radar XMIT/SIL switch . . . . XMIT
4. Adjust search radar for optimum PPI display
5. Doppler LAND/SEA/REF SIG switch (A6A, B, C) . . . . AS DESIRED
6. Velocity correct switch . . . . OFF SAVE
7. Navigation select switch (A-6A, B, C, E) . . . . DR
7A. Navigation select switch (A-6E TRAM) . . . . INERL
8. Doppler select switch . . . . ON-LAND SEA (A-6E KA6D) OR XMIT
9. Monitor Doppler groundspeed and drift angle in windows A3 and A4 (A-6A, B, C), or in
   DDU or Doppler panel (A-6E)

If Doppler Groundspeed and Drift Angle Are Valid:

10. Navigation select switch (except A-6E TRAM) . . . . INERL
10A. Doppler valid code (A-6E TRAM) . . . . ENTER

CONTINUED ON NEXT PAGE

NORMAL PROCEDURES
Shore-Based Procedures (B/N)

AIRBORNE — CONTINUED

If Doppler Groundspeed and Drift Angle Are Not Valid:

11. Doppler select switch .... SILENT/STBY

12. Repeat steps 7-10 after 5 minutes.

BEFORE LANDING

1. Complete landing checklist with pilot using challenge and reply.
2. ICS .... HOT
3. ECM .... STBY/OFF
4. Doppler power switch .... STBY/SILENT
5. Radars .... STBY

A-6C 1, 2, 3

AFTER LANDING

1. Complete after landing checklist with pilot using challenge and reply.

A-6C 1, 2, 3

IN CHOCKS

1. Copy data.
2. PHD power switch .... OFF
3. Radar power switch(es) .... OFF
4. Inertial platform selector button .... OFF

A-6C 1, 2

5. Doppler power switch .... OFF
6. Computer switch .... OFF
7. Panel/console lights .... OFF
8. ECM power switches .... OFF

NAVAIR 01-85ADA-1

NORMAL PROCEDURES
Shore-Based Procedures (B/N)

A-6C PREFLIGHT

1. External airconditioning (if available) .... APPLIED TO POD
2. VDI selector button .... CONT ANALOG
3. TV/IR cooling switch .... RESET (6 SEC) THEN NORM

> **CAUTION**
>
> Without engines running or external air conditioning on, do not set the TV/IR cooling switch to NORM and do not move the IR power switch from OFF.

4. IR power switch .... STBY (OFF if external air conditioning is not available)

Selecting STBY starts IR cool-down.

> **CAUTION**
>
> If external air conditioning is not applied to the pod, leave the TV/IR cooling switch and the IR power switch at OFF until after engines are running and aircraft air conditioning is on.

> **Note**
>
> IR cool-down time is normally 30 minutes. The IR HOT light on the TRIM panel will remain on until cool-down is completed.

5. TV power switch .... OFF
6. Optical platform power switch .... STOW/OFF
7. Optical platform NORM/OVRD switch .... NORM
8. DF power switch .... OFF

Indicator Azimuth Range Multisensor:

9. IARM filter selector .... AS DESIRED

DF Control Panel:

10. DF POWER switch .... STBY
11. DF AUDIO switch .... ON

> **Note**
>
> For the pilot to hear DF audio, the B/N must select ALT 1.

12. DF THRESHOLD and AUDIO GAIN controls .... ADJUST
    Adjust THRESHOLD and AUDIO GAIN controls for a comfortable level of audio in headset.

Bombardier/Navigator's Control Panel

13. Display selector switch .... RADAR (LEFT)
14. Display select button .... PPI
15. PPI RANGE switch .... 5 MILES

NORMAL PROCEDURES
Shore-Based Procedures (B/N)

NAVAIR 01-85ADA-1

A—6C PREFLIGHT — CONTINUED

IN RADAR TURN-UP AREA

16. Search radar power switch . . . . ON
17. Track radar power switch . . . . STBY
18. XMIT/SIL switch . . . . XMIT

DF Control Panel:

19. DF POWER switch . . . . BIT
20. DF THRESHOLD control . . . . ADJUST (100)
21. DF video and audio . . . . CHECK
    a. Observe a DF flag displayed at 10° and 1 1/2 miles on IARM and PHD.
    b. Note 150 pps audio in B/N's and pilot's headsets.
22. DF AUDIO and VIDEO GAIN controls . . . . ADJUST
    Adjust AUDIO GAIN control for a comfortable level in headsets and VIDEO GAIN for a suitable level on IARM and PHD.

Note

It may be necessary to adjust the RANGE MKRS control on the pilot's control panel to obtain a suitable video level.

23. BEACON light . . . . FLASHING
    BEACON light on IARM should flash once per second.
24. DF POWER switch . . . . STBY

Bombardier/Navigator's Control Panel

25. XMIT/SIL switch . . . . SIL
26. Search radar power switch . . . . STBY

TRIM Control Panel:

27. OSP NORM/OVRD switch . . . . OVRD
28. OSP power switch . . . . FWD
29. TV power switch . . . . ON

Bombardier/Navigator's Control Panel:

30. Display selector switch . . . . TRIM (RIGHT)
31. Display select button . . . . TEST
    Observe a test pattern on IARM
32. Display zoom . . . . CHECK
    a. DIS ZOOM button . . . . DEPRESS
       Observe that center set of bars on IARM test pattern is expanded 2:1, demonstrating a 1000-line resolution capability on IARM.

CONTINUED ON NEXT PAGE

A-6C PREFLIGHT – CONTINUED

      b. ZOOM light . . . . ON
      c. DIS ZOOM button . . . . DEPRESS
          Observe that test pattern returns to normal.
      d. ZOOM light . . . . OUT

33. TV/IR BRIGHTNESS and CONTRAST controls . . . . ADJUST
      Adjust for an optimum display on IARM.

Pilot's Control Box

34. VDI selector button . . . . TEST

35. VDI BRIGHTNESS and CONTRAST controls . . . . ADJUST
      Adjust for an optimum display on VDI.

36. Inverted T positioning . . . . CHECK

      a. Enter GLIDE PATH N03000 ALT on keyboard.
          Note that inverted T moves vertically from
          zero position.

      b. Enter GLIDE PATH N00000 on keyboard.
          Note that inverted T returns to zero.

37. VDI selector button . . . . TV
      Observe a television display on VDI.

Bombardier/Navigator's Control Panel

38. Display selector button . . . . TV
      Observe a television display on IARM.

TRIM Control Panel:

39. IR HOT light . . . . OUT

40. IR power switch . . . . ON

Note

IR cool-down normally requires 30 minutes. The IR
HOT light will remain on until cool-down is completed.
The IR power switch may not be set to ON until the
light is out.

Bombardier/Navigator's Control Panel

41. Display select button . . . . IR BLK
      Observe a display of IR targets with hot targets black.

42. IR GAIN control . . . . ADJUST
      Adjust for optimum display of IR targets.

Indicator Azimuth Range Multisensor:

43. IR BLK light . . . . ON

TRIM Control Panel:

44. IR INTENSITY control . . . . ADJUST
      Adjust for optimum IR video contrast.

CONTINUED ON NEXT PAGE

NORMAL PROCEDURES
Shore-Based Procedures (B/N)
NAVAIR 01-85ADA-1

A−6C PREFLIGHT − CONTINUED

45. TV/IR elevation marker brightness control . . . . ADJUST
    Adjust for a suitable brightness at elevation marker on
    left side of IARM display.

46. IR reticle brightness control . . . . ADJUST
    Adjust for a suitable brightness of reticle.

47. Display select button . . . . IR WHT
    Observe a display of IR targets with hot targets white.

Indicator Azimuth Range Multisensor:

48. IR WHT light . . . . ON

Pilot's Control Box

49. VDI selector button . . . . IR
    Observe an IR display on VDI.

50. VDI BRIGHTNESS/CONTRAST controls . . . . ADJUST
    Adjust for an optimum display on VDI.

Bombardier/Navigator's Control Panel

51. IR ZOOM button . . . . DEPRESS
    Observe change to narrow field of view and 4:1 magnification
    on IARM and VDI.

52. IR FOCUS switch . . . . ADJUST
    Adjust for a sharp display on IARM and VDI.

Note

- The IR FOCUS switch functions only when IR ZOOM has
  been selected.
- The focus of the IR ZOOM optics is more easily adjusted
  before takeoff.

Indicator Azimuth Range Multisensor:

53. IR ZOOM light . . . . ON

Bombardier/Navigator's Control Panel

54. IR ZOOM button . . . . DEPRESS
    Observe that display returns to wide field of
    view and IR ZOOM light goes out.

55. Display selector switch . . . . RADAR (LEFT)

Pilot's Control Box

56. VDI selector button . . . . CONT ANALOG

TRIM Control Panel:

57. IR power switch . . . . STBY
58. TV power switch . . . . OFF
59. Optical platform power switch . . . . STOW/OFF
60. Optical platform NORM/OVRD switch . . . . NORM

CONTINUED ON NEXT PAGE

NAVAIR 01-85ADA-1

NORMAL PROCEDURES
Shore-Based Procedures (B/N)

A—6C PRETAKEOFF PROCEDURES

1. OSP indication . . . . STOWED

A—6C AIRBORNE

AFTER TAKEOFF PROCEDURES

1. Optical platform power switch . . . . FWD

Note

When switching from STOW/OFF to FWD there is a 14-second time delay before the turret will rotate to the front. An additional 14 seconds are required for the stowpins to extend.

2. TV power switch . . . . ON

CAUTION

Do not operate the LLL-TV with the sensor pointing into an intense light source.

3. IR HOT light . . . . OUT

Note

The IR HOT light on the TRIM control panel should go out after the FLIR system has been in STBY for approximately 30 minutes.

4. IR power switch . . . . ON
   Do not turn the IR on if the IR HOT light is on.

5. Optical platform power switch . . . . OPERATE

Note

When switching from FWD to OPERATE, there is a 40-second time delay before the turret can be slewed in azimuth and elevation.

A—6C BEFORE LANDING

1. TV power switch . . . . OFF
2. IR power switch . . . . STBY
3. OSP power switch . . . . STOW/OFF

A—6C IN CHOCKS

1. IR power switch . . . . OFF
2. TV/IR cooling switch . . . . OFF

CAUTION

Do not operate the TV or IR or the TRIM pod environmental control system on the ground without engines running and aircraft air conditioning on or external air conditioning applied to the pod.

ASN-31 INERTIAL PLATFORM ALIGNMENT

GROUND ALIGNMENT (COMPASS IN) A-6A, B, C

1. Platform selector button . . . . STBY (5 MIN)
2. MA-1 compass . . . . SYNC AND SLAVE
3. COMPASS switch . . . . IN
4. Doppler SILENT/XMIT switch . . . . SILENT
5. Polar mode switch . . . . AS REQUIRED
6. AUTO/MAN switch . . . . MAN
7. Carrier HEAD/LAT/LONG/SPEED . . . . SET
8. Local MAG VAR . . . . SET
9. Platform selector button (start elapsed-time clock) . . . . ALIGN
10. Monitor alignment on VDI, PLATFORM control panel indicator lights, and align progress meter.
11. Platform selector button . . . . OPER

Note

- To ensure normal alignment operation of the inertial navigation system, a minimum of 5 minutes warmup is required in the STBY position. For cold weather, allow 10 minutes for warmup.

- The FINE ALIGN light should go on approximately 1 minute after selecting ALIGN. If alignment was started with the COMPASS switch at OUT, select IN or MAG/VGI before gyro-compassing begins. This will shorten the time required for alignment; however, the COMPASS switch should be kept at OUT when gusty winds or buffeting of the aircraft occur.

GROUND ALIGNMENT (COMPASS OUT) A-6A, B, C

1. Platform selector button . . . . STBY (5 MIN)
2. COMPASS switch . . . . OUT
3. Doppler SILENT/XMIT switch . . . . SILENT
4. Polar mode switch . . . . AS REQUIRED
5. AUTO/MAN switch . . . . MAN
6. Carrier HEAD/LAT/LONG/SPEED . . . . SET
7. Local MAG VAR . . . . SET
8. Platform selector button (start elapsed-time clock) . . . . ALIGN

CONTINUED ON NEXT PAGE

ASN-31 INERTIAL PLATFORM ALIGNMENT – CONTINUED

9. Monitor alignment on VDI, PLATFORM control panel indicator lights, and align progress meter.

10. Platform selector button . . . . OPER

PRE-SET ALIGNMENT A-6A, B, C, E

Provided the aircraft has not been moved and the COMPASS switch has not been in MAG/VGI:

1. Platform selector button . . . . STBY (5 MIN)
2. Platform selector button . . . . PRESET ALIGN
   (Update erection controller if necessary)
3. FINE ALIGN and READY lights . . . . LIT
4. Platform selector button . . . . OPER

IN-FLIGHT ALIGNMENT (FULL TERM, COMPUTER ON) A-6A, B, C

Note

In-flight alignment is not available with a failure of the left weight-on-wheels switch.

The following checks should be made prior to commencing an in-flight alignment:

1. Computer is navigating correctly with Doppler or velocity-correct inputs (Doppler preferred).
2. Platform selector button . . . . STBY
3. Auto pilot . . . . OFF
4. Compass switch . . . . MAG VGI
5. MA-1 compass . . . . SYNC
6. Man/auto switch . . . . MAN
7. Polar/norm switch . . . . NORM
8. MAG VAR . . . . LOCAL VARIATION SET
9. Norm/gyrocomp switch . . . . NORM

CONTINUED ON NEXT PAGE

NORMAL PROCEDURES
Shore-Based Procedures (B/N)

NAVAIR 01-85ADA-1

ASN-31 INERTIAL PLATFORM ALIGNMENT—CONTINUED

10. Auto pilot .... ON
11. Erection controller panel .... UPDATE LAT, LONG, CARR HEAD AND SPEED (÷10)
    Carrier heading is aircraft true heading, speed is aircraft groundspeed in 10-knot increments.
12. Navigation mode selector .... EMER DOP or DR
13. Platform selector button .... IN-FLIGHT ALIGN (START ELAPSED-TIME CLOCK)
    Observe fine align light after 55 seconds. Observe align progress meter to null shortly
    thereafter, indicating that platform heading is slewed to MA-1 compass. Observe Doppler
    and inertial velocities to converge after approximately 5 minutes.
14. Erection controller panel .... UPDATE LAT & LONG
15. Autopilot .... OFF
16. Compass switch .... IN
17. Navigation select switch .... INERL
    Check VDI for proper attitude display and DVI compass rose for approximate true heading and
    monitor velocities in right-hand unit until readout dials (data position).
18. Auto pilot .... ON
19. Norm/gyrocomp switch .... GYROCOMP
    Fine align and ready light will go out. Alignment will be indicated after approximately
    20 minutes by a null indication on align progress meter, stable inertial velocities,
    proper VDI attitude, and DVI compass rose approximating true heading.

Note

Platform azimuth alignment is suspended (SA) when the aircraft
turns at a rate of 30°/minute or when the Doppler is in XMIT
and memory. SA causes the align progress meter to null.

20. Present position .... CORRECT
21. Platform selector switch .... OPER

IN-FLIGHT ALIGNMENT (SHORT TERM COMPUTER ON) A-6A, B, C

For a short-term computer on inflight alignment, perform steps 1 through 17 of the procedure for full-
term alignment and the following two steps:

18. Update computer present position.
19. Platform selector button .... OPERATE

Note

- Platform level should be accurate and the velocities
  and heading information will be only as accurate as the
  MA-1 compass and the MAGVAR setting.

- A computer-off alignment is accomplished by following the
  same procedures as those listed above for a computer-on
  alignment.

- A computer-off alignment will provide attitude reference
  only.

- Prior to selecting OPER, the VDI should be monitored to
  check the progress of the platform leveling.

CONTINUED ON NEXT PAGE

NAVAIR 01-85ADA-1

NORMAL PROCEDURES
Shore-Based Procedures (B/N)

ASN-31 INERTIAL PLATFORM ALIGNMENT — CONTINUED

GROUND ALIGNMENT (COMPASS IN) A-6E

1. Platform selector button .... STBY (5 MIN MINIMUM)
2. ATTITUDE REF switch .... COMP IN
3. CNI MASTER switch (AFC No. 269 incorporated) .... MA-1 ONLY
4. MA-1 compass selector switch .... SLAVED (3 MIN MINIMUM)
5. ALIGN switch .... OFF
6. Polar mode switch .... AS REQUIRED
7. AUTO/MAN switch .... MAN
8. Carrier HEAD/LAT/LONG/SPEED .... SET
9. Local MAG VAR .... SET
10. MA-1 compass .... SYNC
11. VDI selector button .... CONT ANALOG
12. Platform selector button (start elapsed-time clock) .... ALIGN
13. Monitor alignment on VDI, PLATFORM control panel indicator lights, and align progress meter.
14. Platform selector button .... OPERATE

Note

- To insure normal alignment operation of the inertial navigation system, a minimum of 5 minutes warmup is required in the STBY position. For cold weather, allow 10 minutes for warmup.

- The fine align light should go on approximately 1 minute after selecting ALIGN. If alignment was started with altitude reference switch at COMP OUT, select COMP IN or MAG VGI before gyro compassing begins. This will usually shorten the time required for alignment; however, the attitude reference switch should be kept at COMP OUT when gusty winds or buffeting of the aircraft occurs.

GROUND ALIGNMENT (COMPASS OUT) A-6E

1. Platform selector button .... STBY (5 MIN MINIMUM)
2. ATTITUDE REF switch .... COMP OUT
3. ALIGN switch .... OFF
4. Polar mode switch .... AS REQUIRED
5. AUTO/MAN switch .... MAN
6. Carrier HEAD/LAT/LONG/SPEED .... SET
7. Local MAG VAR .... SET

CONTINUED ON NEXT PAGE

NORMAL PROCEDURES
Shore-Based Procedures (B/N)
NAVAIR 01-85ADA-1

ASN-31 INERTIAL PLATFORM ALIGNMENT – CONTINUED

8. Platform selector button (start elapsed-time clock) .... ALIGN
9. Monitor alignment on VDI, PLATFORM control panel indicator lights, and align progress meter.
10. Platform selector button .... OPERATE

IN-FLIGHT ALIGNMENT (FULL TERM, COMPUTER ON) A-6E

1. Computer is navigating correctly with Doppler or velocity-correct inputs (Doppler preferred).
2. Platform button .... STBY
3. Auto pilot .... STAB AUG OR OFF
4. ATTITUDE REF switch .... MAG/VGI
5. MA-1 compass .... SYNC
6. Erection controller MAN/AUTO switch .... MAN
7. MAG VAR .... LOCAL VARIATION SET
8. ALIGN switch .... OFF
9. Autopilot .... AUTO
10. Erection controller panel .... UPDATE LAT, LONG, CARR HEAD, AND SPEED (±10)
    Carrier heading is aircraft true heading, speed is aircraft groundspeed in 10-knot increments.
11. Navigation mode selector .... EMER DOP OR DR
12. Platform button .... ALIGN (START ELAPSED-TIME CLOCK)
    Observe fine align light after 55 seconds. Observe align progress meter to null shortly thereafter, indicating that platform heading is slewed to MA-1 compass. Observe Doppler and inertial velocities to converge after approximately 5 minutes.
13. Erection controller panel .... UPDATE LAT & LONG
14. Autopilot .... STAB AUG OR OFF
15. ATTITUDE REF switch .... COMP IN
16. Navigation select switch .... INERL
    Check VDI for proper attitude display and DVRI compass rose for approximate true heading; monitor velocities in digital display unit readout dials (data position).
17. Autopilot .... AUTO
18. ALIGN switch .... GYROCOMP
    Fine align and ready light will go out. Alignment will be indicated after approximately 20 minutes by a null indication on align progress meter, stable inertial velocities, proper VDI attitude, and DVRI compass rose approximating true heading.

Note

Platform azimuth alignment is suspended (SA) when the aircraft turns at a rate of 30°/minute or when the Doppler is on and in memory. SA causes the align progress meter to null.

CONTINUED ON NEXT PAGE

ASN-31 INERTIAL PLATFORM ALIGNMENT—CONTINUED

19. Computer present position . . . . UPDATE

20. Platform selector switch . . . . OPER

IN-FLIGHT ALIGNMENT (SHORT TERM, COMPUTER ON) A-6E

For a short-term, computer-on in-flight alignment, perform steps 1 through 18 of the procedure for full-term alignment and the following two steps:

21. Update computer present position

22. Platform selector button . . . . OPER

Note

- Platform level should be accurate and the velocities and heading information will only be as accurate as the MA-1 compass and the MAGVAR setting.

- A computer-off alignment is accomplished by following the same procedures as those listed above for a computer-on alignment.

- A computer-off alignment will provide attitude reference only.

- Before selecting OPER, the VDI should be monitored to check the progress of the platform leveling.

NORMAL PROCEDURES
Shore-Based Procedures (B/N)

NAVAIR 01-85ADA-1

ASN-92 INERTIAL MEASUREMENT UNIT ALIGNMENT

IMU GROUND ALIGNMENT

Note

Before commencing IMU alignment, check the following preconditions:

- HDG SEL switch - CMD TRUE or CMD MAG
- SINS DATA switch - OFF
- VDI - ON, CONTACT ANALOG
- Computer - ON: PRESENT POSITION LATITUDE, LONGITUDE, ALTITUDE ENTERED

1. MODE selector button .... ALIGN
   Note ALIGN light on.

Note

While ALIGN is selected, the VDI PLATFORM light flashes, the landing mode pathway is displayed, the steering symbol and target symbol display the characteristic alignment program motion, and the optical sight moving reticle moves in a 25-mil circle about the fixed reticle.

[handwritten: SOLID PLAT LITE FIRST 4 SEC (UNTIL IMU READY SIGNAL)]

2. Monitor:

   - Elapsed time in DDU window A1 *[handwritten: ≤ PAIP TIME]*
   - ~~Alignment progress in DDU window A3 and on ADF needle of HSI~~
   - Heading in G/S/LONGITUDE window
   - IMU pitch angle in DDU window B2
   - IMU roll angle in DDU window B4

3. INS and breakaway lights .... ON
   The INS and the breakaway lights will come on along with the ALIGN light within 10 minutes, indicating completion of alignment. The INS light will come on in approximately 1 1/2 minute. OPER may be selected at that time, however, remaining in ALIGN until there is a null ~~of the HSI ADF needle~~ *[handwritten: IN HEADING]* will improve the alignment.

4. MODE selector button .... OPER
   Note that ALIGN and INS lights go off.

Note

- If it is necessary to move the aircraft before completion of the alignment (INS light on), select OPER. This will light the TAXI light and suspend the alignment. When the aircraft is parked, the alignment can be recommenced by selecting ALIGN.

- The INS light will flash if the navigation mode selector switch is in a position other than INERL.

CONTINUED ON NEXT PAGE

3-84B Change 2

NAVAIR 01-85ADA-1

NORMAL PROCEDURES
Shore-Based Procedures (B/N)

ASN-92 INERTIAL MEASUREMENT UNIT ALIGNMENT – CONTINUED

IMU IN-FLIGHT ALIGNMENT

1. Computer is navigating correctly with updated present position and velocity correct or Doppler inputs.
2. MODE selector button .... OFF (IF GYRO CAGING REQUIRED)
3. Autopilot .... STAB AUG OR OFF
4. ATTITUDE REF switch .... MAG/VGI
5. Local MAG VAR .... SET
6. Autopilot switch .... AUTO
7. Navigation mode selector switch .... DR (OR EMER DOP)
8. MODE selector button .... ALIGN
   Note that ALIGN light comes on after 45 seconds.
9. INS light .... ON
   The INS light will come on after leveling is complete (approximately 4 minutes).
10. MODE selector button .... OPER
11. Navigation mode selector switch .... INERL
12. ATTITUDE REF switch .... COMP IN

FIXED TARGET GROUND/DISCRETE LOCK-ON TRACKING A-6A,B,C

Note

Those aircraft not incorporating AVC No. 523 (-11 DPU) should perform a track radar optical tracking (TROT) calibration check before using the ground lock-on mode of operation to ascertain the accuracy of the track radar in this mode.

1. Track radar DISPLAY/TRACK/BORESIGHT switch .... DISPLAY
2. Track radar power switch .... ON
3. Track radar mode selector switch .... SELECT A TRACK RADAR DISPLAY ON PHD

Note

If lock-ons are to be attempted, it is recommended that the track radar be operated in a display mode for a minimum of 5 minutes before attempting a lock-on.

4. Sync set .... CHECK
5. Locate fixed target on search radar in PPI 30.
6. Slew control .... POSITION CURSORS OVER TARGET
7. ARE 50/25 .... SELECT (IF DESIRED)

CONTINUED ON NEXT PAGE

Change 2   3-85

NORMAL PROCEDURES
Shore-Based Procedures (B/N)

NAVAIR 01-85ADA-1

FIXED TARGET GROUND/DISCRETE LOCK-ON TRACKING A-6A,B,C—CONTINUED

8. Fixed/moving target switch . . . . FIXED

9. Track radar tone volume control . . . . ADJUST

10. Display/track/boresight switch . . . . TRACK

11. Search radar track switch (RTT) . . . . ON

12. Dislodge switch . . . . DISLODGE

13. Track radar antenna . . . . POSITIONED AUTOMATICALLY
    The track radar antenna should be automatically positioned in azimuth and elevation; however, small adjustments with elevation slew switch may be necessary to obtain a ground lock-on (GLO) light. A valid GLO is achieved when both GLO light and TRACK light are lit and steady.

If lock-on does not occur:

14. Track radar power switch . . . . CYCLE
    Cycle switch from ON to STBY to ON. If there is still no GROUND LOCK light, and TRACK light is on, search-radar-derived altitude data are valid. Proceed, using search radar tracking procedures.

When lock-on is acquired:

15. Tone . . . . B/N WILL HEAR 1200-CYCLE TONE

16. GROUND lock-on and TRACK lights . . . . LIT

17. Fixed/moving target switch . . . . MOVING

18. Velocity correct until target walk-down begins.

Note

If excessive steering wander is noted on the VDI, moving the velocity correct switch to MEMORY POINT will improve steering by added filtering.

If discrete lock-on is desired:

19. Dislodge switch . . . . AFT

20. DISCRETE and GROUND lock-on and TRACK lights . . . . LIT

21. Slew grip . . . . SLEWING IS INHIBITED, CURSORS AUTOMATICALLY TRACK TARGET

To break lock if a new target acquisition is desired:

22. Dislodge switch . . . . FORWARD

23. Slew grip . . . . ACTIVATE AND REPOSITION CURSORS OVER DESIRED TARGET

24. Dislodge switch . . . . AFT

25. DISCRETE and GROUND lock-on and TRACK lights . . . . LIT

MOVING TARGET DETECTION AND ACQUISITION A-6A

1. Search radar display button .... PPI
2. Search sweep range .... 15 NMI
3. Navigation mode selector button .... AS DESIRED
4. Trigger switch .... PRIMARY
5. Antenna pattern .... ADJUST FOR MAXIMUM RETURN
6. Scan angle .... SET ±30.
7. Scan rate switch .... SLOW
8. STC controls .... AS REQUIRED
9. Receiver gain control .... FULL CW
10. AMTI control .... CW FOR OPTIMUM DISPLAY
    Rotating control just out of detent provides maximum cancellation of stationary targets.
    If display was good before turning AMTI on, no further control adjustments should be
    necessary, beyond setting AMTI control for an optimum display.

MOVING TARGET DISCRETE LOCK-ON AND TRACKING A-6A

1. Fixed/moving target switch .... MOVING
2. Track radar power switch .... ON
3. Sync set .... CHECK
4. NAV mode selector button .... UNSTAB NO STEER
5. Locate moving target on search radar.
6. Slew control .... CURSORS OVER MOVING TARGET
7. Computer steering mode button .... OPPORT TGT
8. ARE 50/25 .... SELECT (IF DESIRED)
9. Display/track/boresight switch .... TRACK

CONTINUED ON NEXT PAGE

NORMAL PROCEDURES
Shore-Based Procedures (B/N)
NAVAIR 01-85ADA-1

MOVING TARGET DISCRETE LOCK-ON AND TRACKING A-6A—CONTINUED

10. Track radar antenna . . . . AUTOMATICALLY POSITIONED IN AZIMUTH AND ELEVATION.
    Small adjustments with elevation slew switch may be necessary to obtain a lock-on.

11. Slew grip . . . . MANEUVER CURSORS UNTIL MOVING SIGNAL IS DETECTED
    Moving target signal is audible in headset.

12. DISCRETE lock-on and TRACK lights . . . . LIT
    Monitor moving target velocity in right-hand unit.

13. Slew grip . . . . SLEWING IS INHIBITED, CURSORS AUTOMATICALLY TRACK TARGET,
    MOVING TARGET AUDIO SIGNAL WILL BE STRONG IN HEADSET

To break moving target lock-on:

14. Dislodge switch . . . . DISLODGE

15. Slew grip . . . . ACTUATE AND REPOSITION CURSORS OVER DESIRED TARGET

16. Dislodge switch . . . . AFT

17. DISCRETE and GROUND lock-on and TRACK lights . . . . LIT

SEARCH RADAR TRACKING PROCEDURES (RTT) A-6A

1. Locate target on search radar in PPI 30

2. Slew control . . . . POSITION CURSORS OVER TARGET

3. TRACK light . . . . ON
   TRACK light goes on to indicate that search radar is providing valid target data.

4. ARE 50/25 . . . . SELECT
   For best accuracy, ARE 25 should be used.

5. Track radar power switch . . . . STBY OR OFF

6. S/R track switch . . . . ON

CONTINUED ON NEXT PAGE

SEARCH RADAR TRACKING PROCEDURES (RTT) A-6A–CONTINUED

7. Velocity correct on run to target.

Note

Velocity corrects should not be made after target starts to walk down the display; however, cursor positioning may be improved with the memory point switch at OFF SAVE down to 9,000 feet range to target.

VELOCITY CORRECT PROCEDURES A-6A,B,C

AUTOMATIC CALCULATION OF VELOCITY ERROR

Automatic velocity correct is performed whenever a discrete lock-on is obtained provided that the velocity correct switch is in the MEMORY POINT position. Corrected velocity will stabilize in 12 to 18 seconds.

SEARCH RADAR OR GROUND LOCK-ON TRACKING ONLY

1. Position search radar cursors centered on target in azimuth and just below target in range.
2. Observe cursors for drift for a minimum of 10 seconds
3. Velocity correct switch . . . . MEMORY POINT
4. Slew control . . . . ACTIVATE
   Utilizing slew grip, reposition cursors over target. Repeat as necessary to cancel drift within 120 second time span.
5. Velocity correct switch . . . . OFF SAVE
   Stop velocity correct procedure at target walk down

TRACK RADAR OPTICAL TRACKING (TROT) PROCEDURE (P-7B TRIM)

Overall system tracking accuracy may be determined by making use of the movable reticle of the pilot's optical sight.

1. Acquire a ground lock on a target identifiable both with search radar and visually.
2. Slave pilot's optical sight movable reticle to track radar antenna by depressing pilot's attack commit trigger to the first detent.
3. Establish aircraft in a stable glide so that movable reticle is about 50 miles below fixed reticle.
4. As target becomes visible, read position of movable reticle with respect to target.

Note
- Any mil error in azimuth or elevation should be noted and reported at system debrief.
- Any cursor drift would normally be due to system velocity errors.

CONTINUED ON NEXT PAGE

NORMAL PROCEDURES
Shore-Based Procedures (B/N)

COMPUTER OPTICAL POSITIONING (COP) PROCEDURE (P-8.6)

1. B/N: Position radar cursors on a visually recognizable target in desired tracking mode.

2. Pilot: Depress attack commit trigger to first detent and observe position of optical sight movable reticle in relation to target.

Note

If a COP check is performed on the ground, only azimuth indications are valid.

BORESIGHT MODE
P-7B TRIM

If possible, a velocity-correct should be accomplished within 10 minutes of the time a boresight attack is to be made.

1. Release mode switch .... AUTO
2. Track radar power switch .... STBY
3. Fixed/moving target switch .... MOVING
4. PHD power switch .... ON
5. Optical sight fixed and movable reticles .... ON
6. Optical sight switch .... AUTO
7. Display/track/boresight switch .... BORESIGHT
8. Target altitude .... ENTER
9. Flight mode selector button .... BASE NO AP, PRES TGT NO AP, OR OPPORT TGT
10. Attack mode selector button .... GENERAL OR STRAIGHT
    A general attack with a dive toss release is recommended since it is not required to level off immediately after uncaging to obtain an in-range indication. A straight path attack requires a pitch-up to a more level attitude immediately after uncaging to obtain in-range.
11. G select button .... 4 G
12. Station select switches .... AS DESIRED
13. Fuzing .... AS BRIEFED
14. MASTER ARM switch .... ON
15. Dislodge switch .... DISLODGE
16. Range and azimuth cursor .... PLACE IN TARGET AREA
17. Track radar power switch .... ON
    Ground lock-on should occur automatically as aircraft approaches target. Attack may be be completed on keyboard information if ground lock-on is not acquired.

CONTINUED ON NEXT PAGE

NAVAIR 01-85ADA-1

NORMAL PROCEDURES
Shore-Based Procedures (B/N)

BORESIGHT MODE—CONTINUED

18. Fixed reticle . . . . PLACE ON TARGET
    Pilot maneuvers aircraft into a dive, positioning fixed reticle on target or follows steering to align aircraft with predicted target position as shown by movable reticle. Positioning of movable reticle may be updated by momentarily uncaging, then caging again with fixed reticle on target if range to target is less than 48,000 feet.

    Note

    Reticle alignment should be maintained for a minimum of 1 second above uncaging.

19. Uncage boresight button . . . . DEPRESS
    Null azimuth steering error. B/N call slant range to pilot.

20. Attack commit trigger . . . . DEPRESS

21. Automatic release . . . . OBSERVE
    Observe indications of automatic weapon release.

    Note

    In aircraft incorporating AVC No. 523 (-11 DPU), when making a boresight attack on a waterborne target, the track radar should be detuned for zero crystal current if the sea state is smooth.

(P-8.6)

If possible, a velocity-correct should be accomplished within 10 minutes of the time a boresight is to be made. Present position should be checked and updated as necessary.

1. Release mode switch . . . . AUTO
2. Track radar POWER switch . . . . STBY
3. FIXED/MOVING switch . . . . AS DESIRED
4. PHD power switch . . . . ON
5. Optical sight fixed and movable reticles . . . . ON
6. Optical sight mode switch . . . . AUTO
7. DISPLAY/TRACK/BORESIGHT switch . . . . BORESIGHT
8. Target altitude . . . . ENTER
9. NAV MODE selector button . . . . BASE NO AP, PRES TGT NO AP, OR OPPORT TGT
10. ATTACK mode selector button . . . . GENERAL OR STRAIGHT
    GENERAL is recommended with a dive toss release.
11. G select button 4G
12. Station select switches . . . . AS BRIEFED
13. Fuzing . . . . AS BRIEFED
14. MASTER ARM switch . . . . ON
15. Dislodge switch . . . . DISLODGE
16. Range and azimuth cursors . . . . PLACE IN TARGET AREA
17. Track radar POWER switch . . . . ON
18. Prior to roll-in . . . . STEP INTO ATTACK
19. Movable reticle . . . . PLACE ON TARGET
    Pilot maneuvers into a dive, positioning the movable reticle over target. When moving reticle is on target, pilot should move commit trigger to commit position, pausing momentarily at COP position.

CONTINUED ON NEXT PAGE

NORMAL PROCEDURES
Shore-Based Procedures (B/N)
NAVAIR 01-85ADA-1

BORESIGHT MODE – CONTINUED

20. Attack commit trigger .... DEPRESSED

21. Automatic release .... OBSERVE
    B/N should call altitude and track radar information to pilot throughout run.

TRACK RADAR DISPLAYS A-6A,B,C

E-SCAN

1. PHD power switch .... ON
2. Display/track/boresight switch .... DISPLAY
3. Pilot's horizontal display mode selector switch .... E-SCAN
4. Track radar power switch .... ON
5. Clearance switch .... AS DESIRED
6. Range marker brightness controls .... AS DESIRED
7. Clearance range markers .... ADJUST
8. Flight line control .... ADJUST
9. Track receiver gain control .... ADJUST
10. MRI control .... ADJUST
11. Display scale miles switch .... 5 or 10

TCPPI

1. PHD power switch .... ON
2. Display/track/boresight switch .... DISPLAY
3. Pilot's horizontal display mode selector switch or .... TCPPI
    B/N's display selector button
4. Track radar power switch .... ON
5. Display scale miles switch .... 5 or 10
6. Track receiver gain control .... ADJUST
7. MRI control .... ADJUST
8. Range marker brightness control .... AS DESIRED

EMERGENCY SEARCH

1. PHD power switch .... ON
2. Pilot's horizontal display mode selector switch .... SRCH
3. Display/track/boresight switch .... DISPLAY

CONTINUED ON NEXT PAGE

3-92

NAVAIR 01-85ADA-1

NORMAL PROCEDURES
Shore-Based Procedures (B/N)

TRACK RADAR DISPLAYS A-6A,B,C–CONTINUED

4. Bombardier/navigator's display selector button . . . . EMER SRCH
5. Track radar power switch . . . . ON
6. Display scale miles switch . . . . 5 or 10
7. Track receiver gain control . . . . ADJUST
8. MRI control . . . . ADJUST
9. Elevation slew switch . . . . ADJUST TO CONTROL ELEVATION ANGLE

ATTACK PROCEDURES A-6A,B,C

Note

The attack procedures below are only those required to execute the attack selected, and must be used in conjunction with the procedures for the use of multiple release and for the release of weapons from multiple ejector racks and triple ejector racks.

LAB IP ATTACK PROCEDURES

At any point en route to the initial point (IP), the following settings may be accomplished:

1. Attack mode selector button . . . . LAB IP
2. Station select switches . . . . AS DESIRED
3. Fuzing . . . . AS BRIEFED
4. Release mode switch . . . . AUTO
5. SALVO/TRN/STEP switch . . . . SALVO
   Placing SALVO/TRN/STEP switch in SALVO will release all selected weapons simultaneously.
6. Intervalometer/timer . . . . SET
7. MASTER ARM switch . . . . ON

When aircraft is over initial point (IP), perform the following procedures:

8. Pilot depress and hold commit switch. This starts timer counting down. When timer reaches zero, bomb tone comes, pilot starts 4-g pullup. Store is automatically released at preset angle. At release, bomb tone goes off and station selector flag drops.

LAB TGT ATTACK PROCEDURES

At any point enroute to the target, the following settings may be accomplished:

1. Attack mode selector button . . . . LAB TGT
2. Station select switches . . . . AS DESIRED
3. Fuzing . . . . AS BRIEFED
4. Release mode switch . . . . AUTO

CONTINUED ON NEXT PAGE

NORMAL PROCEDURES
Shore-Based Procedures (B/N)
NAVAIR 01-85ADA-1

ATTACK PROCEDURES A-6A,B,C—CONTINUED

    5. SALVO/TRN/STEP switch .... SALVO

    6. Intervalometer/timer .... SET AS BRIEFED

    7. MASTER ARM switch .... ON

When aircraft is over target, perform the following procedures:

    8. Pilot depress and hold commit switch - Begin 4-g pullup. Store is automatically released at preset angle and station selector flag drops.

Note

Bomb tone comes on when timer reaches zero or the pilot commits, as applicable, and goes off when the weapon is released.

ROCKET ATTACK PROCEDURES

At any point en route to the target, the following settings may be accomplished:

    1. Attack mode selector button .... ROCKET

    2. Station select switches .... ROCKET

    3. Release mode switch .... AUTO

    4. SALVO/TRN/STEP switch .... AS DESIRED

    5. Rocket mode switch .... RPPL or SNGL (AS DESIRED)
       Placing switch to RPPL permits release power to be applied to selected aircraft stations along ripple fire line. Placing switch to SNGL permits release power to be applied to selected aircraft stations along single fire line. RESET position controls operation of weapon release relay, resetting it for a new release cycle.

Note

Unless the jumper cable is installed when a rocket launcher with a stepping switch is loaded, improper use of the rocket mode switch may result in the inadvertent firing of a rocket. Place the MASTER ARM switch to OFF before selecting either RPPL or SNGL.

    6. MASTER ARM switch .... ON

    7. Attack or uncage button .... DEPRESS
       Depressing attack button on slew grip or uncage button on stickgrip places computer in attack mode.

    8. Reselect light .... OFF
       Check that RESELECT light is off. If light comes on, it indicates that no attack solution can be generated because of some incompatible setting of armament switches.

    9. Attack light .... ON
       If attack light remains off, it indicates that ballistics computer has not entered attack mode.

    10. In-range lights .... ILLUMINATE AT MAXIMUM RANGE

CONTINUED ON NEXT PAGE

ATTACK PROCEDURES A-6A,B,C—CONTINUED

11. Zero steering both horizontally and vertically.

    Note

    Release is obtained by the pull-through or line-up techniques. See NAVAIR 01-85ADA-1T.

12. Attack commit trigger . . . . DEPRESS
    When pilot depresses attack commit trigger on his control stick, it informs ballistic computer to fire if within in-range limits and within ±8 mils vertically of electronic center of VDI.

    Note
    - It is possible to commit out of range.
    - When firing rockets, there will be a flag drop with ripple fire, and no flag drop on a single fire. The ripple position of the rocket mode switch uses one computer release pulse to fire rockets at the ripple rate of the package and the system must be reset after each firing.
    - After a rocket attack, ensure that the MASTER ARM switch is OFF prior to deselecting the weapon station. Turning the station select switch OFF with the MASTER ARM switch ON may result in the inadvertent jettison of the rocket pod.
    - For the release of empty rocket launchers or CBU's from MER/TER, set the station-select switch to BOMBS, and release the units as if they were bombs.
    - Vertical steering must be nulled to ±4 mils on the electronic center of the VDI.

HI LOFT ATTACK PROCEDURES

At any point en route to the target, the following settings may be made.

1. Attack mode selector button . . . . HI LOFT
2. Station-select switches . . . . AS DESIRED
3. Fuzing . . . . AS BRIEFED
4. Release mode switch . . . . AUTO
5. G select buttons . . . . DESIRED G
6. SALVO/TRN/STEP switch . . . . SALVO
    Placing SALVO/TRN/STEP switch in SALVO will release all selected weapons simultaneously.
7. MASTER ARM switch . . . . ON

After steps 1 through 7 have been accomplished and the aircraft is within 25 nautical miles of the target, the following procedures must be accomplished:

8. Attack button . . . . DEPRESS
    Depressing attack button on slew grip places computer in attack mode.
9. Reselect light . . . . OFF
    Check that reselect light is off. If light comes on, it indicates that no attack solution can be generated because of some incompatible setting of armament switches.
10. Attack light . . . . ON
    If attack light remains off, it indicates that ballistics computer has not entered attack mode.
11. In-range lights . . . . ON AT MAXIMUM RANGE - HI LOFT PULLUP POINT

CONTINUED ON NEXT PAGE

NORMAL PROCEDURES
Shore-Based Procedures (B/N)   NAVAIR 01-85ADA-1

ATTACK PROCEDURES A-6A,B,C—CONTINUED

    12. Attack commit trigger . . . . PILOT DEPRESS AND HOLD

    13. Bomb tone . . . . COMES ON WHEN ATTACK COMMIT TRIGGER IS DEPRESSED
                                              AND GOES OFF WHEN WEAPON IS RELEASED

STRAIGHT PATH ATTACK PROCEDURES

At any point en route to the target, the following settings may be made.

    1. Attack mode selector button . . . . STRAIGHT

    2. Station-select switches . . . . AS DESIRED

    3. Fuzing . . . . AS BRIEFED

    4. Release mode switch . . . . AUTO

    5. SALVO/TRN/STEP switch . . . . AS DESIRED

    6. Intervalometer timer . . . . SET (AS DESIRED)

    7. Release advance button . . . . ENGAGED (AS DESIRED)

Note

Desired release advance should be reinserted into the ballistics computer before the attack run to insure that the computer is using the proper value.

    8. Desired slant range at release . . . . INSERTED
       Insert desired slant range at release in cruise altitude address with the altitude action key.

    9. G select button . . . . DEPRESS
       Selected g will be used for TDTA computations.

    10. MASTER ARM switch . . . . ON

After steps 1 through 10 have been accomplished and the aircraft is within 25 nautical miles of the target, the following procedures must be accomplished:

    11. Attack button . . . . DEPRESS
       Depressing attack button on slew grip places computer in attack mode.

    12. Reselect light . . . . OFF
       Check that reselect light is off. If light comes on, it indicates that no attack solution can be generated because of some incompatible setting of armament switches.

    13. Attack light . . . . ON
       If attack light remains off, it indicates that ballistics computer has not entered attack mode.

    14. In-range lights . . . . SHOULD LIGHT APPROXIMATELY
                                             9 NMI BEFORE RELEASE

    15. Attack commit trigger . . . . PILOT DEPRESS AND HOLD

    16. Bomb tone . . . . COMES ON WHEN ATTACK COMMIT TRIGGER
                                          IS DEPRESSED AND GOES OFF WHEN
                                          WEAPON IS RELEASED

CONTINUED ON NEXT PAGE

NAVAIR 01-85ADA-1

NORMAL PROCEDURES
Shore-Based Procedures (B/N)

ATTACK PROCEDURES A-6A,B,C—CONTINUED

GENERAL ATTACK PROCEDURES

1. Attack mode selector button . . . . GENERAL
2. Station-select switches . . . . AS DESIRED
3. Fuzing . . . . AS BRIEFED
4. Release mode switch . . . . AUTO
5. G select buttons . . . . DESIRED G
6. SALVO/TRN/STEP switch . . . . AS DESIRED
7. Intervalometer timer . . . . SET (AS DESIRED)
8. Release advance button . . . . ENGAGED (AS DESIRED)

Note

Desired release advance should be reinserted in the
ballistics computer before the attack run to insure
that the computer is using the proper value.

9. MASTER ARM switch . . . . ON

After steps 1 through 9 have been accomplished and the aircraft is within 25 nautical miles of the target, the following procedures must be accomplished:

10. Attack button . . . . DEPRESS
    Depressing attack button on slew grip places computer in attack mode.

11. Reselect light . . . . OFF
    Check that reselect light is off. If light comes on, it indicates that no attack solution will be generated because of some incompatible setting of armament switches.

12. Attack light . . . . ON
    If attack light remains off, it indicates that ballistics computer has not entered attack mode.

13. In-range lights . . . . ON AT MAXIMUM RANGE LOFT PULLUP POINT
14. Attack commit trigger . . . . PILOT DEPRESS AND HOLD
15. Bomb tone . . . . COMES ON WHEN ATTACK COMMIT TRIGGER
                                              IS DEPRESSED AND GOES OFF WHEN
                                              WEAPON IS RELEASED.

Note

- With conventional stores, the computer solves a
  low-loft release with a forced commit at 8°.

- With special weapons, the computer solves a low-
  loft and high-loft in that order.

CONTINUED ON NEXT PAGE

NORMAL PROCEDURES
Shore-Based Procedures (B/N)

NAVAIR 01-85ADA-1

ATTACK PROCEDURES A-6A,B,C—CONTINUED

SYSTEM LAYDOWN BOMBING PROCEDURES

At any point en route to the target, the following settings may be made:

1. Attack mode selector button . . . . STRAIGHT
2. Station-select switches . . . . AS DESIRED
3. Fuzing . . . . AS BRIEFED
4. Release mode switch . . . . AUTO
5. SALVO/TRN/STEP switch . . . . AS DESIRED
6. Intervalometer timer . . . . SET (AS DESIRED)
7. Auxiliary armament panel power selector switch . . . . REL DELAY
8. Release delay . . . . SET
   Set desired release delay on the auxiliary intervalometer timer.
9. MASTER ARM switch . . . . ON

After steps 1 through 9 have been accomplished and the aircraft is at the selected commit point, the following procedures must be accomplished:

10. Attack commit trigger . . . . PILOT DEPRESS AND HOLD
    Depressing commit trigger starts auxiliary intervalometer timer.
11. Bomb tone . . . . COMES ON WHEN ATTACK COMMIT TRIGGER
                                                    IS DEPRESSED AND GOES OFF WHEN WEAPON
                                                    IS RELEASED

Weapon is automatically released at end of selected delay.

GUNNERY ATTACK PROCEDURES

At any point enroute to the target the following settings may be made:

1. Gun switch . . . . READY
   Placing the switch to READY charges all the guns.
2. Station-select switches . . . . ROCKETS/GUNS
   Set the desired station select switches to ROCKETS/GUNS. If BOMBS is selected on a station with a gun pod loaded, pod will be ejected when manual release button is depressed.
3. Optical sight AUTO/OFF/MAN switch . . . . MAN
4. Optical sight movable reticle switch . . . . OFF

When ready to begin the attack:

5. MASTER ARM switch . . . . ON
6. Attack commit trigger . . . . DEPRESS
   When lined up on target, depress attack commit trigger to fire guns.

CONTINUED ON NEXT PAGE

NAVAIR 01-85ADA-1

NORMAL PROCEDURES
Shore-Based Procedures (B/N)

ATTACK PROCEDURES A-6A,B,C—CONTINUED

Note

Firing or clearing the guns will not produce a flag drop indication.

Just before landing or when ready to secure guns (weight must be off wheels):

7. MASTER ARM switch .... OFF
8. Gun switch .... CLEAR, then SAFE

CAUTION

Moving the gun pod switch to the momentary CLEAR position renders the guns inoperative for the remainder of the flight. Do not select READY after selecting CLEAR, as this will result in a jam of the ammunition belt links.

MINING PROCEDURES (P-7B TRIM)

1. Attack mode selector button .... STRAIGHT
2. Station-select switches .... BOMBS
3. Release mode switch .... AUTO
4. SALVO/TRN/STEP switch .... STEP
5. Rocket mode switch .... SNGL
6. Shrike intervalometer or auxiliary intervalometer/timer .... SET
   Set desired interval less 1.5 second.
7. Multiple release quantity select switch .... OFF

Note

With mining mode selected, the multiple release quantity select switch must always be at OFF to get the desired releases.

8. Shrike power switch .... ON
   or
   Power selector switch .... SHRIKE
9. MASTER ARM switch .... ON
10. Mining mode .... SELECT
    a. Aircraft with Shrike panel:
       Target reject button .... DEPRESS
    b. Aircraft with auxiliary armament panel:
       Shrike mode switch .... REJECT, THEN NORM

CONTINUED ON NEXT PAGE

NORMAL PROCEDURES
Shore-Based Procedures (B/N)
NAVAIR 01-85ADA-1

ATTACK PROCEDURES A-6A,B,C–CONTINUED

11. Attack commit trigger .... PILOT DEPRESS/HOLD

12. Pilot's manual release button .... DEPRESS
    First release is initiated when release button is depressed and subsequent releases occur in sequence at interval selected plus 1.5 second. Commit trigger and release button need not be held after first release.

Note

- One release pulse will be generated for each selected station.
- To reset the weapon release system from the mining mode after releases are completed, either the MASTER ARM switch or the Shrike power switch/power selector switch must be cycled to OFF.

MINING PROCEDURES (P-8.6)

1. Attack mode selector button .... STRAIGHT
2. Station select switches .... AS BRIEFED
3. Release mode switch .... AUTO
4. SALVE/TRN/STEP switch .... AS BRIEFED
5. ROCKET switch .... SNGL
6. Shrike power .... OFF
7. Intervalometer .... SET
8. Multiple release switch .... SET AS BRIEFED
9. Computer information .... ENTERED
10. Compute NAV mode .... LAND/GTB
11. MASTER ARM switch .... ON
12. Computer .... IN ATTACK
13. Attack commit trigger .... PILOT DEPRESS/HOLD
14. Release .... OBSERVED
15. MASTER ARM switch .... OFF
    B/N must step computer out of attack after last release.

SPECIAL SIDEWINDER FIRING PROCEDURES
(AIRCRAFT INCORPOATING AFC NO. 332 AND AVC NO. 1433)

1. 1C I-R switch .... COOL/FIRE
2. Station select switch .... ROCKETS/GUNS
3. Release mode switch .... MAN
4. Optical sight AUTO/OFF/MAN switch .... MAN

CONTINUED ON NEXT PAGE

NAVAIR 01-85ADA-1

NORMAL PROCEDURES
Shore-Based Procedures (B/N)

ATTACK PROCEDURES A-6A,B,C—CONTINUED

5. Optical sight movable reticle switch . . . . OFF
6. IC I-R tone volume . . . . AS DESIRED
7. Center fixed reticle on target.
8. Pilot's manual release button . . . . DEPRESS

Note

The above procedure does not constitute authority for carriage or launch. Only those stores listed in the A-6 Tactical Manual, NAVAIR 01-85ADA-1T may be carried and released, singly or in combination to the limits shown.

AN/AWW-1 ELECTRICAL FUZING PROCEDURES

In-flight, enroute to the target, the AN/AWW-1 system should be checked as follows:

Note

- In aircraft incorporating AAC No. 592, the rf fuzing capability has been permanently removed and the system has been redesignated AN/AWW-8.

- The following check should be made no sooner than 20 minutes and no later than 5 minutes before weapon release. Energizing the AN/AWW-1 circuitry in excess of 20 minutes may result in the fuzes charging at options other than that selected. Energizing the AN/AWW-1 circuitry for less than 5 minutes may result in inadequate circuit stabilization.

1. MASTER ARM switch . . . . ON
2. Fuzing power switch . . . . RDY
3. Electrical fuzing button . . . . DESIRED OPTION (A through H)
4. After 30 seconds, note HV DC CHECK button light comes on. (Light must remain on.)
5. Before release, insure that light remains lit, indicating system readiness.

Note

If the light is not lit at weapon release, dud bombs must be anticipated. Duds can also be anticipated if the manual release button is not depressed and held throughout the release sequence.

6. Make desired armament switch selection as listed for attack mode selected.

After weapon release:

7. MASTER ARM switch . . . . OFF
8. Fuzing power switch . . . . SAFE

3-101

NORMAL PROCEDURES
Shore-Based Procedures (B/N)
NAVAIR 01-85ADA-1

TARGET TRACKING PROCEDURES A-6E

CURSOR INTERSECTION TRACKING

1. MODE switch .... TRACK
2. ELEV TRKG switch .... OFF
3. Azimuth-range switch .... DISLODGE (FORWARD)
4. FREQ AGILITY switch .... AS DESIRED
5. Locate fixed/moving target in PPI and proceed as follows:

    a. DISPLAYS button .... PPI OR ARE
    b. PPI RANGE switch .... APPROXIMATELY 20 NMI
    c. Antenna pattern .... ADJUST FOR MAXIMUM RETURN
    d. SCAN ANGLE control .... NARROW (±10°)
    e. SCAN RATE switch .... SLOW
    f. STC SLOPE/DEPTH controls .... ADJUST
    g. AMTI control (for moving target) .... ON, CANCELLATION AS REQUIRED
    h. RCVR gain control .... ADJUST
    j. VIDEO gain control .... ADJUST FOR OPTIMUM DISPLAY

6. Cursors .... SLEW OVER TARGET
7. DISPLAY button .... ARE 60 OR ARE 30
8. Velocity-correct (manual) .... AS REQUIRED

ELEVATION TRACKING

1. MODE switch .... TRACK
2. ELEV TRKG switch .... ON
3. Azimuth-range switch .... DISLODGE (FORWARD)
4. FREQ AGILITY switch .... AS DESIRED
5. Locate fixed/moving target in PPI.
    If moving targets are to be tracked, proceed as follows:

    a. DISPLAY button .... PPI OR ARE
    b. PPI RANGE switch .... APPROXIMATELY 20 NMI
    c. Antenna pattern .... ADJUST FOR MAXIMUM RETURN
    d. SCAN ANGLE control .... NARROW (±10°)
    e. SCAN RATE switch .... SLOW
    f. STC SLOPE/DEPTH controls .... ADJUST
    g. AMTI control .... ON, CANCELLATION AS REQUIRED

CONTINUED ON NEXT PAGE

TARGET TRACKING PROCEDURES A-6E—CONTINUED

    h.   RCVR gain control . . . . ADJUST

    j.   VIDEO gain control . . . . ADJUST FOR OPTIMUM DISPLAY

6. Cursors . . . . SLEW OVER TARGET

7. DISPLAYS button . . . . ARE 60 OR ARE 30 (IF DESIRED)

8. ELEVATION light (under 60,800 feet maximum). . . . . ON

9. Velocity-correct (manual) . . . . AS REQUIRED

AZIMUTH RANGE TRACKING

1. MODE switch . . . . TRACK

2. ELEV TRKG switch. . . . . OFF

3. Azimuth-range switch . . . . DISLODGE (FORWARD)

4. FREQ AGILITY switch. . . . . AS DESIRED

5. Locate fixed/moving target in PPI and proceed as follows:

    a.   DISPLAYS button . . . . PPI OR ARE

    b.   PPI RANGE switch . . . . APPROXIMATELY 20 NMI

    c.   Antenna pattern . . . . ADJUST FOR MAXIMUM RETURN

    d.   SCAN ANGLE control . . . . NARROW (±10°)

    e.   SCAN RATE switch . . . . SLOW

    f.   STC SLOPE/DEPTH controls . . . . ADJUST

    g.   AMTI control (for moving target). . . . . ON, CANCELLATION AS REQUIRED

    h.   RCVR gain control . . . . ADJUST

    j.   VIDEO gain control. . . . . ADJUST FOR OPTIMUM DISPLAY

6. DISPLAYS button . . . . ARE 60 OR ARE 30

7. Cursors . . . . SLEW OVER TARGET

8. Azimuth-range switch . . . . ENABLE (AFT)

9. AZ-RANGE light. . . . . ON
    Slewing is inhibited. Cursors automatically track target.

10. Velocity correct (AUTO) . . . . AS REQUIRED
     If cursors track target, set velocity-correct switch to MEM PT. If cursors
     unstable, proceed with steps 11 and 12.

To Break Lock:

11. Velocity correct switch (if velocity good) . . . . OFF SAVE

12. Velocity correct switch (if velocity bad) . . . . OFF ERASE

13. Azimuth-range switch . . . . DISLODGE (FORWARD)

CONTINUED ON NEXT PAGE

NORMAL PROCEDURES
Shore-Based Procedures (B/N)

NAVAIR 01-85ADA-1

TARGET TRACKING PROCEDURES A-6E—CONTINUED

TRACK-WHILE-SCAN TRACKING

Note

The azimuth-range switch should be left in the forward position until an azimuth-range lock-on is desired.

1. MODE switch . . . . TRACK
2. Locate fixed/moving target in PPI/ARE and proceed as follows:
   a. DISPLAY button . . . . PPI OR ARE
   b. PPI-RANGE switch . . . . APPROXIMATELY 20 NMI
   c. Antenna pattern . . . . ADJUST FOR MAXIMUM RETURN
   d. SCAN ANGLE control . . . . NARROW (±10°)
   e. SCAN RATE switch . . . . SLOW
   f. STC SLOPE/DEPTH control . . . . ADJUST
   g. AMTI control (for moving target) . . . . ON, CANCELLATION AS REQUIRED
   h. RCVR gain control . . . . ADJUST
   j. VIDEO gain control . . . . ADJUST FOR OPTIMUM DISPLAY
3. FREQ AGILITY switch . . . . AS REQUIRED
4. Cursors . . . . SLEW OVER TARGET
5. DISPLAYS button . . . . ARE 60 OR ARE 30 (IF DESIRED)
6. Azimuth-range switch . . . . ENABLE (AFT)
7. AZ-RANGE light . . . . ON
   Slewing is inhibited. Cursors automatically track target.
8. ELEV TRKG switch . . . . ON
9. ELEVATION light . . . . ON
10. Velocity-correct switch . . . . MEMORY POINT

To Break Lock:

11. Velocity-correct switch (if velocity good) . . . . OFF SAVE
12. Velocity-correct switch (if velocity bad) . . . . OFF ERASE
13. Azimuth-range switch . . . . DISLODGE (FORWARD)

VELOCITY CORRECT PROCEDURES A-6E

AUTOMATIC VELOCITY CORRECT

Automatic velocity-correct is performed when the VELOCITY CORRECT switch is at MEMORY POINT and an azimuth-range or track-while-scan lock-on exists. Corrected velocity will stabilize in 12 to 18 seconds.

CONTINUED ON NEXT PAGE

VELOCITY CORRECT PROCEDURES A-6E—CONTINUED

MANUAL VELOCITY CORRECT (CURSOR INTERSECTION OR ELEVATION TRACKING)

1. Position cursors with azimuth cursor centered on target and range cursor just touching leading edge of target.

2. Observe cursors for drift off target (10 seconds minimum).

3. VELOCITY CORRECT switch .... MEMORY POINT

4. Cursors .... REPOSITION OVER TARGET
   Slew cursors to their original position and observe for drift. Repeat as necessary to cancel drift.

5. VELOCITY CORRECT switch .... OFF SAVE

COMPUTER OPTICAL POSITIONING (COP) CHECK A-6E

1. B/N - Position radar cursors on a visually recognizeable target in desired tracking mode.

2. Pilot - Depress attack commit trigger to first detent and observe position of optical sight movable reticle in relation to the target.

Note

- The aircraft should be in a stable dive attitude of 10° to 12° when a COP check is performed for optimum results.
- If a COP check is performed on the ground, only azimuth indications are valid.

ATTACK PROCEDURES A-6E

Note

- The attack procedures below are only those required to execute the attack selected, and must be used in conjunction with the procedures for the release of weapons from multiple ejector racks and triple ejector racks.
- The MASTER ARMT switch should be set to OFF before making any changes to switch selection on the armament control unit.

ROCKET ATTACK PROCEDURES

At any point en route to the target, the following settings may be made:

1. ATTACK mode button .... ROCKET

2. Station select switches .... ROCKETS/MISSILES (DOWN)

3. RELEASE mode button .... ROCKET SALVO

CONTINUED ON NEXT PAGE

NORMAL PROCEDURES
Shore-Based Procedures (B/N)

NAVAIR 01-85ADA-1

ATTACK PROCEDURES A-6E—CONTINUED

4. INTERVAL/QUANTITY/TIME wheels . . . . AS DESIRED

5. MASTER ARMT switch . . . . ON (UP)

6. BOMB TONE switch . . . . AS DESIRED

7. Attack button . . . . DEPRESS
   Depressing attack button on slew grip places computer in attack mode.

8. RESELECT light . . . . OFF
   Check that RESELECT light is off. If light goes on, it indicates that no attack solution
   can be generated because of some incompatible setting of armament switches.

9. ATTACK light . . . . ON
   If ATTACK light remains off, it indicates that computer has not entered attack mode.

10. In-range lights . . . . ON AT MAXIMUM RANGE

11. Zero steering both horizontally and vertically.

    Note

    Release is obtained by the pull-through or line-up
    techniques.

12. Attack commit trigger . . . . COMMIT (SECOND DETENT) AND HOLD
    When pilot depresses attack commit trigger on his control stick, computer is
    directed to fire if within in-range limits and within ±4 mils vertically of electronic
    center of VDI. Bomb tone comes on at commit and goes off when COMPLETE
    light comes on.

    Note

    - It is possible to commit out of range.

    - For the release of empty rocket launchers or CBU's
      from MER/TER, set the station select switch to
      BOMBS/GUNS, and release the units as if they were
      bombs.

HI LOFT ATTACK PROCEDURES

At any point en route to the target, the following settings may be made:

1. ATTACK mode button . . . . HI LOFT

2. Station select switches . . . . UP AS DESIRED

3. Fuzing/arming . . . . AS BRIEFED

4. RELEASE mode button . . . . BOMB SALVO OR BOMB TRAIN

5. INTERVAL/QUANTITY/TIME wheels . . . . SET

6. MASTER ARMT switch . . . . ON (UP)

7. BOMB TONE switch . . . . AS DESIRED

CONTINUED ON NEXT PAGE

ATTACK PROCEDURES A-6E—CONTINUED

After steps 1 through 7 have been accomplished and the aircraft is within 32 nautical miles of the target, the following procedures must be accomplished:

8. Attack button . . . . DEPRESS
    Depressing attack button on slew grip places computer in attack mode.

9. RESELECT light . . . . OFF
    Check that RESELECT light is off. If light goes on, it indicates that no attack solution can be generated because of some incompatible setting of armament switches.

10. ATTACK light . . . . ON
    If ATTACK light remains off, it indicates that computer has not entered attack mode.

11. In-range lights . . . . ON AT MAXIMUM RANGE - HI LOFT PULLUP POINT

12. Attack commit trigger . . . . COMMIT (SECOND DETENT) AND HOLD

13. Bomb tone . . . . COMES ON WHEN ATTACK COMMIT TRIGGER IS DEPRESSED
    AND GOES OFF WHEN COMPLETE LIGHT COMES ON

STRAIGHT PATH ATTACK PROCEDURES

At any point en route to the target, the following settings may be made:

1. ATTACK mode button . . . . STRAIGHT

2. Station select switches . . . . UP AS DESIRED

3. Fuzing/arming . . . . AS BRIEFED

4. RELEASE mode button . . . . BOMB SALVO OR BOMB TRAIN

5. INTERVAL/QUANTITY/TIME wheels . . . . SET (AS DESIRED)

6. REL ADV key . . . . DEPRESS (AS DESIRED)

7. MASTER ARMT switch . . . . ON (UP)

8. BOMB TONE switch . . . . AS DESIRED

After steps 1 through 8 have been accomplished and the aircraft is within 32 nautical miles of the target, the following procedures must be accomplished:

9. Attack button . . . . DEPRESS
    Depressing attack button on slew grip places computer in attack mode.

10. RESELECT light . . . . OFF
    Check that RESELECT light is off. If light goes on, it indicates that no attack solution can be generated because of some incompatible setting of armament switches.

11. ATTACK light . . . . ON
    If ATTACK light remains off, it indicates that computer has not entered attack mode.

12. In range lights . . . . SHOULD LIGHT BEFORE RELEASE

13. Attack commit trigger . . . . COMMIT (SECOND DETENT) AND HOLD

14. Bomb tone . . . . COMES ON WHEN ATTACK COMMIT TRIGGER IS DEPRESSED
    AND GOES OFF WHEN COMPLETE LIGHT COMES ON

CONTINUED ON NEXT PAGE

NORMAL PROCEDURES
Shore-Based Procedures (B/N)

NAVAIR 01-85ADA-1

ATTACK PROCEDURES A-6E—CONTINUED

GENERAL ATTACK PROCEDURES

1. ATTACK mode button . . . . GENERAL
2. Station select switches . . . . UP AS DESIRED
3. Fuzing/arming . . . . AS BRIEFED
4. RELEASE mode button . . . . BOMB SALVO OR BOMB TRAIN
5. INTERVAL/QUANTITY/TIME wheels . . . . SET (AS DESIRED)
6. REL ADV key . . . . DEPRESSED (AS DESIRED)
7. MASTER ARMT switch . . . . ON (UP)
8. BOMB TONE switch . . . . AS DESIRED

After steps 1 through 8 have been accomplished and the aircraft is within 32 nautical miles of the target, the following procedures must be accomplished:

9. Attack button . . . . DEPRESS
   Depressing attack button on slew grip places computer in attack mode.
10. RESELECT light . . . . OFF
    Check that RESELECT light is off. If light goes on, it indicates that no attack solution will be generated because of some incompatible setting of armament switches.
11. ATTACK light . . . . ON
    If ATTACK light remains off, it indicates that computer has not entered attack mode.
12. In-range lights . . . . ON AT MAXIMUM RANGE LOFT PULLUP POINT
13. Attack commit trigger . . . . COMMIT (SECOND DETENT) AND HOLD
14. Bomb tone . . . . COMES ON WHEN ATTACK COMMIT TRIGGER IS DEPRESSED
    AND GOES OFF WHEN COMPLETE LIGHT COMES ON

Note

- With conventional stores, the computer solves a low-loft release with a forced commit at 8°.
- With special weapons, the computer solves a low-loft and high-loft in that order.
- If pull-up steering commands are not followed, the computer solves for and provides a level release.

VISUAL ~~BORESIGHT~~ TARGET ACQUISITION AND ATTACK (E 1.5 PROGRAM)

If possible, velocity-correct within 10 minutes of making a boresight attack.

1. COMPT MODE switch . . . . STEER
2. ADDRESS key . . . . AS DESIRED
   Select any steering mode.
3. Optical sight switch . . . . AUTO
4. MODE switch . . . . BORESIGHT

CONTINUED ON NEXT PAGE

ATTACK PROCEDURES A-6E—CONTINUED

5. ATTACK mode button .... GENERAL OR STRAIGHT OR HI LOFT
   When BORESIGHT is selected, computer uses a general attack regardless of
   ATTACK button depressed.

6. Station select switches .... UP AS DESIRED

7. Fuzing/arming .... AS BRIEFED

8. RELEASE mode button .... BOMB SALVO OR BOMB TRAIN

9. INTERVAL/QUANTITY/TIME wheels .... SET (AS DESIRED)

10. MASTER ARMT switch .... ON (UP)

11. BOMB TONE switch .... AS DESIRED

12. Attack button .... DEPRESS
    Depressing attack button on slew grip places computer in attack mode.

13. RESELECT light .... OFF
    Check that RESELECT light is out. If light goes on it indicates that no attack solution
    will be generated because of some incompatible setting of armament switches.

14. ATTACK light .... ON
    If ATTACK light remains off, it indicates that computer has not entered attack mode.

15. Dislodge switch .... FORWARD

16. ELEV TRKG .... ON
    Elevation track lock-on should occur when validity parameter of ±53° bank angle
    and 2°/second pitch rate are met. Attack may be completed on baro-inertial
    information if elevation track lock-on is not acquired.

17. In-range lights .... FLASHING
    Flashing of in-range lights indicates that computer is using elevation
    tracking data.

18. Movable reticle .... PLACE ON TARGET
    Pilot maneuvers aircraft into a dive, positioning movable reticle on target.
    Movable reticle represents aircraft inertial velocity vector and is 20 mils
    below ADL.

Note

Initial reticle alignment should be maintained for a
minimum of 1/8 second before designating. Subsequent designates require 1/2 second of reticle
alignment.

19. Attack commit trigger .... DESIGNATE (FIRST DETENT)
    To designate a second time, release trigger, and reactuate.

20. Attack commit trigger .... COMMIT (SECOND DETENT)

21. Azimuth and elevation steering .... NULL

22. Bomb tone .... COMES ON AT COMMIT AND GOES OFF
                                                   WHEN COMPLETE LIGHT COMES ON

Note

Flashing of the breakaway lights is the only visual
cue provided to the pilot when terrain avoidance
pullup is indicated in a visual attack.

CONTINUED ON NEXT PAGE

NORMAL PROCEDURES
Shore-Based Procedures (B/N)

NAVAIR 01-85ADA-1

ATTACK PROCEDURES A-6E – CONTINUED

VISUAL TARGET ACQUISITION AND ATTACK (E100 PROGRAM)

If possible, velocity-correct and update system altitude within 10 minutes of making a visual attack.

1. COMPT MODE switch .... STEER
2. ADDRESS key .... AS DESIRED
   Select any steering mode
3. Optical sight switch .... AUTO
4. ATTACK mode button .... GENERAL
5. Station select switches .... UP AS DESIRED
6. Fuzing/arming .... AS BRIEFED
7. RELEASE mode button .... BOMB SALVO OR BOMB TRAIN
8. INTERVAL/QUANTITY/TIME thumbwheels .... SET (AS DESIRED)
9. MASTER ARMT switch .... ON
10. BOMB TONE switch .... AS DESIRED
11. Pilot's attack button .... DEPRESS
    Depressing the pilot's attack button on the stick grip steps the computer into attack and selects the visual mode of target acquisition and attack.
12. RESELECT light .... OUT
13. ATTACK light .... ON
14. ELEV TRKG switch .... ON
15. Movable reticle .... PLACE ON TARGET
    Pilot maneuvers aircraft into a dive, positioning the movable reticle on the target.

Note

Initial reticle alignment should be maintained for a minimum of 1/6 second before designating. Subsequent designates 2/3 second of reticle alignment.

16. ELEV TRKG light .... ON
17. IN-RANGE lights .... FLASHING
    This indicates valid elevation tracking data.
18. Attack commit trigger .... DESIGNATE (FIRST DETENT)
    To designate a second time, release trigger and reactuate.
19. Attack commit trigger .... COMMIT (SECOND DETENT)
20. Azimuth and elevation steering .... NULL
21. Bomb tone .... ON AT COMMIT, OFF WHEN COMPLETE LIGHT COMES ON

CONTINUED ON NEXT PAGE

ATTACK PROCEDURES A-6E – CONTINUED

LAB IP ATTACK PROCEDURES

At any point en route to the initial point (IP), the following settings may be made:

1. ATTACK mode button .... LAB IP
2. Station select switches .... UP AS DESIRED
3. Fuzing/arming .... AS BRIEFED
4. RELEASE mode button .... BOMB SALVO OR BOMB TRAIN
5. INTERVAL/QUANTITY/TIMER wheels .... SET
6. MASTER ARMT switch .... ON (UP)
7. BOMB TONE switch .... AUTO

When the aircraft is over the initial point (IP), perform the following procedures:

8. Attack commit trigger .... COMMIT (SECOND DETENT) AND HOLD
   Pilot depress and hold attack commit trigger. Bomb warning tone comes on for 1/2 second 2 seconds before time countback reaches 0. When time reaches 0, bomb tone comes on, pilot starts 4-g pullup. Stores are automatically released at preset release angle and station release indicators set. When release is complete, COMPLETE light comes on and bomb tone goes off. COMPLETE light goes off when pilot releases attack commit trigger.

LAB TGT ATTACK PROCEDURES

At any point en route to the target, the following settings may be made:

1. ATTACK mode button .... LAB TGT
2. Station select switches .... UP AS DESIRED
3. Fuzing/arming .... AS DESIRED
4. RELEASE mode button .... BOMB SALVO OR BOMB TRAIN
5. INTERVAL/QUANTITY/TIME wheels .... SET
6. MASTER ARMT switch .... ON (UP)
7. BOMB TONE switch .... AUTO

When aircraft is over the target, perform the following procedures:

8. Attack commit trigger .... COMMIT (SECOND DETENT) AND HOLD
   Pilot begins a 4-g pullup when bomb tone comes on. Stores are automatically released at preset release angle and station release indicators set. When release is complete, COMPLETE light comes on and stays on until pilot releases attack commit trigger.

Note

- Bomb warning tone comes on for 1/2 second 2 seconds before time countback reaches 0 if INTERVAL is set to 02.0 or greater. If INTERVAL is set between 02.0 and 01.5, warning tone duration depends on INTERVAL setting. If less than 01.5 is set, there is no warning tone.

- Bomb tone comes on when time countback reaches 0 and goes off when the COMPLETE light comes on.

CONTINUED ON NEXT PAGE

ATTACK PROCEDURES A-6E—CONTINUED

DELAY BOMBING PROCEDURES

At any point en route to the target, the following settings may be made:

1. ATTACK button . . . . DELAY
2. Station select switches . . . . UP AS DESIRED
3. FUZING . . . . AS BRIEFED
4. RELEASE button . . . . BOMB SALVO OR BOMB TRAIN
5. INTERVAL/QUANTITY/TIME wheels . . . . SET (AS DESIRED)
6. MASTER ARMT switch . . . . ON (UP)
7. BOMB TONE switch . . . . AUTO

After steps 1 through 7 have been accomplished and the aircraft is at the selected commit point, the following procedures must be accomplished:

8. Attack commit trigger . . . . COMMIT (SECOND DETENT) AND HOLD
   Depressing commit trigger starts ACU timer.
9. Bomb tone . . . . COMES ON WHEN ATTACK COMMIT TRIGGER IS DEPRESSED
   AND GOES OFF WHEN COMPLETE LIGHT COMES ON
   Weapon is automatically released at end of selected delay.

GUNNERY ATTACK PROCEDURES

At any point enroute to the target, the following settings may be made:

1. RELEASE mode button . . . . GUNS
2. GUN switch . . . . READY
   Placing switch to READY charges all guns.
3. Optical sight AUTO/OFF/MAN switch . . . . MAN
4. Optical sight movable reticle switch . . . . OFF

When ready to begin the attack:

5. Station select switches . . . . BOMBS/GUNS (UP)
6. MASTER ARMT switch . . . . ON (UP)
7. Attack commit trigger . . . . DEPRESS (SECOND DETENT)
   When lined up on target, depress attack commit trigger to fire guns.

Note

Firing the guns will produce a release indication on the stations selected.

Just before landing or when ready to secure the guns (weight must be off wheels):

7. MASTER ARMT switch . . . . OFF
8. Gun switch . . . . CLEAR, (DOWN) THEN SAFE

CONTINUED ON NEXT PAGE

NORMAL PROCEDURES
Shore-Based Procedures (B/N)

NAVAIR 01-85ADA-1

ATTACK PROCEDURES A-6E—CONTINUED

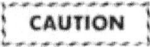

Moving the gun pod switch to the momentary CLEAR position renders the guns inoperative for the remainder of the flight. Do not select READY after selecting CLEAR as this will result in a jam of the ammunition belt links.

MINING PROCEDURES

1. ATTACK mode button .... STRAIGHT
2. Station select switches .... BOMBS/GUNS (UP)
3. RELEASE mode button .... BOMB TRAIN
4. INTERVAL/QUANTITY/TIME wheels .... AS DESIRED
5. MASTER ARMT switch .... ON (UP)
6. BOMB TONE switch .... AS DESIRED
7. Steering .... SELECT TARGET AND GRD TRK
8. Attack commit trigger .... COMMIT (SECOND DETENT) AND HOLD
9. Bomb tone .... COMES ON AT COMMIT AND GOES OFF WHEN COMPLETE LIGHT COMES ON

NAVAIR 01-85ADA-1

NORMAL PROCEDURES
Carrier-Based Procedures (B/N)

part 6 — Carrier-Based Procedures (B/N)

CARRIER ALIGNMENT (AUTOMATIC) A-6A,B,C

1. Electrical power on the aircraft and SINS cable connected.
2. SINS ICS switch . . . . AS DESIRED

   Note

   The SINS ICS switch must be ON to communicate with SINS personnel on ICS.

Doppler/platform panel:

3. Platform selector button . . . . STBY (allow 5 minutes for warmup)
4. Compass switch . . . . OUT

Right-hand unit:

5. MAG VAR . . . . SET
   Set magnetic variation to angle between aircraft and carrier true heading. If aircraft heading is to the left of carrier heading, set in a west reading. If aircraft heading is to right of the carrier heading, set in an east heading.

   Note

   The time required to complete the alignment is dependent upon an accurate spotting angle being inserted in the MAG VAR window before starting alignment.

Platform in-flight alignment panel:

6. NORM/GYROCOMP switch . . . . NORM

Erection controller panel:

7. Polar mode switch . . . . NORMAL
8. AUTO/MAN switch . . . . AUTO
9. Latitude switch . . . . SET LOCAL LATITUDE

Doppler/platform panel:

10. Platform selector button . . . . ALIGN

Erection controller panel:

11. Observe CARR SPEED AND CARR HDG readouts correspond to carrier's speed and handling.
12. Observe that LATITUDE window is updated to carrier's latitude as alignment progresses.
13. Fine align indicator . . . . LIGHTS APPROXIMATELY 1 MINUTE AFTER GOING TO ALIGN.

CONTINUED ON NEXT PAGE

NORMAL PROCEDURES
Carrier-Based Procedures (B/N)

NAVAIR 01-85ADA-1

CARRIER ALIGNMENT (AUTOMATIC) A-6A,B,C—CONTINUED

15. Ready light . . . . LIGHTS BETWEEN 10 AND 20 MINUTES (9 TO 14 MINUTES WITH AVC NO. 1342) AFTER GOING TO ALIGN

16. Align progress meter . . . . CHECK THAT INDICATOR IS AT A NULL ± ONE DIVISION FOR 30 SECONDS.

Note

The ready light in item 15 above is not required provided the following criteria have been met:

- The align progress meter indicates a null ±1 unit for at least 55 seconds before going to operate.
- At least 15 minutes (10 minutes with AVC No. 1342) have been spent in align.
- Actual carrier velocities (within 3 knots) are read out in the right-hand unit after going to operate and no velocity drift is observed.

Additional time will be required for optimum alignment if needle is not at or near a null.

17. Platform selector button . . . . OPERATE

Note

Accurate present position latitude must be inserted into the ballistics computer for proper systems operation.

18. Compass switch . . . . IN

Note

A better alignment can be obtained by aligning the inertial platform sufficiently early in order to be in OPER before the ship maneuvers into position before launch.

19. MAG VAR . . . . SET TO LOCAL MAGNETIC VARIATION
Set local magnetic variation at any time after FINE ALIGN light is lit.

CARRIER ALIGNMENT (MANUAL) A-6A,B,C

A manual carrier alignment may be performed in the same manner as an automatic alignment with the following exceptions:

1. Electrical power . . . . CONNECT

2. SINS ICS switch . . . . ON

Note

The SINS cable must be connected and the SINS ICS switch ON to communicate with SINS personnel on ICS.

3. Auto/man switch . . . . MAN

CONTINUED ON NEXT PAGE

CARRIER ALIGNMENT (MANUAL) A-6A,B,C—CONTINUED

12. Manually set in carrier speed and heading.

    Note

    - Continue updating of carrier speed and heading from the SINS center is necessary for an accurate alignment.

    - Turns of the carrier of 30°/minute or more will suspend the alignment and cause the align progress meter to indicate a null when the SINS cable is not connected.

    - The ready light criteria for manual alignments are the same as for automatic with the addition of the requirements that the 15-minute (10-minute with AVC No. 1342) alignment time must be exclusive of suspend-align time and there must be positive indication that a suspend-align condition is not existing during the 55-second meter null.

CARRIER ALIGNMENT (AUTOMATIC) A-6E

ASN-31 INS

1. Electrical power on aircraft and SINS cable connected.

2. ALIGN switch . . . . SINS ICS

3. Platform selector button . . . . STBY (allow 5 minutes for warmup)

4. ATTITUDE REF switch . . . . COMP OUT

5. MAG VAR . . . . SET
   Set magnetic variation to angle between aircraft and carrier true heading. If aircraft heading is to left of carrier heading, set in a west reading. If aircraft heading is to right of carrier heading, set in an east reading.

    Note

    The time required to complete the alignment is dependent upon an accurate spotting angle being inserted in the MAG VAR window prior to starting alignment.

6. AUTO/MAN switch . . . . AUTO

CONTINUED ON NEXT PAGE

NORMAL PROCEDURES
Carrier-Based Procedures (B/N)

NAVAIR 01-85ADA-1

CARRIER ALIGNMENT (AUTOMATIC) A-6E—CONTINUED

7. Latitude switch . . . . SET LOCAL LATITUDE

8. Platform button . . . . ALIGN

9. Observe CARR SPEED AND CARR HDG readouts correspond to carrier's speed and heading.

10. Observe that LATITUDE window is updated to carrier's latitude as the alignment progresses.

11. Fine align light . . . . GOES ON APPROXIMATELY 1 MINUTE AFTER GOING TO ALIGN

12. Ready light . . . . GOES ON BETWEEN 10 and 20 MINUTES (9 to 14 minutes with AVC No. 1342) AFTER GOING TO ALIGN

13. Align progress meter . . . . CHECK THAT INDICATOR IS AT A NULL ± ONE DIVISION FOR 30 SECONDS

Note

The ready light in item 12 above is not required provided the following criteria have been met:

- The align progress meter indicates a null ±1 unit for at least 55 seconds prior to going to operate.

- At least 15 minutes (10 minutes with AVC No. 1342) have been spent in align.

- Actual carrier velocities (within 3 knots) are read out in the DDU after going to operate and no velocity drift is observed.

Additional time will be required for optimum alignment if needle is not at or near a null.

14. Platform selector button . . . . OPER

CONTINUED ON NEXT PAGE

CARRIER ALIGNMENT (AUTOMATIC) A-6E—CONTINUED

Note

Accurate present position latitude must be inserted into the computer for proper inertial operation.

15. ATTITUDE REF switch . . . . COMP IN

Note

A better alignment can be obtained by aligning the inertial platform sufficiently early in order to be in OPER prior to the ship maneuvering into position before launch.

16. MAG VAR . . . . SET TO LOCAL MAGNETIC VARIATION
    Local magnetic variation may be set at any time after FINE ALIGN light is lit.

ASN-92 IMU

Note

The computer must be operating for either an automatic or a manual carrier alignment.

1. COMPT MODE switch . . . . STEER
2. Navigation mode selector switch . . . . AS DESIRED
3. Data link . . . . ON, FREQ SET
4. SINS ICS switch . . . . AS DESIRED
5. SINS DATA switch . . . . D/L
6. HDG SEL switch . . . . CMD TRUE OR CMD MAG
7. MODE selector button . . . . ALIGN
    Note that ALIGN light comes on. Flashing of the D/L light indicates that the data link was not turned on; a steady D/L light indicates data link failure.

Note

While ALIGN is selected, the VDI PLATFORM light flashes, the steering symbol and target symbol display the characteristic alignment program motion, and the optical sight moving reticle moves in a 25-mil circle about the fixed reticle.

8. Confirm that SINS data are being received. These data may be read out in the DDU.
9. Monitor:

    - Elapsed time in DDU window A1
    - ~~Alignment process in DDU window A3 and on ADF needle of HSI~~
    - IMU pitch angle in DDU window B2
    - IMU roll angle in DDU window B4

CONTINUED ON NEXT PAGE

NORMAL PROCEDURES
Carrier-Based Procedures (B/N)

CARRIER ALIGNMENT (AUTOMATIC) A-6E—CONTINUED

10. INS and breakaway lights .... ON
    The INS and breakaway lights will come on along with the ALIGN light indicating a completed alignment. The INS light will come on in approximately 4 1/2 minutes. OPER may be selected at that time; however, remaining in ALIGN until there is a null of the HSI ADF needle will improve the alignment.

11. MODE selector button .... OPER
    Note that the ALIGN and INS lights go off.

Note

- If it is necessary to move the aircraft before completion of the alignment (INS light on), select OPER. This will light the TAXI light, and suspend the alignment. When the aircraft is parked, the alignment can be recommended by selecting ALIGN.

- The INS light will flash if the navigation mode selector switch is at a position other than INERL.

CARRIER ALIGNMENT (MANUAL) A-6E

ASN-31 INS

1. Electrical power .... CONNECT
2. ALIGN switch .... SINS ICS
3. Platform selector button .... STBY (allow 5 minutes for warmup)
4. ATTITUDE REF switch .... COMP OUT
5. MAG VAR .... SET
   Set magnetic variation to angle between aircraft and carrier true heading. If aircraft heading is to left of carrier heading, set in a west reading. If aircraft heading is to right of carrier heading, set in an east heading.

Note

The time required to complete the alignment is dependent upon an accurate spotting angle being inserted in the MAG VAR window prior to starting alignment.

6. AUTO/MAN switch .... MAN
7. Latitude switch .... SET LOCAL LATITUDE
8. Platform button .... ALIGN
9. Manually set in carrier speed and heading.

Note

- Continuous updating of carrier speed and heading is necessary for an accurate alignment. SINS information is preferred.

- Turns of the carrier of 30°/minute or more will suspend the alignment and cause the align progress meter to indicate a null when the SINS cable is not connected.

10. Fine align light .... GOES ON APPROXIMATELY 1 MINUTE
    AFTER GOING TO ALIGN

CONTINUED ON NEXT PAGE

CARRIER ALIGNMENT (MANUAL) A-6E—CONTINUED

11. Ready light . . . . GOES ON BETWEEN 10 and 20 MINUTES
(9 to 14 minutes with AVC No. 1342)
AFTER GOING TO ALIGN

12. Align progress meter . . . . CHECK THAT INDICATOR IS AT A NULL ± ONE
DIVISION FOR 30 SECONDS

Note

The ready light in item 12 above is not required provided the following criteria have been met:

- The align progress meter indicates a null ±1 unit for at least 55 seconds with positive indication that a suspend align condition is not existing prior to going to operate.

- At least 15 minutes (10 minutes with AVC No. 1342) have been spent in align exclusive of suspend align time.

- Actual carrier velocities (within 3 knots) are read out in the DDU after going to operate and no velocity drift is observed.

Additional time will be required for optimum alignment if needle is not at or near a null.

13. Platform selector button . . . . OPER

Note

Accurate present position latitude must be inserted into the computer for proper inertial operation.

14. ATTITUDE REF switch . . . . COMP IN

Note

A better alignment can be obtained by aligning the inertial platform sufficiently early in order to be in OPER prior to the ship maneuvering into position before launch.

15. MAG VAR . . . . SET TO LOCAL MAGNETIC VARIATION
Local magnetic variation may be set at anytime after FINE ALIGN light is lit.

ASN-92 IMU

1. SINS ICS switch . . . . ON

2. SINS DATA switch . . . . MAN

3. Navigation mode selector switch . . . . AS DESIRED

4. COMPT MODE switch . . . . ENTER

5. Alignment data . . . . ENTER
Keyboard entries are required for present position latitude and longitude as well as carrier heading and speed entered as present position bearing and velocity. Longitudinal and athwartship lever arms may be entered in feet in PRES LOC/DIST.

6. HDG SEL switch . . . . CMD TRUE or CMD MAG

CONTINUED ON NEXT PAGE

CARRIER ALIGNMENT (MANUAL) A-6E—CONTINUED

7. MODE selector button .... ALIGN
   Note that ALIGN light comes on.

   Note

   While ALIGN is selected, the VDI PLATFORM light flashes, the steering symbol and target symbol display the characteristic alignment program motion, and the optical sight moving reticle moves in a 25-mil circle about the fixed reticle.

8. Monitor:

   - Elapsed time in DDU window A1
   - Alignment process in DDU window A3 and on ADF needle of HSI
   - IMU pitch angle in DDU window B2
   - IMU roll angle in DDU window B4

9. INS light .... ON
   The INS light will come on along with the ALIGN light indicating a completed alignment in approximately 4 1/2 minutes. OPER may be selected at that time; however, remaining in ALIGN until there is a null of the HSI ADF needle will improve the alignment.

10. MODE selector button .... OPER
    Note that the ALIGN and INS lights go off.

    Note

    - If it is necessary to move the aircraft before completion of the alignment, select OPER. This will light the TAXI light, and suspend the alignment. When the aircraft is parked, the alignment can be recommenced by selecting ALIGN.

    - Changes to the ship's heading will somewhat degrade the alignment; a new heading is calculated. However if the ship's speed changes a new entry should be made.

    - The INS light will flash if the navigation mode selector switch is in a position other than INERL.

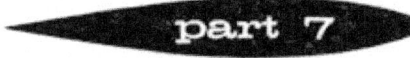 **Degraded System Operating Procedures (A-6A,B,C)**

INTRODUCTION

Since the weapons system is integrated, (that is, one in which all components are interdependently united to accomplish the various navigation and attack solutions) it is evident that failure in any one component must necessarily degrade the overall effectiveness of the system. In order to still be able to accomplish the mission, various backup modes have been included for use in the event of in-flight failure of one or more of these components. Inasmuch as circumstances surrounding such failures may vary widely depending on the type of mission, and the stage at which the failure occurs, hard and fast procedures cannot be set down which will fit every case. It is the purpose of this section merely to point out the existing backup modes and recommended procedures.

SEARCH RADAR FAILURE

If the search radar should fail, the BNCB meter is the most convenient means of troubleshooting, as both MAG CUR and XTAL CUR can be monitored.

AUTOMATIC FREQUENCY CONTROL (AFC) FAILURE

Procedure for Manual Tuning of the Search Radar

Under normal operation, the AFC/MAN RCVR TUNE selector is in the AFC position. With the search radar ON and the METER XTAL CUR button depressed, proper tuning will be indicated by a peak meter reading, generally .6 to .8 on the meter. If the meter needle is sweeping, or if there has been a loss of target returns as a result of zero XTAL CUR, the following procedures are necessary to manually tune the radar:

1. Place AFC/MAN RCVR TUNE selector to MAN.

2. Depress meter XTAL CUR button.

3. Select ECHO CHK.

4. Operate INCR/DECR toggle switch for maximum echo check return, (remember this is coarse tuning only).

5. Turn off echo check and use fine tuning knob (inside control of the AFC/MAN selector) to adjust for optimum video.

Note

When using the INCR/DECR toggle switch to acquire the echo check presentation, adjust in small increments.

Procedure for Manual Tuning of the Track Radar

Under normal operation, the track radar AFC/MAN RCVR TUNE selector is in the AFC position. With the track radar on and the TRACK METER XTAL CUR button depressed, proper tuning will be indicated by a peak meter reading, generally .6 to .8 on the meter. If the needle is sweeping or if there is no video due to a zero XTAL CUR reading, the following procedures will be necessary to manually tune the radar:

NORMAL PROCEDURES
Degraded System Procedures A-6A, B, C

1. Select EMER SRCH display. (E-SCAN or TCPPI may also be used, however, EMER SRCH will prove to be the easiest on which to obtain video.)

2. Place track AFC/MAN RCVR TUNE selector to MAN.

3. Depress TRACK XTAL CUR button.

4. Operate inside control of track AFC/MAN RCVR TUNE selector until a peak meter reading is obtained.

5. Operate inside control of track AFC/MAN RCVR TUNE control until maximum video return is observed on scope, or maximum audio is heard on track tune circuitry.

Note

The MRI and tone volume controls must be adjusted to appropriate levels in order to accomplish step 5.

MAGNETRON RESET BUTTON-SEARCH/TRACK

Each pushbutton switch merely overrides protection circuitry provided to protect the magnetron. Momentarily engaging the reset button will bypass the protection circuitry and allow the magnetron to fire. If the malfunction is temporary, momentarily depressing the switch will restore performance. In an emergency or when operation of the radar is necessary, disregarding the possible damage incurred by the equipment from bypassing the protection circuitry, the button may be locked in by depressing and rotating clockwise. This procedure should be reserved for circumstances when the safety of the crew or the outcome of an important mission is dependent on the operation, even temporary, of the radar. (Such as during the final phase of a mission bombing run, or on a penetration when other navigation equipment is inoperative.) It should be kept in mind that there is no way of determining in advance how long the system will continue to function in the override condition. Complete failure of the magnetron may be imminent. Moreover, the radar picture available may be degraded in quality in this condition.

An internal light in the MAG RESET button comes on when the button is depressed, and remain lit while the button is locked in.

CAUTION

It should be remembered that operation in this condition may result in damage to the equipment over extended periods of time. The system should be returned to normal operation, using the protection features of the reset buttons as soon as practicable, to prevent equipment damage.

Note

In aircraft incorporating the search radar track switch, the track magnetron reset button is deleted. The track radar magnetron may be reset by cycling the track radar power switch to STBY. There is no override capability in these aircraft.

TRACK RADAR EMERGENCY SEARCH OPERATION (EMER SRCH)

In the event of complete failure of the search radar equipment, the track radar may be utilized to accomplish an emergency search function. This is done by using a limited track display.

In the emergency search mode of operation, the track radar operates essentially as a backup search radar system if the search radar system fails. In this mode, the system is used to display approximately 30° of azimuth scan, with antenna elevation angle manually controlled by the B/N. The positioning of the antenna assembly and ground area being scanned by the antenna is adjusted with the track radar elevation slew switch on the slew grip.

LIMITS TO USE OF EMERGENCY SEARCH MODE OF OPERATION

Because of the backup nature of this display, the resulting scope presentations are somewhat limited both as to coverage and degree of definition. Figure 3-13 represents a typical emergency search radar display.

EMERGENCY SEARCH MODE CHARACTERISTICS

In the emergency display, the presentation affords approximately 30° PPI presentation of the target area in a somewhat distorted presentation. This distortion is created by the increase in the transmitted beam width to approximately twice that of the search radar. However, as indicated in the display, the presentations still afford adequate definition for tracking of the prominent points, i.e., bridges, rivers, land water contrast, and small towns. During operation in the emergency search mode, it should be remembered that a number of previously available functions no longer are operative. These include:

1. Moving target detection and tracking

2. Automatic fixed target tracking

3. Selection of either E-Scan or TCPPI by the pilot will override emergency search selection, as the modes are not compatible and cannot be displayed simultaneously.

In addition, the presentation is limited as follows:

1. Range is limited to 5 or 10 nautical miles.

EMERGENCY SEARCH RADAR PRESENTATION

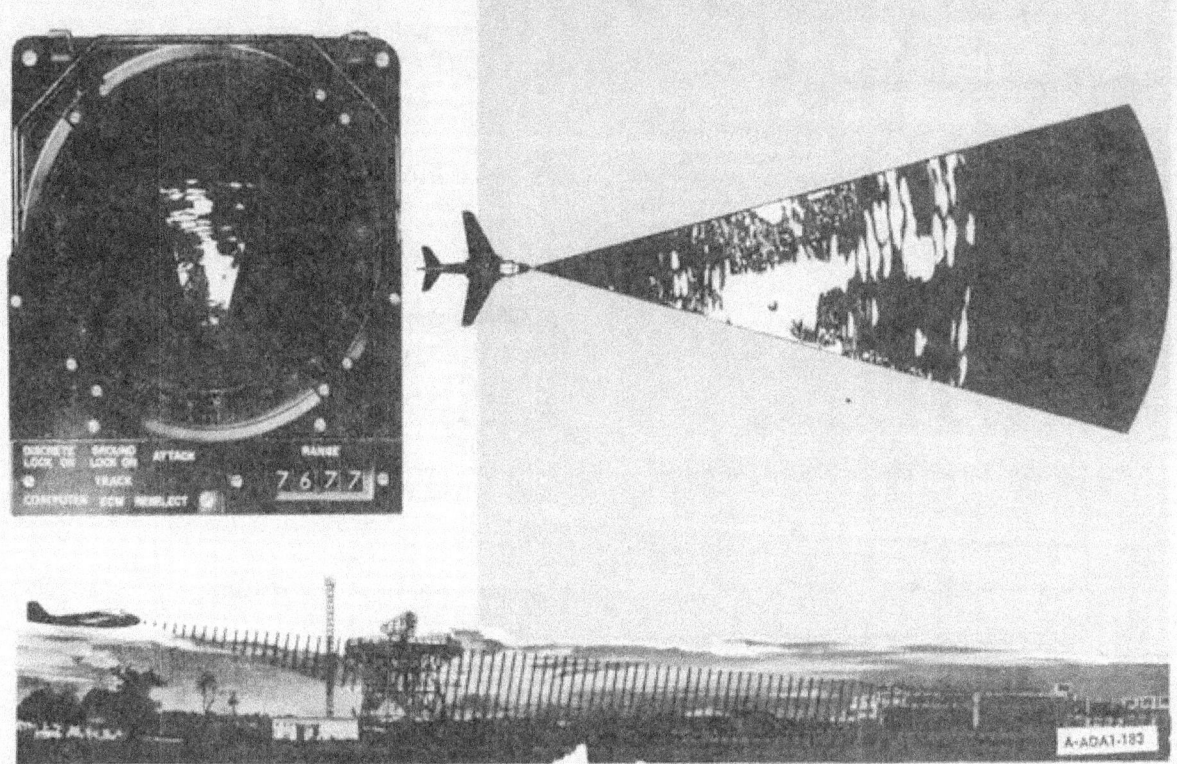

Figure 3-13

2. Antenna azimuth scan is automatically centered about the aircraft armament datum line modified by drift angle.

3. No cursors are displayed.

4. When the digital computer is off, the antenna scan is centered about the ADL of the aircraft.

5. Azimuth slew is not available, however elevation slew may be accomplished by use of the slew stick elevation thumbwheel. Release of the thumbwheel will return the antenna to its original position.

WEAPON DELIVERY IN MANUAL MODE

If, during the mission, it becomes evident that the computer has failed entirely, navigation and target acquisition may be accomplished by means of manually controlled search radar. This will thereby provide the B/N with the basic information necessary to successfully conclude the delivery of the assigned weapon. The bombardier/navigator's control panel includes the necessary controls and indicators required to establish the navigation, target acquisition, and weapon delivery functions.

When a computer malfunction demands that the delivery be accomplished manually, and providing the search radar equipment is operating, the B/N will place the computer/manual (CMPTR/MAN) switch on the bombardier/navigator's control panel to the MAN position. The inputs from the computer components are disabled, and the information developed for delivery uses search radar and platform adapter inputs for the display. To accomplish the actual weapon delivery, the bombardier/navigator will crank into the range readout window on the bombardier/navigator's control panel the slant range from release point to the target for the particular weapon being delivered.

NORMAL PROCEDURES
Degraded System Procedures A-6A, B, C

Note

The range information will vary with different weapons, airspeeds, and altitudes, and should be provided as a part of the mission briefing before departure of the aircraft from the base.

Manual Range Line Calibration

Due to inherent errors in the mechanization of the manual range counter and associated equipment, the bombardier/navigator should ascertain the specific values to be read in the range window for the desired range calculation for each weapon on board the aircraft. Manual range line calibration procedures are as follows:

1. Flight mode selector - FLIGHT
2. Search radar displays - PPI
3. PPI range - as desired (30-5 NMI)
4. Navigation mode selector - UNSTAB-NO STEER
5. Search radar - ON
6. CMPTR/MAN switch - CMPTR
7. Slew range line to within 50 feet of computed release/pullup range.
8. Insert computer release/pullup range into range window by use of manual range knob.
9. Switch CMPTR/MAN switch to MAN, noting range line displacement on DVI.
10. Adjust manual range knob so as to make the two range lines coincident when CMPTR/MAN switch is cycled.
11. Note new readout on range counter and direction of movement of last manual range knob adjustment (cw or ccw).

Procedures For Manual Radar Delivery

1. Insert precalculated release or pullup slant range. This range is inserted into range readout window using manual range knob (MAN RANGE) on bombardier/navigator's control panel.
2. Computer/manual switch - MAN
3. Station select switches - BOMB
4. Armament panel set for manual release, LAB IP, or LAB TGT.
5. Locate target on search radar PPI display.

6. MASTER ARM switch - ON
7. Azimuth scan angle - CCW (narrow scan)
8. Scan rate - FAST

   Azimuth cursor switch ACTUATE
   Position azimuth cursor dead ahead by moving CW or CCW.
   Bombardier/navigator start and stop all turns with verbal instructions to pilot.
   Target will move down azimuth line as range to go decreases, maintain target's left-right position.
   When target reaches range line, initiate pullup or release as applicable.

NONSYSTEM LAYDOWN BOMBING

A backup capability for nonsystem automatic laydown bombing against nonradar-significant targets is provided. Use of this mode does not permit azimuth displacement; therefore, run-in heading must coincide with IP/target heading.

Laydown bombing is selected by setting the auxiliary armament panel power selector switch on the B/N's right console to REL DELAY. The desired release delay is set on the timer on the auxiliary armament panel.

With the master arm switch ON, and the release mode switch set to AUTO, when the pilot commits, a release pulse is sent to the selected store stations at the end of the delay set on the timer.

Weapon delivery may be made using either a visual or radar IP. If visual techniques are used, the delay set should be the time from the visual IP to the computed release point. If a radar delivery is used, release slant range should be set on the manual range line and the time from the radar IP to the target should be set on the auxiliary armament panel timer.

PROCEDURES FOR RADAR DELIVERY

1. Insert precalculated release slant range. This range is inserted in range readout window by manual range knob (MAN RANGE) on bombardier/navigator's control panel.
2. Computer/manual switch - MAN
3. Station select switches - BOMB or BOMBS/GUNS
4. Armament panel set for automatic release
5. Locate IP on search radar PPI display
6. MASTER ARM switch - ON
7. Auxiliary armament panel power select switch - REL DELAY

NORMAL PROCEDURES
Degraded System Procedures A6A, B, C

8. Computed release delay - SET
9. Azimuth scan angle - CCW (narrow scan)
10. Scan rate - FAST

    Azimuth cursor switch - ACTUATE

    Positive azimuth cursor dead ahead by moving cw or ccw

    Bombardier/navigator start and stop all turns with verbal instructions to pilot.

    IP will move down azimuth line as range-to-go decreases, maintain IP's left-right position.

    When IP reaches range line, commit. Tone comes on if selected, and at end of selected delay, release is initiated, and tone stops.

WEAPON DELIVERY WITH LOSS OF AIR DATA (EMERGENCY STRAIGHT PATH) (P-7B TRIM)

Loss of air data due to airspeed, pressure altitude, temperature probe, or angle-of-attack probe will not prevent a computer delivery of weapons. A straight path level attack can be made by manually entering altitude and mach number.

When it is determined that air data is faulty and the backup mode of attack is elected, aircraft true altitude (bombing altitude) is entered through the keyboard under present location and a command mach number is set into the computer by depressing the G buttons in accordance with the following schedule:

G Button	Mach
3.0	.60
3.5	.65
4.0	.70
4.5	.75
5.0	.80

The TAS window on the bombardier/navigator's attack-navigation panel and the command airspeed index on the pilot's mach/airspeed/command airspeed indicator will read the true airspeed for the mach number and altitude selected. For a successful attack, the aircraft must be flown at the altitude and mach number selected.

ATTACK PROCEDURES WITH LOSS OF AIR DATA

1. Flight mode button - PRE FLT
2. Error code switch - ERASE

    Note

    The error code 999 will appear in the DOPPLER GROUND VELOCITY window when the backup bombing mode is selected, the data select switch is at C, and the system is in attack. In addition, the VDI pathway changes to a three-line type as in the landing mode.

3. Mach number - SELECT

    Select desired mach number by depressing appropriate G button.

4. Address key - DEPRESS PRESS LOCA

NORMAL PROCEDURES
Degraded System Procedures A-6A, B, C

Enter aircraft true altitude under present location.

5. Armament panel - SET

    Set armament panel for a straight path level attack for either bombs or rockets.

    Note

    Rockets may be fired at a low grazing angle by selecting a rocket attack rather than a straight path attack.

Bombardier/navigator perform procedures for straight path attack. All tracking functions are available.

Pilot fly the aircraft to obtain selected indicated mach number and maintain altitude entered in the computer, ignoring vertical steering commands generated by the vertical position of the steering symbol.

For accurate bombing in the backup mode, it is more important to maintain a constant airspeed than precisely maintain the selected mach number. Variations in airspeed late in the run due to chasing the selected mach number may introduce transients into the solution that will adversely affect accuracy.

Acquisition of a discrete or ground lock-on will improve the bombing altitude and therefore the accuracy of the release. A track lock-on will eliminate the necessity for accuracy in entering aircraft altitude and target altitude.

WEAPON DELIVERY WITH SELECTIVE DATA REPLACEMENT (NOMATS) (P-8.6)

Loss of sensor input data due to mach (M), angle-of-attack (A), temperature (T), or static pressure (S) failure will not prevent a computer release of weapons. A straight path level attack can be made by selective replacement of failed sensor data. A failure of all these sensors can be accomplished by selecting EMERGENCY BOMB on the FLT MODE selector panel.

Procedures for replacing data for a failed sensor may be found in Section VIII, Weapons Systems.

LAB IP AND LAB TARGET DELIVERY

Two automatic loft deliveries are provided for release of store at preset release angles from 0° to 90° (LAB IP) (figure 3-14) and 90° to 135° (LAB TGT). These angles are preset in the platform adapter. The angles to be used for a nuclear weapon or Shrike missile can be found in the A-6A Tactical Manual and supplement. Whereas the LAB IP and LAB TGT modes of delivery for the Shrike missile are primary modes of delivery and are discussed in detail in the A-6 Tactical Manual, the LAB IP and LAB TGT modes are degraded modes of delivery when used in conjunction with nuclear and conventional weapons. Procedures for target acquisition and steering commands are the same as for manual laydown, but the range set in the manual range window will now correspond to pullup range for a medium angle loft (LAB IP). For LAB TGT, where pullup is initiated over or beyond the target, range may be set at zero only if the target can be acquired visually. Otherwise, range must be

3-123

NORMAL PROCEDURES
Degraded System Procedures A-6A, B, C

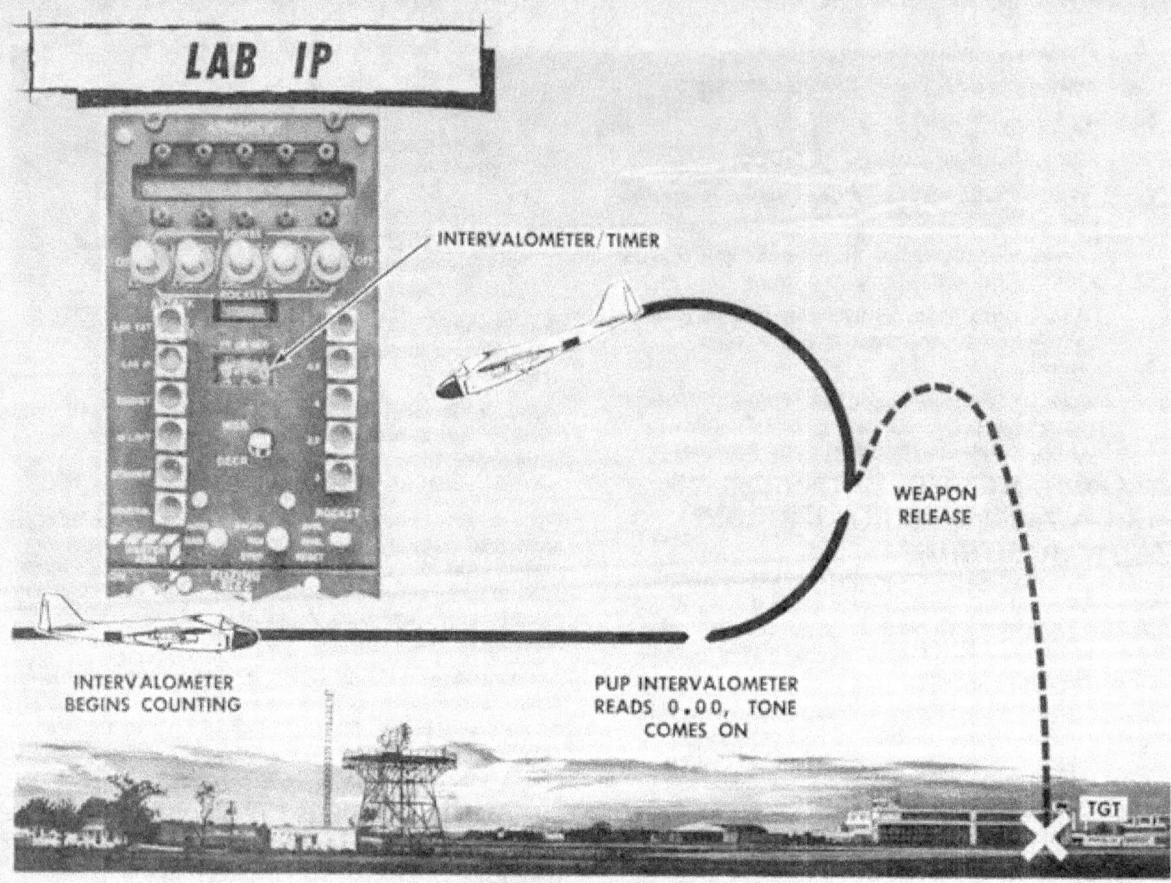

Figure 3-14

set at some distance that will allow the B/N to acquire the target on radar. During either of these maneuvers, the intervalometer timer may be used to establish a pullup for release at the optimum preset release angle. In either of these modes, the range readout window reflects the ground range from pullup point to the target or IP, and represents the directional/range index for this particular release (see figure 3-14).

When executing a LAB IP or LAB TGT maneuver, the weapon can be released either automatically or manually, depending upon the position of the release mode switch. With the switch set at AUTO, the weapon will be released automatically upon arriving at the preselected release angle set in the platform adapter provided that the station-select and MASTER ARM switches have been set and the pilot has depressed the attack commit trigger. A manual release can be accomplished by either the pilot or the bombardier/navigator.

With the release mode switch set to MAN, the pilot can release the weapon by depressing the manual release button when the aircraft reaches the desired release point. A manual release may be obtained with the release mode switch in AUTO; however, the attack commit trigger must be depressed for release.

With the release mode switch set to AUTO and the pilot depressing the manual release button, but not the attack commit trigger, the bombardier/navigator can release the weapon by switching the release mode switch from AUTO to MAN when the aircraft reaches the desired release point.

In aircraft equipped with the Mk-4 gun pod controls, the release mode switch is deleted but the pilot still has the option of selecting either manual or automatic release. With the MASTER ARM switch at ON, and a station selected, the pilot may obtain a manual release at any time by depressing the manual release button on the stick grip or he may select an automatic release by depressing the attack commit trigger on the stick grip. He may override an automatic release by depressing the attack commit trigger and the manual release button.

VALID DATA INTERPRETATION AND USE

Mechanization of valid data logic throughout the attack run acts as a master caution for the system and thereby increases the probability of a successfully executed automatic release since:

1. System failure or inability to release accurately is determined before run-in allowing system analysis and alternate attack mode selection.

2. Positive protection against improper attack geometry is provided.
3. Long-term warning for use of manual override is more adequately displayed.

Preattack run assessment of automatic drop accuracy and reliability is obtained by the vertical display indication of pathway on or off. After attack is selected, there is no computer error light test since all of the basic quantities required for successful weapon release are directly or indirectly checked in the valid data logic. Pathway-off indication means that the computer is incapable of an accurate release due to system malfunction or improper attack conditions.

Common causes of sustained path-off indication due to improper attack conditions are:

1. Underdiving the target in straight path attack.
2. Violent jinking or erratic maneuvering (including turbulence).
3. Large changes of cursor position late in the run.

In a straight path attack, a pull-through (accelerated maneuver) will yield unpredictable results. Valid data indication is designed to remind the pilot, before pull out, that underdiving the target is invalid and the run is impossible. The logic is such that the pilot can judge the amount of maneuvering he can use on the run-in and still obtain accurate weapon release; i.e. he must revert to stabilized flight before release and pathway-on indicates an acceptable stabilized condition.

A discrete lock, over flat terrain, or at low grazing angles, will sometimes result in erroneous or erratic elevation angle data. In either case, valid data logic will indicate the need for alternate target data technique, or alternate attack geometry; i.e. ground lock or cursor intersection data, or higher dive angle.

Common causes of pathway-off due to system malfunctions are:

1. Erroneous vertical velocity.
2. Normal accelerometer failure (except in straight path).
3. Air data computer failure.
4. Almost any encoder failure.

In practice, the pilot is afforded an early assessment of any of these possible failures by selection of attack before entering the target area, thus avoiding an aborted run in heavily defended areas. His alternatives in case of valid data logic are:

1. Assess the vertical display symbol position and motion for failure clues, isolate the failure source, and take appropriate action.
2. Assume the valid data indication is the result of momentary failure and use manual override at release indication.
3. Select alternate attack mode; i.e. emergency straight path.

A series of momentary losses of pathway is usually not serious during the initial run-in and can be considered to be a caution; it should not constitute a down weapon system. Pilot communication of momentary valid data occurrence to the bombardier/navigator under these conditions serves to alert the bombardier/navigator to possible troubles in somewhat the same way that a master caution light functions for the pilot.

SEARCH RADAR DELIVERY

All navigation and attack modes can be accomplished without using the track radar. In all attack modes, the degradation is loss of radar ranging, target depression angle, and target velocity to the ballistics computer. However, these inputs from the track radar are replaced by others, namely, slant range and ground range from the search radar. Search radar, altitude and vertical velocity from the inertial platform, and target velocity are computed as wind by the use of the velocity-correct feature of the ballistics computer. The landing mode is accomplished by using the offset capability on a known fixed target near the landing runway.

COORDINATES SYSTEM BOMBING

If the search and track radars are lost on the mission, weapon delivery may still be accomplished on a preplanned target, provided the inertial or Doppler navigation system and computer are functioning properly.

BOMBING PROCEDURES

The procedures for a coordinate system delivery are as follows:

1. Establish aircraft on known line of latitude or longitude intersecting a release point.
2. Fly cardinal course to release point.
3. Navigation data switch - PRES POS
4. Steering mode - AS DESIRED
5. Enroute - CHECK PRESENT POSITION LATITUDE AND LONGITUDE WHEN TRANSITING A KNOWN VISUAL CHECKPOINT FOR NAVIGATIONAL ACCURACY. UPDATE POSITION IF REQUIRED.
6. Set armament panel for automatic release.
7. Monitor present position tape dial readouts.
8. Attack button - DEPRESS AT 10 MILES TO GO.
9. Attack commit trigger - DEPRESS WHEN IN RANGE.

Note

If track radar only is available, the bombardier/navigator may first locate the target using emergency search, then attempt to make a lock-on using the 1,200-cycle tone. Without lock-on, this is the least accurate means of delivery available, and should be used as a last resort means of mission completion navigation.

RELEASE OVERRIDE

In order to provide the pilot with a fast and positive override in case of automatic release failure, manual release with the release mode switch in AUTO can be made by simultaneously depressing the commit trigger and the manual release button.

In aircraft equipped with the Mk-4 gun pod controls, the release mode switch is deleted but the pilot still has the option of selecting either manual or automatic release. With the master arm switch at ON, and a station selected, the pilot may obtain a manual release at any time by depressing the manual release button on the stick grip or he may select an automatic release by depressing the attack commit trigger on the stick grip. If the computer is in attack, manual override may be accomplished by depressing the attack commit trigger and the manual release button.

Care must be taken in the use of the release override capability to avoid spurious or wild release or premature override of a legitimate automatic release. Pilot assessment of the VDI situation for credibility and continuity is all improtant. If, for example, the attack has progressed smoothly up to the point of release, but release does not occur, the pilot should override. On the other hand, if the position of the release marker is erratic or if steering is not smooth, then use of override is likely to produce unpredictable results.

ALTERNATE MODES OF NAVIGATION AND STABILIZATION

There are several alternate or degraded modes of navigation, heading, and stabilization within the weapons system. The subsystems concerned here are: the inertial system, Doppler radar, MA-1 compass, VGI, air data computer, and the ballistics computer and its velocity-correct feature. (See figure 3-15).

Beginning with a full system as pertains to navigation and stabilization, the following procedures apply.

LOSS OF INERTIAL PLATFORM VELOCITIES

Shift to emergency Doppler navigation mode and continue to use the platform for heading and stabilization. Under these conditions, the Doppler is used for navigation and will continue to damp the platform for heading and stabilization utilization.

1. Altitude input will be provided by the air data computer (ADC). The velocity-correct function of the computer (figure 3-15) does not affect horizontal velocities (wind and groundspeed) when operating in the emergency Doppler mode. With a track radar lock-on, the velocity correct function will apply corrections to vertical velocity (altitude), an especially critical function in attack and/or terrain clearance situations.

2. In the DR navigation mode of computer operation, the automatic correct function (track lock-on) will introduce corrections to the computer in both horizontal and vertical axes (groundspeed, wind, and altitude). Velocity-correct (automatic or manual) is, in DR, a requirement for accurate navigation and attack.

3. Even though horizontal velocities may appear valid without further corrections, present position altitude should be monitored, and automatic velocity-correct performed, if necessary, for vertical input.

LOSS OF INERTIAL AND DOPPLER NAVIGATION VELOCITIES

Shift to DR navigation mode and continue to use the platform for heading and stabilization. Use the velocity-correct feature of the ballistics computer to maintain accurate wind information in the computer. This information will be used with the air data system to generate groundspeed and drift. The DR velocity will also be used to damp the platform for heading and stabilization utilization.

LOSS OF INERTIAL PLATFORM VERTICAL VELOCITY (ALT)

Shift to emergency Doppler or DR navigation mode as applicable. This removes the inertial vertical velocity from the system and uses air data altitude information instead.

LOSS OF INERTIAL PLATFORM

Shift to the MAG/VGI mode of operation for heading and stabilization information. Shut the platform off, and shift the navigation mode to emergency Doppler or DR (velocity-correct) as applicable.

Note

- The magnetic variation switch on the navigation control panel must be kept updated in the MAG/VGI mode to provide accurate true heading information to the ballistics computer.

- If the platform is lost during flight and is to be shut down, place platform selector switch to ALIGN for 10 seconds before going to OFF to prevent system damage.

LOSS OF ALL STABILIZATION AND HEADING INFORMATION TO THE COMPUTER

If all stabilization and heading information to the computer is lost:

1. Platform selector button - OFF

2. Compass switch - MAG/VGI

DR navigate to target area using search radar, (fixed antenna method), and the MA-1 compass. Use emergency straight path or manual mode for weapons delivery.

Note

Search radar presentation will be degraded or lost if aircraft wings are not level.

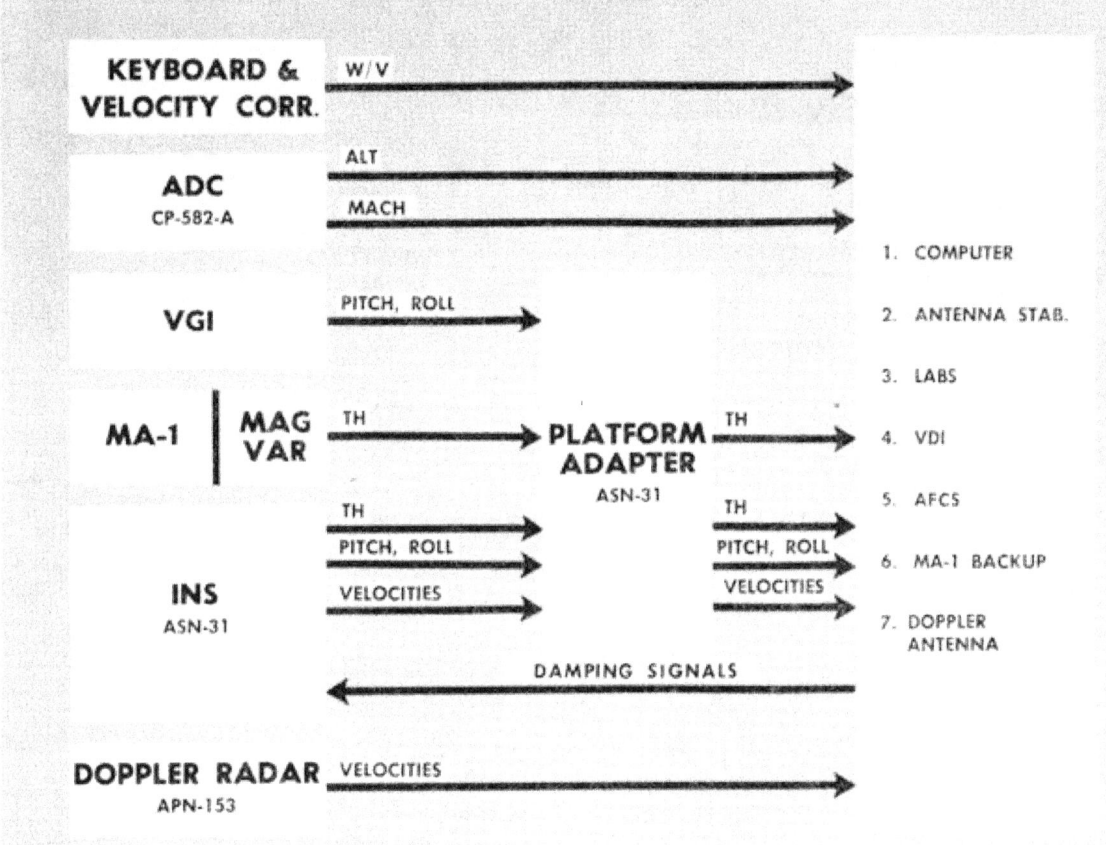

Figure 3-15

NORMAL PROCEDURES
Air Refueling Procedures

NAVAIR 01-85ADA-1

part 8   Air Refueling Procedures

AIR REFUELING PROCEDURES KA-6D

Note

Air-refueling shall be conducted in accordance with the NATOPS Air-Refueling Manual.

INTERNAL AIR REFUELING SYSTEM OPERATION

Before Refueling

1. AFCS .... AUTO NOT ENGAGED
2. Drogue jettison switch .... SAFE
   On ground, drogue jettison switch is deactivated through left weight-on-wheels switch. When airborne, drogue jettison switch is deactivated when drogue is stowed and DROGUE RET/EXT switch is in RET position with refueling POWER switch in ON position.
3. Drogue switch .... RET
4. Refueling power switch .... ON
   Placing refueling power switch on pressurizes wing tanks to 12 psi and opens aft fuselage fuel tank shutoff valve.

   a. Hose-reel position indicator .... STOW
   b. HYD PRESS low warning light .... ON
      The HYD PRESS low warning light indicates hydraulic pressure is less than 1800 psi.

5. Pounds scheduled counter .... SET
   When quantity of fuel to be transferred to receiver aircraft is set on LBS SCHED counter, internal switching is set to provide fuel flow transmitter information.

6. Pounds delivered counter .... RESET
   Set pounds delivered counter to zero.

7. Lights switch .... BRT(Day) DIM(Night)

8. External refueling panel .... CHECK

   a. Ship tank switch .... FROM STORE
   b. Drogue position indicator .... RET
   c. Hose jettison switch .... NORM
   d. Transfer switch .... OFF
   e. Hose extend/retract switch .... RET
   f. Refueling master switch .... OFF

CONTINUED ON NEXT PAGE

NAVAIR 01-85ADA-1

NORMAL PROCEDURES
Air Refueling Procedures

AIR REFUELING PROCEDURES KA-6D—CONTINUED

9. Drogue switch . . . . EXT

   a. HYD PRESS low warning light . . . . OUT
      Placing drogue switch to extend pressurizes hose-reel hydraulic system to extend hose.
      Hydraulic pressure in excess of 1800 psi causes HYD PRESS low warning light to go out.

   b. Hose-reel position indicator . . . . BARBER POLE
      Hose reel position indicator shows barber pole while hose is in transit from fully retracted
      to fully extended position.

   c. Hose-reel position indicator . . . . TRAIL
      When hose reel reaches full extended position, hose reel position indicator shows TRAIL.

   d. READY light . . . . ON
      READY light will come on 5 seconds after TRAIL indication.

10. Fuel transfer switch . . . . AUTO

WARNING

Tanking operations should not be attempted without
a READY light unless special procedures in Section V
are followed.

Note

Tanking operations (as a tanker) with the AFCS in the
AUTO mode is not recommended. Due to attitude
reference source difference in the KA-6D, continuous
corrections by the AFCS in the AUTO mode causes
excessive hose/drogue movement and increases the
number of off-center engagements.

Response Test

In order to properly complete the response test, steps 1-10 of Before Refueling must be completed.

1. Response switch . . . . TEST
   Hold response switch in TEST position for 5 seconds and release. This action initiates a rewind
   signal to hose-reel hydraulic motor, causing a rapid hose rewind, which checks response mode of
   operation.

   a. Hose-reel position indicator:

      (1) Aircraft not incorporating AFC No. 298 . . . . TRAIL
          Hose-reel position indicator continues to show TRAIL when hose leaves full trail
          position.

      (2) Aircraft incorporating AFC No. 298 . . . . BARBER POLE
          Hose-reel position indicator shows barber pole when hose leaves full trail position.

   b. READY light . . . . OUT
      READY light will go out between 5 and 25 feet from full trail.

CONTINUED ON NEXT PAGE

NORMAL PROCEDURES
Air Refueling Procedures

NAVAIR 01-85ADA-1

AIR REFUELING PROCEDURES KA-6D–CONTINUED

    c.   HYD PRESS light . . . . REMAINS OUT

    d.   VALVE OPEN light . . . . ON
          VALVE OPEN light comes on in refueling range when refueling shutoff valve opens.
          Transfer-and-dump pumps come on.

2.   Response switch . . . . RESET
      Hold response switch in RESET position for a minimum of 5 seconds and release. This action
      establishes a new hydraulic reference pressure and hose and drogue extend to full trail.

    a.   Hose-reel position indicator . . . . TRAIL

    b.   READY light . . . . ON
          READY light will come on 5 feet from full trail after 5 seconds.

WARNING

Do not actuate REEL RESPONSE switch unless receiver aircraft is positively clear of area aft of drogue.

Note

A response test is required for functional check flights.

During Refueling

After the receiver aircraft is cleared to engage by the tanker pilot:

1.   Engagement and fuel transfer.
      Response action of hose reel due to receiver aircraft engagement causes hose to rewind to
      refueling range. On aircraft not incorporating AFC No. 298, hose reel position indicator will
      continue to show TRAIL. On aircraft incorporating AFC No. 298 hose reel position indicator
      will show barber pole when hose leaves full trail position.

    a.   Refueling range 5 to 25 feet from full trail.

    b.   READY light out.
          READY light will go out between 5 and 25 feet from full trail.

    c.   VALVE OPEN light on.
          Refueling shutoff valve opens and both transfer-and-dump pumps are energized.

    d.   FUEL FLOW light on.
          Opening of refueling shutoff valve allows fuel flow to commence, actuating fuel flow
          transmitter internal switch, causing FUEL FLOW light to come on.

    e.   FUEL FLOW and VALVE OPEN lights out.
          Fuel flow continues until forward and aft transfer-and-dump pumps are shut down by one
          of the following: pounds delivered equaling pounds scheduled, which actuates fuel flow
          internal transmitter switch to OFF position; drogue traveling outside 5 to 25 foot refueling
          range, positioning refueling range switch to not-fueling position or placing FUEL TRANS
          switch OFF.

CONTINUED ON NEXT PAGE

AIR REFUELING PROCEDURES KA-6D—CONTINUED

2. Advisory lights .... MONITOR

3. Pounds delivered counter .... MONITOR

OVERRIDE/Manual Mode

The override/manual mode of operation is the same as automatic except that placing the FUEL TRANS switch to OVRD manually opens the refueling shutoff valve, starts both fuel cell transfer-and-dump pumps, and energizes the fuel flow transmitter to operate the counters in the fuel flow totalizer. THE VALVE OPEN and FUEL FLOW lights will come on. The LBS SCHED counter must be monitored to stop fuel transfer to the receiver aircraft when required LBS SCHED is delivered. The FUEL TRANS switch is then placed at OFF, closing the refueling shutoff valve and stopping the fuel transfer-and-dump pumps. The VALVE OPEN and FUEL FLOW lights will go out.

> **CAUTION**
>
> The receiver aircraft should never attempt a disconnect while green fuel flow lights are on, as exceptionally high disconnect forces will be experienced.

After Refueling is Complete

1. Receiver aircraft .... DISCONNECT
   Receiver aircraft action causes hose to trail back to full trail position (46 feet extended) and causes it to become disconnected from drogue. READY light will come on.

2. Fuel transfer switch .... OFF

3. Drogue switch .... RET
   Hose and drogue will retract.

   a. READY light .... OUT

   b. Hose-reel position indicator will show barber pole while hose and drogue are retracting and STOW when retraction is complete and reel drum is locked in stowed position.

   c. HYD PRESS low warning light .... ON
      Hydraulic pressure low warning light will come on when drogue is fully retracted.

4. Refueling power switch .... OFF
   When refueling power switch is placed at OFF, HYD PRESS light goes out and hose-reel position indicator displays barber pole.

5. Offload report .... AS REQUIRED

Note

If refueling system malfunctions are encountered, refer to Air-Refueling Emergency Procedures in Section V.

NORMAL PROCEDURES
Air Refueling Procedures

NAVAIR 01-85ADA-1

AIR REFUELING (TANKER) PROCEDURES D-704 STORE

> **CAUTION**
>
> In the KA-6D the use of an external air refueling store is prohibited unless IAFC No. 296 or AFC No. 296 is incorporated in the aircraft. If IAFC No. 296 or AFC No. 296 is installed and it is decided to transfer fuel utilizing the D-704, the TO STORE switch on the centerline refueling store panel shall remain in the OFF position until the fuel quantity in the centerline refueling store is less than 500 pounds. When the fuel in the centerline refueling store reaches 500 pounds or less, move the centerline refueling store switch to the TO STORE position to replenish the store. Monitor fuel quantity indicator closely so that switch may be returned to the OFF position as soon as the fuel quantity indicates 1,500 pounds. If the tanker fuel transfer/dump pump starting relay is malfunctioning, the fuel transfer rate to the refueling centerline store could be fast enough to cause store failure if the indicated fuel level in the store is permitted to go above 1,500 pounds.

BEFORE TAKE-OFF

1. Ship tank switch . . . . OFF
2. Drogue position switch . . . . RET
3. Refueling master switch . . . . OFF
4. Fuel transfer switch . . . . OFF
5. Light switch . . . . (Day) BRT
   (Night) DIM
6. Gallons delivered 000
7. Hose jettison switch . . . . OFF

DROGUE EXTENSION

1. Refueling master switch . . . . ON
2. Airspeed . . . . 300 KIAS or less
3. Drogue switch . . . . EXT
   Drogue indicator will read EXT when drogue reaches full trail position.
4. SHIP TANK switch . . . . TO STORE

CONTINUED ON NEXT PAGE

AIR REFUELING (TANKER) PROCEDURES D-704 STORE—CONTINUED

RECEIVER HOOKUP AND REFUELING

After the receiver aircraft engages and moves forward in relation to the tanker enough to turn off the amber lights on the store, the drogue position indicator will read TRA. The bombardier/navigator then places the fuel transfer switch to TRANS to start the flow of fuel.

Stopping Fuel Transfer

Fuel transfer may be stopped at any time by placing the fuel transfer switch to OFF. Refueling will stop if the receiver aircraft backs off enough for the amber light to come on or if the probe disengages, in either case, the drogue position indicator windows will change from TRA to EXT.

> **CAUTION**
>
> Refueling cannot be stopped by placing the refueling master switch in the OFF position. Lack of hydraulic pressure will cause whiplash to occur in the refueling hose.

To stop transfer to the store, turn the SHIP TANK switch to OFF.

If hose tensioning or reel-in features are inoperative, the hookup should be discontinued immediately and the cause determined. If the hose does not reel in properly, a recycling of the hose by the tanker may remedy the malfunction.

DROGUE RETRACTION

1. Fuel transfer switch . . . . OFF
2. Airspeed . . . . 250 KIAS OR LESS

> **WARNING**
>
> Field arrestment or carrier landing with drogue extended is not recommended. Guillotine drogue in clear or uninhabited area.

3. Drogue switch . . . . RET

Note

If the drogue cannot be fully retracted at about 250 KIAS, reducing airspeed to 230 KIAS or less should permit full retraction.

CONTINUED ON NEXT PAGE

AIR REFUELING (TANKER) PROCEDURES D-704 STORE—CONTINUED

4. When drogue position indicator reads RET, place refueling master switch to OFF.

TRANSFER FROM STORE TO TANKER

If it is desired to transfer fuel from the refueling store to the tanker, place the ship tank switch to FROM STORE.

BEFORE LANDING

1. SHIP TANK .... OFF
2. Drogue switch .... RET
3. Drogue position indicator .... RET
4. Refueling master switch .... OFF
5. Fuel transfer switch .... OFF

JETTISONING REFUELING STORE

The air-refueling store may be jettisoned electrically in the same manner as other external stores.

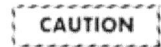

Do not jettison refueling stores above 300 KIAS.

Tanker Safety Precautions

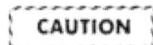

- Do not start the turbine or extend or retract the drogue when over populated areas or when other aircraft are close abeam or behind.
- Do not extend the drogue when a store hydraulic leak has been observed.
- Do not actuate the speed brakes during any part of the refueling operation.
- Once the hose jettison switch is actuated, do not return it to the OFF, position. In advertent cycling of this switch will cause a dangerous condition in the store.

CAUTION

Do not jettison refueling stores above 300 KIAS.

AIR REFUELING STORE LIMITATIONS

1. Maximum speed for unfeathering is 300 KIAS. For extension of drogue and refueling, maximum speed is 300 KIAS or 0.80 IMN.
2. Maximum speed for drogue retraction is 250 KIAS.

CONTINUED ON NEXT PAGE

NAVAIR 01-85ADA-1

NORMAL PROCEDURES
Air Refueling Procedures

AIR REFUELING (TANKER) PROCEDURES D-704 STORE—CONTINUED

3. The air refueling store must be empty for catapult launches if it is suspended from the AERO 7A rack. Catapult launches with a full store are permissible if the AERO 7A rack is used.

4. Maximum gross catapult weight with an air refueling store on the AERO 7A rack is 52,500 pounds due to possible trail bar slap.

5. The air refueling store must be empty for arrested landings.

WARNING

- When the SHIP TANK switch is placed to FROM STORE to empty the air-refueling store prior to carrier arrestment, do not select landing gear down until the SHIP TANK switch is placed from FROM STORE to OFF. When the landing gear is lowered, the air-refueling store depressurizes and, if FROM STORE is selected, the shutoff valve remains open, allowing reverse flow back into the air-refueling store. Fuel flow to store will be accelerated if FUSELAGE DUMP is also selected.

- When receiving fuel from a KC 135, the drop tanks may be filled but the maximum internal fuel shall not exceed 14,000 pounds of JP-4 or 15,000 pounds of JP-5. The A-6 has no surge relief provisions between the probe and the refueling gate valve; therefore, the receiver aircraft must discontinue fueling by disengaging from the refueling drogue.

part 9 — SATS Procedures

SATS LIMITATIONS

In addition to the aircraft limitations given in Section I, part 4 of this manual, the following restrictions are applicable for A-6A SATS catapult launches:

a. CG limits: 23% MAC to 29% MAC

b. Gross weight: 30,000 lb to 54,000 lb

c. The D-704 refueling store may not be carried on the fuselage station.

d. No fuselage stores may be carried on multiple stores racks

e. Density altitude between -2320 to +3000 feet

f. Crosswind not to exceed 15 kts

WARNING

Failure to adhere to the above restrictions will result in damage to the catapult, aircraft, or both.

PREFLIGHT

DAY

A normal preflight inspection should be made with particular attention given to the landing gear, tires, hook, and underside of the fuselage for previous damage. The aircraft gross weight and drag count should be determined and written (grease pencil, etc.) in a place visible to the catapult crew.

CAUTION

SATS launch end airspeeds are functions of aircraft gross weight and drag count. These parameters must be known if a safe launch is to be accomplished.

NIGHT

In addition to the normal cockpit preflight, ensure that external light switches are positioned to dim, the taxi light is definitely off, and that interior lights are prepositioned as desired.

TAXI

Taxiing on duty SATS matting is analagous to taxiing on any dry, hard surface area with the exception that the matting will give slightly under heavy loads. Taxiing into or out of revetted areas presents no difficulties except that particular attention to plane director's signals is required due to the small clearances provided.

Taxiing on wet or oily SATS matting is hazardous at best due to a greatly reduced coefficient of friction. Keep speed under control at all times by judicious use of the brakes. At light gross weights, it may be advisable to use only one engine, starting the other just before positioning for takeoff.

LAUNCH PROCEDURES

Proper positioning on the SATS catapult requires particular attention to the plane director's signals. All functional checks must be performed before taxiing into the catapult. Assure that the following is done:

FLAPS:	TAKE-OFF
TRIM:	RUDDER: 0
AILERON:	0
LONGITUDINAL:	4 units aircraft nose-up

Use nosewheel steering for initial positioning as required. Approximately 80% to 90% rpm will be required to taxi over the arrester ropes and up the dolly ramp. Once the ground handling crew has lowered the launch bar and it is engaged in the lead-in track, release the nose-gear steering and refrain from differential braking. Taxi forward slowly to avoid engaging the launch bar retract mechanism and overstressing the tension bar.

Before launch verify that the takeoff checklist has been completed. Upon receipt of the "tension-up and release brakes" signal, release brakes and watch the catapult officer for two-finger turn-up signal. When this signal is received, advance power to military, grasp and extend the catapult grip, check flight and engine instruments, and when satisfied that the aircraft is ready, give an exaggerated salute to the catapult officer.

CAUTION

If the catapult grip is not extended throughout the launch cycle, the nose strut will not be stiffened and unsatisfactory airplane pitch oscillations may develop during the launch.

After the salute and prior to launch, ensure that the head is back against the headrest and that the control stick is held in a neutral position. Normally, there will be a 2- to 6-second delay before the catapult actually fires. During the actual launch, observe the green cutoff light changes to amber. Upon perceiving the amber light, initiate normal aft stick movement and rotate the airplane to a takeoff attitude.

The front section of the launch dolly will pitch up during the power stroke, causing the aircraft to assume a nose-up attitude. At the end of the programmed launch sequence, as the tow force decays, the front section of the dolly will drop back onto the matting and the aircraft nose-up attitude will decrease. The dolly will be first on the deck and the launch bar will separate from the dolly at approximately the same time the cutoff light changes to amber.

WARNING

Do not apply brakes during launch. Do not use nosewheel steering during launch.

The aircraft will leave the catapult at or near the optimum airspeed for flight. Avoid overrotation but establish a positive rate of climb at 6° to 10° nose-up, cross reference with AOA, vertical speed, and indicated airspeed. Retract the landing gear when safely airborne and flaps below 250 KIAS.

WARNING

Extreme caution should be exercised during flap retraction at heavy gross weights. Do not retract the flaps below 170 KIAS for weights up to 50,000 lb. At heavy gross weights under high ambient temperature conditions, acceleration and climb performance are marginal and it may be impossible to reach 185 KIAS. If 185 KIAS cannot be obtained, reduce external store weight in order to accelerate to 185 KIAS before flap retraction.

NIGHT

Taxi onto the catapult with external lights off. When ready to launch, place the external light master switch on. As in daytime launches, closely monitor AOA, airspeed, vertical speed, and nose and wing position after launch.

CATAPULT EMERGENCIES

If the launch bar separates from the dolly prematurely, the pilot will feel a sudden loss of acceleration but the dolly will continue to accelerate and move ahead of the aircraft. As soon as the dolly can be seen in front of the aircraft, the pilot should maneuver to the side of the matting to avoid contacting the rebounding dolly. If abort or takeoff is not possible and speed of 100 KIAS has been attained, EJECT.

A cold shot can result from a catapult malfunction. If the dolly moves ahead of the airplane, maneuver to the side of the matting so as to avoid contact with the rebounding dolly. If abort or takeoff is not possible and a speed of 100 KIAS has been attained, EJECT.

RECOVERY

SATS traffic and landing approach patterns are generally in accordance with the procedures outlined for normal landings in section III, Part 3 of this manual. Maximum arrested landing weight is 36,000 lb. Begin the approach by turning approximately 5 to 8 seconds past the arresting-gear position in order to have a 1-mile wings-level groove. Report the 180° position with side number and fuel state, and hung ordnance as appropriate.

At approximately the 90° position, 450 feet of altitude, the meatball will appear in the center of the lens; correct the rate of descent as required to keep the meatball centered. Glide slope corrections should be made smoothly with combined power and attitude changes so as to maintain optimum approach AOA and a centered meatball. Pay particular attention to line-up, correcting for cross-wind as required so as to land in the center of the runway.

Upon landing, apply full military power and retract the speed brakes. As soon as arrested, place the throttle to idle and raise the flaps. Allow the aircraft to roll back to disengage the arresting gear, then raise the hook when signalled to do so.

CAUTION

Do not raise the tailhook while engaged so to prevent damage to the hook bumper cable.

WAVE-OFF/BOLTER

Wave-offs and bolters are readily accomplished by application of full military power, retraction of speed brakes, and rotation to a fly-away attitude. To preclude any possibility of engaging the terminal and dolly arrested ropes, retract the tailhook immediately after becoming airborne or safely stopping the rate of descent.

WARNING

Inadvertent engagement of the dolly arrester ropes will result in extensive damage to the aircraft and catapult.

NORMAL PROCEDURES
Functional Checkflight

NAVAIR 01-85ADA-1

 **Functional Check Flight Procedures**

FUNCTIONAL CHECKFLIGHT REQUIREMENTS

Checkflights will be performed when directed by, and in accordance with, OPNAVINST 4790.2 series and the directions of NAVAIRSYSCOM Type Commanders, or other appropriate authority. Functional checkflight requirements and applicable minimums are described below. Functional checkflight checklists are promulgated separately.

CONDITIONS REQUIRING CHECKFLIGHTS

Checkflights are required under the following conditions (after the necessary ground check and prior to release of the aircraft for operational use):

A. At the completion of aircraft rework and all aircraft acceptances (all checkflight items required are prefixed A).

B. After the installation of an engine, or engine fuel control, or any components which cannot be checked in ground operation (minimum required are prefixed B).

C. When fixed or movable flight surfaces or flight control system components have been installed or reinstalled, adjusted, or rerigged, and improper adjustment or replacement of such components could cause an unsafe operating condition (minimum required are prefixed C).

CHECKFLIGHT PROCEDURES

The items which follow provide detailed descriptions of the functional checks, sequenced in the order in which they should be performed. In order to complete the required checks in the most efficient and logical order, a flight profile has been established for each checkflight condition and identified by the letter corresponding to the purpose for which the checkflight is being flown; i.e., A, B, or C, as shown above. The applicable letter identifying the profile prefixes each check both in the following text and in the Functional Checkflight Checklist. Checkflight personnel will familiarize themselves with these requirements prior to each flight. NATOPS procedures will apply during the entire checkflight unless specific deviation is required by the functional check to record data or ensure proper operation within the approved aircraft envelope. A daily inspection is required before each checkflight.

PRETAKEOFF

TAXI CHECKS

Before Taxi

PROFILE

AC 1. Wing-Fold System - SPREAD WINGS.
Check that WING FOLD control handle is locked out when control stick is not in neutral. Control stick is laterally restricted when WING FOLD handle is not stowed (except when autopilot is engaged). Flaps, slats, and flaperon pop-up circuits are open with wings unlocked. Wings cannot be cycled with flaps and slats extended and control stick out of neutral. Wings spread smoothly in approximately 20 seconds.

AC 2. Flight Controls - CHECKED.

a. Flaperons: Check for smooth lateral control stick movement and flaperon operation. Check mutual lock-out of flaperon and wing-fold mechanism. Position FLAPERON POP UP switch to ARM; flaperons should pop up. Check for limited lateral control stick movement. Return FLAPERON POP UP switch to OFF; flaperons should return to normal; check trim operation three units left and right. Full travel in 11 1/4 seconds.

b. Horizontal Stabilizer: Check for smooth operation with flaps up. STAB position indicator should show CLEAN indicating normal stabilizer throw. Lower flaps and recheck. Position indicator will show a symbol of a stabilizer indicating that extended throw is available. Check full travel of trim operation (3 units nose down to 12 units nose up).

PRETAKEOFF—CONTINUED

PROFILE

    c. Rudder: With flaps down, check for smooth rudder pedal movement. Extended rudder throw should be available. Raise flaps and recheck; rudder throw available should return to normal (4° either side of neutral). Check full travel of trim operation (4 units left and right).

    d. Assist-Spin Recovery: Activate assist-spin recovery system. RUD THRO caution light should light and extended rudder and horizontal stabilizer throw should be available. Return ASSIST SPIN RECOV switch to OFF; controls should revert to normal throw and caution light should go out.

    e. Wing Flaps and Slats: Select LAND; flaps extend to 40° down and slats to full down 27.5°. Select UP; flaps return to full up and slats return to full up. Select TAKEOFF; flaps extend to 30° down and slats to full down. Cycle times, flaps 10 to 12 seconds, and slats 6 to 8 seconds.

    f. Wing Flap and Slat Indications: FLAP window indicates UP position; displays 30° and 40° flap positions, barber pole when flaps are in transition or power is OFF. SLAT window displays slat when slats fully extended and IN when slats are retracted; barber pole when slats are in transition or power is OFF.

    g. Emergency Operation of Flaps and Slats: Emergency switch in desired position, electric operation shall have priority over hydraulic operation. Electric emergency switch shall be actuated only with wings spread and locked.

    h. Wing-Tip Speed Brakes: Operate smoothly during fully closed to fully open (120°) operation and incremental partial extension.

AC   3. Automatic Flight Control System - CHECKED.
       Check for engagement in all modes and for positive disengagement. With AUTOPILOT switch OFF, deflect control stick through full lateral throws.

AB   4. Air Conditioning - CHECKED.
       Check air conditioning maintains constant temperature and airflow. Check HOT and COLD switch positions - (Auto and Manual). Check for proper equipment cooling, no warning lights.

AB   5. Vent Suit or Cushion Airflow - CHECKED.
       Check for constant temperature and airflow, and controlability.

AB   6. Anti-G System - CHECKED.
       Press g-suit test button. Pressurization shall commence immediately.

AB   7. A-6C: Check for proper operation of pod air conditioning, no warning lights.

AB   8. Windshield-Washing System - CHECKED.
       Check that spray is even on windshield.

AB   9. Rain-Removal (Anti-Ice) System - CHECK BRIEFLY.
       Reach over top of windshield; check temperature and airflow.

A   10. Lighting Systems - CHECKED.
       Satisfactory illumination control on all lighting systems.

A   11. Oxygen System - CHECKED.
       Check quantity gage; oxygen for flight in accordance with NATOPS Flight Manual for altitude and duration of flight. Check LOX/FUEL press-to-test and proper operation including caution light. Supply satisfactory regulated between 100% O_2 and diluter-demand (GRU-5). Supply satisfactory (GRU-7).

NORMAL PROCEDURES
Functional Checkflight

NAVAIR 01-85ADA-1

PRETAKEOFF–CONTINUED

PROFILE

A 12. Communication, Navigation, Identification equipment (with CNI master switch at ON except A-6E TRAM) - CHECKED.

   a. Intercommunications Set (ICS): Operates satisfactorily in all modes. COLD position of MIC SEL (ICS/MIC, A-6E TRAM) switch allows transmission only when ICS switch is depressed. HOT position allows transmission at any time.

   b. UHF: Operates satisfactorily; channel and frequency-select all functions smoothly. KA-6D and A-6E TRAM: Same check for UHF No. 1 and UHF No. 2.

   c. NAV Beacon sidetone - CHECKED.

   d. AUX UHF: (Except A-6E TRAM): Operates satisfactorily; large needle on HSI indicates magnetic bearing (±10°) to station unless UHF - ADF is selected.

   e. TACAN (Except A-6E TRAM): Controls satisfactorily. With SEL switch in REC position, bearing displayed. With SEL switch in T/R, both bearing and range are indicated. Identification signal is heard in headsets when selected and volume is controllable. Range and bearing displayed on HSI with no undersirable excursions. With antenna select switch in any position, lock-on occurs within 30 seconds of station selected. KA-6D: Ensure TACAN is selected on VDI control panel. TACAN (A-6E TRAM): BIT

   f. Bomb Tone: Check satisfactory tone quality. Except A-6E TRAM, place TRAN SEL switch to U, TONE switch to BOMB, and BOMB TONE switch to MAN. A-6E TRAM, place BOMB TONE switch to MAN, check tone with TRANSMIT switch at BOMB TN 1 and BOMB TN 2.

   g. ECM Warning Tone - CHECKED.

   h. IFF/SIF: Proper response to interrogation signal in each mode. I/P provides identification transmission when switch is actuated plus an additional 15 to 30 seconds after switch release. MIC same as I/P switch but answers interrogation when microphone button is depressed.

A 13. Vertical Display Indicator - CHECKED.

   a. Contrast/Brightness: (Except KA-6D.) Acceptable variable control.

   b. Impact Point: (Except KA-6D.) Approximately circular and located near or at center of scope (minimum drift and angle of attack). Bright shading and thick black line on right edge of symbol.

   c. Target Symbol: (Except KA-6D) Solid white 1/4-inch square.

   d. Steering Symbol: (Except KA-6D) Hollow white 5/8-inch square.
      A-6B Mod 1: Not displayed in TIAS mode.

   e. Pullup Marker: (Except KA-6D) Black line extending from left outline of path to middle of path when visible.

   f. Release Marker: (Except KA-6D) Horizontal black bar ended by short vertical bar extending to right side of display. Left edge of symbol shall be right of center of display. Horizontal member, located at vertical display center in test, is visible only when IN RANGE light is on or in test.

   g. Flight Path: (Except KA-6D) Perspective black vertical lines converging at a point on indicator, A-6A, B, C Centering is equidistant between the two-lines during takeoff mode.
      A-6B Mod 1: Not displayed in TIAS mode.

   h. Horizon: Interface between ground shading and sky shading. Dark shading at horizon becoming lighter at bottom of raster.

   i. -30° Pitch Line: Line parallel to horizon and extending across display approximately midway between horizon and bottom of raster; black shading.

NAVAIR 01-85ADA-1

NORMAL PROCEDURES
Functional Checkflight

PRETAKEOFF–CONTINUED

PROFILE

j. +30° Pitch Line: Line parallel to display horizon and extending across display above horizon; black shading.

k. +60° Pitch Line: Line parallel to display horizon and extending across display above +30° pitch line; black shading. Line is approximately twice thickness of -30° and +30° pitch lines.

l. +90° Pitch Line: Dashed line (3 to 6 dashes) parallel to display horizon and extending across display above +60° pitch line; black shading. Line is same thickness as +60° pitch line.

m. Clouds: Semiflattened, irregularly curved outline, and black lines on right edges. Bright shading against medium light sky.

n. Ground Texture: Rows of ellipses emanating from horizon line constant in size and rate of movement. Dark shading on background.

o. Electronic Roll Marker: White line extending approximately 3/4 inch down from top of screen perpendicular to horizon line; bright shading.

p. Pitch Trim Markers: Two movable vertical lines extending in approximately 3/4 inches from sides of display and parallel to horizon line; bright shading.

q. Command Heading Lines: Three black lines minimum, four maximum. Apparent convergence point shall be approximately 3/8 inch above path apex. Apparent point of convergence shall be centered horizontally within 3/16 inch of path apex point.

r. Roll Index: Centered on roll pointer ±2°.

s. KA-6D: MA-1 Compass slaved; observe lateral motion of clouds and ground texture.

A 14. KA-6D: Vertical Gyros - CHECKED.
Switch VERT REF from No. 1 to No. 2 and observe attitude input to VGI and VDI.

A 15. KA-6D: Navigation Computer ASN-41 - CHECKED.

a. Function selector switch - STBY

b. Function selector switch - D2 (set destination 2 latitude and longitude)

c. Function selector switch - D1 (set destination 1 latitude and longitude)

d. Function selector switch - STBY (set present position latitude and longitude)

e. Local magnetic variation - SET

f. HSI mode switch - NAV COMP

g. Function selector switch - D1 (check correct bearing and distance)

h. Function selector switch - D2 (check correct bearing and distance)

i. Function selector switch - TEST
Wind direction should read 91° ±1° and windspeed should read 231±3 knots.

A 16. Search Radar Terrain Clearance (SRTC) Presentation - CHECKED.

A 17. Internal In-Flight Refueling System - CHECKED.

a. Refueling power switch - ON

b. Pounds scheduled - SET (some quantity)

3-141

NORMAL PROCEDURES
Functional Checkflight

PRETAKEOFF—CONTINUED
PROFILE

    c. Drogue switch - EXT
       Drogue ejects 1 to 2 feet and STOW/TRAIL indicator shows barber pole.

    d. Hose-reel ground test switch - FULL TRAIL
       Hold until STOW/TRAIL indicator shows TRAIL and READY light comes on.

    e. Fuel transfer switch - AUTO

    f. Hose-reel ground test switch - FUEL RANGE
       Valve open and fuel flow lights come on and pounds scheduled decreases.

    g. Reel response switch - TEST (hold for 5 seconds)
       Drogue retracts.

    h. Drogue switch - RET
       STOW/TRAIL indicator shows STOW.

    i. FUEL TRANS switch - OFF

    j. Refueling power switch - OFF

A   18. A-6C: TRIM TV Presentation - CHECKED.

    a. Reticle: Open center cross in center of field of view, brightness is controllable.

    b. Inverted T: White symbol, 0.63 in. wide, 0.63 in. high.

    c. Vertical Speed Chevron: White inverted or upright chevron 0.63 in. wide, 0.63 in. high. During taxi, climb, or dive, no chevron may be displayed.

    d. Horizon Line: A broken white line 6 in. long consisting of two 2 in. segments separated by a 2 in. space.

    e. +30° Pitch Line: A dashed white line (three dashes) 2 inches long parallel to the horizon line extending across the middle third of the display above the horizon line.

    f. -30° Pitch Line: A white line 2 inches long parallel to the horizon line extending across the middle third of the display below the horizon line.

    g. -60° Pitch Line: A white line 4 inches long parallel to the horizon line extending across the middle two thirds of the display below the -30° pitch line.

A   19. Pilot's Horizontal Display - CHECKED.

    a. Command Steering Bug: Functions smoothly and is positioned dead ahead ±0.5° in UNSTAB/NO STEER and agrees with electronic azimuth cursor within ±2°.

    b. Tape Dials: Windows show range and bearing to cursor intersection.

    c. Variable Filter Installation: Satisfactory day/night control.

    d. Controls: Satisfactory brightness, contrast, persist, and marker control. Persist shall be capable of holding through two full scans on all search displays. Adjustment for blooming may be necessary to obtain usable display.

    e. One Scan: While in silent display, one scan of video on next left-to-right sweep.

    f. Erase: Momentary display similar to no-persist.

NAVAIR 01-85ADA-1

NORMAL PROCEDURES
Functional Checkflight

PRETAKEOFF— CONTINUED

PROFILE

A   20. Optical Sight - CHECKED.

       a. Accuracy: Align movable reticle to fixed reticle. Elevation wheel must be within ±3 mils of zero. Fixed and movable reticle lines must not be displaced by more than one line width.

       b. Controls: In-range and breakaway brightness control operate satisfactorily. FIL 1 and FIL 2 control operate satisfactorily in fixed and movable reticles.

       c. Test: In-range and breakaway displays are present.

       d. Elevation Thumbwheel: Functions satisfactorily.

       e. Displays: Fixed reticle has satisfactory display with manual control of masking. Movable reticle has satisfactory display of steering information.

       f. Parallax: Maximum allowable at 0.0 lead angle is ±3 mils.

A   21. A-6E: Complete search radar/computer turn-on and BIT checks.

A   21A. A-6E TRAM, KA-6D with AFC 161: Complete ARA-63 and ASW-25 BIT checks.

During Taxi

A   22. Brakes - CHECKED.
Check wheel brakes for smooth operation and no pulling tendencies.

A   23. Nosewheel Steering - CHECKED.
Check steering just after leaving chocks, for smooth operation and satisfactory shimmy damping.

A   24. Antiskid - CHECKED.
Check antiskid system for proper functioning. ANTI-SKID caution light shall light if a brake release signal exceeds 3.5 seconds.

A   25. Auxiliary Brake System - CHECKED.
Auxiliary brake cycle gage shall indicate and hold 14 cycles.

A   26. INS - CHECKED.

       a. A-6E: Taxi speed in window A1 approximates aircraft speed.
A-6A, B, C: Bearing = Aircraft true heading +180° ±3°.

       b. Altitude holds steady (±32 feet) during taxi run.

       c. Velocities go to zero to 3 knots when aircraft comes to a stop.

       d. Note heading, velocity, and altitude.

A   27. Doppler Radar
A-6E, KA-6D:
After 5-minute warmup in STBY: Set 20° L or R drift angle and 350 knots groundspeed.

       a. Mode Selector Switch - TEST
Groundspeed should read 121±5 knots and drift 0° ±2°.

       b. Return mode selector to STBY.

A-6A, B, C

       a. VEL: Reference signal on and XMIT/SILENT/OFF switch at XMIT, windspeed shall read 116 to 126 knots.

       b. BRG: Wind direction shall read aircraft true heading +177 to 183°.

Change 2   3-143

NORMAL PROCEDURES
Functional Checkflight

NAVAIR 01-85ADA-1

PRETAKEOFF— CONTINUED

PROFILE

A

Note

Computer must be on.

28. Search Radar - CHECKED.
    A-6A, B, C

    a. ANT. PATT.: Smooth and in phase with switch; meter can be driven to zero.

    b. MAG. FREQ.: Check for smooth transition in phase with switch.

    c. MAG. CUR.: It should not take more than 7 minutes or less than 4.5 minutes for magnetron current to time in. Check that it adjusts with INC-DEC switch to 0.8; adjust to 0.7 at 2,400 prf and must not vary by more than ±0.2 as prf is varied.

    d. XTAL CUR.: Adjusts with INC-DEC switch in manual mode. Check that it can be coarse-tuned for target at any MAG. FREQ. in manual mode. It shall be locked and stable with prf change in AFC mode within two antenna sweeps.

    e. Echo Check: Check that there are at least three pulses visible.

    f. AZ STAB.: ON - Sweep follows AZ cursor; OFF - Sweep stabilized about ADL.

    g. XMIT/SIL: Reduction of video (clutter) when switched from XMIT to SIL and no TC video in silent.

    h. Video: Check that there is uniform focus, and noise and spoking are at acceptable level.

    i. SRCH TRIG: No change or loss of video when switch is cycled from PRI to SEC. Switch shall be cycled to STBY before switching from SEC to PRI.

    j. DIFF GAIN: Satisfactory control.

    k. STC SLOPE/DEPTH: Reduces gain of close-in targets and allows display optimization.

    l. PPI Display: All modes must be operationally functional.

    m. PPI-150: Range markers at approximately every 25 nmi (five or six range markers may be visible). Sweep length approximately 140 to 160 nmi. AZ line may shift slightly from sweep to sweep but must not interfere with mission performance.

    n. PPI-75: Range markers at approximately 25 and 50 nmi. Sweep length approximately 70 to 80 nmi. Radar mapping shall be in excess of 30 miles. AZ line may shift slightly from sweep to sweep but must not interfere with mission performance.

    o. PPI-30: Range marker on both sides of AZ line, less than half total scan width at approximately 10 and 20 nmi. Sweep length at 26 to 29 nmi. Radar mapping shall be 25 miles. AZ line shall be a single, sharp, clear, and continuous uniform line.

    p. Rubber Range: Check that it varies display smoothly from at least 29 nmi to 5 nmi with PPI range control.

    q. Expanded Displays: Switching Criteria - When in WAC, switch to SECT automatically occurs when range cursor drives to less than 44 nmi; then automatically switching to ARE-50 at 27.5 nmi. When in SECT, switch to ARE-25 automatically occurs at 27.5 nmi. Manual switching performs satisfactorily. In ARE-50 Video and Display - Operationally functional with quality equal to PPI-30. In WAC Video and Display - Operationally functional with quality equal to PPI-150.

PRETAKEOFF – CONTINUED

PROFILE

    r. DVRI indicator lights: Satisfactory operation.

    s. DVRI bug: Operates smoothly and drives dead ahead ±1/2° in UNSTAB/NO STEER and agrees with electronic AZ Cursor within ±2°.

A   29. A-6C: DF Set Bit - CHECKED.
Set DF POWER switch to BIT and observe proper indications.

A   30. A-6C: Optical Sensor Platform Operation - CHECKED.

    a. Set OSP mode selector switch to OVRD and OSP power switch to FWD. Platform position indicator will display a barberpole indication immediately and will change to a forward chevron in 14 seconds.

    b. Set CMPTR/MAN switch to MAN and note that OSP can be slewed in azimuth with azimuth cursor switch. Note that OSP can be slewed in elevation by means of elevation slew switch on slew stick.

A   31. A-6C: FLIR Receiver - CHECKED.

    a. IR cool-down normally requires 30 minutes. After cool-down is complete, IR HOT light will go out and system can be checked.

    b. IR BLK display: Observe proper display.

    c. IR WHT display: Observe proper display.

    d. IR intensity: Acceptable variable control.

    e. IR gain: Acceptable variable control.

    f. Depress IR ZOOM button, observe 4:1 magnification.

    g. IR focus: Acceptable variable control when IR ZOOM is engaged. Depress IR ZOOM button, normal display returns.

    h. TV/IR brightness/contrast: Acceptable variable control.

A   32. A-6C: OSP landing gear interlock control - CHECKED.
Set NORM/OVRD switch to NORM, displays will go blank and OSP position indicator will display a barber pole, than an aft chevron in 14 seconds.

A   33. Computer - CHECKED.

A-6A, B, C:

    a. Depress UNSTAB/NO STEER button, cursors go to dead ahead at range selected on the six buttons.

A-6E:

    a. Depress UNSTAB button, cursors go to dead ahead at range entered in keyboard.

A   34. A-6A, C: Track Radar - CHECKED.

    a. Track MAG CUR: It shall not take more than 7 minutes nor less than 4.5 minutes for magnetron current to time in. Adjustable and stabilized at 0.8.

    b. RCVR Tune: AFC will lock on within two sweeps of BNCB meter in track XTAL CUR. Man adjustable by B/N for peak video plus stable operation.

    c. SYNC Set: Adjust until cursor position is constant with T/R in both STANDBY and ON in UNSTAB/NO STEER mode.

    d. Slew Control: Satisfactorily controls track antenna AZ and EL.

NORMAL PROCEDURES
Functional Checkflight

NAVAIR 01-85ADA-1

PRETAKEOFF — CONTINUED

PROFILE

e. Fixed Target Track: Lock and track to gimbal limits good point target at more than 14 nmi. With a good lock, maintain steady tone to gimbal limits. Ground lock, discrete lock, and lock-on indications functioning satisfactorily. AZ cursor shall remain approximately centered on target. Slew capability inhibited after discrete lock. TROT, 5 mil or better circular track accuracy on a point source target at less than 5 mils.

f. TCPPI: Range marker shall be sharp at 2.5 nmi. Video shall present from close range to 5 nmi and shall not shift in AZ from scan to scan.

g. Emergency Search: Video is present from close range to greater than 5 nmi. Video does not shift in AZ from scan to scan.

A 35. A-6B Mod 1: TIAS - CHECKED.
Initiate TIAS in accordance with NATOPS procedures. Press SCP TEST button. PHD and DVI shall display correct test pattern and a go indication.

A 36. Inertial Navigation System (INS) - CHECKED.
Note velocity and altitude.

A 37. Communication, Navigation Identification equipment - CHECKED.

a. Intercommunications Set (ICS): Operates satisfactorily in all modes. COLD position of MIC SEL (ICS/MIC, A-6E TRAM) switch allows transmission only when ICS switch is depressed. HOT position allows transmission at any time.

b. Bomb Tone: Activated upon commit, indicates release of weapon in ATTACK and OFF at release. Satisfactory tone quality during check.

A 38. ECM Test - CHECKED.

IN-FLIGHT

TAKEOFF CHECKS

Before Takeoff

PROFILE

A 39. Compass System - CHECKED. (Except KA-6D)

a. Standby compass shall be accurate to ±5° MAG HEAD when compared to corrected true heading from DVRI.

b. MA-1 compass shall be accurate to ±2° when compared to corrected true heading from DVRI.

ABC 40. Complete Before Takeoff Checklist.

AB 41. Throttle stagger 1/2 inch maximum mismatch with engines in sync at MAX POWER; 1/4 inch maximum mismatch at 86% RPM.

AB 42.

Engine	P-8A, P-8B
RPM%	98.5 ±1.5
EGT	640° to 660° C
Fuel Flow	6,500 to 8,500 pph
Oil Pressure	40 to 50 psi
Power Trim	(In Band)
Hydraulic Pressure	(In Band)

NAVAIR 01-85ADA-1   NORMAL PROCEDURES
Functional Checkflight

IN-FLIGHT—CONTINUED

After Takeoff

PROFILE

AB   43. Monitor engine RPM and EGT.

A   44. Counter-pointer/servo barometric altimeter: Operates smoothly; 0 to 500±50 feet, 500 to 1,000±75 feet, and 1,000 to 5,000±150 feet.

AC   45. Check for proper retraction of main gear, nose gear, flaps, slats, and stabilizer (including transition lights, warning lights, and integrated position indicators).

10,000-FOOT CHECKS (LEVEL CRUISE)

A   46. Flight Indicators - CHECKED.

     a. Angle-of-Attack Indicator: Operating smoothly; OFF indication when no power to indicator. Calibration - read 9.5 to 10 units with clean aircraft at 350 knots.

     b. Mach/Airspeed Indicator: Operating smoothly; 10,000 feet, 0.63 IMN at 340 to 360 KIAS.

     c. Rate of Climb Indicator: Operates smoothly and indicates in zero band in level flight.

     d. MD-1 Turn-and-Bank Indicator (Except A-6E TRAM, KA-6D with AFC 161): Operates smoothly; needle width deflection produces 360° of turn in 4 minutes.

     e. ID-1791/A Turn-and-Slip Indicator (A-6E TRAM, KA-6D with AFC 161): Operates smoothly; needle width deflection produces 360° of turn in 4 minutes.

     f. B-6 Accelerometer: Operates smoothly; the two telltale pointers shall remain at maximum readings until reset (±10% tolerance).

     g. G-Meter (Except A-6E TRAM): Operates smoothly (±10% tolerance).

     h. Horizontal Situation Indicator: Operates smoothly with no excessive excursions.

A   47. IFF/SIF (all modes) - Proper response to interrogation in each mode. I/P provides identification transmission when switch is actuated plus an additional 15 to 30 seconds after switch release. MIC same as I/P switch but answers interrogation when microphone button is depressed.

AB   48. Pressurization - Check at minimum rpm at which level flight can be maintained and with defog OFF. Cabin pressure should be 8,000±750 feet.

AB   49. Air Conditioning - Auto air conditioning operates smoothly, manual maintains selected position.

A   50. Doppler Radar - Checked.

     a. Memory: Memory light goes out when Doppler is within ±10% of inertial groundspeed. Out of memory within 2 minutes in flight.

     b. Attitude Limits: Roll - remains out of memory up to ±33°. Pitch - remains out of memory up to 20° (NU) minimum and -24° (ND) minimum.

     c. Accuracy: Groundspeed and windspeed agree to within ±7 knots of known good inertial velocities. Wind direction agrees within ±5° of known good inertial wind direction provided windspeed is greater than 15 knots.

A   51. Computer - CHECKED.

     a. Steering Presentation: Steering presentation shall be free of perturbations on all displays. Movable reticle, steering symbol, and PHD shall all display compatible steering to preselected targets.

Change 2   3-147

NORMAL PROCEDURES
Functional Checkflight

NAVAIR 01-85ADA-1

IN – FLIGHT – CONTINUED

PROFILE

b. Computer Errors: No error codes or lights observed in navigation or attack.

A 52. Search Radar - CHECKED.

   a. All Displays: All modes must be operationally functional.

   b. One Scan: While in silent display, one scan of video on next left-to-right sweep.

   c. Erase: Momentary display similar to no-persist.

A 53. A-6C: TRIM DISPLAYS - CHECKED.

   a. DF Set: Operates satisfactorily; BEACON light flashes, target flag, (1/8 in. wide 1/2 in. high) displayed on IARM and PHD when target received.

   b. FLIR: Operates satisfactorily; IR WHT and IR BLK displays are satisfactory on IARM and VDI; brightness, contrast satisfactory and controllable. TRIM symbols operate properly. Display ZOOM and IR ZOOM function correctly.

   c. LLLTV: Operates satisfactorily; TV display satisfactory on IARM and VDI, brightness, contrast satisfactory and controllable. TRIM symbols operate properly. Display zoom functions correctly.

A 54. A-6C: OSP positioning - CHECKED.

   a. OSP position responds to slew stick inputs in azimuth and elevation when CMPTR/MAN switch is at CMPTR. Slew rates are satisfactory, movement is smooth. OSP position responds to movement of AZIMUTH CURSOR switch and elevation slew switch when CMPTR/MAN switch is at MAN.

   b. With a track radar lock-on, OSP tracks target in azimuth and elevation.

AC 55. Control trim check (After excessive loads in flight or on landing)

   a. With directional and lateral trim in takeoff position, wings held at level attitude, airspeed increased in 50 knot increments from 250 to 550 knots, maintaining 10,000 feet. Note ballwidths off-center from turn and slip indicator at each 50-knot increment. Ballwidths off-center must be 3/4 or less.

   b. Maximum lateral stick force to hold wings level is 3 pounds.

40,000—FOOT CHECKS (LEVEL CRUISE)

AB 56. Pressurization - Check at minimum rpm at which level flight can be maintained and with defog OFF. Cabin pressure should be 15,850 to 17,690 feet.

AB 57. Defogging System - Check proper operation.

AB 58. Engines - CHECKED.

   a. Full Power:

      (1) RPM - Note
          94% to 98% rpm

      (2) EGT - Note
          630° to 660°C maximum

      (3) Fuel Flow - Note
          2,300 to 2,700 pph

IN—FLIGHT — CONTINUED

PROFILE		
	b.	Idle (for two engines without PPC 185) (Check engines alternately):
		(1) RPM - Note
		(2) EGT - Note
		(3) Fuel Flow - Note
	c.	Low engine speed (for engines with PPC 185) (75% RPM):
		(1) RPM - Note
		(2) EGT - Note
		(3) Fuel Flow - Note
A	59.	Mach Airspeed Indicator - CHECKED. Operates smoothly; 40,000 feet, 0.84 IMN at 255 to 265 KIAS.
A	60.	Search Radar Maximum Range - Note

20,000—FOOT CHECKS (LEVEL CRUISE)

A	61.	AUX UHF (Except A-6E TRAM) - CHECKED. Operates satisfactorily; large needle on HSI indicates magnetic bearing (±10°) to station unless UHF-ADF is selected.
A	62.	TACAN - CHECKED. Controls operate satisfactorily with SEL switch in REC position, bearing data are displayed. With SEL switch in T/R, both bearing and range are indicated. Identification signal is heard in headsets when selected and volume is controllable. Range and bearing displayed on HSI with no undesirable excursions. With antenna select switch in any position, lock-on occurs within 30 seconds of station selected.
AC	63.	Automatic Flight Control System - CHECKED.
		a. Stability Augmentation (300 KIAS): Check for proper operation. Engage and disengage trim shifts not to exceed ±.6°/sec in pitch or roll. Rate damping satisfactory about all axes. Engage transient shall be nonobjectionable in nature.
		b. Roll Attitude-Hold (ASW-40; HDG OFF): Tolerance ±1° limited by readability. Effective from 3° to 7° to 60° -3°, -6° from left and right bank. If engaged beyond 60° -3°, -6° limit, the aircraft will return to 60° -3°, -6°. Control stick disconnect-automatic reengage after release of lateral stick commands.
		c. Pitch Attitude Hold: Tolerance ±1° limited by readability. Effective from -60° +6°, -1° to +25° +1°, -4°. Out-of-limit engagements will return aircraft to stated limits. Control stick disconnect-automatic reengage after release of longitudinal stick commands.
		d. Heading Hold (ASW-40 - Heading Switch in NORM): Automatic whenever roll attitude is less than 3° to 7°. Tolerance ±1/2° limited by readability. Control stick disconnect-automatic reengage after release of lateral stick commands.

NORMAL PROCEDURES
Functional Checkflight

NAVAIR 01-85ADA-1

IN – FLIGHT – CONTINUED

PROFILE

    e. Altitude Hold: Altitude hold shall not be engaged with climb or dive rates in excess of 1,000 feet/min. Tolerance for bank angles less than 30°, ±45 feet. With 5% rpm change, note that altitude hold conforms to the above tolerance. Period of oscillation shall not be greater than 30 seconds. Control stick disconnect-automatic reengage after release of longitudinal stick commands.

    f. Mach Hold: Stable flight engage-hold aircraft within ±0.02 mach of that mach that existed at engagement (for bank angles less than 30°). Flight check - from cruise to idle descent from 20,000 feet. Change in mach number shall be ±0.02 mach and stable in descent. Control stick disconnect - automatic reengage after release of longitudinal stick commands.

    g. Roll Command (ASW-40; N/A KA-6D): Accepts computer-derived roll angle command to null steering. Limited to 30° left and right banks.

    h. Automatic Carrier Landing (ASW-40): Engages smoothly. Control stick disconnect - reverts to STAB AUG after manual input of 10 pounds fore-and-aft or 7 pounds laterally.

A   64. Mach/Airspeed Indicator - CHECKED.
    Operates smoothly; 20,000 feet, 0.54 IMN at 245 to 255 KIAS.

AB   65. Anti-G - CHECKED.
    Automatic inflation of g-suit for test; suit begins at 2.2 g's.

A   66. Search Radar - CHECKED.

    a. SEARCH TRIG: No change or less of video when switch is cycled from PRI to SEC. Switch shall be cycled to STBY before switching from SEC to PRI (A-6A, B, C).

    b. RNG: Satisfactory control.

A   67. Fuel System - CHECKED.

    a. Totalizer: Reads ±300 lb +2% of actual fuel except that totalizer shall never read less than zero. The preceding criteria apply only when selectable needle is set on a station that has a fuel tank attached. When selectable needle is set to an external station that does not have a fuel tank attached, the following criteria will apply: (±600 lb +4% of the actual fuel), except that totalizer should never read less than zero.

    b. Fuel Quantity Gage: Large pointer reads quantity in main tanks. Small needle indicates quantity of fuel in tanks selected on fuel management panel.

    c. Transfer: Capable of transfer of all wing fuel. When main tank drops below 6,500 to 7,500 lb, automatic transfer begins raising the quantity in main tank between 7,000 lb and 8,000 lb. Uneven transfer rates will be allowed to maximum of one mark wing heaviness.

    d. Fuel Dump: Briefly check wing dump and fuselage dump.

5,000-FOOT CHECKS (LEVEL CRUISE)

A   68. KA-6D: Internal In-Flight Refueling System - CHECKED.

    a. Refueling power switch - ON

    b. Drogue switch - EXT
    STOW/TRAIL indicator shows barber pole in transit and TRAIL when fully extended. Hydraulic pressure light will go out and READY light will come on.

    c. Fuel transfer switch - AUTO

    d. Pounds scheduled - SET (some quantity above 100 pounds)

NAVAIR 01-85ADA-1

NORMAL PROCEDURES
Functional Checkflight

IN—FLIGHT — CONTINUED

PROFILE

    e. Reel response switch - TEST (hold for 5 seconds)
READY light will go out, and valve open light and fuel transfer light will come on. On K1 thru K52 not incorporating AFC No. 298, STOW/TRAIL indicator continues to shown TRAIL, on K53 and on and those incorporating AFC No. 298, STOW/TRAIL indicator shows barber pole when hose leaves full trail position.

    f. Reel response switch - RESET
Fuel flow and valve open lights go out, and fuel READY light comes on.

    g. Drogue switch - RET
Hose retracts, indicator shows barber pole when in transit and STOW when retracted. Hydraulic pressure light will come on.

    h. Refueling power switch - OFF.

A   69. Ram-Air Turbine (RAT) - CHECKED.
A maximum force of 70 lb is acceptable for operation of the ram-air turbine control.

AC   70. TRIM - CHECKED.
Tolerance from TRIM indicator zero reference - lateral ±1/2 unit and rudder ±1/8 unit.

A   71. Angle-of-Attack Indicator - CHECKED.
Operates smoothly - reads to ±1/2 units. In a (power approach) landing configuration (takeoff flaps), 4,000 lb fuel, 84% rpm, AOA reads 20 units at 111 ±3 KIAS. For every 500 lb of fuel, add or subtract .84 KIAS.

A   72. Search Radar - CHECKED.

    a. STC SLOPE/DEPTH: Reduces gain of close-in targets and allows display optimization.

    b. SRTT: (A-6A, B, C): Lock-on at 5 nmi - track light SR on, track switch on, and track radar power switch on.

A   73. A-6A, C: Track Radar - CHECKED.

    a. Fixed Target Track: Lock and track to gimbal limits good point target at more than 14 nmi. With a good lock, maintain steady tone to gimbal limits. Ground lock, discrete lock, and lock-on indications functioning satisfactorily. AZ cursor should remain approximately centered on target. Slew capability inhibited after discrete lock. TROT, 5 mil or better circular track accuracy on a point source target at less than 5 mils.

A   74. Computer - CHECKED.

    a. Attacks: Check for satisfactory performance, including COP check.

    b. Bomb tone in manual.

    c. PPI displays

    d. Expanded displays

    e. Lock-ons.

A   75. AMTI: MAX range check and tracking.

3-151

NORMAL PROCEDURES
Functional Checkflight

NAVAIR 01-85ADA-1

IN—FLIGHT — CONTINUED

500—FOOT AGL CHECKS

PROFILE

A
76. AAU-19 Altimeter and Radar Altimeter - CHECKED.
With AAU-19 altimeter in STANDBY and a corrected barometric setting, maximum allowable difference compared with radar altimeter at 500 feet and 300 KIAS is 85 feet. Attitude limits for radar altimeter determined over flat terrain are: roll ±30° and pitch ±50°.

A
77. SRTC - CHECKED.

    a. Ten shades of grey.

    b. Ten range contours.

    c. Clearance accuracy.

    d. Selectable range coding.

A
78. E-Scan - CHECKED.

    a. Video: It shall be possible to adjust the pilot's control so as to provide a clean, continuous video return between 1/8 inch and 1/4 inch from minimum slant range, out to a range of 5 nmi or more.

    b. Flight Line: Sharp usable dotted line extending across the display.

    c. Range Markers: Clean and sharp - one at every 2.5 nmi (the range markers occurring at start and end may not be visible).

    d. Controls: All display controls operate satisfactorily.

A
79. TCPPI - CHECKED.

    a. Range Marker: Sharp at 2.5 nmi.

    b. Display: ±15° and centered on CRT.

    c. Control: MRI and RCVR gain control satisfactory.

    d. Video: Present from close range to 5 nmi. Video does not shift in azimuth from scan to scan.

    e. Qualitative Check: Video is lost when aircraft is pitched up and returns when aircraft is pitched down (scans about aircraft velocity vector).

A
80. Low Altitude Warning System (LAWS) - CHECKED.
Whenever aircraft radar altitude penetrates the low limit index (set on radar altimeter) a 2 +1.0, -.25 second tone alternating at 1.5 to 2.5 cps between approximately 700 and 1,700 cps will be heard.

AB
81. Approach Power Compensator System (APCS) - CHECKED.

    a. System Engagement: Place aircraft in approach configuration. Place throttle friction lever to OFF. Set RH and LH engines to approach speed. Place temperature switch in appropriate position for ambient temperature (HOT - temperature greater than 80° F/26.7° C; STANDARD - temperature between 80° F/26.7° C and 40° F/4.4° C; COLD - temperatures less than 40° F/4.4° C). Set control switch to STBY. Note that APCS STBY light is lit. Engage system. Upon release of control switch, switch shall remain in ENGAGE position and APCS STBY light should be out. Engagement of system can be checked by making pitch changes and noting throttle movement. (A micro switch on friction lever shall cut out APCS when friction lever is advanced in increase friction direction.)

3-152

NAVAIR 01-85ADA-1

NORMAL PROCEDURES
Functional Checkflight

IN-FLIGHT — CONTINUED

PROFILE

b. System Disengage: Place control switch to STBY. Throttles shall be free for manual use and APCS STBY light shall come on.

c. Override Check: Manually override system by opening each throttle individually. Control switch shall drop to STBY and STBY light shall come on. Manual override forces should be 8 to 12 lb.

d. Off Speed Engagement: Engage system at 5 knots indicated airspeed above and below referenced AOA (22 units) airspeed. Temperature switch to appropriate outside air temperature. Airspeed shall return to within 2.0 KIAS of approach speed within 4 seconds after engagement.

e. Limit Checks: Perform pullups to hold AOA greater than 22 units. Throttles shall drive to maximum stop 96 to 100% rpm. Perform pushover to hold AOA less than 22 units. Throttles shall drive to minimum stop 71 to 79% rpm.

f. Approach: Observe APCS capability to maintain reference AOA 22 units during FCLP approach. Observe disengagement of touchdown.

A 82. INS NAV accuracy, check the following:

a. INS VEL

b. MVC VEL

c. AVC VEL

d. DOPPLER VEL

A 83. Present Position Update - CHECKED.
A-6A, B, C: Encoder Check if Required - CHECKED.

a. Pitch

b. Roll

c. Heading

LANDING

LANDING CHECKS

PROFILE
AC 84. Landing Gear - CHECKED.

a. Warning Lights: WHEELS warning light flashes when all three gears are not down and locked and both throttles are less than 85% and flaps are extended. Wheels transition light shall light during all gear transitions until all landing gears are locked.

b. Position Indicator: UP in window when all gears are up and locked and doors closed. Picture of wheel appears when all gears down and locked. Barber pole when gear is not locked or door is not closed. Nose-gear indication will indicate TOW LINK if tow link is down or nose gear is cocked (indexer will flash).

c. Arresting Gear: Hook transition warning light shall be on when hook is cycling between stow and trail or trail and stow positions. Approach lights and approach light indexer will flash until hook is released to trail position with landing gear down and hook bypass switch in ARREST.

d. Flaperon Pop-Up - CHECKED.

Change 2   3-153

NORMAL PROCEDURES
Functional Checkflight

LANDING — CONTINUED

PROFILE

A
- e. Wing Flaps and Slats - CHECKED.
- f. Wing-Tip Speed Brakes - CHECKED.
- g. Antiskid - CHECKED.

85. Landing Mode - CHECKED.
   - a. Steering: Check that accurate vertical and horizontal steering commands are provided.
   - b. OAP: Check steering with OAP selected.

PRIOR TO SHUTDOWN

A
86. INS - CHECKED.
   - a. Altitude: Holds steady during taxi run.
   - b. Velocities: Note when aircraft comes to a stop, after OFF ERASE selected.

section IV
FLIGHT PROCEDURES

TABLE OF CONTENTS

PART 1 OPERATING TECHNIQUES	4-2
Familiarization and Transition	4-2
Engine Operation	4-2
Compressor Stalls	4-2
Engine Ratings	4-3
Exhaust Gas Temperature	4-3
Flameout	4-3
Burner Can Blowout	4-3
Cooling Before Shutdown	4-4
Smoke After Shutdown	4-4
Fuel Management	4-4
Wing-Tank Purging System	4-4
Aerodynamic Braking	4-4
Approach Power Compensator Technique	4-4
PART 2 FLIGHT CHARACTERISTICS	4-5
Climb Characteristics	4-5
Normal Stalls	4-5
Deep Stall Penetration	4-5
Accelerated Stalls	4-5
Post Stall Gyrations	4-10
Spins	4-10
Erect Spins	4-10
Erect Spin Recovery	4-11
Inverted Spins	4-11
Inverted Spin Recovery	4-12
Spin Recovery on Instruments	4-12
Flight Controls	4-13
Level Flight	4-13
Pilot-Induced Lateral Oscillation	4-13
Dives	4-13
Speedbrake Blowback	4-13
Single-Engine Operation	4-13
Single-Engine Flight Characteristics	4-13
Single-Engine Flight Performance	4-18
Flight With External Loads	4-18
Backup Flight Controls Hydraulic System	4-18
Longitudinal Control Rate Limiting	4-18
Trim Changes	4-18
Dihedral Effect	4-18
PART 3 FORMATION AND TACTICS	4-19
Formation Takeoff	4-19
Rendezvous	4-19
Turning Rendezvous	4-19
Circling Rendezvous	4-19
TACAN Circling Rendzvous	4-21
Running Rendezvous	4-21
ADF Running Rendezvous	4-21
ADF Circling Rendezvous	4-21
Low-Visibility Rendezvous/Rendezvous On Different Model Aircraft	4-21
Safety Rules for Rendezvous	4-21
Formation	4-22
Free Cruise Formation (4 Aircraft Division)	4-22
Parade Formation	4-22
Formation Instrument Approach	4-22
PART 4 AIR REFUELING	4-24
Air Refueling Receiver Technique	4-24
Pilot Tanking Technique (Receiver)	4-24
Night Refueling	4-24

FLIGHT PROCEDURES
Operating Techniques

NAVAIR 01-85ADA-1

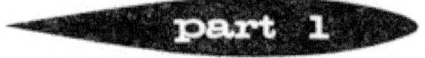 # Operating Techniques

INTRODUCTION

The information for this section was supplied by flight observations of test pilots. As an overall assessment of the flight characteristics of aircraft, the aircraft is fully controllable in all normal speeds and maneuvers. The stall warnings are generally characteristic of slower, conventional aircraft, and landing speed is relatively slow. The A-6 is adequately powered, which is reflected in its takeoff and climb acceleration, and in its ability to carry a substantial external stores load, safely.

FAMILIARIZATION AND TRANSITION

Procedures for the accomplishment of transition and familiarization training are promulgated by the Unit Commander through the Operations Officer. The amount of time required to complete transition and familiarization will vary, depending upon the experience level within each crew category. The training of each crew and each squadron should be directed toward improving crew coordination in the complete mission system.

The training syllabus will be in accordance with the outline in Section II.

ENGINE OPERATION

COMPRESSOR STALLS

Compressor stalls result when one or all of the compressor blades are operating at too high an angle of attack. Normally, the compressor blades are kept in a desirable angle of attack by maintaining air velocity in proportion with engine rpm. Hence, anything that would affect inlet air velocity or engine rpm will either increase or decrease the possibility of compressor stall. In the J-52 P-8A/B engine, compressor stalls are minimized automatically by the compressor bleed system and the fuel control system, but pilot technique can also directly affect the possibility of a compressor stall.

Stall Warnings

Compressor stall warnings vary greatly in degree and intensity. Pulsations through the airframe and retorts from the engine are the most obvious warnings. The noises from the engine can vary from low-intensity pops to loud bangs. The most subtle indication is the inability of the engine to respond to forward throttle movement.

Minimizing Compressor Stalls

The engine bleed control system is used to maintain a desirable angle of attack on the compressor blades by maintaining a proper relationship between inlet air velocity and engine rpm.

When the bleed control senses an unstable pressure ratio, twelfth-stage compressor bleed air pressure is transmitted to a series of 15 intercompressor bleed valves, opening the bleed valves. Air from the low compressor discharge section is then dumped into the engine compartment, tending to restore the air inlet velocity/rpm relationship. The bleed override control automatically locks out any signal from the pressure ratio bleed control below approximately 0.5 IMN, allowing the compressor bleed valves to remain closed. Another automatically operated safeguard against a compressor stall is contained in the engine fuel control system. Since the engine is more susceptible to compressor stalls at low inlet-air temperature and at certain rpm's, it is necessary to limit acceleration fuel flow schedules to avoid a stall. If fuel is introduced at a rate that will increase pressure before the inlet pressure, air flow, and rpm increase, the burner pressure will increase to a point where airflow in blocked through the engine, causing the compressor to stall. The engine fuel control senses the condition of rpm and inlet temperature and schedules a correct amount of fuel.

It would seem that these automatic functions for preventing a compressor stall would be enough to eliminate a stall. However, the engine was set up only for normal operation. One variable not covered by engine adjustments is pilot technique. When operating in conditions marginal for compressor stalls, the responsibility remains with the pilot to aid the automatic functions rather than to rely on them. The flight conditions which can cause a compressor stall must be kept in mind and erratic or abrupt throttle movements must be avoided. An in-flight refueling hookup is a good example where throttle technique could be overlooked. During flight attitudes that affect air inlet flow, throttle technique is even more important due to the added factor of distortion at the air inlet. If poor throttle technique, marginal flight attitudes, and uncoordinated flight are combined, the conditions are ideal for a compressor stall.

Lessening the Stall Effect

Several techniques can be employed to reduce a compressor stall effect. If a rising EGT accompanies an rpm drop, this is an indication of a stall. Retard the throttle to prevent engine damage. If the stall is eliminated, then slowly advance the throttle to the desired thrust level. Avoid erratic throttle movements. If the stall resulted from excessive distortion of airflow at the air inlet, and a drop in rpm without a rising EGT is observed, increasing the thrust setting to about 90%, or increasing the airspeed by decreasing rate of climb, or by dropping the nose will usually eliminate the stall. Be especially careful to maintain coordinated flight. If the stall is uncontrollable, shut down the engine. Although a compressor stall is not normally dangerous, if the stall continues, it could cause engine damage.

ENGINE RATINGS

Engine ratings were not set up as limits which, if exceeded, would result in the engine falling apart. Overall engine life for a particular installation is first determined. This life is broken down into percentages which reflect the time used at different thrust settings. With this information, allowable limits are set. In normal engine life, when engine time is used up, the engine is ready for overhaul. The overhaul times are used to plan logistical support of the aircraft. If premature breakdowns occur, this can seriously affect squadron strength by causing shortages of necessary items. A better understanding of engine ratings will prevent a pilot from inadvertently exceeding engine limits and will bring into focus the real reason engine limits are set.

EXHAUST GAS TEMPERATURE

Excessive temperature causes deformation of sheet metal parts and, if allowed to persist, will result in sagging and subsequent structural failure. Consequently, exhaust gas temperature (EGT) is the most important factor in engine durability. This does not mean that EGT is to be used as a limit in place of a time at maximum thrust settings. However, always reduce a thrust setting to maintain an EGT limit.

In its normal function, the exhaust gas temperature conveys information on how well the engine is performing at a desired thrust setting. Normally, EGT will be kept within limits by the fuel control. If temperatures still increase or stabilize at too high a temperature, retard the throttle. Whenever the EGT becomes uncontrollable, shut down the engine. Excessive temperatures should be noted for maximum reached and for the length of time at the overtemperature. The temperature should be reported as a discrepancy for appropriate maintenance action.

CAUTION

The J52 P-8A/B engine fuel control will not maintain EGT within limits above 35,000 feet at military power. It is therefore necessary that pilots monitor EGT carefully under these conditions and maintain EGT within limits by retarding the throttle.

Exhaust Gas Temperature and Inlet Icing

Exhaust gas temperature will begin to increase in an icing condition usually as a result of decreased airflow through the engine. The decreased airflow is sensed by the fuel control, resulting in an increased fuel flow to the combustion chamber. This causes the EGT to rise. Since a rise in EGT follows the buildup of ice, EGT is a reliable indication of the beginning of ice formation at the air inlet.

FLAMEOUT

A single-engine flameout is not normally a dangerous situation. Nevertheless, the cause of the flameout should be ascertained to prevent a similar occurrence at critical altitudes and airspeeds. A flameout usually occurs if the fuel-air-ratio is either too rich, or too lean to maintain combustion. The fuel control unit automatically responds to varying conditions; however, severe changes in normal flight conditions, such as those which result in compressor stalls, heavy moisture ingestion, or excessive throttle movements at altitude, can exceed the fuel control's ability to react, and will probably result in a flameout.

Indications of a flameout are a loss of thrust, dropping EGT, and dropping rpm; an air start should be initiated as soon as possible while engine rpm is still high. Attempt to avoid the conditions that set up the flameout initially. If the flameout occurs during an icing condition, or during moisture ingestion, use the air start switches and anti-icing for the duration of the condition. However, the starting ignition should not be used indiscriminately, because premature breakdown of the igniter plugs will result. If it is determined that the flameout resulted from an engine malfunction, shut down the engine.

BURNER CAN BLOWOUT

Burner can blowout is an engine condition where one or more nozzles of the four-nozzle cluster have been blown out and failed to relight. One or more burner cans may be affected.

This condition may occur in aircraft with PPC No. 185 incorporated. During idle power, slow-speed descents (below 250 KIAS) or idle power, constant-altitude aircraft decelerations, the burner can blowout condition is characterized by an idle droop. This may result in engine hangups of up to 10 seconds duration during subsequent engine acceleration.

Burner can blowout may also occur during high-speed (in excess of 350 KIAS) idle power descents. In this case, the engine may enter a sub-idle

FLIGHT PROCEDURES
Operating Techniques

condition (20%-30% rpm), which will require shutdown and subsequent relight in order to regain normal operation. If the engine does not enter a sub-idle condition, acceleration hangups may still occur; however, they will probably clear within 3-5 seconds. There will be no warning of burner can blowout or of an impending sub-idle condition during a high-speed descent.

COOLING BEFORE SHUTDOWN

Before shutdown (except for emergency or operational necessity), the engines should be operated at idle for 3 to 5 minutes to allow engine temperature to stabilize, and then at 75% rpm for 30 seconds to permit oil scavenging.

Note

If operating conditions preclude oil scavenging at 75%, no damage will result; however, the possibility of oil overflow from the accessory gear box exists.

SMOKE AFTER SHUTDOWN

If smoke is emitted from the engine after shutdown, determine the cause. White vapor indicates fuel vaporization. This does not harm the engine, but is potentially dangerous because of the fire hazard in the immediate area. If heavy black smoke is emitted, this is indicative of burning oil or fuel. If the GTC is available, crank the affected engine. If the smoke persists, use firefighting equipment to extinguish the fire.

FUEL MANAGEMENT

Since fuel transfer occurs as the result of differential air pressure within the fuel tanks and gravity flow, fuel management is directly related to pressure regulation. Overall fuel management is handled automatically when the wing drop-tank transfer switch is in the normal position. It has been found however, that by controlling fuel from the drop tanks, the range of the aircraft can be increased.

By using fuel from two drop tanks at a time, and then jettisoning the empty tanks, the aircraft reaches a cleaner configuration in the shortest time. The wing drop-tank transfer switch (WING DROP TANK TRANS) selects the transfer from the wing drop tanks. Fuel can be selectively transferred from either the outboard or inboard tanks, or all drop tanks simultaneously.

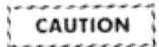
CAUTION

Tests have indicated that possible overpressurization may occur if all four drop tanks empty simultaneously.

Through the use of the wing-tank pressure switch on the fuel management panel, the wing and drop tanks can be pressurized on the ground or transfer can be stopped in flight. The switch positions and their functions are covered in Section I.

WING-TANK PURGING SYSTEM

Wing tanks may be purged by placing the wing dump switch to DUMP. Purging will continue as long as the wing switch remains in DUMP.

Spring-loaded, zero-leak check valves are used for purging. The valves are set to open at 0.5 psi pressure differential. When air is sensed in the wing-tank shutoff valves, a signal is sent to the wing-tank pressure regulator, shuttling off pressure to the wing tanks. When the check valve sense the preset pressure differential, the valves open, purging the tanks. The fuel vapors are evacuated through the wing dump valves, which are electrically opened when the wing dump switch is actuated.

AERODYNAMIC BRAKING

After touchdown and flaperon pop-up activation, raise the nose to 21 units angle of attack and allow the aircraft to decelerate. As indicated airspeed approaches 80 knots, smoothly lower the nose to the runway and commence normal braking as necessary to slow aircraft to taxi speed.

APPROACH POWER COMPENSATOR TECHNIQUE

The technique required for an APC (aircraft incorporating AFC No. 199) approach differs from a manual approach in that all glide slope corrections are made by changing aircraft attitude. Since this technique violates the basic rule that altitude is primarily controlled by throttle, practice is required to develop the proper control habits necessary to use APC. For the APC to perform satisfactorily, smooth attitude control is essential. Large abrupt attitude changes result in excessive thrust changes. Close-in corrections are very critical. A large attitude correction for a high-in-close condition will produce an excessive power reduction and can easily result in a hard landing. If a high-in-close situation develops, the recommended procedure is to stop meatball motion and not attempt to recenter it. A low-in-close condition is difficult to correct with APC and usually results in an over-the-top bolter. It may be necessary to manually override APC in order to safely recover from a low-in-close condition. Throughout the approach, the pilot should keep his hand on the throttles in the event it is necessary to manually override the APC.

Flight Characteristics

CLIMB CHARACTERISTICS

A typical climb schedule for the basic aircraft is 310 KIAS to .70 IMN. For best fuel consumption, military power should be maintained during a climb. Longitudinal stability is positive throughout the climb regime.

STALLS

NORMAL STALLS

The following stall description is applicable to normal 1-g stalls approached at a deceleration rate of approximately 1 to 2 knots per second. At greater deceleration rates, pilot perceptibility of stall warning buffet as well as the time available for reaction to prevent the stall is reduced and stall penetration tends to be deeper. Stall characteristics do not appreciably change with the addition of wing and/or fuselage stores or as a result of assymmetrical power, speed brake position, or STAB AUG engagement.

Stall warning in flaps/slats down configurations (takeoff, wave-off, power approach, and land) occurs 10 to 15 knots prior to stall and is characterized by light buffet at onset, increasing to moderate buffet as stall is approached. Flaperon effectiveness decreases as stall is approached; however, sufficient control authority is available to maintain wings-level flight up to the stall. Rudder is effective for roll control during the approach to the stall and at stall. The use of the flaperons alone to maintain wings-level flight during the approach to the stall may induce a lateral oscillation due to high roll inertia and decreasing lateral control effectiveness. This characteristic is particularly noticeable when carrying wing stores. Stall in the flaps/slats down configuration is defined by a loss of longitudinal control characterized by the aircraft breaking in and out of stall while holding aft stick. In the takeoff and wave-off configurations with military power, a mild longitudinal pitch-up is experienced at stall; however, this phenomenon is only momentary and does not create a dangerous situation.

Stall warning in flaps/slats up configurations (power, cruise, and glide) is characterized by wing rock and a gradual loss of lateral control effectiveness beginning approximately 20 to 25 knots prior to stall followed by light buffet at 7 to 10 knots prior to stall. Stall in the flaps/slats up configurations is defined by a complete loss of lateral control with the aircraft in a sideslip and roll maneuver. Stall recovery in either the flap/slats up or down configuration is immediate and is achieved by applying forward stick to reduce angle of attack and increase airspeed. No excessive altitude loss is encountered during recovery except in the high gross weight/high drag loadings where slow aircraft acceleration increases the time and altitude required to effect a safe recovery.

WARNING

During NATC flight testing under controlled conditions and using optimum recovery technique, up to 2,000 feet of altitude was required for recovery from land configuration stalls in the heavy gross weight/high drag loadings.

DEEP STALL PENETRATION

Three factors combine to make the aircraft highly susceptible to deep stall penetration and progressive stalls during the recovery:

  a. With power reduction or nose-up attitude change, rapid deceleration occurs at heavy gross weight/high drag loadings. In addition to the rapid deceleration, the stall speed increases approximately 12 knots with power reduction from military to idle rpm.

  b. Good longitudinal control effectiveness (pitch response with longitudinal control stick movement). This is particularly evident with extended control travel.

  c. At stall, light longitudinal stick forces induce a tendency to overcontrol aircraft attitude prior to attaining sufficient airspeed for recovery.

Note

To prevent entering a progressive stall, the angle-of-attack indicator should be used as the primary stall recovery instrument.

Stall airspeeds for various configurations are plotted as a function of gross weight in figures 4-1 through 4-4.

ACCELERATED STALLS

Accelerated stalls are preceded by light airframe buffet 30 to 40 knots prior to stall, increasing progressively to moderate buffet at stall. Lateral instability in the form of wing rocking is coincident

FLIGHT PROCEDURES
Flight Characteristics
NAVAIR 01-85ADA-1

STALL SPEEDS

P-8 ENGINE

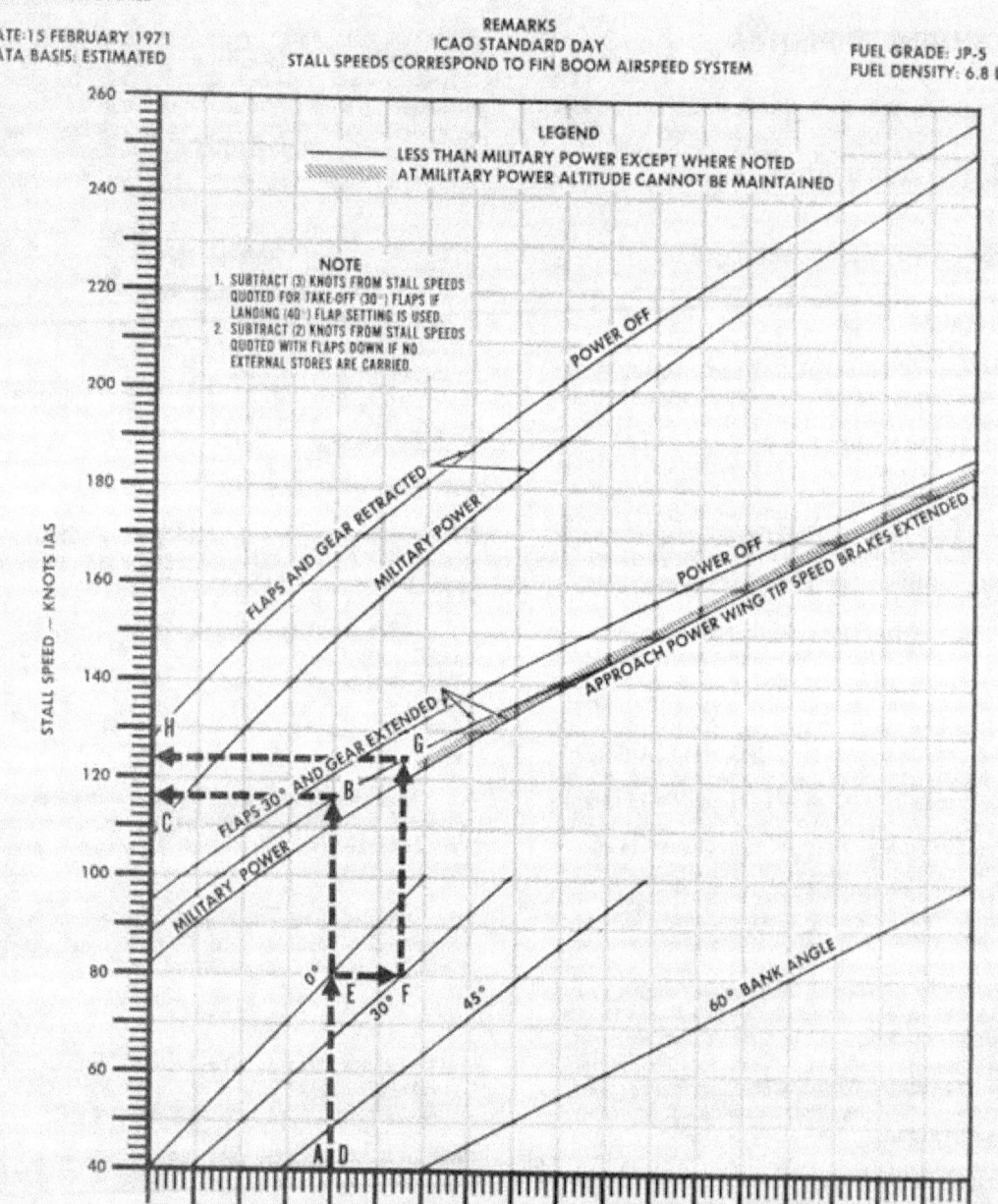

Figure 4-1

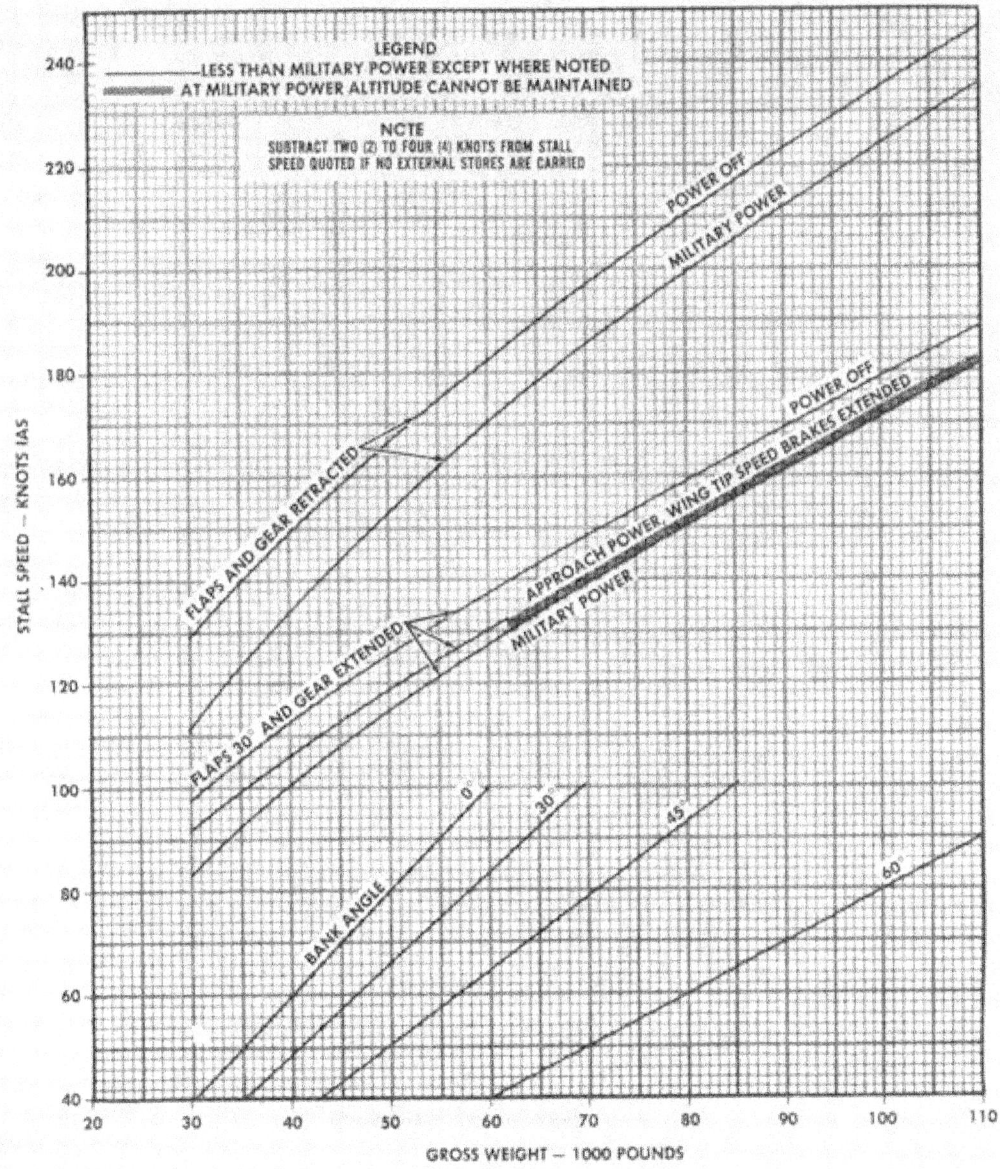

Figure 4-2

FLIGHT PROCEDURES
Flight Characteristics

NAVAIR 01-85ADA-1

STALL SPEEDS

P-8 ENGINES

NO EXTERNAL STORES
5000 FEET
POWER OFF

AIRCRAFT CONFIGURATION:
FLAPS UP, GEAR UP

DATE: 18 OCTOBER 1965
DATA BASIS: FLIGHT TEST

REMARKS
ICAO STANDARD DAY

FUEL GRADE: JP-5
FUEL DENSITY: 6.8 LB/GAL

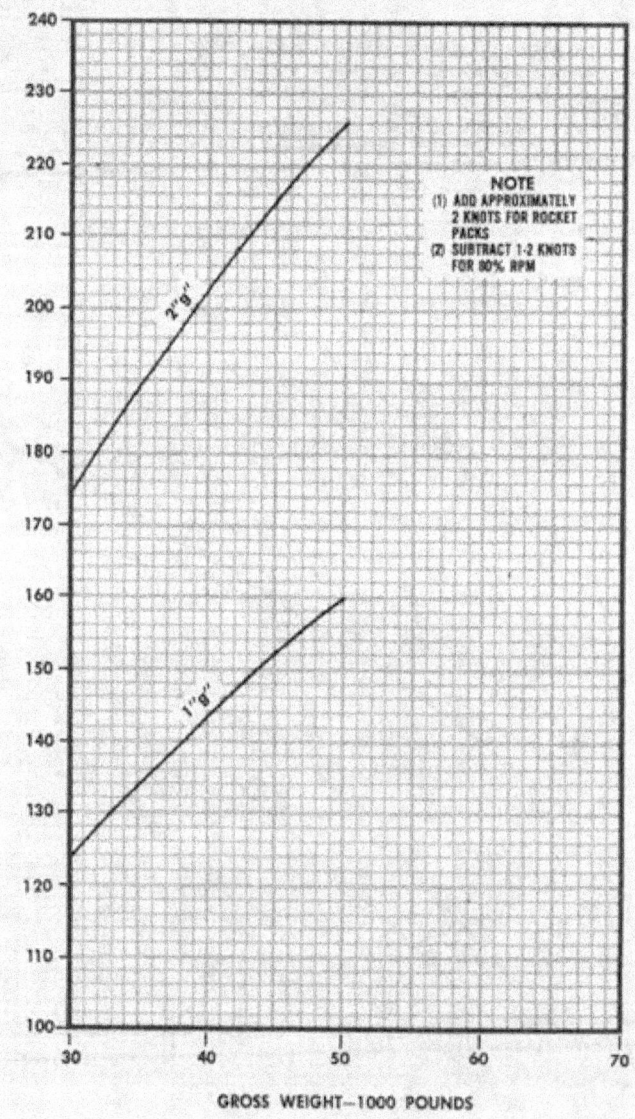

Figure 4-3

NAVAIR 01-85ADA-1

FLIGHT PROCEDURES
Flight Characteristics

P-8 ENGINE
A-6C

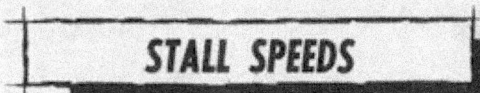
STALL SPEEDS

NO EXTERNAL STORES
5000 FEET
POWER OFF

AIRCRAFT CONFIGURATION:
FLAPS UP, GEAR UP

DATE: 1 APRIL 1970
DATA BASIS: FLIGHT TEST

REMARKS
ICAO STANDARD DAY

FUEL GRADE: JP-5
FUEL DENSITY: 6.8 LB/GAL

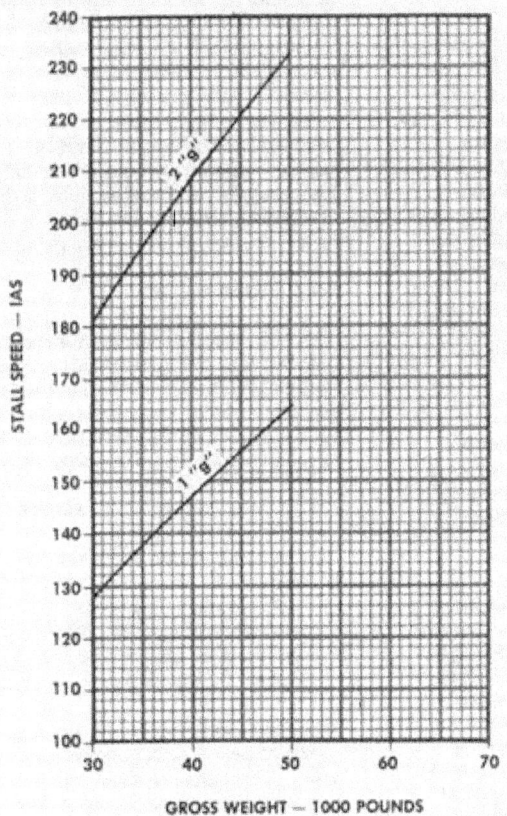

NOTE
(1) ADD APPROXIMATELY TWO (2) KNOTS FOR EXTERNAL STORES

A-ADA1-587

Figure 4-4

FLIGHT PROCEDURES
Flight Characteristics

with airframe buffet but remains at a low level and is correctable with flaperons. In a gradual approach to a 2-g accelerated stall, a decrease in lateral control effectiveness beginning approximately with onset of stall warning buffet provides additional warning of a near-stall condition. However, during high-g high angle-of-attack maneuvering, later control loss will most likely not be noticed and normal prestall airframe buffet will be the primary warning of an impending accelerated stall. If stall warning is not recognized or normal acceleration is not reduced, the aircraft will enter an accelerated stall characterized by a yawing and rolling maneuver. Increasing the rate of aft stick displacement will increase the magnitude and rate of yaw at the stall. Stall recovery is instantaneous and is achieved by applying forward stick to reduce aircraft angle-of-attack and increase airspeed.

POST STALL GYRATIONS

The aircraft exhibits excellent stall recovery characteristics, and post stall gyrations commonly experienced in other swept wing aircraft are not displayed. However, following either a normal 1-g stall or an accelerated stall, if angle of attack is not reduced by releasing back stick pressure, the longitudinal and lateral oscillations will increase in amplitude and the aircraft will roll and pitch to a 50° to 60° dive angle. Pitching then decreases but the lateral oscillations increase varying from gentle rolls to snap rolls as the airspeed builds up. These lateral oscillations will continue as long as the stick is held aft.

Note

The aircraft does not exhibit any tendency to spin from a normal 1-g stall or an accelerated stall. However, application of spin recovery technique during post stall gyrations will induce a spin.

Post stall gyrations entered from vertical stalls are preceeded by wing rocking and a back slide. As the aircraft stalls, it pitches down to a 70° to 80° dive angle with the airspeed increasing rapidly. When the aircraft is stalled with a vertical flight path angle less than 90°, it pitches nose down erect and when the flight path angle is greater than 90°, it pitches down inverted. The negative load factor in the inverted maneuver causes the CSD/S warning lights (L or R SPD DR) on the annunciator panel to come on. These lights will go out when the load factor becomes positive. The aircraft exhibits the same post stall characteristics as those experienced in normal 1-g stalls and accelerated stalls with the stick held full aft.

Note

The aircraft will not spin from a vertical stall unless pro-spin controls (full aft stick, full rudder, and neutral flaperons) with extended throws are applied.

SPINS

The aircraft is not prone to enter unintentional spins. To attain a spin, the controls must be intentionally held in the pro-spin positions (full aft stick, full rudder, and neutral flaperons). During spin testing at NATC, erect spins induced with cruise control throws were achieved only on 12.5% of the attempts. These spins were all from normal 1-g stall entries. Erect spins could not be induced from vertical, inverted, or accelerated stall entries with cruise control throws. Erect spins were induced on 95% of the spin attempts using extended control throws in vertical and 1-g entries.

ERECT SPINS

The erect spin requires approximately 1 1/2 turns to become fully developed. The initial 1 1/2 turns comprising the incipient spin phase (or post stall gyration) are more disorienting than the fully developed spin due to the rolling, pitching, and yawing motions in conjunction with a rapidly changing load factor. This gyration is what will be experienced in most instances rather than a spin and is the same whether or not a spin develops and regardless of the control throws (cruise or extended) used. Recovery is normally effected by neutralizing or releasing all controls, but in some cases lateral stick deflection is necessary to stop rolling motion.

Spin Characteristics

The fully developed erect spin is a low-speed, high angle-of-attack, autorotative spin characterized by the airspeed indication fluctuating around 100 KIAS, the turn needle indicating a steady full needle deflection turn in the direction of the spin, and the accelerometer showing 0 to +0.3 g.

Note

Aircraft oscillatory motion in the spin is sufficient to cause the ball in the turn-and-slip indicator to slide back and forth and to be of no use to the pilot. The turn needle should be used as the primary instrument to determine the direction of the spin.

Airframe buffet level in the spin is very low and the predominant aircraft motion apparent to the pilot is yaw. The spin rotation rate is 3.5 to 4.0 sec/turn, the angle-of-attack is 60° to 65°, and the pitch attitude oscillates from 30° to 50° nose down once during each turn. The forces exerted on the pilot are mild and an erect spin with the shoulder-harness inertia reel unlocked presents no problems. All cockpit switches can be easily reached and full cockpit control throws can be accomplished.

During the fully developed spin, engine compressor stalls at the rate of approximately 10 per second are audible, and EGT will increase rapidly to over 700°C if engine rpm is greater than 88% to 90%. The engine rpm will drop to below flight idle, resulting in loss of the aircraft electrical system if engine rpm is less than 80%. The ram-air turbine will not operate in an erect spin. The automatic flight control system, speed-brake position, or aircraft CG location do not noticeably affect the spin characteristics. However, asymmetrical power assists in inducing erect spins. The approximate 6° cant of the exhaust nozzles out from the fuselage centerline results in an addition to the spin moment when the engine on the inside of the spin is developing more thrust than the one on the outside. Erect spins, with the exception of asymmetrical power spins, are recoverable with cruise control throws but may require up to three turns to effect.

WARNING

The aircraft will not recover from an erect spin with assymmetrical power using cruise control throws for recovery.

An assist-spin recovery switch has been provided to permit the attainment of the landing configuration control throws (+35° rudder and 24° stabilizer leading edge down) while in the clean configuration. Use of extended control throws provide a recovery in 1 to 1 1/2 turns from all spins.

CAUTION

- Operation of the assist-spin recovery switch may impose an additional acceleration which, during an accelerated maneuver, may overstress the aircraft, or when operating at minimum airspeeds may pitch the aircraft up into stall or heavy buffet conditions.

- Reselection of cruise control throws after spin recovery should be done below 300 KIAS while anticipating a nose-down pitch change.

- The assist-spin recovery switch should not be activated with the flaps down. Activation can cause damage to the extended throw mechanism.

The altitude lost in the fully developed erect spin is 1,300 to 1,500 feet per turn. The altitude lost from the initiation of recovery to level flight is approximately 9,000 feet with 2.5 to 3.0 g roundout.

ERECT SPIN RECOVERY

The first step in recovery from all spins is to determine if the aircraft is in a spin. Since post stall gyration can be extremely disorienting, it is relatively easy to assume the aircraft is in a spin when in fact it is not. Application of spin recovery technique during post stall gyration may force the aircraft into a spin. Upon entering a post stall gyration, controls should be neutralized to effect recovery. If it is determined that the aircraft is in a spin, determine the direction of the spin by reference to the turn needle; then initiate recovery according to the following sequence:

1. Apply full rudder pedal deflection in direction opposite to spin (rudder opposite direction that turn needle is indicating).

2. Hold control stick full aft and neutral laterally.

3. Simultaneously with application of spin recovery controls, or as soon as possible, select extended control throws with assist spin recovery switch.

4. Adjust throttles to provide 80% to 85% rpm. Adjusting throttles to a point where they are parallel to pilot's vertical axis results in desired power setting without requirements to monitor rpm indicator.

5. When rotation ceases, immediately neutralize rudder and move control stick forward to at least neutral position. Failure to neutralize controls as soon as spin rotation has ceased will result in violent lateral snaps, causing the aircraft to assume a steeper nose-down position and require more altitude for recovery to level flight.

6. Return assist spin recovery switch to cruise control throw position after return to level flight and at or below 300 KIAS.

Recovery will occur in 1 to 1 1/2 turns at a 70° or greater nose-down attitude. If turn reversals are encountered while neutralizing the controls, release the controls and the aircraft will fly itself out. The flaperons are not effective during erect spins.

WARNING

Wind tunnel tests on spin characteristics of swept wing aircraft have shown that asymmetrical loads on the order of 10,000 to 12,000 foot-pounds or higher produce an undesirable flattening of the spin. A-6 spin characteristics with asymmetrical stores have not been tested. If a spin occurs with asymmetrical stores, use the emergency jettison button to jettison all stores.

INVERTED SPINS

Inverted spins have been unobtainable (contractor demonstration and NATC tests) with the normal cruise control throws, but have been induced by using the extended control throws. The inverted spin requires 1 to 1 1/2 turns to become fully developed. Recovery from the initial 1 to 1 1/2 turns, the incipient spin phase, is effected by neutralizing or releasing the controls, but in some cases lateral stick deflection is necessary to stop the rolling motion.

The fully developed inverted spin is a low-speed high negative angle-of-attack, autorotative spin characterized by the airspeed indication fluctuating from less than 80 KIAS up to 100 KIAS, the turn needle indicating a steady full needle deflection turn in the direction of the spin, the ball remaining in the side of the cage opposite to the direction indicated by

FLIGHT PROCEDURES
Flight Characteristics

the turn needle, and the accelerometer indicating a steady -1.0 g. In the fully developed inverted spin, airplan pitch attitude oscillates from $0°$ to $35°$ below the horizon once very turn, the spin rotation rate is 3.5 to 4.0 sec/turn, the aircraft angle-of-attack in a steady $-55°$, and airframe buffet is non-existent. The main force felt by the pilot is the negative load factor. If the seat belt is not tight and/or the seat is raised, difficulty may be experienced in reaching and actuating the assist spin recovery switch. With the seat belt properly secured, all cockpit switches can be reached and full cockpit control throws accomplished. Yaw, pitch, and roll rates are relatively steady, resulting in a physically comfortable spin. Determination of spin direction by observing the terrain traverse in the windscreen is difficult due to disorientation. However, spin direction can be immediately determined by referring to the turn needle. Engine compressor stalls occur as described for erect spins. The ram-air turbine will operate satisfactorily in inverted spins. All inverted spins are recoverable with cruise control throws but may require up to 3 1/2 turns. Use of extended control throws provides recovery in 1/2 to 1 turn. The altitude lost during a fully developed inverted spin is 1,000 to 1,300 feet per turn. The altitude lost from the initiation of recovery to level flight is approximately 9,000 feet with a 2.5 to 3.0 g roundout.

INVERTED SPIN RECOVERY

Determine the spin direction by reference to the turn needle, then take the following steps:

1. Apply full rudder pedal deflection in direction opposite to spin.

2. Hold control stick full forward and neutral laterally.

3. Simultaneously with application of spin recovery controls, or as soon as possible, select extended control throws with assist-spin recovery switch.

4. Adjust throttles to 80% to 85% rpm.

5. Neutralize controls as soon as spin rotation ceases.

6. Return assist spin recovery switch to cruise control throw position after return to level flight and at or below 300 KIAS.

Recovery will occur in about one turn in a $70°$ to $90°$ nose-down attitude. Turn reversals have not been encountered during forward stick recoveries from inverted spins. The flaperons are not effective during inverted spins. The CSD/S warning lights on the annunciator panel will go on during the spin but will go out following spin recovery without corrective action being taken.

SPIN RECOVERY ON INSTRUMENTS

Recovery on instruments from erect and inverted spins can be effected using the following technique:

1. Determine direction of spin by reference to turn needle. Determine if spin is inverted or erect by reference to the angle of attack. If the angle of attack is pegged upward, the spin is erect. If the angle of attack is pegged downward (low angle of attack), the spin is inverted.

2. Apply full rudder pedal deflection in direction opposite to turn needle.

3. Apply full aft stick for recovery from an erect spin and full forward stick for recovery from an inverted spin.

4. Simultaneously with application of recovery controls, or as soon as possible, select extended control throws.

5. Adjust throttles to 80% to 85% rpm.

6. Hold spin recovery controls for a count of 3, or 3 seconds; then release controls to neutral. Monitor airspeed, turn needle, accelerometer, and gyro horizon for indication of spin recovery.

7. Return to level flight using gyro horizon and turn needle for attitude reference.

8. Select cruise control throws after return to level flight and at or below 300 KIAS.

Recovery from all inverted spins will normally occur when the controls are released to neutral. The recovery from all erect spins will occur within one turn after release of the controls to neutral.

After activating the assist spin recovery switch, the flight controls must be held in the spin recovery position for a count of 3, or 3 seconds, and then released to neutral because the inherent lag in the turn-and-slip indicator is too great for it to be used to determine when spin rotation has ceased. Holding the spin recovery controls for 3 seconds provides about one spin recovery turn, which is enough to cause the spin recovery to progress to a point where the aircraft will recover hands-off within an additional one-half turn. Waiting until the turn needle begins to move toward the centered position before neutralizing the controls results in a series of reversals and the aircraft will not recover due to the late neutralization of the flight controls.

A momentary loss of electrical power will not adversely affect the performance of the gyro horizon or the turn-and-slip indicator. The turn needle will continue to indicate the correct direction of turn for 9 seconds after electrical power failure.

FLIGHT CONTROLS

A movable slab stabilizer, flaperon wing spoiler, and a conventional rudder provide effective control over the operational range of the aircraft. The control surfaces are positioned by irreversible hydraulic actuators linked to the stick and rudder pedals by a proportional followup linkage. Control force feel is provided entirely by mechanical devices such as bungees and bobweights, and requires no mach or "q" compensation. Control trim is accomplished electrically by shifting the feel system neutral position in each system.

The stabilizer travel is increased for flaps-down flight in a programmed manner so that trim change with flap deflection is minimized. Stabilizer shift is accomplished by a cable drive from the flap motor and is designed to remain at either full flaps down or flaps up gearing, should the shift cable fail. Stabilizer travel is 1.5° leading-edge-up, to 9.6° leading-edge-down in the flaps-up configuration, and 1.5° leading-edge-up to 24° leading-edge-down for flaps-down operation, with full stick travel. Selection of the assist-spin recovery drives the same shift mechanism.

> **CAUTION**
>
> Operation of the assist-spin recovery switch may impose additional acceleration, which during an accelerated maneuver may overstress the aircraft, or when operating at minimum airspeeds may pitch the aircraft up into a stall or heavy buffet condition. Reselection of cruise control throws after spin recovery should be done below 300 KIAS, while anticipating a nose-down pitch change.

Rudder travel either side of neutral is increased for flaps-down flight by withdrawing stops in the rudder control linkage. Rudder travel is reduced to 4° with flaps up, and increases to 35° flaps down, or with the assist-spin recovery selected. Rudder travel is proportional to rudder pedal deflection in each case.

The rudder stops shift to full open if the cable fails. Selection of the assist-spin recovery switch accomplishes the stop withdrawal by the same mechanism as (full) flap extension.

After landing, the flaperon pop-up feature, as well as the flaps and slats, act together to effectively kill lift and increase drag to decrease landing roll.

LEVEL FLIGHT

No unusual characteristics will be noted in level flight. Control response is excellent. Longitudinal stability is positive up to .84 IMN, where a reverse stability regime is gradually entered. This transonic trim change of tuckunder is common to swept wing jets of this type and is considered mild and completely controllable. Positive stability is regained at .92 IMN and above.

Loss of either engine will not compromise control or stability. Engine thrust lines pass close to aircraft cg. and minimum single-engine control speeds are within 3 to 5 knots of the normal two-engine stall speeds. Single-engine control speed is limited by prestall buffet, slight lateral and longitudinal oscillations, and nearly full lateral and directional control deflections.

Note

When operating under single-engine conditions, ensure that the speed brakes have been retracted.

> **CAUTION**
>
> Restricted stabilizer travel at low speed could result in inadequate pitch control and full stabilizer travel at high speed could cause structural failure.

PILOT INDUCED LATERAL OSCILLATION

With the AFCS operating in STAB AUG at airspeeds in excess of 450 KIAS, moderately abrupt lateral stick displacement or reversal may induce an oscillation in roll of 20° to 30° per second. This oscillation is sustained by the pilot displacing the stick and may be stopped immediately by neutralizing the stick. The lateral oscillation increases in intensity from 450 KIAS to limit speed but is not divergent or destructive throughout the flight envelope. The oscillation will not normally be experienced in maneuvering flight.

DIVES

Dive entries may be either pushovers or split-s type. In either case, transition through the transonic trim changes will be rapid. At about .90 IMN, reduced lateral control effectiveness and slightly negative dihedral effect will be encountered. The latter phenomenon will not be noted unless rudder deflections are made. The basic airframe is not restricted in dive angle or maximum speeds but certain store configurations may require limits. Dive recoveries may be made either clean or with speed brakes. Trim changes with speed brakes are slight, but it should be remembered that as speed is reduced, trim changes and/or gusts may add to the existing g's during pullouts at the bottom of the dives. See figures 4-5 through 4-8.

SPEED BRAKE BLOWBACK

The speed-brake system is so designed that the speed brakes will blow back when the speed-brake actuator load is equal to 20,300 pounds. This is equal to the 3,400 psi cracking pressure of the relief valve, or 3,560 psi at full flow, with the speed brakes positioned at 55°. The wing-tip speed brakes will blow back at .80 IMN, level flight.

SINGLE ENGINE OPERATION

SINGLE-ENGINE FLIGHT CHARACTERISTICS

For all flight configurations ample lateral and directional control is available for achieving and maintaining straight flight with maximum asymmetrical engine thrust. Minimum single-engine control speeds are defined by attaining the full maximum trimmed lift coefficient of the aircraft. Single-engine stall characteristics are essentially the same as those obtained in normal operation with similar flap settings.

4-13

FLIGHT PROCEDURES
Flight Characteristics

NAVAIR 01-85ADA-1

DIVE RECOVERY CHART - 3g

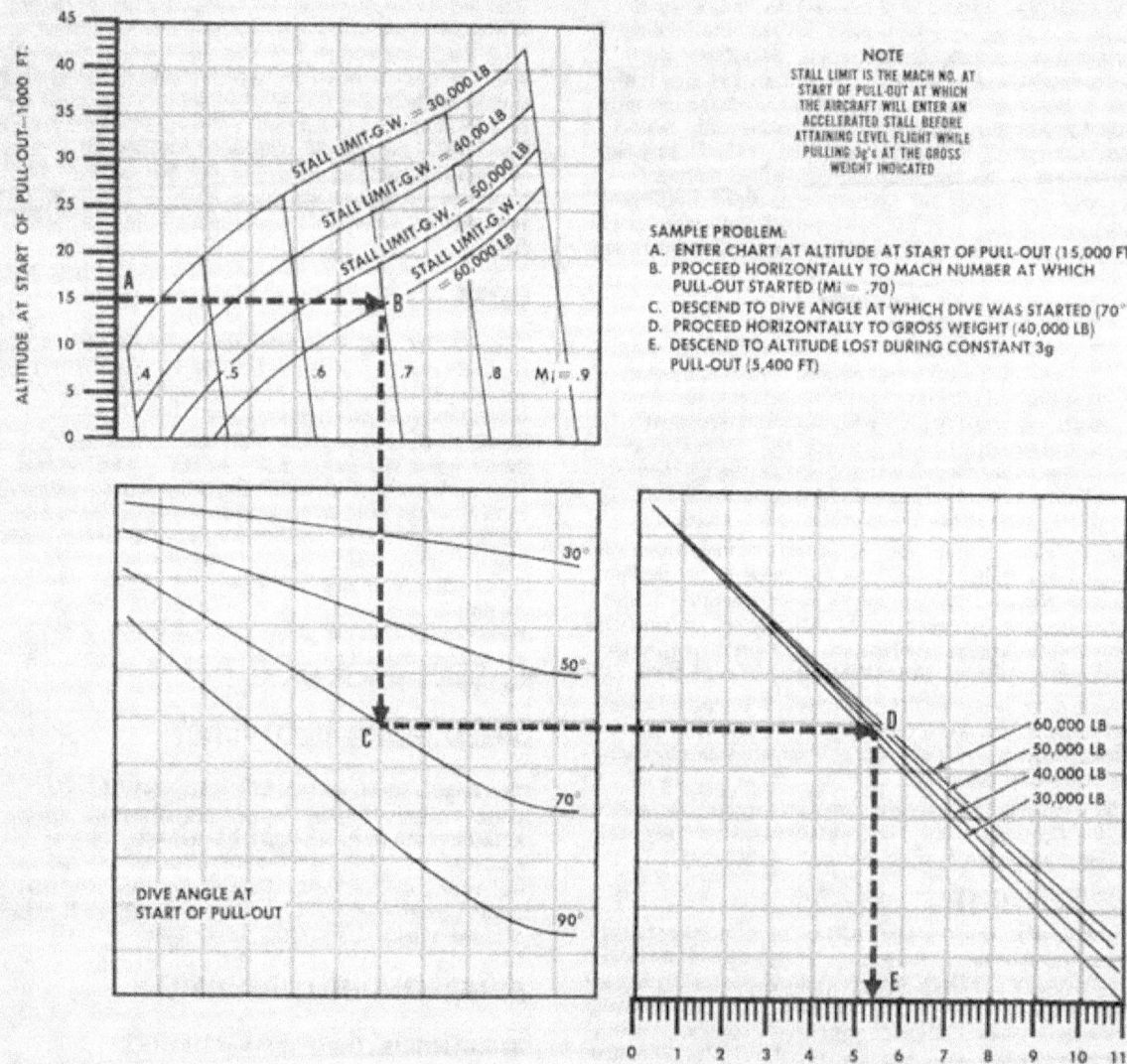

Figure 4-5

NAVAIR 01-85ADA-1

FLIGHT PROCEDURES
Flight Characteristics

DIVE RECOVERY CHART - 4 g

CONFIGURATION:
NO EXTERNAL STORES

DATE: 1 DECEMBER 1972
DATA BASIS: ESTIMATED

REMARKS
WING TIP SPEED BRAKES EXTENDED
80% RPM
ENGINE (S) : (2) J52-P-8

FUEL GRADE: JP-5
FUEL DENSITY: 6.8 LB/GAL

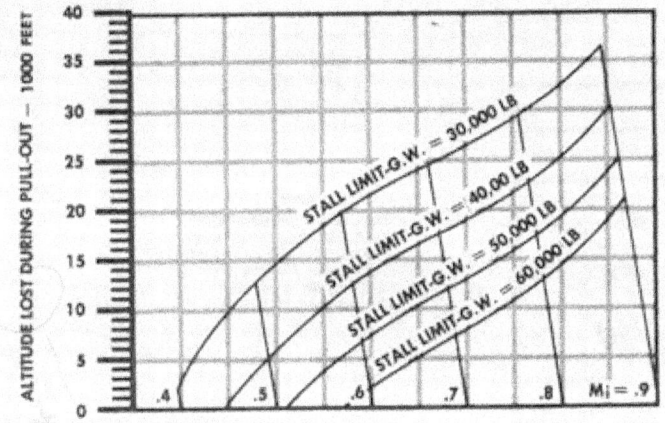

NOTE
STALL LIMIT IS THE MACH NO. AT START OF PULL-OUT AT WHICH THE AIRCRAFT WILL ENTER AN ACCELERATED STALL BEFORE ATTAINING LEVEL FLIGHT WHILE PULLING 4 g's AT THE GROSS WEIGHT INDICATED.

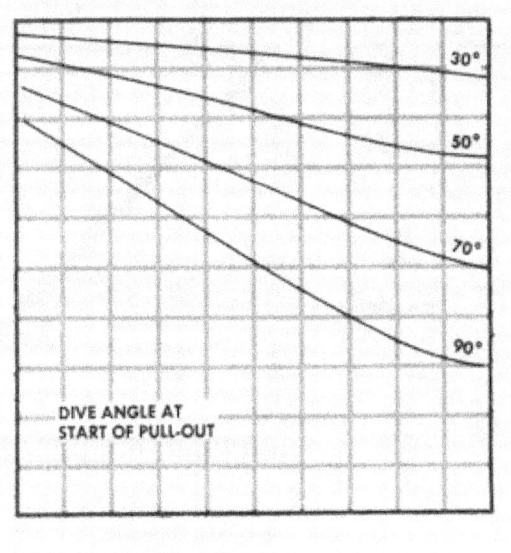

DIVE ANGLE AT
START OF PULL-OUT

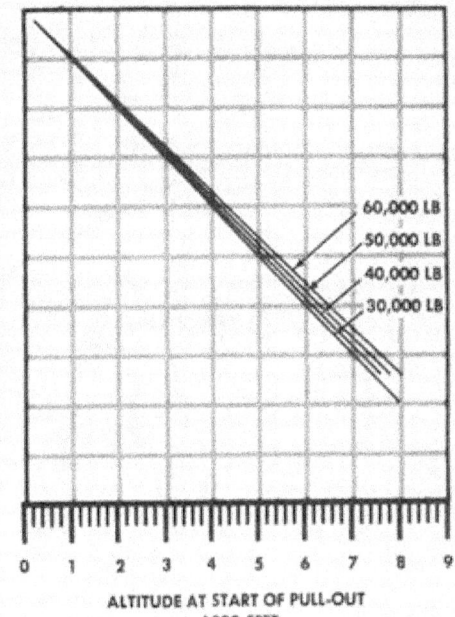

ALTITUDE AT START OF PULL-OUT
— 1000 FEET

C-ADA1-163

Figure 4-6

FLIGHT PROCEDURES
Flight Characteristics

NAVAIR 01-85ADA-1

DIVE RECOVERY CHART - 5g

CONFIGURATION: NO EXTERNAL STORES

DATE: 1 DECEMBER 1972
DATA BASIS: ESTIMATED

REMARKS
WING TIP SPEED BRAKES EXTENDED
80% RPM
ENGINE (S) : (2) J52-P-8

FUEL GRADE: JP-5
FUEL DENSITY: 6.8 LB/GAL

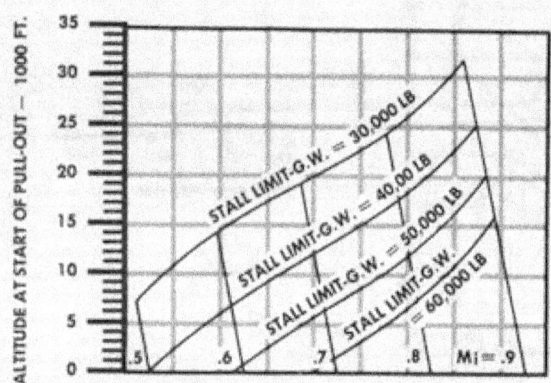

NOTE
STALL LIMIT IS THE MACH NO. AT START OF PULL-OUT AT WHICH THE AIRCRAFT WILL ENTER AN ACCELERATED STALL BEFORE ATTAINING LEVEL FLIGHT WHILE PULLING 5 g's AT THE GROSS WEIGHT INDICATED.

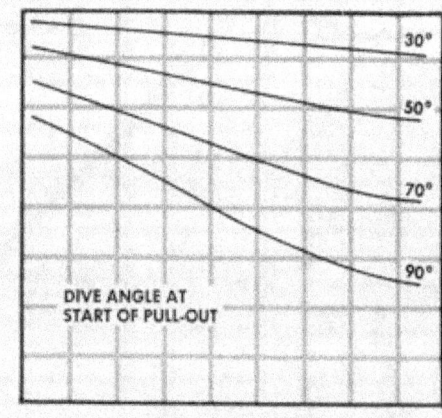
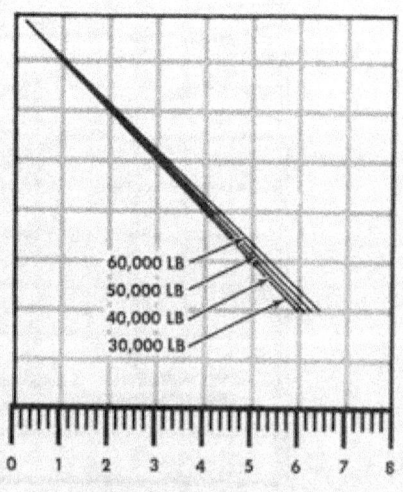

Figure 4-7

NAVAIR 01-85ADA-1

FLIGHT PROCEDURES
Flight Characteristics

DIVE RECOVERY CHART - 6.5g

CONFIGURATION: NO EXTERNAL STORES

DATE: 1 DECEMBER 1972
DATA BASIS: ESTIMATED

REMARKS
WING TIP SPEED BRAKES EXTENDED
80% RPM
ENGINE (S) : (2) J52-P-8

FUEL GRADE: JP-5
FUEL DENSITY: 6.8 LB/GAL

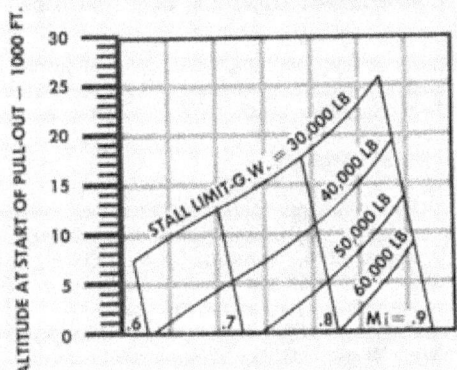

NOTE
STALL LIMIT IS THE MACH NO. AT START OF PULL-OUT AT WHICH THE AIRCRAFT WILL ENTER AN ACCELERATED STALL BEFORE ATTAINING LEVEL FLIGHT WHILE PULLING 6.5 g's AT THE GROSS WEIGHT INDICATED.

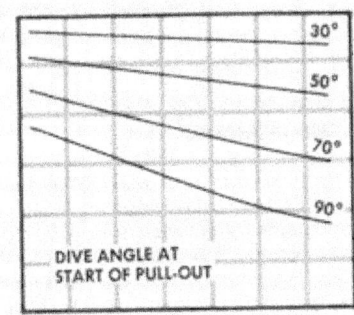

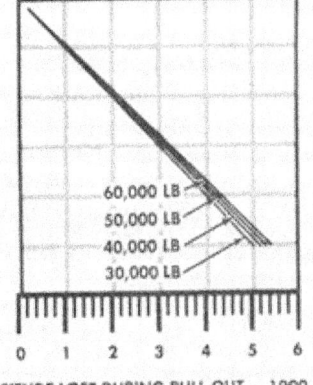

Figure 4-8

FLIGHT PROCEDURES
Flight Characteristics

The only flap setting for single engine operation is 30° (T/O). The single-engine rate of climb as a function of gross weight, pressure altitude, and temperature is presented in Section XI.

> **CAUTION**
>
> Extension of the speed brakes drastically reduces performance.

SINGLE ENGINE FLIGHT PERFORMANCE

Refer to Section XI, for qualitative single-engine performance information.

> **WARNING**
>
> An engine failure will produce a rate of descent in excess of 700 fpm in takeoff configuration at maximum operational takeoff weight: 60,400 pounds sea level standard day. Upon failure of an engine, the pilot should immediately jettison all external stores to reduce gross weight and drag sufficiently for positive rate of climb. The landing gear and flaps can be retracted and excess fuel dumped if desired. Refer to Section XI.

Note

External stores cannot be jettisoned until 70% of the aircraft weight is off the wheels.

FLIGHT WITH EXTERNAL LOADS

Handling qualities of the aircraft with stores loaded vary with their weight, shape, and distribution. Spanwise loading increases roll inertia noticeably, with accompanying reduction in roll acceleration. For all store configurations, lateral control is still satisfactory. Longitudinal control and stability is least affected by addition of stores.

Stores with large diameters, such as fuel tanks and the air-refueling pod, cause added airframe buffet during flight above normal cruise speeds, and during increased g loads.

BACKUP FLIGHT CONTROLS HYDRAULIC SYSTEM

In aircraft 371 and subsequent and aircraft incorporating AFC No. 183, upon complete hydraulic failure, a backup flight control system is activated, which provides horizontal stabilizer control through longitudinal stick movement and rudder control through pedal movement. Flaperon control is not provided.

The backup flight control hydraulic system provides the capability of unusual attitudes recovery, and, under optimum conditions, field landings. Refer to Section V for recommended flight procedures using the backup flight control system.

Flight on the backup flight controls hydraulic system may be simulated by using only rudder for roll control with STAB AUG at OFF. Training should include cruising flight, recovery from unusual attitudes, and no-flap landings, all without the use of flaperons.

LONGITUDINAL CONTROL RATE LIMITING

In the cruise configuration, aircraft pitch response is high, requiring surface rates well below the actuator saturation limit. Aircraft pitch response to longitudinal stick inputs is identical to normal flight control response.

In the power approach configuration, as the speed decreases, the pitch response is reduced, requiring large stabilizer rates to obtain a given g per unit time. Aft stick surface rate limiting occurs first and is more critical and noticeable to a pilot who, during the landing approach, is attempting to recover from a rapidly induced pitch-over. Longitudinal stick rate limiting becomes apparent at about 150 knots and increases in severity as the speed decreases. This condition is not hazardous if rate limiting is anticipated and moderate, unexcessive longitudinal control inputs are effected.

TRIM CHANGES

Gear extension or retraction produces no appreciable trim change and can be easily controlled. Flap extension can result in a significant roll-off in either direction. This is a result of assymetric floating of the flaperons due to flap extension. The degree of assymetry is unpredictable; therefore, it is recommended that the flaps not be extended when controlling the aircraft with the backup system only.

DIHEDRAL EFFECT

Attempts to yaw the airplane with rudder will produce roll in the same direction as yaw. This dihedral effect becomes more pronounced at high angles of attack. The use of rudder inputs to produce yaw and in turn generate roll, with provide the highest attainable roll rates at high angles of attack. The rudder must be used judiciously, however, since excessive rudder inputs will induce excessive yaw.

 **Formation and Tactics**

FORMATION TAKEOFF

All aspects of the takeoff must be prebriefed by the flight leader such as use of nosewheel steering, power changes, power settings, and signals for landing gear and flaps.

Section takeoff will not be performed with dissimilar type aircraft, nor with a crosswind component in excess of 10 knots. The section leader will position his aircraft on the port side of the runway. Aircraft will line up on a parade bearing with enough lateral clearance to provide separation between aircraft in case the leader experiences a blown tire, or is required to abort the takeoff. When the section is in position, the B/N of the lead aircraft will give a two-finger turn-up signal at the command of the flight leader. Next, both pilots will turn up to military power and make all final checks from the check list. The lead B/N will carefully check the second for leaks, trim settings, flap settings, and flaperon position, at which time the second aircraft pilot will make the same checks of the lead aircraft. After airframe and instrument requirements are met by both aircraft, the lead B/N and wingman will show a raised hand to indicate they are both ready for take-off. At the command of the lead pilot, the lead B/N will drop his hand smartly out of view to signal brake release and commencement of takeoff roll. The lead pilot will reduce his power approximately 2% on each engine before giving the brake release command. The wingman will adjust his power to maintain relative position through the takeoff roll. Normal takeoff techniques will be utilized with respect to the nosewheel steering and lift-off speed.

When the section is comfortably airborne and has established a positive rate of climb, the lead B/N at the command of the lead pilot will signal for the landing gear to be raised. When the section has attained safe altitude and airspeed, the lead B/N will give the appropriate signal and the flaps will be raised (again at the command of the lead pilot).

Turns into the wingman will not be made at altitudes of less than 500 feet AGL. The first section must be airborne before the second section commences its takeoff roll. See visual communication procedures in Section VII.

CAUTION

- In the event of an aborted takeoff, the aircraft aborting must immediately notify the other aircraft. The aircraft not aborting should add maximum power and accelerate ahead and out of the way of the aborting aircraft. This will allow the aborting aircraft to steer to the center of the runway and engage the arresting gear.

- It is imperative that the wingman always be alert for an overrunning situation and take timely steps to preclude such an occurrence. Should an overrunning/overshooting situation develop after becoming airborne, the wingman should immediately move laterally away from the lead and, if feasible, reduce power in order to maintain safe wing position. Safe flight of both aircraft must not be jeopardized in an attempt to maintain formation. The leader should detach the wingman if he is experiencing loss of thrust and flying speed. The wingman should detach and add power if unable to maintain a safe wing position on the lead.

RENDEZVOUS

TURNING RENDEZVOUS

The turning rendezvous is made at 300 KIAS (unless otherwise briefed). After all aircraft are in a loose-trail position, the leader commences a 180° turn, using 30° of bank. Each member of the flight waits until the aircraft ahead passes through a 30° bearing from his 12-o'clock position, and then rolls into a 45° banked turn to the inside of the leader's turn. When the leader bears 40° relative to the joining aircraft, wingmen ease turn as necessary to maintain the 45° bearing until joined either on the preceding aircraft or of the flight. Wingmen may add power to gain no greater than a 10-knot speed advantage over the leader, to avoid overshooting. As the aircraft approach the leader, the closure rate is adjusted so as to join on the man ahead or on the inside of the leader's turn. After joining on the inside of the leader, a crossunder is made to the outside, assuming normal wing positions.

CIRCLING RENDEZVOUS

A circling rendezvous is used when aircraft are separated by extended or indefinite distances or time intervals. The pattern is normally a port, nonstandard orbit, using 30° of bank around a geographic fix. Altitude must be specified and airspeed will be 300 KIAS (unless otherwise briefed). Upon arrival, each aircraft flies directly over the fix, slightly below the rendezvous altitude, to provide altitude separation upon entry into the pattern. The first aircraft to arrive should establish the orbit. Subsequent aircraft should be able to sight other aircraft in the circle from directly over the fix. When sighted, a hard turn in the direction of the orbit turn should be made to establish a 45° bearing relative to the joining aircraft. Vary the bank as necessary to maintain the bearing until joined. Do not use an airspeed advantage in excess of 15 knots. As the leader is closed, check closure rate so as to stop on the inside of the turn; then cross under to a normal wing position on the outside (figure 4-9.)

FLIGHT PROCEDURES
Formation and Tactics

NAVAIR 01-85ADA-1

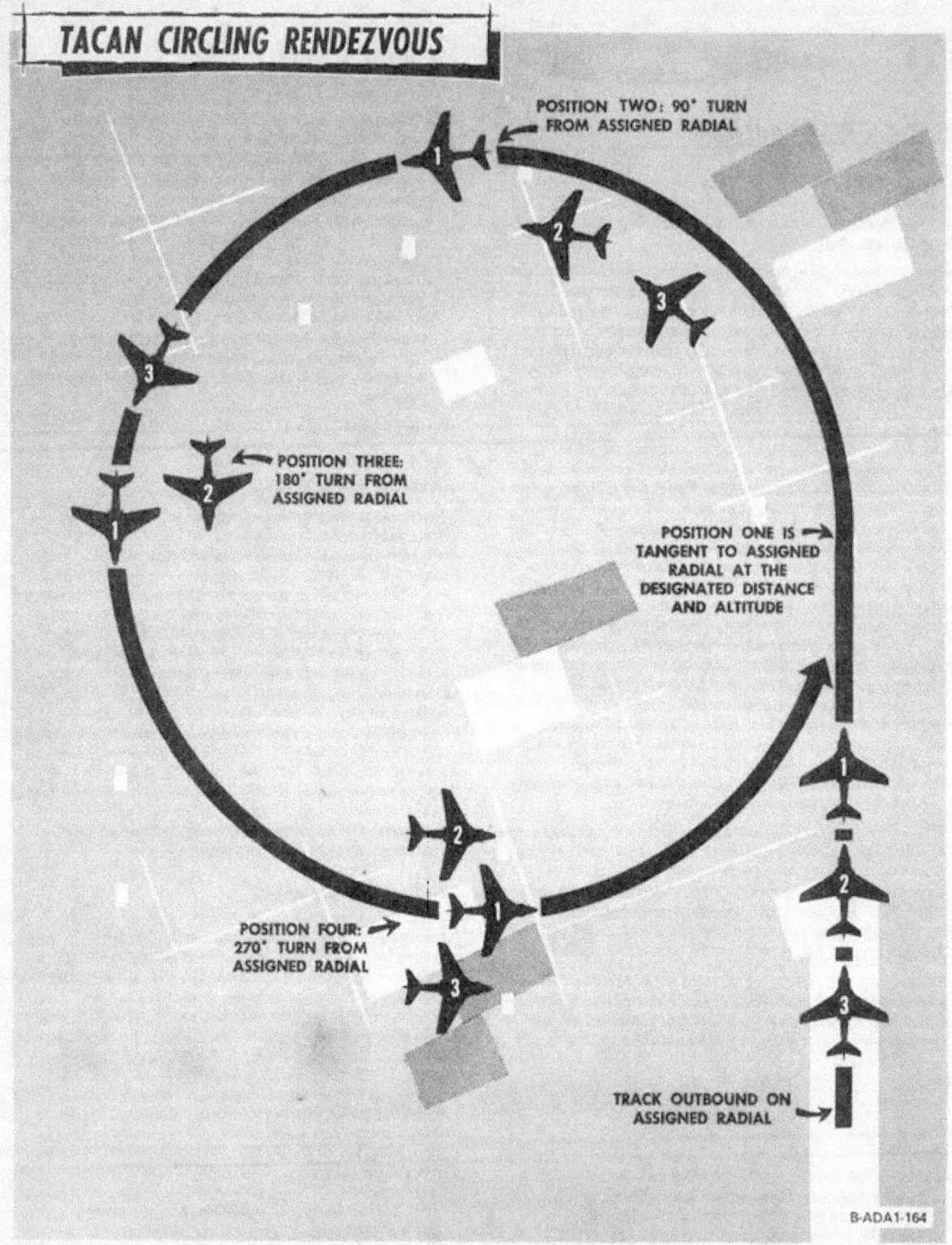

Figure 4-9

TACAN CIRCLING RENDEZVOUS

A TACAN circling rendezvous is used when aircraft are separated by extended or indefinite distances or time intervals and it is not possible to use a geographic fix (at sea or above an overcast). The pattern will be a starboard orbit tangent to the designated TACAN radial, at a specified distance and altitude. Normally, each pilot flies outbound on the assigned radial, maintaining the briefed climb schedule or rendezvous speed. Upon reaching the join-up circle, each pilot commences a starboard orbit, using 30° of bank (or more) until visual contact is made with the flight leader. If necessary, request for the leader's position. The leader will state his position around the orbit, using figures 1, 2, 3, or 4, corresponding to 000°, 090°, 180° and 270°, respectively, relative to the designated radial, as shown in figure 4-9. Each pilot then plans his turn to cut across the orbit for rendezvous. ARA-25 may be used to assist in picking up the leader.

RUNNING RENDEZVOUS

A running rendezvous is effected by closing from the rear on a prebriefed heading or radial. This rendezvous should be accomplished with the leader climbing at 300 KIAS and approximately 95% (unless otherwise briefed). If it is to be made level, the leader should normally be at 300 KIAS at the designated altitude.

ADF RUNNING RENDEZVOUS

The ARA-25 rendezvous is useful for joining aircraft under all conditions, and particularly during a straight course running rendezvous. The procedure to be used for the latter is as follows:

1. Trailing aircraft select ADF position on UHF control.

2. The flight leader will transmit a short count every minute, and when climbing, include passing altitude.

3. Trailing aircraft will position themselves so that as leader transmits short counts, No. 1 needle points 5° left or right of nose position. The No. 2 aircraft will hold leader to his left, No. 3 to his right, etc.

4. As trailing aircraft approach flight leader, they will turn to keep him 5° (left or right respectively) off nose position. The amount of turn required to maintain leader in this position will increase as separation is reduced. Continue until visual sighting is obtained.

ADF CIRCLING RENDEZVOUS

If a circling rendezvous is to be made, the flight leader will maintain prebriefed airspeed, 30° of bank, a specified altitude, and broadcast a short count and heading every minute. The trailing aircraft will correct heading to keep the No. 1 needle on the nose when the leader transmits. From the change in azimuth of the No. 1 needle between short counts, approaching aircraft will be able to determine their proximity to the lead aircraft. Approaching the flight leader, the needle will change more degrees in azimuth between counts, requiring larger corrections to keep the leader on the nose. At this time, the leader can probably be detected visually and a standard rendezvous completed.

LOW VISIBILITY RENDEZVOUS/RENDEZVOUS ON DIFFERENT MODEL AIRCRAFT

This type of rendezvous should be performed in emergency situations only when directed by higher authority or when the urgency of the mission dictates. The rendezvous aircraft should be flown at a safe maneuvering airspeed. The initial procedures will be as previously described for standard rendezvous. However, the latter stages should be modified as outlined below.

1. Establish radio contact, if possible, and determine indicated airspeed and intended flight path of aircraft to be joined.

2. Place all lights on BRIGHT (if applicable).

3. Rendezvous about 1,000 feet out, slightly aft of abeam (4 or 8 o'clock) lead aircraft.

4. Cautiously close, while assuring constant nose-to-tail clearance. Maintain a constant relative bearing. Changes in relative bearing will cause foreshortening or lengthening of aircraft fuselage and make determination of closure rate difficult.

5. A rendezvous on a different model aircraft and or in low-visibility conditions is extremely conductive to vertigo. A high degree of caution and good judgment must be exercised throughout the rendezvous. At no time should a rapid-closing situation be allowed to develop.

SAFETY RULES FOR RENDEZVOUS

1. During all rendezvous, safety shall be the prime consideration.

2. Keep all aircraft ahead constantly in view and join in order.

3. During rendezvous, only enough step-down should be used to ensure vertical clearance on aircraft ahead.

4. When necessary, a wingman should abort rendezvous by leveling his wings, sighting all aircraft ahead, and flying underneath them to outside of formation. He should then remain on outside until all other aircraft have joined.

5. To avoid overshooting, all relative motions should be stopped when joining on an inside wing position. A crossunder to outside may then be made.

FLIGHT PROCEDURES
Formation and Tactics

6. During a running rendezvous, use caution in the final stage of join-up, as relative motion is difficult to discern when approaching from astern.

FORMATION

FREE CRUISE FORMATION (4 AIRCRAFT DIVISION)

This formation (figure 4-10) will normally be employed for all operations away from home base, unless another formation is signaled. Within each section, the wingman's position is 45° aft the section leader's beam, with sufficient distance abeam to clear the wingtips, and sufficient distance astern to clear the tail of the lead aircraft.

The vertical step-down of the wingman will be sufficient to clear the leader's aircraft and jet wash. The second section leader's position is approximately 45° abaft the division leader's beam and slightly stepped down. The second section leader must maintain a distance out on the assigned bearing line which will provide clearance with the lead section wingman and which will also permit visual communications between division and section leader. During steep turns or hard maneuvering, the second section and wingmen within each section are free to slide as necessary to avoid large power changes.

PARADE FORMATION

This formation (figure 4-10) will normally be employed when the flight is operating in the vicinity of home base and in conditions of low visibility. The parade formation position is obtained by the wingmen and sections leader maintaining a position slightly stepped down with 3 to 5 feet of lateral clearance between wingtips on a bearing matching the sweep back of the wing leading edge. Sliding during turns is not permitted.

FORMATION INSTRUMENT APPROACH

1. Wingman follows all configuration changes of the leader.

2. When runway OLS is sighted, leader signals lead change to wingman. When wingman considers he can safely continue approach unaided, he accepts lead.

3. After passing lead, the leader turns away from wingman, and then back to final approach heading and observes wingman's progress.

4. In case of a wave-off or bolter, and a VFR pattern is not feasible, the wingman rejoins leader for another approach.

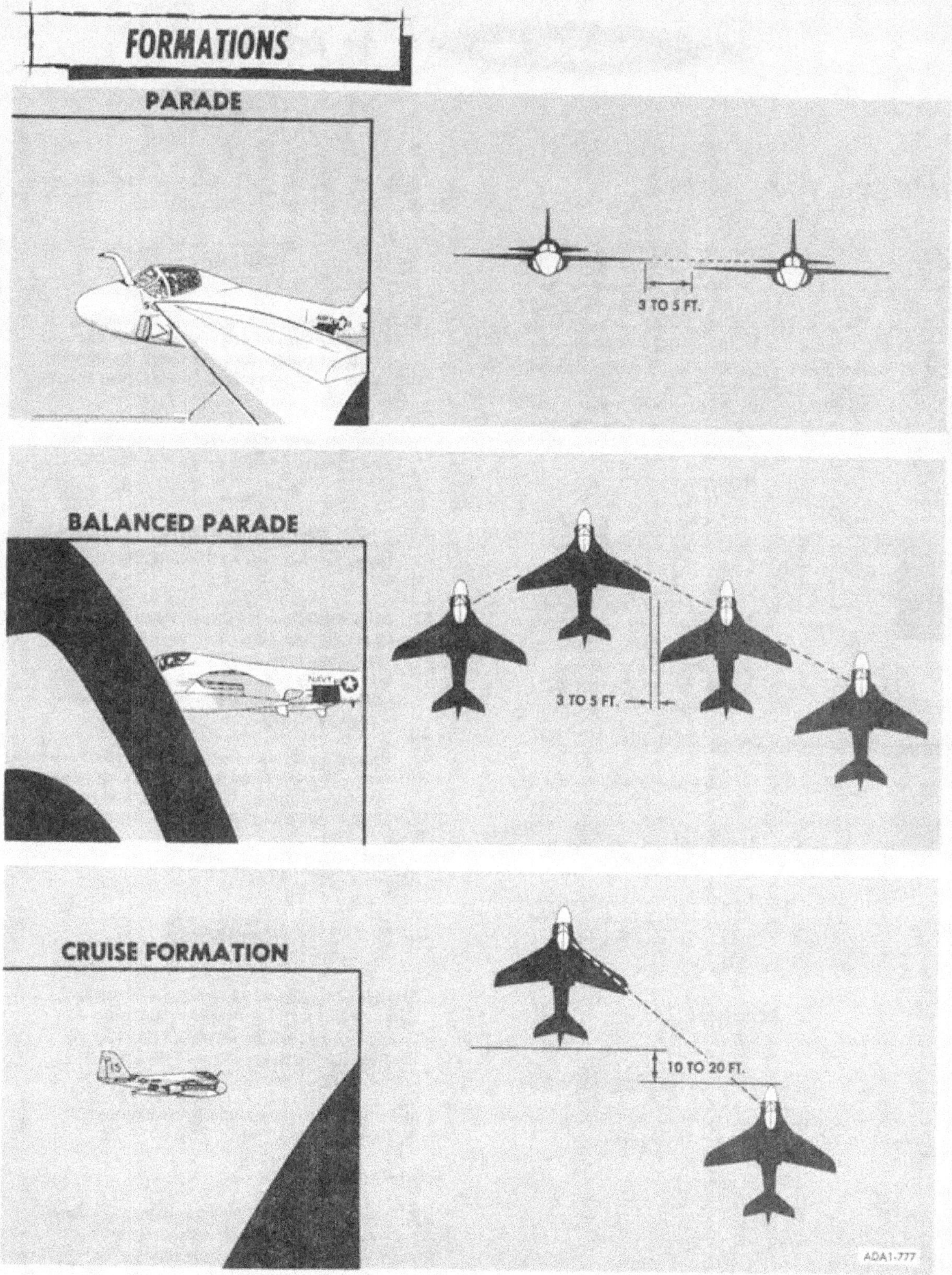
FORMATIONS
PARADE
3 TO 5 FT.
BALANCED PARADE
3 TO 5 FT.
CRUISE FORMATION
10 TO 20 FT.
ADA1-777

Figure 4-16

part 4 — Air Refueling

AIR REFUELING RECEIVER TECHNIQUE

Air refueling can be accomplished within a wide range of altitude and airspeed. Successful engagements have been made between sea level and 35,000 feet at airspeeds between 190 and 300 KIAS. The optimum airspeed for engagement is approximately 230 KIAS. Use of optimum airspeed will assist the receiver in escaping heavy buffeting caused by the tanker slipstream and jet exhaust. Prior to engaging the drogue of a tanker aircraft, the FUEL READY switch on the fuel management panel must be positioned to FLT to depressurize wing and drop tank.

Note

When refueling from KC-130 tanker aircraft, at other than high gross weight conditions, takeoff flaps may be used to maintain position with the drogue. Under high gross weights or high drag counts, use of flaps is not recommended because it will reduce power available to establish sufficient closure speed. Refueling with extreme high gross weight and high drag count combination would be operationally unfeasible.

PILOT TANKING TECHNIQUE (RECEIVER)

The following discussion is applicable to the KA-6D and the D-704 refueling store. All other tanking evolutions are dependent on the type of tanker being utilized. For proper hand signals during the air-refueling operations, refer to Section VII.

1. Receiver pilot should move into a position 20 feet behind and slightly below drogue. The amber light on tanker store should be lit, indicating store may be engaged.

CAUTION

If amber light is not lit do not engage drogue until signaled by tanker aircraft, as hose-reel response may be inoperative, causing damage to tanker and receiver aircraft.

Trim receiver aircraft slightly nose-down to remove any slack or breakout force from horizontal stabilizer control system, and move forward and up until the tip of the refueling probe is approximately 5 to 10 feet behind and 2 to 3 feet below drogue. Pause momentarily, long enough to stabilize the aircraft. Then add enough power to close and engage the drogue at a closure speed of 3 knots. Probe and drogue are primary visual references during this evolution.

CAUTION

o Closure speeds in excess of 5 knots and off-center engagements may cause the refueling-probe valve assembly to become distorted and prevent successful fuel transfer.

o Misalignment at high closure speeds may cause damage to the radome or canopy.

Note

If the drogue is missed, stay below the drogue and back straight out until the drogue is in sight.

2. After engaging drogue, amber light goes out and green light will come on when in refueling range and fuel is being transferred. During refueling, maintain a position directly behind and slightly below tanker aircraft.

3. Disengagement is accomplished by receiver reducing power in order to open from tanker at about 3 knots. Back straight away and down, following flight path of tanker.

When receiver aircraft is clear of area behind hose and drogue, call "Clear".

CAUTION

All disengagements must be made straight back, parallel to the tanker flight path and descending along the natural trail angle of the hose. Disengagements from below the natural trail position of the drogue may cause the refueling-probe valve assembly to become distorted and prevent successful fuel transfer.

NIGHT REFUELING

Night refueling is performed in the same manner as during the day. The tanker should have all exterior lights DIM and the anticollision lights off. The centerline store lights should be on DIM. The amber lights on the outboard pylons of the tanker aircraft are used for reference during night refueling. A

FLIGHT PROCEDURES
Air Refueling

white light in the under side of the tanker fuselage will illuminate the refueling hose.

Prior to assuming position for approach to the drogue, receiver aircraft may turn on the probe light. Take up an initial position on the tanker and use the same procedures described in this section for day refueling. When in position aft of the drogue, correct altitude can be determined by referring to the amber pylon lights. The receiver aircraft lights should be on BRIGHT and the anticollision light ON.

The tendency in night in-flight refueling is to start the approach too far aft. This makes it very difficult to judge relative motion and usually results in a high closure rate.

CAUTION

Do not engage the AUTO mode of the AFCS during air-refueling.

Section V
EMERGENCY PROCEDURES

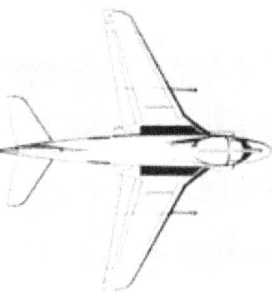

TABLE OF CONTENTS

INTRODUCTION	5-2
PART 1 GROUND EMERGENCIES	5-3
Emergency Entrance	5-3
Engine Starting Malfunctions	5-3
Emergency Engine Shutdown	5-4
PART 2 TAKEOFF EMERGENCIES	5-5
Aborted Takeoff Arrestments	5-5
Engine Fire/Failure - Takeoff Aborted	5-5
Fire Warning Light/Takeoff Continued	5-5
Engine Failure/Takeoff Continued	5-6
Stores Jettison	5-6
Strut Lock Light	5-7
Tow Link/Nose Gear Cocked	5-7
PART 3 INFLIGHT FAILURES	5-8
ENGINE FAILURES	5-8
Single-Engine Flight Characteristics	5-8
Single-Engine Failure During Flight	5-8
Double-Engine Failure During Flight	5-8
Air Starts	5-10
FIRE	5-10
Fire/Bleed-Air System Failure	5-10
Fire Warning Light Lit	5-11
NWW TEMP Light Lit (Aircraft Incorporating AFC 268)	5-11
AFT TEMP Light Lit	5-12
Temp Cont/Computer Overheat Light Remains On	5-12
Steady COMPUTER Light No TEMP CONT Light (A-6E)	5-12
AFT BLEED Light Lit (A-6E TRAM)	5-12
Electrical Fire/Smoke or Fumes in Cockpit	5-12
Air Conditioning Full Hot	5-12A
OIL SYSTEM FAILURES	5-13
Loss of Oil Pressure	5-13
High Oil Pressure	5-13
Low-Oil Warning Lights	5-13
If Normal Oil Pressure Cannot Be Maintained	5-13
FUEL SYSTEM FAILURES	5-14
Engine Fuel Pump Failure	5-14
Fuselage Boost Pump Failure	5-14
Transfer Pump Failure	5-14
Fuel Transfer Failure (Wing/Drop-Tank Pressurization)	5-14
Fuel Filter Light Lit	5-14
Fuel/Air Adapter Malfunction	5-15
Emergency Fuel Dumping (RAT Only Power)	5-15
Throttle Linkage Failure	5-15
ELECTRICAL SYSTEM FAILURES	5-15
Single Generator Failure	5-15
Double Generator Failure	5-16
Loss of Essential DC Bus	5-16
Complete Electrical Failure	5-18
SPD DR Light On	5-18
Loss of Trim Button	5-18
HYDRAULIC SYSTEM FAILURES	5-19
Single Hydraulic Pump Failure	5-19
Flight or Combined Hydraulic System Failure	5-19
Loss of Flight and Combined Hydraulic System	5-20
Complete Hydraulic System Failure	5-21
SPEED-BRAKES SYSTEM FAILURE	5-21
FLAPS/SLATS MALFUNCTION	5-21
Flaps/Slats Fail to Retract	5-21
Flaps/Slats Fail To Extend Normally (Failure Other Than Hydraulic)	5-22
FLAPERONS POP-UP IN FLIGHT	5-22
WEIGHT-ON-WHEELS SWITCH FAILURE	5-23
AIRSPEED INDICATOR FAILURE	5-23
DAMAGED AIRCRAFT	5-23
LANDING-GEAR SYSTEM MALFUNCTIONS	5-23
Landing-Gear Handle Cannot Be Raised	5-23
Landing-Gear Handle Up, Indicates Unsafe	5-25
Landing Gear Down With Unsafe Indications	5-25
PART 4 AIR-REFUELING SYSTEM EMERGENCIES	5-28
Refueling With Single Generator	5-28
Hose-Reel Drive Failures	5-28
Fuel Leaking From Aft Bay During Refueling	5-28
Fuel Leaking From Aft Bay During Refueling Hose Will Not Retract	5-28
Hose Fails to Retract	5-28
Combined Hydraulic System Failure Hose Extended	5-29

EMERGENCY PROCEDURES　　　NAVAIR 01-85ADA-1

TABLE OF CONTENTS

Hose Break/Loss of MA-2 Coupling and Drogue	5-29
Hose Break at Coupling On Reel	5-29
No Ready Light or Fuel Transfer Failure	5-30
Refueling-Hose Jettisoning	5-30
PART 5 LANDING EMERGENCIES	**5-31**
Single-Engine Landing	5-31
Single-Engine Landing (Compounded By Hydraulic Failure)	5-33
No Flaps/No Slats Landing	5-33
Flaps Takeoff/No Slats Landing	5-33
No Flaps/Slats Down Landing	5-33
Stabilizer Shift Failure	5-33
Arresting-Hook Malfunction	5-34
Barricade Arrestment	5-34
Field Arresting Gear	5-34
Blown Tire	5-38
Wheel-Brake System Failure	5-38
Forced Landing	5-39
Ditching	5-39
PART 6 EJECTION	**5-42**
MK GRU-5 SEAT	5-42
Ejection Capability Chart	5-42
Low-Altitude Ejection	5-42
High-Altitude Ejection	5-42
Manual Bailout	5-42
Normal Parachute Descent	5-43
Water Landing	5-43
MK GRU-7 SEAT	5-43
Ejection Capability Chart	5-43
Low-Altitude Ejection	5-43
High-Altitude Ejection	5-43
Manual Bailout	5-43
Normal Parachute Descent	5-52
Water Landing	5-52

INTRODUCTION

Knowledge of the aircraft and emergency procedures must be reviewed on a regular basis to insure that the crew will take the correct course of action when faced with difficulties. The initial training should be thorough in this respect. Above all, the crew must recognize and admit the emergency situation, then take positive steps in accordance with recommended procedures and good airmanship. Due to the many situations that can arise concerning emergencies, it is impossible to set an absolute policy. The crew must weigh all the factors of a given situation and then take appropriate action for the particular situation. This manual discusses and preplans some likely courses of action and the recommended way of handling certain emergencies. The emergency procedure section should be referred to on a continuing basis. Reference to emergency procedures promulgated in NWP-41 is also required.

Note

As soon as possible, the pilot should notify the bombardier/navigator of the emergency and discuss the intended action.

Part 1 — Ground Emergencies

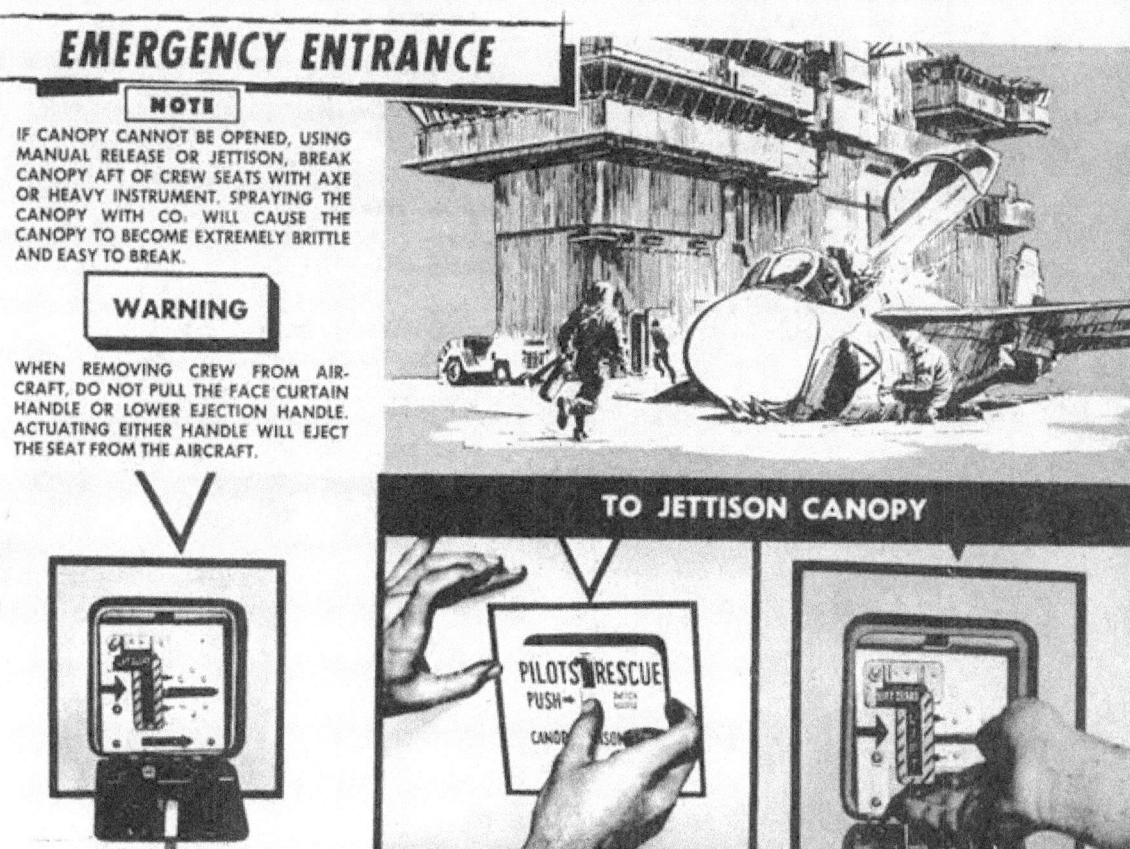

Figure 5-1

For emergency entrance to aircraft, see figure 5-1.

ENGINE STARTING MALFUNCTIONS

If any of the following indications occur during an engine start, a malfunction exists and immediate action is required.

- Wet start (no light-off within 10 seconds of placing throttle to IDLE)
- Hot start (EGT exceeds 455°C)
- Hung start (rpm fails to accelerate to IDLE)

Proceed as Follows:

1. Throttle (affected engine) . . . . OFF
2. Allow engine to continue cranking for 30 seconds minimum if starter mode is still engaged. CSD starter mode automatically disengages at 48% to 50% rpm

EMERGENCY PROCEDURES
Ground Emergencies

Note

If CSD/S starter mode has disengaged, it may be reengaged when rpm has decreased to 10% or below.

Note

Hot Start - Engine windmill should continue until EGT is stabilized. If the maximum start EGT peak of 455°C has not been exceeded, attempt restart only if cause is determined to be other than an engine malfunction.

Wet Start - As much as 5 min. or more of engine windmill may be required to clear fuel from engine/tailpipe after a wet start.

3. Engine/Fuel Master Switch . . . . OFF

4. Prior to attempting restart, an engine/tailpipe inspection should be accomplished by qualified ground crew.

EMERGENCY ENGINE SHUT DOWN

In an emergency, i.e. fire or fire warning indications or if any of the following indications occur during engine start, the engines should be shut down expiditiously.

- Abnormal engine noise or sound
- Oil pressure fails to rise to 35 psi within 30 seconds
- No hydraulic pressure on respective engine
- Speed drive light remains on above 40% rpm

Proceed as Follows:

1. Throttles . . . . OFF

2. Engine/Fuel Master Switches . . . . OFF

part 2 Takeoff Emergencies

The takeoff phase of flight is critical in that it affords the pilot a very short period of time in which to decide whether to continue or abort the takeoff. The crew must have fixed firmly in mind the best course of action to be taken in any given situation. Before each flight the crew should know:

1. Lift-off airspeed and takeoff ground roll
2. Refusal speed and distance; line check speeds and distances
3. Single-engine performance
4. Availability and location of arresting/abort gear
5. Surrounding terrain and obstructions

WARNING

During any takeoff emergency where a safe abort cannot be accomplished and takeoff is impossible, ground-level ejection is possible at any speed (GRU-7). GRU-5, ejection is possible above 100 KIAS.

ABORTED TAKEOFF ARRESTMENTS

Where the aircraft takeoff must be aborted, a roll-in type engagement of all arresting gear is recommended to prevent overrun. The aircraft is cleared up to the maximum takeoff gross weight specified in the Aborted Takeoff column of figure 5-12. Additionally, the data provided in the Long Field Landing column may be used for lightweight aborted takeoff, where applicable.

ENGINE FIRE/FAILURE — TAKEOFF ABORTED

If a fire warning light comes on or if either engine fails during the takeoff run, abort immediately if sufficient runway is available.

1. Throttles/speed brakes . . . IDLE/EXTEND
2. Brakes . . . . APPLY
3. Bleed-air isolation valves (aircraft incorporating AFC No. 268)
   a. NWW . . . . . . ⎫
   b. CSD . . . . ⎬ GANG-BAR OFF
   c. AIR COND . . . ⎭
4. Throttle (affected engine) . . . . OFF

Note

Use caution when securing the right engine to prevent inadvertent shutdown of both engines. If both engines are secured, antiskid, nosewheel steering, flaperon pop-up, and normal braking will be lost.

5. Engine and fuel master switch (affected engine) . . . . OFF
6. Nosewheel steering . . . . ENGAGE
7. Emergency calls . . . . ACCOMPLISH

If an Arrested Rollout is To Be Made:

8. Arresting hook . . . . DOWN
9. Steer for center of runway/engage arresting gear parallel to the centerline

FIRE WARNING LIGHT/TAKEOFF CONTINUED

If a warning light comes on immediately after takeoff, without other visual or audible confirmation, the pilot's first concern is to maintain safe flight.

The fire warning light is reliable.

Before each flight, it is essential that the crew know the single-engine climb speed for his configuration.

If this speed has not been attained, the following steps are considered optimum for continuing safe flight.

1. Engines . . . . MAX. THRUST
2. LANDING GEAR . . . UP, AFTER AIRBORNE
3. External stores . . . . . JETTISON (IF NECESSARY)
4. a. Bleed-air isolation valves (aircraft incorporating AFC No. 268)

EMERGENCY PROCEDURES
Takeoff Emergencies

NAVAIR 01-85ADA-1

NWW . . . .
CSD . . . .   } GANG-BAR . . . OFF
AIR COND . .

4. b. Air-conditioning master switch (aircraft not incorporating AFC No. 268) . . . . . . OFF
5. Establish single-engine climb . 22 units AOA
6. Wing and fuselage fuel . . . . DUMP
7. Throttle (affected engine) . . . . . . OFF
8. Engine and fuel master switch (affected engine) . . . . OFF
9. Climb to safe altitude: DO NOT ATTEMPT restart on affected engine
10. Fly straight ahead. Attempt no turns until a safe airspeed and altitude are attained (terrain permitting).
11. Flaps. UP (after safe airspeed/altitude is attained) See Takeoff and Climb Charts, Section XI, Part 2.
12. If fire indications are positive . . . . EJECT Some positive indications might be explosion, vibration, abnormal engine instrument readings, smoke or fumes in the cockpit, burning odor in oxygen mask, trailing smoke, or verification from another aircraft or control tower.
13. If fire indications are not positive . . . . LAND AS SOON AS POSSIBLE (Refer to Single Engine Landing Procedures)

ENGINE FAILURE/TAKE OFF CONTINUED

The pilot's reaction and his ability to maintain directional control, altitude, or climb depends upon the gross weight of the aircraft, air density, ambient temperature, and the thrust of the good engine. Prior to each flight it is essential that the crew know the single-engine climb speed for their aircraft configuration. The following steps are considered optimum to maintain safe flight:

1. Operating engine . . . . MAX THRUST
2. Landing gear. . . . UP, AFTER AIRBORNE
3. External stores .JETTISON (IF NECESSARY)
4. Establish single-engine climb. .22 units AOA
5. Wing and fuselage fuel . . . . DUMP
6. Failure other than mechanical. . . . ATTEMPT AN AIR START
7. Fly straight ahead. Attempt no turns until safe airspeed and altitude are attained (terrain permitting).

8. Flaps . . . . UP (after safe airspeed/altitude is attained) See Takeoff and Climb charts Section XI, Part 2.

For Obvious Mechanical Failure

9. Throttle (failed engine) . . . . OFF
10. Engine and fuel master switch (failed engine) . . . . OFF
11. Climb to safe altitude; land as soon as practicable. (Refer to Single-Engine Landing Procedures.)

STORES JETTISON

EMERGENCY JETTISON

WARNING

Prior to emergency stores jettison of nuclear stores, ensure that the safe button on the fuzing control panel has been depressed (safe light on and air and ground buttons locked). This prevents the possibility of jettisoning an armed store.

To Jettison All Stores Simultaneously:

1. Emergency stores jettison button. . DEPRESS Hold button down for 1 second, or until separation is felt.

Note

- When jettisoning stores with the emergency jettison button, it is possible to avoid unnecessary expenditure of drop tanks and other salvable stores by first pulling the respective stores jettison circuit breakers on the main panel between the crewmembers.

- 70% of the weight must be off the wheels for emergency jettisoning of external stores.

Selective Jettison:

1. Fuzing . . . . SAFE
2. Appropriate station select switches . . . . BOMBS/GUNS
3. SEL JETT button (A-6E) . . . . . DEPRESS
4. Master ARM switch . . . . ON
5a. Manual weapons release button (A-6E) . . . . DEPRESS
  b. Selective stores jettison switch (A-6A/B/C/KA-6D) . . . . JETTISON

Note

The port forward main landing-gear door must be closed before stores will be released using SEL JETT system.

STRUT LOCK LIGHT

If the STRUT LOCK light comes on with the landing gear down, this indicates that the nose strut is still locked. The landing gear may be safely retracted. During the landing phase, a minimum rate of descent field landing is preferred.

LAUNCH BAR DOWN/NOSE GEAR COCKED

- Tow link in nose-gear window.
- Flashing indexer (hook bypass in touch-and-go or hook bypass in arrest with hook in down position)

1. Obtain a visual check

If Nose Wheel Cocked:

2. Do not retract gear. Make a normal carrier landing or normal field landing. Use aerodynamic braking and then place nose firmly on deck.

If Launch Bar is Down and Nose Wheel is Straight:

3. Gear handle . . . . RAISE

Inflight Emergencies

ENGINE FAILURE

See figure 5-2 for velocity required for maximum glide.

SINGLE-ENGINE FLIGHT CHARACTERISTICS

WARNING

At certain gross weights and ambient temperatures, the aircraft will NOT fly on one engine in the takeoff or landing configuration. The applicable single-engine graphs should be referred to before each flight.

Because of the location of the engines relative to the centerline of the aircraft, only a slight rudder deflection is required to prevent a yaw toward the failed engine at normal speeds. Minimum single-engine control speed varies with gross weight, flap setting, and the landing-gear position. The aircraft is designed so that no one system (hydraulic, bleed-air, electrical, etc.) is dependent on a specific engine. Therefore, loss of an engine will not result in a loss of any complete system. Refer to Section XI for single-engine performance data.

SINGLE-ENGINE FAILURE DURING FLIGHT

It is possible to inadvertantly lose an engine due to a malfunction of the fuel control system or to incorrect technique used during certain critical flight conditions. If engine failure can be attributed to some obvious nonmechanical failure, proceed as follows:

1. Positively determine failed engine
2. Attempt air start if feasible. (See Air Start procedure.)

If No Relight:

3. Throttle and engine/fuel master switch (affected engine) . . . . OFF
4. Land as soon as practicable (Refer to Single-Engine Landing procedures.)

DOUBLE-ENGINE FAILURE DURING FLIGHT

The possibility of a double-engine failure during flight is very remote; however, if such a situation should occur, proceed as follows:

1. Convert excess airspeed to altitude.

WARNING

If both engines fail below 1,500 feet AGL and 250 KIAS . . . . EJECT

2. RAT handle . . . . PULL
3. EMER IGN circuit breakers . . . CHECK IN
4. Attempt air start - (see air start procedure).

WARNING

150 KIAS must be maintained to ensure adequate engine windmill rpm for hydraulic pressure.

If repeated relight attempts are not successful between 20,000 and 10,000 feet, eject by 10,000 feet AGL.

If still on first or second relight attempt when passing through 10,000 feet AGL and it appears that a relight is likely, air start attempt may be continued to a minimum of 5000 feet AGL.

If both engines are still flamed out below 10,000 feet AGL, zoom to convert excess airspeed to altitude. Attempt a normal air start as time permits. If the peak altitude is 5000 feet AGL and the air start attempt is not successful, eject no lower than 5000 feet AGL. If the peak altitude is below 5000 feet AGL and an air start attempt is made during the zoom and there is no evidence of a relight, eject at the peak altitude. If no air start attempt is made, eject at the peak altitude.

If the decision to eject is made at high altitude, it is recommended that the aircrew eject at a minimum of 10,000 feet AGL.

VELOCITY REQUIRED FOR MAXIMUM GLIDE

AIRCRAFT CONFIGURATION
(1) D-704 + (4) 300 GALLON TANKS

DATE: 15 FEBRUARY 1971
DATA BASIS: ESTIMATED

FUEL GRADE: JP-5
FUEL DENSITY: 6.8 LB/GAL

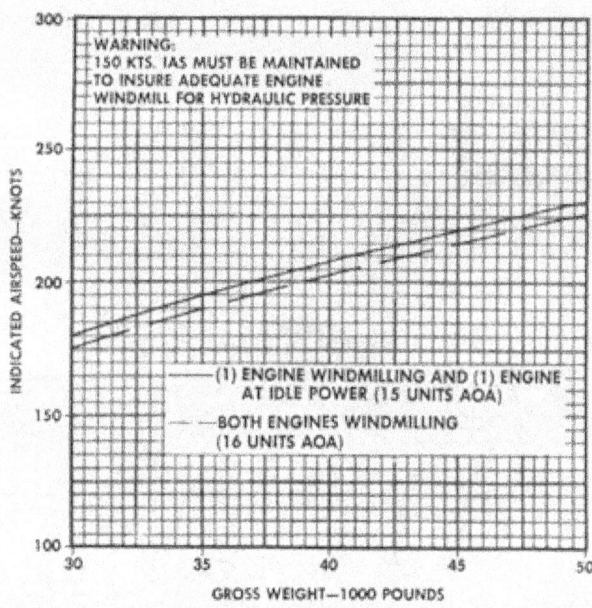

Figure 5-2

EMERGENCY PROCEDURES
In-Flight Emergencies

AIR STARTS

In general, air start capability is increased by higher airspeeds and lower altitudes. Refer to figure 5-3. No damage will occur to the engine if starts are attempted outside the envelope. However, unsatisfactory starts on the low-speed side of the envelope may result in an increase in EGT towards the start limit (455°C) due to a hung start. Care should be taken not to exceed this limit.

Do not delay in the air start attempts.

If Less Than 10 Seconds Have Elapsed:

1. Air start button . . . . DEPRESS AND HOLD
   With air start button depressed, wait for indication of a start by monitoring RPM, EGT, and fuel flow.

If More Than 10 Seconds Have Elapsed:

2. Throttle (failed engine) . . . . OFF

3. EMER IGN circuit breakers. . . . CHECK IN

4. Air start button . . . . DEPRESS AND HOLD

5. Throttle (failed engine) . . . . IDLE
   Go around the horn with air start button held depressed; wait 60 seconds for indication of a start monitoring RPM, EGT, and fuel flow.

FIRE

FIRE/BLEED AIR SYSTEM FAILURE

A fire warning light accompanied by any or all of the following are indications of a probable bleed-air system failure:

a. Loss of hydraulic pressure indications
b. CSD/S or generator failure

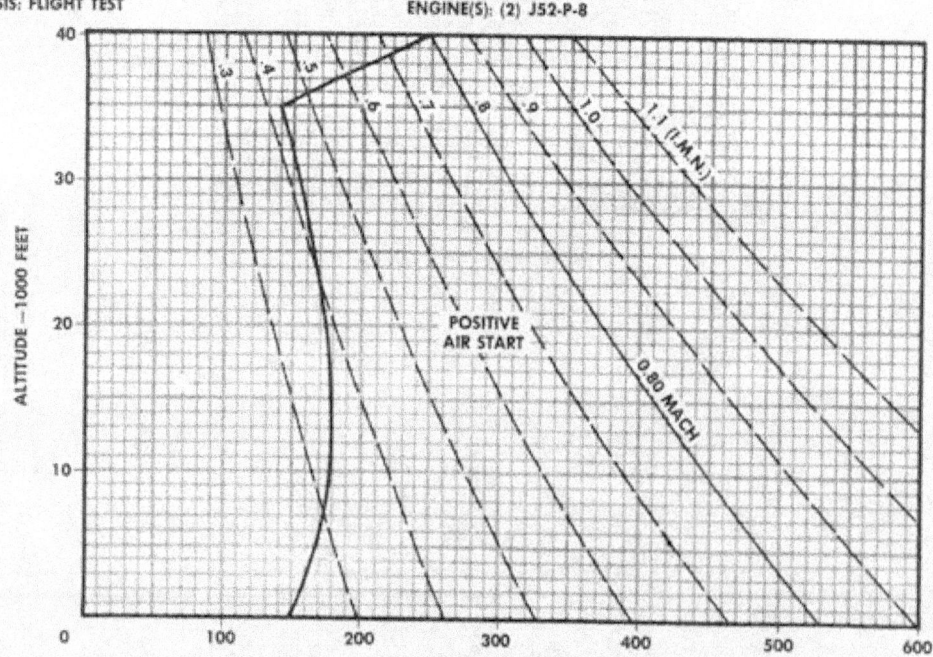

Figure 5-3

NAVAIR 01-85ADA-1

EMERGENCY PROCEDURES
In-Flight Emergencies

c. Unsafe nose gear
d. Noticeable thump at time of failure
e. Loss of wing pressurization
f. Multiple unrelated electrical failures
g. Unusual odors in the cockpit

FIRE WARNING LIGHT LIT

1. Throttle (affected engine) . . . . OFF
2. Engine and fuel master switch (affected engine) . . . . OFF
3. a. Bleed-air isolation valves (aircraft incorporating AFC NO. 268):
   NWW . . . . ⎫
   CSD . . . . . ⎬ GANG BAR . . . OFF
   AIR COND . . ⎭
3. b. Air-conditioning master switch aircraft not incorporating AFC NO. 268 . . . . OFF

Note

If fire warning light is extinguished by securing the air conditioning system, the fire indicator may have been caused by a bleed air leak from the environmental system into the starboard engine bay only.

4. If fire indications are positive . . . . EJECT
   Some positive indications might be explosion, vibration, abnormal engine instrument readings, smoke or fumes in the cockpit, burning odor in oxygen mask, trailing smoke, or verification from another aircraft or control tower.

5. If fire indications are not positive . . . . . .
   . . . . LAND AS SOON AS POSSIBLE
   (Refer to Single Engine Landing Procedures.)

WARNING

- If the fire warning light goes out, DO NOT ATTEMPT restart of affected engine or re-open bleed-air system isolation valves, UNLESS windshield air is required for landing in heavy precipitation. Then the NWW switch must be placed in AUTO to enable windshield air. This should be done only during the final phase of the landing approach and the NWW switch should be repositioned to OFF as soon as possible after landing. This procedure is hazardous and should be performed only if absolutely essential.

- Possible substantial loss of thrust from the remaining engine will result in marginal or no wave-off capability. A BARRICADE IS REQUIRED FOR SHIPBOARD RECOVERY.

- A wave-off is extremely hazardous due to minimum rate of climb available and increased possibility of fire damage.

- In the event of unsafe gear indications, perform emergency landing-gear extension procedures on final approach and LAND on the FIRST PASS regardless of landing gear indication.

Note

In aircraft incorporating AFC 268, if the fire warning light goes out, consideration should be given to the systems lost as a result.

Right Engine Shut Down—Systems Lost:

- Right Generator
- Air Conditioning
- Rain Removal
- TRIM POD Cooling (A-6C only)
- Aft (equipment cooling) Air Cycle Unit (A-6E TRAM)

No equipment cooling will soon cause overheating of all electronic equipment, except (in aircraft thru A-6E 159579 and A-6E Mod M120) the CNI equipment, which is provided with an alternate cooling blower. Therefore, unless absolutely needed for flight, all electronic equipment except the CNI equipment should be turned off. In A-6E 159895 and ON and A-6E Mod M121 and ON, the UHF radios are cooled by cabin air, the TACAN has a cooling blower, and the IFF transponder has no alternate cooling.

Left Engine Shut Down—Systems Lost:

- Left Generator
- Rain Removal
- TRIM POD Cooling (A-6C only)
- Aft (Equipment Cooling) Air Cycle Unit (A-6E TRAM)

NWW TEMP LIGHT LIT (AIRCRAFT INCORPORATING AFC 268)

Lighting of the NWW TEMP light indicates a leak in the bleed-air ducting in the nosewheel well or radome areas. Therefore, damage to electrical/electronic and hydraulic components in those areas should be suspected, even if the NWW isolation valve was closed promptly. With the NWW isolation valve closed, the rain-removal and vortex-removal systems have been lost.

1. NWW bleed-air isolation valve . . . . . . OFF
2. Windshield rain removal . . . . OFF

If NWW TEMP Light Goes Out:

3. LAND AS SOON AS POSSIBLE

If NWW TEMP Light Remains On:

4. Bleed-air isolation valves:
   CSD . . . . . . ⎫
   AIR COND . . ⎬ GANG BAR . . . . . . OFF

Change 2   5-11

EMERGENCY PROCEDURES
In-Flight Emergencies

    5.   Right throttle . . . . OFF

    6.   Right engine and fuel master switch . . OFF

    7.   If positive indications of fire exist . . . EJECT

If NWW TEMP Light Goes Out:

    8.   Land as soon as possible.

AFT TEMP LIGHT LIT (A-6E TRAM AIRCRAFT)

Lighting of the AFT TEMP light indicates a possible leak in the bleed air ducting to the aft equipment bay area. Damage to electrical/electronic and hydraulic components in the area should be suspected even if the AIR COND isolation valve was closed promptly. With the AIR COND isolation valve closed, all air conditioning and equipment cooling have been lost; therefore, unless absolutely needed for flight, all electronic equipment should be turned off. The UHF radios are not specially cooled; they receive cockpit air through louvres in the side of the center console, and may be safely operated. The TACAN has a cooling blower; however, its location in the aft equipment bay indicates restricted operation in this case.

    1.   AIR COND bleed-air isolation valve . . OFF

IF AFT TEMP Light Goes Out:

    2.   LAND AS SOON AS POSSIBLE

IF AFT TEMP Light Remains On:

    3.   Bleed-air isolation valves:

        CSD . . ⎫
               ⎬ BANG BAR . . . . OFF
        NWW . ⎭

    4.   Right throttle . . . . OFF

    5.   Right engine and fuel master switch . . OFF

    6.   If positive indications of fire exist . . . EJECT

IF AFT TEMP Light Goes Out:

    7.   LAND AS SOON AS POSSIBLE

TEMP CONT (A-6E)/COMPUTER OVERHEAT LIGHT (A-6A,B,C)

    1.   Check computer pedestal area for hot air-flow around pedestal base or excessive heating of pedestal area.

If Excessive Heat is Detected:

    2.   CMPTR EMER COOL switch . . . . ON

    2A.   EQUIPMENT switch (TRAM aircraft) . . COLD

TEMP CONT/COMPUTER Overheat Light Remains On and if Pedestal Area Remains Hot:

    3.   Computer . . . . OFF

    4.   AIR COND master . . . . OFF

NAVAIR 01-85ADA-1

> **CAUTION**
>
> Operation of avionics system (radar, etc.) requires air conditioning. Operating with air conditioning off for periods in excess of 5 minutes may damage equipment.

Note

(A-6E) In addition to the TEMP CONT light, the COMPUTER light may be expected to come on.

    5.   Land as soon as practicable.

STEADY COMPUTER LIGHT, NO TEMP CONT LIGHT (A-6E)

This indicates an overheat condition, greater than 230°F, which may be occurring in components in or outside the cockpit.

    1.   Computer . . . . OFF

    2.   Land as soon as practicable.

Note

Cooldown period required to turn the COMPUTER light off may be more than 1 hour.

AFT BLEED LIGHT LIT (A-6E TRAM)

Lighting of the AFT BLEED light with the AIR COND bleed-air switch at on indicates that the aft bleed-air shutoff valve has closed due to an overheat condition in the duct to the aft air-cycle refrigeration unit, shutting off the equipment-cooling system. All electronic equipment except the UHF radios, which are cooled by cockpit air, and the TACAN, which has a cooling blower, should be shut off to prevent damage.

    1.   Electronic equipment . . . . OFF

    2.   Land as soon as practicable.

ELECTRICAL FIRE/SMOKE OR FUMES IN COCKPIT

To eliminate smoke and fumes from the cockpit, proceed as follows:

    1.   Oxygen . . . . Insure ON/100%

    2.   Air-conditioning COCKPIT switch . . RAM AIR

    3.   MAN/RAM AIR switch . . . . COLD

    4.   Descend to below 25,000 feet

    5.   CABIN DUMP switch . . . . ON

If the cause of the malfunction cannot be immediately determined, further steps may be necessary. These will depend on the intensity of the smoke and the circumstances under which the aircraft is operating.

NAVAIR 01-85ADA-1

EMERGENCY PROCEDURES
In-Flight Emergencies

Should symptoms of an electrical fire occur, and the cause cannot be determined, proceed as follows:

6. Computer, search radar, track radar, VDI, and PHD .... OFF
7. AIR CONDitioning MASTER switch .... OFF
8. Unnecessary electrical equipment .... OFF

If Symptoms of Fire Persist:

9. RAT handle .... PULL
10. GENerators .... OFF

Note

The possibility exists that the RAT may be inoperative, and may not assume that electrical load of the essential bus. The best indication of this is failure of the generator caution lights to come on.

11. AIR CONDitioning MASTER switch ... ON

The possibility exists that smoke and fumes symptomatic of an electrical fire may have originated in the air-conditioning system.

12. Necessary electrical equipment ..... ON
13. Circuit breaker (affected equipment)........ PULL IF AVAILABLE
14. GENerators .... ON

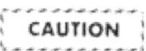

Do not attempt to reset the affected equipment circuit breaker until the cause of the fire has been determined and corrected by qualified maintenance personnel.

15. Land as soon as practicable.

CAUTION

Without AFC No. 268 incorporated, operation of the CNI package requires air conditioning. If operated with air conditioning off for periods in excess of 5 minutes, equipment may be damaged.

AIR CONDITIONING FULL HOT

If cabin temperature goes full hot, perform the following immediately:

1. ENVIRONMENT/SEATS circuit breakers................... IN
2. MAN/RAM AIR switch ..... FULL COLD

Change 2   5-12A/(5-12B blank)

EMERGENCY PROCEDURES
In-Flight Emergencies

If Temperature Remains Hot:

3. AIR CONDITIONING COCKPIT switch . . . . RAM AIR

4. MAN/RAM AIR SWITCH. . . . . FULL COLD

5. AIR COND MASTER switch . . . . OFF

If Temperature Remains Hot:

6. a. In aircraft incorporating AFC No. 268

   1. AIR COND bleed-air switch . . . . OFF

   2. Right throttle . . . . OFF

   3. Right engine and fuel master switch . . . . OFF

6. b. In aircraft without AFC No. 268

   CABIN DUMP switch . . . . ON

7. Canopy. . . . . OPEN OR JETTISON (AS NECESSARY)

WARNING

The canopy must be fully closed or jettisoned before ejection.

8. Foot heat control . . . . CLOSED

9. All unnecessary electrical equipment. . OFF

10. Land as soon as possible.

Note

Ram air will provide sufficient cooling for wing-tank pressurization system in flight.

OIL SYSTEM FAILURES

An oil system failure is recognized by a decrease of, or a complete loss of oil pressure. If an oil system malfunction has caused prolonged oil starvation of engine bearings, the result will be a progressive bearing failure and subsequent engine seizure. This progression of bearing failure starts slowly and will normally continue at a slow rate up to a certain point at which the progression failure accelerates rapidly to complete bearing failure. The time interval from the moment of oil starvation to complete failure depends on such factors as condition of bearings prior to the starvation, operating temperatures of bearings, and bearing loads. Bearing failure due to oil starvation is generally characterized by a rapidly increasing vibration. When the vibration becomes moderate to heavy, complete seizure will occur in seconds. In order to minimize engine damage and conserve re-maining operating time for possible emergencies, the affected engine should be shut down upon first recognition of an oil system failure.

Note

Normal oil pressure is 40 to 50 PSI. Except at idle, oil pressures between 35 and 40 PSI are undesirable and should be tolerated only for the completion of the flight, preferably at a reduced throttle setting. Oil pressures below normal should be reported as an engine discrepancy and should be corrected before the next takeoff. Oil pressures below 35 PSI are unsafe and require that either the engine be shut down or a landing be made as soon as possible, using the minimum thrust required for safe flight.

Upon first recognition of sustained oil system failure (above or below oil pressure limits), perform the following:

LOSS OF OIL PRESSURE

1. Throttle (affected engine) . . . . OFF

2. Engine and fuel master . . . . OFF (affected engine)

3. Land as soon as practicable. (Refer to Single Engine Landing Procedures.)

HIGH OIL PRESSURE

1. Reduce power on affected engine.

If unable to maintain oil pressure within limits:

2. Throttle (affected engine) . . . . OFF

3. Engine/fuel master (affected engine) . . . . OFF

Note

If the engine is secured for oil pressure malfunctions, it may be desirable to relight the engine for use during critical flight evolutions e.g. carrier landings, etc.

4. Land as soon as practicable.

LOW-OIL WARNING LIGHT

CAUTION

Consideration should be given to securing the engine. If engine is allowed to run until oil pressure starts to fall, severe engine bearing damage will result. The engine may be relit for critical flight evolutions e.g. carrier landing, etc.

IF NORMAL PRESSURE CANNOT BE MAINTAINED

1. Throttle (affected engine) . . . . OFF

EMERGENCY PROCEDURES
In-Flight Emergencies

NAVAIR 01-85ADA-1

2. Engine and fuel master
   (affected engine) . . . . OFF

3. Land as soon as practicable.
   (Refer to Single Engine Landing Procedures.)

FUEL SYSTEM FAILURE

ENGINE FUEL PUMP FAILURE

Failure of the entire two-stage engine fuel pump will result in engine flameout due to fuel starvation. Gear stage (high-pressure pump) failure will result in a flameout; failure of the centrifugal stage (low-pressure engine boost pump) alone will have little or no effect on performance, and will not be evident to the pilot since the fuselage boost pump will continue to supply adequate pressure to the inlet side of the high-pressure pump except at higher altitudes (above 20,000 feet). At higher altitudes, failure of the centrifugal stage may reduce pressure at the inlet of the gear stage to below 12-14 psi, lighting its respective FUEL PSI light. Should either FUEL PSI light come on, either power reduction on affected engine or descent to a lower altitude is recommended.

> **CAUTION**
>
> DO NOT DEPRESS BOOST PUMP TEST BUTTON IN FLIGHT, as an engine will flame out if the centrifugal stage of an engine-driven fuel pump has failed.

FUSELAGE BOOST PUMP FAILURE

If the electrically driven fuselage boost pump fails, fuel will still be supplied to the engine fuel pump by suction feed (below 20,000 feet). If the fuel flow demands of the engines cannot be met by suction feed, loss of thrust may result when above 20,000 feet. Insufficient pressure will be indicated by the L and R FUEL PSI lights coming on when pressure to the inlet of the gear stage of the engine fuel pump drops to 12-14 psi. Power reduction or descent is recommended to restore engine performance.

TRANSFER PUMP FAILURE

Failure of one transfer pump will result in a 50% reduction of fuel flow for either fuselage fuel transfer to the air refueling store or fuselage fuel dumping. If both transfer pumps fail, fuselage dumping and fuselage fuel transfer to the air refueling store cannot be accomplished.

FUEL TRANSFER FAILURE (WING/DROP TANK PRESSURIZATION)

For fuel to transfer from the drop and wing tanks, the drop tank shutoff valves and wing-tank fueling and transfer and shutoff valves must be in the open position. These valves are energized to the closed position by primary 28 V DC power with WING DUMP selected, the FUEL READY switch in FLIGHT, FUEL RDY in GROUND with the ground refueling panel in FUEL or DEFUEL positions, or the landing gear extended. In the event of a total electrical failure, fuel will transfer normally from the drop and wing tanks.

If Fuel Transfer Does Not Occur, Proceed as Follows:

1. FUEL READY Switch . . . . . . CHECK OFF

If unable to affect fuel transfer of wing and drop-tank fuel through normal or override pressurization and wing pressure lights are still on, and if fuel considerations dictate:

2. RAT handle . . . . PULL

3. Right and left generators . . . . OFF

Monitor for fuel transfer.

> **CAUTION**
>
> Shutting down the generators is not recommended under IFR conditions unless absolutely necessary. If the RAT is inoperative, securing both generators will result in the loss of all attitude and navigation systems.

Note

If pressurization indications are normal but fuel is not transferring, a non-modulating pilot valve failure may be suspected. Attempt to free the valve by applying positive and negative g.

If Fuel Still Does Not Transfer:

4. Right and left generators . . . . ON

5. Land as soon as possible

Note

In the event the transfer failure is electrically caused, the RAT may be stowed with both generators secured, in VFR conditions. This ensures opening of the drop-tank and wing fuel transfer and shutoff valves. Fuel transfer may then be monitored by redeploying the RAT or turning on a generator periodically until safe landing is assured.

FUEL FILTER LIGHT LIT

Lighting of the Left or Right fuel FILTER light indicates that the fuel filter for the respective engine is contaminated. Proceed as follows:

1. Throttle (affected engine) . . . . . . RETARD

2. Avoid large or unnecessary throttle movements.

3. Land as soon as practicable.

NAVAIR 01-85ADA-1

EMERGENCY PROCEDURES
In-Flight Emergencies

FUEL/AIR ADAPTER MALFUNCTION

Malfunction of fuel/air adapters can lead to loss of drop-tank fuel transfer or fuel leaks in the area of the adapters. To stop the fuel leak, proceed as follows:

1. WING DROP TANK TRANSfer switch . . . INBD OR OUTBD AS REQUIRED TO SECURE DROP TANK PRESSURE

If jettisoning of the drop tank/store is required for landing, proceed as follows:

2. Insure fuel leak has stopped. . . . . . . OBTAIN VISUAL CHECK

3. Selectively jettison affected tank/store.

WARNING

Jettison of a tank/store with fuel still leaking from the area of the fuel/air adapter may result in an in-flight fire.

EMERGENCY FUEL DUMPING (RAT ONLY POWER)

A/C Without AFC 352 Incorporated:

If the situation necessitates fuel dumping with double generator failure and the ram-air turbine is operating, it is possible to dump only from the outboard wing panels.

Wing drop tanks and the centerline drop tank or air-refueling store can be jettisoned. Fuselage and inboard wing fuel dumping is not possible and any weight reduction of remaining fuel must be through burn-down.

A/C With AFC 352 Incorporated:

When dumping fuel with a double generator failure and the ram-air turbine is operating, it is possible to dump the inboard and outboard wing panels and the wing drop tanks. Fuselage and center line drop tank fuel dumping is not possible and any weight reduction of fuselage and centerline drop-tank fuel must be through burn-down.

THROTTLE LINKAGE FAILURE

No provisions are incorporated for automatic positioning of the fuel control in the event of throttle linkage failure. The affected engine may stabilize at any rpm between cutoff and military power. If this should occur proceed as follows:

1. Land as soon as practicable.

Note

The APCS electromechanical actuators are located on the engines, and the throttle linkage failure may have occurred between an electromechanical actuator and the throttle. If so, the APCS switch may be held in the ENGAGE position and the desired throttle position obtained by varying AOA and releasing the APCS switch when set. Desired throttle positions may be set in this manner throughout the flight for all portions of the profile. The APCS should also be available for a normal landing approach.

During a wave-off or bolter, the APCS will be disengaged and a rapid power change on the affected engine may occur.

Prior to Entering Landing Pattern:

2. Dump/burn down to single-engine approach gross weight.

3. Make a normal or single-engine approach as necessary (depending on engine power available).

Note

Engine rpm may change with any change in fuel control vibration. If necessary, due to fluctuating or excessively high power, shut the affected engine down prior to the approach.

After Landing:

4. Throttle (affected engine) . . . . OFF

5. Engine and fuel master switch (affected engine) . . . . OFF

ELECTRICAL SYSTEM FAILURE

See figure 5-4 for emergency power distribution

See figure FO-11 for annunciator caution lights.

See figure 5-5 for key cockpit circuit breakers.

SINGLE GENERATOR FAILURE

Failure of one generator will be noted by lighting of either the L-GEN or R-GEN caution light on the annunciator panel. The light will indicate which generator has failed. Failure of either generator will result in loss of the monitor bus power. If a generator fails, proceed as follows:

1. Affected generator switch . RESET, then ON

5-15

EMERGENCY PROCEDURES
In-Flight Emergencies

Note

Repeated attempts may be made to reset generator. In flight at a reduced power setting, resetting the CSD/S may enable the resetting of the failed generator.

If Generator Caution Light Remains Lit:

2. Affected generator switch . . . . . . OFF

3. AFCS (KA-6D) . . . . . DISENGAGED FOR REFUELING

4. Land as soon as practicable.

For instrument/night approach,

5. RAT handle . . . . PULL
   The extended RAT ensures the reliability of electric power supply to the essential busses.

WARNING

Do not engage AFCS during single generator refueling operations. Voltage transients may induce abrupt control deflection.

CAUTION

KA-6D Only - Utilizing the air-refueling system package is not recommended. (See refueling with single generator.)

DOUBLE GENERATOR FAILURE

When both generators fail, both generator caution lights will be out and all ac power will be lost. All dc power except battery power will also be lost. Upon the loss of both generators, immediately perform the following:

1. RAT handle . . . . PULL

2. Check GEN caution lights lit

3. Generator switches . . . . RESET, Then ON

4. COMPASS/ATT REF switch (A-6A, B, C, E only) . . . . MAG/VGI
   Check heading and attitude instruments for proper indications.

If the GEN caution lights remain lit:

5. Land as soon as practicable.

CAUTION

As the fuselage boost pump in inoperative under RAT only power, possible thrust loss may be experienced above 20,000 feet.

Note

- Minimum airspeed to maintain RAT power is 110 KIAS.

- With a double generator failure, when operating on RAT only power, the WHEELS warning light will continue to flash during approach with gear down, and the hydraulic indicators and backup hydraulic pump will not function.

LOSS OF ESSENTIAL DC BUS

If the external number one essential dc bus circuit breaker pops, the entire number one essential dc bus will be lost even though both main generators remain operative and power the primary and monitor buses. Major items lost include: speed brakes, normal and emergency flaps/slats, normal gear operation, AOA, integrated position indicator, CNI package including ICS, annunciator lights, MA-1 compass system, weapons release, normal and emergency stores jettison, approach indexer, fuel-gate valve, cabin dump, emergency flap brake, flight instrument lights, turn and slip, and master caution and warning lights. If it is suspected that the number

EMERGENCY POWER DISTRIBUTION

SINGLE GENERATOR FAILURE (LOSS OF MONITORED BUS) EQUIPMENT LOST			
INSTRUMENTS OAT, ACCELEROMETER SYS, "G" METER, POWER TRIM	**AVIONICS** ECM, VTR (A-6C/A-6E), GCB, DOPPLER, DATA LINK	**EXTERIOR LIGHTS** DROGUE LIGHTS, POSITION LIGHTS, FORMATION LIGHTS, PYLON LIGHTS, TAXI/PROBE LIGHTS	
FUEL & OIL FWD. TRANS. PUMP (EXCEPT KA-6D)		**INTERIOR LIGHTS** CONSOLE LIGHTS, DVRI LIGHTS	
DOUBLE GENERATOR FAILURE (ESSENTIAL BUS ONLY) EQUIPMENT REMAINING			
ENGINE INSTRUMENTS FUEL QUANTITY, FUEL FLOW, EGT, OIL PRESSURE, % RPM	**FLIGHT CONTROLS** LAT. TRIM, LONG. TRIM, RUD. TRIM, FLAPS/SLATS (NOR), FLAPER POP-UP, SPIN ASSIST	T-375 WEAPONS MONITOR & CONTROL, ESS ARM FEEDER, MAN WEAP RELEASE, GUN CLEAR	
FLIGHT INSTRUMENTS ALTIMETER (BAR), HSI, MA-1 COMPASS, VGI, AOA, INT. POS. IND., APPR. INDEXER, TURN & SLIP, A/S	**RADIO** ICS, CNI	**AIR COND** RAM AIR, CABIN DUMP VALVE, BLEED AIR ISOL. VALVES	
	ENGINE CONTROL AIR START, CSD/S	**LIGHTS** FIRE WARNING & TEST, FLIGHT INSTRUMENT ANNUNCIATOR PANEL, APPROACH LIGHTS, FLOOD LIGHTS, UTILITY LIGHTS, MAP LIGHT, PILOT'S SPOTLIGHT, B/N INSTRUMENT, CAUTION DIMMING, WHEELS WARNING, WHEELS TRANSITION	
LANDING AND ARRESTING GEAR LANDING GEAR, ARRESTING HOOK	**FUEL** DUMP (OTBD WG ONLY), WG & WG DROPS WITH AFC 352, AIR REFUEL (MAN), NORMAL TRANS.	
	ARMAMENT MECH FUZING, STORES JETTISON, ELEC. FUZING (A-6E)		

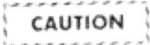 EXCEPT A-6E 159895 AND ON, A-6E MOD M121 AND ON

Figure 5-4

KEY COCKPIT CIRCUIT BREAKERS

CIRCUIT BREAKER PLACARD	BUS	LOCATION	ITEMS ON CIRCUIT BREAKER
LAT/LONG TRIM	ESS AC	MAIN	AIR COND RAM AIR SWITCH AIR NAV COMPUTER (A-6A)
GEAR/HOOK	ESS DC #1	MAIN	SPIN ASSIST WEIGHT ON WHEELS SWITCH
L. SPD DR	ESS DC #1	MAIN	LEFT ENGINE FUEL MASTER LEFT CSD/S
R. SPD DR	ESS DC #1	MAIN	RIGHT ENGINE FUEL MASTER RIGHT CSD/S
CNI/MA-1 [1]	ESS AC	MAIN	HSI (TACAN) MA-1 ASQ-57 POWER
CAUTION LTS	ESS DC #1	MAIN	LOW ALTITUDE WARNING LIGHT (A-6E) APN-141/APN-194 INDICATOR (A-6E) WARNING LIGHTS TEST SWITCH MASTER LIGHT PANEL ANNUNCIATOR PANEL INTEGRATED POSITION INDICATOR
ANGLE OF ATTACK	ESS DC #1	MAIN	ANGLE OF ATTACK INTEGRATED POSITION INDICATOR (A-6A,B,C/KA-6D) ELECTRIC FLAP DRIVE (A-6A, B, C/KA-6D) EMERGENCY BRAKE RELAY (A-6A, B, C/KA-6D) WHEELS WARNING SWITCH (A-6E)
INST LTS	ESS AC ESS DC #1	MAIN	INSTRUMENT LIGHTS ACLS [3]
TURN/SLIP [1] TRIM/IND [2]	ESS DC #1	MAIN	TURN AND SLIP INDICATOR RUDDER TRIM INDICATOR STABILIZER TRIM INDICATOR LOW FUEL CAUTION LIGHT IF C/B POPPED
26V INST XMFR #2	ESS AC	MAIN	MA-1 COMPASS AND CARD EGT/FF/RPM INDICATORS
26V INST XMFR	PRIM AC	B/N	L/R HYDRAULIC PRESSURE INDICATORS SEARCH RADAR RADAR RECORDER
ADC/OPT SIGHT	PRIM AC	B/N	ADC OPTICAL SIGHT CONTROL SPEED BRAKE NULL DETECTOR
TSEC CONT	ESS DC #1	B/N	KY-28
AUTO PILOT	PRIM DC	B/N OBSERVER	ADC AUTO PILOT ASQ-61 (A-6A) ASN-31 (A-6A)
MISSILE (A-6A, B, C/KA-6D)	PRIM AC	B/N OBSERVER	ICS
3 PH MSL PWR (A-6E)	PRIM AC	B/N	ICS JUNCTION BOX ARMAMENT PANEL (AWE)
PRARS ADPT PH A [1]	PRIM AC	B/N	A/D CONVERTER INS ADAPTER (A-6E)
CNI [1]	ESS AC	B/N	ASQ-57 RECEIVER AMPLIFIER POWER ARC-75 TRANSMITTER (A-6E)

[1] A-6, B, C/KA-6D AND A-6E 158041 THRU 159579 AND MOD M1 THRU M120

[2] A-6E 159895 AND ON, A-6E MOD M121 AND ON

[3] AIRCRAFT WITH A F C 230

Figure 5-5

EMERGENCY PROCEDURES
In-Flight Emergencies

one essential dc bus circuit breaker is disengaged, proceed as follows:

1. RAT handle . . . . PULL

If power is not restored to essential flight instruments and equipment by this action:

2. Both generators . . . . OFF

Note

- Unless absolutely necessary, do not secure main generators if not in VFR conditions. If the RAT is inoperative, securing both main generators will result in loss of all attitude and navigation systems.

- Minimum airspeed to maintain RAT power is 110 KIAS.

COMPLETE ELECTRICAL FAILURE

If both generators fail, and electrical power to the essential bus is not restored when the RAT is deployed, proceed as follows:

Night/IFR

Maintain controlled flight if possible, or attempt to gain and maintain outside visual reference. If unable to maintain controlled flight . . . . EJECT

Note

Instruments remaining are the vertical speed indicator (VSI), airspeed indicator, pressure altimeter, cabin pressure altimeter, standby compass, and auxiliary brake gage.

VFR

Attempt to join another aircraft, and use HEFOE signals to indicate extent of problems. Use PRC emergency radio if available.

Note

- If failure occurs on takeoff, it will be impossible to raise the landing gear and flaps or jettison stores.

- Landing gear must be lowered by emergency method (visual check by LSO/tower/wingman is desirable).

- Fuel state must be estimated using power setting, airspeed, altitude, and time (fuel quantity gage pointers will freeze at the last fuel indications before power loss).

- Flaps/slats, antiskid, flaperon pop-up, trim, and nose-wheel steering will not be available. Normal wheels brakes WILL be available.

- If available, plan to make field arrested landing.

- Battery-powered spin assist may be selected before landing, to gain extended rudder throw for additional directional control.

WARNING

Extreme caution must be used when utilizing normal braking without anti-skid at high landing speeds.

SPEED DRIVE FAILURE

Lighting of the L or R-SPD DR light on the annunciator panel indicates a failure of the constant-speed drive/starter (CSD/S). A steady light indicates high oil temperature, low oil pressure, or CSD/S failure in aircraft with 30 kVA generators. A bright flashing light (2 to 3 second interval) indicates CSD/S overspeed. A random, dim, flickering light at altitudes above 30,000 feet indicates low oil pressure due to altitude. If the constant-speed drive starter malfunctions perform the following:

If SPD DR Light Steady/Flashing

1. Reduce rpm - Reset SPD DR

If Light Remains On Steady/Flashing:

2. SPD DR switch (affected CSD/S) . . . . OFF

If at High Altitude and SPD DR Light Flashes Brightly (2-3 sec. int.):

1. Reduce both engine rpm's to 75% - Reset SPD DR.

Note

Attempts to reset the CSD/S at high engine rpm and high altitude may cause undamped CSD/S overspeed.

If SPD DR Light Continues to Flash Brightly:

2. Descend to lower altitude - Reset SPD DR

If SPD DR Light Continues to Flash Brightly:

3. SPD DR switch (affected CSD/S) . . . . OFF

SPD DR Light Flickers Dimly:

1. Descend to lower altitude.

Note

If the SPD DR light is allowed to continue flickering, loss of CSD/S control and generators may result.

LOSS OF TRIM BUTTON

1. LAT/LONG TRIM circuit breaker. . . . . PULL

WARNING

Should the trim button become dislodged, human contact with the exposed probe with electrical power on can result in incapacitation/unconsciousness.

Note

Pulling LAT/LONG TRIM circuit breaker de-energizes the ram air switch. Should ram air be desired, reset the LAT/LONG TRIM circuit breaker long enough to select RAM AIR.

HYDRAULIC SYSTEM FAILURE

SINGLE HYDRAULIC PUMP FAILURE

The loss of any one hydraulic pump will be indicated on the hydraulic pressure indicator and will not present any flight control problems.

CAUTION

Failure of one pump may result in failure of the other pump in the same system.

1. Land as soon as practicable.

FLIGHT OR COMBINED HYDRAULIC SYSTEM FAILURE

Loss of either the flight or combined hydraulic system allows the one operating system to assume full control of the stabilizer, rudder, and flaperons.

Note

Either the combined primary or the flight hydraulic system alone will power the flight controls throughout the flight envelope except at high IMN; above approximately 0.70 IMN, diminished control effectiveness can be expected.

The internal refueling package (KA-6D) is operated from the combined hydraulic system. The maximum extension limit of the refueling hose is maintained by creating a hydraulic lock in the associated combined system lines. Should the hose be pulled beyond this limit during refueling, a failure of the combined system is likely to occur. To minimize the possibility of a complete hydraulic failure, refueling using the internal refueling package should not be attempted following failure or malfunction of the flight hydraulic system.

WARNING

In the event of flight hydraulic system failure or malfunction, immediately discontinue refueling operations using the internal refueling package. A subsequent malfunction of the refueling package that causes complete loss of the combined system fluid will result in a complete hydraulic failure.

With a failure of either hydraulic system, hydraulic operation of the following systems will not be available:

*Canopy	*Landing Gear
*Wing Slats	Nose-wheel Steering
*Wing Flaps	Antiskid
Flaperon Pop-Up	*Normal Brakes
Wing Fold	Arresting Hook
Strut Lock	(retraction)

*Alternate means of actuation available

With a flight hydraulic system failure, the AFCS will also be inoperative.

With a combined hydraulic system failure, the following will also be inoperative.

Speed Brakes
Assist Spin Recovery
RAT Retraction
KA-6D Hose-Reel Assy Operation
A-6C TRIM Pod Operation

If Either Flight or Combined Hydraulic System Fails, Proceed as Follows:

1. Land as soon as practicable.

Note

Advise tower of intentions prior to landing.

Just Prior to Landing:

2. Fuel . . . . DUMP TO APPROPRIATE LANDING WEIGHT

3. Slow to 180 KIAS

4. Flap lever . . . . TAKE OFF DETENT

5. Flaps/Slats . . . . . . EXTEND ELECTRICALLY TO TAKE-OFF (30°) POSITION, THEN OFF

EMERGENCY PROCEDURES
In-Flight Emergencies

> **WARNING**
>
> Emergency extension of the flaps to takeoff may result in extension beyond the T/O position. Due to time differential between flap and slat retraction, an attempt to return to T/O position will result in a partially or fully retracted slat condition. Accept whatever flap indication exists following the initial extension to obtain takeoff (30°) flaps.

6. Slow to 150 KIAS

7. Landing gear . . . . LOWER BY EMERGENCY SYSTEM

8. Brake selector handle . . . . . TURN 90° CW

9. Auxiliary brake gage . . CHECK AT 15 CYCLES

Note

Except with complete loss of combined hydraulic system fluid, the brake accumulator can be recharged. Availability of fluid may readily be determined by operating the handpump and noting an increase on the brake pressure gage or back pressure on the pump handle. The bombardier/navigator shall assist the pilot in this operation.

10. Arresting hook . . . . AS REQUIRED
    A short field arrestment is recommended.

11. Make a normal landing approach.

After Landing (No Arrestment):

12. If there is less than a 10-knot crosswind, use aerodynamic braking to decelerate.

13. Use minimum number of brake applications. (Bombardier/navigator actuate auxiliary hydraulic pump to replenish brake accumulator as necessary.)

14. Clear runway. DO NOT attempt to taxi.

15. Insert landing gear ground safety locks prior to securing engines.

LOSS OF FLIGHT AND COMBINED HYDRAULIC SYSTEM (AFC 183 BACKUP HYD SYSTEM ONLY)

Failure of either flight or combined hydraulic system will energize the backup hydraulic pump and light the BACKUP-HYD caution light.

Note

The backup hydraulic pump is not available on RAT only power.

If the RUD THRO caution light also lights, this indicates loss of normal hydraulic system pressure in both systems with flight controls limited to rudder and stabilizer using the backup flight control system. This provides rudder control through rudder pedal movement and horizontal stabilizer control through longitudinal stick movement. Flaperon control is not provided.

In cruising flight, nose attitude is easily maintained by normal stick control. Straight flight and gentle turns can be performed by the use of smooth rudder input.

Recovery From Unusual Nose-High Attitudes:

1. Maintain angle of attack below 20 units.

2. Gently roll the aircraft upright using only as much rudder as necessary.

> **WARNING**
>
> Full rudder authority (35°) is provided automatically upon loss of flight and combined hydraulic system pressure. Use of excessive rudder at low speeds and high angles of attack may induce a spin.

Recovery From Unusual Nose-Low Attitudes:

1. Reduce power to idle.

2. Use rudder gently to roll the aircraft upright.

3. As soon as bank angle is less than 90°, apply aft stick to raise nose to horizon. Continue to roll aircraft to wings-level attitude.

> **WARNING**
>
> Full rudder authority (35°) is provided automatically upon loss of flight and combined hydraulic system pressure. Use of excessive rudder deflection above 190 KIAS should be avoided because resulting loads on the vertical stabilizer may exceed available strength. If rudder is used at speeds above 200 KIAS, observe the following limits to prevent possible catastrophic failure:
>
> Full pedal to 190 KIAS
> One half pedal (1 1/2 inch) to 250 KIAS
> One quarter pedal (3/4 inch) to 365 KIAS
> One eighth pedal (3/8 inch) above 365 KIAS

In addition, apparent dihedral effect (the ability to roll the aircraft with rudder) is sharply reduced to zero above .84 MACH. If airspeed exceeds .80 MACH, lateral control on backup hydraulic power using rudder or assymetrical thrust is severely limited.

NAVAIR 01-85ADA-1

EMERGENCY PROCEDURES
In-Flight Emergencies

Under optimum conditions, field landings are possible using the backup flight control system.

If a Field Landing is to be Attempted:

1. Lower landing gear at safe altitude using emergency method.

2. Leave flaps and slats . . . . UP

WARNING

Asymmetrical flaperon float exists when the flaps are lowered in flight following complete hydraulic failure. Asymmetry may cause uncontrollable rolling moment in either direction.

3. Conduct slow flight at safe altitude using 18 units angle of attack, 150 KIAS, or minimum controllable speed, whichever is higher.

4. Plan for a straight-in approach using speed determined in step 3.

Note

- If fuel permits, one or more practice approaches may be made prior to landing.

- For go-around, avoid rapid large longitudinal control inputs. The bombardier/navigator should monitor the BACK-UP HYD light and alert the pilot if the light goes out, indicating pump capacity has been exceeded.

- Longitudinal control rate limiting (decreased pitch response) may occur in the power approach configuration while using the backup hydraulic system.

5. Brake selector handle . . . . . TURN 90° CW

6. Plan arrested landing since flaperon pop-up and antiskid braking will not be available.

7. Use smooth control movements; do not attempt to damp the aircraft dutch roll.

COMPLETE HYDRAULIC SYSTEM FAILURE

If complete hydraulic system failure occurs, all normal flight controls will be inoperative. Upon initial detection of hydraulic pressure loss or gage fluctuation, the pilot shall reduce airspeed and attempt to establish level flight. If aircraft is uncontrollable, EJECT.

SPEED BRAKE SYSTEM FAILURE

If an electrical system failure occurs with the speed brakes extended, they will be automatically retracted by combined hydraulic system pressure. If a combined hydraulic system failure occurs, the speed brakes will be retracted by air loads when the speed-brakes switch is moved forward. When the electrical and combined hydraulic systems both fail, the speed brakes will retract by air loads.

FLAP/SLAT MALFUNCTIONS

FLAPS/SLATS FAIL TO RETRACT

If a Barberpole Indication Should Occur on The Flaps/SLATS Indicator:

1. Climb to a safe operating altitude (do not exceed flap extension limit of 250 KIAS).

2. Maintain a safe airspeed/angle of attack and a high thrust setting.

WARNING

Extreme caution should be exercised during flap retraction under heavy gross weight conditions. To avoid aircraft stall or settling due to flap retraction, do not retract the flaps below 170 KIAS for weights up to 50,000 pounds and not below 185 KIAS for weight above 50,000 pounds. At the heavier weights and under high ambient temperature conditions, acceleration and climb performance are marginal and it may be impossible to reach 185 KIAS. If 185 KIAS cannot be reached, it is recommended that external store weight be reduced in order to permit acceleration to 185 KIAS prior to flap retraction.

Note

Remedial action for barberpoled flaps/slats may include any or all of the following steps at speeds above the minimum for flap/slat retraction and up to a maximum of 250 KIAS.

3. Place flap lever to the TAKEOFF position. After flaps/slats have extended, place flap lever . . . . UP

4. If the indicator barperpoles, apply 0 g momentarily.

5. If it still barberpoles, momentarily actuate the flap lever to TAKEOFF. As the flaps/slats begin to extend, immediately return the lever to UP.

6. If it still barberpoles, momentarily actuate the emergency flap switch to DN. As the slats begin to extend, immediately set the switch to UP and then OFF.

7. If it still barberpoles, maintain airspeed above the minimum retraction speed and extend the flaps/slats partially and then retract. As the flaps/slats approach the fully closed position, momentarily apply slight negative g.

8. If it still barberpoles, return to base and land.

5-21

EMERGENCY PROCEDURES NAVAIR 01-85ADA-1
In-Flight Emergencies

FLAPS/SLATS FAIL TO EXTEND NORMALLY (FAILURE OTHER THAN HYDRAULIC)

Above 180 KIAS (approximately), the flaps may not extend to the TAKEOFF (30°) position. Above 140 KIAS (approximately), the flaps may not extend to the full down or LAND position. In either situation, the flap indicator may indicate a barberpole situation until the airspeed is reduced.

Note

Flaps and slats may fail to extend normally as a result of hydraulic or electric malfunctions. If the cause is determined to be hydraulic, follow procedures as outlined for flight or combined hydraulic system failure. If the malfunction is not hydraulic, proceed as follows:

1. FLAP/SLAT circuit breaker . . . . . PULL

Pulling the flap/slat circuit breaker isolates the normal flap/slat position switches, allowing any flap position to be selected electrically. If the circuit breaker is not pulled, TAKEOFF flaps cannot be selected electrically, since the flaps may return to the up position hydraulically as soon as the emergency flap switch is repositioned to OFF.

2. Slow to 180 KIAS

3. Flaps/slats . . . . EXTEND FLAPS ELECTRICALLY TO TAKEOFF (30°) POSITION, THEN OFF.

WARNING

Emergency extension of the flaps to TAKE-OFF may result in extension beyond the T/O position. Due to time differential between flap and slat retraction, an attempt to return to T/O position will result in a partially or fully retracted slat condition. Accept whatever flap indication exists following the initial extension to obtain TAKE-OFF (30°) flaps.

Note

After landing, and the flaps and slats have been raised, the FLAP/SLAT circuit breaker must be reset, the flaps/slats visually checked up, and the normal flap handle checked in the UP position prior to folding the wings.

FLAPERONS POP UP IN FLIGHT

1. Throttles . . . . MILITARY
2. External stores . . . . JETTISON (AS NECESSARY)
3. Flaperon pop-up switch . . . . OFF

Note

Turn flaperon pop-up OFF to preclude pop-up if failure is due to a weight-on-wheels switch malfunction. If pop-up is required for crosswind or short field landing, it may be armed shortly after touchdown.

4. Return flap lever to original position if applicable.

Note

If the flaperons pop up at the start of flap/slat transit (from up or down), and did not retract with application of power, the failure is then of a hydraulic check valve, which ports fluid to the pop-up valve any time the flaps/slats are in transit up or down.

LANDING IF FLAPERONS HAVE POPPED UP IN FLIGHT

If flaperons popped up in flight due to a failure of the weight-on-wheels switch, then make a normal landing insuring the flaperon pop-up switch is OFF.

If landing with a suspected check valve failure, proceed as follows:

1. Landing gear . . . . . EXTEND NORMALLY

CAUTION

Actuation of the flaps/slats hydraulically may cause re-activation of flaperon pop-up.

2. Slow to 180 KIAS, leaving flap handle up.
3. FLAPS/SLATS circuit breaker . . . . PULL
4. Flaps/Slats . . . EXTEND ELECTRICALLY TO TAKE-OFF (30°) POSITION, THEN OFF.

WARNING

Emergency extension of the flaps to takeoff may result in extension beyond the T/O position. Due to time differential between flap and slat retraction, an attempt to return to T/O position will result in a partially or fully retracted slat condition. Accept whatever flap indication exists following initial extension to obtain TAKEOFF (30°) flaps.

5. Flap lever . . . . TAKEOFF DETENT

Note

After landing, the FLAPS/SLATS circuit breaker must be reset prior to folding wings.

WEIGHT-ON-WHEELS SWITCH FAILURE

LEFT WEIGHT-ON-WHEELS SWITCH

Failure of the left weight-on-wheels switch to actuate to the in-flight position may be readily identified in the cockpit by the landing-gear handle lock remaining engaged. Additional systems affected are as follows:

- Flaperon pop-up enabled
- AOA indexer lights/approach lights disabled
- AOA/total temperature probe heat disabled
- Power trim indicators remain unmasked
- Radar altimeter indicating a constant value between 0 and 10 feet
- Emergency jettison disabled
- Gun charging and clearing disabled
- Refueling store hose-jettison disabled
- Tow link and strut-lock indications disabled
- ALE-29/39 Sequencer disabled
- Electric fusing disabled
- Step solenoid for wing-tank pressurization disabled
- Approach power compensator disabled
- Shrike guidance disabled (NA KA-6D)
- In-flight alignment disabled (NA KA-6D)
- NWW valve remains open (AFC No. 268 only)

The landing-gear handle can be released by lifting the override lever.

RIGHT WEIGHT-ON-WHEELS SWITCH

Failure of the right weight on wheels switch to actuate to the in-flight position will cause no in-flight losses. Failure of the switch to actuate to the on-deck position will cause the loss of nosewheel steering and antiskid braking.

CAUTION

With anti-skid selected and the right weight-on-wheels switch failed to actuate to the on-deck position, normal braking is not available. To regain normal braking, deselect anti-skid.

AIRSPEED INDICATOR FAILURE

Figure 5-6 presents angle of attack for various flight conditions for use in the event of airspeed indicator failure.

DAMAGED AIRCRAFT

Loss of structural integrity may result from a mid-air collision, exceeding structural limits, bird strikes, canopy losses, or battle damage. The following procedure generally applies:

1. Determine whether adequate control of the aircraft is available; if not EJECT.

2. If at low altitude, ZOOM to convert airspeed to altitude. Maintain airspeed as required.

3. If FOD damage is suspected:

    a. TO ONE ENGINE - Secure the engine.

    b. TO BOTH ENGINES - Reduce power to minimum required for maintaining level flight or a slow climb.

4. If practicable, climb to at least 10,000 feet and proceed to an uninhabited area in the vicinity of intended landing.

5. When possible, obtain a visual inspection by another aircraft to assist in evaluating the damage.

6. Cabin pressurization . . . . DUMP
   (if above 8,000 feet)

7. Landing-gear handle . . . . DOWN

8. Flaps/Slats . . . . TAKEOFF/DOWN

9. Perform slow flight to determine minimum safe airspeed to be used during landing approach. If insufficient lateral control is available, flaps and slats down, or if flaps or slats fail to extend fully, make a flaps/slats up landing. (Refer to No Flaps/No Slats Landing Procedure.)

10. Approach speed should be the minimum speed obtained on slow flight check plus 10 knots.

LANDING GEAR SYSTEM MALFUNCTIONS

LANDING GEAR HANDLE CANNOT BE RAISED

Note

If the landing-gear handle cannot be raised, it may be due to failure of the landing-gear handle lock solenoid, the left weight-on-wheels switch or a popped GEAR HOOK circuit breaker.

1. Flaperon pop-up . . . . OFF

To raise the landing gear:

2. Landing-gear OVERRIDE lever . . . . . LIFT

3. Landing-gear handle . . . . RAISE

EMERGENCY PROCEDURES
In-Flight Emergencies

NAVAIR 01-85ADA-1

AIRSPEED INDICATOR FAILURE

FLIGHT CONDITION	ANGLE OF ATTACK (UNITS)
CATAPULT	
TRANSITION FROM CATAPULT (30° FLAPS, GEAR DOWN)	22
L/D$_{MAX}$ DIRTY	
30° FLAPS/SLATS DOWN DRAG INDEX = 0	19
30° FLAPS/SLATS DOWN DRAG INDEX = 100	21
L/D$_{MAX}$ CLEAN	
DRAG INDEX = 0	15
DRAG INDEX = 100	16
MILITARY POWER CLIMB	
30° FLAPS/SLATS DOWN GEAR UP	17
FLAPS/SLATS AND GEAR UP DRAG INDEX = 0 ... SEA LEVEL	10
COMBAT CEILING	14
DRAG INDEX = 100 ... SEA LEVEL	13
COMBAT CEILING	16
MAX RANGE CRUISE AT ALTITUDES BELOW 20,000 FT. (ALL GROSS WEIGHTS)	
DRAG INDEX = 0	12
DRAG INDEX = 100	14
MAX RANGE CRUISE AT OPTIMUM CRUISE ALTITUDE	
DRAG INDEX = 0	12
DRAG INDEX = 100	13
ENDURANCE AT OPTIMUM ENDURANCE ALTITUDE	
DRAG INDEX = 0	15
DRAG INDEX = 100	16
DESCENTS (LOW TO MEDIUM GROSS WEIGHTS)	
MAX. RANGE DESCENT (IDLE POWER)	18
NORMAL DESCENT (80% RPM, WING TIP SPEED BRAKES OPEN)	14
GEAR AND FLAP EXTENSION	
SAFE GEAR EXTENSION (WITH FLAPS UP)	15
SAFE 30° FLAP EXTENSION (WITH FLAPS/SLATS UP)	15
STALL WARNING	
FLAPS/SLATS UP	21
FLAPS 30° SLATS DOWN (WITHOUT AFC 287/WITH AFC 287)	26/27
STALL	
FLAPS UP, GEAR UP	25
FLAPS 30°/SLATS DOWN GEAR DOWN WITHOUT A.F.C. 287/WITH A.F.C. 287	28/30 PLUS
APPROACH (FINAL ON SPEED APPROACH)	
GEAR DOWN, FLAPS 30°, WING TIP SPEED BRAKES OPEN	22
GEAR DOWN, FLAPS UP/SLATS DOWN	22
GEAR DOWN, FLAPS/SLATS UP	20
WAVE OFF	
SINGLE ENGINE	23
NO FLAP/NO SLAT	20
BOLTER	
SINGLE ENGINE	20
NO FLAP/NO SLAT	20

NOTE
- DUE TO THE BASIC INACCURACY OF SETTING UP FLIGHT CONDITIONS (OTHER THAN LANDING APPROACH) BY REFERENCE TO THE ANGLE OF ATTACK INDICATOR, THE INFORMATION INCLUDED IN THIS TABLE SHOULD BE USED ONLY IN AN EMERGENCY SITUATION.
- THE ANGLES SHOWN FOR ANGLE OF ATTACK VERSUS DRAG INDEX, WHILE NOT ENTIRELY LINEAR, MAY BE INTERPOLATED LINEARLY FOR PRACTICAL PURPOSES.

Figure 5-6

EMERGENCY PROCEDURES
In-Flight Emergencies

LANDING GEAR HANDLE UP, INDICATES UNSAFE

With the landing-gear handle in the UP position, if the wheels transition light comes on, and/or the integrated position indicator displays a barber pole for any of the three landing gear, the unsafe indication may be due to electrical or mechanical failure. Such a failure will normally first be observed when the landing gear is raised immediately after takeoff; cycling the gear may correct the problem. Repeated cyclings are not recommended. Observe 200 KIAS limit for gear retraction.

1. Obtain a visual check if possible.

2. If both flight and combined hydraulic system pressure is available, isolation valve switch - LDG.

3. Landing gear handle . . . . RECYCLE

CAUTION

- When cycling the gear from the up position, allow sufficient time (approximately 7 seconds) for the landing gear to complete a half cycle (i.e. from full up to full down) before attempting a reversal. If the direction is reversed before the door is fully opened, the gear linkage will not have completed its travel and the forward gear door may fail.

- If either flight or combined hydraulic system pressure is not available, or gear continues to indicate unsafe with the isolation valve in the LDG position - Observe gear extension speed limit (250 KIAS).

LANDING GEAR HANDLE DOWN, INDICATES UNSAFE

Gear extension failures may be due to electrical, hydraulic, mechanical, or cabin pressurization malfunctions. The gear will not extend normally if combined secondary hydraulic system pressure or 28 V dc essential bus electrical power is not available. Without 28 V dc power, the wheel transition light will be inoperative and the wheel position indicator will show a barberpole unsafe condition. Whenever the landing-gear handle is selected down and all the wheels do not extend and indicate positively down and locked, accomplish the following as necessary:

1. Gear/hook circuit breaker . . . . CHECK IN

2. Cabin dump switch . . . . ON

3. Reduce airspeed to 200 KIAS.

4. Landing gear. . . CYCLE AS NECESSARY TO OBTAIN DOWN INDICATION
Leave gear handle DOWN after completion of landing-gear cycling.

CAUTION

When cycling the gear, allow sufficient time (approximately 7 seconds) for the landing gear to complete a half cycle (i.e. from full up to full down) before attempting a reversal. If the direction is reversed before the door is fully opened, the gear linkage will not have completed its travel and the forward gear door may fail.

5. With flaps up, accelerate to a maximum of 250 KIAS and apply positive and negative g, and yaw the aircraft.

Note

For NOSE GEAR unsafe indications, the trade-off between increased airloads and g available must be accepted.

CAUTION

In the flaps/slats down configuration g is limited to 2 positive g, zero negative g.

6. Flap/Slats . . . . TAKEOFF/DOWN

7. Have a visual gear position check made by another aircraft or by the tower on a fly-by. (See figure 5-7.)

Note

- If a landing gear indicates unsafe and is visually checked down after executing the above procedures, a short field arrested landing or carrier arrestment is recommended.

- The nose gear indicator in the integrated position indicator, the wheels warning light, the nose gear door anti-collision light (out), and the approach indexer/approach lights all sample the nose gear down and locked Micro Switch. Since all of these indicating systems are subject to malfunctions of their own, their activation, singly or collectively, does not necessarily constitute an unsafe nose gear situation.

- Valid mechanical down and over center for the landing gear can be ascertained using index tapes (if installed) or by close visual inspection of the respective over center mechanism. See figure 5-7.

8. If the indicating system is suspect, make a normal carrier arrestment/field arrestment, pinning the gear prior to further aircraft movement.

NOSE AND MAIN LANDING GEAR OVER CENTER MECHANISM

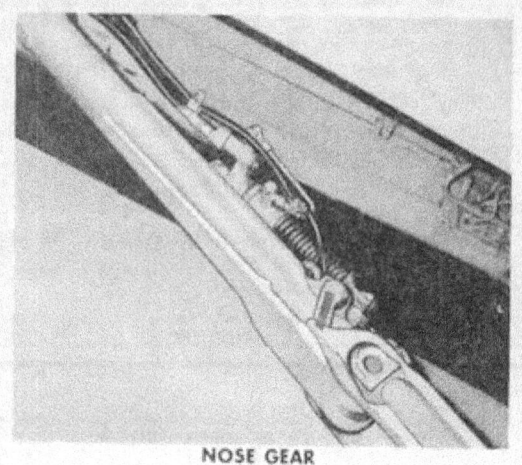
NOSE GEAR

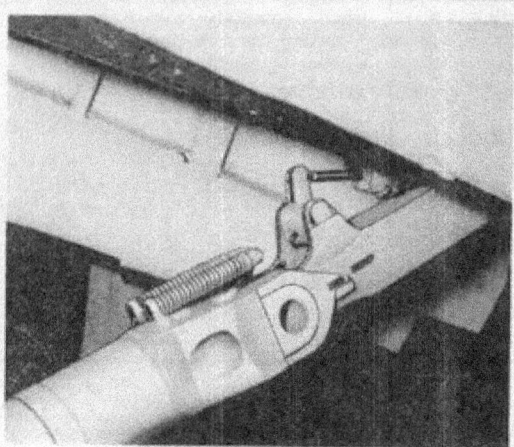
MAIN GEAR

Figure 5-7

9. If one or more gear are still unsafe, steps 4, 5, 6, and 7 may be repeated, and the following steps commenced:

10. Reduce airspeed to 150 KIAS.

Note

- The alternative of landing aboard ship with one or more gears not down, vice proceeding to a suitable divert airfield, must be considered prior to attempting gear extension by the emergency means, since the possibility exists that the offending gear may remain not down after such action is taken, and any feasible divert fields attainable in a clean configuration may then be beyond range.

- The landing gear, once extended by the emergency means, cannot be retracted while airborne.

11. With gear handle DOWN (any configuration), push handle in, rotate 90° clockwise, then pull out.

Note

- The landing gear handle must be pulled out with sufficient force and extension to ensure actuation of the emergency air bottles. Extension of the gear handle may be in excess of 3 inches depending on control rigging.

- When it is necessary to lower the landing gear by the emergency extension system (for other than a hydraulic failure/malfunction), there is no loss of the full operation of normal braking, anti-skid, flaperon pop-up, or nosewheel steering.

12. If necessary, steps 5, 6, and 7 may be repeated.

Note

After landing, pin gear prior to further aircraft movement if unsafe indication still exists.

13. When landing with any gear unsafe, figure 5-8 provides recommended courses of action. These recommendations are based on available information and experience to date. They are subject to operational and pilot/crew consideration existing at the time.

LANDING GEAR EMERGENCY

FINAL CONFIGURATION	CARRIER LANDING APPLICABLE NOTES	FIELD LANDING APPLICABLE NOTES
ALL GEAR UNSAFE	3, 4, 5, 6, 8, 9, 10, 16, 17, 18, 19	1, 2, 3, 4, 5, 6, 7, 8, 9, 10, 14, 17, 19
NOSE GEAR UNSAFE	3, 4, 5, 6, 7, 8, 9, 10, 17, 18, 19, 20	1, 2, 3, 4, 5, 6, 7, 8, 9, 10, 11, 12, 17, 19, 20
ONE MAIN UNSAFE	3, 4, 5, 6, 7, 8, 9, 10, 17, 18	1, 2, 3, 4, 5, 6, 7, 8, 9, 10, 13, 15, 17
BOTH MAINS UNSAFE	3, 4, 5, 6, 7, 8, 9, 10, 17, 18	1, 2, 3, 4, 5, 6, 7, 8, 9, 10, 14, 17
ONE MAIN NOSE GEAR UNSAFE	3, 4, 5, 6, 7, 8, 9, 10, 17, 18, 19	1, 2, 3, 4, 5, 6, 7, 8, 9, 10, 11, 15, 17, 19

NOTES

1. Request Foam on Runway.
2. Utilize Arresting Gear and LSO, If Available.
3. Lighten Aircraft by Dumping and Burning Off Excess Fuel.
4. Retain External Tanks, If Empty.
5. Jettison Other External Stores (If the Gear Has Been Lowered the Emergency Jettison System Must Be Used to Jettison Stores. Pull Appropriate Emergency Stores Jettison Circuit Breakers to Retain Empty Drop Tanks).
6. Flaps Down, If Available.
7. Arresting Hook Down.
8. Canopy Closed.
9. Wingtip Speedbrakes Out, If Available.
10. Flaperon Popup Off.
11. Fly Reduced Rate of Descent Utilizing LSO If Available. Do Not Let The Nose Fall Through.
12. Touch-Down Short of the Arresting Gear on Runway Centerline with Power On. Maintain 90 KIAS Nose High Attitude with Aft Stick Until Arresting Gear is Engaged.
13. If Arresting Gear Is Not Available, Land on Side of Runway Opposite the Failed or Unsafe Main Gear.
14. Touch-Down Just Short of the Arresting Gear on Runway Centerline.
15. Touch-Down Just Short of Arresting Gear on Runway Centerline with Power On. Maintain Flying Speed (105-115 KIAS) Until Arresting Gear Is Engaged. Be Prepared to Go Around If Arresting Gear Is Missed.
16. Hook Up Landing Is Recommended to Prevent Possible Crew Injuries As the Result of Excessive Nose Slapdown Loads.
17. Throttles and Engine Master Switches Off (After Engaging Arresting Gear, or After Touchdown, If No Arresting Gear Is Available).
18. Barricade Required.
19. Tank Pressurization Switch OFF.
20. Touch and Go Permitted to Achieve a Gear Down Indication.

Figure 5-8

EMERGENCY PROCEDURES
Air-Refueling System Emergencies

NAVAIR 01-85ADA-1

part 4 — Air Refueling Emergencies

Note

- If any emergency condition occurs with a receiver aircraft in the refueling or pre-contact position, the tanker pilot will immediately inform the receiver to move to the observation position to insure adequate separation of aircraft.

- Refueling operations shall not commence or be reinitiated unless the pilot can ascertain that NATOPS safety procedures will not be compromised.

WARNING

- Any emergency that may affect the ability to fly formation, such as loss of an engine or flight control malfunction, requires an immediate breakaway before initiating any other emergency procedures.

- In the breakaway, the tanker aircraft climbs straight ahead at maximum power to the top of the refueling block. The receiver descends to the bottom of the block. Both aircraft attempt to maintain visual contact during the breakaway. Notify controlling agency of intentions as soon as practicable.

REFUELING EMERGENCIES

REFUELING WITH SINGLE GENERATOR

Actuation of the air refueling system package with only one generator operating is not, in itself, inherently dangerous. However, such utilization is not recommended and should be tempered with an assessment of the reliability of the remaining generator. The following procedures apply:

1. RAT handle . . . . PULL
2. FUEL TRANSFER switch . . . . . check OFF

CAUTION

Simultaneous actuation of fuel transfer pumps and reel response circuits may overload the remaining generator, causing it to drop off the line with subsequent loss of reel response, and possible damage to receiver aircraft.

3. Receiver aircraft . . ENGAGE DROGUE (when cleared in)
4. FUEL TRANSFER switch . . . . AUTO

HOSE REEL DRIVE FAILURES

Failures of the hose-reel drive and their corrective actions are shown in figure 5-9.

FUEL LEAKING FROM AFT BAY DURING REFUELING

1. Terminate refueling; receiver disconnects.
2. FUEL TRANSFER switch . . . . OFF
3. RET/EXT switch . . . . RET
4. Refueling power panel switch . . . . . OFF
5. Secure all unnecessary electrical equipment.
6. Land as soon as practicable.

FUEL LEAKING FROM AFT BAY DURING REFUELING, HOSE WILL NOT RETRACT

1. Terminate refueling, receiver disconnects.
2. FUEL TRANSFER switch . . . . OFF
3. Secure all unnecessary electrical equipment.
4. Land with hose trailing, as soon as practicable.
5. Do not guillotine hose since pyrotechnics may cause explosion or ignite fuel/fumes.
6. Bingo if fuel state permits. If an arrested landing is absolutely necessary, yaw aircraft before lowering tail hook in order to prevent hose-hook interference. An arrested landing could cause hose to whip forward, damaging aircraft.

HOSE FAILS TO RETRACT

1. Reduce airspeed to decrease drag on drogue and attempt retraction.

If Hose Fails to Retract:

2. HOSE JETTISON switch . . . . . . JETTISON

If Hose Fails to Jettison:

3. A field arrested landing is recommended.

CAUTION

A shipboard arrestment with a trailing air refueling hose is not recommended.

HOSE REEL DRIVE SYSTEM FAILURES

FAILURE	EFFECT	CORRECTIVE ACTION IN FLIGHT
Loss of one engine or engine-driven hydraulic pump.	Slight reduction in response rate.	No corrective action required.
Reel arming valve failed closed.	No operation of reel system.	None, use D-704 if available.*
Reel arming valve failed open.	None, except reel lock will not engage.	After retraction of hose, leave refueling panel power ON and EXT/RET switch in RET for remainder of flight and landing.
Failure of reel drive motor or servo valve.	No operation of reel system.	None, use D-704 if available.*
Electrical failure of power supply to reel system.	No operation of reel system.	None, use D-704 if available.*

*AIRCRAFT INCORPORATING A.F.C. No. 296

Figure 5-9

COMBINED HYDRAULIC SYSTEM FAILURE, HOSE EXTENDED

Note

The hose cannot be retracted if the combined hydraulic system fails.

1. Refueling panel power . . . . OFF
2. Airspeed 220 - 320 KIAS
3. HOSE JETTISON switch. . . . . JETTISON
   If hose fails to jettison, refer to Failure of Hose to Retract, step 3.

An arrested landing is recommended with the hydraulic failure. A shipboard landing with a trailing hose is not recommended.

4. Leave refueling panel switches in their present positions.
5. Follow procedure for combined hydraulic system failure.

HOSE BREAK/LOSS OF MA-2 COUPLING AND DROGUE

1. Refueling panel power . . . . OFF
   Immediately place power OFF in order to snub hose and prevent severed end from damaging interior of aft bay. Hose reel will make scheduled number of turns regardless of length of hose remaining.

Jettison remaining hose.

2. Hose Jettison switch . . . . JETTISON

Note

Integral electrical/hydraulic provisions will shut down the hydraulic and fuel systems.

HOSE BREAK AT COUPLING ON REEL

Note

The STOW/TRAIL indicator shows TRAIL until hose-coupling failure, then shows barber pole. The READY light will go out. Response is not possible. The hose will be snubbed in the guillotine.

1. FUEL TRANSFER switch . . . . OFF

EMERGENCY PROCEDURES
Air-Refueling System Emergencies

2. EXT/RET switch . . . . , . . EXT

3. Refueling panel power . . . . OFF

NO READY LIGHT OR FUEL TRANSFER FAILURE

Failure of the READY light may be due to a response failure or to a failure in the ready light circuitry.

1. FUEL TRANSFER switch . . . . AUTO

WARNING

Before attempting refueling with no READY light or with a fuel transfer failure, ensure that receiver pilots are briefed to engage and disengage the drogue only when cleared by the tanker pilot. Should the receiver aircraft attempt to disengage while the fuel transfer switch is in OVRD, both aircraft may be damaged.

2. Receiver aircraft . . . . ENGAGE DROGUE
   (when cleared)

If No Fuel Transfer:

3. FUEL TRANSFER switch . . . . OVRD

After Transfer Complete:

4. FUEL TRANSFER switch . . . . OFF

5. Receiver aircraft . . . DISENGAGE DROGUE
   (when cleared)

REFUELING HOSE JETTISONING

Internal Refueling System

1. POWER switch . . . . OFF

2. Airspeed . . . . 220 to 320 KIAS

3. DROGUE JETT switch . . . . JETT

WARNING

If the hose has been jettisoned, moving the DROGUE JETT switch from the JETT position with the POWER switch ON will restore power to the hose-reel assembly and the severed hose seal may be broken.

External Refueling Store

1. Refueling master switch . . . . OFF

2. Airspeed . . . . 300 KIAS (MAX.)

3. Hose jettison switch . . . . CUT

WARNING

Once the CUT position has been selected, do not return the switch to NORM, as the turbine will unfeather and cause the hose to be pulled from the guillotine crimper, spilling fuel in the store and creating a fire hazard.

Landing Emergencies

If the situation necessitates an approach speed above normal, or affects slowing or control of the aircraft after landing, an arrested landing shall be considered. Satisfactory field and carrier approaches can be made in abnormal approach configurations. For optimum angles of attack for various approach configurations, see figure 5-10.

EMERGENCY APPROACH CONFIGURATION AOA/AIRSPEED

CONFIGURATION	OPTIMUM AOA (UNITS)	OPTIMUM APPROACH SPEEDS GROSS WEIGHT 33,500 KIAS
FLAPS UP SLATS OUT	22	141
FLAPS 30° SLATS IN *	19	118
FLAPS UP SLATS IN	20	147
SINGLE ENGINE FLAPS 30° SLATS OUT	21	113

NOTES
1. FOR EACH 1000 LBS ADDED TO ABOVE GROSS WEIGHTS, ADD 2 KIAS TO OPTIMUM APPROACH SPEED.
2. DATA IN ABOVE CHART IS THE RESULT OF CARRIER SUITABILITY FLIGHT TEST EVALUATION CONDUCTED BY THE NAVAL AIR TEST CENTER, PATUXENT RIVER, MARYLAND.

* WARNING
- DO NOT ATTEMPT TO FLARE THE LANDING. THIS MAY RESULT IN A SEVERE PITCH UP.
- DURING WAVEOFF OR BOLTER IN THIS CONFIGURATION, OVERROTATION MUST BE AVOIDED DUE TO PITCHUP OCCURING AT 20 TO 22 UNITS AOA.

Figure 5-10

SINGLE ENGINE LANDING

A single-engine landing is basically the same as a normal landing, except that the pattern is expanded slightly to avoid steep turns. Performance at high gross weights and high ambient temperatures is critical. Single-engine landing, wave-off, or bolter may be accomplished safely up to gross weight and temperature limits as shown in figure 5-11.

WARNING

Do not use LAND flaps for single-engine landing.

During wave-off, the optimum technique is to select military thrust, and rotate to 23 units AOA. After wave-off, decrease AOA to 18 units to provide adequate excess thrust margin for maneuvering flight. Bolter techniques consist of selecting military thrust, rotating to 20 units AOA. During acceleration, decrease AOA to 18 units. External fuel tanks have a negligible affect on thrust required and need be dropped only if necessary for gross weight considerations.

Single Engine Landing Proceed as Follows:

1. Fuel . . . . DUMP/BURN DOWN to minimum acceptable level

2. External stores . . . JETTISON (as necessary)

WARNING

High weight/drag stores will considerably reduce wave-off and bolter capability.

3. Speed brakes . . . . IN
4. Landing gear . . . . DOWN
5. Flaps/slats . . . . TAKEOFF/DOWN
6. Maintain a shallow, slightly fast approach speed (21 units) AOA
7. Make a normal touchdown and roll out.

EMERGENCY PROCEDURES
Landing Emergencies

NAVAIR 01-85ADA-1

SINGLE ENGINE CARRIER LANDING
GROSS WEIGHT VS TEMPERATURE

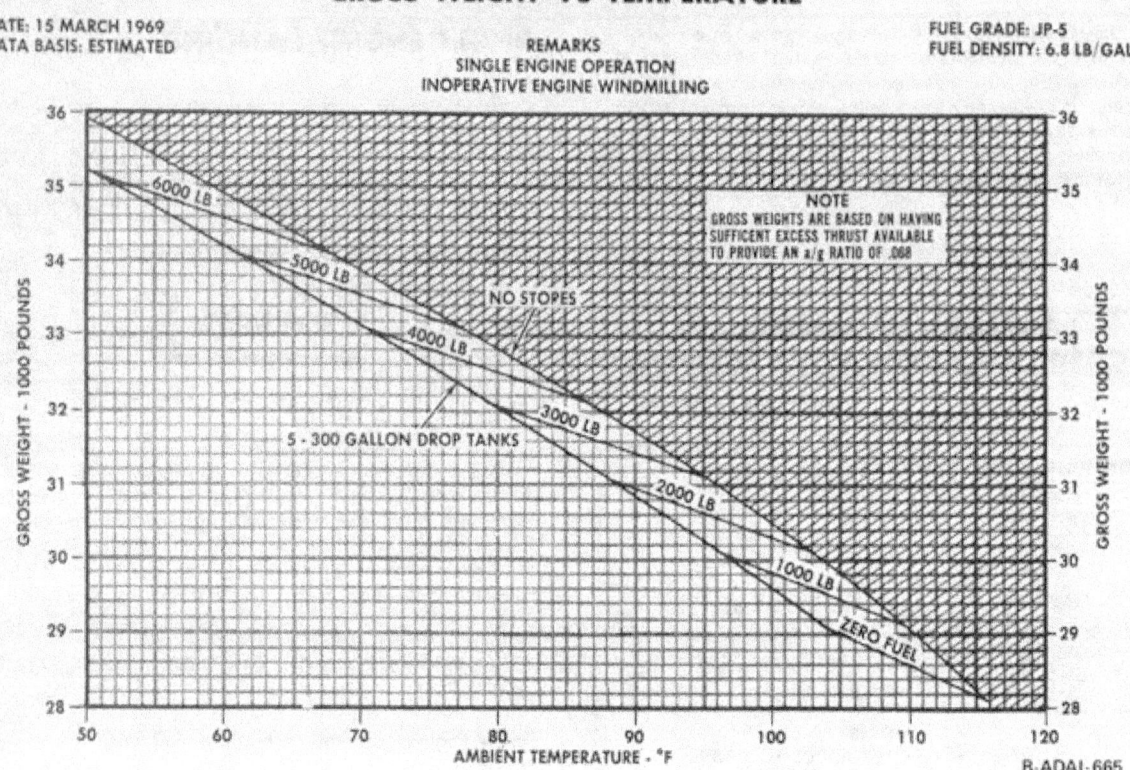

Figure 5-11

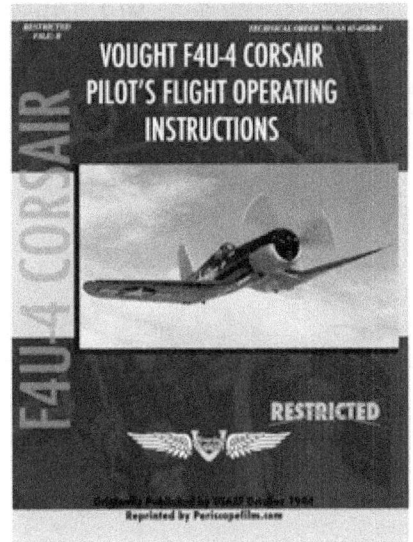
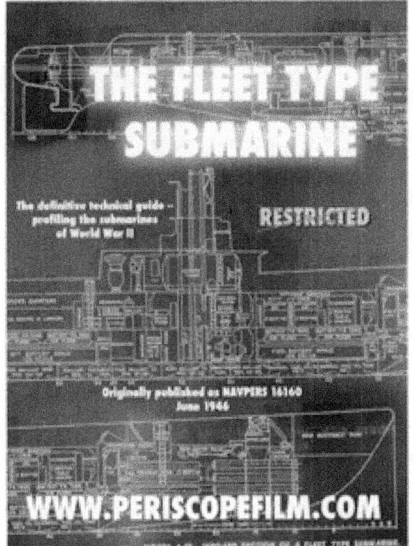
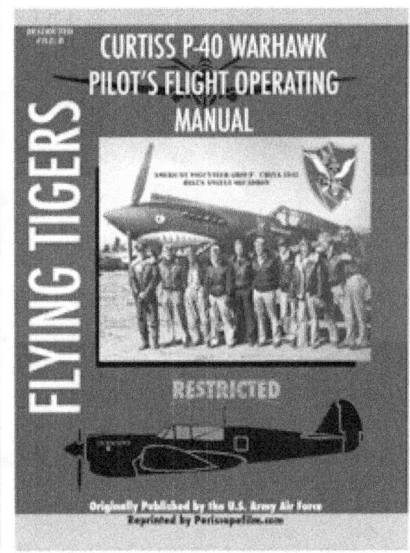

ALSO NOW AVAILABLE FROM PERISCOPEFILM.COM

This manual is sold for historic research purposes only, as an entertainment. It is not intended to be used as part of an actual flight training program. No book can substitute for flight training by an authorized instructor. The licensing of pilots is overseen by organizations and authorities such as the FAA and CAA. Operating an aircraft without the proper license is a federal crime.

Copyright ©2009 Periscope Film LLC
All Rights Reserved
ISBN #978-1-935327-76-9   1-935327-76-3

www.ingramcontent.com/pod-product-compliance
Lightning Source LLC
Chambersburg PA
CBHW082025300426
44117CB00015B/2356